The Complete Guide to Executive Compensation

The Complete Guide to Executive Compensation

Bruce R. Ellig

McGraw-Hill

New York Chicago San Francisco Lisbon Madrid
Mexico City Milan New Delhi San Juan
Seoul Singapore Sydney Toronto

Library of Congress Cataloging-in-Publication Data

Ellig, Bruce R.
  The complete guide to executive compensation / Bruce R. Ellig
    p. cm.
  Includes index.
  ISBN 0-07-137629-1 (acid-free paper)
    1. Executives—Salaries, etc. I. Title

  HD4965.2.E438 2001
  658.4'0722—dc21   2001044887

McGraw-Hill

A Division of The McGraw·Hill Companies

    3 4 5 6 7 8 9 0 AGM/AGM 0 9 8 7 6 5 4 3

ISBN 0-07-137629-1

Production services by CWL Publishing Enterprises, Madison, WI, www.cwlpub.com.

Printed and bound by Quebecor Martinsburg.

This publication is designed to provide accurate and authoritative information in regard to the subject matter covered. It is sold with the understanding that neither the author nor the publisher is engaged in rendering legal, accounting, or other professional service. If legal advice or other expert assistance is required, the services of a competent professional person should be sought.
—From a Declaration of Principles jointly adopted by a Committee
of the American Bar Association and a Committee of Publishers

McGraw-Hill books are available at special quantity discounts to use as premiums and sales promotions, or for use in corporate training programs. For more information, please write to the Director of Special Sales, McGraw-Hill, 2 Penn Plaza, New York, NY 10121. Or contact your local bookstore.

This book is printed on recycled, acid-free paper containing a minimum of 50% recycled de-inked fiber.

Contents

Dedication

This book is dedicated to:

… my parents, Robert and Lucille, for all they did while I was growing up,

… my son, Brett, for all I hope he will be, and

… especially my wife, Janice, for all she is—lover, best friend, and soul mate

Preface

his book is somewhat immodestly titled *The Complete Guide to Executive Compensation*, for that was its objective from the beginning. It is to be a book that compensation professionals, members of management, and directors of the boards can use to find useful information for understanding the issues involved in coming up with a sound executive compensation package that effectively blends salary, benefits, perquisites, short-term, and long-term incentive, while taking into account government regulations, tax law, organization and exective needs, and the rewarding of performance.

I was fortunate to have input and suggestions from a number of outstanding people who are listed in the acknowledgments. While I have made every attempt to be accurate and current, it is important to realize this is not a book that professes to provide expert information on accounting, SEC, tax, or other professional service matters. For that, you need to seek appropriate counsel. Nevertheless, I believe the material in this book provides a good understanding of most executive compensation issues and will help you formulate good questions for those discussions.

While I've made every attempt to avoid errors in this book, I regret if any exist. I am very interested in comments and suggestions that will make the next edition more useful and come closer to really becoming the complete guide to executive compensation. Send these to me in care of the publisher at Two Penn Plaza, New York, NY 10121.

ACKNOWLEDGMENTS

First, and foremost I wish to thank three people without whom this book would never have happened: my editor, Mary Glenn, for her faith in me from the very beginning and helpful assistance all along the way, Cathy Catalano who, with her wordprocessing skills, converted my illegible scribblings into an electronic manuscript, and, once the book was written, John Woods and his team at CWL Publishing Enterprises, who turned it into the book you now hold.

A special thank you to the following for their thoughtful comments and suggestions: Larry Bickford (SEC), Bob Birdsell (life insurance). Peter Chingos and Fred Cook (long-term incentives), and Wally Nichols (performance management). Thank yous also to the following for input on the history of executive compensation: Larry Bickford, Lou Cheek, Peter Chingos, Fred Cook, Bud Crystal, Mike Davis, Ed Goff, Tim Haigh, Vic Iannuzzi, Les Jackson, Ira Kay, Jim Kuhns, Greg Lau, Fred Meuter, Pearl Meyer, Wally Nichols, Alan Ritchie, Sandra Sussman, Nat Winstanley, and Gordon Wolf.

And thank you also to John England for encouraging me to do this book by updating my earlier book on executive compensation.

Several people were very helpful to me early in my career, one that resulted in a strong passion for the field of compensation. They include: the late Professor Alton Johnson, who got me interested in the field of compensation while at the University of Wisconsin, the late Bill Stuart, who hired me at Pfizer and lived the values of business partner and employee champion, the late Don Lum who followed Stuart as Vice President, Personnel and was my boss and big supporter while there, Chairman and CEO Ed Pratt, who gave me the top HR job at Pfizer (the third in the company's history) and made it enjoyable while demanding, and Bill Steere, who continued to make my job challenging and very rewarding.

Thank you all!

And while Brucell and other proper names in the book are fictitious some bear a striking similarity to members of my family.

Chapter 1

Executive Compensation Framework

As the title of this book suggests, this is a handbook or reference tool on executive compensation. You can read it cover to cover, chapter by chapter, or access it selectively for definitions and examples of various programs. It is intended to be useful to several different audiences: executives, approvers of executive compensation programs, designers, and administrators of executive pay delivery systems, and those who write and report on executive pay. Each group will understandably have a different degree of interest as well as different perspectives.

Executives, as the recipients of pay plans, will find this book useful both in describing what they don't have and for reviewing plans in which they participate. *Approvers* of executive pay plans will not only find valuable definitions and descriptions of various type plans, but also useful insight as to the conditions under which they might be used. Thus, this book offers independent input to that provided by the recommenders of the pay plan. Hopefully, *designers* and *administrators* will find details and examples that will trigger their own creativity; and for those who *report* about executive pay plans, this book will not only provide useful background, but also help form a better understanding of the topic.

Having defined how various readers will find the book useful, it is important to indicate what the book does not purport to do. Specifically, you should not rely on accounting, tax, Securities Exchange Commission, or other potentially legally binding statements in this book. Seek appropriate professional counsel for such guidance. The statements made in this book are offered as illustrations to help readers understand principles and practices. You should consult with appropriate counsel before making any binding decisions.

WHO IS AN EXECUTIVE?

For the purposes of this book, it is important first to define the *executive* I will be covering. My definition of executive is not that provided by the Fair Labor Standards Act, which exempts from overtime pay those supervising at least two full-time subordinates in a position customarily requiring the exercise of independent judgment and discretion. We can define executive by one of six methods: salary, job grade, key position, job title, reporting relationship (organization level), or a combination of two or more of these methods.

Salary

Using salary to identify eligibility is fairly simple, once the appropriate salary level is identified; however, it has several drawbacks. First, it gives a false degree of finiteness to eligibility, for example, $100,000 and up "yes" vs. $99,999 and below "no." Second, considerable pressure will be exerted to move people above the magic cutoff. Third, the cutoff must be adjusted annually in relation to compensation adjustments; otherwise, the size of eligible candidates will continually increase.

Job Grade

The use of *job grade* to determine who is an executive—like salary—also has a misleading degree of precision. The rationale is simple: the value of a job to the organization was already determined when each job was placed in a job grade. The approach is superior to use of salary in that it relates to the job, not to the person's earnings. However, it places a similar pressure on the compensation program—pressure to upgrade positions into the eligible group.

Key Position

Using the *key position* approach means examining each job for appropriateness (e.g., only those positions with "bottom-line" responsibility). Or it may be restricted to include only corporate officers or *insiders* as defined by the SEC. Administratively, this practice has two drawbacks. First, it is possible that two jobs in the same job grade will be treated differently. Second, it will be necessary to review the list of eligible candidates on almost an annual basis for appropriate additions and deletions. This approach is generally more prevalent among smaller organization than larger ones. When used, it normally results in staff jobs being included.

Job Title

Eligible candidates could be determined by job title (e.g., vice presidents and above). The problem with this method is that the lowest-level vice president may have less responsibility than the highest-level director. It also raises the issue of organizational comparisons. For example, are divisional vice presidents as important as corporate vice presidents? Or even, are vice presidents in Division A as important as vice presidents in Division B? This might lead to a multitiered job title list as shown in Table 1-1.

Reporting Relationship

Reporting relationships are used by some to determine who is an executive (e.g., the top three organization levels in the company). The problem is the inclusion of "executive assistants" and "assistants to" whose degree of importance to the position is better represented by their job grade than their organization level.

Organizational Unit	Title
Corporate Office	Vice President and up
Group	Executive Vice President and up
Division	President

Table 1-1. Example eligible executive titles by organizational unit

Combinations

Because each of these five approaches has one or more disadvantages or shortcomings, the best approach may be a combination of two or more definitions. For example, using the definition of anyone in Grade X or higher within the top three levels of the organization takes pressure off job re-grading and the need to include "assistants" and "assistants to."

HOW MANY ARE EXECUTIVES?

For many, an executive is probably an individual in the highest-paid two to three percent of the company's total employee population or the highest-paid five percent of the exempt portion of the workforce. However, these percentages are only rough guidelines. The percentages would probably be lower in centralized companies and higher in decentralized organizations. The relative percentage of executives to the company's total employment is compared and contrasted with size and type of organization in Table 1-2.

One might expect a higher percentage of executives in a capital-intensive than a people-intensive organization because equipment rather than people dominate the lower levels of the organization. In people-intensive companies, decision-making has to be pushed further down in the organization; otherwise, the company will be a slow plodding bureaucracy.

Revenue Size	Company Structure	
	Centralized	Decentralized
Large	Low	Moderate
Small	Moderate	High

Table 1-2. Percentage of executives to total employment relative to revenue and structure

Table 1-3 is a generalization contrasting the percentage of executives to total employment in centralized and decentralized capital-intensive and people-intensive organizations. As one would expect, the lowest percentage would be found in centralized, people-intensive organizations (i.e., large workforces but all major decisions made by a handful of executives at the top of the organization). Whereas a decentralized, people-intensive organization would have a moderate percentage of executives relative to total employment because executive decision-makers would be at all levels, with a relatively small workforce. With a centralized, capital-intensive organization, there would be fewer executives and, therefore, a moderate ratio. Moving from a people-intensive to a capital-intensive organization, the number of executives decreases more slowly than the non-executive population. The reverse is also true in moving from a capital-intensive to a peo-

	Capital-Intensive	People-Intensive
Centralized	Moderate	Low
Decentralized	High	Moderate

Table 1-3. Percentage of executives in centralized and decentralized vs. capital-intensive and people intensive organizations

ple-intensive organization. This generalization will not apply in many situations because of the various definitions used for executives—some being more liberal than others.Nonetheless, capi-tal-intensive vs. people-intensive is a factor in determining the weighting of executives to non-executives in an organization.

WHAT IS COMPENSATION?

Extrinsic vs. Intrinsic Compensation

It may be easier to think of pay as a form of extrinsic compensation while work environment, type of work, learning, developmental opportunities, and extent of recognition form intrinsic compensation—often called psychic income. Other forms of intrinsic compensation include autonomy and power. Combined, extrinsic and intrinsic compensation constitute the total reward structure.

Organizations that are visibly successful may be providing some intrinsic compensation to their executives (i.e., a pride in membership). Since such organizations usually pay at least com-petitively, the intrinsic pay reinforces the retention capability of direct pay. Conversely, less suc-cessful organizations, which may be unable to afford fully competitive pay, place additional pressure on the pay package since intrinsic compensation may actually be low to negative and must be offset to retain the individual.

As shown in Figure 1-1, all jobs have a combination of intrinsic and extrinsic compensa-tion. I believe that to the extent the job does not have a desired level of intrinsic compensation, an offsetting level of extrinsic compensation is required. This could explain why garbage col-lectors earn almost as much pay as some college professors. No one will ever mistake garbage collecting for a job with high levels of intrinsic compensation. Conversely, the intrinsic appeal of being a college professor or a prominent politician (e.g., U.S. senator) explains why the extrinsic pay in these professions seems low as compared with other jobs.

Executives are somewhere in the middle of the curve, either shedding intrinsic needs due to positive pay-performance situations (e.g., for-profit sector) or increasing searches for high intrinsic compensation because the direct pay-performance link is not sufficiently strong (e.g., non-profit sector). In addition to seeking a position that has sufficient extrinsic compensation to meet ego and other needs, most are looking for work that is high in intrinsic compensation—personally meaningful and satisfying. Executives more than others in the corporation usually have sufficient flexibility in organizational issues to be able to organize their work, at least in part, to meet their intrinsic needs; however, their accountability may be in areas of low interest. The emphasis in this book is on extrinsic compensation, although even extrinsic pay has intrin-sic aspects.

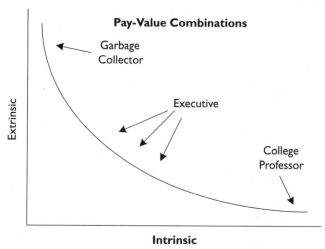

Figure 1-1. Extrinsic vs. intrinsic pay

The Compensation Elements

There are five basic compensation elements: salary, employee benefits, short-term incentives, long-term incentives, and perquisites. As shown in Figure 1-2, only salary and employee benefits are a factor at the lower portion of most organizations; however, all five are present at the CEO level—each of the other three being phased in at different points in the organization.

Salary

The objective of the salary element (Chapter 5) is to reflect extent of experience and sustained level of performance for a job of a particular level in importance to the organization. Many times it is also the basis on which the other four elements are determined. Salary is the income level

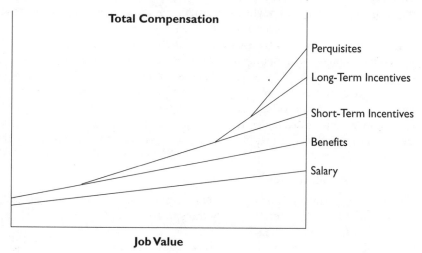

Figure 1-2. Total compensation (five element curves)

that will allow the executive to meet some, but not all, of his or her lifestyle objectives. A more extensive and expensive lifestyle can be supported through the short- and long-term incentive plan payouts. The latter keeps the executive "at risk." Essentially salary is a no-risk form of pay since it is rarely if ever reduced. However, since incentives are essentially nonexistent in some industries and in non-profit organizations, the salary program takes on added importance in adequately reflecting short- and long-range contributions to the organization. When this is true, it is important that salary be competitive in the marketplace with annual cash compensation (i.e., salary plus annual incentives) at levels comparable to similar positions in other companies. However, the extent to which a company chooses to be directly competitive on salaries is a function of the degree of risk/reward it wants to build into its program.

Employee Benefits and Perquisites

The *employee benefits* (Chapter 6) element deals with providing time off with pay, employee services, awards (other than performance), health care, survivor protection, and retirement coverage to all employees in the organization. Cost effective to both the organization and the executive because of economies of large-scale coverage, employee benefits meet many needs the executive otherwise would have to pay for from his or her own pocket. The extent of coverage is typically determined by years of service and/or level of pay. Also covered in Chapter 6 are *perquisites*, namely, employee benefits that are designed only to apply to executives and, therefore, also called *executive benefits*. In some instances, they merely supplement employee benefit coverage (often that limited by law), in other instances, they provide coverage that does not exist in the employee benefit program. Some executive benefits take the form of intrinsic or psychic income (e.g., a large, well-furnished office).

Short-Term Incentives

Short-term incentives (Chapter 7) are designed to include both downside risk and upside potential, rewarding the extent of accomplishment of a short (normally, yearly) target. Typically, the amount of payment goes up and down each year in relation to performance, thereby lowering costs to the organization when performance is low while providing the executive an opportunity to attain significant rewards for achieving or exceeding objectives. An example of the degree of risk identified in the salary element above is shown in Figure 1-3. The more darkly shaded area represents the short-term incentive opportunity. As risk increases, salary (the lighter shaded area) decreases, but it is more than proportionately replaced by incentive opportunities.

Objectives may be group and/or individual in nature and should be tied to annual business targets in a way that provides clear line-of-sight (i.e., one should not have to look around corners in an attempt to see the connection). Financial results are typically major components of short-term plans. Incentive pay increases as a percentage of salary as salary increases, thereby providing ascending reward opportunities. Some identify this as the *progressivity principle*.

Long-Term Incentives

This element (Chapter 8) is similar to short-term incentives in objective except the performance period is multi-year in nature (typically three to 10 years). Normally, there is no individual performance component in long-term incentives, only some definition of group. The incentive award (which is typically significantly larger than the annual incentive) by definition means the executive has a portion of pay placed "at risk" with degree of attainment of business objectives.

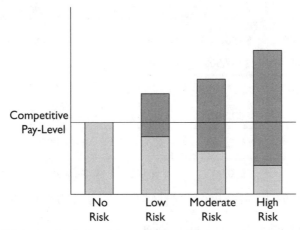

Figure 1-3. Risk/reward relationship to market data

Not meeting the expected target calls for no payment or a low payment—a form of punishment short of termination of employment. The multi-year nature of long-term incentives provides some holding power over the executive if the payout will be significant later on. The progressivity principle defined in short-term incentives also applies here. Pay is typically based on shareholder value and/or financial performance of the defined unit (e.g., company, sector, or division).

Combinations

As depicted in Figure 1-2, but perhaps more clearly in Table 1-4, these elements of compensation take on different emphasis at different pay levels in the organization.

For example, salary might be 75 percent of total compensation at the $100,000 level but only 20 percent at the $5-million level. Conversely, long-term incentives might only be 2 percent at $100,000 total pay but 50 percent at the $5-million level. Table 1-5 converts these percentages to dollars. Thus, at the $500,000 total-pay level, the 40 percent salary shown in Table 1-4 reflects $200,000 as reported in Table 1-5.

Element	Total Compensation				
	$100,000	**$250,000**	**$500,000**	**$1,000,000**	**$5,000,000**
Salary	75.0%	55.0%	40.0%	30.0%	20.0%
Employee Benefits	15.0%	11.0%	8.0%	6.0%	4.0%
Perquisites	——	1.0%	2.0%	4.0%	6.0%
Short-Term Incentives	8.0%	13.0%	16.0%	18.0%	20.0%
Long-Term Incentives	2.0%	20.0%	34.0%	42.0%	50.0%
Total	**100.0%**	**100.0%**	**100.0%**	**100.0%**	**100.0%**

Table 1-4. Possible compensation distribution (total pay = 100%)

	Total Compensation				
Element	**$100,000**	**$250,000**	**$500,000**	**$1,000,000**	**$5,000,000**
Salary	$75,000	$137,500	$200,000	$300,000	$1,000,000
Employee Benefits	$15,000	$27,500	$40,000	$60,000	$200,000
Perquisites	—	$2,500	$10,000	$40,000	$300,000
Short-Term Incentives	$8,000	$32,500	$80,000	$180,000	$1,000,000
Long-Term Incentives	$2,000	$50,000	$170,000	$420,000	$2,500,000
Total	**$100,000**	**$250,000**	**$500,000**	**$1,000,000**	**$5,000,000**

Table 1-5. Possible compensation distribution in dollars

At higher levels of total compensation, decreasing emphasis is applied to salary and benefits, whereas an increasing emphasis is given to short-term incentives, long-term incentives, and perquisites. The reason for the decreasing emphasis on salary at the expense of short- and long-term incentives is that it is more advantageous to the company to relate reward to performance, and, in some cases, it is more advantageous to the individual to receive the reward in a form other than cash.

The limitations imposed in many benefit plans (e.g., maximum pension) and the non-income-related programs (e.g., medical and dental insurance) account for the decrease in benefits as a percentage of total compensation as that figure grows. In many situations, however, this decrease is offset by perquisites (e.g., chauffeured car, financial counseling, and supplementary pensions).

One further variation of the relationship is shown in Table 1-6. There all elements are expressed as a percentage of salary.

Employee benefits are often expressed as a percentage of salary; however, this is frequently

	Total Compensation				
Element	**$100,000**	**$250,000**	**$500,000**	**$1,000,000**	**$5,000,000**
Salary	100%	100%	100%	100%	100%
Employee Benefits	20.0%	20.0%	20.0%	20.0%	20.0%
Perquisites	—	1.8%	5.0%	13.3%	30.0%
Short-Term Incentives	10.7%	23.6%	40.0%	60.0%	100.0%
Long-Term Incentives	2.7%	36.4%	85.0%	140.0%	250.0%
Total	**133.4%**	**181.8%**	**250%**	**333.3%**	**500%**

Table 1-6. Percentage relationship of elements to salary

misleading, especially at the executive level. This is because short-term incentives are often included in the definition of pay for determining benefit coverage. This point is illustrated in Table 1-7 where employee benefits as a percentage of salary is constant as pay increases, but when expressed as percentage of salary plus short-term incentives, it declines. However, when perquisites are added to benefits, the downward trend is reversed. In this example, there is a very heavy emphasis on the perquisite, or executive benefit package.

The relative importance of each element at the different income levels would, of course, vary from industry to industry and even within a given industry from company to company. It will also be different for privately held companies and non-profits.

Element	Total Compensation				
	$100,000	**$250,000**	**$500,000**	**$1,000,000**	**$5,000,000**
Salary	$75,000	$137,500	$200,000	$300,000	$1,000,000
Short-Term Incentives	$8,000	$32,500	$80,000	$180,000	$1,000,000
Total	$83,000	$170,000	$280,000	$480,000	$2,000,000
Employee Benefits	$15,000	$27,500	$40,000	$60,000	$200,000
% of Total	18.1%	16.2%	14.3%	12.5%	10.0%
% of Salary	20.0%	20.0%	20.0%	20.0%	20.0%
Benefits and Perquisites	$15,000	$30,000	$50,000	$100,000	$500,000
% of Total	18.1%	17.6%	17.9%	20.8%	25.0%
% of Salary	20.0%	21.8%	25.0%	33.3%	50.0%

Table 1-7. Employee benefits in relation to salary and short-term incentives

DESIGN CONSIDERATIONS

Having defined *executive* and described *compensation,* let's identify the factors that impact the design of the pay program. Design considerations are covered in significant detail in Chapter 9 but it is important to highlight some of the basic factors at this point. They are illustrated in Figure 1-4. First, we have the *stakeholders.* They consist of the executive, other employees, shareholders, customers, suppliers, and the community. Within the community are the *rule-makers,* who limit the design and amount of pay. In the United States, at the federal level, they are Congress, the IRS, the SEC, and the Financial Accounting Standards Board (FASB). The stakeholders and rulemakers are covered in some detail in Chapter 4. A subset of the shareholders is the Board of Directors (and its Compensation Committee); they are not only expected to be shareholders but also to act on behalf of the shareholders. The Board and the Compensation Committee are discussed in Chapter 10.

We have already highlighted the five compensation elements indicating where they will be reviewed in more detail: salary (Chapter 5), employee benefits and perquisites (Chapter 6), short-term incentives (Chapter 7), and long-term incentives (Chapter 8). The performance

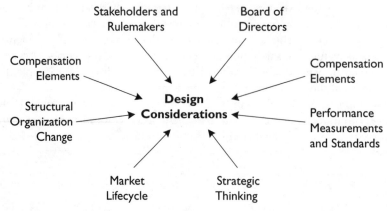

Figure 1-4. Design considerations

measurements that can be used in the design of the executive pay program are also reviewed (Chapter 2). Also included is a write-up on current vs. deferred compensation (Chapter 3).

That leaves us to review strategic thinking, market lifecycle, organizational structure change, and type of company, which together form the basis for new design considerations (Chapter 9).

STRATEGIC THINKING

In this rapidly changing world where technological advances are coming faster than some can absorb and customer needs are ever changing, it is difficult to believe that *strategic planning* (looking ahead five to 10 years) can be anything more than an interesting exercise resulting in a beautiful book that will have little resemblance to what actually unfolds.

That does not mean companies should sit back, watch things happen, and hope to make the right decisions. Companies must engage in *strategic thinking*, always looking to the direction and rate of change. In doing so, a company must decide if it wishes to be a pacesetter or one that capitalizes on established changes. The first probably emphasizes product innovation. The second looks to operational effectiveness and customer identification. The steps in the process are shown in Figure 1-5.

The Vision

Although sometimes belittled, many are successful because they start with a dream. It is analogous to the child who determines what he or she wants to be when he or she grows up. This is the *vision* or description of the desired future of the organization. Perhaps the company's vision is "to thrive on exceeding our customer communication needs." To the extent this comes after pertinent input, it enhances the probability of relevance. Saying at the age of seven that you want to be a doctor—unaware of the requirements—is a lot different than if a few years later, after having talked with a doctor, you still want to become such a professional.

The Mission

Since there is a recognizable gap between the now and the vision, the *journey* needs to be described. This is the *mission*, or how one achieves the vision. Building on the above described

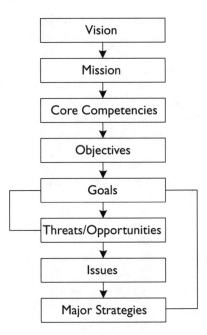

Figure 1-5. Strategic thinking process

vision, perhaps the mission is "to earn the trust every day of thousands of new customers while retaining the trust of existing customers, never having lost one because of violated trust."

Core Competencies

Core competencies are the things a company is very good at doing. They must align with the mission and vision. If not, either the vision and mission must be altered to conform to core competencies or the latter must be changed to enable achievement of the mission and vision. Obviously, it is much easier to do the former than the latter, i.e., to develop a business plan.

Companies sometimes stray from focusing on core competencies and seek to diversify their investments and/or capitalize on perceived resulting synergies. However, investors often do not concur with this boardroom logic—if they want to construct a diversified portfolio, they will do it by selecting an appropriate mix of companies themselves. Companies that attempt to replicate a diversified portfolio within their organizational structure may find that the composite is worth less than the sum of its parts. The result has been companies selling off non-core businesses and returning to focus on what they do best. By being the best in their industry segment, they hope to be the selection of every investor who wishes to put money in that market sector.

However, even companies apparently in the same sector are often significantly different. For example, in the insurance sector, property and casualty companies require large amounts of capital to respond to natural catastrophes whereas life insurance companies must balance a lump sum payment protection of dying too soon vs. an annuity payment of living too long.

Objectives and Goals

The mission is further refined in terms of qualitative targets, or *objectives*. The objectives are broken down into quantitative targets, or *goals*. An example of an objective might be "to bring to market products that enhance the customer's quality of life." A goal that might relate to this objective could be "to introduce product 'A' in all of North America by the second quarter next year and in the European community by the first quarter of the following year at a price recapturing cost and return on investment within three years." Some reverse the terms, calling the goals the qualitative and the objectives the quantitative. For this reason, confusion sometimes exists when talking to someone from another company. Hopefully, there are no such confusions within the company. Defined goals and objectives could also be identified as *critical success factors* (CSF). Performance standards tied to these CSFs must be put in place with a measurement basis if a pay delivery system is to be a reinforcement of desired outcome. The performance measurements are reviewed in Chapter 2 and should be tied closely to the *core competencies* so critical to success.

Threats and Opportunities

Goals may be easier or more difficult to attain based on perceived *threats* and *opportunities* identified by an environment scan of not only what is happening, but what is likely to occur.

Let's highlight examples of the type of information one would examine to determine the presence of eight kinds of threats and opportunities as shown in Table 1-8.

	Threats and Opportunities	
	External	**Internal**
Economy	A	B
Business	C	D
Law	E	F
Culture	G	H

Table 1-8. Scan for threats and opportunities

Economy. External economic (A) factors would include *population*, both customer and workforce. The size and financial ability of the customer base is critical to the organization's success in selling its products and services. The size, composition, and education of the workforce has an impact on the ability of the organization to meet its internal, core-competency staffing needs (B). Are needed skills available or in short supply? Are recruiting pay premiums needed? An internal assessment of skill base of employees is a related matter, along with the ability to retain key talent. *Capital* is another key external factor. What is the availability of either borrowing or equity financing? What are short- and long-term interest rates? Is the publicly traded stock market in a *bull market* (increasing stock prices) or *bear market* (falling stock prices) cycle? Internally, what is the company's cash flow ability to meet its needs?

Business. An external scan (C) would define market size for current and future products and major competitors. Internally (D), the focus will be the ability to meet customer requirements of quality, availability, and price.

Law. A look to the outside also examines what is present and likely to happen with *legal* requirements (E) imposed on the organization. Legislation, regulation, and litigation are more prevalent in some parts of the world than others. In addition to state and federal laws, a number of alphabet soup organizations dramatically affect how an organization will do business. In the U.S., they include the EEOC, EPA, FASB, IRS, and SEC, to name a few. Internally (F), the organization has to determine what it needs to meet these requirements and prescribe a code of conduct.

Culture. An external look (G) examines the type of society present. Depending on the country, it ranges from autocratic to democratic to socialistic. The type of government and its stability is a key consideration in determining whether or not to enter that market and, if so, at what pace. What are the mores and values of the society in question? How do they relate to the organization's products and services? An internal review (H) should focus on the company's culture.

What is company culture? The organization's *culture* is the composite of values and beliefs that it considers core to its existence. It is the way it does business. It is the way it treats people. Companies operating in different countries must be careful not to export a country-of-origin culture. While it is important to hold on to core values, it is also important to adapt to the local culture within a universal code of conduct. As shown in Table 1-9, these values can be expressed in both *hard* and *soft* terms, internally and externally. It is obviously more difficult to measure the qualitative (soft) than the quantitative (hard).

Where Found	Measurements	
	Hard	**Soft**
Internal	Operating Income Net Income Revenue	Talent Depth Talent Ability Employee Satisfaction
External	Stock Price Market Share Peer Performance	Talent Availability Customer Satisfaction

Table 1-9. Measurements of the organization

To ensure conformance, company culture rewards compliance and penalizes shortfalls. Thus, it is not simply results, but also the process and behaviors that are important. The compensation system is one of the most powerful vehicles for reinforcing desired values.

To illustrate, assume customer satisfaction is considered to be a key desired value. First, we need to identify *who* the customers are and *what* they want. Following this, the focus might be on continuous improvement, while the drivers of change might be price, quality, service, and timely delivery. It would be difficult to be successful with a pay program emphasizing salary and benefits. Rather, an annual incentive plan focused on decreasing costs, response time, and returns, or a long-term incentive plan based on increasing market share, would be more logical.

Culture clash is a major reason why acquisitions and mergers (M&As) that appear so logical, nonetheless, fail. Imagine reconciling the differences between a culture that considers its employees to be assets, spending considerable time and expense to optimize their growth and development, with another that views them as expenses, frequently terminating their services through periodic downsizings to improve the earnings statement. Similarly, there is a distinct

Element	Importance	
	Egalitarian	Distinctive
Salary	Low	Moderate
Employee Benefits	High	Low
Short-Term Incentives	Moderate	High
Long-Term Incentives	Moderate	High
Perquisites	Low	High

Table 1-10. Cultural differences in pay elements

difference in the importance of the pay element in an egalitarian vs. a *distinctive*, or class system, as highlighted in Table 1-10.

A *performance-driven* culture would be similar to a *distinctive* one except that perquisites would be dropped to a low importance. Hence, rewards are differentiated in a meaningful manner because a good assessment system with meaningful metrics is tied to demanding standards, not to organization level.

Culture can also be defined in terms of rewarding risk vs. compliance, creativity vs. conformity, and values vs. results. Therefore, it is critical to define the current culture and determine whether to maintain or change it. Namely, is it consistent with the vision and mission? A highly regulated culture that penalizes failure would have a difficult time succeeding if product innovation were key to success. If changed, the direction and degree of change must be clearly articulated. How does the organization differentiate itself from its competitors? How is work organized? How is the organization structured? How are employees treated? How are resources allocated? What gets communicated and how? Are these consistent across organizational units? What is the *line of sight* between individual and group objectives and goals?

Is it surprising that a pay plan that may be very successful in one organization would be a failure in another? Of course not, if they had different cultures. Company culture is a major factor in designing pay delivery systems since it reinforces desired behavior and outcomes.

Another way of looking at how these various components come together is shown in Figure 1-6. Degree of success is shown on the "Y" axis and time on the "X" axis. Starting with where a company is now, compare it to its vision of the future. The difference is addressed by the mission, or how to achieve the vision. Having assessed the threats and opportunities along the way, the company has developed a major business strategy with supporting objectives and goals. The next step is to operationalize the process.

Strategies

The word *strategy* is derived from the Greek word "strategos" which means commander or general, the one who decides on action taken to defeat one's enemies. It is a fitting meaning in the business world. Business strategies capitalizing on threats and/or opportunities to achieve goals and objectives would include: product additions and deletions; centralization vs. decentralization; acquisitions and divestitures; quality and process positioning; and expansion and downsizing. However, these strategies are subsets of an overall major business strategy. As shown in

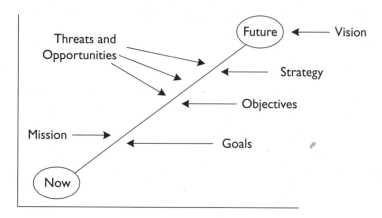

Figure 1-6. Strategic thinking illustration

Figure 1-7, there are six different types of strategies, each focused on one of the earlier described stakeholders. They are:

- **Product/Service Innovation** focuses on creating new markets with new or existing products/services.
- **Employee Intimacy** focuses on an Employer of Choice objective, creating a work environment where individuals want to come to work and to give their best efforts.
- **Customer Satisfaction** means providing reliable products/services at prices the customer considers excellent value. The emphasis is both on getting new customers and getting existing customers to buy more.
- **Shareholder Return** means increased dividends and rising stock prices to create shareholder wealth.
- **Operational Optimization** focuses on productivity (cost, quantity, and quality).
- **Community Partnership** means providing plenty of good paying jobs and not contaminating the environment.

Most companies engage in at least several of these business strategies. In designing an executive incentive plan, it is important to prioritize and weight their respective importance, recognizing that some are more in conflict than complementary—a fact that will become obvious

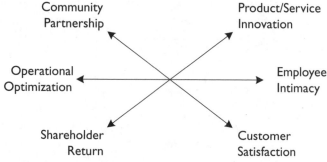

Figure 1-7. Strategy focus

later in the book when reviewing design of incentive plans.

It can be argued that the flow chart for business success often begins with a product or service followed by a review of potential market and customers. Prototypes are then tested and refined. This is illustrated in Figure 1-8.

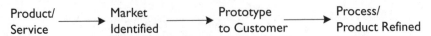

Figure 1-8. Product seeking a customer model

Figure 1-9 illustrates how major business strategies can support desired outcomes resulting from market analysis.

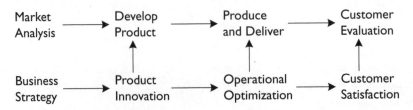

Figure 1-9. Business strategies supporting major actions

Aids to product planning can be developed based on market and financial factors. A simple version of this is shown in Figure 1-10. The two criteria are "dollar return" and "market performance."

Obviously, the grid could be more refined; however, even this simple version shows where a combination calls for certain actions:

- **Combination A:** This ideal situation is a prime candidate for additional investment, assuming industry is in the threshold or growth stage.
- **Combination B:** Investment needs are directed to improving strength of market per-

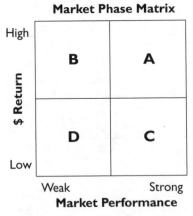

Figure 1-10. Market phase—dollar return vs. market performance

formance. However, this must be assessed in terms of probable success; investment without improved market performance may turn this into a D combination.

- **Combination C:** Probably not likely to be a candidate for additional investment, this situation could provide a source of capital for other projects.
- **Combination D:** This is a prime candidate to be deleted; continuation is based on the extent to which deletion would adversely affect the product line (and/or currently absorbed, overhead charges) and lower other products to C or D combinations.

This type of analysis is very helpful since it places each product in perspective as well as showing where new products are needed and what to do with the current product line. Suffice it to say that from these reviews, issues will be identified and strategies described on how to overcome the obstacle or maximize opportunities to achieve the goal.

The relationship between objectives and goals and the executive compensation program, especially incentives, must be clear and understood by all stakeholders. Naysayers claim that pay for performance would do nothing to motivate employees to work any harder. They are already going "full speed." This is probably true. Pay for performance would do little to increase their efforts, but it will do a lot to *focus* their efforts. It will reward them for achieving their goals and penalize them (by withholding pay) for not achieving them. Pay for performance is not about working harder—it is about working smarter.

Typically, companies will select one business strategy as their dominant theme with another as a supporting strategy. What one does to excel is the business strategy. How one excels in this strategy is based on the organization's core competencies.

It is critical that an organization have core competencies that support its intended strategy. Operational optimization will require strengths in producing products and services; product/service innovation will require strengths in research and development; and customer satisfaction requires strong sales and marketing competencies. It is easy to see the difficulty in shifting from one strategy to another because of the changes required in developing new core competencies. Only by linking the organization's core competencies with an appropriate strategy does the organization have a chance at achieving a sustainable competitive advantage.

Companies typically start out with a single product or service. Only over time do they expand their base. Often this is done without clearly defining their strengths. As a result, the market may penalize their stock value. As organizations seek new products and/or markets, it is critical they be consistent with core competencies and strategies. If not, one or the other must be changed. Constant discipline and communication is essential. New products, services, and competitors require a review of business strategy to ensure optimal targeting.

Downsizing may produce financial savings; however, sustained growth requires increasing the capital- and employee-resource base while also increasing the productivity of both. Companies that have focused on downsizing may have weakened their effectiveness. Reduced labor costs may improve the income statement, but is the company able to maintain, much less expand, its market share? Has cost cutting positioned the company for sustained productivity enhancement, or is it simply making do with less? Is sufficient investment being made in research and the development of intellectual capital? It is difficult to grow to greatness from a shrinking base.

Annual Planning Process

An example of a schedule that might be employed in a planning and review process is found in

January	Previous year's business plan results: i.e., strategies, objectives and goal(s) completed
February	Business and support staff complete scan of internal and external issues identifying those pertinent to the organization
March	Issues are prioritized and responsibility for each assigned along with review of compensation objectives
April	Drafts of next year's business plan including strategies, objectives, and goals are prepared and compensation objectives updated
May	Vision and mission statements reviewed and modified if necessary, as is the proportionate balance of the five compensation elements
June	Drafts are reviewed by appropriate parties and a draft of a modified pay plan is prepared
July	Mid year review of current year business and compensation plans completed
August	Modifications to next year's business and compensation plans completed
September	Final reviews of both plans completed
October	Plans submitted to Management Committee for review
November	Committee review completed
December	Modifications incorporated and approved by Board of Directors with both plans communicated

Table 1-11. Annual planning and review process

Table 1-11. As one can see, it is a never-ending loop. The one shown is annual. It could be condensed into a fraction of that time.

Although the strategic thinking process is critical in positioning the design of an executive compensation program, it is not sufficient. Where the company is in its market cycle must also be determined.

MARKET LIFECYCLE IMPACT

There are four stages in the market lifecycle: threshold, growth, maturity, and decline. They are shown in Figure 1-11.

The market cycle for a company is simply a consolidation of its products and where they are in their respective market cycles. By the same logic, a company and/or industry can be described by stage of lifecycle. Recognize that a product could be in the growth phase while the market for such products is in decline. Shown in Table 1-12 are the 16 possible combinations of a product's lifecycle vs. the lifecycle of the market for the product. Indicated for each combination are possible actions.

By aggregating the products for a company particular to an industry, one can come up with a similar analysis. Contrast a company in the growth phase but in a declining industry with one in a maturity phase in a growth market. The first will quickly find itself in maturity or even decline unless it grows faster than the market declines. The other company finds that its revenues are increasing simply by retaining market share in a dramatically increased market.

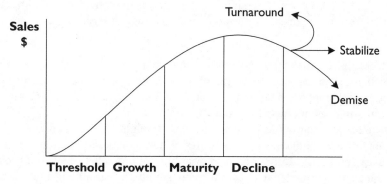

Figure 1-11. Four-stage market cycle

However, mergers, acquisitions, and divestitures can significantly alter where the organization is positioned on the market lifecycle, as will be reviewed later in this chapter.

Given the difference between company and industry in terms of stage in market cycle, more emphasis should be placed on industry. Thus, if the company is in the maturity phase while the industry is in the growth stage, the latter should be the primary reference since the company should be able to realize new crests (due to established market position) as the industry reaches maturity. Conversely, if the company is in the growth stage and the industry in the maturity phase, it will be more difficult for the company to improve its current level of success.

An organization often consists of strategic business units (SBUs) in different stages of the market lifecycle. Thus, while the company may be categorized as the composite of its SBUs, it is important to remember each has different characteristics and needs and should not be smothered by an overarching corporate pay plan not in sync with different market stages. This argues for both corporate and SBU pay plans. Each needs to be reviewed annually and quickly adjusted as necessary. Ongoing review is likely to result in minor modification, reducing the likeli-

Market for Product	Company Action			
Decline	Why bother?	Watch margins	Milk it	Milk it
Maturity	Look elsewhere	Increase market share	Look for the second wave	Milk it
Growth	Invest heavily	Stay the course	Increase market share	Hold market share
Threshold	Risky	Invest cautiously	Maintain position	Look for change
Company Product Lifecycle Stage	**Threshold**	**Growth**	**Maturity**	**Decline**

Table 1-12. Product vs. market cycle position

hood of radical changes necessitated by ignoring the plan for too long. Let's examine the characteristics of each stage in the market cycle and what they suggest regarding programs.

Threshold

During this stage, the company probably has a limited range of closely related products. Distribution of these products may be primarily in a regional area; the company may have attained a position of dominance in a small industry; sales are probably under $50 million; and managers are exploring new markets for products.

Decisions are made by individuals, often with little thought or delay and usually on intuition, as there are few, if any, policies and procedures. Written job descriptions and organization charts do not exist and relative duties and responsibilities of individuals have not been clearly identified. A high degree of overlap in apparent responsibilities exists among a number of jobs. There is no depth of management.

The tone is casual with everyone on a first-name basis, and the dress code emphasizes comfort rather than appearance. Survival of the products has the full attention of everyone. Cash is scarce and cash-flow problems periodically occur, with management often deferring its own salary payments to ease the crunch. It is a time of high risk in order to survive. Increased sales and sufficient cash flow to meet needs are key.

Growth

This phase marks the period of tremendous growth as the threshold company emerges with strong success in new venture areas as well as becoming a national influence by challenging established leaders in market share. An increase in product lines probably has increased the diversity and complexity of related management processes. The number of employees increases along with sales, and management may shift from the original owners into the hands of professional managers, as the company must cope with different problems brought on by apparent success. Coordination needs are greater and communication more formalized to ensure consistent interpretation; relative priorities need major review to ensure optimal success. Return on shareholder equity is very strong and increasing significantly during this phase.

During this period, the company is likely to state its nature of business too broadly, venturing into product lines for which it lacks expertise. This often results in a level of performance far short of expectations; however, success in main lines overcompensates.

Cash and available time both seem to be in short supply as full energy is directed to maximizing product success and reinvesting in the business. Little time exists for formalizing job descriptions, although individual responsibilities are better understood as greater specialization is required. Written policies and procedures start to emerge. The depth of management is very thin; however, some replacements and new positions can be staffed internally by juggling. Decision-making has become more formalized (and therefore slower) and alternatives are viewed in light of precedents set during the threshold stage. White shirts, rolled up at the sleeves, have replaced sport shirts; however, the tone is still informal and essentially on a first-name basis.

To stay in the growth phase, the company must continually find new uses for existing products and/or introduce new products. This requires a careful analysis of available capital for manufacturing and marketing to optimize return on investment.

Maturity

This phase is marked by little change in market position (some slippage may be offset by new products—mainly interpolation or minor extrapolation of existing products rather than new breakthroughs). Emphasis is probably on maintaining current market penetration and servicing existing customers rather than adding new customers. Market share is more likely to gain by lowering prices than by increasing investment. Administrative expenses become an increasing percentage of total costs as productivity improvements chip away at direct expenses. However, staff functions are increasing faster than the reductions in direct labor. Reducing costs is important, especially if sales revenues have flattened out; however, cash flow (because of various deductions) may be stronger than ever.

Job descriptions and organization charts have appeared, as have management succession charts to ensure adequate depth of management to meet organization needs. Corporate policies have been written to cover the full gambit of business issues, and an extensive financial record-keeping system has been developed. Managers find their freedom to act restrained by both. Due to policy limitations or dollar ceilings, the manager must now recommend, rather than decide. Such recommendations require considerable time to prepare and justify. Committees have become popular during this phase and are often part of the decision-making process, resulting in both a slowdown of this process and a diffusing of individual responsibility. Transactional rather than transformational behavior is dominant.

Companies in a mature stage often undergo a "consolidation" whereby they trim their management ranks and narrow their marketing focus. Usually, the latter is focused on their high-profit product lines in a more concentrated area. Product areas where the company sees little hope for increasing low profit margins are abandoned or spun off. Many conglomerates in the mature stage return to the businesses in which they have excelled. Others expand in acquired business lines. The need to develop new products or find new markets for existing products has surfaced. Productivity improvements are critical, especially those lowering costs; however, in some situations cash flow is aided by depreciation write-offs.

Decline

This phase is the period during which market share is falling and/or the market itself is disappearing due to technological obsolescence. Cost-improvement programs take on strong importance, many times in the form of amputation of unprofitable operations. The need to develop new products or find new markets for existing products is now critical. The focus is on survival.

Procedural manuals exist on almost every topic, specifying the preparation of forms to get approval on everything from a dozen pencils to a multi-million-dollar capital investment. Form has become more important than substance. Commitment to the process has replaced commitment to results. Bureaucracy rules.

The organization is more formal in tone than in earlier phases, and first names are rarely used, regardless of how well known the person. Individuals are oblique and obtuse in their statements, and the manner of presentation has become more important than the substance. Although the *Titanic* is listing badly, some crew members are methodically rearranging the deck chairs, oblivious to the fact that the ship is sinking! Putter clutter rules!

Embedded costs are high but, paradoxically, cash is more likely to be available during this phase than most others, due to cutbacks in research and marketing expenses or the sale of part of the business. In capital-intensive companies the strong cash position could be the result of depreciation allowances that have not been reinvested in newer equipment. Also, the book value of the stock may very well exceed its market value. Or even more dramatically, net working capital (assets less all liabilities including preferred stock) may exceed the aggregate market value for the company's common stock.

In this stage, many companies will be forced to diversify simply by nature of their product line. Mining, oil, and gas companies facing a dwindling natural resource must look to supplementary business lines. The projected exhaustion point can be set back by new discoveries, but they delay, rather than alter, the inevitable results. For some, this will mean other forms of geological exploration (such as minerals); for others, it will mean entering businesses where its products are an essential part of business (such as chemicals). Others may reach outside of the related business worlds and enter a completely new field. The decision to leave the energy business may not be related to demand, but rather to supply.

The problem with food companies is the reverse one of leveling demand in many countries (related to population). Here the desire to diversify within the field leads some to different, higher-profit product lines or alternative preparations (such as fast-food outlets). For others, vertical expansion to include growing, breeding, and shipping may be a more logical approach.

To avoid taking the company into oblivion, the CEO and board of directors are looking to "catch a wave" as the surfers would say. They are looking for a market coming out of the first stage and beginning to explode in growth. By moving to an industry in this early stage, the company is able to reinvent itself by applying its expertise, shifting itself back to a growth phase. Sometimes the industry will do it by itself. Some argued years back that the pharmaceutical industry was in the maturity phase. There were no product breakthroughs remaining. Talk about being wrong! An explosion of new novel products repositioned the industry back into the growth stage.

Ideally, the time to make this retro move is while in the late stage of growth or early maturity. It is far riskier to wait until decline sets in, not only because revenues are declining (although cash flow may be increasing), but because the organization is becoming more rigid and less able to respond to a dramatic shift. This is a time when CEOs and other senior executives are most at risk as their board of directors may think them incapable of making the daring but necessary move for survival. They have been part of the problem rather than part of the solution. Failure to anticipate and act would be an indication of poor strategic thinking.

Turnaround, Sale, or Demise

The decline phase leads to one of three positions: turnaround, sale, or demise. *Turnaround* is clearly the more attractive alternative. It is intended to reposition the organization to an earlier stage, preferably growth, and could begin earlier (e.g., in the maturity phase). *Sale* is when the organization believes a turnaround to be unlikely, and begins the search for a buyer before the situation gets worse. This is often done under the guise of "exploring strategic alternatives"— most believe this means the company is looking to sellout. Efforts will be made to reduce costs in an attempt to make the business more attractive to a buyer—dressing it up for sale. *Demise* means the company has been unsuccessful with the other two alternatives, or may not have even had the foresight to attempt them, and goes out of business, resulting in a bankruptcy Chapter 7 liquidation. If the company believes it can work its way back, it may go into a Chapter

11 reorganization, holding back the creditors as it tries to return to a profitable state.

There are many possible explanations for a company moving into a decline phase. They may be internal, external, or both. Internal factors would include poor management decisions, rising costs and declining prices, and a non-productive workforce. External factors might include new competitors, new technology, declining markets, and/or a redefined market. Overnight carrier service companies soon learned that the fax machine would redefine the movement of hard copy. This market in turn was redefined by e-mail.

To prevent demise, the organization must cut expenses. This includes: shutting facilities, terminating employees, and writing-off non-productive assets. Fixed costs such as salaries and benefits are reduced where possible but, at the minimum, are frozen. Salary increases are replaced by variable pay plans with upside potential and downside risk. Substantial investments in company stock may be required of executives to reinforce the company's commitment to survival. It must then return to its core competencies (it probably does not have enough time to develop new ones), identifying products and markets that will help it to a brighter future. Time is of the essence but the business must be viable: buggy whips, 33 rpm records, and manual typewriters would be difficult businesses to turn around.

Combination Lifecycles

Because companies have SBUs that may be in different stages of the lifecycle, programs must be customized to reflect those differences. Programs should also reflect not only current stages, but the future the company is positioning towards. Because of the fluidity of changing events and resulting strategies, it is critical to continually review the composition of a pay program to ensure it is consistent with objectives.

Changes in Lifecycle Stages

In any of the four stages, there are five possible events: remain, advance, sellout, turnaround, and bankruptcy. These are illustrated in Table 1-13 along with probability values. The latter are best viewed not in absolute terms but relative to each other. For example, in the threshold stage, bankruptcy is probably the most likely occurrence—a large percentage of start-ups fail. Advancing (or selling out to someone else) is probably more likely to occur in the threshold stage than remaining put.

Action	Probability of Action			
	Threshold	**Growth**	**Maturity**	**Decline**
Remain	Low	Low	Low	Low
Advance	Moderate	High	High	None
Sellout	Moderate	Low	Moderate	High
Turnaround	—	Low	Moderate	Moderate
Bankruptcy	High	Low	Moderate	High

Table 1-13. Action probabilities in various market lifecycles

Company Size

While companies tend to grow larger as they move from threshold to later stages of development, that does not mean all companies become large. Some will remain small, others will become only moderate in size. One way to categorize company size is by sales (revenue); another way is by size of market capitalization. Regardless, while there would be differences in emphasis on each of the five pay elements based on absolute size of the company, differences are more likely to be influenced by stage in the market cycle. However, there are ways to dramatically increase or decrease a company's size. These will be reviewed next.

ORGANIZATIONAL STRUCTURE CHANGE

Virtually all companies begin as startups with the founders financing the capital needs of the company by taking out loans and mortgages as necessary. The next stage is when venture capitalists are willing to put up money for an equity position in the company. By now, the founders have given themselves large stock-option grants, hoping for a run-up in price when the stock goes public. However, these stocks can not be sold for a stated period of time after an initial public offering (IPO)—typically 180 days. This is called a *lock-up period*. Later, a company may decide to acquire or merge with another company, or it may want to divest all or a portion of its business. These phases are listed in Table 1-14. All have executive pay implications.

Initial Public Offering

If the company decides to undertake an *initial public offering*, it must first select an underwriter. Typically, this is done after reviewing proposals from interested candidates. The selected underwriter analyzes the firm's financial data, comparing them with rivals, to set a preliminary value for the company. This leads to setting a preliminary stock price. After the company agrees with the initial price range, meetings are set up with institutional investors to get an indication of interest. Typically, this is a grueling several weeks of cross-country (perhaps cross continent) travel with several meetings a day with various fund managers. This travel, usually called a "road show," is set up only after long hours of polishing the presentation and preparing responses to anticipated questions.

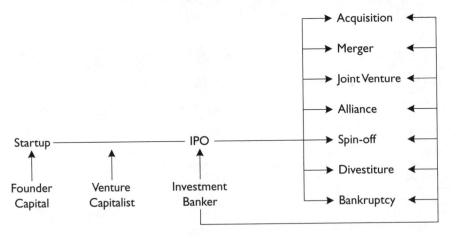

Table 1-14. Structural change of an organization

Based on this information, the underwriter sets the final IPO stock price the day before trading is to begin. Setting the IPO price is important—too high and investors are turned off, too low and the company is losing money. The lowest offering price acceptable to the IPO company is typically called a *collar*. A *prospectus*, filled with financial data as well as special risks and how the company intends on using the money, is prepared for filing with the SEC. A draft prospectus preliminary to the actual offering is called a *red herring* (because of the red ink on the top of the page). An agreement with underwriters that they can buy up to a specified percentage more of company stock during the first month of trading is referred to as a *green shoe*. When shares begin trading, they often do so at a premium to the initial offering price. Essentially, this is the result of an imbalance, namely, there are more buyers than sellers on the first day. It is not uncommon to see a 50 percent gain in the stock price on the day of the IPO. Those interested in a quick profit *flip* (or sell) their shares. For some companies, the rapid rise is a short-run phenomenon as sellers begin to outnumber buyers. If this happens during the *lock-up period* when insiders cannot sell their stock, they see their profits disappear. A small gain in the stock price of a failing company is sometimes called a *dead cat bounce* (with apologies to animal rightists).

For their work, investment bankers will probably get about 7 percent of the IPO proceeds, with the lead underwriter getting about half of that amount. The lead underwriter not only sells the greatest number of shares but also arranges the deal and prices the stock. The higher the price, the more money the company and underwriter make. Secondary offerings in later years because of the need for more capital can also generate underwriting activity.

An IPO of a self-standing company typically occurs during the threshold stage whereas an IPO from a parent organization is typically done in the latter part of the growth stage or in maturity. After the IPO is completed, it is important that the company increase revenues so it can reinvest in the business. Some companies attempt this solely by internal actions, often called *organic growth*. Others look externally for ways to expand the scope of their business, namely, through mergers and acquisitions.

Mergers and Acquisitions

A merger is the joining together of two companies to form a new organization. Typically, these companies are of comparable size and a new stock is created, whereas with an acquisition, one company clearly buys out the other. Acquisitions are easier to finance if the acquirer's stock has been on the ascent and the stock of the company being acquired has been dropping. However, the latter is likely to be quickly reversed by speculative investors. Until mid-2001, wherever possible, pooling-of-interest accounting was attempted. This meant both income statement and balance sheets were combined, unless the acquisition was deemed to be performing poorly, then the asset had to be written down because of an impaired value. However, to qualify for pooling, companies are required to use their common stock (not cash) for the acquisition and are limited for two years in stock buybacks and selling acquired company assets. Under *purchase accounting*, the acquired company's assets are written up to reflect current market value. The increase over book value of the acquired company is considered *goodwill* and must be amortized, thereby diluting earnings. In accord with Accounting Principles Board 16 "Conditions of Pooling of Interest Methods of Accounting for Combination," pooling rules must be used if they apply. If not, purchase accounting must be used and the difference between purchase price and net assets amortized or written off over a 40-year period. However, that changed in 2001 when FASB eliminated pooling but gave some relief on the treatment of resulting goodwill.

Companies planning mergers or acquisitions would look to investment bankers to structure the deal. In return, the bankers would likely receive fees ranging from 0.5 percent to 1.5 percent, depending on size, with the highest fees going for the smaller deal. An offer to buy a company that is not welcomed is called an *unfriendly takeover* by a *black knight*. If another organization considered more attractive by the company being pursued enters the scene, it is sometimes referred to as a *white knight* (charging to rescue the fair maiden). The takeover could be by a company or by venture capitalists who see the breakup value of the company exceeding its market price.

During discussions, both sides typically sign *confidentiality agreements* to prevent the other from using confidential information should the talks fail, as many do. However, even with enforcement of these agreements, companies gain a better understanding of their own competitive strengths and weaknesses.

M&As could occur in any stage of the market lifecycle although the later rather than the earlier stages are more likely. The key issue is which is better—to build, or to buy? Among the considerations are: key product portfolios, research and development opportunities, time to market improvements, cost-reduction opportunities, management depth, culture, and the expected rate of return on capital before and after the merger or acquisition. Is the focus on cost reduction or revenue growth? Diversification by customer, products, and/or geography may also be factors.

In a merger, it may be appropriate to design new pay programs; with an acquisition, the issue is whether to bring employees into the acquirer's programs or permit them to continue with their current plans. Whether an acquisition or merger, stock options will be recast based on the stock prices of the two companies before they were combined. Executives in both probably have employment contracts specifying severance agreements.

At some stage in the market lifecycle, typically maturity, although it could be earlier or later, the company looks to shed certain businesses, typically, because they do not fit with core competencies. This divestiture is either done through a sale to another company or a spinoff to the company shareholders.

Joint Ventures and Alliances

A *joint venture* is when two companies form a third, either with each owning half or with one having a majority stake. An *alliance* is a formal agreement between companies on respective responsibility without forming a new company.

When two companies have different complementary strengths (e.g., one has a strong research portfolio and the other manufacturing capabilities), it may be appropriate to set up a joint venture or JV. The new organization is staffed with individuals from both organizations and one of the requirements will be to set up an executive compensation program. Coming to agreement may be difficult, especially if the partners have equal votes and different views. Another problem to be addressed is what happens to the pay plans when the JV is dissolved (as most eventually are). Exit strategies should be agreed upon at time of formation, not at time of dissolution.

An alliance is a contractual agreement specifying respective responsibilities over a period of time without forming a new company. They are formed to either increase revenue and/or reduce costs. For example, a company recognized for its marketing excellence might be approached by another with a new product and reluctant to take the time and expense to expand its own sales force. Assuming the marketing leader has the available resources and the commission arrangement is attractive, a co-marketing alliance will be formed. Similarly, a company may choose to form an alliance with a research organization rather than expand its own research capabilities. In return for the investment, the investor will have rights of first refusal on marketing any discoveries through an agreed-upon royalty arrangement.

Alliances are far less costly than acquisitions or mergers and can be just as successful (if not more so) in many situations. Since the organizational structure of each company has not been altered, there is little effect on the executive pay plans. Nonetheless, alliances must be continually reviewed to ensure they are appropriate and properly aligned with organizational needs. Most importantly, exit strategies identifying when and how companies will end the relationship (before they commit to the deal) are essential. For example, the return of trademarks to the parent organization in a JV is critical; otherwise, a third party may end up using them.

Divestitures (Sales and Spin-Offs)

The divestiture-sale of one company is the acquisition of another. The sale ranges from brand names only to full businesses (including plants, buildings, and people). A divesting company has an obligation to protect its employees transferring to a new owner. The sale may be for cash and/or stock.

In a *spin-off*, the divested business is given (not sold) to existing shareholders. This is done by creating a new stock. If the transaction is carefully done, it should be able to qualify as a tax-free exchange, meaning the shareholder has no income-tax liability. It is hoped that the sum of the two stock prices will exceed that of the original company. If that does not happen, some companies do a *spin-in*, simply reversing the action.

With a spin-off, care must be taken in crediting or protecting existing pay programs while designing a new pay program for the spin-off, based on a newly defined survey peer group. Stock options from the former company are typically converted on an equivalency basis, namely, (1) no reduction in ratio of exercise price to market price, (2) the option spread is not greater, and (3) the vesting and other option terms remain the same. This is described more fully in Chapter 8 on long-term incentives.

A key difference between a spin-off and the earlier-described initial public offering is that with an IPO, stock is sold to new shareholders. With a spin-off, stock is given away to existing shareholders.

The objective of an IPO is typically to raise capital enabling the organization to invest in buildings, equipment, and people. However, it might also be to reverse an *LBO* (Leveraged Buy Out), taking down debt and liquefying investor holdings. A spin-off is frequently done to sharpen the focus and direction of an organization, capitalizing on its core competencies, and, hopefully, increasing shareholder value.

MARKET CYCLE AND COMPENSATION ELEMENTS

A comparison of the different stages of the market cycle goes a long way to explain stock price movement. When companies are in the development and growth stage, higher multiples are given to their earnings in anticipation of higher future profits, thereby resulting in rising stock prices. Companies in the mature phase can expect a sluggish market for their stock, and those in decline are likely to see their stock price head in the same direction. However, projections of the future based on past company performance are subject to significant error since the rate of growth is likely to be greater or less than in the past. This degree of miscalculation is compounded by the number of years used in the projection.

As emphasized earlier, a particular company may have units in different phases of the market cycle. Thus, while it may be possible to generalize as to a company's stage in the market cycle, there are different needs for different parts. For this, different divisional pay programs may need to be developed. Shown in Figure 1-12 are Brucell's eight divisions in relation to market stage and profitability. The size of the circles reflects relative size one to another. One only has to contrast "1" (high profit in the threshold stage) with "8" (low profit in a decline phase) to see that one plan will not fit both situations.

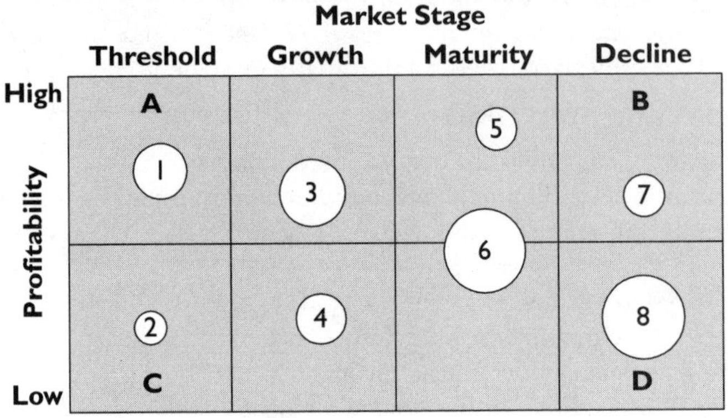

Market Stage

	Threshold	Growth	Maturity	Decline
High	A		5	B
	1	3		7
			6	
	2	4		8
Low	C			D

Profitability (vertical axis label)

Figure 1-12. Market stage vs. profitability

As compared with company plans, however, divisional incentive plans suffer a great disadvantage. Only rarely is a common stock traded on the market for a subsidiary; by financial definition there is no common stock for a division. But one could set up a phantom stock plan for a division and a common stock plan for a wholly owned subsidiary if its stock is publicly traded.

Even a true profit is often difficult to ascertain for a division or subsidiary (due to decisions made by corporate, not divisional, management on cross-divisional pricing, assigned products, and assessments). Thus, the range of design possibilities for long-term divisional incentives is severely limited—often so greatly that a corporate plan is the de facto decision.

Determination of market phase is also an important frame of reference for viewing the importance of each of the compensation elements as shown in the matrix on Table 1-15.

Threshold

As Table 1-15 shows, the most important element in the *threshold* phase is the long-term incentive, essentially for two reasons. First, the need to reinvest earnings for marketing and production requirements places a heavy curtailment on direct cash outlays. Second, the potential for the company's stock prices to rise as it enters the growth phase should help it retain its top people. The latter is a strong case for the use of stock options.

Startups may literally begin in a garage or basement. When the product or service is considered viable, the individuals seek and receive backing from venture capitalists and from attorneys. As key contributors are selectively added, they may receive stock or stock options due to the scarcity of cash. As staff expands and money is more readily available from financial backers, cash compensation for selected executives is more available. However, equity participation

Compensation Element	Emphasis by Market Stage			
	Threshold	**Growth**	**Maturity**	**Decline**
Salary	Low	Moderate	High	High
Employee benefits	Low	Moderate	Moderate	High
Perquisites	Low	Low	Moderate	High
Short-term Incentives	Low	Moderate	High	Moderate
Long-term Incentives	High	High	Moderate	Low

Table 1-15. Compensation element vs. market stage

is still the dominant form of compensation. New hires and ongoing employees both receive grants considerably larger than employees in growth stages. Equity awards, typically in stock options, are allocated on the basis of percentage of company or percentage of available pool.

The promise of probable future success shifts the attention from venture capital to an initial public offering. One or two years before this is likely to occur, the organization focuses on putting in place formal policies based on competitive analysis. This would include more formalized stock-option-grant guidelines, namely, eligibility, size, frequency, and vesting.

With the intent of giving executives an opportunity to participate in stock price appreciation from date of IPO, stock would be a key component of the pay program. This stock is typically described as *founder's stock* and, as such, may be narrowly defined as that awarded/granted to the entrepreneurs who founded the company or more broadly defined as any pre-IPO stock. A stock award perhaps equal to one times salary with a five-year cliff vest along with a mega stock-option grant equivalent to three to five years of normal grants would address the objective of retention, tying the executive to the organization for five years. This might be supplemented with an employment contract protecting both the executive and the company.

Growth

During the *growth* stage, capital investment needs are still strong, but the company is in a good position to improve salaries and benefits (especially profit sharing) and set up some type of annual incentive plan. Long-term incentive plans, however, still have the major emphasis, as there is a strong interest in capital income programs tied to company growth. The period is identifiable as one during which pay plans become more structured and complex. During this phase, annual cash incentives tied to financial targets are becoming popular while stock options continue to be dominant for long-term incentives. However, various types of three- to five-year performance plans are emerging. Perquisites are becoming more popular.

Maturity

By the time the company shifts into the *maturity* stage, the time ranges for investment opportunities typically become shorter than in the growth phase. Emphasis on cost containment as a major way to improve earnings becomes important. This is reflected in more emphasis on short-term than on long-term incentive plans. Return on investment becomes more important than product innovation. Budgets and internal financial measurements take on more importance than stock price and shareholder return, making performance-share and performance-unit plans more attractive than stock options. Long-term incentives start to shift from stock market to non-market valuation techniques as price earnings multiples start to slide. Perquisites start to increase in importance as psychic income becomes a partial trade-off for a decline in real income from incentive plans. There is increased emphasis on salaries, leading to increased importance of wider structural ranges because promotional opportunities (and their big pay increases) are less likely. Executives remain in job grades longer.

Decline

During the *decline* phase, the company must move aggressively to reduce expenses, not only shrinking the employee population, but also reducing salaries and perquisites while introducing short-term incentives that will reward cost efficiencies. Assuming the company hopes to turn-around, it will replace performance-share and performance-unit plans with stock options, or it may concentrate solely on internal financial measurements for the long-term plan since book value probably exceeds market value. Either method may be supplemented with restricted stock to ensure retention of key executives.

TYPE OF COMPANY

There are a number of ways to describe an organization, namely, publicly traded vs. privately held, for-profit vs. not-for-profit, or new economy vs. old economy.

For-Profit vs. Not-for-Profit Companies

Not-for-profit or non-profit companies receive favorable tax treatment and must meet the requirements specified in the Internal Revenue Code to qualify. While non-profits do not intend to make money, they will get a lot of attention from the IRS if they show a significant residue left after paying all their expenses. Lacking a profit incentive removes many of the incentive opportunities (both short- and long-term) available to the for-profits.

Privately Held vs. Publicly Held Companies

Publicly traded companies are those that are required by the Securities Exchange Act of 1934 to register their issues because of an offering to the public, as described in the Securities Act of 1933. A company not meeting these requirements is considered to be a private (or privately held) company. Where much of the stock is in the hands of a few, it is considered to be *a close-ly held, private company. Subchapter S* (Section 1361 of the Internal Revenue Code) is a version of a small, privately held company. Here the stockholders are taxed on the company's earnings proportionate to the percentage of stock they own. This avoids the double taxation of dividends of other corporations.

Being privately held is sometimes so attractive that a large shareholder of a publicly traded company proposes to take the company private by buying out the stock held by others. Since the individual wishes to do so at the lowest possible cost, such plans frequently result in law-suits by other shareholders wanting a better price for their stock.

Two other versions of privately held companies are co-ops and mutual organizations. A *co-op* is a company owned by its customers or suppliers, such as one selling agricultural products. A *mutual* is another example of an organization owned by its customers, such as one selling life insurance.

One might expect privately held companies to pay higher salaries than their public counterparts due to the absence of publicly traded stock and capital gains opportunities. However,
this is far from a general rule—the reverse may even be true. Short-term incentives for both are
very comparable using both internal and external measurements, although privately held companies may use less of the latter. Long-term incentives are similar in design, but the absence of
a public stock market restricts the attractiveness of equity issues in private companies. Owners
not wishing to diffuse ownership are another reason for limited use. Shares are typically subject
to a buyback requirement stipulating that they must be offered for sale to the company (or
named major shareholder) before selling or otherwise transferring ownership to someone else.
This would occur at the time of leaving the company, disability, death, or other completion of a
period of employment. These situations require the company to periodically arrange for an
impartial appraiser to value the stock.

Both private and public companies vary not only by type of industry, but to the extent the
industry is or is not heavily regulated. Where it is heavily regulated pay programs (especially
incentive pay plans) are likely to be subjected to a close review by the regulatory body before they
can be implemented. This, of course, changes dramatically when the industry is deregulated.

Tables 1-4 through 1-7 attempted to identify the relative importance of each compensation
element in a *for-profit, publicly held* organization not subject to close regulatory review. However,
as suggested above, these values would not be appropriate for either a privately held or not-for-
profit organization. Neither has stock traded on a major exchange, thereby dramatically affecting the incentive plan programs. Furthermore, not-for-profits have to be very careful in structuring an incentive plan to ensure there is no undue emphasis on *net asset change* (i.e., the
remainder after expenses have been subtracted from revenue, or what for-profits would call *profit*). The three types of organizations are contrasted during the growth phase in Table 1-16. Note
the reversed positions in privately held and publicly traded companies in incentive types
because common stock is not available to the privately held company. And for the not-for-profits, the absence of long-term incentives places more emphasis on salary and perquisites. If the
privately held company chose to develop a phantom stock plan based on internal measurements, it might more closely mirror the publicly held company's mix in the growth phase,
although it is unlikely the premium the stock market would place on the stock could be
matched with an internal plan.

Compensation Element	For Profit		Not-for-Profit
	Publicly Traded	**Privately Held**	
Salary	Moderate	Moderate	High
Employee benefits	Moderate	Moderate	Moderate
Perquisites	Low	Moderate	High
Short-term Incentives	Moderate	High	Moderate
Long-term Incentives	High	Moderate	—

Table 1-16. Compensation elements by type of company in growth phase

Not included in this analysis is the public sector, which in many cases has less emphasis on the pay elements than even the not-for-profits because of the scrutiny of the voter. Typically, salaries are low and short- and long-term incentives are nonexistent. Employee benefits are pretty good but probably not more than moderate in importance because of the shortness of service. How many make a career as mayor or governor, much less president? Perquisites are definitely high—both extrinsic and intrinsic forms.

Recognizing that a number of factors outside the company's control can and do significantly affect the market value of its stock, some might argue that the relationship of stock prices to book value (i.e., shareholder equity divided by number of shares issued and outstanding) is as shown in Table 1-17. Note that during the growth stage, market price significantly exceeds book value; during maturity, the relationship is reversed; and during decline, book pulls significantly away from market value.

Type Plan	Market Stage			
	Threshold	Growth	Maturity	Decline
Market Value	Very High	High	Moderate	Low
Book Value	Low	Moderate	High	Very High

Table 1-17. Stock value vs. market stage

New vs. Old Economy Companies

Much is being made of the difference between the new economy (high tech) and the old economy (long-established, traditional companies). This difference between the "clicks" and "bricks" is often described in terms similar to that shown in Table 1-18. Whereas the old economy has high emphasis on salary, employee benefits, and short- and long-term incentives (except for a low emphasis on stock options), the new economy is virtually the reverse situation with broad-based stock-option plans going deep into the organization. They also would use larger grants for new hires and persons promoted.

Pay Element	Emphasis In	
	Old Economy	New Economy
Salary	High	Low
Employee benefits	Moderate	Low
Perquisites	Moderate	Low
Short-term Incentives	High	Low
Long-term Incentives Stock Options Other	 Low High	 High Low

Table 1-18. Pay elements in new vs. old economy companies

Actually, these are not so much differences in economies, as differences in the two represented by their stage in the market cycle. The new economy mirrors the compensation element emphasis in the threshold stage of development, whereas the old economy is representative of a combination maturity/decline phase (see Table 1-15). There are some exceptions but this is a typical view of where new and old economy companies are positioned in the market cycle.

Old economy companies (positioned in maturity/decline) that attempt to change their pay practices to more closely align with new economy companies are advised to use this to implement a turnaround, not simply to reformat pay practices.

SUMMARY AND CONCLUSIONS

The opening chapter looked at the various ways one could define an executive, namely, by salary, job grade, key position, job title, reporting relationship, or some combination. It then went on to introduce the five elements of compensation to be described more fully in later chapters, namely, salary (Chapter 5), employee benefits and perquisites (Chapter 6), short-term incentives (Chapter 7), and long-term incentives (Chapter 8).

Having defined both *executive* and *compensation*, the chapter moved on to the important considerations in executive compensation. *Strategic thinking* was defined in terms of vision, mission, objectives and goals, threats and opportunities, strategies, and core competencies. The various stages of the *market lifecycle* (threshold, growth, maturity, decline, and turnaround, sale, or demise) were reviewed. *Organizational structure change* was positioned in terms of IPOs, mergers and acquisitions, and divestitures (sales and spin-offs). The various *types of companies* (for-profit vs. not-for-profit, private vs. public, and new economy vs. old economy) were defined and contrasted. The five compensation elements' importance was viewed in the terms of stage of market lifecycle and type of company. Additionally, the chapter introduced topics to be covered later in the book, namely, performance measurements (Chapter 2), current vs. deferred compensation (Chapter 3), stakeholders (Chapter 4), design considerations (Chapter 9), and the board of directors (Chapter 10).

Note: You should not rely on accounting, tax, SEC, or other professional service statements in this chapter. You need to seek appropriate professional counsel for such guidance. Statements made in this chapter and elsewhere are offered as being illustrative to help you frame such further investigations with the help of counsel.

With that let's move to Chapter 2 and the measurements of performance that are in use in the executive pay program.

Chapter 2

Performance Measurements and Standards

 Before going any further, it is important to take time to identify and describe measurements and standards of performance that can be used in compensating executives. A *standard*, or stated objective, is intended to improve performance (typically, by a stated amount).

UNDERSTANDING PERFORMANCE MEASUREMENT

The *performance measurement* is an outcome-based metric that determines the extent the objective has been achieved. Linking outcome to pay results in *pay-for-performance*. There are two types of measurements: quantitative and qualitative. Quantitative measures are financial and non-financial. Either may be internal to the company or external.

Whose Performance?

Performance measurements can be based on total company performance, individual performance, or an identifiable unit between the two extremes. Financial measurements dominate company performance and sub-units thereof, whereas individual performance is more likely to be measured in non-financial goals and/or objectives. It is not uncommon for an executive's performance rating to be a combination of: his or her own performance, the performance of his or her division/department/strategic business unit (SBU), and overall company performance.

Measurement Types

As indicated, there are two *measurement types*: financial and non-financial. We'll begin with the financial measurements internal to a company. Financial measurements date back hundreds of years. And keep in mind that whether addressing the income statement, the cash-flow statement or the balance sheet, they are all historical numbers and not by themselves predictive of future performance. Nonetheless, they are undoubtedly the most common performance measurements for executive pay purposes.

Two Sets of Books

We've all heard about the illegal practice of keeping one set of books for the auditors and another that reflects the true status of the business. This practice is not only illegal, it will get one a rent-free accommodation in a confined facility. However, the company does maintain separate records for bonafide reasons.

Accounting vs. Tax Requirements. Accounting records are driven by Generally Accepted Accounting Principles (GAAP) and statements by the Financial Accounting Standards Board (FASB). Tax records reflect the Internal Revenue Code (IRC) and proclamations by the Internal Revenue Service (IRS). A reconciliation of the two is called "deferred taxes," which appears on the accounting balance sheet.

Accrual vs. Cash Accounting. Another difference in financial reporting appears when an action is reflected on a financial statement. Under accrual accounting, a sale is realized when the product is shipped or the service performed; under cash accounting, it is reflected when the cash is received. The same is true for items purchased by the company. Under accrual accounting, they are recognized when ordered; under cash accounting, they are recognized when paid.

Executive Pay Considerations. Given these differences, it is important to know what records are being used as measurements for executive pay. Typically, accrual accounting is used, and that is where most of the emphasis will be in this chapter.

Financial Measurements Within the Company

There are numerous financial measurements that can be used in the design of executive pay plans, especially short- and long-term incentives. They fall into various categories: (1) relative return on a financial measurement expressed in percentage terms; (2) increase or decrease in absolute dollars, (3) relative value or percentages other than returns on income, and (4) various combinations of the first three.

There are three financial statements that are the source of most of the financial measurements of a company. They are the income statement, the cash-flow statement, and the balance sheet. Each of these will be examined, and then various measurements from them will be identified and described. The balance sheet reportedly has been in existence for over one hundred years, the income statement for little less than half that time, and the cash-flow statement of rather recent origin. However, double entry bookkeeping goes back some five hundred years and is attributed to Luca Pacioli, a Venetian mathematician and monk (a little something for your trivia data bank).

Income Statement. This is a statement of income and expenses for a prescribed period of time. It is prepared monthly and usually issued to shareholders on a quarterly and year-end basis. The three-month statements are both self-standing and cumulative year-to-date. Thus, the fourth quarter will show the full year results in addition to the fourth quarter only. For most companies, the business year is the same as the calendar year; however, some companies have a fiscal year with a different twelve-month period (e.g., July 1st through June 30th). Such companies select the twelve-month period most representative of their business year.

Shown in Table 2-1 is a hypothetical *income statement*, sometimes called a *profit and loss statement*. It is also called an *earnings statement*. Expenses are identified as a *charge to earnings* since they lower income. Such amounts are expressed over the time periods incurred—not necessarily when paid. The top line of the income statement is typically *net sales*, or revenues ($101,546,400 in the example). This is gross sales less any returns, discounts, and allowances.

Net Sales (Revenue)		$101,546.4
Cost of Goods Sold	$37,459.7	
Gross Margin		$64,086.7

Operating Expenses
  Research and Development
  Sales and Marketing
  General and Administrative
  Total
	$17,366.5
	16,954.7
	5,398.4
	$39,717.6	

EBITDA
  Depreciation
  Amortization of Good Will
  Total
	$1,387.6
	2,624.8
	$4,012.4
		$24,367.1

Operating Income (EBIT)
  Interest Expense
  Other Income
  Total
	$3,845.7
	(1,764.9)
	$2,080.8
		$20,354.7

Income Before Provisions for Income Taxes and Extraordinary Items Provision for Income Tax	$6,714.8	$18,273.9
Income Before Provisions for Extraordinary Items Extraordinary Items (Net of Tax)	$418.5	$11,559.1
Income from Continuing Operations Discontinued Operations (Net of Tax)	$1,481.8	$11,140.6
Net Income		$9,658.8

Earnings per Common Share–Basic
  From Continuing Operations
  Net All Operations
	$0.73
	$0.63	

Earnings per Common Share–Diluted
  From Continuing Operations
  Net All Operations
	$0.69
	$0.59	

Weighted Average Number of Shares–Basic	15,250.0	
Weighted Average Number of Shares–Diluted	16,250.0	

Table 2-1. Income statement (in thousands)

If there is other business income (e.g., alliances and co-marketing ventures), it probably has a separate line directly under net sales. This is followed by the *cost of goods sold*, or cost of sales ($37,459,700), namely, what it cost to make or buy the product (e.g., cost of materials used and other manufacturing expenses such as pay and overhead). The reduction of sales by cost of goods sold leaves *gross margin* ($64,086,700). This is a useful measurement for manufacturing and retailing pay plans. The next category of expenses is *operating expense*. In this category are found research and development ($17,366,500), sales and marketing ($16,954,700), and general and administrative expenses ($5,398,400).The latter includes compensation and benefit costs (except for those directly involved in the cost of goods sold) including all executive compensation costs. If a company uses its own employees to construct a fixed asset (e.g., a building), the compensation and benefits costs will be added to the value of the asset and depreciated over time. Incentive plans to be paid out after year-end have the estimated payment accrued quarterly over the year with the final amount "trued-up" when payment is made. To be eligible to charge the expense during the year, even though paid after the year, the payment must generally be within 75 days of the close of the year. Multi-year plans with payment only after the end of the multi-year period similarly have their estimated payout accrued over the year, with the estimated amount calculated quarterly. Again, the final quarter before payment will have the accrual trued-up to match the actual expense.

Netting operating expenses from gross margin results in *EBITDA* (Earnings Before Interest, Taxes, Depreciation, and Amortization). In this example, the amount is $24,367,100. Some choose to use this amount for SBU incentive plans as it includes expenses within the control of the unit. However, it is not usually appropriate at the company-wide level, as senior corporate management should be held accountable for capital expenditures and acquisition expenses. The category also includes *depreciation* ($1,387,600) for the period on equipment, building, and property, as well as *amortization of goodwill* ($2,624,800), and patents and franchise fees, if any. When all operating expenses have been removed, *operating income* ($20,354,700) remains, sometimes referred to as *EBIT* (Earnings Before Interest and Taxes). Those who believe CEOs and other key corporate executives should neither be rewarded nor penalized for changes in tax rates (which are out of their control) will use EBIT in their incentive plan calculations; however, doing so also gives them a "free ride" on interest charges.

Next, one includes *interest expense* ($3,845,700) and *other income* (e.g., gains or losses on investment sales, fixed assets, and affiliate earnings—a loss of $1,764,900 in this example). This results in income before provision for income taxes and extraordinary items, often referred to as pretax income — $18,273,900 in the example — which is probably better for CEOs and other top corporate executives than EBIT. Reducing this amount by the *provision for income taxes* for the year ($6,714,800) results in *income before extraordinary items* ($11,559,100). Extraordinary items net of tax are sometimes referred to as "Acts of God," perhaps an uninsured loss from an act of nature (e.g. avalanche, earthquake, fire, or flood). Subtracting this amount of $418,500 leaves income from *continuing operations* ($11,140,600), a figure usually of high interest to financial analysts and investors. Subtracting the effect of *discontinued operations* net of tax ($1,481,800) leaves *net income* ($9,658,800). This is also called *net earnings, net profit*, or the *bottom line*. Many argue that this figure should be used for incentive calculations at the corporate level as it includes all the costs.

Cash-Flow Statement. Income is not synonymous with cash, and therefore, a *cash-flow state-*

ment showing the source and amount of cash receipts and payments is a useful supplement to the income statement. A company will record a sale when it is delivered to a customer, but since few customers pay cash at that precise moment, there is a time lag before a company receives the cash. Additionally, the company may have investing and financing activities. The cash-flow statement is thus a report of the cash received and spent during the business year.

First, cash flow from operations is determined. There are two methods: direct and indirect. The indirect method, shown in Table 2-2, begins with net income for the year ($9,658,800) increased by expenses that did not require the expenditure of cash such as depreciation and amortization ($4,012,400), reduced by payment of deferred taxes ($1,703,800), and increased for the tax benefit of the stock plan ($9,165,400). Changes in working capital (with the exception of marketable securities) are also reflected in this section of the cash-flow statement. This includes accounts payable (+$858,200), accrued—but not paid—compensation (+$6,164,200), other accrued liabilities (+$5,643,000), other taxes payable (–$3,389,700), inventories (–$1,907,200), prepaid expenses (–1,374,800), and accounts receivable (–$3,517,900). The net amount ($23,608,600) is *net cash provided by operating activities.*

The next step in a cash-flow analysis is to determine the amount of cash used in investment activities. This section reflects the acquisition or divestiture of assets used in the production of the firm's goods or services. Cash would be increased from the proceeds of business sales ($42,398,500 in Table 2-2) and redemption (receipts) for short-term ($6,181,500) and long-term ($5,406,200) investments. Cash would be decreased for purchase of: short-term ($3,486,500) and long-term ($4,176,200) investments; property, plant, and equipment ($18,649,300); licenses ($3,916,500); purchase of business ($37,183,700); and other liability activities ($1,374,900). Subtracting the outflow from the inflow of cash would result in *net cash used in investment activities* ($14,800,900).

The third category of a cash-flow analysis is to determine the cash flow from financing activities. This section deals with the debt and equity financing of the company. Cash would be increased with sale of common stock ($23,719,600 in Table 2-2) and issuance of long-term debt ($7,524,200). It would be decreased with the payments on short- and long-term debt ($654,300 and $15,704,900, respectively), purchase of common stock ($16,175,100), and cash dividends paid ($6,953,600). The difference between increases and decreases result in the *net cash used in financing activities* ($8,244,100).

Subtracting the net cash used in investing ($14,800,900) and financing ($8,244,100) activities from the net cash provided by operating activities results in the increase or decrease in cash/cash equivalents for the year. In Table 2-2, this is an increase of $563,600. Cash-flow statements also report the cash position at the beginning and end of the year ($6,197,600 and $6,761,200, respectively).

The other method of constructing a cash-flow statement is the *direct method.* Rather than beginning with net income (as done in the indirect method), the inflow and outflow of cash provided by operating activities is reported directly as shown in Table 2-3. Note that the total net cash provided by operating activities is the same as shown in Table 2-2 ($23,608,600). However, the items listed and their amounts are different. They include cash received from customers ($96,630,000) and from interest received ($1,764,900) versus cash paid to: employees ($36,625,700), suppliers ($27,600,100), and for interest ($3,845,700) and taxes ($6,714,800). Cash flow used in investing and financing has not been repeated since it is the same as shown in Table 2-2.

Operating Activities		$9,658.8
Net Income		
Adjustments to reconcile net income to net		
cash provided by operating activities		
• Depreciation and Amortization	$4,012.4	
• Deferred taxes	(1,703.8)	
• Tax Benefit for Stock Plan	9,165.4	
• Changes in Operating Assets and Liabilities		
Accounts Receivable	($3,517.9)	
Inventories	(1,907.2)	
Prepaid expenses and other assets	(1,374.8)	
Accounts Payable	858.2	
Income taxes payable	(3,389.7)	
Accrued compensation	6,164.2	
Other accrued liabilities	5,643.0	
Net Cash Provided by Operating Activities		$23,608.6
Investment Activities		
Purchase of Short-Term Investments	($3,486.5)	
Proceeds for Redemption of Short-Term		
Investments	6,181.5	
Purchase of Long-Term Investments	(4,176.2)	
Proceeds from Redemption of Long-Term		
Investments	5,406.2	
Purchase of Property, Plant, and Equipment	(18,649.3)	
Purchase of Licenses	(3,916.5)	
Purchase of Businesses	(37,183.7)	
Proceeds from Sale of Businesses	42,398.5	
Other Liability Activities	(1,374.9)	
Net Cash Used in Investment Activities		($14,800.9)
Financing Activities		
Payments of Short-Term Debt	($654.3)	
Proceeds from Issuance of Long-Term Debt	7,524.2	
Payments of Long-Term Debt	(15,704.9)	
Issuance of Common Stock	23,719.6	
Purchase of Common Stock	(16,175.1)	
Cash Dividends Paid	(6,953.6)	
Net Cash Used in Financing Activities		($8,244.1)
Net Increase/Decrease in Cash and Cash Equivalents		$563.6
Cash and Cash Equivalents at Beginning of Year		$6,197.6
Cash and Cash Equivalents at End of Year		$6,761.2

Table 2-2. Consolidated cash-flow statement (in thousands)—indirect method

Operating Activities		
• Cash Received From:		
Customers	$96,630.0	
Interest	1,764.9	
• Cash Paid:		
To Employees	($36,625.7)	
To Suppliers	(27,600.1)	
For Interest	(3,845.7)	
For Taxes	(6,714.8)	
Net Cash Provided by Operating Activities		$23,608.6

Table 2-3. Consolidated cash flow statement (in thousands)—direct method

As shown in Table 2-4, paying the executive in cash is negative cash flow while paying the person in stock is positive because the fair market value (less any dollars paid by the executive) is tax deductible. Therefore, if the corporate tax rate is 35 percent, there will be an increase in cash of 65¢ for every $1 of net stock value given to the executive.

Cash Flow Impact	Cash	Stock
Positive		✔
Negative	✔	

Table 2-4. Cash flow impact of cash vs. stock

Some choose to not simply analyze a company's annual cash-flow statement but will make assumptions on future statements (maybe no more sophisticated than the current cash flow projected into the future and then discounted by some definition of the cost of capital, including the payment of all debt). Comparing what is left with shareholder equity (as shown on the balance sheet) provides a view as to whether shareholder equity is over- or understated in terms of value. And comparing such an analysis each year indicates whether or not the company is adding value, and if so, at what rate.

Balance Sheet. This is a snapshot at a point in time of the company's financial health. It consists of assets, liabilities, and shareholders' equity. This statement is prepared monthly and usually issued to shareholders on a quarterly or year-end basis. It is called a balance sheet because total assets must equal (or be in balance with) total liabilities plus shareholders' equity. An example is shown in Table 2-5.

Assets are sometimes described as *current* (short-term) and *non-current* (long-term). Short-term assets include cash and other items that could be converted to cash within a year. Long-

Assets	$330,997.9	Liabilities	$193,920.5
		Shareholder Equity	137,077.4
Total	$330,997.9	Total	$330,997.9

Table 2-5. Balance sheet (in thousands)

Current Assets		
Cash and Cash Equivalents	$18,738.2	
Short-Term Investments	14,833.8	
Short-Term Loan Receivables	4,559.4	
Accounts Receivable	18,678.6	
• Gross	$19,463.2	
• Doubtful Accounts	784.6	
Inventories	14,095.3	
• Finished Goods	$6,576.4	
• Work in Process	4,981.7	
• Raw Materials and Supplies	2,537.2	
Prepaid Expenses and Other Assets	8,396.2	
Total Current Assets		$79,301.5
Non-Current Assets		
Long-Term Investments	$28,347.7	
Long-Term Loan Receivables	4,679.3	
Land	47,065.4	
Buildings and Equipment (Net of Depreciation)	76,980.5	
Goodwill (Net of Amortization)	89,836.8	
Prepaid Expenses and Other Assets	4,786.7	
Total Non-Current Assets		$251,696.4
Total Assets		$330,997.9

Table 2-6. Balance sheet—assets (in thousands)

term assets include items with values and uses extending beyond a year. The former includes *working capital*, or current assets that are available to meet current obligations, namely, current liabilities ($23,683,100 in Table 2-7). In the example Table 2-6, *current (short-term)* assets of $79,301,500 include: cash and cash equivalents ($18,738,200), short-term investments ($14,833,800), short-term loans ($4,559,400), accounts receivable ($19,463,200 less doubtful accounts of $784,600 or $18,678,600), inventories [($14,095,300) consisting of finished goods ($6,576,400) plus work in process ($4,981,700) plus raw material and supplies ($2,537,200)], and prepaid expenses ($8,396,200). In Table 2-6, current assets total $79,301,500. Thus, working capital is $55,818,400 ($79,301,500 less $23,683,100). Also shown in Table 2-6 are representative *non-current (long-term)* assets. They include: long-term investments ($28,347,700), long-term loans ($4,679,300), land ($47,065,400), buildings and equipment (net of depreciation of $76,980,500), goodwill (net of amortization of $89,836,800), along with other longer-term, prepaid expenses and other assets ($4,786,700). In the example, these total $251,966,400, resulting in a combined total of $330,997,900 for current and non-current assets.

Liabilities are similarly described in terms of *current* (short-term) and *non-current* (long-term). As shown in Table 2-7, current liabilities would typically include: short-term borrowing (including current portions of long-term debt of $4,813,100), accounts payable ($1,304,600), income taxes payable ($7,928,200), and accrued compensation ($9,637,200). In the example,

Current Liabilities		
Short-Term Borrowing (including current portion of long-term debt)	$4,813.1	
Accounts Payable	1,304.6	
Income Taxes Payable	7,928.2	
Accrued Compensation	9,637.2	
Total Current Liabilities		$23,683.1
Non-Current Liabilities		
Long-Term Debt	$126,763.9	
Deferred Compensation	19,630.5	
Deferred Tax Liabilities	23,843.0	
Total Non-Current Liabilities		$170,237.4
Total Liabilities		$193,920.5

Table 2-7. Balance sheet—liabilities (in thousands)

these total $23,683,100. Non-current liabilities include: long-term debt ($126,763,900), deferred compensation ($19,630,500), and deferred tax liabilities ($23,843,000). In the example, these total $170,237,400, resulting in a combined total of $193,920,500 for current and non-current liabilities.

Shareholder equity is what is left for shareholders after liabilities have been subtracted from the assets as shown in Table 2-8. More specifically, it consists of par value (the original stated value of the stock at the time of capitalization adjusted for stock splits) of common stock outstanding ($152,500) and additional paid in capital (dollars received for sale of company stock less par value, or $119,113,200). Thus, when a stock option is exercised, the proceeds from the option are split between the par value and additional paid in capital accounts. If the par value is $.01 and the option price is $10, the par value account would receive $.01 and the other $9.99 would go to the additional paid in capital account. Retained earnings are the cumulative effect of net income minus paid dividends ($24,173,900). Dollars paid to buy back company stock ($6,362,200), which becomes *treasury stock* (795,200 shares), are also shown. In Table 2-8, total shareholder equity is $137,077,400.

A more detailed analysis of the use of the company's common stock is shown in Table 2-9. The shareholders had earlier approved the use of 30,000,000 shares of common stock. As of the date of the Annual Report, there were 15,250,000 shares outstanding, leaving 14,750,000 shares

Common Stock (par value of $.01) 1,525,000 shares issued	$152.5	
Additional Paid-in Capital	119,113.2	
Retained Earnings	24,173.9	
Treasury Stock (at cost) 795,200 shares	(6,362.2)	
Total Shareholder Equity		$137,077.4

Table 2-8. Balance sheet—shareholder equity (in thousands)

	Number of Shares	% Outstanding
Shares Authorized	30,000,000	
Shares Outstanding	15,250,000	
Shares Approved for Use	1,500,000	9.8%
Shares Granted	1,000,000	6.6
Exercised	750,000	4.9
Forfeited	100,000	0.7
Not Exercised	150,000	1.0
Vested	50,000	0.3
Not Vested	100,000	0.7
Shares Available for Use	600,000	3.4
Shares Not Exercised and Available for Use	750,000	4.9

Table 2-9. Company common stock analysis

available for use by the company. Of these, 1,500,000 have been set aside for compensation purposes of which 1,000,000 shares were granted, but since 100,000 of these were forfeited, there are still 600,000 shares available for use (i.e., 1,500,000 − 1,000,000 + 100,000). Combining these 600,000 with the 150,000 still not exercised results in a total of 750,000 shares either not exercised or available for use. This is called the *overhang*. The overhang percentage is determined by dividing overhang (750,000 shares) by the total shares outstanding (15,250,000), or 4.9 percent in this example.

For many years, an overhang of more than 5 percent was not looked upon favorably by stock analysts. But this has crept up to 10 percent or more in recent years for a number of reasons. Factors include:

1. Companies in the threshold stage of development have higher overhang rates because stock options are used much more extensively than in any other stage in the market cycle.
2. Those using stock options will use greater numbers of shares than those using only stock awards. In Chapter 8 (Long-Term Incentives), this will be discussed in greater detail. But a ratio of three-to-one is not uncommon (i.e., three stock options being of comparable value to one stock award).
3. Those pushing stock options all the way down in the organization will use more shares than those who do not.
4. When the company stock has not shown any appreciable gains for a long period of time, there will be a greater number of unexercised stock options than if there were appreciable appreciation.
5. If reloads and repriced stock options (Chapter 8) are not returned to the pool for reuse as new grants, the shares available for use will more quickly be depleted. The same is true for forfeited shares unless returned for use.
6. If all shares used are from shareholder-approved plans, the overhang will be greater than if stock used had been purchased from the open market, as the latter reduces the denominator in the calculation.

The balance sheet is typically understated in terms of the fair market value of such things as property, which is reported on a cost basis. The problem with *Fair Value Accounting*, favored by some to replace the *historical cost basis*, is that it is virtually impossible to determine the "fair value." Is it based on a tax assessor's amount? Or on what similar property sold for recently? If the latter, to what extent are conditions (e.g., exact locations, space, interest rates, and lapsed time) the same? For such reasons, historical cost remains the financial model for recording non-current assets.

Definitions and Formulas. Following is a listing of various financial definitions and measurements used in executive pay plans.

- **Accounting Principles Board (APB)** This overseer was the successor to the American Institute of Public Accountants (in 1959), and predecessor (in 1973) to the Financial Accounting Standards Board, for establishing Generally Accepted Accounting Principles. See Financial Accounting Standards Board and Generally Accepted Accounting Principles.

- **Accruals** Income and expenses are charged on an estimated basis against the period when incurred on the income statement regardless of when paid. The final accrual is "trued up" when paid so that the accrual matches the actual income or expense.

- **Actual vs. Budgeted Performance** This scorecard measures the year-end results vs. those established as the budget or target for the year. Typical measurements would be in terms of sales, net income, or any other quantifiable measurement.

- **Amortization** This is the cost allocation to the income statement of a non-tangible, non-current asset such as franchise fees, patents, and goodwill (resulting from an acquisition at more than fair value) on the balance sheet. The amount is determined annually in accordance with GAAP and reported on the income statement. In Table 2-1, an amount of $2,624,800 is shown. Tax regulations may differ from GAAP.

- **APB 25 ("Accounting for Stock Issued to Employees" [1972])** This established the Measurement Date Principle; namely, that the compensatory value of stock is measured on the first date on which both the number of shares and the price is known. If this is known at date of grant, the accounting is set or fixed at that date; if not known until a later date, then variable accounting is in effect.

- **Arbitrage** This is the taking advantage of an imbalance of prices for an item in at least two places by simultaneously buying at the lower price and selling at the higher price, thereby making a profit.

- **Bear Market** A stock market with falling stock prices.

- **Bond** This is a long-term debt obligation of the company, issued for business investments requiring the payment of a stated amount of interest annually and the full amount borrowed at the end of a stated period of time (see debenture). A *high-yield* or *junk bond* is a company debenture with low or below-investment-grade rating, assigned by a rating service and resulting in the payment of a significantly higher interest rate because of the high risk of forfeiture.

- **Book Value** This is the shareholders' equity ($137,077,400 in Table 2-8) and sometimes called the break-up value of the company.

- **Book Value to Earnings Ratio** This is the book value per share divided by the earnings per share (see Book Value Share Price). In Table 2-1, with book value at $8.99 per share and an EPS (earnings per share) of 63¢ , this would result in a ratio of 14.3 to 1.

- **Book-Value Increase** Book value at the end of the business year divided by the book value at the end of the previous year equals the percentage change; book value at the end of the year minus book value at the end of the previous year equals the dollar change. This formula is typically used by privately held companies that have no common shares outstanding as well as by companies that have relatively flat stock-price appreciation (perhaps because they are in the late stages of maturity or worse). In the example, if year-end book-value share prices were $8.39 and $8.99 for the previous year and current year, respectively, the increase would be 60¢, or 7.2 percent.

- **Book Value to Price Ratio** This is book-value share price divided by market price of the stock. In the example, with book value at $8.99 and market price at $10 per share, the ratio would be .90 to 1.

- **Book-Value Share Price** This is shareholder's equity divided by the average shares outstanding during the year. In the example, this is $137,077,400 (Table 2-8) divided by 15,250,000 (Table 2-1), or $8.99.

- **Bull Market** A stock market with rising stock prices.

- **Burn Rate** This is the speed at which expenses will use up all available cash.

- **Capital Employed** This is shareholder's equity ($137,077,400 in Table 2-8) plus long-term debt ($126,763,900 in Table 2-7), or $263,841,300. Some choose to use total non-current liabilities ($170,237,400 in the example) instead of long-term debt to see how management has used these available dollars. Capital Employed is equal to Total Capital.

- **Capital Expenditures** These are the dollars invested in non-current (long-term) assets ($251,696,400 in Table 2-6).

- **Cash Flow** As the words suggest, this is the net effect of cash received vs. cash paid out during the year. Assets and expenses are a use of cash; liabilities, equity, and income are a source of cash. An important cash-flow figure is the net cash provided by (or used by) the business ($23,608,600 in Table 2-2). Another interesting figure is the net cash provided by (or used by) financing (outflow of $14,800,900 in Table 2-2) vs. that used for investment (outflow of $8,244,100 in Table 2-2). In other words, to what extent is the organization taking on debt to expand the business? The financing and investment segments better relate to corporate than divisional measurements.

- **Commercial Paper** This is the short-term debt (typically 90 days or less) of a company.

- **Commodities** Theses are raw materials such as cocoa, gold, oil, and wheat.

- **Common Stock** This is the stated number of shares of ownership in the company. For publicly traded companies, stock price is set by buyers and sellers on a listed stock exchange. Each share has a voting right and may be eligible for a dividend, although it is neither fixed nor guaranteed. In Table 2-1, there are 15,250,000 shares of common stock outstanding.

- **Compounding** This is earning interest on the interest already earned, in addition to the original investment.

- **Debt** The amount owed by the company that must be paid at sometime in the future. Typically, it is described in terms of short-term (portion due within a year) and long-term (portion to be paid in more than a year from the date of this balance sheet). In Table 2-7, these are $23,683,100 and $170,237,400 respectively, or a total of $193,920,500.

- **Debenture** This is a bond backed by the company's general credit (rather than a lien against specific assets). *Convertible Debenture* is a bond issued by the company that permits the holder to convert it into shares of common stock at specified terms (e.g., dates and prices).

- **Default** When the company does not pay the interest and/or the principle due on its debt, it defaults.

- **Depreciation** This is the systematic and rational allocation of the cost of a fixed (non-current) asset over its useful life. Buildings and equipment listed on the balance sheet as non-current assets ($76,980,500 in Table 2-6) are reduced annually in accordance with GAAP by expensing them on the income statement as a depreciation expense ($1,387,600 in Table 2-1). Tax regulations differ from GAAP.

- **Derivative** A financial contract on the direction and amount of change in any item that can be measured quantitatively (e.g., interest rates, bond value, stock price, or commodity). A derivative could be used to hedge against possible adverse consequences.

- **Derivative Security** Any security that may become a share of the company's common stock. In addition to stock options, this would include all convertible securities (e.g., convertible debentures and convertible preferred stock).

- **Dilution** This is EPS before issuing additional shares of stock minus EPS after issuing the additional shares divided by EPS before stock issuance. In Table 2-1, the *basic EPS* for all operations is 63¢ per share (i.e., $9,658,800 net income divided by the weighted average number of shares outstanding, namely, 15,250,000) vs. 73¢ for continuing operations (i.e., $11,140,600 divided by 15,250,000 shares). *Diluted EPS*, in accord with Financial Accounting Standard (FAS) 128, increases the number of shares outstanding by the dilutive effect of all "in-the-money" outstanding stock options and awards. In this example, that number is a million shares (Table 2-1), resulting in an EPS of 69¢ for continuing operations and 59¢ for all operations. This four-cent reduction is a dilution of 5.5 percent for continuing operations (i.e., 4¢ divided by 73¢) and 6.3 percent for all operations (i.e., 4¢ divided by 63¢).

- **Dividend** Payment by the company to any owner of a share of company stock. For common stock, the amount is typically adjusted from time to time. For preferred stock, the amount is typically preset at time of issuance. It could be expressed as the dividend for the last or next quarter; it could be the actual dividend paid for the past 12 months; or it could be the current quarterly dividend projected for the next 12 months.

- **EBIT (Earnings Before Interest and Taxes)** Also called *Operating Income*; many argue that this definition makes the most sense in measuring executives as it includes all expenses other than income taxes (over which executives have no control) and interest charges (over which they may have some control). In Table 2-1, this is $20,354,700.

- **EBITDA (Earnings Before Interest, Taxes, Depreciation, and Amortization)** This is gross margin less operating expenses or, stated another way, it is EBIT (Operating income) with depreciation and amortization added back in. EBITDA is not usually found as a line item in many company annual reports, but it may be useful in incentive plans if the board of directors believe management should not be held accountable for borrowing and acquisitions decisions. However, many believe executives should be held accountable for achieving an income in excess of these amounts, and therefore, it would be more logical to use EBIT than EBITDA. In Table 2-1, EBITDA is $24,367,100.

- **Earnings Charge** Also called *charge to the earnings statement*, this is an expense item that reduces earnings.

- **Earnings Per Share (EPS)** Net income divided by the average total number of shares outstanding equals earnings per share. In Table 2-1, this would be $9,658,800 divided by 15,250,000, or 63¢. However, this excludes the diluted effect of outstanding stock options. Factoring in stock equivalents (i.e., the net increase of the exercise of all "in-the-money" stock options outstanding after buying back as many shares as the option proceeds would enable) would result in *diluted earnings per share*. In Table 2-1, this would be $9,658,800 divided by 16,250,000, or 59¢. Both figures are shown in Table 2-1 for continuing and all operations. These can be compared current year vs. previous year. In Table 2-1, the 63¢ would be an increase of 5¢ per share since the previous year was 58¢.

- **Economic Profit (EP)** This is what remains after the cost of capital is subtracted from net operating profit after taxes (NOPAT). The cost of capital is the interest paid on debt plus a return to the shareholders. The latter may be defined as dividends paid or an expected return such as the risk-free rate of return on a government debt obligation plus a risk premium of say 6 percent. However, in the example, with NOPAT of $20,110,400 (see NOPAT definition), interest expense of $3,845,700 (Table 2-1), and dividends paid of $6,953,600 (Table 2-2), the economic profit is a gain of $9,311,100. Alternatively, a cost of capital could be determined by determining the current short- and long-term borrowing rates and what the investors look to receive beyond a risk-free rate of return. Assume for illustration this is 10 percent. This might be multiplied by capital consisting of net current currents: in other words, current assets minus current liabilities, or $55,618,400 in the example ($79,301,500 less $23,683,100) plus other assets ($251,696,400), or a total of $307,314,800. Applying the 10-percent rate to this would result in a capital charge of $30,731,480. Subtracting this from NOPAT would result in an economic loss of $10,621,080. Because of the equity element, this measurement is most likely to be found only on the corporate level.

- **Economic Profit Equity Adjusted (EPEA)** This is net operating profit after tax (see NOPAT definition) minus after-tax cost of debt plus a reasonable return on equity. It is also called *economic profit modified*. If this is positive, shareholder value is appreciating beyond an expected return on investment. If it is negative, one must look to Economic Profit Refined (EPR) to see if any value is appreciating. If NOPAT is $20,110,400, and after-tax cost of debt is $2,499,705 (see Return on Capital definition) with an expected 10 percent return on equity of $13,077,400 or $187,077,400 (Table 2-8), then EPEA is $3,902,955.

- **Economic Profit Refined (EPR)** This is NOPAT(see definition) minus the after-tax interest on debt plus a comparable value for net assets and an appropriate return on equity. By including net current assets, one has also charged it with their use, assume 7 percent (see Net Assets definition), or $21,512,036 on net assets of $307,314,800. The formula would be $20,110,400 (NOPAT) − [$2,499,705 (after-tax debt cost) + $21,512,036 (net asset charge) + $3,902,915 (EPEA)] = -$7,804,296.

- **Economic Value Added** This is another version of calculating economic value (see EP, EPEA, and EPR). EVA® has been trademarked by Stern, Stewart.

- **Equity** *See* Shareholder Equity.

- **Expense Budget** This is the allocation of dollars for business use, typically defined by category (e.g., supplies, business travel, and executive incentive pay).

- **Financial Accounting Standard (FAS) 123 "Accounting for Stock-based Compensation" (1995)** This provides a company with a choice of either reflecting a present-value charge to the financial statements with a formula such as Black-Scholes, or continuing to use APB 25, but reflecting impact of the present value on net income and earnings per share in financial footnotes.

- **Financial Accounting Standards Board (FASB)** This is a non-governmental regulatory board that establishes accounting principles. It is the successor to the Accounting Principles Board. Its actions are subject to oversight review by the Securities Exchange Commission (SEC) for publicly traded companies.

- **Generally Accepted Accounting Principles (GAAP)** The principles set down by the FASB, which SEC-affected companies are expected to follow.

- **Goodwill** This is the amount the purchase price of an acquired company exceeds its market-adjusted net assets. It appears as an asset on the balance sheet ($89,836,800 in Table 2-6) and is amortized (charged to the income statement) over a stated period of time in accord with GAAP, currently up to 40 years, at the discretion of management. Tax regulations differ. It appears as $2,624,800 in Table 2-1.

- **Gross Margin** This is income after subtracting the direct costs of goods sold ($37,459,700 in Table 2-1) from net sales ($101,546,400 in Table 2-1). This definition is often used for subdivisions of an organization (e.g., a manufacturing division on site) where other expense deductions do not apply (e.g., selling expenses). In Table 2-1, this is $64,086,700.

- **Hedging** The purchase of a forward derivative contract to reduce, if not totally eliminate, gains or losses (typically on foreign currencies) is called hedging.

- **Income** Any of the previous definitions of income could be used to measure absolute dollar increase. They include gross margin, EBITDA, EBIT, and net income.

- **Initial Public Offering (IPO)** This is when the company first sells its stock to the public. Stock sold subsequently to the public is known as a secondary offering.

- **Inventory** This is the cost of goods produced or purchased but not sold. In Table 2-6, this is $14,095,300 and consists of finished goods ($6,576,400), work in process

($4,981,700), and raw materials and supplies ($2,537,200).

- **Inventory Sales Ratio** This is average inventories of $13,100,700 (not the year-ending figure of $14,095,300) from Table 2-6 divided into net sales ($101,546,400 from Table 2-1), or 7.8. While no one wants to have a backlog of unfilled sales orders because of a lack of finished inventory, neither does one want to have a lot of capital tied up in inventories. This ratio could be used as a corporate measure but may be even more important at a divisional level where it is better controlled.

- **Liquidity** This is the extent that short-term assets ($79,301,500 in Table 2-6) exceed short-term liabilities ($23,683,100 in Table 2-7) for the company or $55,618,400 in this example. This is also called working capital.

- **Long-Term Debt Ratio** This is long-term debt ($126,763,900 in Table 2-6) divided into shareholder equity (137,074,400, Table 2-5) plus long-term debt, or 2.1 (to 1). To the extent this ratio is high, it suggests a highly debt-leveraged company that may have borrowing difficulty during a downturn.

- **Margin** This is sometimes a reference to profit but also may refer to a type of stock purchase. If an investor buys stock paying only a portion of the cost in cash with the remainder from a broker loan, it is described as "buying on the margin."

- **Market to Book Ratio** This is the price of the common stock divided by the company's book value per share. In the example, with a market price of $10 a share and book value of $8.99, the ratio is 1.11 to 1.0.

- **Market Capitalization** This is the total number of shares of common stock outstanding multiplied by the price of the stock. Thus, in the example, with 15,250,000 shares (Table 2-1) outstanding and the fair market value of each share worth $10, market capitalization would be $152,500,000.

- **Market Share** This is own total sales divided by the estimated total dollar value of all sales for similar products/services in the marketplace. If the marketplace for the products is estimated to be $500 million, then in the example with sales of $101,546,400 (Table 2-1), this would represent a 20.3-percent market share ($101,546,400 divided by $500,000,000). It can also be calculated by organizational units of the company having sales.

- **Milestones** These are identifiable, key-event completions in a multi-event project. For example, completing the business system study would be a milestone in a project to install a completely new accounting system.

- **Net Assets** These are total assets minus current liabilities. In the example, this is $330,997,900 (Table 2-6) minus $23,683,100 (Table 2-7), or $307,314,800. This is equal to non-current liabilities of $170,237,400 (Table 2-7) plus equity of $137,077,400 (Table 2-7).

- **Net Earnings Growth** This corporate measurement is also called *net income growth*. This is the increase in dollars and/or percent over the previous financial period. If the net income for the previous period were $8,749,620, then compared with $9,658,800 (Table 2-1), the dollar increase would be $909,180, or 10.4 percent. See Revenue Growth.

- **Net Earnings or Net Income** This is income after all expenses have been deducted. Because of the high visibility of this net-net, it is used for many of the traditional "return" formulas. In Table 2-1, this is $9,658,800. It is best used as a company-wide indicator due to a number of expenses that are not easily identified as division-specific. It is also commonly referred to as the "bottom line."

- **NOPAT (Net Operating Profit After Taxes)** This consists of operating income or EBIT ($20,354,700 in Table 2-1) minus taxes ($6,714,800) plus goodwill amortization ($2,624,800) and interest expense ($3,845,700), or $20,110,400.

- **Net Worth Growth** This is the increase in shareholder equity measured by subtracting the previous year total from the current year total. In the example, if the previous year were $125,471,500 and the current year were $137,077,400 (Table 2-8), then the increase would be $11,605,900, or 9.3 percent.

- **Operating Profit** Also called *Operating Income*, this is income before interest and taxes (EBIT). In Table 2-1, this is $20,354,700. It is more likely to be used for a unit of the organization; company-wide corporate income measurements are more likely to be Economic Profit or NOPAT.

- **Overhang** This is the number of common stock shares of all "in-the-money," unexercised stock options (150,000 in Table 2-9) and unvested stock awards (none in Table 2-9) plus the number of shares of stock available for use (600,000 in Table 2-9). This amount (750,000) divided by the total number of common shares outstanding (15,250,000 in Table 2-1) equals the overhang percentage (4.9%). It is another measure of potential dilution. *Potential overhang* is overhang plus the number of additional shares requested by management for option and award use. If the company were requesting an additional 1,500,000 shares, potential overhang would be 2,250,000 (750,000 + 1,500,000), or 14.8 percent.

- **Peer Rankings** This is the result of comparing company performance as defined by any of the absolute or relative performance measurements against a defined list of comparable companies.

- **Phantom Stock** This is a financially defined instrument of varying definitions (often times a book value) other than common stock of the company.

- **Present Value** This is today's value of a payment to be made in the future. Assumptions about future interest rates are used to arrive at this value.

- **Preferred Stock** Like common stock, the price of preferred stock is set by the marketplace and significantly affected by interest rates in relation to the prefixed dividend, which must be paid before dividends are paid on common stock. In case of bankruptcy, preferred shareholders will stand in line ahead of common shareholders. *Convertible preferred stock* (like convertible debenture) permits the holder to convert to common stock at specified terms (e.g., dates and prices).

- **Price Dividend Ratio** This is also called the *yield*. A stock price of $10 with a dividend for the last four quarters of 46¢ would have a ratio of 21.7 to 1 ($10 ÷ 46¢), or 4.6 percent if expressed as a percentage (46¢ ÷ $10).

- **Price Earnings Ratio (PE)** This is the result of dividing the stock price by earnings per share for the last four quarters. In the example, with a stock price of $10 per share and earnings of 63¢ per share, the PE ratio would be 15.9 to 1 ($10 ÷ 63¢). A company with a low rather than high ratio is generally a more attractive potential investment; however, that is very simplistic. Ratios vary by industry and within industry by what the company is doing. For example, the PE ratio may be high because the company has depressed earnings caused by large-scale startup costs, or it might be very low because earnings have been increased through asset sales. It is important to analyze earnings as well as the number of shares of stock outstanding. Is the company issuing a lot of stock to its employees? Is it buying stock back in the open market?

- **Receivables** This is money due the company from sales of products or services to its customers. In Table 2-6, this is $19,463,200 with a reserve of $784,600 for doubtful accounts.

- **Restricted Stock** This is stock with restrictions on when it can be sold. *See* Stock Award.

- **Return** This includes a wide variety of definitions of income in relation to a specified type of investment (e.g., see the various "return" definitions listed in this section). It is important to determine if the "return" formula is for a year or a multiple of years (e.g., three years). The advantage of a multiple-year formula is to smooth out ups and downs. However, it may also mask poor performance. Namely, if the multi-year return is higher than the most recent year, it means performance has deteriorated. Conversely, if the multi-year return is lower than the most recent annual return, the position is improving.

- **Return on Assets (ROA)** This is net income divided by total assets. This formula is not uncommon with capital-intensive companies and financial institutions as a measurement of the return on this definition of capital. In the example, using net income of $9,658,800 (Table 2-1) and total assets of $330,997,900 (Table 2-6), this would give an ROA of 2.9 percent. This percentage excludes the time value of money because non-current assets are carried on the balance sheet at historical cost less depreciation and amortization.

- **Return on Capital** This is synonymous with ROCE.

- **Return on Capital Employed (ROCE)** This is net income plus after-tax interest expense divided by capital employed, namely, shareholder equity and long-term debt. This formula is also called *Return on Capital* and *Return on Total Capital* (ROTC). In the example, this would be shareholder equity of $137,077,400 (Table 2-8) plus long-term debt of $126,763,900 (Table 2-7), or $263,841,300 divided into net income ($9,658,800 in Table 2-1) plus after-tax interest: $3,845,700 (pre-tax interest) in Table 2-1 times 1 minus .35 or .65 (due to 35-percent corporate tax rate) or $2,499,705 (after-tax interest), or 4.6 percent. Some choose to use total non-current liabilities instead of long-term debt ($170,237,400) to see how management has used these available dollars.

- **Return on Equity (ROE)** This is net income divided by total shareholders equity. In the example, this would be $9,658,800 (Table 2-1) divided by $137,077,400 (Table 2-8), or 7.0 percent at the corporate level. It is appropriate with companies that have little or no debt. To the extent assets are undervalued (see Return on Investment), Shareholder Equity will be comparably lowered, thereby possibly distorting any ROE measurements.

- **Return on Investment (ROI)** This is a generic term to describe any of the "return" formulas (e.g., ROA, ROCE, ROE, and others). It may be somewhat misleading if a significant portion of "investment" is in undervalued assets (e.g., land and significantly depreciated assets). In such situations, executives might be reluctant to invest in needed asset replacements since it would make improvement difficult because of a larger "investment."

- **Return on Net Assets (RONA)** This is net assets of $307,314,800 in the example (see Net Assets definition), divided into operating income ($20,354,700 in Table 2-1), or 6.6 percent. Like ROA, it is typically used for capital-intensive organizations. It is frequently used at the SBU level where there is no shareholder equity. Nonetheless, the net effect of the calculation is similar to ROTC and ROCE.

- **Return on Sales (ROS)** This is net income divided by net sales (e.g., sales minus freight and returns). In Table 2-1, this is $9,658,800 divided by $101,546,400, or 9.5 percent. This is frequently used by manufacturing and service sector companies.

- **Return on Shareholder Equity (ROSE)** This is synonymous with ROE.

- **Return on Total Capital (ROTC)** This is synonymous with *Return on Capital Employed* (ROCE).

- **Revenue** This is synonymous with *Sales*.

- **Revenue Growth** This corporate measurement is also called *sales growth*. It is the increase in dollars and/or percent over the previous financial period. If the sales for the previous period were $95,836,700, then compared with the $101,546,400 (Table 2-1), the dollar increase would be $5,709,700, or 6.0 percent. If the percentage increase is greater than that of net earnings growth, it could mean expenses are increasing faster than sales (often times the indication of an expanding business with high marketing and developing costs holding down earnings). If the percentage is lower than net earnings percentage growth, it may mean a shrinking future even though expenses are apparently being controlled. See Net Earnings Growth.

- **Risk-Free Rate of Return** This is the yield or return on the investment in such "safe" investments as securities of the United States.

- **Risk Premium** This is the expected additional return on common stock by shareholders vs. a no-risk instrument such as a government bond.

- **Run Rate** This is the percentage of shares granted annually under option (or award) as a percentage of the total shares outstanding. In Table 2-9, if only 100,000 shares were optioned annually, this would be .7 percent of the 15,250,000 shares outstanding. Percentages of approximately 1 percent are not uncommon.

- **Sales Per Employee** Sales divided by the number of employees in the unit is sometimes used as a measurement of people-intensive organizations.

- **Shareholder Equity** This is what is left after all liabilities have been subtracted from assets. In Table 2-8, this is $137,077,400. It hypothetically is what the shareholders would receive after all debts were paid. Shareholder equity is often called the *book value*, or *breakup value*, of the company—a term well-known to corporate raiders who purchase controlling interest in a company because the breakup value is in excess of market capitalization (i.e., product of number of shares times the price per share of stock).

- **Shareholder Value Increase (SVI)** This is stock price plus the dividend (typically the value of such dividend reinvested in the stock at the time paid) less the price of the stock at the beginning of the year. If the stock price were $9 at the beginning of the year and $10 at year end with 46¢ paid in dividends during the year, the SVI would be $1.46 ($10 - $9 + $0.46), or 16.2 percent ($1 + 46¢ ÷ $9).

- **Shares Authorized** This is the total number of shares of common stock authorized by the shareholders for use by the company. Within this overall total (which is 30 million shares in Table 2-9), there is a total number of shares approved by the shareholders for use in the stock plan (options and awards) for executives and others. In Table 2-9, this is 1,500,000 shares.

- **Shares Available for Use** This is the total number of shares approved for use less the number of shares exercised and not exercised (excluding the number forfeited). In Table 2-9, this is 600,000 shares (i.e., 1,500,000 shares less 900,000 shares).

- **Shares to Sales Ratio** This is the result of dividing net sales ($101,546,400) by the number of diluted shares outstanding (16,250,000), or 6.2 (to 1). Low ratios (compared with comparable companies) might suggest overuse of common stock and/or under performance.

- **Shares Exercised** This is the total number of granted shares that have been exercised and are now in the optionee's hands (or the marketplace if they were sold). In Table 2-9, this is shown as 750,000.

- **Shares Forfeited** These are shares that were either under option or restrictions and have been forfeited because the option period lapsed or the individual left before exercising the option or receiving the award. In Table 2-9, this is 100,000 shares.

- **Shares Granted** This is the total number of shares granted under the stock plan. In Table 2-9, this is 1,000,000.

- **Shares Not Exercised** These are shares either under option or awards under restrictions that have not been earned. In Table 2-9, the total is 150,000 shares. This total consists of vested and non-vested shares. *Vested* shares (50,000 in Table 2-9) have met the time restriction and are exercisable at any time. Non-vested shares (100,000 in Table 2-9) cannot be exercised by the optionee because the earn-out time requirements have not been met.

- **Shares Not Exercised and Available for Use** These are shares available for use (600,000 shares in Table 2-9) plus shares not exercised (150,000 shares), or a total of 750,000 shares. This total is often called the *overhang.* Typically, it is expressed as a percentage of shares outstanding (15,250,000 in Table 2-1), or 4.9 percent in Table 2-9.

- **Shares Outstanding** This is the total number of shares outstanding in the marketplace (15,250,000 in Table 2-1).

- **Stock Award** This is issuance of a stated number of shares of common stock of the company at no cost (other than tax consequences) to the recipient with or without restrictions on when it can be sold. The former is called *restricted stock.*

- **Stock Market** This is where shares of company stock are traded. They are also known as *secondary markets* because shares are bought and sold between investors, using stockbrokers rather than directly by the company. Stocks sold to an investor such as through an *Initial Public Offering (IPO)* would be the *primary market.*

- **Stock Option** This is the right of a person to buy a stated number of shares of common stock of a company at a prescribed price over a specified period of time. They may either be granted by the company to an employee or another (e.g., vendor or non-management director) or sold by investors in the marketplace. In the first instance, the company receives the proceeds from the person buying the stock; in the second situation, an independent investor receives the money. They are similar to warrants.

- **Stock Price** This is the price set by the marketplace (i.e., stock market). In the example, it is $10 per share of common stock.

- **Stock Split** This is when the number of shares is increased by a stated ratio (e.g., two for one) with the stock price appropriately adjusted. For example, a two-for-one split with a stock selling at $100 a share would result in an investor having two shares each valued at $50. A reverse split is when the number of shares is decreased (e.g., one-for-two). This is often done to boost the price of a low selling stock. In this case, a shareholder having two shares of stock worth $10 each would receive one share valued at $20.

- **Total Capital** This is long-term debt (the sum of monies owed by the company that extend beyond a year) and shareholder equity, or $126,763,900 (Table 2-7) and $137,077,400 (Table 2-8), respectively. In the example, this is $263,841,300 (see Capital Employed). Some choose to use total non-current liabilities ($170,237,400 in the example) instead of long-term debt to see how management has used these available dollars.

- **Total Shareholder Return (TSR)** *See* Shareholder Value Increase.

- **Treasury Stock** These are shares of the company's common stock that it has purchased in the marketplace for later use, typically, employee compensation and benefit plans using company stock. They are also called treasury shares. In Table 2-8, the cost of the 795,200 shares purchased is reported to be $6,362,200.

- **Treasury Stock Method** This is the method used to calculate diluted EPS. It assumes that outstanding options have been exercised at the beginning of the year and all restricted stock awards have been released at the same time. The proceeds received are used to hypothetically buy back at the average market price (for the period) as many shares as possible. Proceeds include not only cash from stock option exercises but the cash effect of tax deductions.

- **Warrant** This is the right of an investor to buy a stated number of shares of common stock of a company at a prescribed price over a specified time period. Typically, they are packaged with bonds or preferred stock sold by the company, enabling the investor an opportunity to participate in an increase in the value of the common stock. They are similar to stock options.

- **Working Capital** *See* Liquidity.

- **Yield** This is the rate of return on an investment. For bonds, it is interest received divided by bond cost. For stock, it is annual dividends per share divided by the stock price. If dividends for the year were $.46 ($6,953,600 from Table 2-2 divided by 15,250,000 from

Table 2-1) and the stock price was $10, the yield would be 4.6 percent. Yield increases with rising dividends and falling stock prices and decreases with reduced dividends and increasing stock prices. This enables an easy comparison with alternative investments after adjusting for future growth and investment risk.

Combination Formulas. As indicated at the beginning of this chapter, there are four categories of measurement: (1) relative return on a financial measurement expressed in percentage terms; (2) increase or decrease in absolute dollars; (3) relative value of percentages other than returns on income; and (4) various combinations of the first three. For example, two relative return formulas could be selected (e.g., ROA and ROE) with performance measured in terms of which was greater or which was less. An absolute increase formula (e.g., net income) could be combined with a relative return (e.g., ROE) to determine performance, defined as the extent to which net income exceeded a prescribed ROE minimum. Permutations and combinations abound and more will be illustrated later in this chapter.

Relevance of Financial Measurements. Whereas Old Economy companies have relied on traditional financial measurements more than New Economy companies, how important are earnings in determining a company's stock price? Some will argue that the stock price is the present value of future earnings. Others will argue that it accounts for less than 20 percent. The New Economy provides many examples to validate this view.

While financial measurements are commonly used in short-term and long-term incentive plans, do they really reflect the way an organization measures its performance? They account for financial stewardship, but do they measure value added? Furthermore, they are backward looking not forward focused and therefore do not highlight important changes until after the fact. For these reasons, exclusive use of financial measurements is probably inappropriate. There are non-financial performance measurements that, although more difficult to quantify than financial measurements, may be more appropriate in indicating how an organization is truly performing. However, such measurements lack the definition of consistency of financial measurements, which are prescribed by GAAP.

Other Key Measurements Within the Company. As we have seen, there are a number of financial measurements available; however, they exclude a host of other items that could, and maybe should, be measured. Financial measurements do not include all factors that management looks at when running the company. These factors include non-financial assets and processes that led to the creation of value. Often times these are grouped in a category called *goal sharing* since eligible persons share credit for the extent to which the goal has been achieved. When including non-financial measurements, it is important that each be clearly defined in terms of output and time. Needless to say, the objective must be important to the organization and it must be attainable. Here are some possibilities:

- **Culture** The embodiment of values and beliefs of the workforce on how work is to be done. This is especially important when companies are attempting to change their culture. Attitude surveys and behavioral tests are typical measurements.

- **Intellectual Capital** It has been often cited that an organization's workforce is its only sustainable competitive advantage. The collective and interactive skills of an organization's workforce (and contractors) at all levels of the company are the major factor in determining its creativity, productivity, and customer satisfaction. The first two are obvious, the last less so. But empirical evidence suggests that customers are most likely to be satisfied with a company if the employees (with whom they interact) are also satisfied; the reverse is also true. Dissatisfied employees often result in dissatisfied customers. Therefore, employee work should be evaluated in terms of what they know, what they do, and how they do it. The first is knowledge based, the second is output based, and the third is value based.

Therefore, the motivational model which indicates that effort times ability equals output needs to describe ability in terms of the knowledge (intellectual capital) and traits (value systems) of each individual. Knowledge can be measured in terms of the cost or hours of training (an input) or by skill-level testing. Effort is based in large part on the willingness (i.e., commitment) to optimize one's skills and values. This degree of willingness is based on satisfaction with how the individual is being treated. Demonstrated effort by the company to provide employment—not necessarily job—security is a significant factor. Satisfaction levels can be measured by attitude surveys, as well as by the number of charges of discriminatory treatment, and turnover statistics measuring the loss of people the company wants to retain.

A subset of intellectual capital is a measurement of the depth and readiness of individuals to step up to greater levels of responsibility. At the top of the organization, this would be described as *executive succession* and possibly be a specific performance objective for the CEO.

- **Intellectual Property** How strong are the copyrights and patents of the company? When do they expire? What is the likely impact on revenue and earnings of the company?

- **Organizational Objectives** This covers a wide range of possibilities ranging from business strategies (the "what") to culture (the "how"). Business strategies might include: organizational restructuring (acquisitions, divestitures, mergers, alliances, and/or joint ventures) and planning issues (environmental compliance, product portfolio, technology transfers, executive succession, and workforce diversity). Culture defines how work is done and how people are treated. Ethical behavior is only the first rung in developing a high-performance workplace. People must believe they are treated with dignity and respect and all dealings are open and honest.

- **Product/Service Innovation** New product development can be examined at the corporate as well as the divisional level. Some measure the cost of research and development in relation to sales. This is an input model and does little in measuring the effectiveness of the other expenditures. Some will measure the market potential of new products in the pipeline. This is a market-share model. Others will measure R&D costs over a period of time in relation to new sales (namely, the product of the expenditure). This is an output-cost model. Some will measure the time from discovery (or development) until the product is marketed, namely, how long does it take to bring a product to market? This is a process or calendar model. Others will measure the prevalence of new products as a percentage of total sales (e.g., 20 percent of total sales came from products not sold the previous year, or 80 percent of total sales came from products not sold five years ago). This is a revenue output model. One would expect the percentage to increase with an increase in the period of time measured.

- **Productivity** If output is defined as volume times cost, then productivity increases can come from increasing volume with no increases in cost, decreases in cost with no decrease in volume, or increases in volume and decrease in cost. Productivity can be measured at all levels of the organization.

- **Quality** This is defined in terms of nearness to perfection at any level of the company. Some have chosen the Six-Sigma Standard, in other words, 99.99966-percent perfect. Stated another way, only 3.4 imperfect products for every one million produced. The quality standard selected should be consistent with the requirement, especially if the product is delivered at higher cost; otherwise the lower-cost product would be the obvious choice of the buyer.

- **Quantity** This is volume, or the number of units produced or sold at any level of the company. It excludes cost and price. It is useful in netting out price changes in measuring productivity.

Combination of Financial and Other Key Measurements. It is more difficult to motivate individuals with multi-factor performance measurements than with a single measuring stick because it requires the person to focus on a number of different items, some of which, at least on the surface, may appear to be contradictory. Nonetheless, multi-measurement systems add balance to the process.

It would not be unreasonable to have a measurement combining innovation, productivity, customer satisfaction, employee commitment, and financial results. Designing the most appropriate mix must be company specific. It is also likely that the measurements will change from time to time. At the minimum, they should be reviewed annually to ensure they are still focusing on the key components.

Sub-Unit Measurements. Because of their composition, some measurements are not appropriate for sub-units of the company, whereas all of the ones discussed so far could be used at the corporate level. Shown in Table 2-10 are some that could be used in sub-units of the company. In selecting the ones to be used, make a determination of whether to use the same definition on a company-wide plan as well. For example, if operating income is used for a division plan and the division head will be paid partly on company and partly on division performance, should the company plan also include operating income, or perhaps EBIT, or EBITDA?

Some of these measurements will be more relevant than others. For example, if the sub-unit is dedicated to manufacturing, RONA and gross margin would probably be more relevant than innovation. If it were a research unit, innovation might be key, whereas with a sales unit, customer satisfaction and retention would be high on the list.

External Measurements

Like internal measurements, there are two categories of *external measurements*: financial and non-financial.

Financial Measurements Outside the Company. There are two types: performance of other companies and general economic factors.

- **Performance of Other Companies** These measurements are typically relative to own company performance and could use any of the measurements identified as internal to

Relative Returns	Return on Assets (ROA) Return on Net Assets (RONA) Return on Sales (ROS)
Absolute Changes	EBIT EBITDA Gross Margin
Non-Financial	Customer Satisfaction Customer Retention Expense Budget Innovation Intellectual Capital Productivity Quality Quantity

Table 2-10. Possible sub-unit measurements

the company. The purpose is to show how well the company is doing relative to others. An excellent example of this is the stock chart required to be included in the company proxy statement for publicly traded companies. It could be a company-defined group of companies, an industry sub-set within the appropriate stock exchange, or the composite performance of the entire stock exchange. Such measurements are for shareholder value. However, some companies have designed annual and long-term incentive plan payouts in relation to how well the company has performed against a defined peer group of companies on such factors as earnings per share, economic profit, and return on sales, to mention a few. Valid peer comparisons are very difficult to do because no two companies are alike; however, the objective is to view the comparison from the eyes of an investor trying to decide in which company (in a particular sector) to make an investment.

- **General Economic Factors** Own company performance could be adjusted in light of changes in economic factors. Two key measurements would be the cost of capital and corporate income taxes. One could argue that it is misleading to compare historical performance or even the cost of capital or corporate-taxes change against budgeted expectations when either of these factors is changed. More specifically, one would expect better financial performance if interest rates and/or corporate income taxes decline. Conversely, one would expect poorer performance if the reverse were true. However, some planners attempt to avoid such comparison difficulties by using measurements that exclude their impact. For example, EBIT (earnings before interest and taxes) excludes both, while both are included in net earnings.

Other Key Measurements Outside the Company.

- **Customer Satisfaction** Measured by surveys and/or focus groups, this is an indication of future sales potential company-wide and/or by division. Satisfied customers will buy again; dissatisfied customers will not. Both will tell others; so their experiences also affect future sales. Items measured are quality of product/service in relation to price. Such surveys may also include: delivery of undamaged goods, goods when promised, back-up warranty with fast repair, and fast response to information requests and complaints. When measuring the level of customer satisfaction with own products/services, it is important to put this assessment in terms of customer needs and expectations. Why do the customers who like us value our products/services? What one thing do we do best? What one thing is our greatest opportunity for improvement? Of those who do not value our products/services, what three things must we address to gain their approval? And who are the major competitors and how do they measure up?

- **Customer Retention** This is a measurement of the percentage of customers who come back to buy again. What percentage of first-time customers come back? What percentage keeps coming back? The shorter the interval between their return and the longer the period of continually coming back, the more impressive the indicator.

- **Environmental Compliance** This is a measurement of how well the company is performing in terms of air and water pollution, complying with regulatory requirements. What is the likely financial exposure of non-compliance?

Combination Financial and Non-Financial Measurements

Comparing own financial performance with that of others on earnings per share and stock price could be combined with measurements of customer retention and satisfaction.

Combination Internal and External Measurements

To determine which measurements would be most appropriate, consider the industry, stage of the market cycle, strategy focus, and organization structure. The *industry* will suggest factors on the income statement and balance sheet that will be most significant, as well as the importance of the cash-flow statement. Comments on these were made earlier when reviewing the various financial measurements. As for *market-cycle stage*, as shown in Table 2-11, there is almost a reciprocal relationship between sales and earnings. At the threshold stage, revenue is key as the company looks to establish market position. Profits may be non-existent because of development and marketing costs. In the growth stage, market penetration to increase market share is still key, but profits are becoming important. At maturity, revenue has slowed and profits are high in importance. And in decline, revenue is decreasing but opportunities still exist.

The industry, market stage, strategy focus, and organization structure measurements identified can be measured both for the company itself as well as in relation to identified peer companies. In other words, the internal performance (both financial and non-financial) is assessed and the results compared with external measurements to see how well the company is doing vs. others and in light of major economic factors affecting profitability.

Category	Threshold	Growth	Maturity	Decline
Revenue (Sales)	High	High	Moderate	Low
Profits (Earnings)	Low	Moderate	High	High

Table 2-11. Market stage vs. revenue and profit importance

As described in Chapter 1, *strategy focus* could be community partnership, customer satisfaction, employee intimacy, operational optimization, product/service innovation, and/or shareholder return. Community partnership would measure environmental compliance. Customer satisfaction would measure customer satisfaction and customer retention. Employee intimacy could be measured by employee-attitude surveys, undesirable separations, charges of discriminatory treatment, and improvements in the core-competence knowledge of the workforce. Operational optimization would measure productivity in terms of quality and quantity. Product/service innovation could measure the input, process, and/or output of such efforts (as described earlier in this chapter). And shareholder return would measure the various shareholder return formulas described.

Organizational structure will impact not only the level at which the measurement is made, but given the definition of measurements available, the type most likely used. A centralized organization is likely to emphasize corporate measurements; a decentralized organization is more likely to emphasize measurements at lower levels in the organization. To the extent the latter have no shareholder equity or decisions on taxes and debt, the financial formulas available are even more limited. Nonetheless, a number of possibilities were identified earlier in this chapter.

How Does It Get Done?

Who Determines What Gets Measured?

The measurements for the CEO are typically set by the board of directors and heavily influenced by shareholder input. The measurements for the first level below the CEO are set by the CEO and reflect an allocation of his or her own objectives, in addition to those that the CEO and subordinate also believe appropriate. This breakup and allocation of objectives continues to cascade down through the organization. If done effectively, at lower levels, an employee can see his or her own objectives contribute to the top organizational objectives. This assessment is referred to as *line of sight*, in other words, a straight-line relationship of aggregating performance going up the organization, leading to organization-wide objectives. The performance management process will be described more fully in Chapter 5 (Salary).

There are two types of measurements: input-based and output-based. *Input-based* measurements evaluate what the individual has or possesses. Input consists of knowledge and values and describes what a person can do. *Output-based* defines how a person might do it. Output-based measurements evaluate what was done and how it was done. Input-based measurements are helpful in selecting individuals for work (ranging from initial hire to subsequent promotions); output-based measurements are used for pay actions.

How Are Targets Set?

Targets typically are set in relation to past performance, future expectations, and/or performance of comparable companies. *Historical* (or look-back) targets are improvement-focused in relation to a defined base. *Future* expectations (or look-forward) are described in quantitative ways (perhaps with a look at past performance). *Peer performance* (or look-around) is focused on outperforming organizations in own industry.

Typically, the desired performance level is called the *target*. A predetermined range around it establishes both a *threshold* and a *maximum*. The threshold is the minimum level of performance below which no incentive payment will be made; the *maximum* is the upper limit beyond which no credit will be given for accomplishment.

These three levels of performance are shown in Figure 2-1 along with their respective incentive awards. This concept will be further developed in Chapter 7 (Short-Term Incentives).

Obviously, it is important that whatever is being identified can be measured and that the outcomes are at least influenced, if not totally controlled, by the person being rated. It is equally important to identify those factors outside of the rated person's control and their degree of significance. If setting targets for different measurements and for different parts of the business, the degree of difficulty should be included. These are called *stretch targets*. They should be of equal difficulty rather than equal in *absolute* or percentage improvements.

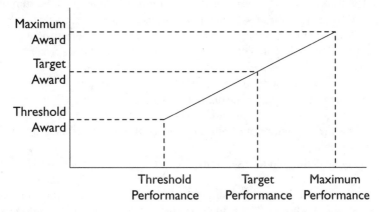

Figure 2-1. Threshold, target, and maximum performance and bonus opportunities

What Is the Performance Period?

The typical *performance period* for executives is the business year (calendar or fiscal depending on the company), although quarterly periods within the year might also be established. While performance is tracked during the period, it is only measured for pay purposes after the performance period has been completed. The emphasis is on results not efforts, although some performance evaluations may include a degree of difficulty factor as well as how the work was done.

How Are Goals Weighted?

If more than one measurement is used, the question is what weight should be given to each? The answer is: it depends. If each is of equal importance, then each is of equal weight. That is the first step in the weighting process. If they are of equal weight, stop. If not, attempt to determine the rough order of magnitude. If, for example, there were four objectives, it might be determined that "A" was four times as important as "D," two times more important than "C," but only slightly more important than "B." However, if "B" were viewed as three times as important as "D," relative weightings would be: A (40 percent), B (30 percent), C (20 percent), and D (10 percent).

What Gets Communicated and When?

Individuals should know *what* is being measured and *how* before the beginning of the measurement period. They should also receive regular reports during the period on progress in relation to the identified target. If these two steps are not performed, how can one expect to motivate performance? People need to know the basis for measuring performance especially as it relates to pay. It is important during the communication phases to show how individual performance is aligned with the identified objectives. This is the *line of sight* alignment. Furthermore, the specific link between performance and pay needs to be clearly described.

How Does Data Get Measured?

This is not a course in statistics, but it is important to quickly highlight some of the more common ways to measure data. Where there is more than one measurable item, data is measured in terms of some definition of average *central tendency* and/or in terms of *dispersion/distribution*.

Central tendency consists of the mean, median, and mode. The *mean* is the sum of the individual items divided by the number of such items. The *median* is the middle value of the data after it has been arrayed low to high in value. The *mode* is the most frequent value, meaning a value must be repeated at least once (thus describing the *frequency* of occurrence). If there were two such most-frequent values, there would be a *bimodal* average.

The mean is the most commonly used, although it is distorted by data significantly higher or lower than the other values being measured. The median is not subject to such distortions but must be arrayed in ascending value in order to be calculated. The mode is easily observable, but only if the data is arrayed with same values clustered. It may not be statistically significant if there are not many data points.

Distribution may be defined in terms of *range* (low to high) or in relation to a measurement of central tendency (typically the mean). This can be shown graphically with a vertical (Y) axis and a horizontal (X) axis. In the example shown in Figure 2-2, the percentage increase in EPS for some 131 companies is shown. The value is shown on the X axis and the number of companies with such a value on the Y axis. This *frequency-distribution* manner of presentation is called a *bar chart*, or *histogram*.

In this example, the data is *skewed positive*. If the data were flip-flopped and 20.1-25.0 the median, the data would be described as *skewed negative*. Had the most common rating been a

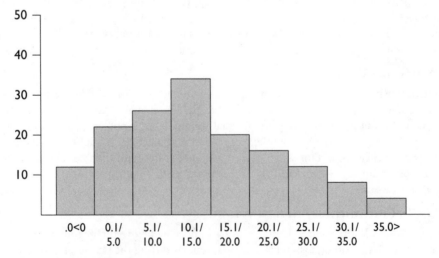

Figure 2-2. Histogram of EPS increase

15.1-20.0 percent increase with ratings both above and below it descending at a comparable rate, the distribution would be described as *normal* or *uniform distribution*. As for central tendency, the median is 10.1-15.0 percent (the 66th company), the mode is also 10.1-15.0 percent (it has the most ratings), and the mean is 12.7 percent [the sum of each rating (1664) divided by the number of ratings (131)]. The standard deviation is the variation from the arithmetic mean. One standard deviation would include all data plus or minus 68.26 percent from the mean. Two standard deviations would be 95.46 percent and three standard deviations would be 99.73 percent of all values.

In Figure 2-3, we show the other common frequency distribution example, a *scattergram*. In this example, the EPS percentage increase (Y axis) is shown in relation to shareholder value percentage increase (X axis). These individual plots could represent survey data for a peer group of companies as well as own results. The line is described as the *line of best fit* (it is an average of the data). It is described as the *least squares line* line of best fit when the values above and below the line are not only equal, but the sum of their squares from the line represents the lowest deviation from the line. A straight line will result using a *linear regression formula*; a curved line will result if a *non-linear regression formula* is used (unless the data is best described by a straight line, then even the non-linear formula will produce a straight line). Additional examples are found in Chapter 5 (Salary), but details on how to calculate these lines can be found in virtually any statistics book.

The relationship of the data on the X and Y axes to the trend line describes the degree of *correlation*. If every plot point were on the trend line, the correlation would be perfect or 1.0. Variations from the line of regression are described in terms of the *standard error of estimate*, as opposed to the standard deviation (which was previously described as variation from the arithmetic mean). One standard error of estimate would include data plus or minus 68.26 percent from the line mean. Two standard errors of estimate would be 95.46 percent, and three standard errors of estimate would be 99.73 percent of all values plotted. Another way to express dispersion is in terms of percentiles, quartiles, and deciles. A *percentile* is 1/100th, the *quartile* is 1/25th, and the *decile* is 1/10th. Thus, if one wanted to be in the 70th percentile, it

Shareholder Value % Increase

Figure 2-3. Scattergram of EPS and shareholder value increase

would mean there would only be 30 percent of the data greater than this value. If there were 50 companies in the study, one would have to rank at least among the top 15 to be in the 70th percentile (i.e., 50 - [.7 x 50]).

When examining data (as well as the measurement of dispersion and central tendency), it is important to remember the distinction between validity and reliability. *Validity* means it is an accurate report of events; *reliability* means you are consistently getting the same answer. Validity without reliability suggests a change in definition; reliability without validity suggests one is not measuring the correct data to accurately describe the situation.

Rater Errors. The more subjective the measurement, the more likely the rating will be subject to rater errors, resulting in an evaluation too negative or too generous. Here are some of the more common problems:

- **Event Influenced** A particular event is used as a generalization of overall performance. This could be a *halo* (everything is good) to *horns* (everything is bad).

- **Person Influenced** Appearance, personality, and potential are used as performance measurements.

- **Time Influenced** Undue emphasis is given to either prior history or most recent event rather than performance over the entire measurement period.

Characteristics of Valid Measurements. In selecting what measures to include when designing the pay program, there are a number of considerations. These include:

- Are the factors being measured the most important ones?
- Are the definitions clear, enabling both a valid and reliable measurement?
- While difficult, are the targets (and even the maximums) attainable?
- Are the factors being measured and the measurements understandable to those being rated?
- Is the degree of difficulty comparable across the organization for similar positions/jobs?
- To what extent are individuals able to achieve the stated performance based on their own efforts? And for group plans, to what extent are the individuals able to at least significantly impact the results?
- Will individuals be able to receive regular feedback on progress?
- Are the raters objective and not subject to bias?
- Has the plan been successfully tested?
- Will the measurements place the company in a cost-effective position with other comparable companies?

Alpha vs. Numeric Ratings. Typically, whatever is being measured is translated into either an alpha or numeric score, thereby enabling not only comparisons with the threshold, target, and maximum values, but also with the scores of others (who may not be measured on exactly the same items). These measurements are then converted into a pay action. This is described in more detail in Chapters 5 (Salary), 7 (Short-Term Incentives), and 8 (Long-Term Incentives).

SUMMARY AND CONCLUSIONS

In designing a pay-for-performance plan, the first and clearly one of the most important steps is to determine what performance will be measured. Will it be financial, non-financial, or a combination of the two? Will it be based on individual, group, or a combination of the two? Will there be a hurdle (minimum level) before payment will be made? Will there be a target? Will the performance relative to other companies in one's peer group be assessed? These are all-important issues to be examined because empirical evidence suggests that what gets measured gets attention. The attention is even greater if it is the basis for earning money.

An additional question that needs to be addressed is will the same measurement(s) be used for salary, short-term, and long-term incentives? Typically, the answer is "no." Individual performance typically is the sole basis for salary actions, while the basis for short-term incentives is often combined with group (up to and including company-wide) performance, and only group performance is the basis for long-term incentive payouts. For example, a salary increase might be for satisfactorily doing the routine, day-to-day work, whereas the short-term incentive might be based on several specific individual objectives as well as the extent a group objective was achieved (e.g., economic profit). The long-term incentive might be tied to earnings per share and shareholder value increase vs. a defined peer group of companies. Chapter 5 (Salary), Chapter 7 (Short-Term Incentives), and Chapter 8 (Long-Term Incentives) will explore these approaches in more detail. A key factor is avoiding paying more than once for a particular measurement over a prescribed period of time.

Note: You should not rely on accounting, tax, SEC, or other professional service statements in this chapter. You need to seek appropriate professional counsel for such guidance. Statements made in this chapter and elsewhere are offered as being illustrative to help you frame such further investigations with the help of counsel.

Chapter 3

Current vs. Deferred Compensation

he five compensation elements described and defined in the previous chapter will each be explained in greater detail in subsequent chapters. *When* the compensation is received is an issue in each instance. Will it be received when earned or deferred to some future date? The first situation is very simple. The latter is not. This chapter will discuss the implication of current vs. deferred compensation, setting the stage in subsequent chapters for the *what* and *how* unique to each of the five elements.

INTRODUCTION

In order to understand the five compensation elements covered in subsequent chapters, it is important first to understand the implications of current vs. deferred compensation. The subject is presented early in order to avoid repetition in later discussions.

Deferred compensation is an agreement between a company and an individual employee that all or a portion of compensation will be paid at a future date. Distribution options typically include: lump sum, installments, and annuity payments. The amount under installments is determined by the number of payments, the amount under annuity is typically determined by mortality tables. The period of deferral can be either short or long term in nature. Deferred payment is similar in result to restricted compensation plans where the executive has to earn out the full rights to ownership, unless the benefits are non-forfeitable. The latter is usually done for the executive's benefit, whereas the former is a form of golden handcuffs benefiting the company.

The objective of deferrals is to shift income from current to future years in order to maximize personal income needs. One should clearly understand that deferring or not deferring is an investment decision, but only after it is determined that money is not needed currently for personal or family obligations (e.g., education and housing). Included in the decision to defer are assumptions about current and future events (e.g., taxes, inflation, risk of forfeiture, investment opportunities, and need for liquidity). Some take the simplistic view that it will always be beneficial to defer dollars (which will be highly taxed now) to a point in the future when income (and tax rates) will be lower. While this may have been true when marginal taxes were as high as 91 percent, it is not true when marginal maximums are 50 percent or less, since the opportunity for a significant reduction is lessened. Furthermore, there is less of an executive need to defer due to improved pension plans and capital accumulation programs, although, as will be shown in the chapter on employee benefits and perquisites, the company typically supplements qualified pension benefits with non-qualified amounts.

VOLUNTARY AND INVOLUNTARY DEFERRALS

Deferred compensation is either voluntary or mandatory in nature, and can be applicable to each of the five compensation elements (i.e., salary, short-term incentives, long-term incentives, employee benefits, and perquisites). Under a mandatory plan, the company unilaterally defers a portion of compensation in accord with a schedule (e.g., equal installments from the short-term incentive award over three years beginning now, or equal installments from a long-term incentive plan over 10 years beginning at retirement). Under voluntary plans, the individual enters into an agreement with the employer to defer a portion of compensation (e.g., salary, short- or long-term incentive payment) for a stated number of years. Such plans range from qualified retirement plans (where deferral is an inherent characteristic of the defined benefit or defined contribution plan) to personalized employment contracts. Thus, the spectrum runs from arrangements open to all to individually negotiated agreements, the latter often in conjunction with employment negotiations.

TYPES OF DEFERRED COMPENSATION

Plans are either funded or non-funded, qualified or nonqualified, and forfeitable or non-forfeitable. As shown in the matrix (Table 3-1), this results in eight possible combinations. We could add voluntary or involuntary; however, that would make it unnecessarily complicated—viewing 16 combinations, many of which are impossible to do.

Type Plans	Forfeitable	Non-Forfeitable
Funded • Qualified • Non-Qualified	 1 2	 3 4
Non-Funded • Qualified • Non-Qualified	 5 6	 7 8

Table 3-1. Type of deferred compensation matrix

Funded vs. Non-Funded

A *funded* plan is one where the benefits promised by the employer are secured by rights to property (e.g., stock, insurance, or some other negotiable item). Distinction may be drawn between informal and indirect funding, and formally funded plans. In the former, the company sets up a reserve or possibly even takes out an insurance contract or invests in a mutual stock fund for the amount of the liability but retains sole control over its application. Thus, in case of financial failure of the company, the employee stands in line as a general unsecured creditor seeking settlement of a claim. In a formally funded plan, the funding of the liability is direct and the payment will be made from the property set aside. A *non-funded* plan is one backed simply by a promise of the employer to pay. The mere promise to pay does not trigger an income tax liability to the recipient as long as such promise does not include earmarked funds that would put the recipient ahead of general creditors of the company according to Revenue Ruling 70-435 by the Internal Revenue Service (IRS).

If the company wishes to fund the payments through a life insurance contract on the executive's life, it will probably use a corporate, variable, universal life policy rather than a retail or traditional whole-life type of policy. The premiums will be invested in mutual funds held inside the policy. This strategy will allow the company to provide the executive with investment options that are similar to those available in a 401(k) plan. A number of insurance companies have developed such policies specifically for the corporate market.

Most policies that have been designed for this market have been priced so that the sponsoring company does not incur a charge to earnings as a result of acquiring such policies, and therefore, they are desirable assets to informally fund the liabilities associated with deferred compensation. This is true because of the tax-free, inside buildup afforded cash values of policies that comply with Section 264 of the IRC.

Companies choosing to employ this strategy often will fund the liabilities in the aggregate rather than attempt to fund liabilities by purchasing specific policies on participants and match assets and liabilities on an individual basis. This strategy further distances the participant from the funding used to support the plan and therefore reduces the possibility of constructive receipt. The policies are owned by the company and all benefits are paid to the company for the purpose of offsetting liabilities associated with the deferred compensation plan. Corporate-owned life insurance is often referred to as COLI or TOLI (trust-owned life insurance).

Conversely, an executive may go to an insurance company for a surety bond that will ensure payment. If the executive pays the premium, there is no tax liability; if the company pays, it is taxable income to the executive. Other ways in which the employer can fund the payments include mutual funds, company stocks (own or others), and/or bonds (governmental or corporate). As will be described later in a discussion of tax treatment, it is important to know who owns the funds. A *secular trust* is one where the assets are for the exclusive use of paying the executive and therefore subject to taxes. A modification is when the executive is given the right to receive the employer contribution directly or have it paid by the employer to the trust. This changes the status to an *employee-grantor secular trust*. As such, the employee is taxed directly thereby avoiding the trust becoming a taxpayer.

Another approach is the SERP swap. This is the exchange by the executive of all or a portion of non-qualified supplement executive retirement plan (SERP) benefits for a split dollar insurance policy with the company paying all or a portion of the premium. In essence, the executive gives up payments that would otherwise be made during his/her lifetime in exchange for more favorable estate and income taxes at the time of death. This assumes payments are for a prescribed period of time. These arrangements must be carefully designed in light of accounting and tax requirements, which, due to their complexity and changing nature, are not discussed here.

A *rabbi trust* (so named for a tax decision dealing with a rabbi's pension plan) may be either an unsecured promise to pay or funded. It is also called a *grantor trust*. However, if it is funded, the funds are available to the company's creditors as well as the executive. The trust is established by the employer entering into an *irrevocable trust* agreement with a trustee responsible for ensuring that the terms of the trust agreement are executed. The trustee is often a bank but could be a designated individual. The tax status of an irrevocable trust is shown in Figure 3-1.

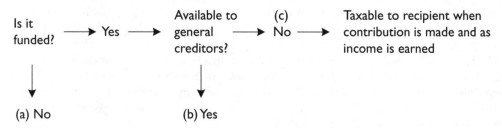

Figure 3-1. Tax status of an irrevocable trust

Example "A" is an unfunded or *dry rabbi trust*. Example "B" is a funded or *wet rabbi trust*, but since the funds are available to general creditors, there is no tax liability to the individual until benefits are actually received. While a properly constructed rabbi trust cannot protect the executive against the company's later inability to pay the promised benefits, it can and should be able to protect the executive against the company's later unwillingness to pay the promised amounts. Example "C" shows that trust benefits are set aside for the beneficiary; therefore, payments made to the trust (when made) and income (when earned) are taxable to the beneficiary. This is a *secular trust* and is defined in Section 402(b) of the IRC. A common form of a "dry" rabbi trust going "wet" is a *springing rabbi trust*; namely, it is funded at time of a change of control of the company. In such event, it is not uncommon the company will gross up the individual's pay to cover the tax liability.

Should the company use company stock to fund a rabbi trust (still keeping it available to general creditors) the company can avoid variable accounting if it pays it out in company stock according to the Financial Accounting Standards Board's (FASB) Emerging Issues Task Force. However, as stated in EITF Issue 97-14, should it be converted to cash, then there will be a charge to the income statement for the appreciation in value over the period.

Qualified vs. Non-Qualified

A *qualified* plan must meet a number of tests dealing with such items as: permanency, non-discriminatory coverage and non-discriminatory benefits (these cannot favor higher-paid employees), and non-recoverability of employer contributions. It is called a qualified plan because it qualifies for favorable tax treatment under the IRC. Namely, the advantage of such plans, covered by Section 401 of the IRC and the Employer Retirement Income Security Act of 1974 (ERISA), is that while the employer receives a tax deduction on the amount of the contribution to the plan, the employee's tax liability is deferred until benefits are actually received. To qualify, plans must meet prescribed eligibility, vesting, funding, fiduciary, and other requirements prescribed by ERISA. Additionally, when the amounts are received, they may be rolled over into another qualified plan thereby deferring taxation to still a later date. A *non-qualified* plan is one not meeting the requirements of Section 401 of the Code; therefore, there is no company tax deduction until the employee receives taxable income and the individual is barred from making a tax-free rollover into a qualified plan. Many of these qualify as a *top hat pension plan* (which deals with payments over a period of more than several years) as opposed to a *top hat welfare plan* (which relates to severance pay and various types of insurance coverage). ERISA limits coverage to a select group of management or highly compensated employees. However, the Department of Labor in 1990 added that this group must have the ability to affect or substantially influence the design and operation of the plan thereby accepting the attendant risks. It is essential that companies ensure they are in compliance with ERISA requirements to avoid problems with the Department of Labor, which is responsible for administering ERISA. Qualified plans, by definition, are non-discriminatory in nature. However, questions to be answered when non-qualified deferrals are permitted include:

1. **Who is eligible?** If not all employees, who is eligible? This goes back to the definition of an executive covered in Chapter 1. Typically, eligible persons would include those who might receive a short-term incentive. However, as the eligibility for such plans is pushed further down in the organization, some additional definition will be required.

2. **What portion of current pay may be deferred?** In addition to short-term (and long-term) incentives, plans may permit deferral of portion of salary. In case of incentives, the full amount may be deferrable, but for salary, there may be a limit expressed either as a percentage of salary, dollar annual amount, or some combination of the two. It may also be stated in terms of amounts in excess of ERISA limits. Section 401 prescribes the limit on pay that may be used for benefits. Section 402 states the limit of pre-tax 401(k) benefits. And Section 415 states the annual limit to defined contribution plans and the annual benefit limit from defined benefit plans.

3. **What portion of deferral is optional vs. mandatory?** Deferrals may be mandatory, voluntary, or a combination of the two. Mandatory deferrals typically apply to a portion of annual incentive, when used, and only for a limited period of time (e.g., three to five years). The rationale is to lock the individual into staying. Such plans are not as frequently used as they once were because companies realized that outstanding performers could always be bought out, leaving them only with locked-in average performers. Voluntary-only deferrals are the most common and are permitted because they are attractive to the executive. A combination of mandatory and voluntary deferral could be designed but is uncommon.

4. **How far in the future is deferral permitted?** Deferrals are essentially of two types: short-term and long-term. The first is for a lump-sum payment or a period of several years while the latter typically either goes to retirement or begins with retirement.

5. **When must election be made?** The safe harbor provision would require deferrals to be made before the first day deferral amounts may be earned. Typically, the executive would make a determination each year on the amount he or she would like deferred and the amount of payment for each year of payout. Conversely, the company may mandate the amount to be deferred each year.

6. **When is the decision made on payout form of the deferral?** The safest point in time would be to make this decision at the same time as deciding how much to defer. Later decisions could trigger tax consequences.

7. **What conditions will be imposed to receive deferred pay?** Must the individual be on the payroll at time payments are to begin? Since these are payments on monies already earned it seems unfair to impose additional requirements for payment.

8. **What appreciation formula will apply to the deferral?** Deferrals that are expressed in shares of stock or stock units have a built-in appreciation factor (hopefully). But cash deferrals will erode in value over time because of lost investment opportunities. Therefore, it is logical to either build in a prescribed appreciation factor or permit the executive to select among a list of possibilities.

9. **Will the deferral be secured and funded?** The company may choose to fund the deferrals through a number of different ways (e.g., stock purchases, insurance contracts, or other purchases), or it may decide simply to keep it on the books as an unsecured liability.

10. **What reports will the executive periodically receive on deferral status?** It is important the executive receive at least annually a schedule of the current status of deferrals, including scheduled payment dates and amounts.

Forfeitable vs. Non-Forfeitable

A *forfeitable* benefit is one that the employee must earn. Typical arrangements would call for a time period—either a stated number of years (e.g., five) or upon retirement. In addition, some plans will require that the employee not engage in any activity that could be viewed by the company as being in competition with its lines of business. A *non-forfeitable* benefit is one in which the executive is completely and immediately 100 percent vested.

Combinations

Now, let's examine the essential characteristics of each of the eight combinations listed in Table 3-1 to determine their degree of plausibility and attractiveness to employer and employee. Note that the numbers below coincide with those on Table 3-1.

1. **Funded, qualified, forfeitable plan.** This type of plan, due to its qualified nature, has very definite limitations on the degree of forfeitability. By definition it cannot be any more severe than that allowed by ERISA (see the section on Retirement in Chapter 6, "Employee Benefits," for a description). These plans are probably not very attractive to the executive because their qualified nature limits the extent of benefits the company is prepared to give—since they must essentially apply to all employees. Other than for the basic retirement benefit, this is not an attractive alternative to either employer (due to cost) or executive (due to limitation on amount of benefit).

2. **Funded, non-qualified, forfeitable plan.** This plan is identical to the one just described except that the employer can tailor the plan to a small group of employees or even one individual. It is the previously defined wet rabbi trust. Payments are secured by a non-qualified trust, insurance contract, or reserve account. Since the payments are subject to a substantial degree of forfeiture, the employee has no income-tax liability until such restrictions are removed. However, the employer is similarly barred from taking a tax deduction until the restrictions are removed. Thus, while this plan may be attractive to the employee, it is not very attractive to the employer (who must set aside non-deductible dollars to fund the benefit).

3. **Funded, qualified, non-forfeitable plans.** This is the same as the first plan described except that employees have 100-percent, immediate vesting. Thus, it is even less attractive to employers than the first alternative, for in addition to all the limitations of a qualified plan, the cost of this type of plan is even greater since there are no forfeitures that can be used to offset funding the non-forfeited benefits. Since employers will be forced to lower benefits in designing such a plan, it is not very attractive to executives either because, of the eight alternatives, it will probably provide the lowest benefit for the highly paid.

4. **Funded, non-qualified, non-forfeitable plan.** While at first glance this plan should be the most attractive to the executive (since risk is eliminated and the nonqualified nature permits a generous benefit design), it is rarely used. The reason being that because it is funded and non-forfeitable, the IRS will consider payments made by the employer to the "fund" to be currently taxable income to the employee if the funds are owned by the executive. Thus, the employee will have a tax liability without the benefit of having received the payments! This is an example of the earlier-described secular trust.

5. **Non-funded, qualified, forfeitable plan.** By terms of ERISA, it is not possible to have a qualified, non-funded plan. To be qualified it must be properly funded. Thus, this alternative does not exist.

6. **Non-funded, non-qualified, forfeitable plan.** Until recent years, this probably was the most typical form of executive deferral. Because this plan is non-qualified, it enables the employer to design a very attractive personal package. Because it is non-funded and forfeitable, the executive accepts the unsecured, tenuous nature of future payments in exchange for no current tax liability. The company has no tax deduction until payments are made, but since it also has no funding requirement, there is no immediate cash flow problem. Among the most common are excess or restorative plans, which deal with Section 415 and 401(k) limits. They are sometimes called *mirror plans* because they mirror, or look like, their qualified-plan counterparts except they begin where the others end, providing the full benefits stated under the company qualified plan before the legal stated cutoffs are imposed.

7. **Non-funded, qualified, non-forfeitable plan.** By terms of ERISA, it is not possible to have a non-funded, qualified plan.

8. **Non-funded, non-qualified, non-forfeitable plan.** This is even more attractive to the executive than number six, since the benefit is 100-percent vested. This is an example of the earlier-described rabbi trust. Although this situation was covered in Revenue Ruling 60-31, for years companies included some degree of forfeiture to minimize any possible claim by the IRS of constructive receipt. Revenue Rulings 64-279 and 70-435 reaffirmed,

as did the Revenue Act of 1978, that a mere promise to pay does not trigger an income-tax liability as long as the recipient is not put ahead of the general creditors of the company. From the employer's point of view, it is a little less attractive than number six since ability to retain the executive is lost with the full vesting. As with other non-qualified plans, the company has no tax deduction until the executive receives payment. Intent on providing a safe harbor from constructive receipt and economic benefit issues, the IRS set up a model rabbi trust in Revenue Procedure 92-64. Anyone creating such a trust would be well advised to examine this procedure very carefully.

TAX TREATMENT

The individual pays taxes on the benefit when received (actual or constructive) in addition to any economic benefit that may have been received. These two principles, *constructive receipt* and *economic benefit*, will be described subsequently, as well as the definition and treatment of restricted property. The company has a tax deduction when paid to the individual (non-qualified deferral) or put into a trust (qualified deferral).

Constructive Receipt

Some bonus plans may call for payments in several annual installments, usually no more than five. The rationale for such an approach on timing is: (1) it cushions the effect of one low-bonus year, (2) it helps to retain executives since the payment of deferred awards is often contingent upon continued employment with the company, and (3) it spreads the tax bite. Concerning this last point, it is imperative that any deferred payments be viewed in light of the IRS doctrine of constructive receipt in order to avoid taxation to the recipient in the year in which granted. This was defined in Revenue Ruling 60-31, which said, "Under the doctrine of constructive receipt, a taxpayer may not deliberately turn his back upon income and thereby select the year for which he will report it."

The *doctrine of constructive receipt* is defined in Section 1.451-2(a) of the Treasury Regulations. It states: "Income, although not actually reduced to a taxpayer's possession, is constructively received by him in the taxable year during which it is credited to his account, set apart for him, or otherwise made available so that he may draw upon it at any time, or so that he could have drawn upon it during the taxable year if notice of intention to withdraw had been given. However, income is not constructively received if the taxpayer's control of its receipt is subject to substantial limitations or restrictions." In other words, if the executive could reach out and take the money (regardless of whether or not he or she did), it will be considered taxable income. This could lead to the disastrous situation where the person is taxed on income not yet received!

The chances of such an interpretation being made is minimized if the individual makes a determination before the amount is earned; some interpret this as before January 1 of the year on which the bonus is calculated, not simply a couple of months before the calculation is made. They cite Revenue Ruling 69-650 that indicates that a decision by December 31 is required in connection with compensation to be earned during the following year. This is the *year-before-the-year principle*. Although this applied to deferral of a portion of salary (not bonus), it is presumably a sound position that the more time between the decision and the event, the less likely there is to be a problem with the IRS. Revenue Procedure 71-19 sets forth the conditions under which the IRS will issue advance rulings in this matter.

In addition, if the executive indicates a preference but final decision is in the hands of a compensation committee, the likelihood of a problem with constructive receipt is also minimized. Thus, in adopting a deferred compensation approach, the issues of "who makes the determination" and "at what point in time" are critical considerations.

It is possible to do a deferral on a deferral. For example, if an executive has deferred a $100,000 bonus for five years, he or she might decide (early enough to avoid constructive receipt) to further defer the amount, perhaps paid out in annual installments of $50,000 until the deferral is exhausted, beginning seven years after the initial deferral. This gives the executive flexibility to meet children's college or other expenses.

Companies must also be careful in permitting earlier payout after the amount has been deferred. To avoid constructive receipt issues, companies impose some type of penalty. This could be in the way of forfeiting a portion of the account balance (e.g., 10 percent) and/or ineligibility to defer in the future for a stated period of time (e.g., two years). This is commonly known as a *haircut provision*, and lacking a ruling by the IRS, such payouts should be approached very carefully. These forfeitures would typically not apply if the company permitted hardship withdrawals. However, a committee would be charged to determine if: (1) there was a severe financial emergency, and (2) it was beyond the control of the deferee.

Economic Benefit

Another tax principle closely allied with the doctrine of constructive receipt is the theory of *economic benefit*. Here the IRS interprets an action by the employer as resulting in something of value being bestowed upon the employee. For example, the mere promise by the company to pay in the future (rather than currently) has no economic, value even though the trust is irrevocable and not accessible to present or future management. This is the earlier identified rabbi trust. This non-qualified trust may or may not be funded. If funded, it must be available to creditors in case of bankruptcy. It is taxable to the recipient at time of receipt of funds, not when the organization makes a contribution. A variation is a dry rabbi trust, which becomes funded at time of a change of contract typically to protect the executive and, therefore, subject to taxation.

Another variation is a grantor trust with a *call provision* that permits the recipient to require early payment by the grantor. This typically would be because the executive feared pending company bankruptcy and therefore an inability by the company to make full payment. Such a provision must be structured very carefully to avoid constructive receipt at time of deferral. The provision should be very limited in the executive's ability to "call" the payment as well as require some form of discount on the paid amount. Additionally, the inability to make other deferrals for a stated period of time if the call right is exercised may be required.

Similarly, if the employer sets up a trust to which the employee has non-forfeitable rights, then the amount of annual contribution will be construed to be an economic benefit, and the employee will be taxed that year on the value of that contribution. This is a *secular trust*. Note that this is not an issue of constructive receipt because the trust specified when in the future the executive will receive payments. However, if there were a substantial risk of forfeiture associated with these payments, then the economic benefit theory would not apply. One should recognize, however, that the IRS may look to an individual's age to determine whether continued employment is really a substantial risk of forfeiture. A 60-year-old executive with 30 years of company

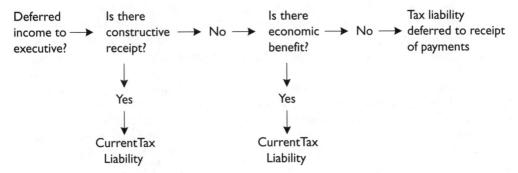

Figure 3-2. Constructive receipt and economic benefit matrix

service (and a handsome pension accruing) is not as likely to depart as, say, a 40-year-old individual with only five years of service. Secular or non-exempt trusts are described in Section 402(b) of the IRC. They are irrevocable, non-forfeitable interest in a trust's assets with payment made upon date of a specified event (e.g., death, termination of employment, retirement, or other reasons). Such trusts are subject to certain provisions of ERISA.

The impact of constructive receipt and economic benefit is shown in the flow chart in Figure 3-2.

Revenue Procedure 93-64 should be consulted as it provides "safe harbor" guidance to avoid constructive receipt and economic benefit problems.

Restricted Property

Prior to the 1969 Tax Reform Act, a number of deferred compensation plans used restricted property. A typical example would be to give an individual shares of stock in the company indicating that the restrictions would lapse according to a schedule. For example, an executive might be given 1000 shares of company stock (then selling at $100 a share) and told that restrictions would lapse at the rate of 100 shares a year for the next 10 years. Not only was there no tax liability at time of grant, but when the restrictions were removed, the value would be subject to the lesser of: ordinary income tax on the fair market value at time of award; or capital gains tax when the restrictions lapsed. Thus, if the value of the stock rose, there was a capital gains opportunity; if it dropped, the tax would be based on the fair market value at time of receipt.

The Tax Reform Act of 1969 added a new section to the Code—Section 83, which deals with the taxation of property. It states that the fair market value of the property will be that when the restrictions lapse, at which time it will be considered ordinary income. To delay recognition of income, the restrictions must include substantial risk of forfeiture. IRC Section 83(c)(1) states: "The rights of a person in property are subject to a substantial risk of forfeiture if such person's rights to full enjoyment of such property are conditioned upon the future performance of substantial services by any individual."

However, the recipient may make a *Section 83(b) election*, not later than 30 days after the date of such transfer, to include in the recipient's gross income for the taxable year, the excess of the fair market value over the amount paid for such property. Notice of such election before end of the 30-day window must be sent to the IRS with a copy to the company. When the executive files the tax return (for the year in which election was made), a copy of the notice filed with the IRS should be included. The stock must also be subject to the risk of forfeiture and be non-transferable. If these requirements are met when the restrictions lapse, the fair market value less the adjusted taxable base will be eligible for long-term capital gains (LTCG) tax if held long enough. However, if the property is forfeited, no deduction will be permitted in respect to such forfeiture except for the amount paid (if any) by the executive to purchase the restricted stock.

The risk of forfeiture also comes into play in determining when to subject the monies to FICA and HI (Health Insurance or Medicare) taxation. The rule is that individuals covered by a nonqualified plan will be subject to such taxation when the amount can be reasonably determined. Namely, it will be taxed when actually or constructively received unless it is not subject to forfeiture, in which case it is taxed at that time.

Thus, said taxation may occur when received or earlier if the risk of forfeiture requirement has not been met. In the latter situation, the individual having been taxed on the amounts set aside will not be again subject to taxation when received. This is the *non-duplication rule*, namely, amounts once taxed (plus any future earnings on such values) will not be subject to taxation when received.

Salary Reduction Plans

In the early 1970s, the "salary reduction" plan became popular. It effectively allowed the employee to have a portion of salary deferred by placing it in a money-purchase-type investment plan.

It worked like this. An executive would be hired at $200,000 but would agree that $20,000 of this would be invested in a Section 403(b) tax-sheltered annuity program. The executive would have $180,000 (not $200,000) of reportable income; however, the company could claim a $200,000 compensation deduction ($180,000 for salary and $20,000 for contribution to the money purchase plan). Effectively, it allowed the company to take a deduction before the executive had a taxable event!

During the mid-1970s, these plans were allowed to continue by the IRS, but new plans lost the attractive tax feature. More specifically, such contributions were considered to be made by the employee; thus the person had $200,000 salary with a $20,000 contribution made from after-tax income. The company had a $200,000 deduction for salary.

The Tax Reform Act of 1976 made deferred compensation generally attractive. It amended the definition of "personal service income" (which it substituted for "earned income") to include amounts received as annuities, pensions, or other deferred compensation. Thus, properly designed, deferred compensation plans are subject to the same maximum tax in effect when the monies are earned. Prior to this act, it might be subject to a 50-percent tax when earned, but if deferred, it could be subject to a 70-percent tax, if received later than the year following the year in which it was earned. The 1-year grace period then in effect was helpful only in exempting short-term incentive awards, usually paid in the first part of the year subsequent to the year in which earned. The 1976 Tax Reform Act allowed both qualified and non-qualified deferred compensation to be subject to the 50-percent personal service income maximum tax. This distinction between "personal service" and "ordinary" income taxes came with the tax act of 1969.

Beginning in 1979, the same favorable tax treatment on salary reduction plans, but with a different requirement, was returned. Qualified profit-sharing plans could again include a provision that would allow the covered employee to elect either to take the employer's contribution in cash or have it contributed to the trust. Tax treatment will be based on the action taken. Thus, if elected to be received as cash, it will be taxed when received; if deferred, the normal rules for payment from a qualified trust apply.

Going back to our example, this would mean hiring the executive at $180,000 salary and indicating that the $20,000 generated by the profit-sharing plan could be received as cash or contributed to the trust. If deferred, the executive has $180,000 of reportable income, the company a $200,000 tax deduction. If received as cash, the employee has $200,000 of reportable income, while the company still has a $200,000 deduction. This is called a *CODA (Cash or Deferred Arrangement)*, section 401(k) of the IRC. Such plans are discussed further in Chapter 5.

TAX AND ACCOUNTING TREATMENT

Company

The company is expected to take an annual charge to earnings equal to that period's obligation to future payment. A reserve on the balance sheet reflects the accumulated liability.

Under the Accounting Principles Board's (APB) Opinion No. 25's *Measurement Date Principle* (which will be described in detail in Chapter 4), since the number of shares of stock and their price is known at the time the restrictions go into effect, then the fair market value of the stock at that time will be expensed over the period of restriction, without regard to changes in the stock price. However, the company will not receive a tax deduction on the full value of the stock until the time the restrictions lapse. If dividends were paid during the period of restriction, they were tax deductible at that time.

If the deferral is in the form of cash, that amount (along with any interest consideration) is expensed over the period of restriction. In this regard, the cash plus interest will require a greater charge to earnings than the restricted stock, whose price is locked in at time of deferral. If the deferral is in the form of stock, it will be dilutive, increasing the number of shares of stock outstanding and therefore decreasing earnings per share; however, the earnings charge would be less since it was fixed at the time of deferral.

If the individual makes an 83(b) election at time of deferral, the company gets a tax deduction equal to the amount of the individual's taxable income. However, the company will not have a tax deduction at the time the restrictions lapse since the executives' gain would be subject to capital gains tax.

Individual

The executive has no accounting issue, only one of taxation. If the individual made a Section 83(b) election, choosing to be taxed at time of award (rather than payment), the gain on the stock price (if any) will receive long-term, capital-gains tax treatment. If no election was made, the full value of the stock received would be taxed as ordinary income, just as if it were cash. A stock award with no 83(b) election is illustrated in Table 3-2. EITF 97-14 states that only by paying the deferred compensation in company stock can the company lock in the charge at time of deferral. If it can be paid in cash, then additional expense must be recognized over the deferred period for this increase in value.

Issues	Award	Paid Out
Time lapse	Now	Five years later
Stock price	$100	$130
Individual income	0	$130
Company • Tax Deduction • Expense*	0 $100	$130 0

*Accrued over period until paid out

Table- 3-2. Tax and accounting example

SEC REQUIREMENTS

Funded, voluntary, non-qualified deferral compensation arrangements are considered securities under the Securities Act of 1933. This requires registration and disclosure in the proxy of the amount deferred for the top officers of the company.

DEFERRAL ADVANTAGES

There are currently a number of advantages to deferring compensation. These include:

1. Unlike many IRS rules requiring no discrimination in favor of higher employees, non-qual-ified deferred agreements can be set up on a highly discriminating, "pick-and-choose" basis. Many companies will limit this to less than five percent of their workforce.

2. If the amount earned is paid interest or otherwise invested, the individual does not experi-ence a loss in value due to inflation. And (if geared to appreciation in interest ratios, the value of stock, or other property reflecting inflation) the amount is allowed to grow at a tax-free compound rate until time of payment, when all dollars are subject to the income tax.
   This is especially advantageous for long-term deferrals. For example, if a $20,000 payment is deferred for five years at 7 percent of pre-tax interest and then paid out, the $28,051 is worth $14,026 after taxes (assuming the entire amount is subject to a 50 percent tax). This is $2,013, or 16.8 percent more than the after-tax value of $20,000 paid out immediately and then invest-ed at 7 percent (because the amount available for investment was $10,000, not $20,000, since it was immediately subject to a 50-percent tax). For 10 years deferral, as shown in Table 3-3, the post-tax values increase to $19,672 and $14,836, respectively, for a $4836 or 32.6 percent variance. This increase in absolute and relative differences is also shown for 15 and 20 years.

3. Deferrals can increase retirement income and thereby offset pension plan weaknesses, espe-cially for executives.

4. Deferred salary and incentives may be included as pensionable earnings for nonqualified pension plans in year *earned*, thereby protecting the pension.

5. In accord with Revenue Rulings 68-99 and 72-25, it would appear that the employer can

Years	$10,000		$20,000		Post-tax Variance	
	Pretax	Post-tax	Pretax	Post-tax	Amount	Percent
5	$14,026	$12,013	$28,051	$14,026	$2,013	16.8%
10	19,672	14,836	39,343	19,672	4,836	32.6%
15	27,590	18,795	55,181	27,590	2,795	46.8%
20	38,697	24,349	77,394	38,697	14,348	58.9%

Table 3-3. Pre- and post-tax comparisons—current vs. deferred with 7 percent interest

fund the deferred compensation obligation without triggering an income liability to the employee if the company owns all policy rights, including designation of beneficiary.

6. If the individual has significant preference income and/or ordinary income currently, the marginal tax rate may be less at a subsequent date. However, the possibility of higher marginal rates in the future through new tax legislation is a high offsetting risk.

7. A non-qualified plan is not subject to ERISA funding requirements (but is probably covered by the reporting requirements) as long as such benefits are in excess of defined benefit or contribution plan limits, and/or deferral arrangements are limited to more highly compensated individuals.

8. Generally, social security benefits are not affected by the amount of deferred payments received. However, care should be taken in developing such arrangements because payment (which permits the company to use the individual as a consultant) may be regarded as wages for the purpose of reducing social security payments. This may be only a short-term issue, however, as individuals age 65 and over are permitted unlimited earnings without reducing social security benefits.

9. If amounts deferred are under risk of forfeiture for executives who leave the company for reasons other than death, disability, or retirement, the individual's inclination to join another company may be retarded. However, many plans will permit a "hardship" withdrawal. Specifically, the executive may withdraw an amount to cover an unforeseen financial emergency.

10. A large portion of the deferred income can be passed on to the beneficiaries through properly designed trusts and supplemental insurance coverage provided by the employer.

11. Short-term deferrals significantly reduce year-to-year fluctuations to incentive payments and smooth out the taxable earnings of the executive. This is important when high marginal tax rates are in effect, thereby enabling the executive to tailor income to meet personal needs.

12. Non-funded, deferred compensation plans enable the company to preserve capital by withholding a portion of compensation to a future date and thereby increase current cash flow. This may be especially important to a threshold or emerging company. However, the Accounting Principles Board (APB) Opinion No. 12, "Deferred Compensation Contracts,"

should be examined carefully to ensure the expensing of future benefits is properly reflected.

13. The company benefits to the extent it recaptures forfeited payments since these would have been lost if paid when earned. In addition, it will benefit to the extent it credits the deferral with a value less than the cost of borrowed capital.

14. It is advantageous to the company for an executive to defer until retirement that portion of pay which otherwise would be nondeductible under Section 162(m) of the IRC which places limits on deductible compensation in excess of $1 million.

DEFERRAL DISADVANTAGES

Conversely, there are a number of disadvantages to deferring compensation. These include:

1. Unless the amount deferred is protected against inflation, it will have significantly less value when received than when earned, even under the most favorable tax circumstances. Or even if it is vested and has less value when received than the executive believes could have been obtained, the executive will not be very happy. The $40,000 deferred over four future years in the earlier discussion would amount to a total of $52,432 if credited at 7-percent interest. Assuming a 50-percent tax is in effect, this amount is reduced to $26,216. Contrast this with the $40,000 paid immediately and half of it paid out for taxes. If the remaining $20,000 were invested in 5.5-percent, tax-free bonds, it would net $24,776 after four years — $1440, or 5.5 percent less than the deferred net payment. Thus, while the deferral is better, it may not be considered sizable enough to be worthwhile. This is especially true if the recipient believes the $20,000, if invested in stocks, real estate, art, or the like, would have a much greater net appreciation (after deducting capital gains taxes at the time of sale).

    Application of a rate of interest to preserve purchasing power is, therefore, very logical, especially during periods of inflation. Approaches include: a specific percentage (e.g., 7 percent), a non-company index (e.g., prime passbook savings or 90-day treasury notes), or a company index (e.g., return on assets, investments, borrowed capital, or shareholder equity). The latter two approaches may make an additional adjustment (e.g., prime rates less 1 percent or one-half the rate of return on shareholder equity). In addition, two or more of these can be placed in a combination (e.g., prime or one-half return on equity, whichever is lower).

    In using rates, it is important to identify when the measurement will be taken and how long it will be in effect. For example, using 90-day treasury notes, one could agree that the averages for the last weeks in March, June, September, and December would be the applicable rates for the respective quarters. For reference to company data, it logically would be calculated after the close of the year.

2. The buildup in deferred compensation resulting from an interest rate or other inflation factor is currently considered compensation when received. However, the increase might be ruled unreasonable compensation and therefore not deductible by the corporation. It would seem the risk of this occurring is greatest when the value increases at a rate significantly greater than an after-tax investment.

3. The tax situation must be thoroughly reviewed on a state as well as federal basis to ensure it results in lower taxes. Beginning in 1996 in accordance with Public Law 104-95, no state

may tax retirement income of a person not a resident of the state. Prior to this law, states taxed the person upon receiving benefit even though the individual no longer lived or worked in that state. Nonetheless, future tax increases may more than offset all other advantages.

4. An unfunded plan makes the executive a general creditor of the company and therefore the executive risks non-payment. While every company expects to exist in perpetuity, there are enough bankruptcies each year to require an assessment of the probability of this occurring to the company in question. Establishing a trust without forfeiture requirements will probably mean the executive will be taxed when money is deposited in the trust; including a forfeiture clause will probably defer income tax liability to the executive; however, the company may not be able to take a tax deduction until monies are paid from the trust (thereby resulting in negative cash flow).

   While bookkeeping reserves may be established, no funds can be set aside to meet the obligation. Furthermore, no annuity contracts or life insurance policies can be purchased for the employee; however, it is possible that such might be accomplished by the employer as long as the latter retained full ownership and the proceeds were not directed toward fulfillment of the deferral obligation.

5. Deferred compensation plans increase the administration requirements of the company. Much of this can be minimized by computer programs unless plans are individually customized.

6. The deferred compensation plan, especially if funded, may come under the definition of a security as defined by the Securities Act of 1933 and the Securities Exchange Act of 1934. If it is deemed a security and a sale is involved, it will mean registration with the SEC, proper disclosure to those covered, and concern that no fraud charge can be directed to the "securities" management.

7. Benefits received are subject to FICA tax either when actually or constructively paid (general rule), or earned and not subject to risk of forfeiture (special rule). The applicable interpretation varies with the form and requirements of the plan and is beyond the scope of this discussion. Suffice it to say that it may be a disadvantage (it is unlikely to be an advantage) and needs to be carefully researched.

8. Since the amount deferred proportionately reduces current total compensation, the executive may be more vulnerable to offers at slightly more than the current total package but with no deferral requirements. This is true during the early years of a short-term deferral program (see Figure 3-3, a 5-year deferral plan) and during all active years under payments deferred until retirement.

9. Conversely, executives may demand more current compensation. To the extent the corporation acquiesces, it will pay more under a deferred compensation plan than if all compensation were paid currently.

10. Due to the partial payment of a number of years of service, it is difficult for the executive to see the impact of performance on the bonus. For example, in the fifth year, as shown in Figure 3-3, the executive received payments totaling $270,000. The following year, the bonus earned dropped $100,000 (from $250,000 to $150,000), but the amount received fell

Year	\$50	\$110	\$150	\$220	\$270	\$250	\$240	Amount Earned
				Amount Paid				
7							\$50	**\$250**
6						\$30	\$30	**\$150**
5					\$50	\$50	\$50	**\$250**
4				\$70	\$70	\$70	\$70	**\$350**
3			\$40	\$40	\$40	\$40	\$40	**\$350**
2		\$60	\$60	\$60	\$60	\$60		**\$300**
1	\$50	\$50	\$50	\$50	\$50			**\$250**
	1	2	3	4	5	6	7	

Figure 3-3. Amount earned vs. paid, under multiple-year plans (in thousands)

only \$20,000 (from \$270,000 to \$250,000). Conversely, the next year, the amount earned rose \$100,000 (from \$150,000 to \$250,000), but the amount paid slipped from \$250,000 to \$240,000. Given such a correlation in amounts earned vs. paid, one must question the extent to which the individual truly receives reinforcement for the level of performance attained under deferred compensation plans.

11. Compensation deferred cannot be considered pay during the period of deferral for purposes of determining benefits under qualified pension and profit sharing plans. In testing compliance, pay must satisfy an IRC Section 414(G) definition, such as W-2 or gross pay. Care should be taken to ensure that life insurance and disability protection is not similarly reduced. Thus, while this has little effect on short-term deferrals (except for installments payable after retirement), it has considerable impact on long-term deferrals not payable until after retirement. The result can be a very significant reduction in the company pension plan payments—the magnitude being a factor of the percentage of earnings deferred. Such a position was described by the IRS in Revenue Ruling 68-454 when it disallowed compensation deferred by certain officer-employees. However, in accord with Revenue Ruling 69-145, it would appear that such compensation could be recognized if all employees were eligible to defer compensation. Revenue Ruling 80-359 added that if the proportion of lower paid employees who made deferrals was equal to or greater than the higher-paid, the basis for calculating benefits would not be viewed as discriminatory in favor of the prohibited group. However, given the low limits on qualified plans, this is only a theoretical disadvantage.

12. Payment beginning at the time of retirement from the company can create another problem, namely, when the individual is "retiring" from company A to join company B. The earnings from the new employer will significantly reduce, if not totally eliminate, any tax advantage the executive hoped to receive on the deferred payments. However, careful planning and specific language in the deferral contract can essentially eliminate this problem. Namely, the con-

tract with company A should indicate that payments begin when the employee ceases full-time employment (not simply employment with company A). In addition, it may be advantageous to indicate that payment should begin the year after the year in which full-time employment ceases. In case of a person retiring late in the year, sufficient earnings may have been accumulated to eliminate favorable tax treatment of any deferral payments that year.

13. Some committees only allow the executive to state preferences (current vs. deferred) in percentages (e.g., 25 percent immediate and 75 percent deferred). This approach does not recognize that the individual's current needs are absolute, not relative. Thus, using the above percentage example, everything would be fine if the total award were $400,000 and the individual's current needs were $100,000. But what if the committee decided the executive should only receive a total of $200,000? In this case the immediate amount ($50,000) would be one-half of the needed $100,000.

    This problem can be overcome simply by allowing the executive (at the beginning of the agreement so as to obviate constructive receipt problems) to indicate the dollar amount desired currently or deferred, with the balance going to the other. Thus, the executive could indicate a preference for the first $100,000 in cash with the rest deferred, or conversely, the first $200,000 deferred with the rest payable currently. An additional refinement would be to combine that absolute and the relative (e.g., the first $100,000 or 25 percent, whichever is greater, payable immediately with the balance deferred).

14. If the deferred payments are designed to continue after the death of the employee, such payments will probably be included in the decedent's estate in accordance with Section 2039 of the Code. In addition, if the payment would have been considered taxable income to the decedent, it may also be considered income to the beneficiary. This double taxation (estate tax and income tax) can cause significant liquidity problems without sufficient life insurance to cover tax liabilities.

15. While deferred compensation plans are often described as golden handcuffs locking the executive to the corporation, often only marginal performers are really shackled to the company. Top-quality performers invariably find someone with the key (namely, comparable compensation to that forfeited). The result is that not only do deferrals not retain the top performer in many situations, but equally undesirable, they make it difficult for a less effective executive to seek alternative career opportunities.

SUMMARY AND CONCLUSIONS

Shown in Table 3-4 is a summary of the tax and accounting treatment for current and deferred income as well as the principles involved.

As the list of advantages and disadvantages would suggest, deferred compensation is not for everyone. From the individual's point of view, it is a needs vs. investment decision. What are my current cash needs? What is the after-tax value of the award today? What is it likely to be at the time the deferral ends? What is the compound rate of return on the investment? What is the projected inflation and value of the dollar at the end of the deferral? The executive must attempt to place future as well as present values on the chart in Figure 3-4 before determining the extent to which deferred compensation is appropriate. The before- and after-tax positions will vary by individual, based on the person's assumptions.

	Individual	Company	
When Paid	**Tax Liability**	**Accounting**	**Tax Deduction**
Current Payment	Now	Now	Now
Deferred Payment	Later	Now	Later
Principle	When received	When known	When paid

Table 3-4. Summary of accounting and tax treatment of current and deferred income

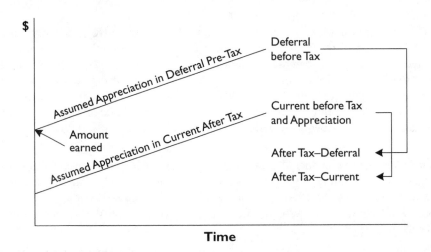

Figure 3-4. Current versus deferred compensation, after-tax comparison

Let's review several of the key issues that impact on the appropriateness of deferring compensation.

First, it must be remembered that, although the amount is being deferred for tax purposes, it is also being deferred for investment purposes! It is logical to defer if the investment growth is judged to be the same for both current and deferred payments. However, the situation must be carefully examined if the growth rate on deferred payments is less than that available through other opportunities if received immediately. In this case, the deferral may actually cost the recipient more than is saved in taxes, even if some form of interest is added to the deferred amount.

Second, the younger executive is usually at an income level that is too low to provide any real tax advantage. Even if this is not the case, he or she by definition has more years in which to build up a post-retirement income. Obviously, the more the deferred income increases through pension annuities, savings, and other forms of deferrals, the higher the income tax and the less the tax saving over current rates.

Third, the recipient may need the money now to meet mortgage and college tuition costs even though the net may be less than in later years. The countering argument is that financial needs will be correspondingly less in post-retirement years.

Fourth, since the main justification for deferring income is to optimize the individual's net income, it is imperative that the act of transferring income from years of employment to years of retirement be carefully examined. Pension and long-term, profit-sharing plans should be examined in relation to the amount deferred until retirement, through salary and incentive plans, to determine the total package available at post-retirement as replacement income. Forgotten considerations include looking at the loss of income in determining retirement annuities—especially those that call for a percentage of the last five or 10 years of earnings. Often overlooked is what the recipient's total post-retirement income will be. Some companies have found that, taken individually, each plan provided a tax savings, but when combined with other plans, the tax savings was either greatly reduced or eliminated. Examples can be found of executives who retired at higher incomes than earned in their last year of employment.

Fifth, not only are deferred bonus arrangements difficult to construct from a value to the recipient's point of view, but they are also complicated from the viewpoint of applicable taxes. To determine when they should begin and how long they should last, a number of assumptions and calculations must be made. Specifically, an estimate must be made of the recipient's income (from all sources) for the years in question and the applicable tax rates at those times (a very tenuous assumption when dealing five, 10, or even 20 years in the future). Due to this high degree of uncertainty in both income and tax rates, deferred compensation payments are logical only if a considerable safety margin exists.

Sixth, the current tax rate is always a given, but the tax structure even several years from now is an unknown. What is known is that we get a new tax law about every other year. Who's to say that the current tax on income will not be increased? Few, if any, recall the 91 percent marginal rate in effect in the early 1960s and the 70 percent rate in the late 1960s. Perhaps an additional tax on deferred compensation, either during the period of deferral or upon receipt, will become law.

Seventh, the longer the period of deferral, the greater the risk that one or more of the assumptions will incur significant deviation (e.g., need for current cash, tax structure, or alternative investment opportunities).

Eighth, the greatest drawback to deferred compensation lies in its motivational appeal, or more properly stated, its lack of motivational appeal. Since the reward is separated in time from the performance of the act, it is often difficult to relate the two. This is especially true when the deferral is until retirement.

Ninth, just as important is that as deferrals build up, there is a natural reluctance to do anything to jeopardize the receipt of such payments. For the truly outstanding performer, this is no problem because he or she will either succeed with the current employer or find another who is willing to "buy off" the deferrals. However, for the maturing executive whose performance has plateaued there is a reluctance to accept risk ventures outside the current employer that would cause the forfeiture of unpaid bonus monies.

Tenth, evaluate answers to the first nine, and you'll have a more thoughtful answer to the question "should income be deferred?"

Note: You should not rely on accounting, tax, SEC, or other professional service statements in this chapter. You need to seek appropriate professional counsel for such guidance. Statements made in this chapter and elsewhere are offered as being illustrative to help you frame such further investigations with the help of counsel.

Having reviewed the matter of current vs. deferred compensation, let's look next at the stakeholders of executive pay. Who are they, and what is their impact?

Chapter 4

The Stakeholders

aving reviewed performance measurements and identified the five compensation elements, I will next examine the stakeholders in executive compensation. They are not only those directly concerned, but also those who impact, to varying degrees, the design of executive compensation—both the "how" and "how much" as shown in Figure 4-1.

The stakeholders are: the *executives* themselves, *other employees*, the *shareholders* (directly and through their representatives on the board of directors who approve the plan), the *community*, the *customers* of the organization, and the *suppliers* to the organization. A subset of three other groups of stakeholders—those whose "stake" is one level removed—would include shareholder watchdogs, the business press, and government regulators. *Shareholder watchdogs* analyze executive pay packages and often advise shareholders and companies on appropriate action. The *business press* is similar in approach, but with the objective of increasing reader circulation. You could say they are a subset of the community. A more involved subset of the community would be the *rulemakers*—those who pass laws and regulations affecting executive compensation. Let's begin with the executives.

THE EXECUTIVE

As stated at the outset, an executive is not simply the CEO, or the corporate officers, or those defined by the SEC as "insiders," but any and all high-level individuals who can have significant impact on the success of the organization. They participate in all five compensation elements. Through their efforts, executives exchange their human capital for pay (or financial capital). The management pyramid is shown in Figure 4-2.

The five compensation elements have different impact on attracting, retaining, and moti-

Figure 4-1. Executive compensation stakeholders and rule makers

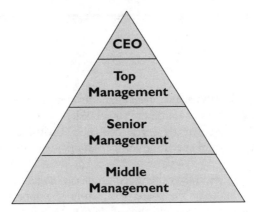

Figure 4-2. Management pyramid

vating the executive—the basic requirements of a positive pay package. Shown in Table 4-1 are the five elements in terms of these three requirements.

Salary is very important in attracting and retaining executives, but it is of little value in motivating them since salary adjustments are usually modest, even for top performers. The salary associated with a promotion, however, is believed to be a positive factor. Thus, while the promotional pay increase may be motivational, it is doubtful that the normal merit pay policy serves as an inspiration. Hiring bonuses are similar to a lump-sum salary payment inasmuch as it is not factored into ongoing salary. Intended to offset what may be lost from a current employer, they are sometimes referred to as the *golden hook*. Salary has little retention ability, unless some portion has been deferred and subject to forfeiture if leaving prior to receipt. Similarly, a hiring bonus has little retention value, unless subject to repayment if leaving before being earned out. For more on deferred vs. current payments, see Chapter 3.

By contrast, a good *employee benefit and perquisite* program usually will have little impact on attracting and motivating the executive (although poor programs may make it more difficult

Compensation Elements	Impact on Individual Executive		
	Attract	**Retain**	**Motivate**
Salary	High	High	Moderate
Employee benefits	Low	Moderate	Low
Perquisites	Low	Moderate	Low
Short-term incentives	High	Moderate	High
Long-term incentives	Moderate	High	Moderate

Table 4-1. Impact of five compensation elements on executives

to interest wanted executives), but may have at least a moderate retention effect. Some factors, such as a final-pay pension plan, may have a considerable holding impact if the executive has not attained a 100-percent vested level.

Short-term incentives can be very attractive and motivational to a top performer, especially if the payout is based on individual rather than group achievement. However, for incentive plans to work, the executive must have a positive attitude toward them and must believe that differences in performance will result in comparable differences in reward. In addition, the required level of performance must be considered not only attainable but also cost effective (i.e., what is received must be deemed worth the time expended).

Long-term incentives, on the other hand, do have some positive aspects in attracting and motivating, but their main strength is usually in retaining the executive, due to the multi-year performance period definition. Long-term incentives are typically based on group, not individual performance and, therefore, are not as motivating as short-term incentives. Multi-year plans stipulate "vesting," or earn-out dates, when the recipient is eligible to receive all or a portion of the award. The longer the vesting period, the greater is the retention feature. Often times, such long-term earn-outs are called "golden handcuffs." Golden because of their extrinsic compensation nature; handcuffs because of their retention feature.

Even if the pay packages do not attract, retain, and motivate as desired, their form and level of reward do serve as reinforcement vehicles to attract and retain a particular type of executive. As an example, a company with a high emphasis on salary (and by definition, low on incentives) is likely to retain a steady performer but not the high-risk acceptor who wishes to be appropriately rewarded for success.

Attracting Executive Talent

While companies usually express a desire to retain solid performers, they often do not pay them as well as new people they hire for comparable jobs. The latter receive a premium to leave a known and move to an unknown—increases of at least 25 percent are not uncommon. The greater the risk of failing in the new job, the greater the required premium to attract the person—pay may even have to be doubled. More and more executives recognize the need to have a written agreement stipulating the pay package while employed, as well as the severance package should employment be terminated by the employer. Employment contracts are discussed in

Chapter 6 (Employee Benefits and Perquisites). Executives recognize their bargaining power will be significantly reduced once they have joined the company.

The greater the need and the more risky the position, the greater the premium expected. Thus, the individual who has moved every four or five years is invariably ahead in compensation, after 15 or 20 years, of the individual who stayed with one organization — even though both started out on the same job at the same pay, and both now have the same responsibilities. Twenty years ago, individuals who had made several job changes were considered suspect, but today the individual who has stayed with the same company is considered the oddity. Organization structure can have a significant impact on the type of executive needed for a particular job. With some companies, the group executive is a significant position, essentially responsible for organizational changes and allocating capital to the appropriate division (based on assessment of need and potential return on assets), and possibly defining markets and sales strategies for the group. In other situations, the group executive is essentially a high-priced liaison between the CEO and a number of autonomous divisions. Needless to say, these two jobs call for different personality makeups and compensation packages.

Executive search firms work under either contingency or a *retainer*. The latter is paid year-round regardless of the level of search, if any. Those who work under a *contingency arrangement* are paid on commission—often a third of more of the pay of the person hired. A combination approach is sometimes called a *container*. Sometimes firms will *unbundle fees* and offer separately the research and interview costs. While obviously interested in the cost of the search, the client is especially interested in the quality of the candidate. To test hiring specifications, firms sometimes send a *stalking horse* candidate to the client.

Sick companies especially are in search of an executive with instant healing powers. Rather than simply the capable problem solver, they want the individual who is able to turn around a crisis situation. Typically, this means controlling costs and increasing productivity in order to turn a losing venture into a profitable operation.

Not only do many individuals look for a 25-percent or greater increase in total pay for making the jump to a new job, but an increasing number also look for a *front-end bonus*. This is used to buy out, at least in part if not in full, forfeited benefits and deferred pay at the former company. Thus, it becomes necessary to project a reasonable payout level under the former company plan and then discount to present cash value equivalency. Some also take into account future equity-based awards and their value. Amounts are paid either in a lump sum or installments, with a repayment required should the executive voluntarily leave within a prescribed time period. Also of interest is the pay contract going beyond the normal two- to five-year employment agreement. This longer-term agreement stipulates a minimum pay level until retirement.

Management should recognize that its pay philosophy in large part determines the type of talent it will attract and keep. For example, a company that says its salary-plus-bonus is competitive with salary-plus-bonus of other companies is more likely to attract a risk taker than a salary-only company who says its *salary* is competitive with salary-plus-bonus of other companies. In the first instance, if the company cuts back bonuses for ineffective performance while giving very handsome awards for top performance, it is likely to get more than its share of results-oriented individuals. Conversely, if the company rarely reduces bonuses or gives significant salary increases, then it is more likely to attract and retain the steady but unspectacular performer. Multi-million-dollar packages are often extended as lures only to those who perceive a small increase in power and responsibility and/or a significantly greater risk of failure (and loss of job).

Retaining Executives

Once executives are inside the organization, the next objective is to keep the better performers. Executives not only expect to be properly paid for their performance and to receive promotions when they have demonstrated ability to assume greater responsibilities, they also expect formal recognition. While pay is a form of recognition, many individuals also need oral and written communication officially recognizing the level of accomplishments. To the extent this is communicated to the individual's peer group, it may disrupt needed teamwork. Nonetheless, such recognition is extremely important to some individuals. If it is not given, the person may be unhappy although very well paid. Lavishing praise for a job well done is a lot less expensive to the company than increasing the compensation. While few would accept official recognition in lieu of a pay change, for many, the amount of the pay changes could be reduced if proportionately offset by an increase in recognition.

Many executives reach a level in the organization where they are comfortable with their responsibility and reward. They have little interest in competing for greater responsibility because for them, the effort and stress are not worth the compensation. For them, the recognition is very important. This may be accomplished in part with a few perquisites (e.g., larger office, more impressive title, and access to the executive health spa). However, further recognition may also be needed, ranging from the simple "Nice job, Brett" to a story in the company magazine.

Another important factor many companies overlook is ensuring that the executive who is likely to figure in a future promotion understands the situation. Many individuals leave because they do not know what the company has planned. A number of companies either believes executives are mind readers or expect them to "trust" the organization. Thus, companies sometimes lose top executives for modest compensation increases simply because someone else provides a well-laid-out plan for career advancement. For talented executives, the golden handcuffs of long-term incentive plans and/or deferred compensation have less retention value than open communication about advancement opportunities. Level of pay, while important, is secondary to relative rate of movement upward through the executive pyramid illustrated in Figure 4-2. An estimated two-thirds or more of executives' pay comes from promotional adjustments, with the remainder from merit increases.

Remember too that incentive compensation is a two-edged sword. It should reward executives handsomely during very successful years and thereby increase the likelihood of retention, but in bad years, it may make a company vulnerable to loss of top executive talent by significantly reducing total pay. This is especially true when incentive pay comprises a large portion of total compensation.

While a company could prune off some deadwood during poor years, it probably has a greater need than ever to ensure it loses no top-caliber executives—for these individuals may be the ones who will help the company again rise to the ranks of the successful.

Reportedly, some companies, in an attempt to minimize being raided, employ executive search firms on a regular basis, since ethical conduct prohibits search firms from raiding clients (at least in the area of the search). In this way, the company purchases additional insurance against losing key executives—insurance that can be very important as more and more companies use search firms to seek out underutilized and under-rewarded executives. These restrictions on candidates is typically called *blockage*. Conversely, after a merger, some executives are given the green light to start looking for a job, either because their job will disappear or an executive from the other company will take it.

Although it is often difficult for a shareholder to evaluate the worth of an executive while with the company, the stock market sometimes reacts to the loss of a Chief Executive or CEO apparent with a sell off of the stock. When an individual leaves and the stock drops $2 a share, with 500 million shares outstanding, one could argue that that person's present value is one billion dollars. Pity the person whose departure is announced, and the stock *rises* $2 a share.

Clearly, the organization wishes to retain effective executives. But these often are not simply those who meet their objectives. Evidence suggests individuals are exited from organizations often times based on *how* they perform, not simply *what* they accomplish. This is consistent with reinforcing desired organizational values. Individuals who are arrogant, insensitive, and disloyal are as likely to get the boot as the dishonest and incompetent.

Motivating Executives

The basic motivational model indicates that *effort times ability leads to outcome,* or performance. Thus, a shortfall in one factor can be offset by a higher value in the other. Many individuals compensate for average ability with a very high level of effort. The amount of energy the individual will expend in a given area is a function of the desirability of the expected outcome versus alternative outcomes from efforts directed toward other areas. In any event, most analysts would agree that there is not a constant relationship between level of effort and performance. Above a certain level of effort, there is a decreasing rate of return. *Pareto's Law* or the *80-20 principle,* avowed by some, is an extension of this philosophy. It states that 80 percent of the desired output can be achieved with 20 percent of the available effort. Anything beyond the 20 percent effort is achieved at a diminishing rate of return.

Some argue that pay does not motivate individuals to work harder. For some, that may be true. Their own need to succeed may be the driving force. However motivational incentives should not focus on working harder, but rather on working smarter, achieving desired results within a prescribed time frame. As such, it will reward success and penalize failure (by withholding pay). The belief is that individuals will repeat behavior that is rewarded and will eliminate actions that are penalized. If there is a focus on the process rather than the outcome, it is on working smarter rather than simply harder. Some make the distinction between intrinsic and extrinsic motivation. One could argue that the best of all worlds is to have both. *Intrinsic motivation* is when the work is the reward because it is satisfying. This may be desired because of a need for an expensive lifestyle per se or as a status symbol to others. More than one CEO has scanned the proxies of other companies to see where he or she stands in the financial pecking order. *Extrinsic motivation* is when the work is seen as the way to achieve the desired pay.

Equity vs. Expectancy. Traditionally, the motivation of pay is explained by two formulas: equity and expectancy. The *equity theory* states that the individual will increase level of performance if level of pay is believed greater than output and, conversely, will decrease performance if level of pay is believed below current performance. Most people will argue that the latter alternative is more plausible than the former. However, it seems that the performance of many sports stars falls, rather than increases, after receiving contract sums that would feed much of the world's impoverished. Of course, the executive who believes his or her performance exceeded the level of pay would first attempt to obtain a pay increase; only if this effort failed would the individual lower performance or, more drastically, leave to accept another job.

Expectancy theory suggests that an individual will increase output in the expectation of receiving an increase in pay. Sports stars often seem to have their best season the year their contract is expiring. For executives, it could be an increase in pay for performing current responsibilities or a promotional increase commensurate with a job reclassification. If the individual does not receive an increase consistent with the level of performance, the person (operating under the equity theory) is again likely to reduce performance or seek a different job.

However, the level of pay can be either a "carrot" or a "stick." The carrot symbolizes higher pay, held out to motivate the individual to work harder. The stick, on the other hand, is a negative symbol, meaning, "Do it right or we'll find someone else." Logically, the carrot works best until the individual's compensation has risen to a level where additional pay no longer has the same motivation, and then the stick takes over. The executive is thus encouraged to continue a high level of performance in order to keep the job and the high level of pay.

Executives typically wear the hats of both subordinate and superior. As subordinates, they are very vocal about the need to *equitably* link pay and performance; as superiors, they often become defensive and describe the problems of *adequately* relating pay to performance.

Obviously, this dual standard is inappropriate. Part of the problem is that executives are often poorly trained in identifying and discussing performance problems with subordinates. The result? To avoid unpleasant discussions, many performance ratings are artificially raised. No wonder the pay delivery system is failing. Those responsible for training and development have not kept up with pay program designs. The latter are usually more sophisticated than the ability of the users, due to inadequate training.

Importance of Effort. As stated above, the classic performance model indicates that effort times ability will equal outcome, or performance. Thus, a lower value in one can be offset by a higher value in the other. For example, a person with average ability could become very successful by expending great amounts of effort. The amount of effort expended is a function of the desirability of the outcome and the capacity for effort.

This is illustrated in Figure 4-3. In this example, the two curves are straight lines; however, either or both could be curves of varying slopes dependent upon the structure of the reward system and the nature of the work. With some combinations, there is an increasing efficiency; with others, efficiency decreases; and still others create a combination, or S curve. In this model, the executive receives a decreasing rate of return on effort (although the variance is positive) up to point A. After that point, although the individual continues to receive more pay, the return for effort is not equitable. Thus, if there were competing opportunities, the individual would probably shift to those after point A. This shift can be offset if the organization increases the slope of the pay line and moves the intersection point farther to the right.

Obviously, it is much easier to demonstrate this type of relationship clinically with a set of curves than for the executive to quantify it personally. However, although the measurements may not be as precise, they nonetheless are made and are used as the basis for altering behavior.

Achievement vs. Pay. While the objective of a sound compensation program is to pay correctly in relation to performance, there are repeated examples of pay not being in concert with achievement—even for those companies that strive diligently to administer in an equitable manner. This can be demonstrated with the matrix in Table 4-2, which compares level of pay with level of achievement. Setting aside the legal issues of equal pay for equal work, there are a number of interesting observations that can be made.

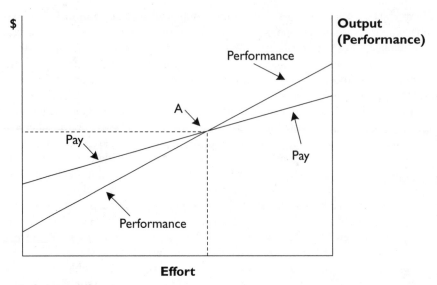

Figure 4-3. Effort—and its impact on performance

While the "correctly paid" column is the pay program's objective, the company should be pleased if it has more overachievers than underachievers in this situation. Level of achievement here is defined as the quantity as well as the quality of accomplishment. Three different individuals could have the same level of quality, but one could produce 80 percent of expected quantity, the second 100 percent, and the third 120 percent. Conversely, all three could produce the same quantity of work but one could do so in a truly outstanding manner, the second in a fully satisfactory manner, and the third in a less than satisfactory fashion. Most performance evaluation programs can deal with the second situation (output is equal) more easily than with the first; however, the level of output can be built into the performance program. Assume three individuals perform at a 3.0 level of performance (using the university 4.0 system). For the overachiever, the adjusted rating is 3.6 (i.e., 3.0 x 120 ÷ 100). The individual attaining the desired level of performance retains the 3.0 rating (i.e., 3.0 x 100 ÷ 100), while the underachiever's rating drops to 2.4 (i.e., 3.0 x 80 ÷ 100). Admittedly, the concept is easier to describe than to apply; nonetheless, it is a workable concept and will be covered again in Chapter 5 (Salary).

Level of Achievement	Level of Pay		
	Underpaid	**Correctly Paid**	**Overpaid**
Underachievement	1	2	3
Desired Achievement	4	5	6
Overachievement	7	8	9

Table 4-2. Achievement vs. pay

Let's look at some of the other interesting combinations and see what they represent:

A **1 (underpaid, underachiever)** is an individual who is paid even less than the poor performance warrants. This appears to be the result of some form of discrimination or recrimination, perhaps for past failures. It may be a management message to the individual: "You are not wanted. Why not leave?" Such a situation would obviate the need for a messy company-initiated severance.

A **2 (correctly paid, underachiever)** has the opportunity to increase pay by elevating outcome.

A **3 (overpaid, underachiever)** may develop out of a 5 or 8 whose performance drops but whose bonus does not, or out of a 4 or 7 who reaps a bonanza in pay but does not keep performance high enough to become a 5 or 8 (many professional sports stars playing under long-term contracts may meet this description). Lack of adequate downside risk in pay programs causes development of many 3s.

A **4 (underpaid, desired achiever)** is similar to a 1 but not as flagrant. Some companies may knowingly or otherwise allow this to happen to some of their older executives, feeling they are unlikely to leave due to all the accrued advantages of long service (e.g., pensions, deferred bonuses, and long vacations). Withholding a portion of pay increases from such executives means more merit dollars are available for other seemingly more deserving persons. However, one does so at risk of being in violation of age discrimination laws.

A **5 (correctly paid, desired achiever)** reflects harmony. It is equity theory in application; pay is consistent with outcomes.

A **6 (overpaid, desired achiever)** is less dramatic, but similar in nature and development, to the 3.

A **7 (underpaid, overachiever)** is usually not likely to remain that way for long. Either the company will correct the inequity, or the individual will correct it (by lowering performance, by directing efforts to other interests outside of the company, or by simply leaving). This is an example of equity *and* expectancy theory in action. Classically, this situation exists in companies that make little effort to truly reward performance. Such a company or division, when faced with a five-percent merit budget, gives adjustments ranging from three percent to seven percent (placing greater emphasis on restoring lost purchasing power to marginal performers than on adequately compensating the overachiever).

A **8 (correctly paid, overachiever)** reflects a situation with more downside risk than upside potential. Any decline in achievement will result in either a 3 or 6, assuming no decrease in pay. A decrease in pay combined with a decline in achievement will result in either a 2 or 5.

A **9 (overpaid, overachiever)** is probably an individual who has been demoted. This overachiever may remain an overachiever in the new position but may have had little or no reduction in pay and thus may be overpaid in relation to the new level of responsibilities.

This analysis provides a way of describing level of pay and performance in relative terms and also shows (contrary to some beliefs) that pay vs. performance can be a fluid and changing relationship. Too many pay technicians are content to simply fall back on their merit guide charts without trying to ascertain the dynamics of particular situations.

Pay-for-Performance Problems. To what extent is the company a *meritocracy*, where people succeed or fail based on their own work performance? An ineffective pay-for-performance program not only does not send the proper signals for good performance, but probably also reinforces poor performance because it does not withhold sufficient pay. This is especially true for companies that have little or no incentive pay, since salaries are rarely reduced. A zero bonus is only a punishment when a minimal level of bonus is needed simply to make pay levels competitive.

Not only must differences in pay relate to differences in performance, but also the executives must believe that the company is administering the program on this basis. A lack of consistency in administration will have a debilitating effort on the most efficacious pay plan. Invariably, in such situations managers will blame the pay system rather than the ability (or desirability) of differentiating. If the pay system provides the basis for significant differences in individual pay, including reducing pay (by lowering incentive payments) when performance drops, the system is not at fault. It is the manager who makes the recommendations, and the person who approves the proposal who are failing to make the necessary differentiation.

When pressed, many managers will indicate they need more objective measurements by which to differentiate pay adjustments. Obviously, these are desirable; unfortunately (or fortunately), the costs of developing, installing, and maintaining sophisticated measuring devices to judge the value of a particular report, decision, or activity are usually prohibitive. The pay-for-performance concept is difficult to effectively administer, but consider the alternative. Not to vary compensation in relation to an objective assessment of performance is de facto to reward mediocrity and to penalize the better performing executive. Thus, either managers work hard to use what is available to make pay differentiations, or they must accept pay for seniority or on some other basis. In either event, they should stop blaming the system when in fact the system provides the opportunity, but they lack the ability.

Incentives work best where the individual has a clearly defined, measurable objective to accomplish—either an objective with few external impacting factors or an objective with factors that can be easily measured. The company must be careful to ensure that incentive plans are not so attractive that they encourage individuals to violate the corporation's standards of business conduct, or worse, commit illegal acts. Not only must falsifying records to show increased production, or sales, or reduced expense, be formally forbidden, but also necessary control procedures must be adopted to officially enforce the rules. In addition, plans must be structured to serve the financial interests of the shareholders, not simply the well being of the professional manager; otherwise, beneficial mergers or acquisitions might be thwarted.

A logical way to motivate the professional manager to take more personal interest in the success and well being of the company is to make that individual a part owner. This has been the main rationale behind the use of stock options and stock awards.

Importance of Pay. Pay is, admittedly, not of equal importance to all executives. As indicated earlier, some have achieved a level that is satisfactory in meeting financial needs. For others, the need is greater, either for direct use of pay or simply as recognition of their importance.

The importance of pay in altering or reinforcing performance is strongly influenced by several factors, including background and current economic status. For those who grew up in an affluent environment and currently have sufficient money, pay has little impact. Conversely, for someone who did not grow up with money and still doesn't have it, but does have high economic desires, pay is very important.

Some have questioned how much the individual is motivated by greed rather than simply need. Envy of the pay level of others is often a factor, but dissatisfaction is often based on perception rather than facts. Since most people probably overestimate the pay of others and also overestimate their own level of contribution, it is not surprising that many are unhappy with their pay programs, regardless of how lucrative. Therefore, a competitive pay program should "toot its own horn," emphasizing how it compares to what other organizations are paying for comparable performance and responsibility.

Executive Qualities

What personal qualities are likely to make an executive effective? Fortunately, there is no one model that can be used to clone replacements. Variances in positions, companies, industries, and stage of the market cycle demand different profiles. Nonetheless, there are certain qualities that seem to exist to some extent in many situations.

The Need to Succeed. If asked, most executives would probably indicate that they got where they are through their own efforts, rather than because of whom they knew. Long work hours have probably kept the individual away from the family more than he or she wanted, but a genuine interest in the job has made this a rational trade-off. The executive's results-oriented philosophy is reinforced by a desire for greater responsibility and balanced by a high level of integrity. While pay-for-performance-oriented, the executive has a higher degree of loyalty than he or she would probably admit. Probably no other employee group is as stereotyped as being believers in the work ethic as are executives: "Work hard, do a good job, and you will be appropriately rewarded."

Although professional or technical competence is highly regarded, the executive probably attributes success more to level of effort than to ability. The executive also probably believes that personal strengths lie in problem-solving situations, circumstances requiring creativity, and/or being able to effectively lead others.

There is a conviction that the job of the executive today is tougher than it has ever been. Government intervention, shareholder dialogue, and visibility of executive compensation are all becoming more evident. Executives realize they must continually prioritize the events impacting upon them—taking only as much time to analyze the data as is cost effective, given the problems facing them. Furthermore, they must be prepared to modify each decision, or alter its impact, as events and additional data make the earlier action inappropriate. Many must continually fight with themselves not to overindulge in an area of their own interest and expertise at the expense of less attractive but more significant issues.

For most executives, there is diminishing time to relax. In spite of how successful they have been in the past, the worry is about the present and the future. There is always pressure. Being successful is difficult enough, but continuing to be successful without experiencing a setback is both an impossibility and a requirement. The euphoria of success contrasts with the humiliation of failure.

The ultimate humiliation is being fired. This is especially traumatic to those in mid-career, since it may be difficult for them to get another job with commensurate pay and responsibilities. The higher placed the individual, the fewer the opportunities. Executives who are fired late in their careers may be able to simply retire (depending on the largess of the separation agreement); those in early career usually have a number of other opportunities available and don't have to fight middle-age discrimination [the Age Discrimination Employment Act (ADEA) notwithstanding].

Many successful executives are apparently motivated by fear of failure. This drive to ensure that their present work is always considered good or, preferably, better than their earlier work, drives them to spend whatever hours are necessary to reduce the risks of failure. As indicated, the ultimate failure is being fired. The worse part of being fired is not so much the economic repercussion (since an alternative job elsewhere is probably available) as the humiliation of defeat. The threat of failure hangs like the sword of Damocles over the heads of successful executives.

For individuals with tremendous drive and a desire to prove to themselves (even more than to others) that they have the ability to overcome virtually impossible obstacles, the objective of the pay delivery system logically is to channel these efforts by rewarding the individual for doing those things the corporation thinks best.

Peer pressure is another factor; many CEOs and other top executives track their pay progress versus their counterparts in other organizations. At the minimum, they consider it necessary to stay even with such individuals, but they would prefer to have their pay progress at a faster rate. Such views are tempered by the extent to which the person believes his or her own responsibilities to be less or greater than the contemporaries' responsibilities. Needless to say, this is easier to do when pay is in the company's proxy statement.

Furthermore, the executive typically believes that his or her own standards of performance exceed the expectations of the organization. Thriving under pressure, the individual is capable of planning and paying attention to detail, as well as successfully executing a decision that is personally not agreeable.

The problem many organizations have with such an executive is not how to motivate the individual to achieve better performance, but rather how to avoid demotivating conditions. Successful recruitment of such an executive by another company will probably be due to the promise of new challenges (with commensurate pay), rather than simply a significant increase in compensation.

Relationship with Superiors. To be successful, the executive must deal effectively with three levels in the organization: above, the same, and below. The executive must remember that superiors control pay increases and promotions. Therefore, being an effective subordinate is probably as important as being an effective manager. Interestingly enough, the emphasis in personal development programs is on the latter. Yet probably as many effective managers are fired because they are poor subordinates as vice versa. To be an effective subordinate, the executive must identify with the company philosophy, which can range from a family atmosphere to one of intense competition and little loyalty. The superior's management style is also important. One of the first facts to determine is whether the boss wants a written memo or a verbal briefing. Some are readers; others are listeners. The readers are handled by sending the memo and following it up with a meeting; the listeners are best approached by having a meeting and then leaving a memo.

Ideally, the executive will both like and professionally respect the superior, although it is more often one or the other. It is doubtful whether the relationship will last if both ingredients are missing, unless the executive is prepared to be a very good actor—and the executive who receives unsatisfactory pay and recognition will probably not keep up the act.

Being too good can be almost as bad as being a poor performer if the superior lacks self-confidence. A possible indicator of this is when the executive's work is signed by the superior and then discussed with others at meetings to which the executive received no invitation.

Executives must assess carefully the likelihood of their being given proper recognition in such situations. In addition, some superiors require a certain amount of stroking by their subordinates, perhaps to compensate for the lack of such recognition coming from their own peers and superiors. In such situations, the executive must acknowledge the superior's accomplishments and show respect for the superior's rank. It is also critical to take criticism without being offended, even if it is delivered poorly. How important is behavior modification? Is this a gentle tap or a threat to continued employment? Probe the statements to make certain you understand the exact nature of what went wrong and the seriousness of a repeat performance. View criticism as an opportunity to be better, not an emotional threat to as one's character.

A successful relationship is often typified as one where the executive brings solutions to the superior, not simply problems—especially after the toothpaste is out of the tube. Preferably, the solutions proposed should be ones that can be implemented smoothly without upsetting others. Few executives (including superiors) openly seek confrontations. In addition, the executive must keep superiors informed of events, including possible significant problems. Many superiors abhor surprises, even pleasant ones. The subordinate must also remember to utilize the superior's time effectively. Time is a finite quality in short supply for all executives.

In some situations, the executive must also "look the part." Here the old adage, "Clothes don't make the man," is not completely true. Some executives spend considerable time and money working with image consultants who focus on speech, mannerisms, and weight, as well as wardrobe. The most effective executive is not always the one who gets the promotion or the big bonus. Unfortunately, in some situations, the bonus goes to the executive who looks good and sounds persuasive. However, unless that image is backed up by performance, it is likely to be a short career. Conversely, if an individual's interactive skills are as exciting as watching paint dry, a charisma implant may be appropriate.

Interacting with Peers. Peer relationships are difficult because they are both competitive and cooperative. The successful executive must be competitive because superiors are examining performance, not simply on the job, but also relative to others in the peer group. Cooperation is a necessity because considerable interaction takes place among those on the same organizational level. Invariably, the respect of peers improves one's functional knowledge and effectiveness. Some executives are more concerned with self-perpetuation than with meeting their assigned responsibilities, a few to the point where they have become legends in their own minds. Others suffer from foot-in-mouth disease, engaging vocal cords while their brain is in neutral. Still others are gunslingers, who shoot from the lip: they may be wrong, but they are never in doubt. Needless to say, such individuals are not very highly respected by their peers.,

Relating to Subordinates. How many executives treat their subordinates as they would want to be treated by their superiors? Probably many fewer than profess to meet this common standard. There is a difference between correcting and humiliating subordinates, which some executives either have not learned or, for some particular reason, choose to ignore. Some apparently thrive on keeping their subordinates in a continual state of anxiety and fear. Others seem to ignore subordinates, allowing them to function completely on their own. A common complaint of the subordinate is that the superior does not spend sufficient time with the individual discussing objectives and performance.

Typically, as an executive rises in the organization, less and less time is available for his or her own work, and more and more time must be directed to the work of others, especially within the unit. This places an inordinate demand on the executive's time. It is thus essential that the executive be able to use time effectively. For most, this means identifying and prioritizing tasks daily, examining the monthly requirements weekly, assessing the yearly commitments monthly, and examining the long-range needs at least yearly. This continual assessment of priorities to ensure proper focus is as important as the expenditure of effort in completing the tasks.

Every executive must maximize the capabilities of subordinates, while limiting their exposure to their limitations. However, in areas of strength, they must be afforded the opportunity to fail! This means rewarding success and punishing failure. However, the risk of failure should be commensurate with the subordinate's ability, and the ability of the unit, to accept failure of that particular task.

Some executives are completely open with their subordinates; others are more obtuse. Some are very objective, others more subjective. Some are directive, others more participative. The effectiveness of the executive in executing a particular style is probably more important than the style itself. Furthermore, each subordinate must be counseled on performance, and the assessment must be based on current work, not past successes or failures. It is also important not to confuse pronouncements by subordinates with performance. When successful, the individual should be complimented *then,* not six months later in the written review. If the individual has not been successful, be candid but kind, not only in highlighting the shortcomings, but also in identifying possible ways in which the person would have been successful. This two-step process—what is wrong and how to be successful—are critical components of an appraisal and coaching program.

Subordinates should believe they are not "being used" by the executive simply to further his or her own career. Subordinates can more effectively sabotage an executive's career growth than the peer group because it is the subordinate's work for which the executive takes credit or blame. Here's a simple piece of advice: Emulate the things one believes own superior does well, and find better ways to do things he or she does not do well.

Problem Areas

Sometimes executives stay in positions that do not match up well with their abilities, including personal values. Believing that their family and others are counting on them, they continue in the position instead of considering alternatives. An objective review might result in a major change, or at least significant refinements, in the current work. Too often, executives focus on the position instead of what is an extension of what they like to do. Individual skills are only part of the whole person. It is the latter that must fit the position.

There are four problem areas that could derail executives' "express to success" and send them in search of other alternatives. They are the impact of stress, becoming a workaholic, facing a career crisis, and burnout. Let's examine each of these.

Impact of Stress. Stress is a part of most executives' lives. Making high-stake decisions with limited resources over long hours of work results not only in high stress, but limited hours of sleep to rest and recover. Engineers talk of stress in terms of the amount of weight a substance can support before it collapses; executives talk in terms of the amount of pressure to perform that can be absorbed without having a breakdown.

Some argue that a little stress is good. It elevates blood pressure and provides the adrenaline needed to move quickly through difficult situations. The key is to thrive, not simply survive, by improving one's capacity to handle stress. Self-confidence, positive thinking, and emotional contentment are key to managing stress. Additionally, recovery time, even brief, is critical to restore the needed energy to continue. Moving back and forth frequently and quickly between stress and recovery (and not trying to do both at the same time) maximizes one's effectiveness. However, stress may also impair the individual's ability to carefully examine alternative courses of action. In addition, stress may cause physical and mental health problems, probably the most common being ulcers and depression.

For some executives, the absence of stress may lower mental acuity. For them, stress is the vitamin needed to be a higher achiever. This might be the reason that a number of corporations have their headquarters in major metropolitan areas. The hassle of the commute gets the blood pumping and the adrenaline flowing. The office routine takes on an accelerated pace—one that might not be achieved in the idyllic forest setting of the suburbs.

The Workaholic. Just as the alcoholic can no longer control the role of alcohol, the workaholic can no longer keep work in perspective. The workaholic is a person obsessed with the good old American work ethic. The individual focuses on one half of the cliché, "Work hard and play hard." The person works hard and makes up for not playing hard by working harder! Some suffer from *career acrophobia*, in other words, the fear of failing and falling from their lofty corporate position.

Long hours of work do not make the executive a workaholic; a true workaholic does not know how to relax. The work effort takes on a meaning of its own, rather than being simply a means of achieving results. This lack of perspective may result in less-than-optimum performance as well as alienating peers and superiors. Individuals who have lost sight of the true reason for work usually are not good planners nor very creative; they don't have the time to devote to such activities. In addition, the workaholic is probably not a believer in delegation, choosing instead to do the work personally.

Few companies really want workaholics. Rather, they want executives capable of expending a great amount of energy, but able to work under control and keep perspective. However, many jealous peers maliciously label a hardworking overachiever as a workaholic in order to minimize some of the competitive threat. Only a small percentage of those labeled workaholics truly fit the definition.

Career Crisis. A crisis could occur early-, mid-, late-, or post-career. When it occurs, the executive believes that he or she has not and/or will not achieve the top rungs of management.

Early-career crisis is arguably the best of the four because there is still enough time to do something about it. The *mid-career crisis* usually occurs sometime around age 40, when the executive recognizes that about half of his or her working career is over. By now, the golden ring should have been reached or clearly within sight. *Late-career crisis* typically occurs after the half-century mark, certainly by age 55, if career expectations appear they will not be realized. *Post-career crisis* is after retirement. Some choose not to accept failure and go on to do something else. Others decide to take out their frustration on a golf ball and/or extended cocktail hours. Some feel trapped within a particular industry due to their particular skills. This would seem more likely to occur to those in line than staff positions, due to the latter's abilities to cross industry lines.

By definition, this trauma is greatest for those who had high expectations but are still a significant way from top management, with no apparent shortcuts in sight. Those who identified their strengths and interests earlier in developing career paths, and have made the necessary adjustments to stay on course, probably have less of a crisis with which to cope.

For those with very significant difficulties, alcohol and emotional concerns may be sufficient to require counseling. Unfortunately, although the facilities exist in many organizations to handle such situations, executives are often concerned that their problems may not be treated in complete secrecy. They may fear that discussions with a counselor will be revealed and used to minimize future promotions. Therefore, they often do not use the facilities available.

Burnout. A problem similar to career crisis is *burnout*. Both problems result in significantly lowered job performance. Whereas career crisis is associated with lack of promotion, burnout is typified by lack of interest in present position. Individuals have lost their enthusiasm for continuing their duties. Reasons cited include disillusionment as to job importance and loss of creativity. The job not only is no longer "fun," it is a depressive form of punishment. In many cases, burnout is caused by gruelingly long hours of work and yet still not enough time to get the work done. The workload has gotten increasingly heavier at all levels of the organization. In many cases, this occurs when organizations downsize without figuring out how to reduce the workload. Twelve-hour days at the office coupled with long commutes and additional work at home have the American executive experiencing a problem common to Japanese management—very little free time. Multiply stress by long hours and it's easy to see why "burnout" is an issue at a much earlier age than it used to be.

Individual Preferences on Pay

Although on the surface perceived value and after-tax value seem to correlate closely, some analysts advance the hypothesis that recipients assign a higher value to deferrals and non-cash forms of payment than to other forms of pay. Such a valuation would presumably be lessened during inflationary periods. While it is important to consider executive preferences in developing a pay package, such preferences might not be optimally appropriate. For example, many companies persisted with qualified stock options for their highest-paid people long after the net cost/net value analysis had relegated these options to a secondary position. In part, this was due to the fact that executives wanted qualified options in order to convert the entire gain to capital gains rather than ordinary income. The statutory limits on their successor, the incentive stock option (ISO), went a long way toward solving this issue. Another example is that many executives place a low value on stock options when the market is depressed and listless. Many financial analysts would counter that such times are precisely when options are attractive and should be used to benefit from a subsequent rally.

There are many problems in considering individual preferences, in particular, developing the appropriate possibilities, determining after-tax cost and value for each executive, avoiding IRS problems of constructive receipt, and maintaining the necessary records. (Constructive receipt was reviewed in Chapter 3 and will be discussed later in this chapter.) In addition, as suggested above, the executive's perception may be misplaced, and it will be necessary to subsequently do a little hand holding.

The Executive Stakeholder: Summary

Ideally, the entire compensation program is designed, developed, and administered in a manner that will motivate the executive to work harder, faster, and smarter. It is therefore important to examine the program to determine the extent to which this is true and, just as important, whether the executives perceive that it is designed in this manner.

Although many executives believe they are worth every penny of the hundreds of thousands of dollars they are paid, not everyone shares this view. The dissidents range from shareholders to lawmakers. With million-dollar-plus compensation packages becoming more common (even below the CEO level), public resentment may initiate confiscatory tax rates for the super-paid. In some cases, executive pay not only looks like a seven digit telephone number, but will soon have an area code!

Compensation should reward executives for taking appropriate business risks. Professional managers do not have the same motivation as owner-managers. Many will agree that no successful company has gone through the perils of the threshold stage without taking a calculated risk on an innovative product. Few professional managers are successful entrepreneurs, and few successful entrepreneurs are successful administrators. Participation and sense of ownership are therefore essential to properly channel the work efforts of the professional manager.

Establishing a perfect reward-for-accomplishment system is a virtual impossibility, since we are dealing with imperfect measurements. Nonetheless, it is imperative to make the system as good as it can possibly be. There aren't so many talented, self-motivated individuals with a strong need to excel that a company can afford to mishandle their pay program.

The entire premise behind well-designed compensation programs is to modify executives' behavior until it is considered optimal by the organization, and then to reinforce continuation of that level of performance. Unless executives are properly compensated, the organization will have a very difficult time in successfully attracting, motivating, and retaining top-quality executives.

As might be expected, the five elements of compensation have attracted varying degrees of executive interest over the years, due in part to the influence of the other stakeholders. Shown in Table 4-3 is their interest level by quarter century. The importance of these ratings is relative rather than absolute. During the first quarter of the twentieth century, interest was primarily on salary and incentives, as the U.S. dominated the world's industrial market with the marvel of mass production. The next quarter century was one of more balance. It was marked by the Great Depression of the 1930s and World War II. The following quarter was again one of U.S. domi-

Time Period	Salary	Benefits	Perks	Incentives	
				Short-term	Long-term
1900-1925	High	Low	Low	High	Moderate
1926-1950	Moderate	Moderate	Moderate	Moderate	High
1951-1975	Moderate	High	High	High	High
1976-Present	High	High	Moderate	High	High

Table 4-3. Executive interest in executive compensation

nance, since much of the world's industry was in rubble from the war. However, Korea and then Vietnam brought industrial opportunities along with high inflation. And the last quarter of the twentieth century was marked with high interest in all forms except perks, which lost their tax effectiveness appeal.

OTHER EMPLOYEES

In years past, employees paid little attention to CEO pay in their company. After all, the CEO was responsible for keeping the company going and ensuring others had jobs.

CEO Pay and Job Security Disconnect

But two things happened beginning in the mid 1980s. First, CEO pay (increasingly tied to the price of the company stock) started to increase at a much faster rate, while individuals began losing their jobs through massive cutbacks and downsizing. If that wasn't enough, some companies professed the reason the CEO got larger stock options than usual was because he or she had announced (or successfully completed) a massive downsizing (which meant a large percentage of the company workforce lost their jobs). Lofty statements of how these "rightsizings" were creating wealth for the economy by reallocating resources from those with excess capacity to those with needs for expansion did little to impress the out-of-work worker or, perhaps even more important to the company, their still-working friends. Many saw the executive as to blame in the first place for allowing the company to get into a position of too many employees. Not surprisingly, employees (and ex-employees) were angry that the CEO apparently prospered at the expense of their jobs. Consistent with this reaction, third party representatives, primarily labor unions, are likely to be very vocal. This anger is expressed in everything from an information page on the Internet, to the introduction of a shareholder resolution to limit the amount and/or alter the forms of executive compensation, or more directly, to an organization-wide effort to unionize the company's workforce.

Executives need to remember that employees have the ability to influence several other stakeholders every day, including customers, the community, and shareholders. It is ridiculous for executives to talk about a "committed workforce" when, by its own pay actions, it alienates the employees. Management must take the time to show how executive pay is tied to company performance. A clear indication that executive compensation *is* pay-for-performance is an important first step in removing employee dissatisfaction over executive pay. Furthermore, unless management wishes to formalize a "we-they" culture, it will also go out of its way to answer questions about how executives are paid. A second step would be to include all (or virtually all) employees in the same type of short- and long-term incentive plans. Admittedly, there will be a major difference in the size of awards (based on job importance), but at least the employees believe they are participating in the same way.

The Pay Gap

The spread between CEO and lower worker pay (however measured) has been widening and is commonly referred to as the *pay gap*. Detractors and proponents both agree that long-term incentives need to be included in comparing executive and worker pay. However, they cannot agree on how to calculate such a value. Some express it in absolute terms (i.e., the dollar difference). High absolute pay is a red flag by itself. For many people, a million dollars is a career earnings target.

Pay Definition	Average			
	CEO	Company	OTE	Lowest Paid
Salary	$200.0	$75.0	$40.0	$20.0
Multiple		2.7	5.0	10.0
Salary + ST/INC	$300.0	$80.0	$42.0	$20.0
Multiple		3.8	7.1	15.0
Salary + ST + LT/INC	$500.0	$100.0	$45.0	$20.0
Multiple		5.0	11.1	25.0

Table 4-4. CEO pay vs. other employees ($ amounts in thousands)

Paying that much or more is a point not to dismiss quickly. Others prefer to express the difference in relative terms (i.e., the percentage difference). This is often described as the *pay multiple*. In doing so, one must understand both the numerator and the denominator. Shown in Table 4-4 are three possible definitions for each. *OTE* is an abbreviation for overtime-eligible, those persons who must receive pay for overtime hours under the Fair Labor Standards Act. Note that multiples range from 2.7 to 25. To make the best case for CEO pay, compare CEO salary with average pay in the company (a 2.7 multiple). To make the worst case, use salary-plus-all-incentives compared to the wages of the lowest paid worker (a 25 multiple).

One can see how the impact of a significant long-term incentive plan could raise the multiple dramatically. It has been said that J.P. Morgan considered a multiple of 20 times average pay appropriate, but since he was likely referring to incomes with little in the way of long-term incentives, his statement is somewhat misleading. Even so, there is no evidence to show that he was including dividends on all of the company stock he owned.

The ratio is also greater for larger than smaller companies. In some cases, the problem has been exacerbated by adding on new long-term incentive plans without reducing or removing others previously in place. Enlightened CEOs tried to address the issue, not by lowering their pay, but by putting in similar pay-for-performance rewards throughout their organization. Stock options, gain sharing, team-based pay, and company performance measurements for defined contribution and incentive plans are examples.

Therefore, employees paid little attention to executive pay as long as they had good-paying jobs. Even during the Great Depression of the 1930s, because many of the "Fat Cats" had been wiped out in the Stock Market Crash of 1929, there was not much attention given to what executives were paid. However, as shown in Table 4-5, all of that changed in recent years as employees took offense that those executives not only kept their jobs while they lost theirs, but they were handsomely rewarded for downsizing other people out of jobs.

THE SHAREHOLDERS

A shareholder is one who has purchased and owns one or more shares in a company. Typically, these are shares of *common stock*, entitling the stockholder to vote on election of directors and other subjects. The other type of stock ownership would be in *preferred stock*, which typically has a better dividend and liquidation right but more limited voting rights. Common stock is by

				Incentives	
Time Period	**Salary**	**Benefits**	**Perks**	**Short-term**	**Long-term**
1900-1925	Low	Low	Low	Low	Low
1926-1950	Low	Low	Low	Low	Low
1951-1975	Low	Low	Low	Low	Low
1976-Present	High	Low	Moderate	High	High

Table 4-5. Employee interest in executive compensation

far the most commonly used—perhaps a good reason for its name. (When the company buys back stock from its shareholders, it goes to its own treasury and is called *treasury stock*.)

Type of Shareholder

Shareholders include: executives, members of the board of directors (elected by shareholders), and others (individuals and groups). Initially, during the threshold stage, executives are also the owners. As they see the opportunity to expand given more capital, they may first turn to venture capitalists, but at some point decide to make the initial public offering (IPO) described in the first chapter. At that point a portion of the business moves from the owner-executive to the investor-owner. By the time the company is well advanced in the growth stage (unless it is privately held), the amount of stock in family hands has not only diminished as a percentage of the total, but the owners are no longer running the company. Professional managers have been hired.

In some situations, the company may not be required to get shareholder approval but must disclose actions taken or being considered to ensure shareholders can make an informed decision on whether to buy, hold, or sell the stock. Some companies even seek shareholder opinion on subjects. This could be by mail, telephone, and/or the Internet.

For many years, the individual owner of record was the most common shareholder, making his or her own decision to buy or sell stock. Now retail brokers hold many shares, buying and selling often times with no more instruction than to achieve an expected return. When shares are in an individual's name, that person retains voting power. Where stock is part of a mutual fund, it is the fund manager who casts the ballot. Pension fund portfolios continue to grow as a proportion of total stock investments. Many of today's shareholders are not *owners* (interested in the long-term return); they are *investors* looking for the best short-term return on their investment. Whether short- or long-term in focus, each is looking for a favorable return on their investment. Shareholder return is typically described as current market price plus dividends received minus original investment cost. Many believe that institutional investors focus more on cash flow and revenue growth than earnings. However, this flies in the face of stock sell-offs when anticipated quarterly-earning targets are not met.

It is not uncommon today for large companies to have more than half of their stock in the hands of institutions. There are the large mutual funds where individuals have accounts in the fund but not individual stocks. The fund manager makes stock selections. Then there are private money managers who invest for individuals directly or indirectly through a company pension fund. Thirdly, there are the public sector retirement funds. CALPERS and TIAA-CREF are examples. Such funds may exist for states and municipalities or for job categories (e.g., law enforcement officers or teachers).

Shareholder Concerns

Shareholders want executive pay to be largely in company stock and variable in relation to performance. They also expect the level of pay to be comparable to that of similar positions with similar performance. Shareholders with significant ownership in a company can be an important voice on issues such as executive pay. More than ever, the focus of major shareholders is not on "how much" but rather on "how" executives are to be rewarded. The view being if the "how" is tied to shareholder value (i.e., stock price and dividends), the executive would not prosper without the shareholder benefiting. Stockholders are also concerned about *dilution* (an increase in the number of shares outstanding) caused by executive pay programs. As stock-option plans typically use about three times as many shares of stock as share award plans, they obviously have a more dramatic effect. As described in Chapter 2 (Performance Measurements), unvested stock awards and "in the money" unexercised stock options divided by shares of common stock outstanding equal dilution.

The *treasury stock method* is used to compute the effect on dilution of outstanding in-the-money stock options (i.e., option price if below market price) and other unvested stock awards. This method assumes all these shares have been converted to outstanding stock at the beginning of the year and the proceeds received (including cash equivalents of tax deductions) are used to buy back as many shares as possible, thereby reducing the number of shares outstanding for dilution impact.

Should a company actually buyback the stock (making it treasury stock), it is advisable that these be specifically earmarked for compensation plans. Shares reacquired without a specific intention for utilization may be considered tainted shares by the Financial Accounting Standards Board, preventing a company from use of the *pooling of interests* for an acquisition for a period of two years or until the reacquired shares were reused. However, that all changed in 2001 when FASB eliminated the pooling method.

Overhang, or *potential dilution,* is calculated by adding the total number of shares available for award/grant to the unvested stock awards and unexercised stock options, and dividing by the total number of shares outstanding, using the above described treasury method. Further increasing the numerator with the addition of shares requested for use (and the same denominator) equals *total potential dilution*. Once the option has been exercised, forfeited, or lapsed, and the restrictions removed from the stock award, they are no longer included in the numerator and, if exercised, are now in the denominator outstanding (having been added to the shares outstanding), thereby having a two-fold dampening effect on future dilution calculations.

With ever increasing overhang percentages, companies are mortgaging more and more of their future with stock-option plans. Companies that buy back optioned shares are doing so at a price. Namely, they are selling low and buying back high. It also means the proceeds are unavailable for investment purposes.

Shareholders traditionally vote on additional stock requests for executive pay in terms of the *5-10 rule*. If the increase in dilution over 10 years is five percent or under, vote "yes" (thereby assuming ½ percent a year use); if it is more than five percent but less than 10 percent, look to its terms before deciding to vote for or against the proposal; and if 10 percent or more, vote "no." With the increased use of company stock throughout the organization, the annual rate is more like one to two percent. Therefore, many argue for a new 10-20 rule, with the same actions applying to now higher percentages. Furthermore, companies in the threshold market stage may have percentages twice as high because of their heavy reliance on stock-option plans.

To oversimplify, shareholders prefer indexed and performance stock options to option prices locked in at time of grant. In addition, they do not like stock options that are either re-priced or reloaded with new options after exercise. They do not like stock awards without performance vesting features but do like such awards based on increases in shareholder value. They typically do not like internally based financial performance plans that do not take into account shareholder value. However, if they had a choice, they would prefer some form of economic profit plan (that would require income to exceed the cost of capital before any incentive payments could begin) to performance-unit or similar type financial plan. This is illustrated in Table 4-6.

Type Plan	Dislike	Like
External (Market)	Reloaded and repriced stock options Plain stock awards	Indexed and performance priced stock options Shareholder value awards
Internal (Financial)	Performance units	Economic profit

Table 4-6. Shareholder interest in incentive plans

Investment Decisions

Some say that to make money buying and selling stock, you only have to be right 60 percent of the time. Why then does an investor decide to buy stock of a particular company? While different reasons motivate different investors, high on the list has to be the belief of a good return on investment, either short and/or long term, through dividends and/or stock-price appreciation. This is sometimes expressed as a quantitative benchmark called the *equity premium*. An equity premium is the additional return (dividends plus stock-price appreciation) over a risk-free investment such as U.S. Treasury bonds. Historically, this has averaged around six percent. Even with federal treasuries one can do an after-tax comparison to municipal bonds (often called *munis*) that are not subject to federal income tax. Thus, a person in a 50-percent marginal tax bracket would have a three-percent after-tax return on a six-percent federal treasury, but a four-percent after-tax return on a four-percent muni.

Stocks are often described as either a *growth* or *value stock*. A *growth stock* is one with a low dividend (and therefore low yield) as the stock price is expected to increase faster than the average of other prices. Conversely, a *value stock* is one with a high yield because of depressed stock prices, which hopefully will rise.

A rise in shareholder value (i.e., dividends plus stock price) and/or a drop in risk-free interest rates would move investors to the stock market. Similarly, a decrease in the expected equity premium might provoke moves in the opposite direction, with investors moving from equity markets to risk-free investments. Few companies could expect to retain a shareholder without meeting his or her return expectations, although high scores for innovation and social responsibility might help. Another comparison that investors examine is the relationship of book value to market value. When book value exceeds market price, takeover specialists are attracted to buying the stock to gain control of a company and then sell off the assets. In the process of acquiring control, they have taken on large amounts of debt. Cash flow becomes critical to meet interest payments, which puts a restraint on investment opportunities. Expense control is critical. Typically, annual incentives focus on return on invested capital, whereas long-term incentives look to shareholder value.

Some investors are particularly interested in the quality of earnings (i.e., those resulting from revenue not tax write-offs), the use of corporate assets, and the strength of the balance sheet. These are the items of most interest to shareholders, not recipients of executive compensation. Nonetheless, resolutions may be put before shareholders to alter the design of pay plans and/or limit payments to the CEO and other executives, but typically, as long as the shareholder is prospering, they are unlikely. Not the case when CEOs are prospering and the stock is languishing. The ability, or lack thereof, of an organization to attract, develop, motivate, and retain people of talent, especially in management and other key roles has a strong correlation with success.

Investors are usually interested in companies that have a recent history of *stock splits*, where the price per share is proportionately reduced by the number of shares increased. For example, a share of stock selling at $100 a share will be selling at $50 a share after a two-for-one stock split, but the total value of stock held is still $100 as each share is worth $50. The reason companies do stock splits (and attract investor interest) is that they are confident the stock price will continue to rise, and without periodic stock splits, the shares would be selling at thousands of dollars each. This would not affect institutional purchases but would limit purchases by the individual investor with a limited asset position.

Investors may choose to buy or sell stock at either market price or a prescribed price. Instructions to a broker for a *market order* means to buy (or sell) stock at the current market price. A *limit order* prescribes the price of the transaction. Believing the stock is going to go up (and wishing to catch it before it falls) an investor might ask the broker to sell the stock at $80, the current price being $75. Conversely, a limit buy would be setting a price below current market believing it is going to go down. For example, setting a limit order to buy at $70, the current price being $75. Limit orders may be overtaken by other events (e.g., a market run-up or sell-off, which could make the decision a poor one).

Stock purchased by a broker can be put in the name of the individual and held by the broker, or the certificate is sent to the new owner. Conversely, the stock could be in the name of the broker, but held for the person. Such a designation is called *street name*.

Investors typically will buy stock through a broker, paying cash for the amount of the stock plus a broker's fee. The fee ranges considerably based on the type of broker. One can expect to pay the greatest fee to a full-service broker, who provides research and other services, and the lowest to a discount broker, possibly one on the Internet. However, some decide to leverage their available assets by *buying on margin*, in other words, paying only a part of the cost, the remainder paid by a loan from the broker. The Federal Reserve Board Requirement (since 1974) has been that the purchaser must put up at least 50 percent of the fair market value (FMV) in cash and that the loan cannot be for more than 50 percent of FMV. Therefore, an investor could pay $50 for a stock selling at $100 with the other $50 in a broker's loan. However, if the stock price drops to $80, the margin has risen to 62.5 percent and the investor must then come up with another $10 cash to cover the margin, or the broker will sell enough stock to bring the loan percentage back to 50 percent. This is called a *margin call*.

In addition to those investors who choose to directly buy or sell stock, there are those who buy and sell options. Options are contracts with the right (but not the obligation) to buy or sell 100 shares of a particular company's stock at a stated price by a prescribed date. Purchasing a *call option* gives the holder the right to buy the stock at the stated price within the prescribed expiration period. A *put option* gives the buyer the right to sell the stock at a specified price within the stated period of time. A *collar* is a put and call on the same stock hedging against a drop in the stock price with acceptance of a maximum rise. The price is called the exercise or *strike price*. If the price of the stock is below the call or above the put, it is *out-of-the-money*. Conversely, if the price of the stock is above the call or below the put, it is *in-the-money*. Option contracts are typically for brief periods, although they may extend for several years.

Shown in Table 4-7 is how such option quotations might be expressed. With a current price of $100 a share, future prices of $90, $95, $105, and $110 are shown. Assuming today is the end of December, an option to buy (or sell) a share before the June expiration date might be $8. If you believe the stock will be above $108 by that time, you would place a *call option*. If you believe the price will drop below $92, you would purchase a *put option* giving you the right to sell the share at $100. Buying a put option without owning a share of stock to sell is called a *naked option*. If the option is not sold before maturation, it will be necessary to purchase stock to cover the option. The Black-Scholes formula [reviewed in detail in Chapter 8 (Long-Term Incentives)] was first developed to set the premium to be paid on such options. It later came to be used for stock options given to executives (rather than those traded on the stock market), which will also be reviewed in Chapter 8.

A *warrant* is similar to a call option in that it is the right to buy a stated number of shares of common stock of the company at a prescribed price over a specified time period. They typically are packaged with bonds or preferred stock sold by the company and enable the investor an opportunity to participate in an increase in the value of the common stock.

Investors are typically identified as either bulls or bears. A *bull* expects the price of a stock (or specified grouping of stocks) to rise in the future and therefore buys stock now. Conversely, a *bear* is a person who believes the stock price will fall and therefore will sell the stock now, expecting to be able to buy it later at a reduced price. A bull would purchase call options to purchase higher priced stock in the future at today's prices; a bear would purchase put options, to sell lower priced

Price per Share		Expiration Date		
Current	Future	January	March	June
$100	$90	$10	$12	$15
100	95	6	8	10
100	100	4	6	8
100	105	2	4	6
100	110	1	2	3

Table 4-7. Market options

stock in the future at today's price. An upward movement in stock prices (typically 20 percent over a year) across a significant portion of the stock market is called a *bull market*; conversely, a broad-gauge decline (of 20 percent or more) in stock prices is called a *bear market*.

The principle of publicly held corporations is that shareholders elect individuals to the board of directors to represent them. Actually, shareholders have three ways to influence companies. They can vote their representation onto the board (thereby voting off the board those they do not want). Secondly, they can introduce and/or vote for resolutions limiting management discretion. And most of all, they either buy or sell the stock based on whether or not they support the management. In the next section (Rulemakers), we'll be looking at an organization focused on protecting shareholders, the Securities and Exchange Commission.

Shareholder Watchdogs

In addition, several watchdog organizations give their opinion on the appropriateness of management proposals to be voted on by shareholders. Among the retirement funds, probably the best known is *CALPERS* (California Public Employees Retirement System) and *TIAA-CREF* (Teachers Insurance Annuity Association-College Retirement Equities Fund). Two other well-known groups are the *Council of Institutional Investors* and the *Institutional Shareholder Service*. Additionally, there are several individuals who assume this responsibility, buying a few shares in many organizations to broaden their impact.

Because there is a significant difference between using the plan-approved number of shares for stock awards vs. for stock options, it is not surprising that some institutions require a company to put an inside limit on the number of shares to be used as awards vs. options in order to get a favorable rating from the institution on the proposal. An extreme example would be limiting the percentage to about one third on the belief that a present value calculation would equate one award to approximately three options.

Takeover Defenses

Few proposals draw more attention than anti-takeover proposals. While management describes them as shareholder-rights plans they are typically called *shark repellents*. They are directed toward proposed changes in the corporate charter and bylaws; typically, they fall into one of the following categories:

Control of Board of Directors

- **Board Size.** To prevent a group that has taken control of a majority of outstanding stock from expanding the number of directors and putting in enough of its own candidates to achieve a majority, some companies have amended their charter requiring a supermajority (e.g., 75 percent or 80 percent of the votes) to agree to the change.

- **Classified or Staggered Board.** Directors are typically divided into three classes or groups each with a three-year term. Electing a third each year makes it more difficult for a takeover bidder to quickly gain control of the board.

- **Cumulative Voting.** Takeover candidates would want to ensure that this is not permitted, as it gives a shareholder the right to vote all of the shares for one board candidate. The number of votes is equal to number of shares owned times the number of board candidates. Thus, if a shareholder had 10,000 shares and there were 10 board candidates, the shareholder could cast 100,000 votes for one director.

Increased Cost of Transaction

- **Convertible Rights.** Shareholders of target company are given the right to convert their shares into shares of takeover company at a ratio unattractive to the bidder.

- **Discount Stock Price.** Shareholders can buy stock in target company at a deep discount (e.g., half price), making it more expensive to bidder when these shares are sold to the bidder.

- **Fair Price.** Bidder must pay all shareholders a price equal to the highest price the bidder paid for any of the stock unless the takeover is approved by the board.

- **Pension Rights.** Surplus pension funds are used for improved benefits to prevent termination of plan and use of excess funds.

- **Poison Pill.** Whether convertible to cash and/or stock of the target company, they increase the acquisition cost through the grant of preferred stock and/or warrants to buy additional stock at favorable costs.

- **Redemption Rights.** Shareholder have the right to sell the target-company stock at a significant premium (may be equal to fair price).

Approval of the Transaction

- **Dead Hand.** Some adopted a requirement that only ousted directors could approve takeover bids. Referred to as the *dead hand*, it ran into difficulty in the courts. The *modified dead hand*, which allowed only those directors in place at the time of a hostile bid to vote, had similar legal problems.

- **Re-incorporation.** If the state in which incorporated makes it difficult to adopt anti-takeover measures, companies may decide to reincorporate in a state more favorable to such actions.

- **Supermajority Requirement.** This requires the approval of at least 75 percent of the voting stock.

- **Unequal Voting Rights.** By creating a separate class of stock, recognizing long-term holders of the stock and/or limiting the votes of those with substantial stock ownership, companies are able to give more votes to those they think will vote for them in a takeover bid.

Some bidders, finding it difficult to achieve a takeover, will attempt to *greenmail* the target company. In other words, they agree not to attempt another takeover for a stated period of time if the company will pay a significant premium above the market price of the stock. Sounds like "blackmail" only with a different color code. Some companies have tried to stop this with a charter amendment stating that the same privilege must be extended to all shareholders.

The objective of all these anti-takeover measures are to "encourage" the takeover company to deal with the target company's board of directors and reach a mutually agreeable position so that the board will not activate the measures. The board is mindful of its responsibility to obtain the highest possible sale price and thereby maximize the benefit to company shareholders. Some have questioned whether anti-takeover measures are intended to do this or simply to ensure top management keep their jobs.

Many CEOs and CFOs are perplexed—they are convinced their company is worth more than the stock market's assessment. Typically, this occurs when a company is a combination of businesses that apparently lack a synergistic reason for their existence. Often times this is because of two reasons. First, the market bases its assessment on the predominant revenue business, thereby undervaluing smaller businesses that may have more income opportunity. Second, the investor may avoid the company altogether, preferring to buy only those companies focusing on one business. The rationale being that the investor wants to make the decision on how to weight his or her portfolio rather than invest in a company that has a predetermined allocation in different businesses, based on its make up.

Strategies for overcoming these shareholder concerns range from selling a portion of a business to selling off the business totally (either to another company, a group of executives who will take it public, or directly to its shareholders). This was discussed in Chapter 1.

The Stock Market

A *stock market* is where shares of company stock are traded. They are also known as secondary markets because shares are bought and sold between investors using stockbrokers, rather than directly from the company to the investor as through an IPO.

The traditional form of a *stock exchange* is a physically located stock exchange. The New York Stock Exchange (NYSE), dating back to 1792 transactions under a button wood tree, is not only the oldest but also the largest in the United States. It is often referred to as the Big Board. The American Stock Exchange is similar to the NYSE but much smaller. Additionally, there are a number of regional stock exchanges in the United States. The NASDAQ (National Association of Stock Dealers Automated Quotation System) is also a stock market, but unlike the above named, has no physical presence.

A *stockbroker* is a person who is authorized to buy and sell stock on a stock exchange on which the broker is a member. Stock not sold through a stockbroker is called *over-the-counter* (OTC) stock, referring to its 19th century origins where owners sold shares of their stock over the counters of their shops directly to a buyer.

In 1896, Charles Dow and Edward Jones established the Dow Jones Industrial Average (DJIA) Stock Index. It used 12 stocks to give the investor a sense of what was happening in the stock market. In 1916, it expanded to 20, and in 1928, rose to 30 where it remains. Companies have been deleted or replaced by others for various reasons and, of those that remained, many have done so under different names, sometimes with different industry focus.

One has to look no further than the list of the original 12 companies in the index to see the difficulty of remaining in business. The companies were: American Cotton Oil, American Sugar, American Tobacco, Chicago Gas, Distilling & Cattle Feeding, General Electric, Laclede Gas, National Lead, North American Co., Tennessee Coal & Iron, U.S. Leather, and U.S. Rubber. See many familiar names?

While a list of some 30 companies, even though representing various industries, is arguably not a very effective indicator of market movement, the rejoinder is that the market capitalization, or market cap for short, of those companies often accounts for 20 percent or more of the entire stock exchange market cap for listed companies. As one might expect, the DJIA is made up of very large cap companies, whereas the Russell 2000 consists of small cap stocks listed on the NASDAQ. A broader-based index is the *Standard & Poors (S&P) 500*, introduced in 1957, consisting of 500 widely held stocks listed on the New York Stock Exchange. However, the Wilshire 5000 Index is probably the broadest measure of the United States stock market as it contains 5,000 different daily priced stocks.

Market capitalization is determined by multiplying the stock price by the number of common shares outstanding. Definitions vary, but representative definitions might be: *micro-cap* (under $100 million), *small-cap* (over $100 million but less than $1 billion), *mid-cap* (over $1 billion, but less than $10 billion), *large-cap* (over $10 billion but less than $100 billion), and *mega-cap* (above $100 billion).

Bear stock market terminology is a function of severity of decline measured within a few days start-to-finish. This might include a routine decline (drop of 5 percent), a correction (10 percent), a severe correction (15 percent), and a crash (20 percent or more). As of this writing, there were only three days when the closing DJIA had a correction of more than 10 percent: October 28, 1929 (12.8 percent), October 29, 1929 (11.7 percent), and October 19, 1987 (22.6 percent).

Not withstanding a few severe declines, all are aware that the stock market has had a long-term successful history, albeit not without a number of negative years (the year end value was less than the beginning-year value). More specifically, for the DJIA, the number of negative years by decade are: 1900-09 (five); 1910-19 (five); 1920-29 (two); 1930-39 (four); 1940-49 (four); 1950-59 (two); 1960-69 (four); 1970-79 (four); 1980-89 (two); and 1990-99 (one).

Significant declines have been far more prevalent then upside adjustments. The greatest relative increase on the NYSE was October 21, 1987—a gain of 10.2 percent. All other increases were less than five percent.

Although the NASDAQ began in February of 1971, the significant increase in stock prices occurred in the 1990s, as shown in Table 4-8.

Milestone	Date	Percent Gain
100 (Inception)	February 1971	—
500	April 1991	400
1000	July 1995	100
2000	July 1998	100
3000	November 1999	50
4000	December 1999	33
5000	March 2000	25

Table 4-8. NASDAQ milestones

The first half of the twentieth century was dominated by the individual shareholder; however, change was underway. By the last quarter of the century, pension and mutual funds were dominant. As shown in Table 4-9, interest in executive pay became very significant. The focus was on *how* not *how much* executives were paid. As long as there were rewards for building shareholder value, the institutions supported their pay program. Not surprisingly, many companies put a great portion of the pay program on stock-based plans. Also not surprising is that with the dramatic rise in the stock market, CEO pay also rose dramatically—correlating strongly with stock prices.

Time Period	Salary	Benefits	Perks	Incentives	
				Short-term	Long-term
1900-1925	Low	Low	Low	Low	Low
1926-1950	Low	Low	Low	Low	Low
1951-1975	Low	Low	Moderate	Moderate	Low
1976-Present	High	Low	Low	High	High

Table 4-9. Shareholder interest in executive compensation

Shareholder Summary

Not surprisingly, shareholders like executive compensation plans that are based on increasing shareholder value (stock value and dividends) with only modest shareholder dilution. Traditional stock-option plans whose grant price remains unchanged over the term of the grant (typically 10 years) can be expected to be less popular with shareholders during a prolonged bull market, since it appears executives do not have to do much to receive large rewards. Hybrids, which ratchet up the grant price, take on more shareholder appeal during such periods. Traditional stock options are most attractive to shareholders during prolonged periods of modest growth. However, no one is very interested in stock options of any type during prolonged bear markets, although one could argue that they would be very useful if given shortly before the market reversed and the bulls resumed control.

Conversely, shareholders do not like plans based on internal financial goals (ignoring shareholder value). Nor do they like restricted stock awards not tied to performance. Obviously, they do not like re-pricing stock options at a lower price than originally granted. Nor do they like *stock option reloads* (replacing exercised grants with new stock options). They are also not in favor of *omnibus plans*, which permit multiple uses of stock without describing what will be used when, nor of *evergreen plans,* which automatically replace stock used with new deposits to the plan.

Some look to the following warning signs to indicate excessive executive pay: interlocking directors (especially on compensation committee), CEO friends on board and key committees, and directors on more than several boards (thereby minimizing the time spent on any one).

In determining whether shareholder approval is needed, check the requirements of: the stock exchange (in order to list shares), the state of incorporation, the IRS (for statutory plans), or the SEC (in accord with the sale of securities).

THE CUSTOMERS

Customers are looking for low prices, high quality, immediate availability, and outstanding services. Until rather recently, customers have played no direct part in the issue of executive compensation nor shown much interest, as seen in Table 4-10. However, their decisions to or not to buy a company's product or service does affect the company's profitability, which in turn affects annual incentive awards and long-term stock plans.

Some organizations now include customer evaluation of products and services, making this

Time Period	Salary	Benefits	Perks	Incentives	
				Short-term	Long-term
1900-1925	Low	Low	Low	Low	Low
1926-1950	Low	Low	Low	Low	Low
1951-1975	Low	Low	Low	Low	Low
1976-Present	Low	Low	Low	Moderate	Low

Table 4-10. Customer interest in executive compensation

a part of the annual incentive plan calculation. Obviously, customers could also be shareholders and thereby influence executive pay in that aspect.

THE SUPPLIERS

The quality, price, and availability of supplier products and services have a direct effect on the ability of the organization to supply its customers, which determines its financial success, which in turn has a direct effect on executive pay. How a company looks at its suppliers is a major issue. Is the focus short term or long term? A short-term focus examines price, quality, and supply time. The long term looks not only to ensuring suppliers stay in business, but that they prosper. There may be a time when the organization will need financial assistance from its suppliers, for example, extended credit if it comes upon difficult times. Companies have found that driving down the price of its suppliers may put many out of business. What happens when there are only one or two left and they can sell their products/services elsewhere?

Although suppliers are looking for long-term, predictable relationships, to date, suppliers have expressed little interest in executive pay, as shown in Table 4-11.

Time Period	Salary	Benefits	Perks	Incentives	
				Short-term	Long-term
1900-1925	Low	Low	Low	Low	Low
1926-1950	Low	Low	Low	Low	Low
1951-1975	Low	Low	Low	Low	Low
1976-Present	Low	Low	Low	Low	Low

Table 4-11. Supplier interest in executive compensation

THE COMMUNITY

The community is truly a stakeholder. It relies on companies to provide a large taxable revenue base (of corporate earnings and employee pay) and plenty of good-paying jobs, all the while preventing any negative environmental impact. It is also the host of the business press and the rulemakers. Both have an impact on executive pay.

Business Press

Business newspapers (or business sections within general information publications), magazines, and television cover special events on executive pay in addition to detailing a compilation of data from proxy statements and reporting who made how much. In some instances, they even discuss the *why*. To make a story on executive pay newsworthy, it often must meet an appearance test of excessive compensation. Often times this is more easily accomplished if the supporting rationale for the numbers is not included.

THE RULEMAKERS

In the United States, the three branches of the federal government (Congress, the executive branch, and the courts) all play a part in influencing executive pay (see Figure 4-4). Space does not permit a discussion of city and state requirements, much less the laws and regulations of other countries. Just highlighting U.S. federal requirements is a major undertaking.

In the *legislative branch* of the federal government (Congress), making laws is a rather lengthy and time-consuming process. A bill is introduced and referred to an appropriate committee where it in turn is forwarded to a specialized sub-committee for study. Hearings are held and a bill reflecting the hearings is sent back to the full committee where additional hearings and revisions are likely. The full committee typically either forwards the bill to its chamber (i.e., House or Senate) recommending approval, or it takes no action, effectively postponing if not completely killing the bill. In the House, the Rules Committee will determine how and when the bill will be debated. In the Senate, the majority leader is likely to determine the course of action. Once before the House or Senate, a bill is debated (possibly amended) and either passed or

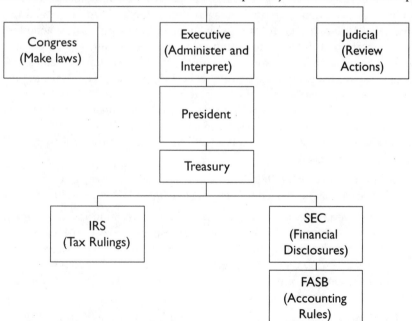

Figure 4-4. The federal government rulemakers

defeated. If it is passed, it moves to the other chamber of Congress and the process is repeated. If the bill is passed again, then it is referred to a joint House-Senate Conference Committee to work out any differences in the two bills. The compromised bill is returned to both houses for approval. If approved, it goes to the President of the United States for approval or veto. If vetoed, it returns to both houses where the veto can be overturned by a two-thirds vote. Lacking such a majority the bill dies. You can find selected laws affecting executive pay, some more significantly than others, in Appendix A.

The *executive branch* essentially exists to approve, interpret, and administer enacted legislation. The President can do this by issuing executive orders; various agencies do this by issuing regulations. Regarding executive compensation, it is the Treasury Department that is the most visible. Within it can be found the *Internal Revenue Service* (IRS) and the *Securities and Exchange Commission* (SEC). The Secretary of the Treasury, like other cabinet officers, reports directly to the President of the United States.

The *IRS* serves to interpret the *Internal Revenue Code* (IRC) and collect taxes. (Selected sections are found in Appendix B.) The IRS issues its interpretations of the IRC in the form of regulations and rulings. With the latter, the first two digits indicate the last two digits of the year of the ruling and the next digit(s) indicate the numerical sequence of the ruling in that year. Thus, Revenue Ruling 03-1 would be the first revenue ruling issued by the IRS in 2003. Appendix C includes a representative list of executive compensation-related Revenue Rulings.

The *SEC* monitors and regulates the registration of publicly traded securities, the disclosure of company financial information, and security trading by those with information not readily available to the general public, or *insiders*. A selected history of executive compensation-related SEC actions is in Appendix D. The FASB is the *Financial Accounting Standards Board*. It is recognized by the SEC as a non-governmental agency with the authority to establish *Generally Accepted Accounting Principles* (GAAP) for publicly traded companies. These actions are usually issued in the form of a financial accounting statement (FAS) also in numerical sequence. Thus, FAS 123 is the one hundred and twenty-third financial accounting statement issued by FASB. The SEC can override a FASB action if it believes it inappropriate. You can find a listing of some important interpretations affecting executive compensation in Appendix E.

The *judicial branch* of the government reviews the constitutionality of enacted legislation. Judicial decisions may be appealed up to the Supreme Court, which may overturn a lower court decision or affirm it, either by refusing to hear the case, or upon hearing the case, by agreeing with the lower court's decision.

The Rulemakers and Executive Pay. During the twentieth century, actions by rulemakers regarding executive pay can be divided into four distinct periods. They are shown in Table 4-12.

Pay Controls. On several occasions, Congress has taken action limiting pay actions. Shown in Table 4-13, the 1942, 1950, and 1970 actions were in response to cost-push inflation concerns. Respectively, they were concurrent with World War II, the Korean conflict, and the Vietnam War. Listed also is the 1993 Omnibus Budget Reconciliation Act; although it was primarily a tax act, it did curtail the amount of pay that would be tax deductible unless performance based. More will be said later about this law.

Tax Considerations. Congress periodically passes legislation that amends the IRC, stipulating what is taxable and at what rate. It also describes what may be excluded from income and what

Period A	1900-1912	Virtually regulation free. They truly were the "good old days."
Period B	1913-1933	Widely fluctuating maximum personal tax rates (after their 1913 introduction) made tax effectiveness very important in plan design.
Period C	1934-1972	Securities Exchange Commission requirements on company stock was added to the tax issues and were coupled with on-again/off-again pay controls, creating a three legged stool with tax policy and SEC requirements.
Period D	1972-Present	The emergence of accounting rules through APB and FASB on stock plans is a dominant feature overshadowing the IRS and SEC, bringing an Orwellian Animal Farm definition to the importance of the three.

Table 4-12. Key regulatory periods

expenses may be deducted from income. The latter is a tax deduction and differs from a tax credit in that a credit may be directly applied to reduce taxes due. *The general rule is that compensation (whether in cash or stock) received by the executive is taxable when received, and the company has a tax deduction at that time for the same amount.* Exceptions to this rule are the capital gains tax and alternative minimum tax, which are not tax deductible to the company.

Essentially there are four levels of tax information. First is the Internal Revenue Code, which is the collection of tax laws passed by Congress. Next are the income tax regulations (ITR), written by the Internal Revenue Service and interpreting the IRC. Third are the Revenue

Act	What It Did
Stabilization Act of 1942	Froze wages and salaries but permitted limited benefit increases
Defense Production Act of 1950	Curtailed wages and salaries but permitted limited benefit increases
Economic Stabilization Act of 1970	Permitted President Nixon to: • freeze pay and benefits for 90 days (Phase I) • establish pay board limiting pay to a 5.5% increase and benefits to a 0.7% increase (Phase II, removed in 1974) • set a period of voluntary compliance (Phase III, removed in 1974) Permitted President Carter to set a 7% ceiling on salary increases in 1978 (lifted 1980)

Table 4-13. Federal wage controls

Rulings made by the IRS to interpret the IRC and/or the ITR. And finally, there are private letter rulings, which interpret the IRC/ITR Revenue Rulings for a specific company.

History of Taxation. Hard to believe that income taxes have not always been a part of the United States economy. Actually, we almost made the first 100 years without such a system by financing the government through the sale of lands and the collection of duties and tariffs. But in 1861, an income tax was introduced to help finance the costs of the Civil War. It was removed in 1872. In 1894, Congress again imposed an income tax, but the U.S. Supreme Court struck it down in 1895, citing a conflict with Article 1, Section 9 of the Constitution, which stated, "Taxes must be in direct proportion to the census or enumeration." That roadblock was removed in 1913 following passage of the 16th Amendment. It states, "The Congress shall have the power to lay and collect taxes on incomes from whatever source derived, without apportionment among the several states, and without regard to any census or enumeration." President Wilson signed into law later that year the first income tax permitted by the new amendment. Tax due was to be calculated and reported on Form 1040 (form numbers were assigned sequentially by the Bureau of Internal Revenue). The form contained four pages—one each for instructions, gross income, deductions, and the income worksheet. The tax was progressive in nature in accord with the schedule shown in Table 4-14. Taxable income was gross income less deductions and either a $3,000 (single) or $4,000 (married) exemption.

Taxable Income	Tax Rate
Over $20,000 up to $50,000	1% plus
Over $50,000 up to $75,000	2% plus
Over $75,000 up to $100,000	3% plus
Over $100,000 up to $250,000	4% plus
Over $250,000 up to $500,000	5% plus
Over $500,000	6%

Table 4-14. 1913 tax schedule

With the average worker at the time earning about $1,000 a year, it was considered a reflection of being somewhat well off if you had to pay a tax. Reportedly, some 350,000 individuals were entitled to such bragging rights. The form along with payment was due March 1, along with an in-person affirmation of the truthfulness of the tax return. Since reportedly all returns were audited, it was important to be both truthful and accurate, just as it is today even though the percentage of returns audited has dropped.

Ever since 1913, an income tax system has been with us in some form or another. Highlights include World War I finance needs that pushed up the maximum rate to 77 percent. A postwar recession saw this cut back to 50 percent and by the late 20s to 25 percent. However, it was back up to 77 percent by the early 1930s; World War II costs sent the top rate up to 91 percent. After the war, it was reduced but raised again with the Korean conflict to 91 percent. In 1964, the maximum was reduced to 77 percent and lowered again in 1969 to 50 percent. The modern-day bottom was reached in 1986 with a top rate of 28 percent. A recap of maximum

Year of Change	Tax Rate
1913	6.0%
1917	77.0%
1920	50.0%
1926	25.0%
1932	77.0%
1944	91.0%
1948	77.0%
1950	91.0%
1964	77.0%
1965	70.0%
1969	50.0%
1986	28.0%
1990	31.0%
1993	39.6%
2001	38.6%
2004	37.6%*
2006	35.0%*
2011	39.6%

*Scheduled to occur before reverting back to 39.6% in 2011

Table 4-15. Maximum ordinary income tax rates

ordinary income tax rates is shown in Table 4-15. It is now estimated that the top one percent of tax filers pay about one third of all income taxes with the top five percent paying about half.

Tax rates are prescribed in the IRC for ordinary income (cash), capital gains (property owned), and an alternative minimum. Ordinary income is taxed at a prescribed rate by income level, capital gains (if held for a period qualifying as long-term) at a lesser rate, and the *alternative minimum tax*, which was introduced in the Tax Reform Act of 1969. It stipulates that individuals should pay the greater of regular income tax or the alternative minimum tax (AMT), which addresses *tax preference income* (TPI). TPI would include adjusted gross income plus non-taxed gains on incentive stock option (ISO) exercises, non-taxed income from tax shelters, and certain otherwise deductible items. The AMT requires planning ahead, identifying how much TPI can be taken in a year without triggering the AMT. The 1997 Taxpayer Relief Act set

Year	Rate
1969	10.0%
1976	15.0%
1986	21.0%
1990	24.0%
1997	28.0%

Table 4-16. Maximum alternative minimum tax rates

the AMT at 26 percent of AMT income up to $175,000, and at 28 percent above that amount. A recap of AMT rates is shown in Table 4-16.

The Alternative Minimum Tax (AMT) was allegedly established to ensure that taxpayers with significant deductions and credits paid their fair share (a corporate AMT exists for the same purpose). However, the elimination of most tax shelters with the 1986 Tax Act and lower tax rates in subsequent years has trapped more and more middle income individuals, since the allowable exemptions (unlike ordinary income) have not been indexed. Individuals living in a high-tax state, with large families, high medical bills, and exercising a lot of incentive stock options are likely to be caught in the snare of the AMT. With fewer deductions available to off-set income, and other items (such as paper gains on the exercise of incentive stock options) being included as tax preference income (AMT), more and more individuals will be subject to the AMT. If the taxpayer does not file an AMT liability, the IRS will send a bill for the amount due with interest and penalties added.

After the end of the calendar year, executives receive a W-2 stating the total amount of *ordinary income* received for the year. This will include cash and its equivalent for stock. The latter includes the spread (or gain between market value and exercise price) on the exercise (purchase) of non-statutory stock options and the market value of stock given outright. It will also report the amount of federal income tax and social security tax withheld from such payments.

Capital gains taxation typically is defined as short-term and long-term. Although it has varied from time to time, the most common definition has been capital gains on property held more than twelve months will be taxed at a lower rate than income taxed as short-term capital gains (i.e., held for twelve months or less). Oh what a difference a day can make! A history of recent long-term capital gains rates is shown in Table 4-17.

Tax Effectiveness. In examining tax impact, it is appropriate to consider what is left after taxes. This after-tax examination can be done for both the executive's income and the company's (*after-tax cost*). To the extent the executive's after-tax value increases or the company's after-tax cost decreases, one has improved the *after-tax effectiveness*.

The company essentially has three situations with regard to a compensation expense: no expense or tax credit, tax deductible (fully or partially), and non-tax deductible. The first says either there is no out-of-of-pocket expense or the expense is a tax credit and therefore reduces dollar-for-dollar its tax liability (truly a no-cost expense since the federal government is paying the full charge). If it is tax deductible, it reduces the company income before taxes dollar-for-

Year	Rate
1944	25.0%
1969	35.0%
1978	28.0%
1981	20.0%
1986	*
1993	28.0%
1997	20.0%

*Taxed at ordinary income rate

Table 4-17. Long-term capital gains tax rates

dollar (here the federal government is a partner in paying the expenses). The worst situation is when the expense is nondeductible for tax purposes. The company therefore receives no tax assistance and bears the full expense of the payment.

The executive's income can fall into one of six categories: not taxable; taxable but 100-percent deductible; taxable and deductible if above stated allowance; taxable above a certain allowance; taxed as long-term capital gains; and taxed as ordinary income or short-term capital gains. The combination of taxability to executive and tax deductibility to the company is shown in Table 4-18. The attractiveness to the executive ranges from 1 (best) to 6 (worst) and for the company from A (best) to D (worst).

Taxable to Executive	Tax Deductible for Company
1. Not Taxable	A. No expense or 100% tax credit
2. Taxable but 100% tax deductible	B. 100% tax deductible
3. Taxable but only deductible above allowance	C. Partially tax deductible
4. Taxable above a certain allowance	D. Not tax deductible
5. Taxable as long-term capital gains	
6. Taxable as ordinary income or short-term capital gains	

Table 4-18. Taxable income and tax deductions

Shown in Table 4-19 are the 24 possible combinations with examples. Not all combinations necessarily will have possible applications. See combination 1C from Table 4-18, 1 (not taxable to the executive) and C (partially tax deductible to the company). An additional factor is the timing of taxation and tax deductibility. Non-tax qualified deferred compensation cannot be taken as a tax deduction by the company until the executive receives the income and has a tax liabili-

Executive	Company	Examples
1	A	Job Title
	B	Matched Gift/Health Care/Scholarship
	C	
	D	ISO Exercise
2	A	
	B	Business Travel
	C	Business Entertainment
	D	
3	A	
	B	Financial Counseling
	C	T&E Allowance
	D	
4	A	
	B	Group Life Insurance
	C	
	D	
5	A	
	B	
	C	
	D	Stock Option Sale (over 12 months after exercise)
6	A	
	B	Cash, Stock Awards, Disqualifying ISO Sales
	C	Pay not Meeting Section 162(m) Requirements
	D	Dividends

Table 4-19. Taxable income and tax deduction combinations

ty. Conversely, tax qualified pension plans permit the company to take a tax deduction when a contribution is made to the plan, while the executive is not taxed until the benefit is received.

Shown in Table 4-20 are possible tax rates on company income. A tax rate of zero is equivalent to a nondeductible item since the government underwrites no portion of the expenditure. Conversely, a tax rate of 100 percent will be comparable to a full reimbursement by the government, only because all the income is turned over to the government. In more typical situations, if the federal tax were 40 percent, the after-tax or net cost to the company would be 60 percent of the expenditure. As company taxes increase, it is less expensive to make tax-deductible expenditures and the reverse is also true. As taxes on company income decrease, it becomes more expensive for such outlays. Conversely, as individual tax rates increase on ordinary income, executives seek alternative forms of pay taxed at lower rates.

The executive's after-tax value is dependent on the manner in which the expense is taxed. In the best situation, it either is not taxed or, if taxable, is fully tax deductible and therefore cancels itself out (i.e., the amount is entered as income but income is then reduced by the same

Company											
Tax Rate	0%	10%	20%	30%	40%	50%	60%	70%	80%	90%	100%
Net Cost	100%	90%	80%	70%	60%	50%	40%	30%	20%	10%	0%

Executive											
Tax Rate	0%	10%	20%	30%	40%	50%	60%	70%	80%	90%	100%
Net Income	100%	90%	80%	70%	60%	50%	40%	30%	20%	10%	0%

Table 4-20. Tax rate effect (net income vs. net cost)

amount). The next best situation is long-term capital gains (i.e., property held longer than a year), where the gain is taxed at a rate lower than the tax on ordinary income. In addition to the capital gains tax, which may lower the tax paid (because it usually is less than the ordinary income tax), there are several situations that will affect tax effectiveness. First is the earlier described alternative minimum tax (AMT), which increases the individual's tax rate (thereby lowering his or her net income). The second is capital gains, which increases the recipient's after-tax value (as it is taxed at a lower rate) but is not deductible to the company. The third is a limit on the amount of compensation that is tax deductible to the company. It thereby increases the after-tax cost to the company. One such limitation is described in Section 162(m) of the IRC. Enacted in 1993 it imposes a one-million-dollar limit on tax-deductible compensation to the chief executive and the next four highest-paid officers of a publicly held company.

Excluded from the one-million-dollar limit are:

- Commissions
- A shareholder-approved stock-option plan that specifies individual grant limits and is administered by a committee of independent directors
- Performance based compensation when:
  - the compensation committee of the board of directors establishes objective performance goals
  - the performance goals and other material terms are approved by shareholders
  - the compensation committee certifies that the performance goals and other material terms have been met before payment is made
- Contract payments in effect prior to enactment (February 13, 1995)
- Tax-qualified retirement plan contribution
- Employee benefits and perquisites not included in taxable income (e.g., healthcare)

Individuals leaving prior to the end of the year are not subject to the limit as the law deals with individuals on the payroll on the last day of the year. Similarly, severance payments and non-qualified, deferred compensation are not subject to the limit. Not surprising, Section 162(m) has increased the amount of compensation deferred to retirement age for affected individuals. It is to the company's advantage to do so and, therefore, some inducement is provided to executives to make it attractive, such as giving an interest rate equivalent.

As indicated earlier, dividing the executive's after-tax value by the company's after-tax cost

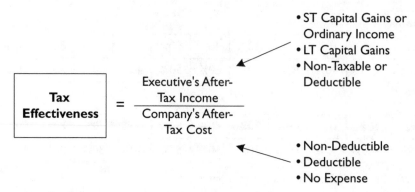

Figure 4-5. Tax effectiveness

gives one a measurement of the tax effectiveness of the form of payment. The higher the value, the more tax effective the payment. Figure 4-5 illustrates the formula.

The tax effectiveness range is from zero to infinity. A zero is the value when the recipient is taxed at a rate of 100 percent on the income, resulting in a zero for the numerator. An infinity value results when the company has zero cost.

Table 4-21 allows one to determine tax effectiveness under a wide range of combinations. This is especially helpful when individual rates may be different. For example, if the company tax rate (CTR) is 40 percent and income on $200,000 is taxed at 50 percent, but at $500,000 is taxed at 60 percent, the tax effectiveness (TE) calculations are .83 and .67, respectfully. In other words, it is less tax effective at the higher income level.

For the same two executives, the tax effectiveness would be .50 and .40, respectively, on stock dividends since they are taxed as ordinary income to the executive and are not tax deductible to the company. The importance of salary not being a non-tax deductible dividend to a small company executive-shareholder is quite apparent. It must also not be deemed unreasonable compensation by the Internal Revenue Service (IRS), for it would then move from .83 or .67 in the two examples to .50 and .40, since unreasonable compensation is not tax deductible to the company while still taxable as ordinary income to the recipient. The IRS challenge is of concern to privately held or closely held organizations, since the IRS view is that unreasonable compensation is really a distribution of profits and, therefore, a dividend—which is not tax deductible.

To generalize, there are three levels of tax effectiveness: low, moderate, and high (as shown in Table 4-22). "Low" means the full value is taxed at ordinary income rates: cash and stock award are examples. "Moderate" is because it is taxed at more favorable assessment valuation. "High" is when the item is not taxed or taxed at more favorable rates (e.g., capital gains). Tax effectiveness is not to be confused with the *effective tax rate*. The latter is the total tax paid divided by total income reflecting the percentage of income paid in taxes. Thus, with total taxes of $300,000 on a $1,000,000 income, the effective tax rate would be 30 percent. This in turn is different from the *marginal tax rate*, which is the tax rate in effect for the next dollar of income. In a progressive tax structure, this would be ever increasing. Needless to say, executives look for legal ways to minimize taxes. This is *tax avoidance*, not to be confused with *tax evasion*.

The lower the tax effectiveness rating, the more attractive it is to revenue collectors.

	0%	10%	20%	30%	40%	50%	60%	70%	80%	90%	100%
Individual Tax Rate											
CTR 0% →											
TE	1.00	.90	.80	.70	.60	.50	.40	.30	.20	.10	0
CTR 10% →											
TE	1.11	1.00	.89	.78	.67	.56	.44	.33	.22	.11	0
CTR 20% →											
TE	1.25	1.13	1.00	.88	.75	.63	.50	.38	.25	.13	0
CTR 30% →											
TE	1.43	1.29	1.14	1.00	.86	.71	.57	.43	.29	.14	0
CTR 40% →											
TE	1.67	1.50	1.33	1.17	1.00	.83	.67	.50	.33	.17	0
CTR 50% →											
TE	2.00	1.80	1.60	1.40	1.20	1.00	.80	.60	.40	.20	0
CTR 60% →											
TE	2.50	2.25	1.00	1.75	1.50	1.25	1.00	.75	.50	.25	0
CTR 70% →											
TE	3.33	3.00	2.67	2.33	2.00	1.67	1.33	1.00	.67	.33	0
CTR 80% →											
TE	5.00	4.50	4.00	3.50	3.00	2.50	2.00	1.50	1.00	.50	0
CTR 90% →											
TE	10.00	9.00	8.00	7.00	6.00	5.00	4.00	3.00	2.00	1.00	0
CTR 100% →											
TE 00 →											

Legend: CTR = Company Tax Rate   TE = Tax Effectiveness

Table 4-21. Tax effectiveness

Amazingly, some legislators still have not recognized that it is not simply the tax rate levied on the individual's income that affects tax revenue. It is the spread between the rates on taxable income to the individual *and* the employer. The effect is illustrated in Table 4-23.

Note that the government is better off with a low 20-percent tax on executive income when

Element	Importance
Salary	Low
Employee Benefits	Moderate-High
Short-term Incentives	Low-Moderate
Long-term Incentives	Low-High
Perquisites	Moderate-High

Table 4-22. Tax effectiveness importance

	Tax Rate			
Executive	50%	40%	30%	20%
Employer	35%	35%	35%	—
Revenue Gain	15%	5%	(5%)	20%

Table 4-23. Tax collector's net gain

there is no offsetting tax deduction, than with a higher 50-percent rate but tax deductible to the employer who pays a 35-percent rate. To illustrate, if the executive receives additional ordinary income of one million dollars (taxed at 50 percent), the individual will pay $500,000 in taxes; however, the employer will take the one million dollars as a tax deduction (thereby lowering the company's taxable income by a like amount) and save $350,000 in taxes. Net effect: government tax revenue of $150,000. But if all one million dollars were long-term capital gains (taxed say at 20 percent), the tax collector would net $200,000 because the company would have no tax deductions.

In addition to direct pay (or fair market value for such things as stock awards), executives must be familiar with several taxable situations described more fully in Chapter 3, especially constructive receipt, economic benefit, and imputed income. *Constructive receipt* occurs when the executive had the right to take the pay currently but chose to defer it or to accept it in some other form. Simply turning one's back on the offered compensation is not sufficient to avoid constructive receipt (i.e., being taxed as if it were received). *Economic benefit* is closely allied with the doctrine of constructive receipt, but it is usually invoked when the company funds a future payment to the executive through an insurance contract or trust. In these situations, the individual will be taxed on the annual value of the employer contributions, even though the principle of constructive receipt was not invoked because the risk of forfeiture has been removed. *Imputed income* occurs when the value of a service is estimated (e.g., personal use of corporate aircraft). The value may be the actual cost to the company or, in some instances, the value of a comparable service through other means (e.g., the cost of first-class commercial airfare). With these considerations in mind, let's move on to the next rulemaker.

SEC Impact

The SEC came into being with the 1933 Securities Act and the Securities Exchange Act of 1934. The intent of Congress was to protect the investor from unscrupulous individuals and firms. The first law focuses on distribution of securities and the second on trading of securities after distribution.

The sale of stock either has to be registered with the SEC or considered to be exempt because: small amounts of capital are involved; raising capital is not the purpose; and/or investors are sophisticated and have information access. The main focus is on disclosure through the establishment of financial accounting and reporting standards for all publicly held companies. Its impact is seen in the annual report of the company with both an income statement and balance sheet, and its proxy statement sent to shareholders prior to the annual meeting. Additionally, the SEC requires publicly held companies to file a *Form 10-K*, which provides financial and related business information, including background on the corporate officers. Both the income statement and the balance sheet are used in identifying measurements to be used in short- and long-term incentive pay. A number of such performance measurements were described in Chapter 2.

American Institute for Certified Public Accountants. To provide a level playing field in financial reporting, the American Institute for Certified Public Accountants (AICPA) issued various interpretative bulletins from 1939 to 1959. Bulletin No. 43 "Compensation Involved in Stock Options and Stock Purchase Plans" prescribed rules for the newly authorized restricted stock options under the 1950 Revenue Act. This bulletin marked an exception to the basic rule that the company must expense the full value of a compensation item, be it cash or stock, over the performance period.

Accounting Principles Board. The Accounting Principles Board (APB) succeeded the AICPA in 1959 and, through it, accounting firms established generally accepted accounting principles (GAAP), which form the basis for consistency in accounting matters. *The basic rule is that compensation is an expense charged to earnings and all stock issued is a dilution.* A landmark ruling affecting executive pay was Opinion No. 25 in 1972 "Accounting for Stock Issued to Employees." It was prompted by the establishment of restricted stock plans (which will be discussed in Chapter 8, Long-Term Incentives).

APB 25 stated that in accounting for stock issued to employees, one either had a *compensatory stock option* or a *non-compensatory stock option*. Non-compensatory plans were considered those intended to raise capital and/or diversify ownership among its employees. The requirements included:

- Substantially all full-time employees must be eligible.
- The stock must be distributed equally per formula to all eligible persons.
- A reasonable time period must be provided to exercise the rights.
- Discount from market price can be no greater than a reasonable offer to shareholders or others.

A compensatory plan is one that does not meet all four of these requirements. Broad-based stock-option plans may meet the definition of a non-compensatory plan, but executive stock-option plans clearly would be compensatory. There are no compensation expenses under the former, but under the latter, an expense equal to the difference between the option price and the market price at time of grant must be charged over the vesting period. This would be zero if there were no discount.

Under APB 25, plans are categorized as either fixed or variable. As the term suggests, with a *fixed plan* the expense is fixed or determined at time of grant (and therefore sometimes called *grant date accounting*). Under a *variable plan,* the expense is determined at the date following grant when both the number of shares and the price per share are known. The former would include traditional, non-discounted stock options (as well as those with a discount at time of grant). It also covers restricted stock awards when the number of shares and latest possible payment date are known. Variable plans essentially cover all other type of stock options and stock awards.

The key principle of APB 25 is the *measurement date principle*, which stated that compensation expense should be measured when the number of shares and price per share is first known. More specifically, "Compensation for services that a corporation receives as consideration for stock issued through employee stock option, purchase, and award plans should be measured by the quoted market price of the stock at the measurement date less the amount, if any, that the employee is required to pay ... if a quoted market price is unavailable, the best estimate of the market value of the stock should be used to measure compensation. The measurement date for determining compensation cost in stock option, purchase, and award plans is the first date on which are known both (1) the number of shares an individual employee is entitled to receive and (2) the option or purchase price, if any." The net result is that there is no requirement for a charge to earnings for stock options that are issued at or above fair market value (FMV) at grant date and vest solely on time. The other exception to the basic rule that came from this ruling is restricted stock. The value of the stock at time of grant is prorated over the vesting period, whereas other multi-year performance stock awards are accrued on the basis of period-ending value, since the stock price and/or the number of shares are not known at time of grant.

Financial Accounting Standards Board. In 1973, the APB was replaced by the Financial Accounting Standards Board (FASB), an independent group financed by the private sector. It currently consists of seven members approved by the Financial Accounting Foundation. The view of some was that industry was so upset with a number of APB Opinions (especially APB 25) that they financed the establishment of a new accounting authority. However, it like its predecessors remained subject to SEC control. Namely, if the SEC did not concur with FASB's actions, it could reverse them. And in turn, the chair of the SEC could be overruled by congressional action.

About 10 years after formation, certified public accountants requested a reexamination of stock plans by FASB. The major issue was stock options. Virtually everyone agreed they were a part of compensation, but under the measurement date principle, there was no recognized expense.

FASB undertook the review of accounting for stock because it believed that plans with similar economic benefits to employees had different accounting treatment. Moreover, not only had a number of new plan types been developed since Opinion 25 in 1972, but new valuation methods for valuing stock options had also been developed.

In the mid 1980s, FASB tentatively decided to adopt a *minimum value method* to determine the accounting cost of employee stock options. The calculation would be the stock's fair market value at time of grant minus the present value of the option price using a risk-free rate of return discounted from the option's maximum term (10 years in most cases). The net amount would then be reduced by the present value of the expected dividends during the same maximum term, also discounted by the same risk-free rate of return. Some argued this was mislabeled, as it was more like a maximum value. Based on a flurry of objections to this approach, FASB explored various adjustments to the model (e.g., date of vesting instead of date of grant).

In 1986, FASB ruled that dividends on restricted stock should be recognized as a compensation expense rather than charged to equity like other dividends.

While FASB was still deliberating on the method for costing stock options, the SEC stated in late 1992 that the stock option/stock appreciation right (SAR)-grant table in the proxy statement could use assumed five-percent and 10-percent appreciations or a present value method such as the *Black-Scholes Formula.*

The formula developed by Fisher Black and Myron Scholes was not the first attempt to measure financial risk—efforts can be traced back to the beginning of the century. However, their formula is the most widely acclaimed for helping investors put a price tag on risk. This mathematical formula published in 1973 was created to value stock options traded on public markets. It looks at a grant date, number of years option is exercisable, the option price, the stock price, volatility, dividend yield, and risk-free interest rate. The formula is further discussed in Chapter 8 (Long-Term Incentives). Based on these values, it estimates the fair value one should pay for an option. However, not everyone agrees with such present value calculations for executive stock options. Unlike stocks on the market, executive stock options are not bought and sold, nor is the time period measured in months. How many executives would be willing to buy their options at a price somewhere around 30 percent of the option price? The one problem with such present value models for a long period of time is that the value will be something other than the calculated value. It could be significantly greater, significantly less, or somewhere in between. Additionally, executives do not accept the logic that a higher price option is worth more than a lower option price. This is generally true when the higher-priced grant preceded the lower-priced grant. For example, the executive received a grant at $75 a share and, one year later, an additional grant at $60 (because the company's stock price dropped). Present value calculations might have put these at $25 and $20, respectively. Even if the executive agreed with the $20 for the $60 option, the person would not see the logic to an option priced $15 higher ($75-$60) to be worth an added $5 ($25 - $20).

In mid-1993, FASB issued an exposure draft that would require an earnings charge for all grants. In 1995 after a decade of deliberation, FASB issued FAS No. 123. It stated companies had a choice. Either continue using APB 25 as before, or determine cost at time of award with a present value formula such as Black-Scholes. However, the company must use the same method for all employee stock plans. And if they used APB 25, they had to show the present value impact in the financial footnotes as if FAS 123 were used. Since stock options issued at Fair Market Value (FMV) have no discount, the cost under APB 25 is zero. Not surprisingly, few companies use FAS 123. A comparison of key points of APB 25 and FAS 123 are shown in Table 4-24.

In 2000, FASB issued Interpretation No. 44. The stated intent was to further interpret, not amend or modify APB 25. It permitted the inclusion of non-employee directors and some leased employees. And it described when stock option re-pricings, reload options, and stock-for-tax withholding result in an earnings charge because of a new measurement date.

Emerging Issues Task Force. FASB's Emerging Issues Task Force (EITF) resolves technical issues interpreting how existing accounting pronouncements apply to new situations. For

Definition	APB 25	FAS 123
Measurement Date	When number of shares and price per share first known	Grant date
Measurement Cost	Market value less cost to buy on measurement date	Present value
Expense Report	Charged to income statement if an expense	Charged to income statement as an expense or as a footnote
Expense Period	Until vested	Until vested

Table 4-24. Comparison of APB 25 and FAS 123

example, it looked at the accounting impact of companies re-pricing underwater stock options following the October 1987 crash. It initially ruled there was no compensation expense if done once. However, a second re-pricing would be considered a variable grant and treated as an SAR for accounting purposes. In 1999, FASB ruled that even the first re-pricing would result in the option being considered a variable grant.

Insider Trading. In addition to overseeing how executive compensation will be reflected in the company's financial statements, the SEC also provides restrictions on purchase and sale of company stock by those with information not available to the general public (i.e., insiders). Highlights of these are found in the 1934 Securities Exchange Act as amended and directly related rules adopted by the Commission.

Section 16(a) defines "insiders" and their filing requirements:

- Insiders are those in policy-making positions (such as executives and board members) and owners of 10 percent or more of the company.
- Insider filing requirements [Forms 1 and 2 are not applicable to 16(a)] include:
  - **Form 3** Beneficial ownership upon attaining insider status filed within 10 days of effective date.
  - **Form 4** Specified changes in beneficial ownership, filed within 10 days of end of month.
  - **Form 5** Annual statement of changes in beneficial ownership not required to be on Form 4 or corrections on Form 4; filed within 45 days of end of fiscal year.

Three copies go to the SEC (one being hand signed) one copy goes to each exchange on which the stock is listed, and one goes to the company corporate secretary or other designated person.

Under **Rule 144** of the 1933 Securities Act, *restricted stock* (shares not registered with the SEC) and *control stock* (defined as stock owned by person or persons who control the company directly or indirectly) must generally be held two years before it can be sold. Notice of such an intended sale must be made to the SEC (on Form 144) when an offer is contemplated. Rules on limitations on amount sold, manner of sale, availability of public information, reporting requirements, and other issues need to be carefully reviewed.

Rule 145 from the same act covers the requirements of sale of company stock resulting from mergers, acquisitions, and other stock issued as the result of stockholder approved reorganizations. As with Rule 144, limitations on amount sold, manner of sale, availability of public information, reporting requirements, and other issues need to be reviewed carefully.

Section 16(b) prevents insiders from profiting on their information. Profits from purchase or sales within a six-month period of each other are to be returned to the company. This includes so-called profits from lower-priced purchases that occur within six months following higher priced sales. These are deemed short-swing profits.

The SEC also ruled in the late 1970s that there is a 10-day period following a public release of company financial statements when insiders may cash out their stock appreciation rights without being in violation of short-swing actions. More specifically, this 10-day period is defined as the third to the twelfth day after the disclosure. This requirement effectively disappeared with the 1991 ruling that stated the "purchase" was at time of grant. Thus, if there were more than six months between date of the grant of the SAR and its exercise, there could be no short-swing issues. Nonetheless, a number of companies use this same 10-day definition for permitting executives to exercise stock options and sell stock. An additional restriction that companies impose (to not be in violation of insider-trading rules) is a *blackout* period, during which insiders are prohibited from any stock transactions.

Section 16(b)3 specifies exceptions to the 16(b) rule and what needs to be done to meet those exceptions. For example, in 1991, the SEC ruled that the grant, not the exercise of a stock option, constituted a purchase. Therefore, if options were exercised more than six months after grant, the acquired shares could be sold immediately without triggering short-swing profits. To comply, the following is required: shareholder approval of the plan (except for certain broad based plans); document must prescribe price and number of shares reserved for calculating number; plan must be administered by disinterested parties; and eligibility must be stated as well as other requirements.

In 1996, the SEC further clarified its 1991 ruling by permitting an exemption for Section 16 equity awards (including options). Previously, only equity awards that were made in accord with a plan approved by shareholders (or issued within twelve months of receiving such approval) were exempted from the six-month purchase/sale rule. The new ruling's focus is on approval of the transaction, rather than approval of the plan. Dispositions of stock sold back to the company can be exempted in basically a similar manner. An exemption will be granted for stock options or awards meeting one of the following conditions:

- The board of directors, a board committee, or two or more non-employee board directors have approved the action. Remuneration for services to company and pecuniary interest dollar limits apply.
- Shareholders have approved the action, either in advance or at the next annual meeting (note the similarity with the old rule substituting specific action for the full plan). Note, however, that delay in getting shareholder approval might result in FASB considering the price at time of shareholder approval and, if higher than at time of grant, considering the option a discounted option requiring a charge to earnings.
- The acquired stock has been held by the insider for at least six months.

Additionally, stock transactions between the company and an insider would be exempt under one of several conditions:

- A *routine transaction* (e.g., employee contribution and matching employer contribution) under a tax-qualified plan (Section 401 and 423 plans) and/or excess plan (restoring limits imposed by Section 415).
- *Discretionary transaction* (e.g., fund switching) if an opposite type transaction were not made within a six-month period.

In 2000, the SEC issued *Regulation FD* (Fair Disclosure) forbidding companies from selectively disclosing material information. Failure in this regard must be promptly corrected with public disclosure so no one is at an advantage regarding a purchase, hold, or sale decision on the company stock. Failure to comply will result in significant penalties. About the same time, the SEC issued *Rule 10b5-1* stating that executives would not be barred from buying or selling their stock regardless of what information they possessed at time of a transaction provided that the transaction was part of a trading plan, formula, or similar established program before the insider was aware of the material non-public information regarding the company.

This is an important exception to Section 10(b)5, which otherwise bars anyone inside or outside of the organization from trading in the security if that person possesses information unknown to the public that could affect the stock price. An example might be a consultant privy to confidential information.

Company Disclosures. The SEC also requires filings from publicly traded companies. A few of the more significant ones are:

- **Form S1.** The registration form for initial and secondary public offerings of the company stock. A prospectus with required information about the company (which includes officer and director compensation data) is included.
- **Form S3.** A shorter version of Form S1, used to sell additional shares by a company that is already public, having successfully registered under Form S1 and not meeting the secondary offering requirement of Form S1.
- **Form S4.** Used if company issues shares for an acquisition or a merger.
- **Form S8.** A very brief registration statement used to register shares for a stock plan.
- **Form 8K.** Anything of significance that would be reported in the next 10K or 10Q should be reported here and not delayed until the issuance of those reports.
- **Form 10K.** Annual report on financial and related business information, including background on corporate officers.
- **Form 10Q.** An abbreviated version of the 10K, filed after the completion of each of the company's first three fiscal quarters.

The SEC also requires that publicly traded companies notify shareholders of the annual meeting (or other shareholder meeting) in a document identified as the *proxy statement*. This document must also disclose matters to be voted on at the meeting (e.g., election of directors and some approvals of acquisitions and mergers), a ballot for voting, and significant information reporting the pay of the Chief Executive Officer (CEO) and the next four highest-paid officers. In late 1992 the SEC laid down new executive compensation disclosure rules.

The proxy must include detailed compensation for persons who served as CEO during the year (regardless of employment at year end) as well as the next four most highly compensated executive officers, plus up to at least two other such officers who would have been listed if still employed at year end. Requirements are set forth on how to report annual and long-term com-

Year	Name/ Title	Salary	Bonus	Other Awards	Restricted Stock	Options SAR	Payment LTIP	All Other
xxxx	xxxx/xx	xxxx	xxx	xxx	xxx	xxx	xxx	xxx
xxxx	xxxx/xx	xxxx	xxx	xxx	xx	xx	xx	xxx
xxxx	xxxx/xx	xxx	xx	xx	xxx	xx	xxx	xx

Table 4-25. Summary compensation table, past year and two years prior

pensation, as well as perquisites and potential retirement amounts.

Generally, actual compensation has to be specific by individual for the year completed and the two prior fiscal years as shown in Table 4-25. Definition highlights are: salary is amount earned or credited, bonus is amount earned, other awards include perquisites, and restricted stock reflects value at time of grant while only the number of shares for those covered by options/SARs need to be disclosed. The long-term incentive plan (LTIP) shows value earned, while "all other" covers anything not reported elsewhere but credited or accrued to the executive.

A detailed table is also required for the top five, detailing stock options and SARs granted during the year. Among other requirements, this includes number of shares and share price. Potential realizable value is also required, using either the Black-Scholes option pricing formula or a five percent and 10 percent compared annual growth over the term period.

In addition to the table detailing grant activity described above another one requires the reporting of shares exercised with value realized by the top five executives, as well as the number and value of unexercised Options/SARs must be shown separate for exercisable vs. non-exercisable:

A fourth table (if applicable) is required to list again for the top five executives any other long-term grants made during the reporting period. This includes stating the number of shares (or other measurable amounts if granted in dollar-denominated units), the performance period, and three levels of payout threshold (minimum other than zero), target and maximum. An explanation of the performance required to generate payments is also required.

The SEC also decided that since shareholder value is one way the investor can see a correlation with executive pay, a stock performance graph is also required. This entails a graphic presentation for the five most recent years of: the company's stock performance, a broad based market index (if listed in Standard and Poor's 500, that index must be used) and an appropriate peer group with each reflecting market capitalization weighted stock values plus reinvestment of dividends.

In addition to the compensation tables and performance graph, a report from the compensation committee explaining the executive pay principle in general and, specifically, how the CEO's pay was determined must be included—namely, the specific relationship between company performance and the executive pay package must be explained. The committee report is expected to be specific and not general and vague in its writings. It should fairly report what one would have heard if present at the committee meetings. If any of the incentives are not excluded from the million-dollar cap of Section 162(m), the committee should report that fact.

In addition to rules set down by the SEC (and appropriate states), for publicly traded companies, the exchange on which a particular company's stock is listed may also have requirements. For example, in 1998, the New York Stock Exchange ruled that most stock-option plans do not need shareholder approval for the company to continue to be listed on the Exchange. Remember too that security laws in many situations also exist at the state level. Also, 162(m) and incentive stock-option plans require stockholder approval as stated in the Internal Revenue Code.

Rulemaker Summary

Rulemakers interest in executive compensation was low during the first quarter of the twentieth century, as seen in Table 4-26, but moved into high gear in the next quarter with wage controls, high tax rates, and SEC action. Pay guidelines and controls came back in the third quarter century along with higher taxes. Much of the third period also had high tax rates before being dramatically reduced near period end. In the last period, tax law, SEC requirements, and accounting standards all focused on one or more components of the pay package.

				Incentives	
Time Period	**Salary**	**Benefits**	**Perks**	**Short-term**	**Long-term**
1900-1925	Low	Low	Low	Low	Low
1926-1950	High	Low	Low	High	High
1951-1975	High	Moderate	High	Moderate	Moderate
1976-Present	High	Moderate	High	High	High

Table 4-26. Rulemakers interest in executive compensation

SUMMARY

The stakeholders significantly affect the design of pay programs as they have different, sometimes conflicting, objectives. For example, employees look for employment as well as good pay, shareholders want a good return on their investment, the rule makers prescribe regulations to be followed, suppliers look for purchases of their goods and services, customers look for quality-priced products/services when needed, and executives look to be paid handsomely for achieving all of the above to the extent possible.

Table 4-27 recaps and summarizes the previously described stakeholder interest in executive pay by time period. One would expect the interest of customers, employees, shareholders, and suppliers to be linked inversely to how well they are faring. The rulemakers' interest seems to be continually increasing, making it more and more difficult to design pay programs that do not cause serious problems with one or more rulemaking authorities. And of course, executive interest is high, especially since risk (contractual employment) seems not to decrease but only get riskier.

Some suppliers and companies in the threshold stage find it mutually advantageous for the company to "pay" in the form of stock options. More than one celebrity took a large stock option in such a company instead of a significant fee to promote the company product. Fee consultants have done the same.

Companies get themselves in difficulty because they do not focus on all of their stakeholders or meet the requirements of the rulemakers. Really successful companies nurture their rela-

	1900-25	1926-50	1951-75	1976-Present
Executive	High	Moderate	High	High
Employees	Low	Low	Moderate	High
Shareholders	Low	Low	Moderate	High
Customers	Low	Low	Low	Low
Suppliers	Low	Low	Low	Low
Rulemakers	Low	Moderate	Moderate	High

Table 4-27. Stakeholder historic interest in executive pay

tionships with their shareholders, their community, their suppliers, *and* their employees. Similarly, the executive has a number of stakeholders: family, friends, community, work associates, and employer. Like the employer, the executive must keep these relationships in balance.

For years the view shared by many was that the shareholder was the most important stakeholder. That view has changed over time. A number of very successful companies now believe that employees should come first, followed by customers, suppliers, community, and then the shareholders. The rationale is simple. The unique competitive advantage that a company has is its workforce. Treated with respect, fairness, and honesty, the company stands a good chance of gaining a committed workforce—one that likes to work for the company. This positive attitude rubs off on the customer, supplier, and community. This in turn should lead to financial success, which means that shareholders will get a return on their investment, and the company will have funds available for reinvestment in the business.

While shareholders may invest a portion of their financial capital in the stock of a company, it is the employees (executives included) who invest all of the human and intellectual capital. Both expect to be compensated for their investments. If not, they will look elsewhere. Also, when discussing shareholders, distinguish between an *investor* (ready to quickly buy or sell the stock depending on its short-term outlook) versus an *owner* (who is committed to the long-term success of the organization). Shareholder value is an end result for the investor; it is an interim measuring stick for the owner.

Note: You are again reminded not to rely on accounting, tax, SEC, or other professional service statements in this chapter. You need to seek appropriate professional counsel for such guidance. Statements made in this chapter and elsewhere are offered as being illustrative to help frame such further investigations by the reader with counsel.

A compensation plan must strike an appropriate balance among all interested parties. Having set the stage, let's review of the five compensation elements, beginning with salary.

Chapter 5

Salary

e have all heard the expression, "He's worth his weight in gold." You may also have heard the expression, "She's worth her salt." Some lexicographers trace this back to ancient times when salt—a natural preservative—was at least as valuable as gold. Salary, another valuable asset, may also trace its roots to salt, deriving from the Latin "sal."

Today, salary is the cornerstone of the compensation program. It is the base upon which the other elements of compensation are built. This justifies its other name—*base pay*. Some refer to *base salary*, which would suggest that there are other parts of salary. However, with the possible exceptions of lump-sum merit increases and geographical differentials (both will be discussed later), the term is redundant. Salary *is* the base.

INTRODUCTION

Typically, the amount of salary an executive is paid is a function of the value of the individual's responsibilities to the organization and how well the individual is discharging these responsibilities. The value of an individual's responsibilities is typically determined by job analysis, job evaluation, salary surveys, and the resulting salary structure adjustments. Individual pay actions result from promotion and how well the executive performs the assigned risks.

The probable importance of the salary element is dependent on whether the company is a non-profit or for-profit, publicly held or privately held. This is illustrated in Table 5-1. For privately held companies, the lack of market-based, long-term incentives places greater emphasis on salary. While salary is less important for publicly traded companies in the threshold and growth stages, it grows in importance in the maturity and decline stages, except perhaps in turnaround situations when stock options may be significant. The not-for-profits, because of the visibility of salaries probably have them in the moderate importance category, although that might shift to high importance in growth and beyond, again because of the lack of incentives.

Type Company	Market Stage			
	Threshold	**Growth**	**Maturity**	**Decline**
For-Profits • Publicly Traded • Privately Held	Low Moderate	Moderate High	High High	High High
Not-for-Profits	Moderate	Moderate	Moderate	Moderate

Table 5-1. Importance of salary by type of company and market stage

Job Analysis

The objective of job analysis is to obtain information about a job and summarize it in a manner that sets it apart from other jobs within the organization. Typically, such information is obtained through an interview with the executive, or the job incumbent completes a questionnaire. The focus at this point is on reporting relationships within the organizational structure as well as on the principal responsibilities. Therefore, it is important to obtain information on the extent of planning required, the degree of involvement and responsibility for specified tasks, and the type and extent of contacts within and outside the organization.

Job vs. Position

A *task* is a separate, definable portion of the job; it is the most basic, simplified portion—the element. Following this analogy, the *job* is a compound consisting of various elements or tasks existing in varying degrees.

The supervisor, the job incumbent, and/or the personnel representative will write the *job description*. Technically, a distinction can be made between a job and a position. More than one person performs a job, whereas only one person fills a position. This forms the distinction between a job description and a *position description*. However, in this book the two will be used interchangeably.

Job Title

In writing the job description, tasks are listed either in a logical work sequence or in descending order of frequency of occurrence. If listed in work-flow sequence, typically, the percentage of time spent on each task is shown at the end of each statement. From these statements, a summary of one or two sentences is constructed and placed at the beginning of the description to give the reader a quick synopsis. And finally, a *job title* is selected (if one does not already exist). It should be only several words in length and indicate the basic nature of the work as well as the organizational level (e.g., vice president—corporate human resources or corporate vice president—human resources). The first may be a divisional position; the latter most likely is a corporate officer. Be careful not to get caught up in title inflation where it seems almost everyone is a vice president. Guidelines must be in place. For example, divisional vice presidents may report to corporate vice presidents (who are officers of the company). However, neither divisional nor corporate vice presidents should report to someone with the same VP identification unless that person has a modifier such as senior or executive or group.

It is important that jobs be carefully and accurately described because they form the basis for the subsequent evaluation of the job's relative worth. Rater bias coupled with organizational politics will otherwise distort valid comparisons.

Few organizations undertake job analysis at all levels of the organization. Typically, it includes those below group or division president level; few position descriptions exist for company chief executive officers. If the CEO does not believe a job description is necessary, the board of directors may think otherwise. The rationale for sidestepping job analysis is that it is not necessary above a certain organizational level. After all, we all know what a company CEO does, don't we? Interestingly, these same people may question the compatibility of survey data when only a job title is used.

JOB EVALUATION

The objective of job evaluation is to array jobs described in the job analysis phase in a manner that will best reflect their value to the organization and their relationship to similar jobs in other companies.

There are literally thousands of different job-evaluation plans in existence throughout the country at the executive level. Probably, no two companies have exactly the same job evaluation program. However, these many plans can be categorized into essentially five types: ranking, classification, point factor, maturity, and market pricing.

Whatever system is used, it must correlate strongly with what the company perceives as important; otherwise, it will surely fail. In addition, the executives being evaluated must view it as being valid; otherwise, it will similarly fail. Thus, to be workable, it must be acceptable to both the evaluator and the evaluated.

Ranking

The ranking approach is by far the simplest; it is a non-quantitative method of arraying jobs in order of importance. This array is accomplished by comparing two jobs with one another and determining which is more important. The third job is compared with the first two, and its position with respect to the first two is determined. The process is repeated until all jobs have been slotted into the array.

One difficulty encountered in such a plan is deciding whether a group executive with four different divisions (each with $50 million in sales) should be worth more than a division head with $200 million of business. The argument "for" focuses on the additional layer of management in a centrally managed company; the argument "against" says the real value rests with the division managers in a decentralized organization.

The simplicity of the ranking approach to job evaluation is its greatest virtue: little preparation is required and it works well when not too many jobs are involved. Unfortunately, simplicity is also its greatest drawback. Many find it difficult to think in terms of the whole job. Therefore, there is a natural tendency to rate each job on the basis of its dominant characteristic(s). Such an approach will definitely affect the resulting hierarchy.

Another drawback of the ranking method is that the array reflects absolute rather than relative differences. In other words, there is no way of knowing whether the difference between the vice president of human resources and the director of compensation and benefits is equal to, greater than, or less than the difference between the director of compensation and benefits and the manager of compensation. Ranking will simply report the sequence in the ascending hierarchy—not the relative differences between the various jobs.

Classification

Whereas the ranking method requires comparing jobs directly with each other, the classification method calls for comparing each job with a set of written standards. For example, if 35 grades were in effect, each grade would have a set of standards describing the type of job that should be classified in that grade.

The advantage of this approach is that grade levels are predetermined, and identifying the grade for the job simply requires matching the most appropriate descriptors. Unfortunately, this also means a significant investment of time and effort in developing these standards, which must be sufficiently generic to be relatable to any type of job and yet sufficiently specific to allow direct comparison with a particular position. Obviously, the greater the number of grades, the greater is the difficulty in separating and identifying distinctions.

Another problem with the classification method is its inflexibility (i.e., the number of grades). As the organization matures and more levels of management are introduced, it may not be possible to adequately reflect organizational differences. This may mean adding additional grades or completely rewriting the standards. Too few organizational levels exist when insufficient compensation growth (i.e., too small a number of grades) exists between levels. A practical test of this hypothesis is to determine when the differences in compensation midpoints no longer adequately reflect promotional growth.

Point Factors

Point factor plans are similar to the classification method in that they require the comparison of a job to an impartial measuring stick rather than directly with other jobs. However, rather than develop a composite standard for each grade level, the point factors begin at the opposite end of the spectrum. They indicate the separate factors that make up the composite and identify degree statements describing various levels of requirement, assigning each degree statement a number of points. Thus, if work experience needed to satisfactorily learn the job is one factor, it might be broken down into the various degree statements shown in Table 5-2. Therefore, a job requiring six months to learn would be given 75 points, while a job requiring five years would receive 150 points.

Most factor plans focus on responsibilities and the knowledge needed to perform the tasks. Within these two major categories, a number of separate factors can be constructed (e.g., separate factors of responsibility for sales, profit, equipment, and employees). Such plans typically have from five to 10 factors. The more factors, the more suspect the evaluation plan, as it is very likely that several factors are measuring the same value in only a slightly different manner.

Developing the Structure. By examining the job factor by factor and assigning the correct number of points to the most appropriate degree statement within the factor, it is possible to sum the points assigned and array the jobs on their point totals. These point totals, along with the current pay of each person in that job, are typically displayed in a *scattergram* using an X (job points) and Y (pay) axis as shown in Figure 5-1.

This data is then converted into grades by first identifying the cutoffs on the X axis which would seem consistent, given any clustering of similarly valued jobs, as shown in Figure 5-2.

Next, a *regression analysis* is performed on the data to describe the line of best fit. This may

Amount of Experience Needed	Job Points
Under 3 months	25
At least 3 but less 6 months	50
At least 6 but less than 12 months	75
At least 1 but less than 2 years	100
At least 2 but less than 4 years	125
At least 4 but less than 8 years	150
At least 8 but less than 15 years	175
15 years or more	200

Table 5-2. Point factor example of educational requirements

Figure 5-1. Pay and job value scattergram

be either a linear formula (which will force a straight line regardless of the format) or a nonlinear formula (which will describe the simple curve best reflecting the data). A nonlinear formula will result in a straight line only if all the plots truly describe a straight line. We will not take the time to perform the necessary calculations; the specific methodology for calculating the line (or curve) may be found in almost any statistics book. However, it is important to know the formula values.

The formula for a linear regression analysis is $Y = a + bX$. The a is the value on the vertical or Y-axis when X equals zero. The b describes the scope of the curve, in other words, the extent of increase in the Y-axis (e.g., compensation) resulting from a stated change in value of the X-axis (in this case job points).

The nonlinear formula is $Y = a + bX + cX^2$. The value of c indicates the rate of change in the slope of the curve. A positive value indicates an increasing rate of change; a negative or minus c value indicates a decreasing rate of change.

The difference between the plot points and the curve is measured vertically and is identified as the *deviation*. The line of best fit will, by definition, minimize the degree of deviations

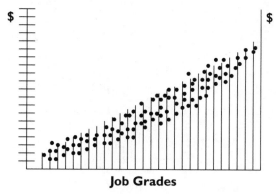

Job Grades

Figure 5-2. Conversion to job grades

existing. The sum of the squares of these deviations will not only be equal above and below the line, but the sum of the squares of these deviations will be the lowest possible value. This is called the *least squares method.*

Employing the nonlinear formula to test for the presence of a curve results in the line shown in Figure 5-3—a curve with a positive slope.

By establishing the line value as the midpoint for each grade, it is possible to construct the salary ranges shown in Figure 5-4. Typically, these range widths increase as one progresses

Job Grades

Figure 5-3. Nonlinear pay curve with job grades

through the structure. This is a simple reflection of decreasing promotional opportunities due to the organization's pyramid shape. Thus, ranges must be wide enough to accommodate longer periods of residence.

Therefore, while ranges of plus and minus 15 percent from the midpoint might be appropriate to construct the range minimum and maximum at the bottom of the structure, ranges of plus or minus 25 percent may be appropriate at the top. Ranges of plus and minus 33.3 percent or more may be necessary in the absence of short- and long-term incentives. Table 5-3 shows the relationship of plus and minus deviations from the midpoints to the normal manner in which ranges are described, in other words, spread between minimum and maximum values.

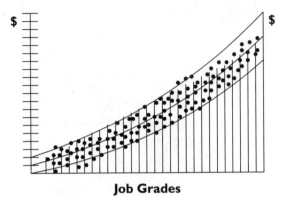

Job Grades

Figure 5-4. Job grades with pay ranges

Thus, a plus and minus deviation from the midpoint of 16.7 percent will construct a range with a maximum over minimum spread of 40 percent.

Table 5-4 shows an example of a salary schedule for the salaried, exempt jobs in an organization. Note that this schedule has positive slope to the curve with the increase in midpoints, beginning at seven percent at the bottom and progressing in an arithmetic progression to 14 percent at the very top. In addition, the range spread (maximum over minimum) also increases in a progression, beginning with 50 percent at grade 1 and increasing to 78 percent for grade 35. This schedule might typify a salary-only type of compensation program. In Chapter 7 (Short-Term Incentives), this schedule will have its range maximums lowered to include an annual incentive plan.

Grades vs. Curves. The problem with the typical grade structure is that it does not consistently result in increased pay for increased job points. Shown in Figure 5-5 are three jobs: A, B, and C. Note that the difference between A and B is much greater than the difference between B and C,

Plus-Minus Adjustment to Range Midpoint of Percent	Equals the Following Maximum over Minimum Spread, Percent
50.0	200.0
40.0	133.3
33.3	100.0
30.0	85.7
25.0	66.7
20.0	50.0
18.4	45.0
16.7	40.0
15.0	35.3

Table 5-3. Plus–minus midpoint adjustment vs. maximum–minimum ranges

Grade	Minimum	Lower 1/3	Upper 1/3	Maximum	Midpoint
35	1,000.7	1,260.8	1,521.0	1,781.1	1,390.9
34	884.1	1,111.0	1,337.8	1,564.7	1,224.4
33	785.2	984.1	1,183.1	1,382.0	1,083.6
32	695.5	869.4	1,043.2	1,271.1	956.3
31	617.5	769.8	922.2	1,074.5	846.0
30	548.7	682.2	815.8	949.3	749.0
29	489.1	606.5	723.9	841.3	665.2
28	436.8	540.2	643.6	747.0	591.9
27	391.4	482.7	574.1	665.4	528.4
26	350.8	431.5	512.1	592.8	471.8
25	315.9	387.5	459.1	530.7	423.3
24	285.1	348.8	412.4	476.1	380.6
23	257.1	313.6	370.2	426.7	341.9
22	233.0	283.5	333.9	384.4	308.7
21	210.6	255.5	300.5	345.4	278.0
20	189.7	229.6	269.4	309.3	249.5
19	172.3	207.9	243.5	279.1	225.7
18	156.0	187.7	219.5	251.2	203.6
17	142.2	170.6	199.0	227.4	184.8
16	129.9	155.4	181.0	206.5	168.2
15	118.9	141.9	164.9	187.9	153.4
14	108.6	129.3	149.9	170.6	139.6
13	99.8	118.4	137.0	155.6	127.7
12	92.3	109.2	126.0	142.9	117.6
11	84.3	99.5	114.7	129.9	107.1
10	78.0	91.8	105.6	119.4	98.7
9	72.1	84.6	97.0	109.5	90.8
8	66.8	78.1	89.5	100.8	83.8
7	62.2	72.6	83.0	93.4	77.8
6	58.0	67.7	77.3	87.0	72.5
5	54.2	63.2	72.2	81.2	67.7
4	50.4	58.8	67.2	75.6	63.0
3	47.0	54.9	62.7	70.6	58.8
2	43.6	50.9	58.1	65.4	54.5
1	40.6	47.4	54.2	61.0	50.8

Table 5-4. Thirty-five-grade salary schedule (in thousands)

and yet A and B are in the same grade, whereas C is in the next higher grade.

Therefore, some companies, especially those who really believe in the efficacy of their factor point plans, do not establish arbitrary point cutoffs to form grades. Rather, the maximum and minimum are, like the original midpoint value, a set of curves. As shown in Figure 5-6, the

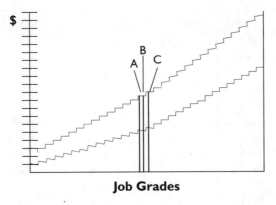

Job Grades

Figure 5-5. Job grade inequities (three-job comparison)

pay relationship of jobs A, B, and C is essentially the same as their job value. While this may be a more accurate basis for establishing pay, the addition of even one point will result in a higher pay range; thus, there may be numerous requests by management to review the points assigned to certain jobs. Conversely, under the grading approach, such requests will essentially be limited to those jobs that are close to the point cutoff for the next higher grade.

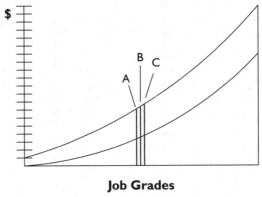

Job Grades

Figure 5-6. Pay ranges without grades (three-job comparison)

Maturity Data

The maturity method of job evaluation is similar to the point factor approach, except that instead of establishing points for separate factors only one measurement of job value is used—time. Thus, the X-axis is defined as time (e.g., years since B.S., years of experience, or age). This method of job evaluation is rarely used for executives, since its greatest appeal is in those instances where there are a large number of employees who are performing essentially the same work, and it is almost impossible to draw lines of distinction establishing separate jobs. Frequently, this method is used for engineers and chemists, with separate curves for each discipline as well as separate curves for supervisors and non-supervisors.

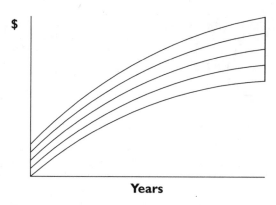

Figure 5-7. Maturity data

As shown in Figure 5-7, individuals automatically move up one notch on the X-axis each year, rather than await a re-evaluation as under the more traditional point factor method. Note that the curve has a descending rate of growth rather than the ascending one shown earlier. This occurs for at least two reasons: (1) pay increases are usually more pronounced during the first years of assignment, following a typical learning curve pattern, and (2) many of the top performers have left the job after a number of years (e.g., they were promoted or they quit to accept a better job elsewhere).

Note that the maturity data shown has four bands or ranges within the minimum and maximum values. These could be used to distinguish between levels of performance on the job.

Market Pricing

The traditional methods of job evaluation begin with an establishment of job value based on some method of internal equity. This hierarchy is then measured in terms of survey data to determine the competitive level of pay for comparable positions, in order to establish external equity. The problem is that any attempt to measure items using two different methods stands a very good chance of reaching dissimilar conclusions. Invariably, the survey results will suggest that several jobs are either over-graded or under-graded by one or more levels under the internally oriented job evaluation plan. This places the company in the uncomfortable position of knowingly either underpaying or overpaying certain jobs in relation to the market, or overriding the job-evaluation plan based on market results.

The market-pricing method of job evaluation begins with the labor market as the basis for evaluating jobs. Jobs for which no survey data exists are then evaluated by the ranking method. For example, as illustrated in Table 5-5, assume the president of the Brucell Division is assigned grade 23, the vice president of sales and marketing grade 20, and the plant manager grade 17— all based on survey data. The vice president of production (for which no survey data exists) is probably grade 19, 20 or 21, depending on the perceived internal value in relation to the vice president of sales and marketing.

Many will argue that it is possible to be more precise and accurate in classifying jobs using the market-pricing method at the lower end of the structure where there is a greater likelihood of similar jobs existing in other companies. The difficulty in market pricing the executive posi-

Grade	Salary Midpoint	Job	Survey Data
23	$341,900	Division President	$346,800
22	308,700		
21	278,000		
20	249,500	VP Sales & Marketing	251,000
19	225,700		
18	203,600		
17	184,800	Plant Manager	186,300

Table 5-5. Market pricing example

tions is that, with the possible exception of functional division heads, there is a great divergence of differences in specific responsibilities. While this may make job matching more suspect, it may be possible to obtain meaningful data through multiple regression studies as will be discussed subsequently.

After the initial structuring, the need for extensive surveys is minimized since the structure is adjusted periodically on an assessment of the rate of compensation growth over the previous period. Therefore, only those jobs that have not moved at the same rate would be re-graded, probably by not more than a grade.

Table 5-6 shows a listing of market-pricing principles that might be appropriate.

Market-Pricing Principles
1. In using survey data, consideration will be given not only to measures of central tendency (simple or adjusted for scope measurement) but also to raw data where available (viewing its dispersion from reported measurement of central tendency). Other reported compensation correlates will be examined (e.g., total compensation and five-year average return on investment) where appropriate and believed significant.
2. Survey results will be factored up or discounted to the extent it is believed the position is heavier or lighter than the position surveyed.
3. Market data will also be tempered by the lack of necessity of replacing the job incumbent from a particular industry (i.e., sales and marketing positions would relate very strongly to industry survey data, whereas staff positions would primarily be based on cross-divisional data and internal factors).
4. In structuring the grade for a job with a market-oriented compensation program, it can always be placed higher than market dictates (in order to preserve internal relationships), but it cannot be placed lower without running the risk of turnover.
5. When survey data older than 1 year is used in ranking jobs, a factor will be added to equate it with other data used.

Table 5-6. Marketing pricing principles

6. Survey problems (e.g., small sample and significant dispersion from reported averages) will require a closer look at internal job relationships.

7. In viewing relative positions of jobs, at least a two-grade differential is needed in order to talk of a significant difference (i.e., a likely promotion). Furthermore, at least a two- or three-grade difference would normally be expected when talking of reporting relationships.

8. Market data on average compensation paid for the position dictates the job grade. The performance of the individual within the job determines the position within the range.

9. Staff and line positions are both sensitive to size of unit served (as a general indicator of extent of responsibility); however, staff positions are much more sensitive to the individual in the position. There is, therefore, usually a greater range on competitive compensation data for staff positions.

10. When evaluating a position, it is important to determine how jobs with similar responsibilities interact with the one in question. Decentralization causes some duplication; it is important to determine to what extent this affects the rating of a particular job.

11. Structural compensation (i.e., range and midpoint), when available, is a helpful aid in pricing jobs inasmuch as actual compensation is a product of the maturity of the job incumbent. One would expect, for example, a person with more job experience to be paid more.

12. The best way to rank jobs relative to market data and assure comparability is to "lock in" on job comparability for the lowest and highest levels and then to work toward the middle.

13. A practical test of overstructuring in an organization is to determine when the differences in compensation midpoints no longer adequately reflect a normal promotional increase.

14. To ensure compensation adequate to attract and retain qualified persons, the primary equity must be with the marketplace. Therefore, when there are two jobs considered to be equal by internal standards but unequal by external standards (compensation surveys), the latter should prevail unless there are unusual circumstances.

Table 5-6. Continued

SALARY SURVEYS

Whether market pricing is used to evaluate jobs, or the more traditional method of internal equity followed by selectively pricing the structure is employed, information on what other companies are paying executives in comparable jobs is needed.

While a plethora of executive compensation surveys exist today, this was not always true: even before 1950, they were nonexistent. Early efforts were directed to reviewing the data submitted to the Securities and Exchange Commission (SEC) on the highest-paid executives; today such data is available through a number of studies conducted by associations, consulting firms, and other companies. Although, as we've seen in Chapter 4, the SEC has expanded the disclosure requirements on the highest-paid five executives, so that with a little effort you can determine exactly how much they are paid and in what form.

Indeed, if there is a problem today, it is that there are too many surveys done by individual companies, each drawing on its own sample of a defined population. Considering the costly inefficiencies of generating and producing results, the amount of duplication of efforts is appalling. Here is where impartial third parties such as consulting firms can provide an effective cost-benefit product.

Defining the Community

Before undertaking a survey or examining existing studies, it is important first to define the survey community appropriate to this company. Typically, companies will look to companies in the same or similar industries that are approximately the same size. The larger the company, the greater is the problem in this respect, since there are only a limited number of companies of comparable size.

An industry analysis is especially appropriate for jobs that are industry-sensitive, in particular, sales and marketing, and to some extent, production and research. However, functions such as finance, legal, and human resources are less industry-sensitive, and it is appropriate to look across industry lines to determine the competitive level of pay for executives in these functions. Whether intra- or inter-industry, the companies selected must be looking for comparable-level people. For example, perhaps there are only five companies within a particular industry that consistently hire only those individuals in the 90th percentile of qualified candidates.

Selecting the Jobs

Unfortunately, not all jobs can be surveyed (due to a combination of magnitude of effort and lack of comparability). However, a careful attempt should be made to ensure that the survey has a good balance of horizontal and vertical representation. Horizontal representation requires the inclusion of the various organization functions (e.g., research, production, marketing, sales, finance, legal, and employee resources). The vertical requirement focuses on promotional career paths within a particular function (e.g., plant manager to general production manager to vice president of production). The number of jobs to be surveyed is a function of availability (and extent of cooperation of the surveyed companies) as well as the method of evaluation. Point factor plans require surveying only a few key jobs representing the various levels, whereas market pricing requires surveying as many jobs as possible, perhaps 25 percent or more.

Job Comparability

Before obtaining any data, it is important to determine the manner in which the surveyed companies will be reporting on comparable jobs. Essentially, there are three methods: job matching, job evaluation, and multiple regression.

Job Matching. Job matching is the most common method of ensuring comparability of data. It requires matching jobs to ensure that similar responsibilities exist. This is important because job content can vary significantly between two organizations, even though the jobs may have the same title. For this reason, organization charts showing reporting relationships along with job descriptions are included to maximize good job matches.

Nonetheless, it becomes increasingly difficult to find companies with similar positions at senior levels. In many instances, the differences in job content for the same job title in different companies are as great as, if not greater than, those for jobs with dissimilar titles.

Further, the implicit assumption is that like responsibilities will be valued comparably by other organizations. Unfortunately, there are too many instances where this is simply not true. Be it a formal job-evaluation plan or a simple ranking program, different companies come up with different perceptions of the importance of different disciplines. Thus, even if two jobs in two different companies were identical, the pay practices of the companies would differ if they placed different values on the position.

Another difficulty many companies have is matching up to a company with either fewer or more management levels. For example, assume a survey has data on the top functional heads at the corporate, group, and division levels. How does a company with four levels—corporate, business, multi-division, and division—relate to this data? The answer: by matching first those most comparable (namely, corporate and division) and then interpolating (e.g., between corporate and group for business, and between group and division for multi-division). Obviously, less confidence should be placed in data that have to be massaged in this manner than in data that match well.

Another technique that may be employed in job matching is adjusting for degree of deviation. For example, the data received from each company could be weighted based on degree of closeness of fit with the survey job. Therefore, as shown in Table 5-7, a company that had a job either noticeably heavier or lighter would be given a weighting of 0.5, whereas those that were only slightly different would be given a weighting of 0.8. This technique is typically called *survey leveling*.

Degree of Comparability	Data Weighting
Noticeably heavier	0.5
Slightly heavier	0.8
Good match	1.0
Slightly lighter	0.8
Noticeably lighter	0.5

Table 5-7. Survey leveling

A variation is to adjust the reported compensation based on the match. Some job-evaluation plans have built values around 15-percent multiples, believing that the difference in responsibilities between two jobs is recognizable in multiples of 15 percent. Table 5-8 illustrates the effect on *leveling reported pay* data for four companies all reporting the same data as the surveying company, E. A noticeable variation is either .85 (heavier) or 1.15 (lighter). Two variations are .723 (much heavier) and 1.323 (much lighter). For example, Company A is reporting pay of $100,000 for a job much heavier than Company E's. This would suggest it might pay about $72,300 if it had a perfect match. This would be calculated by the formula .723 ($100,000) = $72,300. Conversely, Company C's job is reportedly "lighter" than Company E's. This would suggest that if Company C had a comparable job, it would pay $115,000 based on the formula 1.15 ($100,000) = $115,000.

In this example the variances have essentially offset each other; however, one can see the dramatic effect had the variances all been skewed in one direction.

Company	Actual Pay	Job Match	Adjusted Pay
A	$100,000	Much Heavier	$72,300
B	$100,000	Heavier	$85,000
C	$100,000	Lighter	$115,000
D	$100,000	Much Lighter	$132,300
Average	**$100,000**		**$101,150**
E	$105,000		

Table 5-8. Leveling reported pay

A technique that may be employed to test the possible existence of lack of comparability is the *survey ratio*. This is simply the division of the lowest salary reported for a position into the highest (after the data has been arrayed high to low). If this value is much above 1.5, it is appropriate to examine the data more closely, since it indicates that there is over a 50-percent difference in the amount being paid to individuals allegedly performing the same job.

Another refinement in job matching is to stratify the data based on a meaningful measurement of scope, such as that shown in Table 5-9 for plant managers. Whenever this is done it is important to be certain the measurement is essentially meaningful. Size of workforce for plant managers would not be very useful if the survey data consisted of a mixture of capital-intensive and labor-intensive operations.

An extension of the stratified example is where the actual data (e.g., the number of employees in the plant) are given along with the compensation data. As will be seen in the later section on analysis of survey data, this information can be displayed on a scattergram and run through a regression analysis in a manner similar to the techniques used to develop salary ranges.

Job Evaluation. A variation to determining what companies pay for comparable jobs is to determine what they would pay *if* they had jobs similar to the ones in the survey. This requires identifying those positions most similar to the survey for each company and then evaluating these

Number of Employees in Plant	Report for Plant Manager, Job Number
5,000 and up	6
2,500 to 5,000	5
1,000 to 2,500	4
500 to 1,000	3
100 to 500	2
Under 100	1

Table 5-9. Survey job match based on number of employees in plant

positions using a common job evaluation plan, probably a version of the point factor plan. This is simply a more refined version of the leveling process described in job matching. However, it requires an extensive effort in time to collate and evaluate the appropriate job data.

Multiple Regression. The power of the computer has made possible the *multiple regression analysis*. Instead of simply comparing compensation to one independent variable, it is possible to compare two or more. While single regression results can be plotted using the typical X and Y-axes, it is not possible to plot three or more. It is even difficult attempting to visualize more than a three-dimensional chart; nonetheless, the analysis is possible.

By employing a *step-progression analysis*, the computer orders the independent variables studied (e.g., sales, assets, profits, age, and length of service of job incumbent) in terms of single regression analysis values and picks the one which, when combined with the first analysis, will produce the highest two-measurement prediction. This is not simply the single regression analysis with the second highest value, since it could be accounting essentially for the same values as the first if they are strongly related (e.g., age and years of experience). Thus, sales might account for 55 percent of the variance in pay within the community for the CEO position, but when combined with incumbent's years of service, the total might be 75 percent. Then a third variable is combined with the first two, and so on.

Some suspect that this approach brings a level of analysis to the issue far greater than the data warrants, or than the executive is interested in attempting to absorb. Nonetheless, it is a device that enables a refined method of job matching.

What to Survey

Having determined what to survey and what jobs to include, determine next what questions to ask. At the minimum this would include: number of incumbents, salary structure, average actual salary, short-term incentive maximum, average actual short-term incentive pay, and total salary and short-term incentive. It may also be appropriate to include questions on long-term incentive plans; Chapter 8 will describe how to place a value on such plans. The inclusion of perquisites may be appropriate for very senior positions. They are usually common to certain levels of positions. Thus, if several division-president positions were surveyed, it would not be surprising to find they were all eligible for essentially the same perquisites. A study of employee benefits limited to retirement and survivor protection may be helpful in identifying companies significantly above or below the average in level of coverage.

For those interested solely in the highest-paid five executives within an organization, the company proxy statement may be sufficient. But be sure to read the footnotes very carefully as well as obtain at least the previous year's copy, due to the relationship of the respective columns.

It is important to remember that if a company has few or no incentives, it will be establishing a less-than-competitive position when comparing its salaries only with the salaries of other companies. It must attempt to include salary and incentive pay of the community in order to be competitive. Since incentive-paying companies typically pay more than non-incentive companies (one would hope only during profitable years), it may be more logical to average the short- and long-term incentives paid in the community over a period of time to reduce the fluctuations.

Plan payout periods are important to know in long-term incentive plans, since one company may pay interim awards annually, while another pays only after three full years. In two of the three years, the first company will appear to be paying more than the second; in the third year, the second company will appear to be paying significantly more than the first company.

If a regression analysis (single or multiple) is going to be performed, the appropriate data is also required. As indicated earlier, this might include sales, assets, profits, stockholder equity, number of employees, age, and length of service for the job incumbent.

How to Analyze

Essentially, there are two basic approaches to analyzing the data: average pay only or average pay in relation to one or more independent variables. Shown in Table 5-10 is an example of average pay only. In this hypothetical study for a CEO, we see that the average total compensation for the community is $1,986,300 vs. $1,878,000 for the Brucell Company. Note in this example that Brucell would be even further below the average except for its long-term incentive plan.

All in all, it's not too bad. But note the wide range in total compensation reported. Is the average really meaningful? Let's examine the same data in relation to sales volume. As shown in Figure 5-8, a significant amount of this variation is explained by the relative size of the organizations. (Brucell is identified by a star.)

Rank	Company Code	Salary	Short-Term	Long-Term	Total
1	J	$1,231.5	$651.0	$592.8	$2,475.3
2	M	825.0	1,152.3	397.2	2,434.5
3	B	1,134.0	802.5	466.5	2,403.0
4	Q	1,650.0	697.2	0	2,347.2
5	E	1,312.5	658.8	330.6	2,301.9
6	H	1,446.6	801.0	0	2,247.6
7	A	1,179.0	543.6	501.9	2,224.5
8	M	1,227.3	786.0	189.0	2,208.3
9	R	1,260.0	517.5	412.5	2,190.0
10	D	1,158.0	609.0	403.8	2,170.8
11	G	1,095.6	701.4	339.0	2,136.0
12	T	1,017.9	782.1	303.0	2,043.0
13	C	993.0	993.0	0	1,986.0
14	I	1,140.0	525.0	61.0	1,848.0
15	S	795.0	444.0	378.0	1,617.0
16	P	879.0	487.5	173.1	1,539.0
17	F	930.0	531.0	0	1,461.0
18	L	1,014.9	404.1	0	1,419.0
19	O	1,380.0	0	0	1,380.0
20	K	1,296.0	0	0	1,296.0
Survey Average		$1,145.4	$598.8	$242.1	$1,986.3
Brucell (14th)		1,050.0	453.0	375.0	1,878.0

Table 5-10. Survey pay data for CEO, thousands

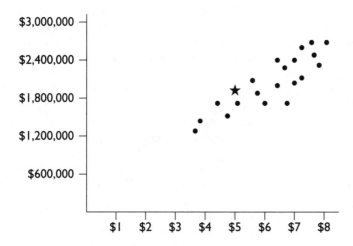

Figure 5-8. Scattergram pay for CEO

Since such an approach can result in literally hundreds of pages of graphs, a logical way to summarize the results is shown in Table 5-11. This hypothetical table is for divisional positions. Similar tables could be constructed for multi-division, multi-business, and corporate levels. The numbers in the matrix reflect grades appropriate for the Brucell Corporation. These were calculated from the comparison reading at the appropriate sales level by identifying the grade midpoint that was closest to the survey data. This midpoint would be either salary or total compensation, depending on what the survey reported.

Problems with Independent Variables. Sales are probably the most common independent

Sales (Millions)	Vice President, Marketing	Vice President Sales	President
$500	24	22	30
$250	22	20	28
$150	21	20	27
$100	20	19	26
$75	19	19	25
$50	18	18	24
$25	17	17	23
$10	15	15	21
$5	13	13	19

Table 5-11. Survey suggested divisional grades

variable used in regression analysis studies of compensation. Probably, for this reason more than any other, it also usually has the highest correlation with compensation. The reason is simple: Because many companies are using sales data to set their pay policies, individual executives see their rate of salary change slowed if they are high relative to the regression value (at their sales volume), or accelerated if they are low. It could be argued, therefore, that the primary emphasis is on increasing sales rather than increasing profits within an organization. It is dubious how many shareholders would agree with such an objective.

Similarly, surveys that include number of employees supervised and number of organizational levels reporting to the position reward bureaucratic empire building. They penalize the top-performing executive who is accomplishing the same results with a smaller organization! Unfortunately, short of a massive organizational study with significant value judgments, this variable cannot be explained away. Thus, while its impact cannot be fully assessed, its existence cannot be completely ignored.

Another example of a questionable correlation is one that compares size of research budget with pay of the research head. The obvious message here is: Justify a larger budget in order to get a pay increase! Completely lacking is a measurement of performance.

Impact of Rate of Change on Independent and Dependent Variables. How often have there been surveys describing the rate of compensation change (dependent variable) in terms of a constant independent variable (e.g., sales) over a period of time?

As shown in Figure 5-9, this would suggest the increase in CEO pay at the $100-million sales level as the difference of A minus B. This assumes the same sales volume of surveyed companies in successive years—a very questionable assumption. If, for example, the average increase in sales was 10 percent, then the comparison should really be between $91 million and $100 million (points A and C), which is obviously a much more significant increase.

Therefore, in evaluating compensation in terms of an independent variable, it is essential to understand the impact of the rate of change of each. There are three situations: (1) compensation and sales increase at the same rate, (2) compensation increases faster than the rate of sales, and (3) compensation increases more slowly than the rate of sales. Each of these situations is described below:

1. As shown in Figure 5-10, if compensation and sales increase at the *same rate*, the slope and Y intercept of the curve are *unchanged* over time. Assume the average pay for presidents of $100-million divisions is $200,000, and both sales and pay increase 10 percent for the year. While the average pay for $100-million divisions will be $200,000, so too will the average pay be $200,000 at $100 million for division presidents who the previous year were paid $182,000 for running $91-million divisions. Thus, the $200,000/$100-million coordinate is unchanged. (The abbreviations TY and LY represent "this year" and "last year," respectively.)

2. If the rate of compensation increases *faster* than the rate of increase in sales, the curve *rises*:
   a. *Without change in slope*, if rate of compensation increase is the same at all levels. For example, if the average rate of increase in sales is 10 percent and the average increase in compensation is 15 percent, the $100 million in sales last year is worth $110 million this year, but the $200,000 level of pay last year has increased to $230,000. Similarly, last year's $91 million division increased to $100 million this year, while average pay increased from $182,000 to $210,000. Thus, the reading at $100 million in sales increased from $200,000 to $210,000, as shown in Figure 5-11.

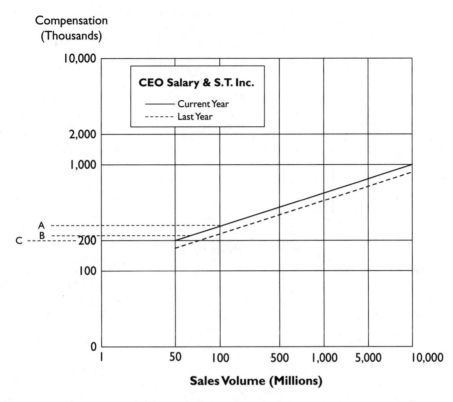

Figure 5-9. CEO pay last year vs. current year

  b. With a *slope increase,* if pay rate changes are greater relative to sales growth as sales volume increases. For example, assume the average rate of increase in sales ranges from 10 percent at the low end to five percent at the upper end of the curve, and the average increase in compensation is 15 percent. The result, described in item 2a above, is repeated at the $100 million level of sales, but the increase in compensation becomes more dramatic with increases in sales volume. This is highlighted in Figure 5-12. A similar result is attained if sales increase at a constant percentage, but the rate of compensation increases faster than sales.
  c. With a *slope decrease,* if pay rate changes are lower relative to sales growth as sales volume increases. For example, assume the average rate of increase in sales ranged from five percent at the low end to 10 percent at the upper end of the curve, and the average increase in compensation was 15 percent. Then the result, described in items 2a and 2b, might be repeated; however, the increase in compensation would be slowed with further increases in sales volume. This is highlighted in Figure 5-13. A similar result is attained if sales increase at a constant percentage, but the rate of compensation increase drops with increases in sales.
3. If compensation increases at a rate *slower* than the increase in sales, the curve is *lowered:*
  a. *Without change* in slope, if rate of compensation increase is the same at all levels. Thus,

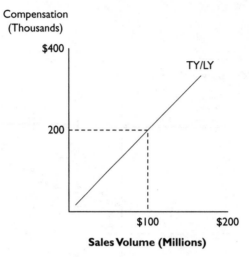

Figure 5-10. Sales vs. compensation, same curve

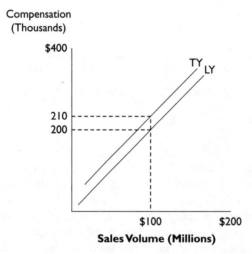

Figure 5-11. Sales vs. compensation, same slope but TY higher

assume the average sales increase at all volumes is 15 percent vs. a 10-percent average increase in compensation. The $100-million division increases to $115 million and the average pay for division presidents at this level increases to $220,000. Similarly, the $91 million-division increases to $105 million and the average pay for division presidents increases from $182,000 to $200,000. Thus, the $200,000 reference has been increased from $100 million to $105 million, reflecting a lowering of the compensation curve as shown in Figure 5-14.

b. With a *slope increase*, if rate of sales growth *decreases* as sales volume increases. Therefore, assume the average level of pay increases 10 percent at all levels, but the

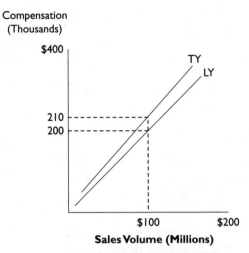

Figure 5-12. Sales vs. compensation, TY higher and ascending

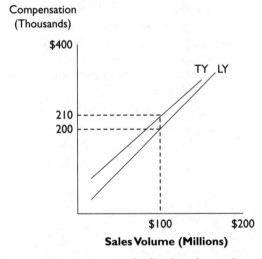

Figure 5-13. Sales vs. compensation, TY higher but descending

increase in sales range from 25 percent at the low end to five percent at the high end of the curve. This could mean that last year's $91 million increased 20 percent to $109 million, while the $100 million increased 15 percent to $115 million. The result is a lower but more sharply rising compensation curve, this year vs. last. This is reflected in Figure 5-15. A similar result is attained if sales increase at a constant percentage, but the rate of compensation increases with an increase in sales.

c. With a *slope decrease,* if rate of sales growth *increases* as sales volume increases. Thus, assume the average level of pay increased 10 percent at all levels of sales, but the increase

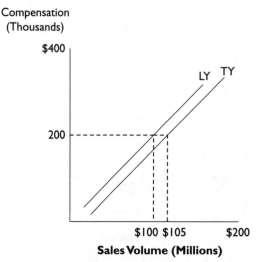

Figure 5-14. Sales vs. compensation, same slope but TY lower

in sales ranged from 15 percent at the low end to 25 percent at the upper end of the curve. This might mean that last year's $91 million increased 15 percent to $105 million, while the $100 million increased 20 percent to $120 million. The result is a lower and flatter compensation curve, this year vs. last year, as shown in Figure 5-16. A similar result would be obtained if the growth in sales was constant, but the increase in compensation decreased with an increase in sales.

The above-described changes in slope and position of the compensation curve from one year to another for the survey community must be examined in relation to one's own increase

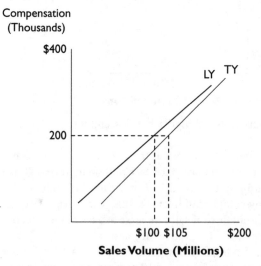

Figure 5-15. Sales vs. compensation, TY lower but ascending

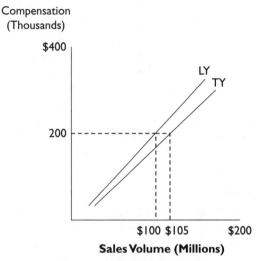

Figure 5-16. Sales vs. compensation, TY lower and descending

in sales and structural midpoint to determine the probability of having to re-grade the position. The matrix in Table 5-12 identifies the probable result, recognizing that the degree of difference in the rate of change increases or decreases the likelihood of re-grading.

Sales increase in relation to survey community	Structure increase in relation to survey community		
	Less than	**Equal to**	**Greater than**
Less than	No change	Possible lowering	Probable lowering
Equal to	Possible increase	No change	Probable lowering
Greater than	Probably increase	Possible increase	No change

Table 5-12. Probability of re-grading based on sales and pay changes

Multi-Factor Analysis. The simple regression analysis illustrated in Figure 5-8 and Table 5-11 explained away a significant portion of the variation found in Table 5-10. If other data had been collected, it would be possible to rerun a multiple regression analysis that might explain 90 percent or more of the variances in pay.

Thus, studies can determine the level of competitive pay, given a host of financial factors. The results, however, express various levels of success in terms of significantly different risks. Without carefully examining the strategies of each company over the previous years and quantifying on a common scale these risk variances (a practical impossibility), it is not possible to include risk analysis in a study of competitive pay. However, it is possible to measure company size and success.

Company size can be measured in *absolute* terms (e.g., sales, net profits, total assets, stockholders equity, and total number of employees). Company success can also be expressed in *rel-*

ative terms (e.g., return on investment, return on shareholder equity, and net income as a percentage of sales). Measurements can cover one year or compound averages over two or more years. Performance measurements were covered in some detail in Chapter 2.

Personal factors of the executives (e.g., age, education, years in position or related positions, and years of service) can be examined in relation to themselves and to the company financial factors by use of multiple regression analysis, thus permitting an important quantification of each of the pay elements.

In short, given the appropriate data, the analytical techniques available are capable of making very sophisticated measurements of the interaction of pay determinants. In fact, these measurements are probably more sophisticated than most people are really comfortable with in analyzing the data.

Indexing Pay Relationships

A frequently-employed survey-reporting format is the percentage relationship of pay for the top three executives. Setting the pay of the highest compensation as 100, the second and lowest paid are expressed in numbers such as 70 and 39, as shown in Table 5-13, for Company A.

	Company A		Company B		Average	
	Pay	**Index**	**Pay**	**Index**	**Pay**	**Index**
Highest Paid	$1,000	100	$800	100	$900	100
Second Highest Paid	700	70	650	81	675	75
Third Highest Paid	390	39	590	74	490	54

Table 5-13. Indexing pay of highest-paid three (in thousands)

What is the value of this format in viewing the competitiveness of these three executives? Not very much, if only the index values are reported, since they can mask very significant differences! Note the variance between the two companies on the third highest paid. The index value of 54 may be statistically accurate, but it is certainly not representative, masking index numbers of 39 for Company A and 74 for Company B.

Furthermore, these numbers only express pay relationships; they do not indicate anything about level of pay unless the actual pay values are also reported. For example, assume that company C's second and third highest-paid executives receive 83 percent and 61 percent of the CEO's pay, respectively. Versus survey averages of 75 and 55, one might be tempted to conclude that these two executives are overpaid vs. the market. Not true! As seen in Table 5-14, it is the CEO who is underpaid, while the other two are paid at the competitive level. Thus, if the absolute pay levels are not known, the relative percentage relationships are of little value. Furthermore, remember that it is also unlikely that the second and third highest positions are the same jobs in the survey community. This is an excellent example of an attempt to compare apples and oranges.

Aggregating Pay Relationships

A variation to the indexing method is aggregating the pay for the top three, four, or five executives of a company and comparing it with one's peer group. Since job matches for other than the CEO are spurious at best among the top paid executives, the aggregate method addresses the

	Company C		Survey	
	Pay	**Index**	**Pay**	**Index**
Highest Paid	$800	100	880	100
Second Highest Paid	660	83	660	75
Third Highest Paid	484	61	484	55

Table 5-14: Indexing pay of highest-paid three, company C vs. survey (in thousands)

cost of managing the company by the top three, four, or five individuals. For example, in Table 5-15 we see that Company D's CEO is paid virtually at the survey average. However, the aggregate of the other four is over 15 percent below the comparable average. This would suggest a further review of the four jobs to see if they are paid appropriately.

		Company D	
	Survey	**Actual Pay**	**% Survey**
CEO	$880	$900	102
Other 4 Highest	2,500	2,100	84
Total	$3,380	$3,000	89

Table 5-15. Aggregating pay, CEO and other four highest-paid (in thousands)

Updating the Survey Data

Since survey data is actual as of a point in time, it is by definition historical in nature and at least several months old. This raises the question of whether or not to update the information and if so, to what point in time using what factors?

Breaking this question down, the problem is whether to project the survey data to the date of intended adjustment and, if so, how much further the projection should be extended. For example, assume the survey used for determining job grading has an effective date of March; it is now September, and the individual pay increases using these new ranges will take place in January (and will not be reviewed again until the following January).

It seems logical to first project the survey community to January 1. If it is assumed that the survey community will be increasing pay at an annual rate of 10 percent, then it is logical to add 7.5 percent to the reported rate (i.e., 10 percent times 3/4 year). Assume it is also assumed that pay increases next year for the survey community will be increasing at a 10 percent annual rate. There are essentially three choices: (1) Make no additional projection, recognizing that pay will begin to slip competitively shortly after January 1 and will be trailing 10 percent by the following January; (2) increase the survey data an additional 10 percent (on top of the 7.5 percent adjustment) thereby placing the company theoretically 10 percent ahead of the survey on the date of adjustment, recognizing that this will deteriorate and by next January will approximate community pay; or (3) take a compromise position between "no increase" and "full increase" (e.g., use five percent, recognizing that this will place the company five percent ahead of the community on the date of adjustment, equal to the community average at midyear, and five percent behind the community by the following January). Which of these three positions to take is a matter of company philosophy regarding competitive position in the marketplace.

Actions based on projections need to be adjusted (plus or minus) when the actual numbers are known. If the estimate proved too high, the next adjustment should reflect this overestimate. For example, assume the estimate a year earlier had been for a six percent market growth, but the actual increase in pay proved to be five percent. The following year's projection would be reduced by one percent to offset the incorrect adjustment. The same would apply in reverse. If the estimate was six percent but it turned out to be seven percent, then one percent would be added to the estimated market growth. This type of adjustment means the data is never off more than one year.

STRUCTURAL ADJUSTMENTS

While most companies use survey data to adjust their pay structures, they differ as to how often they make those adjustments. Companies that review everyone in the same period usually adjust annually, while those that use individual review dates, such as anniversary date of employment, may adjust on a quarterly or biannual basis. If a company does not update its *structure* at least annually, it will face pressure to increase *grades* in response to pay increases in the marketplace.

Adjustments reflect a company's beliefs about increases at varying job levels in the marketplace. For some, this is a simple action of adjusting the structure by a specific percentage (e.g., eight percent) based on what the non-exempt employees have received in the way of increases. For most, it is a more sophisticated analysis.

Assume the company last adjusted its structure September 1. Further assume that all the survey data suggests that lower management jobs have increased at the rate of about nine percent, whereas top management has increased by seven percent. One could stop at this point and develop a new schedule, with increases of nine percent at the bottom tapering consistently down to a seven percent adjustment at the top. While such an action per se probably will not cause any problems, continual movement of this type will continue to compress or reduce the relative differential between executives and their subordinates, as shown in Figure 5-17. The impact of such a result is that the pay incentive to accept promotions is reduced.

Thus, flattening the curve and introducing compression must be examined when adjusting the structure. Empirically, it seems that differentials of 20 to 25 percent are needed between supervisor and subordinate to provide sufficient financial incentive for a subordinate to accept the responsibilities of supervisor. Such evidence has been seen in production operations—line supervisor and skilled operator. One could argue that because of the progressive tax structure and the increased visibility (and resulting risk of failure) of higher-level positions, this relationship should increase progressively through the pay structure, and there is some evidence at very senior levels of management to support this hypothesis.

Position vs. Survey Community

In developing a structural adjustment, consider where the company wants to be positioned competitively, and at what point in time. Many companies simply indicate they want to be competitive (or about equal to the average) with the companies in their surveys. Others will take a

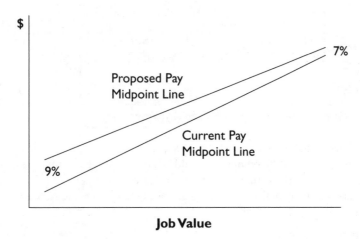

Figure 5-17. Structural change in midpoints

more aggressive posture such as in the 75th or 90th percentile. The importance of the salary element should be factored in as outlined at the introduction of this chapter when determining position in regard to the community. For example, if the importance relative to the other four elements is "high," then one would expect to have a higher community position than for those who ranked it "low" or "moderate." Conversely, if the community is made up of companies with similar importance ratings then one would expect the community position to be about the 50th percentile, unless the company deliberately sought a premium position.

The impact of the timing reference can be illustrated with a brief example. Assume that the company is seven percent behind at all pay levels in its defined survey community. Further, assume that all indicators are that competitive pay at all levels will increase by eight percent over the next 12 months. If the company wishes to be about equal to the survey community, how much should it increase its salary ranges? The obvious answers are eight percent or 15 percent, depending on whether the company is satisfied with its current market position (i.e., a 7-percent discount) or wishes to equal the market. If the latter, one choice is to increase the ranges now by seven percent, and then by 0.67 percent every month for the next year. However, this does not seem realistic since the community average is probably not increasing in a straight-line progression during the coming year.

Increasingly, companies are answering the timing issue by compromising between adjusting only for the immediate lag and including the full year's growth. In our example, this would mean an 11-percent adjustment. The large jump vs. market data occurs only the first time this action is taken. To illustrate, assume that one year later we found our foresight was 20-20 and pay did increase by eight percent—thus placing us currently about four percent behind the market. Assuming pay is estimated to increase at the rate of eight percent during the coming year, we should increase the schedule by eight percent to retain the same relationship. In other words, after the first adjustment for projecting pay for the community, the schedule is subsequently adjusted simply by the full amount of the estimated future community growth, plus or minus adjustments to the extent the previous estimate was less or more than actually occurred. This is illustrated in Table 5-16, using index numbers for comparative purposes.

	Current	Next Year				1 Year Later		
		Est. Increase	Actual	New Rate	Survey vs. Co.	Est. Increase	New Rate	Survey vs. Co.
Survey	107	8%	8%	115.6	} 4.1%	8%	124.9	} 4.1%
Company	100	11	11	111.0		8%	119.9	

Table 5-16. Structural change, company vs. survey community

If the first year's actual increase for the survey community were nine percent instead of the estimated eight percent, then the company would adjust the ranges by nine percent the following year (eight percent for the estimated future growth and one percent for the adjustment to last year's estimate). If the actual proved to be seven percent, then the new adjustment would be seven percent using the same logic.

Use of Average Increases in Pay

Many are confused by apparent conflicts in average increases in executive salaries as reported by different surveys. For example, three different studies might report figures of eight, nine, and 10 percent and yet be completely compatible.

Taking them in reverse order, the last study may have examined the average increases only of those who received adjustments, whereas the second might have examined the average increase in all salaries. Thus, if 90 percent received an average increase of 10 percent, the data would be comparable to the 10 percent number reported by the first. Finally, the first study might have been looking at the increase in payroll after one year. This is similar to the second study except that it is "net" of all additions and terminations to payroll as well as measuring the promotional adjustments. To the extent replacements are hired at lower pay than those being replaced and/or the workforce is being expanded at a pay level below the average payroll (i.e., total payroll divided by number of employees), this will not only offset promotional increases but may offset a portion of the average increase in salaries as well.

Therefore, when examining reported average increases in pay, look closely at the definition(s) used. In the above illustrations, the results were comparable; however, a different company mix, the timing of the study, and poor survey techniques might have resulted in widely divergent data in apparently comparable studies.

Must All Jobs Have Grades?

Formal minimums and maximums for jobs are more likely to be found in mature organizations than those in the threshold or emerging stages. However, even some mature organizations have no official grades for their very senior executives. Their position is usually that grades at that level have no meaning since compensation is very personalized. Perhaps. But compensation committees (as will be discussed in Chapter 10) are showing increasing interest in knowing whether such individuals are overpaid or underpaid in relation to the market. Once the job has been placed in a grade based on a study of competitive levels of compensation, such a concern is rather easily resolved. However, those totally flexible, ungraded situations are much more difficult for compensation committees to address. Furthermore, the lack of grades is totally inconsistent with a philosophy of adjusting individual pay in relation to performance and competitive pay levels. Without a grade reference, the latter is not readily apparent. Therefore, lacking a formal structure that is updated for market conditions, the pay of individual executives is more likely to be adjusted in relation to the average increases reported in the marketplace than on the basis of individual contributions. In such instances, an executive's level of pay is more likely to be a function of length of service than degree of accomplishments. Rather than delete job grades altogether, some organizations have gone to *broad-banding*. Typically, four to six (maybe more) grades are collapsed into one grade or band, as shown in Figure 5-18. Therefore, instead of having 25 to 50 grades, a company may have six to 10.

A move to broad-banding is logical at the time a company is de-layering the organization and emphasizing cross-functional (horizontal) movement, not hierarchical (vertical) structures. Broad-banding minimizes issues of promotions or demotions, facilitating movement.

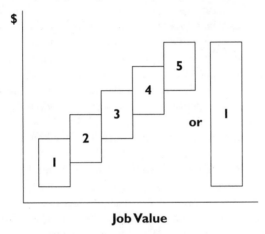

Figure 5-18. Traditional vs. broad-band grades

Must All Grades Have Jobs?

Some are troubled when they examine a pay structure and find grades with no positions. Their immediate response is to request that the structure be collapsed to eliminate these situations. Most, however, recognize that job grades have been developed with either a constant increase in midpoint (e.g., 10 percent) or a progression (e.g., 5.0 percent, 5.1 percent, 5.2 percent, etc.). The latter approach partially takes into consideration the need for fewer grades at the upper executive levels, since they may be more than 10 percent apart, while allowing for more fine tuning at the lower, exempt levels, where job comparisons with survey data are more dependable and less subject to validity questioning. It is not expected that every grade will have a job; however, it is likely that future re-gradings may result in some empty grades being filled.

Geographical Differences

Some surveys demonstrate a definite difference in level of pay for comparable positions in different parts of the country. Therefore, to ensure the organization is not overpaying in lower pay areas or underpaying in higher pay areas, some companies have adopted area pay differential policies. It should, however, be noted that while such differences admittedly still exist, the degree of difference seems to be diminishing over time (a reason holding back a number of companies from adopting such a policy). The main reason for not adopting such a policy, however, is that there is usually insufficient data on level of pay in different areas to adopt geographic differentials, and therefore the company must switch from a level-of-pay basis to a cost-of-living basis. This works on the presumption that level of pay will follow—and be dependent on—the cost of living. However, it brings the cost of living into prime focus—a difficult point for those working hard to sever any linkage of their pay program with this factor. Even where geographical differentials exist, they are likely to be found only in lower grade levels. The exception would be country-pay differentials for overseas assignment of executives.

Cost of Living. Let's take a moment to contradict popular opinion. The *consumer price index* (CPI) is *not* a measurement of the cost of living as commonly believed. It is merely the weighted change in the movement of prices for various products and, therefore, considered an indication of inflation. Inflation without a corresponding increase in pay is considered a reduction in pay. While the weighting is based on total U. S. usage, it does not apply to any one family. The family of four used by the Department of Labor describes a "typical," perfect, average family that does not exist. How can it? Furthermore, the CPI includes conflicting situations such as both the cost of renting and the cost of buying a home. Additionally, it does not include changes in the quality of the product, merely its price. Therefore, to the extent price increase is partially offset by quality improvement, the CPI is overstated. We are obsessed with movements in the CPI. Why? Because there is always a desire to seek a simple answer to complex issues—even when it is shown to be wrong. Nonetheless, an unexpected increase in inflation transfers income from the lender to the borrower, since the latter pays back the debt with dollars of reduced purchasing power. Conversely, a lower-than-expected rise in inflation transfers money from the borrower to the lender, since the returned dollars have greater-than-previously estimated purchasing power. This applies to anyone on either side of a debt transaction. Returning to the issue of geographic differentials, essentially, there are two approaches: develop separate salary structures or pay separate premiums.

Separate Salary Structures. This might result in two or more different schedules to cover communities ranging from New York City to Manitowoc, Wisconsin. The structure might bear a consistent percentage difference (e.g., schedule B is 90 percent of schedule A, schedule C is 80 percent of schedule A, etc.) or some other mathematical basis consistent with the intent of recognizing differences in pay levels. Therefore, a person who moves from the area C schedule to the area A schedule is able to receive a significant promotional increase due to the more liberal structure. Unfortunately, it similarly means that moving from area A to area C will mean little salary growth, if not an actual reduction in pay. One way to minimize these issues is to keep the portion of the salary that reflects the geographical differential in a separate check. This practice does not remove the problem, but it does keep the differential payments very visible.

Separate Pay Premiums. Some companies take a simpler view of area differentials and simply structure premium percentages by area or city (e.g., New York—10 percent, Chicago—5 percent, etc.). This approach is more prevalent in companies headquartered outside the highest premium-percentage markets. As with separate schedules, the adjustment can be folded directly into salary or, more logically, kept as a separate monthly payment. An additional advantage of the percentage approach is that it can be phased out. In other words, if the rationale for paying the premium is to help the individual get adjusted, the payment could be structured to phase out over a period of time (e.g., 15 percent the first year, 10 percent the second, five percent the third, and zero thereafter).

Where geographic differentials exist, they normally do not apply fully to executives. This is accomplished by either completely excluding those above a certain salary level (e.g., $100,000) or applying the differential to only a certain portion of pay (e.g., 10 percent on the first $100,000 of salary, thereby effectively giving a five-percent premium to an executive earning a $200,00 salary). It should also be remembered that differentials apply only to salary, and thus, a company with a high short- and long-term incentive opportunity would have a higher percentage differential than a company with little or no short- and long-term incentive plans, assuming both were approximately the same in total compensation.

INDIVIDUAL PAY ACTIONS

Job analysis, job evaluation, salary surveys, and structural adjustments are all keyed to determining how much to pay a particular job. The individual pay actions are determined within this set of parameters. The range may be open or have incremental values. The increments may be either reference points for merit increase values (e.g., breakpoints for lower, middle and upper one-third of range) or fixed rates for pay increases. If the latter is used, there is no opportunity to use non-listed values. In some situations, the two approaches may be combined (e.g., fixed increments for the lower one-third or one-half of the range with an open range for the remainder). Fixed increments are more likely to be found in non-profits, especially the public sector, than in the private sector. Because of their importance relative to incentives, salary ranges are likely to be wider in the public sector than in the private, with the exception that executive salary ranges are likely to be wider at the executive level than lower in the organization since executives are likely to remain in their range longer (due to decreased promotional opportunities).

Typically, executive pay is determined in relation to performance over a period of time and position within the salary range. An indication of how these two interrelate is illustrated in Figure 5-19. Note the reference to *compa-ratio*; this is simply actual pay divided by structural control point (midpoint of range for most companies). Thus, a person earning a $90,000 salary in a grade with a $100,000 control point has a compa-ratio of 0.90. The compa-ratio enables the reviewer to relate position in range of one executive to another, as well as doing a grade-by-grade analysis.

As can be seen, the width of the structural compensation compa-ratio increases with management level. This is consistent with our earlier discussion that ranges might be 50 percent (maximum over minimum) at the low end of the structure, but would increase with management level.

As seen in Figure 5-19, executives with only "brief" experience and "acceptable" levels of performance (combination E) should be low in the lower one-third of the range. Conversely, only individuals with "extensive" experience who have been consistently judged as "outstanding" performers (combination A) should be paid near or at the range maximum.

The middle one-third of the range is appropriate for those individuals who have the "optimal" experience and have been consistently rated as "good" (combination C). However, experience and performance levels can offset each other. Combination C can also reflect an executive with "extensive" experience who has been consistently judged as "acceptable," or an individual with only "brief" experience who is rated as "outstanding." Additional experience and performance combinations suggest positions in the range shown by the letters D and B.

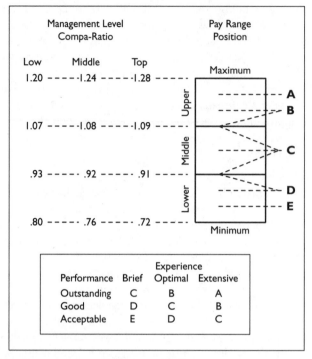

Figure 5-19. Position in pay range—experience/performance

Performance Appraisals

Differentiating pay by performance, by definition, necessitates the evaluation of executive performance. While this may be nothing more than a five-minute reflection by the manager in some instances, most organizations are more formalized in their appraisals. However, small, threshold companies are likely to have a greater degree of informality than the larger, more mature organizations. In some instances, formality can retard the growth of an organization, as the bureaucracy of the process takes on a goal of its own.

Not uncommon is a lack of formal performance appraisals at the very senior levels of management. The common reply is that the individuals know how they are doing simply by examining their unit's performance vs. the operating plan for the period. Admittedly, that indicates how the unit is doing, but is the executive aiding or hindering the level of performance?

Interestingly, a number of executives hold two divergent views about performance appraisal. They don't believe appraisals are necessary for people who report immediately to them (as there is enough interaction and data to make structured appraisal unnecessary); however, they want to have their own performance reviewed by their superior! Under such circumstances, the most satisfied individual is the one receiving a performance appraisal (hopefully positive) who is not required to formally review the performance of his or her own subordinates. Conversely, the most frustrated executive is the one who is told to have formal review sessions with subordinates but is not given a session by a superior. A large number of executives still fall into the latter category although the situation is improving.

CEOs often times find that they must continually remind their direct reports to complete performance appraisals on their subordinates for the CEO's review. A more drastic way of gaining compliance than cajoling is to inform them their salary checks will be withheld until the appraisals have been completed. This form of mandatory deferral not only can cause cash flow problems for the affected, it also sends a very strong message throughout the organization: Performance reviews are important.

Appraisal Types. There are two types of appraisals: *input-based* and *output-based.*

Input-Based. This consists of what a person has or possesses. It consists of knowledge and values; it describes what a person can do and how likely he or she is to do it. It is helpful in selecting individuals (ranging from hire to promotion), but not of much use in pay actions as it does not measure performance. When used for pay actions, it is likely to raise questions of legality. Input-based factors are often identified as competencies.

Output-Based. This type of appraisal (also called performance-based) is one of three types: what, how, and a combination of the two. The "what" approach is a detailed list of what is to be done when. An example of a grid that might be used to evaluate each assignment in terms of timeliness and quality is shown in Table 5-17.

A brief description of an objective, or goal-oriented, performance management process, sometimes called *management by objective,* is shown in Table 5-18. It is a process, not simply a program: A program is something of limited time frame; a process is an ongoing event.

The advantages of a performance-based measurement include:

- Outcome expectations can be clearly defined for the person.
- The organization's strategy can be parceled out to individuals so that the composite constitutes the entire strategy.

Quality	Final Completion Date				
	Not Finished	**Very Significantly Late**	**Significantly Late**	**Slightly Late**	**On or Ahead of Schedule**
Perfect	1.0	2.0	2.8	3.7	4.0
Outstanding	0.7	1.7	2.5	3.3	3.8
Superior	0.4	1.4	2.2	2.9	3.4
Very Good	0.1	1.1	1.8	2.5	3.0
Good	0.0	0.8	1.4	2.0	2.5
Acceptable	0.0	0.5	1.0	1.5	2.0
Marginal	0.0	0.2	0.6	1.0	1.5
Very Marginal	0.0	0.1	0.3	0.5	1.0
Unacceptable	0.0	0.0	0.1	0.2	0.5

Table 5-17. Performance matrix, quality vs. timelines

1. Identification and written description of specific goals to be accomplished (including timetable and basis of measurement) by supervisor.
2. Vertical linkage of individual with group goals is carried out.
3. The subordinate makes a commitment to meeting the objectives.
4. Horizontal balance must be assured by the supervisor to ensure equal stretch by subordinates in achieving goals.
5. Real-time assessments and feedback are given to the subordinate by the supervisor, assessing the degree of accomplishments in relation to the stated objectives.
6. Closure at year-end measures the extent of achievement on each goal and aggregates these component parts for the job as a whole.
7. The overall appraisal is "leveled" by adjusting for rater strictness or leniency, and is then expressed in numerical or key word form for the purpose of determining the appropriate size of pay adjustment.
8. The process begins all over again.

Table 5-18. Goal-oriented performance management process

On the other hand, frequent disadvantages include:

- Goals may not be realistic nor of comparable difficulty to those of others.
- Goal attainment may be dependent on performance of others.
- Changing conditions require frequent adjustments to goals and timetables.
- Routine responsibilities of the job may not be included and therefore not appraised.
- Expected behavior is typically absent.

The last disadvantage is negated if a *how factor* is included. The "how" assesses behavior, or the manner in which the work is done, in other words, adding an input-based component. Some call this the *culture* or the set of company values. Regardless of what it is called, poor "how" performance probably gets more executives fired than poor "what" performance. Because of the subjectivity in "how" measurements, multi-rater systems are typically employed. Customers, peers, and/or subordinates may be queried in some form to determine their degree of satisfaction with how the results were achieved. Multi-rater systems provide views from different perspectives and, therefore, are more likely to be complete in the whole.

When subordinates, peers, and managers are included, the process is sometimes called a *360 review.* However, use this "view from all sides" carefully. Typically, they are used for developmental issues, not pay actions, because peers and those supervised can exert positive or negative bias depending on their relationship with the rated person. Some companies will allow the ratee an opportunity to identify persons to serve as raters, while still retaining the right to modify the list. The manner in which results are conveyed to the rated range from unedited comments to edited versions (to retain anonymity). Usually, the rated is encouraged to meet individually with the raters to focus on how to improve. A 360 review is illustrated in Figure 5-20.

Regardless of the outcome-based approach used, it typically details expectations before the beginning of the performance period. Ideally, these reviews have been jointly prepared. However, if they have been rater-imposed, they must be clearly communicated to the rated. How else can

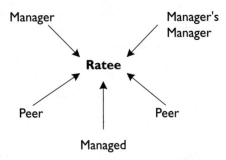

Figure 5-20. 360 performance review

the person meet expectations? During the performance period, the rater tells the ratee how performance is proceeding so there is time to make adjustments and also that there are no surprises at year-end. These rater comments during the year and when the final evaluation is made are called "feedback." It has to be done, it must be done right. While shortcomings must be exposed, it should be a developmental opportunity rather than a tortuous infliction of a thousand cuts.

Performance-management systems can be structured for either consequences or development. In addition, for use in determining pay, a *consequence* objective results in actions to terminate, retrain, or promote. A *development* objective would focus on performance improvement and possible preparation for positions of greater responsibility. A 360 review is useful when the objective is development. However, it is not ideal for pay actions because of the possible impact of favoritism or perceived favoritism.

Performance-management systems can assess a single individual, a defined group, or the entire company. This is highlighted in Table 5-19. The number of "groups" will vary by organization, with more in larger companies than smaller ones. Groups may be defined by team type, ad hoc or long-standing, as well as project vs. process. As shown, salary actions are typically based only on the individual's performance, while short-term incentives are based on three types of performance appraisals (individual, group, and corporate). Long-term incentives typically use only corporate performance.

Yet, another appraisal method is called a *critical incident* approach. It is a look-back at a specific event, with feedback on the extent to which the "what" and the "how" met or did not meet expectations.

Regardless of the method, the process must lead to an overall rating for pay purposes. Typically, this means giving a weight to each performance objective. This begins with giving

	Type of Performance		
	Individual	**Group**	**Corporate**
Salary	✔		
Short-Term Incentives	✔	✔	✔
Long-Term Incentives			✔

Table 5-19. Level of performance rating vs. pay element

each an equal weighting and then making adjustments. For example, if there were 10 objectives, each would start with a weighting of 10 percent and then be adjusted to the extent it was more or less significant than the average. In addition, the process must establish a rating scale to assess the level of performance.

By multiplying the performance rating by the assigned weighting for each objective and dividing by the total number of points, it is possible to calculate an overall performance rating. For example, such a system might use the university-based 4.0 system with the results summarized in a verbal manner, as shown in Table 5-20. Note that any score between 2.6 and 3.5 would be considered "superior." This rating might be further subdivided so that 2.6 to 3.0 was "very good" while 3.1 to 3.5 would be "superior." However, the difficulty in identifying key words that clearly describe differences in performance levels has caused some people to simply stay with the numerical results.

Descriptor	Rating
Outstanding	3.6-4.0
Superior	2.6-3.5
Good	1.6-2.5
Marginal	0.6-1.5
Unacceptable	0.0-0.5

Table 5-20. Key word vs. numerical performance rating

An alternative is the seven-level rating scale shown in Table 5-21. Here both a numeric and verbal rating are identified along with a brief, descriptive definition. Note that there are two variables identified: degree of attainment and degree of difficulty.

A variation of Table 5-21 is shown in Table 5-22. Here a "promotability" factor has been added, also resulting in scores ranging from 0 to 6. This works better below the executive ranks. For most highly ranked executives, the possibility for additional promotion is slim. For the chairman and CEO, it is non-existent.

Another way to build difficulty into the rating process is to factor the rating up or down, based on stretch or lack thereof in the goal. Typically, goals when totaled equal 100. If they are too easy, the manager might mark them down to total 95 or 90. Conversely, for a person with more difficult stretch goals, the total might be 105 or 110. In both situations, the totaled scores are divided by 100. The impact is shown in Table 5-23. The example shows two different individuals but it could be the same person after having decided to be more aggressive, taking on the more difficult goal E and adding in goal F.

Objectives vs. Goals. When defining performance expectations, typically, one describes objectives and goals. Objectives are usually *qualitative* targets, while goals are usually *quantitative* targets, although some companies reverse the two. (The confusion may be due to origin. Sports minded individuals know goals are scores in football, hockey, and soccer. Military types think in terms of objectives, such as "take that hill.") The first step is to define an objective, or qualitative target; for the CEO, this might be "restructure the company to emphasize core business."

Rating		Objective Attainment
Numeric	**Verbal**	**Objective Attainment**
6	Outstanding	Significantly surpassed or Surpassed over major obstacles
5	Superior	Surpassed over obstacles or Achieved over major obstacles
4	Very Good	Surpassed or Achieved over obstacles or Almost achieved over major obstacles
3	Good	Achieved or Almost achieved over obstacles or Partially achieved over major obstacles
2	Acceptable	Partially achieved or Little accomplishment over major obstacles
I	Marginal	Little accomplished or Nothing accomplished over major obstacles
0	Unacceptable	Nothing accomplished

Table 5-21. Performance ratings, seven-scale

The goals, or quantitative targets, are a subset of the objective, and must be defined next. In this case, a goal might be "divest business A before end of year. The key is to express the quantitative target in sufficient detail to determine the extent to which it was or was not achieved.

In reviewing the performance management process, it is appropriate to use a template with questions such as these to determine if it needs adjusting:

- Are objectives and goals clear?
- Are objectives and goals appropriately linked vertically and horizontally to others?
- Are the right people involved at the right time?
- Is there sufficient discussion in setting goals and reviewing achievements?
- Are the metrics appropriate for measuring both quantitative and qualitative targets?
- Are multi-year targets set where appropriate?

Linking Goals and Objectives. In setting the objectives and goals, the CEO will want to ensure that his or hers are also reflected in the direct reports. This is the vertical link, sometimes called the *line of sight*, which the direct reports will also parcel out to their direct reports. Directly or indirectly, these are financial goals. For line executives, the targets would obviously include: revenue, net income, return on assets, percentage of market share, and other similar goals and objectives. Staff executives may have some of these same targets in their own write-ups to promote cross-functional collaboration. However, most of their targets will be non-financial in nature, although linked to improving performance on financial targets. In categorizing goals and objectives, they are probably one of three types: initiatives (new), maintenance (continuing), and development (personal growth).

Rating		Objective Attainment
Numeric	**Verbal**	**Objective Attainment**
4	Outstanding	Significantly surpassed or Surpassed over major obstacles
3	Superior	Surpassed over obstacles or Achieved over major obstacles
2	Very Good	Surpassed or Achieved over obstacles or Almost achieved over major obstacles
I	Good	Achieved or Almost achieved over obstacles or Partially achieved over major obstacles
0	Acceptable	Partially achieved or Little accomplishment over major obstacles
0	Marginal	Little accomplished or Nothing accomplished over major obstacles
0	Unacceptable	Nothing accomplished
2	Excellent	Likely for more than one promotion
I	Good	Likely for one promotion

Table 5-22. Performance and "promotability" ratings

Executive A			Executive B		
Goal	**Weight**	**Score**	**Goal**	**Weight**	**Score**
A	20	4	A	20	4
B	25	3	B	25	3
C	10	3	C	10	3
D	20	3	D	20	3
E	15	3	E	25	3
			F	25	3
Total	90	290		110	350
Average		2.9			3.5

Table 5-23. Adjusted goal total impact

In addition to the vertical link, some goals and objectives will be shared horizontally between two or more individuals reporting directly to the CEO or lower in the organization. An example of a horizontally shared goal (or objective depending on definition) would be "design and implement new pay-for-performance plan by first of next year. Include significant upside potential and downside risk for CEO and direct reports, based on performance vs. industry peer group." It is fairly clear that the CFO, chief legal officer, and chief human resources officer could share this goal. Another example would be "launch product A in second quarter in markets X and Y, capturing at least 10-percent market share before year end." Development, production, marketing, and sales executives would each have specific responsibilities and timelines to meet this target. If it were major enough, it might be included in the write-ups of the CEO and the reporting business head.

How Much Detail? Sufficiently detailed performance appraisals minimize disagreement between supervisee and supervisor on the level of performance. When appraising, be specific. Such information could be several well-chosen paragraphs describing the performance, or it could list objectives for the year and the extent to which they have been accomplished and are on time. Many programs fail because they require either too little or too much detail. The optimum program would balance simplicity with validity to attain an acceptable compromise position.

When Shall Appraisals Be Conducted? Performance appraisals that are conducted shortly prior to an anniversary merit review are subject to great pressure to be positive enough to justify an appropriate compensation action. When using anniversary review dates, it may be appropriate to have two reviews: one on a common date for all employees and the second prior to an adjustment. The first is needed to minimize heavy skewing to the top performance levels, and the second is required to justify the compensation action. The two should be reasonably close in outcome. If they are not, it would be appropriate to have a discussion with the supervisor. A common merit review date, and thus only one performance review, may be more logical. It has the advantage of placing the compensation actions directly within a prescribed merit budget. Within these two approaches, there will likely be project performance review schedules focused on key milestone dates as well as project completion dates.

Who Is Involved? The extent of interaction and participation is a function of how closely the subordinate and manager see eye-to-eye on the performance level. Where there is an appreciable difference (invariably the manager having the lower opinion), frequent discussions during the year on specific project performance are necessary. When the year-end wrap-up session is held, there is little opportunity for the individual to be "surprised" by the supervisor's rating. Another technique that is useful is requesting the ratee to prepare and give to the rater a self-appraisal before the review session. Regardless of the rating definitions, there is a built-in bias to go above an average rating. Everyone believes they are "above average." One way to side-track this is to state up front that "average" company standards are above-average community standards. In fact, "meets company standards" could substitute for "good." Qualify with appropriate modifiers such as "exceeds" or "does not meet."

At the minimum, the manager's manager should see the performance write-up (along with the individual's self-assessment if one is prepared), preferably before and after the review with the individual. By showing the write-up to the manager's manager before the meeting, the manager has an opportunity to obtain the boss's agreement: Nothing is worse than to have the manager's manager later agree with the ratee that the rater was incorrect in the rating. It is also logical for the manager's manager to review it after the performance review session, especially when the individual is allowed to add written comments to the appraisal. This session forms the basis for ensuring that an appropriate follow-up course of action is agreed upon. It is common knowledge that some raters are more generous than others in rating their subordinates. Unless there is a level playing field, ratees of the generous rater will receive heftier pay increases than those under a stricter reviewer. One way to balance the ratings is to have the CEO subordinates sit together and review each other's ratings of their subordinates. Under peer scrutiny, the "hard" marker may ease off and the "easy" marker may lower assigned ratings. It may not completely level the playing field but it will help. More will be said of performance standards and definitions in the chapters on short-term and long-term incentives.

Distribution of Performance Ratings

Some companies mandate that distribution of performance ratings fit a prescribed pattern, usually a bell-shaped normal distribution curve. This is called *forced distribution*. Others *suggest* such a distribution but do not force it; this may skew the distribution negatively, as shown in Figure 5-21, reflecting a "drift" to higher performance ratings. The *normal distribution* is shown as a dotted curve.

Forced distribution by grade usually is impossible because of the few individuals involved; however, it is possible to develop bands of management as indicated in Table 5-24, thereby achieving some normalcy in ratings except to the extent unit performance legitimately suggests overall higher or lower ratings. This distribution could be a guideline or require mandatory compliance with exceptions requiring top management approval. Mandatory forced distribution systems are like mandatory pay contributions, they do not work too long (if at all) as they ignore size (and composition) of group and group performance. Unfortunately, they are a substitute for effective management of performance ratings.

Ideally, performance distributions comparing one division to another should reflect differences in performance rather than differences in raters. In many cases, however, what the distributions really show is a range from the "softie" to the "hard marker." While an objective performance appraisal can help to minimize such differences, it can never completely eliminate them.

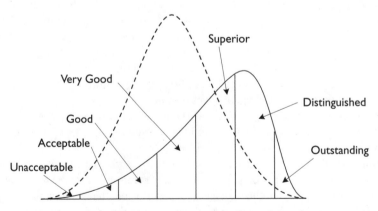

Figure 5-21. Distribution of performance ratings, normal vs. skewed

	Distribution of Performance Ratings						
Top Management	4	8	16	44	16	8	4
Senior Management	4	8	16	44	16	8	4
Middle Management	4	8	16	44	16	8	4
Lower Management	4	8	16	44	16	8	4
Rating	0	1	2	3	4	5	6
Company-Wide	4	8	16	44	16	8	4

Table 5-24. Distribution of performance ratings—bands

A rather dramatic attempt to solve this imbalance would be for the boss of the division head to tell the division head that his or her assessment of the overall division performance is a "4" (superior). Assuming the weighted average of performance ratings in the division (which includes everyone except the division head) is a "5" (distinguished), the performance of the division head must have been less than "4," meaning he or she has negatively affected the division's overall performance. Unless the division head can refute the boss' ratings, he or she is in a very awkward position.

There is another leveling approach that some may choose to use, although it too requires a high degree of self-confidence and intestinal fortitude. The boss brings in each of his or her division heads with the performance ratings for their immediate subordinates. Each rating is then open to constructive criticism by the other division heads, who will use critical incidents (typically illustrating poor results) to challenge the seemingly high performance rating in another division. Such sessions have such colorful terms as a "bloodbath" or an "arrow slinging session."

In attempting a rational distribution of performance within a division, watch out for the "high grade/high performance" syndrome. This is evidenced when the top performance ratings are awarded to the executives in the highest job grades, forcing lower rankings to those in the lower grades (as illustrated in Figure 5-22). This is a manifestation of the "my best people are in those top grades" philosophy. While this statement may be true, it is not pertinent. A higher salary range rewards top-graded jobs for their associated greater responsibility. The issue is whether or not the individuals are meeting these higher standards.

As an example of how this syndrome occurs, assume that an individual is a grade 20. Because he or she is a "distinguished performer," exceeding the standards of the position, management decides to incorporate these higher standards into the job description, making them the normal requirements. The position now merits a grade 23 rather than 20. Unless performance is further elevated, the individual should not be judged above "very good"—he or she is simply meeting, not exceeding, the new and higher job standards. Using Table 5-4, assume a current salary of $250,000 and merit increases as shown in Table 5-25. As a result of the new job grade, the hypothetical employee's 11-percent salary increase for "distinguished" performance in the middle one-third of grade 20 becomes the same increase, but for "very good" performance in the below-minimum range of grade 23. The increase is equal (11 percent), but the "distinguished" performance rating is lost.

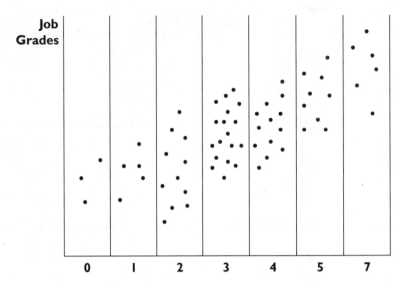

Figure 5-22. High grade/high performance syndrome

Performance Level		Percentage Increase Based on Position in Range				
Alpha	Numeric	Below Minimum	Lower 1/3	Middle 1/3	Upper 1/3	Above Maximum
Outstanding	6	21	16	13	11	0
Distinguished	5	17	13	11	9	0
Superior	4	14	11	9	7	0
Very Good	3	11	9	7	5	0
Good	2	8	6	5	4	0
Acceptable	1	6	4	3	2	0
Unacceptable	0	0	0	0	0	0

Table 5-25. Merit pay matrix—performance vs. position in range

Note that no pay increase is normally expected for a person above the range maximum. However, after one or two years with no adjustment, most such individuals fall back within the range, simply as a result of annual structural adjustments. These over-maximums, typically identified as *red circles*, are the result of individuals having been demoted from higher-graded responsibilities.

Developing an annual incentive structure on top of the salary structure (for those companies wanting both) will be covered in Chapter 7 (Short-Term Incentives). With incentive compensation, salary-increase guidelines might need to be different for those under a "salary only" structure than for those participating in an annual incentive plan, *if* there is a significant increase

Performance Rating		Minimum	Below Minimum	Lower 1/3	Middle 1/3	Upper 1/3	Above Maximum
6	Salary Only		21.0%	16.0%	13.0%	11.0%	0
	Both		14.1	10.7	8.7	7.4	
5	Salary Only		17.0%	13.0%	12.0%	9.0%	0
	Both		11.4	8.7	8.0	6.0	
4	Salary Only		14.0%	11.0%	9.0%	7.0%	0
	Both		9.4	7.4	6.0	4.7	
3	Salary Only		11.0%	9.0%	7.0%	5.0%	0
	Both		7.4	6.0	4.7	3.4	
2	Salary Only		8.0%	6.0%	5.0%	4.0%	0
	Both		5.4	3.0	3.4	2.7	
1	Salary Only		6.0%	4.0%	3.0%	2.0%	0
	Both		4.0	2.7	2.0	1.3	
0	Salary Only		0%	0%	0%	0	0
	Both		0	0	0	0	0

Table 5-26. Comparative merit pay increase guidelines—salary only vs. salary plus annual incentives

in upside potential. Table 5-26 reflects the schedule in Table 5-25 for salary only and introduces lower guidelines for those with "both" salary and annual incentives. In this example, the latter is two-thirds the former. More or less emphasis on the annual incentive would change this ratio.

Timing of Salary Action

In many companies, the pay review is related to the anniversary of employment, but in some, it occurs at a common time during the year. Different portions of the company may have reviews on their own separate dates, or the entire company may have a common adjustment date.

The advantages of a common review date include: (1) maximum utilization of management time in the review process, (2) a minimal need for separate budgetary controls, (3) easy adjustment to economic conditions, and (4) promotion of internal equity. The disadvantages are that such a system is less personalized in nature, and it enables individuals to make easier comparisons on how well they did.

The advantages and disadvantages of distributed adjustments are essentially the mirror image of the common-date system. The advantages are that management can be more personalized in deciding and communicating adjustments, and that the making of pay comparisons is diffused. The disadvantages include: (1) the demands on management time are greater since the manager must "come up to speed" on each situation; (2) budgetary game playing (namely, deferring the increase to later in the year in order to give a bigger percentage without incurring more expense for the year) is made possible; (3) it is more difficult to respond equitably to rapidly changing economic situations (consider those who just missed versus those who got caught by the last set of federal pay guidelines); and (4) it is more difficult to ensure equitable pay treatment throughout the organization.

Frequency of Salary Reviews

Determined by Job Grade. Some companies vary the time interval between salary reviews, normally stretching out the period for upper-level positions. Thus, while entry-level positions might be reviewed every six months for the first several years of employment, middle management positions would be on an annual or 18-month basis and the very senior executives on a biennial review.

These longer intervals mask a slowing down in compensation (e.g., a 10-percent pay increase after 18 months is really just a little more than a six-percent annual adjustment). Furthermore, increasing the time interval for a stated percentage adjustment as one moves further up the organization automatically contributes to the compression problem (i.e., lack of sufficient pay differential between supervisor and subordinates).

Determined by Position in Job Grade. Another approach is to increase the normal time interval as the executive progresses within the salary range. An example of this is found in Table 5-27. The percentages are the annual target amounts; thus an "outstanding" performer below range minimum might receive anything from about seven percent five to eight months after the last change to about 13 percent after eight months with the target being 10 percent after six months. Table 5-27 also illustrates the type of merit program that establishes ceilings within the range. Note that an "acceptable" performer is not expected to move above the lower one-third, and "good" and "very good" performers are held to the middle one-third of the range. Only "superior," "distinguished," and "outstanding" performers are permitted to reach the full range maximum. Furthermore, the two highest performance ratings permit token increases for those above range maximum, but on less than a yearly basis.

Another possibility is to hold the percentage increase constant and simply vary the frequency of adjustment based on performance. This is illustrated in Table 5-28, with an eight-percent adjustment. Actually, the amount is higher when compounding is considered.

Performance Rating	Position in Salary Range				
	Below Minimum	Lower 1/3	Middle 1/3	Upper 1/3	Above Maximum
Outstanding	20% / 5-8 mos	16% / 6-9 mos	13% / 8-12 mos	10% / 12-18 mos	5% / 18-24 mos
Distinguished	17% / 5-10 mos	13% / 7-12 mos	11% / 9-15 mos	8% / 15-21 mos	3% / 25-36 mos
Superior	14% / 6-12 mos	11% / 8-15 mos	9% / 10-18 mos	6% / 18-24 mos	
Very Good	11% / 7-14 mos	9% / 9-18 mos	7% / 11-21 mos		
Good	8% / 8-15 mos	6% / 10-20 mos	5% / 10-20 mos		
Acceptable	6% / 9-18 mos	4% / 12-24 mos			
Unacceptable					

Table 5-27. Merit pay matrix—amount vs. timing

Performance	Frequency of Adjustment, Months	Annualized Effect of 8% Increase
Outstanding	3-4	25-32%
Distinguished	5-8	12-19
Superior	9-12	8-11
Good	12-18	5-8
Marginal	18-24	5-5
Unacceptable	25-30	3-4

Table 5-28. Frequency of review varied by performance

De-emphasizing Salary. The classic problem with the salary program is the difficulty of truly rewarding performance with a large salary increase. This is especially a problem with companies that have limited incentive plan opportunities. One approach is to employ a lump sum. Rather than build the increase into the ongoing salary, the amount is annualized and paid as a one-time award. A variation would be to build in a portion of the award as a salary increase (e.g., the first five percent of pay). Where incentives are available, many are de-emphasizing salary as they put more emphasis on the annual and long-term incentives. Some go so far as to freeze salaries (especially at the CEO level) due to the earlier mentioned Section 162(m) limit. However, they make a major mistake if they disallow promotional increases or salary adjustments for expanded responsibilities. Freezing these people perpetuates a salary inequity and underpays the incentives (which are percentages of salary).

Developing the Merit Budget

For companies using a common review date, it is a simple matter to model the population (and each of its units) in terms of position in range and desired performance against a merit grid (such as the one in Table 5-25) to develop salary increase funds or pools. These funds constitute an allowable total amount of annualized salary dollars that are available for use. For those units that distribute increases throughout the year, the same principle is involved, but the data must be time-weighted in relation to the anticipated date of adjustment.

Several approaches to developing the control total include: (1) projection of most recent actual performance by individual, (2) weighting individual performance in accord with desired performance distribution, and (3) using the described average performance rating.

Using the Most Recent Performance Rating. Projection of the most recent actual performance rating assumes that each individual will have the same rating as last year. Thus, if the person was "outstanding" last year and a current salary of $360,000 placed the individual in the middle one-third of grade 24, a 13-percent increase, or $46,800, is suggested. Repeating the process for all employees generates a total (which can be increased or decreased by top management in accord with willingness and ability to pay). The problems with this approach are (1) its static nature, assuming neither an increase nor a decrease in performance one year to the next, (2) the lack of a previous rating for newly hired individuals, and (3) the questionable use of a rating at a lower grade for a recently promoted person.

Weighting Based on Desired Distribution. The second approach in developing the control total is assigning probable performance weights to each individual in accord with a desired distribution of performance. This is illustrated in Table 5-29, again using the same example. Note that the 6.96-percent increase would generate a $25,056 increase on a $360,000 salary. Repeating the process for other employees and summing the dollar increases would generate a raw control table.

Performance Rating	Raw Percentage	Assigned Weighting, Percent	Adjusted Percentage
Outstanding	13	4	0.52
Distinguished	11	8	0.88
Superior	9	16	1.44
Very Good	7	44	3.08
Good	5	16	0.80
Acceptable	3	8	0.24
Unacceptable	0	4	0.00
Total		**100**	**6.96**

Table 5-29. Weighting performance based on desired distribution

Using the Average Performance Rating. The third approach in developing a control total is an extension of the second. However, rather than assign probable weightings to each performance rating, the expected mean value is used. Following this approach, one might conclude that "very good" is the average performance rating. Using Table 5-25, all individuals below their salary-grade minimum would be projected for an 11-percent increase; those in the lower one-third would rise nine percent; those in the middle one-third would rise seven percent; and those in the upper one-third would rise five percent. To calculate the control total, identify the appropriate percentage based on each person's position within the salary range and multiply it by the person's salary and then sum the dollar increases for each person, resulting in a control total dollar of salary increases.

Adjusting for Unit Performance

A simple way to adjust for unit performance is by identifying a division's performance and adding the value on that line of the grid to the basic simulation, as illustrated in Table 5-30. Thus, using the simple average performance rating approach, if the division's performance were adjudged "superior," the "below minimum" guideline percent for everyone in that division would be increased 0.75 percent to 11.75 percent, the "lower one-third" would move up 0.63 percent to 9.63 percent, the "middle one-third" would be incremented by 0.5 percent to 7.5 percent, and those in the "upper one-third" would have a 0.38 percent higher amount, or 5.38 percent.

A simpler approach, but one that does not take into consideration position in range, is plus or minus a stated amount from the "very good" performance, as shown in Table 5-31. After the basic simulation, if a division had a weighted average allowable increase of 7.4 percent, but a performance of "superior," it would be allowed a merit-pool average of 7.9 percent (i.e., 7.4 + 0.5).

	Below Minimum	Lower 1/3	Middle 1/3	Upper 1/3	Above Maximum
Outstanding	2.25%	1.88%	1.5%	1.13%	0.0%
Distinguished	1.50	1.25	1.0	0.75	0.0
Superior	0.75	0.63	0.5	0.38	0.0
Very Good	0.00	0.00	0.0	0.00	0.0
Good	-0.75	-0.63	-0.5	-0.38	0.0
Acceptable	-1.50	-1.25	-1.0	-0.75	0.0
Unacceptable	-2.25	-1.88	-1.5	-1.13	0.0

Table 5-30. Adjusting for unit performance and position in range

Performance	Percent
Outstanding	+1.5
Distinguished	+1.0
Superior	+0.5
Very Good	No adjustment
Good	-0.5
Acceptable	-1.0
Unacceptable	-1.5

Table 5-31. Adjusting only for unit performance

Rather than use the qualitative definitions shown in Table 5-31, one might establish quantitative adjustments reflecting the extent to which the unit has achieved its financial targets. Shown in Table 5-32 is a formula that adjusts the merit budget based on sales and income performance above and below target. However, credit for increased sales cannot exceed the income increase. Note that below-target performance is penalized five times more than increases above target are rewarded. Perhaps this is too severe, but conceptually, missing target should be penalized more than exceeding target. Some would argue there should be no increase if target is not achieved, however, this is too severe and provides no money for those who did an exceptional job.

Shown in Table 5-33 through Table 5-36 are adjustments to a six-percent merit pay budget based on varying sales and income results for the unit. In this example, the maximum increase or decrease for each is 25 percent. This is illustrated in Table 5-33 (maximum increase) and Table 5-36 (maximum decrease). Illustrating that sales-increase adjustments cannot exceed income increases is shown in Table 5-34. In Table 5-35, we see a slight adjustment both above income target and below sales target.

Adjustment Per 1%	Sales	Income	Maximum
Above Target	1%	1%	25%
Below Target	5%	5%	25%

Table 5-32. Adjusting for unit sales and income performance

Adjustment Per 1%	% Target	Adjustment	
Sales	140	25%	(Maximum exceeded)
Income	130	25%	(Maximum exceeded)
	Total	50%	6% (1.50) = 9%

Table 5-33. Adjustment for sales of 140% and income 130% of target

Adjustment Per 1%	% Target	Adjustment	
Sales	110	8%	(Limited by income 8% increase)
Income	108	8%	
	Total	16%	6% (1.16) = 7.0%

Table 5-34. Adjustment for sales of 110% and income 108% of target

Adjustment Per 1%	% Target	Adjustment	
Sales	99	-5%	
Income	101	1	
	Total	-4%	6% (.96) = 5.8%

Table 5-35. Adjustment for sales of 99% and income 101% of target

Adjustment Per 1%	% Target	Adjustment	
Sales	94	-25%	(Maximum exceeded)
Income	92	-25	(Maximum exceeded)
	Total	-50%	6% (.50) = 3.0%

Table 5-36. Adjustment for sales of 94% and income 92% of target

Adjusting Merit Increase Guidelines

Many companies work very hard to disassociate the size of their merit budget from the assigned level of inflation. They focus instead on their own ability and willingness to pay as well as the assumed compensation growth in other companies.

Except in those situations where government controls artificially restrict the average pay increase for exempt employees, the merit budget, expressed either in dollars or percent of salaries, while normally at least equal to the annual rate of inflation, provides decreasing opportunity to reward meritorious performance as inflation increases. This is shown graphically in Figure 5-23, where the merit budget is a constant three percentage points above inflation.

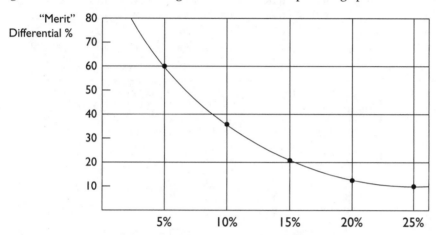

Figure 5-23. Merit pay vs. rate of inflation

Thus, while a company may set a merit budget of eight percent with a five-percent inflation assumption, it may also set an 18-percent budget with a 15-percent increase in the CPI. While the absolute difference is identical (i.e., three percentage points), the relative difference has been reduced from a 60-percent increase (i.e., eight percent/five percent) to a 20-percent increase (i.e., 18 percent/15 percent). Thus, the opportunity to truly differentiate in pay levels has been lessened.

Needless to say, this places great pressure on pay planners to devise effective pay delivery systems that maximize the utilization of available dollars in times of high inflation. During inflationary periods, increased pressure tends to restrain growth in executive pay. By holding executive pay increases to slightly below the average, a greater proportion of the remaining exempt employees receive higher percentage increases.

Each year, the matrix has to be re-examined in terms of appropriateness. The matrix in Table 5-25 reflects the position that a "very good" performer in the middle of the salary range should keep pace with the increase in competitive pay in the marketplace (here assumed to be seven percent). The remaining matrix is expanded on the double premise that (1) those lower in the range should move faster than those higher up and (2) increase should vary directly with performance. After the matrix is constructed, it has to be tested under varying structural-increase assumptions to track the rate at which different-level performers move through the salary range.

Table 5-37 shows an example of how this type of simulation can be performed. The seven performance ratings are expressed in numerical form (6 = high and 0 = low). In this illustra-

Year	Range Minimum	Performance Rating							Range Maximum
		0	1	2	3	4	5	6	
0	0.71	0.71	0.71	0.71	0.71	0.71	0.71	0.71	1.29
1	0.71	0.67	0.71	0.72	0.74	0.76	0.78	0.81	1.29
2	0.71	0.63	0.71	0.74	0.78	0.80	0.84	0.89	1.29
3	0.71	0.60	0.71	0.75	0.80	0.84	0.89	0.97	1.29
4	0.71	0.56	0.71	0.76	0.82	0.88	0.95	1.03	1.29
5	0.71	0.53	0.71	0.76	0.85	0.92	0.99	1.10	1.29
6	0.71	0.50	0.71	0.76	0.87	0.96	1.04	1.15	1.29
7	0.71	0.47	0.71	0.76	0.90	0.99	1.09	1.21	1.29
8	0.71	0.45	0.71	0.76	0.92	1.02	1.14	1.27	1.29
9	0.71	0.42	0.71	0.76	0.95	1.05	1.17	1.29	1.29
10	0.71	0.40	0.71	0.76	0.96	1.08	1.21	1.29	1.29

Performance Rating	Below Minimum	Lower 1/3	Middle 1/3	Upper 1/3	Above Maximum
6	21%	16%	13%	1%	0
5	17	13	11	9	0
4	14	11	9	7	0
3	11	9	7	5	0
2	8	6	5	4	0
1	6	4	3	2	0
0	0	0	0	0	

Table 5-37. Position in range after merit adjustment (mid 1/3 = 0.90 - 1.10)—82 percent spread

tion, a range of $71,000 to $129,000 is tested for a six-percent annual structural increase for 10 years. The issue is how quickly a person currently at the minimum ($71,000) will progress through the range if the structure is adjusted annually by six percent.

Note that performance rating of 0 drops progressively further below minimum; however, this effect is purely academic, since such an unacceptable performer would soon be terminated. Rating 1 just stays even with the minimum, whereas rating 2 achieves a very limited growth. Rating 3 does not move to the middle one-third until the seventh year, whereas rating 4 reaches this level in the fifth year, rating 5 in the fourth year, and rating 6 in the third year. Only ratings 5 and 6 move into the upper one-third—the former after eight years and the latter after five years.

These progressions must be examined in terms of what appears reasonable. Assuming the norm is performance rating 3, should such an executive take seven years to move to the middle one-third (i.e., to perform in a fully satisfactory manner)? Probably not. It may be concluded that for this particular level, four or five years is more logical.

Another reason salary ranges get wider as one progresses through the organization is the recognition that it will take longer to attain a level of fully satisfactory performance. There are four ways to improve this rate of progression: (1) lower the structural increase percentage, (2) increase the merit percentage amounts, (3) narrow the range, or (4) shorten the interval between increases.

Assuming the structural pay increase is a reasonable assessment of market increase, logic dictates not to lower it. On the other hand, increasing the merit amounts sets a troublesome precedent. A compromise strategy would allow the desirable position to be attained over several years, and thereby, minimize significant up-down repercussions.

Narrowing the range can have a significant impact. In the earlier example, the maximum-over-minimum spread was 82 percent; by lowering this to 50 percent (and thereby starting our hypothetical employee closer to the midpoint) the impact is noticeable as shown in Table 5-38. Note that for most performance classifications, it has meant movement into the middle and upper portions of the range several years sooner.

Year	Range Minimum	Performance Rating							Range Maximum
		0	1	2	3	4	5	6	
0	0.80	0.80	0.80	0.80	0.80	0.80	0.80	0.80	1.20
1	0.80	0.75	0.80	0.82	0.84	0.86	0.88	0.91	1.20
2	0.80	0.71	0.80	0.83	0.83	0.90	0.94	1.00	1.20
3	0.80	0.67	0.80	0.85	0.90	0.94	1.00	1.07	1.20
4	0.80	0.63	0.80	0.86	0.93	0.99	1.05	1.14	1.20
5	0.80	0.60	0.80	0.86	0.95	1.03	1.10	1.19	1.20
6	0.80	0.56	0.80	0.86	0.98	1.06	1.15	1.20	1.20
7	0.80	0.53	0.80	0.86	1.01	1.09	1.19	1.20	1.20
8	0.80	0.50	0.80	0.86	1.02	1.13	1.20	1.20	1.20
9	0.80	0.47	0.80	0.86	1.03	1.16	1.20	1.20	1.20
10	0.80	0.45	0.80	0.86	1.04	1.17	1.20	1.20	1.20

Table 5-38. Position in range after merit adjustment (mid 1/3 = 0.93 - 1.07)—50 percent spread

Shortening the time interval between adjustments also creates faster movement through the structure. For example, changing adjustment frequency from once a year to once every six months for everyone in the lower one-third of the range has a very dramatic impact, as seen in Table 5-39. Note that with the 82 percent spread, performance rating 3 moves to the middle one-third in three years (compared to seven years in the first grid using only annual increases), and rating 6 (the top performer) gets into the middle one-third in one year and the upper one-third in four years.

Table 5-40 reflects the compound effect of reducing the range spread from 82 percent to 50 percent and reviewing pay every six months for those in the lower one-third of the structure. Rating 3 is now in the middle one-third after two years, the same time frame it takes rating 6 to move into the upper one-third. Management philosophy will dictate the optimum construction of range spread, merit matrix, and review frequency.

Promotion Increases

Promotional-increase guidelines are just as important as merit-increase policy. Few companies structure their pay programs to properly compensate the promoted individual. Too often, a promotion is rewarded with a flat percentage increase (e.g., 10 percent) even though the same logic that applies to merit increases also applies to promotional adjustments. For an individual receiving a significant increase in responsibilities, a 10-percent increase may still be far short of the new job's pay minimum; conversely, it may be a modest organizational change and therefore 10 per-

Year	Range Minimum	Performance Rating							Range Minimum
		0	1	2	3	4	5	6	
0	0.71	0.71	0.71	0.71	0.71	0.71	0.71	0.71	1.29
1	0.71	0.67	0.74	0.77	0.81	0.85	0.89	0.94	1.29
2	0.71	0.63	0.77	0.81	0.85	0.89	0.94	1.00	1.29
3	0.71	0.60	0.78	0.86	0.93	0.93	0.99	1.07	1.29
4	0.71	0.56	0.80	0.91	0.94	0.96	1.04	1.14	1.29
5	0.71	0.53	0.82	0.91	0.95	0.98	1.08	1.19	1.29
6	0.71	0.50	0.83	0.91	0.96	1.01	1.14	1.25	1.29
7	0.71	0.47	0.85	0.91	0.97	1.04	1.17	1.29	1.29
8	0.71	0.45	0.87	0.91	0.98	1.07	1.20	1.29	1.29
9	0.71	0.42	0.88	0.91	0.99	1.10	1.24	1.29	1.29
10	0.71	0.40	0.90	0.91	1.00	1.13	1.27	1.29	1.29

Table 5-39. Position in range after six-month merit adjustment (mid 1/3 = 0.90 - 1.10)—82-percent spread

Year	Range Minimum	Performance Rating							Range Minimum
		0	1	2	3	4	5	6	
0	0.80	0.80	0.80	0.80	0.80	0.80	0.80	0.80	1.20
1	0.80	0.75	0.83	0.86	0.91	0.96	1.00	1.06	1.20
2	0.80	0.71	0.87	0.92	0.94	1.00	1.04	1.13	1.20
3	0.80	0.67	0.88	0.97	0.97	1.03	1.09	1.20	1.20
4	0.80	0.63	0.90	0.97	0.99	1.06	1.15	1.20	1.20
5	0.80	0.60	0.92	0.97	1.00	1.09	1.18	1.20	1.20
6	0.80	0.58	0.94	0.97	1.01	1.12	1.20	1.20	1.20
7	0.80	0.53	0.96	0.97	1.02	1.15	1.20	1.20	1.20
8	0.80	0.50	0.94	0.97	1.03	1.16	1.20	1.20	1.20
9	0.80	0.47	0.94	0.97	1.04	1.17	1.20	1.20	1.20
10	0.80	0.45	0.94	0.97	1.05	1.18	1.20	1.20	1.20

Table 5-40. Position in range after six-month merit adjustment (mid 1/3 = 0.93 – 1.07)—50-percent spread

cent would be overly generous (e.g., pay is already well within the middle one-third of the new job's pay grade). Remember that position in grade is the company's best assessment of the individual's worth vis-à-vis the marketplace and other individuals within the company. Following such logic, a guide could be constructed such as the one shown in Table 5-41, with varying percentages of increase depending on position in the new job's salary structure.

Below Minimum	Lower 1/3	Middle 1/3
25%	15%	5%

Table 5-41. Promotional guidelines

To test the quality of the adjustment, one could ask, "What would I offer this individual to accept this job if he or she came from another company?" Under such an examination, most internal promotional pay actions pale by comparison.

A well-thought-out promotional pay policy is essential to retaining internal equity, not to mention its value during a period of federal pay controls when promotional increases are usually easier to accomplish than merit adjustments.

SUMMARY AND CONCLUSIONS

Salary is the compensation element on which the other four elements are layered. It is therefore critical that a person's salary be reflective of organizational importance, viewed both internally and externally. As shown in Figure 5-24, job evaluation sets the minimum and maximum to be paid for a position. The employee's performance combined with experience is the basis for determining the rate of movement through this structure. Lower in the organization, this may be based on a time factor (e.g. time in job or since degree) or level of knowledge/skills. At the executive level, it is based solely on performance.

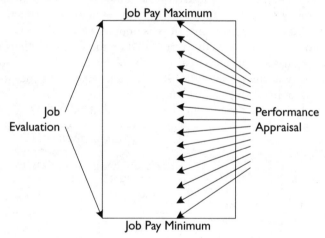

Figure 5-24. Job evaluation vs. performance appraisal

A promotion to a higher job grade may also result in a salary increase. Indeed, the greatest opportunity for increased salary is through promotions. A CEO's current salary consists primarily of prior promotional increases, not performance adjustments. The latter are relatively modest because there is no downside risk—salaries are rarely if ever reduced. Therefore, incentives, not salary, are the primary vehicles for implementing pay-for-performance. When incentives are available, the salary element may be used to reward ongoing work, while incentives reward achievement of specific goals or objectives. When incentives are not available, the salary element must attempt to do both.

Poor to mediocre performers must be identified and counseled. If counseling, skill development, and reassignment to other jobs are not successful measures, terminate employment. Such individuals cost the company multiples of their pay, after factoring in hiring costs, support costs, mistakes, and lost opportunities. The cost of severance pay may be a bargain.

When marginal tax rates increase, executives may experience a reduction in net income since few companies adjust salaries for tax increases. On the other hand, *lower* tax rates do not provoke salary decreases. For a period of time up to 1964, we had a marginal tax rate of 91 percent for income in excess of $400,000 (married person filing joint return). This later dropped to 70 percent, then 50 percent, and even 28 percent. Know of anyone who reduced salaries to reflect the increase in take-home pay?

Wage controls such as existed in 1971 to 1974, typically restrain salary more than the other four pay elements, while formulas in place are allowed to generate increases far in excess of salary limits. More recently, legislation has slowed salary increases to top-paid executives. Salary is reportable as earned income to the individual and tax deductible to the company up to $1 million a year. To the extent that salary exceeds $1 million, the tax effectiveness is reduced because of the non-deductible portion. The tax effectiveness of salary was described in Chapter 4. This annual limit applies not simply to salary, but to all annual pay that does not meet section 162(m) of the Internal Revenue Code. The Omnibus Budget Reconciliation Act of 1993 added this section. This limit will be discussed further in Chapters 7 and 8. Ways will be described whereby amounts in excess of $1 million can be deducted by the company. However, there appears to be no way to exclude the salary portion of annual pay from the Section 162(m) limit.

In addition to tax deductibility restraints, there is another very good reason for putting a restraint on the salary of the CEO. It effectively puts a lid on the salary of others in the organization, permitting the emphasis on incentive pay (which will be discussed in Chapters 7 and 8). For example, setting salary at the twenty-fifth percentile and salary plus incentive pay at the fiftieth percentile permits a major shift to incentives.

The accounting and tax treatment of salary is highlighted in Table 5-42.

Paid	Individual Tax Liability	Company	
		Expense Charge	**Tax Deduction**
Currently	Now—Ordinary Income	Now	Now
Deferred	Later—Ordinary Income	Now	Later
Principle	When Received	When Known	When Paid

Table 5-42. Summary of accounting and tax treatment of current and deferred salary

Note: You are again reminded not to rely on accounting, tax, SEC, or other professional service statements in this chapter. You need to seek appropriate professional counsel for such guidance. Statements made in this chapter and elsewhere are offered as being illustrative to help frame such further investigations by the reader with counsel.

With the salary element behind us, we move to the next compensation element—employee benefits and perquisites

Chapter 6

Employee Benefits and Perquisites

his chapter combines two compensation elements—employee benefits and perquisites—since executives participate in both. Perquisites (perks for short) begin where employee benefits leave off and for that reason the two are combined in this chapter.

Importance by Type of Company

Like the salary element described in Chapter 4, the importance of employee benefits and perquisites in the compensation package depends on whether the company is non-profit or for-profit, publicly held or privately held. This is illustrated in Table 6-1 and Table 6-2. The relatively higher importance of employee benefits and perquisites for not-for-profit companies is caused by restrictions on use of incentive pay. Thus, employee benefits and perquisites have to pick up some of the slack.

Eligibility

Employee benefit eligibility typically applies to all full-time and part-time employees. However, eligibility for perquisites is very selective. Typically, it is the most exclusive of the five pay elements and applies only to executives as defined in Chapter 1. Key position, salary, job grade, title, reporting relationship, or some combination of these can define an "executive."

Employee Benefits vs. Perquisites

The *employee benefits* element deals with providing time off with pay, service programs, health care, survivor protection, and retirement coverage to all employees in the organization. The word distinguishing employee benefits from perquisites is "all." Perquisites are available only to executives and could be called *executive benefits*. They are given to only a select few executives

	Market Stage			
	Threshold	**Growth**	**Maturity**	**Decline**
For-Profits • Publicly traded • Privately held	 Low Low	 Moderate Moderate	 Moderate Moderate	 High High
Not-for-profits	High	High	High	High

Table 6-1. Importance of employee benefits by type of company

	Market Stage			
	Threshold	**Growth**	**Maturity**	**Decline**
For-Profits • Publicly traded • Privately held	 Low Low	 Low Moderate	 Moderate High	 High High
Not-for-profits	High	High	High	High

Table 6-2. Importance of perquisites by type of company

based on organization level (and perhaps to some extent, past performance). However, like benefits they have a low risk factor because degree of participation is not varied with performance. In addition, once given, they are rarely taken away. Perks are either restorative (replacing an employee benefit taken away by law) or additive (given in addition to the employee benefit received by all). Perquisites begin where employee benefits end. However, employee benefits are important to the executive as part of the total compensation package.

Some perks, such as supplemental pension plans, are of significant dollar value to the executive. Others are more status symbols where the intrinsic (or psychic) income is of greater value than the extrinsic (dollar) value. Cost effective to both the organization and the executive because of economies of large-scale coverage, perks meet many needs the executive otherwise would have to provide personally. For this reason, perks are an important element of executive compensation. The extent of coverage in benefit plans is typically determined by years of service and/or level of pay, whereas with perks it is a function of organization level.

Initially, employee benefits were identified as *fringe benefits*—a term denoting peripheral importance. With many companies today expending over a third of their payroll on this element, it is certainly no longer an item of peripheral importance. Employee benefits have risen in importance and cost because: (a) businesses want to provide competitive packages; (b) trade unions use them as a bargaining chip in negotiations with employers; and (c) many benefit programs get favorable tax treatment. The latter is especially important. Namely, employee-benefit expenses are usually tax deductible to the employer and, when deferred, are not taxed to the employee until received. In some cases, they are not taxed at all.

Many perks simply supplement the basic benefit program by lifting or completely removing dollar maximums. This applies essentially to disability, retirement, and survivor protection plans.

A prime advantage of such supplemental plans is that the company can be selective in determining participation, extent of coverage, forfeiture and vesting provisions, and period of protection. The disadvantage is that the company receives no tax deduction until the benefit is paid. The advantage is that the executive receives a greater benefit than otherwise available, at reasonably attractive income-tax rates. However, frequently the benefit is lower than comparable after-tax cash value. Thus, perquisites must be structured very carefully, especially since employees will press for extended coverage of existing programs and the addition of new ones for top executives.

Because the main appeal of perquisites is their restricted use, they either (1) identify a group more exclusive than that covered by the long-term incentive plan or (2) reinforce the distinction between those covered under long-term incentives and all others, by defining eligibility as participation in the long-term plan.

Although some forms of employee benefits can be traced back a hundred years or so, due to their limited application, employee benefits truly were "fringe" in nature until World War II. The Stabilization Act of 1942 froze wages and salaries but allowed limited benefit improvements; needless to say, there were almost limitless "limited-benefit improvements." Then, after the war, the U.S. Supreme Court ruled that pension plans were negotiable items for collective bargaining agreements. Shortly thereafter, inflationary pressures caused by the Korean conflict forced the Defense Production Act of 1950, which again allowed "limited" benefit improvements. Within 10 years, "fringe benefits" exploded into "employee benefits."

To provide employee benefits, companies have turned to group insurance plans rather than individual plans. By clustering individuals under a group plan, the carrier minimizes "adverse selection," in other words, that someone will receive a payment far in excess of premiums paid. Individual risk is dispersed through a large group. This permits the insurance carrier to provide a lower premium per person than under individual contracts. Reduced administrative and selling expenses are also a factor in the lower rate per employee.

Designing benefit plans raises a number of questions. What benefits should be provided? Who will be eligible? What will be covered? Will there be degrees of coverage? How will it be administered? What portion of the cost will employees pay? How will the plan be funded (e.g., insurance contract, trust agreement, or self-administered)? What program balance is consistent with the organization's culture?

Cost Definitions

Before proceeding any further, let me stress the importance of *carefully* defining benefit costs as a percentage of pay. While variations are numerous dependent on what is and what is *not* a benefit, essentially there are three major definitions.

1. Total cost for all benefits (numerator) divided by gross pay or W-2 (denominator). On the surface, this appears sound and logical. The problem is that a number of benefits are *cash benefits*, which are reflected in the W-2, and thus, present in both numerator and denominator. When such benefits increase (e.g., vacation pay), benefit costs may show less increase than costs for non-W-2 items. To illustrate, assuming total benefit costs of $30 million and total payroll of $100 million, we have a benefit rate of 30 percent ($30 million divided by $100 million). If a benefit improvement of $1 million is implemented for a non-W-2 item, the total benefit cost is 31 percent ($31 million divided by $100 million). However, for improvements also counted in the denominator, the final tally is 30.7 percent ($31 million divided by $101 million).

2. Total cost for all benefits (numerator) divided by base pay for time actually worked (denominator). The numerator is the same as in the earlier definition, but the denominator consists only of base pay for time actually worked. This is probably the optimal formula, because all items are accounted for and only once. To illustrate, assume the $100 million in the previous example consisted of $90 million for base pay and $10 million for time not worked. The $10 million would be subtracted from the denominator but *not* added to the numerator, as it is already included in the $30 million. The benefit rate, therefore, would be 33.3 percent ($30 million divided by $90 million).

3. Benefits costs excluding time off with pay (numerator) divided by gross pay (denominator). Of the three, this approach will reflect the lowest benefit percentage, simply because it has the highest denominator and lowest numerator. It occurs in companies that lack payroll records that record lost time with pay—invariably for those on the monthly payroll. Based on the previous example, this would result in a benefit rate of 20 percent ($20 million divided by $100 million). The numerator is only $20 million because the lost-time pay has not been included.

The variations in these three formulas demonstrate the importance of clearly understanding the definition of benefit costs. Using the same data, but changing definitions, we calculated three different rates: 30 percent, 33.3 percent, and 20 percent.

Accounting, Tax, and SEC Implications

Accounting rules concerning the cost of benefits and perquisites are basically simple and straightforward. Generally, any costs expensed by the company must be taken as a charge to earnings (found in the income statement under an item usually identified as "selling, general, and administrative expenses"). For those items that extend beyond one year, an accrual is established to retire a liability charge on the balance sheet.

As was discussed in the tax section of Chapter 4 (Stakeholders), the tax effectiveness varies for both the executive and the company. Shown in Table 6-3, the tax effectiveness of the employee benefit or perquisite for executives ranges from a "1" (best) to a "5" (worst). For the company, it ranges from an "A" (best) to a "D" (worst). An additional factor is timing of taxation and tax deductibility. Tax-qualified pension plans, for example, permit a company to take a tax deduction when a contribution is made to the plan, whereas employees are not taxed until they

Employee	Company
1. Not taxable	A. No expense
2. Taxable but 100% tax deductible	B. 100% tax deductible
3. Taxable but deductible if above allowances or taxable above certain allowances	C. Partially tax deductible
4. Taxed as long-term capital gains	D. Not tax deductible
5. Taxed as ordinary income or short-term capital gains	

Table 6-3. Taxation and tax deductions

receive the benefit. The taxability and tax-deduction availability will be reviewed throughout this section.

The Securities and Exchange Commission (SEC) disclosure rules typically apply only to those executives named in the proxy. As these are updated from time to time, it is important to determine what needs to be reported and in what format. Typically, the requirements deal with perquisites rather than with employee benefits, although such items as pension size may be a combination of both.

Plan Types

Benefit programs can usually be classified under one of five categories: time off with pay, service programs, health care, survivor protection, and retirement. How important a specific benefit is to an executive depends on category and program limits, but benefits could be generally classified as of low, moderate, or high importance.

TIME OFF WITH PAY

As the phrase implies, this is payment for time not worked. It ranges from coffee breaks and meal periods on one extreme to sabbaticals and termination pay on the other. Programs covering paid time off are the opposite of pay-for-performance. They are pay-for-non-performance! Some employers avoid overlaps in coverage of this benefit either through managed time-loss programs and/or flexible employee benefit programs, as will be discussed later in this chapter.

Paid time off often takes rather subtle forms. For example, executives who are members of a board of directors of another company rarely take a vacation day to attend the board meeting. Rather, they charge it off as a business day. Even for those who do use vacation time, how many use company time to read reports and recommendations preparatory to attending the board meeting? How often are business meetings scheduled at resort facilities with half-day business agendas? Who really watches late arrivals and early departures? Because most executives put in 60-70 hour workweeks, such paid time off may be a phantom benefit—available but rarely used. This is probably true for the hard-driving, results-oriented individuals but no so for those who no longer reenact the Charge of the Light Brigade. Perhaps the most accurate conclusion is that the use of this benefit is in proportion to the lack of effectiveness of the executive. With few exceptions, this benefit is taxed as ordinary income to the executive and, therefore, 100 percent tax deductible to the company.

Holidays

The executive, like everyone else in the company, is eligible to take a specified number of *paid holidays*. For most companies, these holidays are equivalent to two to three weeks (i.e., 10 to 15 days). In addition to the basic six (New Year's Day, Memorial Day, Fourth of July, Labor Day, Thanksgiving, and Christmas), common additions include: Martin Luther King Day, President's Day, Columbus Day, Veteran's Day, Election Day, and the employee's birthday. In addition, holidays called "floaters" may be provided. These are either predetermined by the company (such as the Friday after Thanksgiving) or left to employee choice. If left to employee choice, they may be sufficient in number to substitute for other popular holidays and are especially helpful for individuals wishing to take a religious holiday (e.g., Good Friday or Yom Kippur). Sometimes holidays are welcome respites; more often, they mean the executive works at home instead of in the office. As such, holidays are of moderate importance to executives.

Vacations

More important than paid holidays are paid *vacations*, which usually depend on the length of service with the company. A typical vacation benefit would allow two weeks after the first year of work, three weeks after five years, four weeks after 10 (or 15) years, five weeks after 20 (or 25) years, and perhaps six weeks after 30 (or 35) years of service. Such a schedule is reasonable for the executive who has been with the company 10 or more years. However, not many newly hired executives will be content with two weeks vacation, even workaholics who are unlikely to take the full allowance. Thus, even if the executive is unable to take more than two weeks vacation a year, he or she will want the option. To resolve such situations, some companies adopt a minimum age as an alternative eligibility criterion for all employees. For example, regardless of years of service, persons age 40 to 49 will receive four weeks, 50 to 59 will receive five weeks, and 60 or more will receive six weeks.

It is not unusual for companies to provide liberalized vacations for certain executives, identified by organization level and/or title. This may be a flat four- or six-week minimum regardless of service (important to the executive recently hired who is in mid-career), or it may be a supplement (e.g., two weeks) to the basic policy so that the executive will always have more vacation than other employees with the same service. In addition, the company may pay part or all of the executive's vacation expenses, or the vacation may be combined with a business trip. Another perquisite is to allow executives to accumulate any unused portion for one or more years—thus providing the opportunity to take a mini-sabbatical, to phase in to retirement, or to soften the blow of termination. (The accounting impact of this policy should be carefully reviewed.) The perceived value of vacations is probably moderate for the all-employee portion and somewhat higher if supplemental and carryovers are permitted.

Court Duty

Companies typically supplement the allowance provided for jury or witness duty. In other words, the company pays the individual as usual but expects the employee to sign over to the company any pay received. Some companies allow the employee to retain any allowance provided. Periods of absence extend from a couple of days to months if serving on a complex case. The longer the absence, the more difficult it is for the executive to stay current with work and, therefore, the benefit is of low executive importance.

Workers' Compensation and Disability

Accident or illness is covered by *workers' compensation* if work-related or *disability pay* plans if non-occupational in nature. Although there have been instances of suits for workers' compensation coverage in cases of heart attack (on the grounds that work stress contributed to the attack), executives are typically more concerned with disability benefits than workers' compensation. Disability plans are short-term or long-term, depending on the length of absence. Normally, the short-term plan will cover the first six (sometimes 12) months of absence at full salary (possibly including annual incentive). While paid sick leave is a variation of short-term disability pay, it differs in that at the end of the year, any unused sick leave is paid in cash. Disability pay is expressed in the maximum number of days or weeks that absence for medical reasons will be paid. Sick leave is usually described in the number of days permitted each year. The difference is that disability pay is given only if absent; unused sick leave at year-end is typically paid in cash. Long-term disability (LTD) benefits begin when short-term benefits expire. Unlike short-term benefits, they are typically integrated with Social Security. In other words, LTD benefits are added to social security payments to reach a specific pay target such as two-thirds of pay. In addition, other statutory benefits and other plans in which the employer pays all or a portion of the expense may offset them. However, LTD benefit amounts are not usually affected by additional insurance benefits purchased independently by the employee. Normally, LTD benefits run for two years if the individual is unable to return to the same job he or she previously held. After that, payments are contingent upon ability to work in any field of suitable employment.

Since a significant portion of plan benefits are after-tax and gross pay is pretax, plan benefits rarely exceed about two-thirds of gross pay. In addition, a number of expenses associated with work (e.g., transportation) are suspended, further reducing the needed income-replacement level. From the company's viewpoint, benefits should not be so high they discourage a return to work.

Typically, broad-based LTD benefit plans discriminate against higher-paid employees in two ways: (1) incentive pay is often excluded as a definition of pay, so the formula becomes two-thirds of salary rather than two-thirds of earnings, and (2) there is a maximum monthly benefit (e.g., $3,500). Thus, as shown in Table 6-4, the percentage of pay replaced progressively decreases at upper income levels. However, it is not uncommon to supplement short- and long-term disability payments by: (1) increasing or completely removing the dollar maximum on benefits and/or (2) increasing the time period of benefits (both for partial or full pay). Some companies choose to allow the executive to take out separate LTD coverage and then reimburse the individual at the end of the year. If the company pays the premium, the proceeds are taxable to the executive; if the executive pays the premium costs, the proceeds are tax-free. The all-employee disability may be of low importance to the executive because of the restrictions cited; however, a generous supplement is of high importance to the executive as it potentially protects against income loss.

Family and Medical Leave

The 1993 Family and Medical Leave Act (FAMLA) legally mandated what some employers had been providing voluntarily—time off to tend to family issues and/or recover from a medical problem. FAMLA requires job-protected, unpaid time off for up to 12 weeks in a 12-month peri-

Salary		Monthly LTD Benefit	Percntage of Pay
Annual	Monthly		
$50,000	$4,166.67	$2,791.67	66.7%
75,000	6,250.00	3,500.00	56.0
100,000	8,333.33	3,500.00	42.0
250,000	20,833.33	3,500.00	16.8
1,000,000	83,333.33	3,500.00	4.2

Table 6-4. LTD benefit vs. salary

od. Preexisting medical coverage also must be continued. Some companies will consider at least a portion of the lost time as paid time off. The job protection aspect may be of moderate importance to an executive worried about being replaced.

Funeral Leave

Funeral leave (or bereavement pay) is typically limited to about three days' salary at time of death of a person in the immediate or extended family. The latter is a more generous definition of coverage than the former. Since an executive will most likely be expected to make up for lost time, funeral leave is of low importance.

General Leave and Sabbaticals

In addition to the aforementioned leaves, some companies allow a general leave of absence for other reasons such as volunteer work. This leave of up to one year, depending on length of service is typically unpaid, although some companies pay a portion of the period.

Executive sabbaticals are more generous than leaves available to others in the organization. A typical executive sabbatical would be a six-month period, fully paid (or fully supplemented), during which the individual undertakes a civic responsibility, volunteer work, pursues an advanced degree, or simply "gets away from it all" in order to return to work with fully recharged batteries. Conceptually, sabbaticals are logical and meet an apparent need, but many executives are afraid to take advantage of the benefit. Some are concerned that old job may not be there when they get back, especially if the sabbatical is for a year or more. Like generous vacation policies, it is of at least moderate importance.

Flexible Work Schedules

In response to a growing need among employees to balance work and family, many companies have adopted flexible work schedules for those interested. While such schedules do not provide additional pay for lost time, they increase flexibility in the workweek schedule. Flexible scheduling includes variable start/stop times, variable workdays, and job sharing (e.g., two half time workers equally share one full time position). It also includes work at home, frequently referred to as telecommuting because of the electronic movement of the work rather than the physical movement of the individual. Not only does it eliminate transportation costs, evidence suggests it improves morale and increases productivity. For executives, the flexible work schedule also means working *while* commuting, whether being driven to work or back, or in the air. Transportation provides another opportunity for the executive to extend his/her workweek.

Flexible work schedules for the executive's staff may make work more difficult because invariably the person the executive wants to see is not in. However, the flexibility to work late in exchange for coming in later than scheduled may be of moderate importance to the executive. Another option is working longer during the workweek to free up some weekend time for family.

Employment Contract

For most employees, the employment contract is a *social* not a legal commitment. For decades, the social contract between companies and their employees implied that as long as workers did their job well, the company would keep them employed. No longer. The prevailing "contract" is that in lieu of a job guarantee, the employer provides opportunities to acquire new job skills. As long as an employee's skills are needed and performance requirements met, the individual will have a job. When either is no longer true, the individual is discharged to find work elsewhere but with newly acquired skills. In other words, the long-standing "employment-at-will" principle is truer now than ever before. In the absence of an employment or union contract, a company may terminate employment whenever it wishes as long as termination is not discriminatory as defined by law. (With the number of discrimination cases going to court, some companies are looking at insurance contracts to cover associated legal costs.)

Executives taking on new responsibilities and/or new employees should seek a written employment contract. Such a contract will typically specify the period of time for which it is in effect, what constitutes acceptable performance, and what the executive will receive in the way of pay (e.g., salary, short- and long-term incentive amounts, and specific benefit and perquisite coverage). In addition, it may include an automatic annual renewal unless notified by the other party within a specified time period before the end of the contract. A contract period of three to five years is common, along with the automatic renewal clause (probably terminating in case of disability, retirement, or death). A process for resolving disputes is also a common feature. The contract will typically include a clause barring the executive from disclosing confidential information, often for an indefinite period. Additionally, a clause may be inserted that prevents the executive from engaging in any activity considered competitive to the employer. This *non-compete* clause usually extends beyond the contract term and is linked to eligibility for severance payments. Violation of this requirement not only results in the loss of future payments but may require the return of previous amounts (including exercised stock options for a prescribed period of time) if a *claw-back clause* has been included. While companies prefer a broadly defined, long-term non-compete clause, they are difficult to enforce. The courts are inclined to be restrictive in both definition and term. Companies may be more aggressive in enforcing contracts when the executive has defected to a competitor. A clause may also be included to permit renegotiation upon mutual agreement of the company and the executive. In addition to stipulating pay during the period of employment, the contract will also often include a *signing bonus* and specify the terms and conditions of severance pay. The signing bonus is intended to cover what the executive is leaving behind. This includes at least the current value of forfeited pay and benefits. It may also include the present value of anticipated future appreciation of both outstanding awards as well as those not yet received by the executive. The form of payment may be cash, stock options, and/or restricted stock. Additionally, a package of other perquisites such as those described in this chapter may be put together. (Perhaps executives should employ an agent to negotiate their contracts, as do prominent sports figures. Few would argue that the use of agents has not been successful for the men and women who are being paid whopping amounts of money to continue to play games learned as children.)

The employment contract is most prevalent in smaller organizations, although larger companies have used them to obtain key executives or retain an executive (after a successful acquisition or merger). There is no tax effectiveness rating in a contract per se, and its component parts are taxed in the manner they would normally be taxed. The value to the executive is continued employment for a prescribed period of time and a very clear understanding of the compensation to be received; the value to the company is that it has increased its probability of retaining a key executive (especially if the contract includes a non-compete clause and protection of confidential information if the executive leaves). Even those not covered by an extensive employment contract may be required to sign a confidentiality agreement at the time of hire or along with a significant change in responsibilities. The content of the agreement may vary from one unit to another within the company; however, typically it would require the executive not to disclose any confidential information to those outside the company without explicit permission.

The employment contract should also define how much severance pay (if any) is added on to the unworked, paid period of the contract. An employment contract is of very high importance to those taking on new responsibilities and/or a new employer. Without such protection, executives and employees must rely on the company's severance pay policy. However, the terms of severance pay will likely include prorated incentive payments and vested stock-option grants.

Severance Pay

Performance and Organizational Restructuring. The employee who does not perform satisfactorily or who is no longer needed may receive another form of pay for time not worked—*severance pay*. Conceptually, severance pay is intended to bridge the period of unemployment, and supplements unemployment compensation provided by state and federal governments. Initially, the state benefits were not subject to income taxes; however, they are no longer completely excludable. Section 85 of the Internal Revenue Code (IRC) limits the amount that may be excluded. This amount is sufficiently low that most executives will pay tax on unemployment benefits if they have any other income that year, since benefits are added to any other gross income during the year.

Many years ago, it was not uncommon for the boss to tell a worker on Friday afternoon, "You're fired! Don't come to work on Monday." In lieu of advance notice, the company might give two weeks' pay. Over the years, trade unions negotiated an additional week per year of service, thereby making a distinction between short- and long-service employees.

The 1987 Worker Adjustment and Retraining Notification (WARN) Act addressed the issue of prior notice. It required employers with 100 or more workers to give at least 60 days advance notice of a plant closing or mass layoff. During the two-month period between notification and effective date, the individual was to be paid (and assumedly would work). Enlightened companies use the same schedule for individual actions as well. Companies are usually lenient during the notification period, especially with executives, in allowing time off for job searches. Additionally, the amended Age Discrimination in Employment Act (ADEA) of 1967 prohibits termination based solely on age if over age 40.

A typical company severance plan for all employees might be two weeks pay plus two weeks for every year of service. Therefore, an individual with 12 years' service would receive 26 weeks, or about six months' pay. Some companies distinguish between individual and group actions in their formulas. Thus, they may give two weeks plus two-weeks of pay for every year of service for an individual whose performance is no longer acceptable, but will give two weeks plus three weeks for every year of service when an installation is being closed or a department within a site phased out. Such payments occur only after all attempts to otherwise place affected employees elsewhere within the company have failed, since the individual is being terminated due to organizational restructuring not poor performance. Some companies add an additional week for every year of service if an employee signs a waiver indicating he or she accepts the severance as full settlement and will not pursue legal options. Where waivers are used, their legality should be carefully reviewed. Among other requirements, waivers must comply with the 1990 Older Workers' Protection Act (OWPBA). This act requires: (1) the waiver be clear and understandable; (2) the rights being waived for compensation must be stated (future acts of age discrimination cannot be waived) and must refer to rights and claims protected by the ADEA; (3) advising the employee to review the waiver with an attorney own; and (4) the individual have at least 21 days (45 days if the termination is part of a group action) to determine whether or not to accept and at least seven days after signing to change mind and revoke the contract.

In designing severance pay formulas, consider not only years of service but also age and what might be available from the pension plan. For example, a person being severed with 30 years of service at age 65 probably has less financial need (being eligible for a full pension) than a 55 year old also with 30 years service. The second individual might be able to retire, but the pension may be significantly discounted or reduced for early retirement. While considering age in this situation seems logical, it is difficult to do because of age discrimination rules.

The Department of Labor (DOL) has also looked at the pension/severance issue in light of the Employee Retirement Income Security Act (ERISA). It concluded in 1979 that for severance payments not to be considered a pension plan and come under all of its requirements, severance benefits must not exceed two years of pay, and payment must be completed within two years of termination (or after normal retirement date if early retirement benefits were elected). In determining the amount of severance, all compensation including employee benefits should be considered. While some all-company severance plans are rather generous, few exceed two years' pay. To illustrate, a formula providing four weeks plus three weeks per year of service for a person with 30 years would still be eight weeks short of two years. Nonetheless, the Multiemployer Pension Plan Amendments Act of 1980 amended the DOL restrictions and permitted the Secretary of Labor to establish rules by which severance plans could be treated as welfare rather than pension plans under ERISA, thereby increasing flexibility in design and funding.

Most broad-based severance plans are of only moderate importance to executives since the protected pay period (i.e., weeks of pay) is likely to be insufficient. It typically takes longer for higher-paid individuals to find a new job simply because there are fewer of them. It is possible to devise a formula to address this problem. A simple one would be one day of severance pay for every $1,000 of earnings or alternatively develop a graduated scale such as:

- Up to $50,000—one week per every $25,000
- $50,000 - $100,000—one week per every $20,000
- $100,000 - $250,000—one week per every $15,000
- $250,000 and up—one week per every $10,000

The graduated scale and the flat formula of one day for every $1,000 of earnings are illustrated in Table 6-5—both with and without an additional factor of two weeks per year of service. As stated earlier, anything over 104 weeks would be capped at the two-year maximum. The flat formula without a service add-on could result in a very large severance for short service. The graduated formula seems to reflect a nice balance of service and pay considerations. However, under the flat formula a person with 10 years service paid $250,000 would receive 50 weeks (70 weeks if there was a service add-on of two weeks per year of service); however, the same executive would receive only 14.5 weeks under the graduated formula, but 34.5 weeks with a service adjustment. Note that under $50,000, severance pay is two weeks plus two weeks per year of service.

Less egalitarian companies may adopt a more traditional two or three weeks per year of service for all employees except those whose pay is determined by the company's compensation committee. Disclosing the severance pay policy in this manner effectively cloaks the benefits that will be paid to executives.

Flat Formula					
Pay	No Service Add-on	Plus Two Weeks Per Year of Service			
		5 Years	10 Years	20 Years	30 Years
$500,000	100	110	120	140	160
$250,000	50	60	70	90	110
$100,000	20	30	40	60	80
$50,000	10	20	30	50	70
Graduated Formula					
$500,000	39.5	49.5	59.5	79.5	99.5
$250,000	14.5	24.5	34.5	54.5	74.5
$100,000	4.5	14.5	24.5	44.5	66.5
$50,000	2.0	12.0	22.0	42.0	62.0

Table 6-5. Flat vs. graduated severance formula

In addition to level of compensation, another factor in severance pay formulas is the general marketability of the departing executive. Other things being constant, the person with experience in several industries has an advantage over a person who has spent all of his or her life in one industry. Similarly, a person who has management experience in several functional disciplines is more marketable than a person who has specialized in one area. While these factors might not be as easily reduced to a formula as age, years of service, and level of compensation, they are just as important and could be considered in increasing or decreasing the payment.

Furthermore, companies are likely to be more generous with an individual who: has given all the outward appearances of trying; still makes consistently loyal statements about the organization; has made a significant contribution earlier in his or her career; and/or knows the location of a few skeletons. A cynic would argue these are all forms of conscience money; the pragmatist would indicate that any severance pay formula merely quantifies the agreed-to values for determining the amount of pay. The reason for a formula is consistency in application. The formula should adequately compensate for past service contributions without overly penalizing failure to perform.

Since severance pay is somewhat analogous to alimony, some argue for companies to make regular payments (not a lump sum which could be rapidly squandered). However, regular payments could serve as a disincentive for the individual to seek other job opportunities. Some argue that payments should not cease when a new job is found, for such an approach only encourages the employee to "cheat on the company." It is better, they say, to consider the remainder a bonus for getting the new job faster than anticipated. Others more logically argue that severance payments are transition awards until new employment is gained. Even when lump-sum payments are used, it may be advantageous to the individual whose employment is terminated later in the year to have a significant portion of the payment deferred to the subsequent year for tax purposes. Such arrangements must be carefully orchestrated to avoid constructive receipt issues.

Executives are terminated for failures in performance and/or the inability to mesh with decision-makers. As a matter of fact, the less-than-competent executive may keep the job if he or she is well liked by those responsible for making the termination decision, whereas a topflight performer might be terminated for making waves (and being seen as a personal challenge to the authority of others). Thus, in spite of many of the teachings of results-oriented management, what matters in some organizations is not how well one performs but the extent to which one's personality is compatible with others. Nonetheless, consistent failure to meet short-term objectives and/or long-term goals will lead to termination.

Termination for poor performance requires the individual be aware of the performance problem and be given an opportunity to correct it before the termination action. A company that uses its bonus plans to acknowledge performance can communicate to an executive very clearly about poor performance simply by cutting back or eliminating the bonus. In such companies, it would be unlikely that a person would have back-to-back zero-bonus years and still be around. In companies with modest variation in compensation adjustments, there is greater need for a face-to-face discussion with the executive about performance improvement. This is unlikely to happen since it is this same inability to deal with problem cases that causes modest compensation adjustments! This situation usually deteriorates until management finally fires the person, or convinces him or her to retire if that is a reasonable option.

Because of the potential loss of future income, severance pay benefits are of high importance to executives. It is always nice to know there is a good safety net. While severance pay is offered after termination due to ineffective performance of duties, it is not usually offered for terminations due to violation of company rules (e.g., gambling or drinking on the job) or insubordination. Additionally, committing an illegal act would be considered termination "for cause," providing no severance benefits.

Change of Control Contracts. These employment agreements specify pay and benefits that the executive will receive if the executive loses his or her position following a defined *change of control* (COC) of the company. The control change could be defined as: (1) a specific percentage of the voting shares that have been acquired by a person or organization (typically not less than 20 percent); (2) a merger; (3) a sale of a stated portion of the company's assets; (4) a specified change in the composition of the board of directors (composition of directors may be described as an unapproved change both in stated portion of the board and prescribed time period); and/or (5) liquidation or dissolution of the company. Depending on the language, the contract may be activated at time of shareholder approval or later when the transaction is completed. Typically, these are called *golden parachutes*.

There are two types of contracts that will trigger payment: single and double. A *single trigger contract* typically permits the covered executive to leave voluntarily within 30 days following a change in control and receive all the benefits stated in the contract. A *modified single trigger* contract provides severance benefits for a voluntary termination (typically within 30 days after a one-year anniversary of the defined change of control). Sometimes called a *walk-away,* it is in essence a delayed single trigger contract. Its purpose is to retain key executives for a stated period to ensure a smooth transition of leadership. A *double trigger contract* requires both a change in control and termination, either involuntary (being asked to leave) or constructive (providing good cause for the executive to leave within a specified period following the change of control). Typically, this period is two to three years. Double trigger contracts are more prevalent. A *hybrid* is a modified trigger that permits voluntary termination with full benefits typically for a brief period after one year in addition to being a double trigger for the first two to three years.

Change of control packages typically provide the maximum allowable under Section 280G of the IRC (Golden Parachute Payments) to be tax deductible, in other words, less than three times the base amount. The latter is defined as average annual W-2 compensation for the five preceding years. Amounts of three times or more this base average will trigger an excise tax described in Section 4999 of the IRC of 20 percent of the amount received in excess of the base average amount. Additionally, the company will lose its tax deduction on amounts in excess of the base period amount. Some contracts insert language indicating that in no event will payments exceed the amount allowable under law to receive a tax deduction. If the parachute payment is in excess of that provided in Section 280G, then any amount in excess of one time (not three times) the person's base amount is considered an *excess parachute payment* and is not tax deductible to the company. Reasonable compensation is tax deductible under Section 162.

Since the five-year average is the base for calculating the allowable golden parachute payment, it favors individuals who had significant W-2 earnings during this period. Namely, it would be advantageous to have large stock option exercises, big incentive payouts, and no deferrals of pay. It would also favor a person who had relatively flat earnings during this period as opposed to a person who had a rapidly increasing total pay package during the five years since it would result in a higher percentage of most recent pay. Conversely, no stock option exercises, low or no bonus payments, significant deferral of pay, and rapidly increasing earnings at the end of the five-year period would hurt the executive in a five-year formula.

Some companies promise to gross up the payment to executives to ensure they receive the annual net of any excise taxes. In doing so, the company may also include other items in the contract. The most common is immediate vesting of all unvested stock options and stock awards. It may further require immediate payout. If options are vested in the COC contract, the paper profit is most likely to be considered compensation under Section 280G. For stock options, profit would be the appreciation (i.e., current market price less option price). Typically, the vesting action is tied to a single trigger definition. Payout more likely is tied to a double trigger event. Additionally, some double trigger contracts provide enhanced retirement benefits. The most liberal being crediting service to age 65 and providing a benefit not discounted for age. Reimbursement of all legal fees might also be added in addition to the continuation of some benefits (e.g., medical and life insurance) and perquisites (e.g., automobiles, financial counseling, as well as outplacement counseling) for a limited period of time. Some may give a cash bonus of sufficient size to cover the exercise cost of all outstanding stock options. Parachutes that are significantly more liberal than the IRC-defined "golden parachutes" are often called *platinum parachutes*. Although COC contracts may be exempt from the reporting and disclosure requirements of ERISA (as a top hat plan), companies need to review carefully to ensure compliance.

The value of a golden parachute to an executive is clear: it is a good severance package. The value to shareholders is that since executives are protected financially, they should not be worried about losing their jobs and, thereby, be free to negotiate the best possible arrangement for shareholders.

The extent to which the above is applicable is often a function of organization level. The

CEO and perhaps the next level of senior executives may have the most lucrative contracts. The contracts of executives one level below are slightly less lucrative, and so on down the line. If the same contract does not cover all executives equally, then it could gradually de-liberalize for lower-level executives smoothly transitioning pay into that provided for non-executives.

At the time of a takeover, some companies have extended to all employees the type of severance benefits usually reserved for executives. The all-employee protection plan is often called a *tin parachute*. An example would be a plan that would double the normal severance benefit. Thus, a company that normally provided two weeks per year of service would now provide four weeks per year of service for any employee who lost his or her job within a prescribed period of time (e.g., one year) after the takeover had been completed.

In designing or reviewing golden and tin parachutes, it is useful to compare the two payouts as well as comparing them to a standard termination schedule. Shown in Table 6-6 are three possible standard termination formulas: a tin parachute of four weeks per year of service;

Type Formula	Years of Service				
Standard Termination	**5 Years**	**10 Years**	**15 Years**	**20 Years**	**25 Years**
3 months + 3 weeks per year	.54	.88	1.12	1.40	1.69
2 months + 2 weeks per year	.44	.63	.83	1.02	1.21
2 weeks + 2 weeks per year	.23	.42	.62	.81	1.00
Tin Parachute	.38	.77	1.15	1.54	1.92
Golden Parachute					
2.99 x 5%	2.69	2.69	2.69	2.69	2.69
10%	2.45	2.45	2.45	2.45	2.45
20%	2.00	2.00	2.00	2.00	2.00
1.99 x 5%	1.79	1.79	1.79	1.79	1.79
10%	1.63	1.63	1.63	1.63	1.63
20%	1.33	1.33	1.33	1.33	1.33
.99 x 5%	.89	.89	.89	.89	.89
10%	.81	.81	.81	.81	.81
20%	.66	.66	.66	.66	.66

Table 6-6. Severance pay in years

and golden parachute multiples of 2.99, 1.99, and .99 of the previous five years' W-2 average. Increases during this five-year period of 5 percent, 10 percent, and 20 percent are shown. The higher the rate of increases, the lower the payment as a percentage of current pay. The five-year average W-2 salary and bonus typically is lower than current-year income; however, long-term incentive payments (including gains on exercised non-qualified stock options) will increase the base period average.

Since parachutes are not length-of-service sensitive, they pay extremely well for short service; however, the traditional severance formulas may pay better for longer service. This analysis would suggest the policy pay under the more liberal of the two formulae.

Outplacement Assistance

As described in the previous section, severance pay is intended to cover the bridge of unemployment linking former job and new employer. Outplacement assistance is the help provided the employee in getting a new job. This includes preparing (or updating) a job resume and circulating that resume to those who might be hiring. This is done first within the company to eliminate the need for severance pay and permit the individual to continue the company benefit plans. If this fails, an external search is undertaken. Assistance is also provided in qualifying for unemployment compensation.

The former employer provides many terminated executives more deluxe assistance at time of severance. The executive is counseled either by company consultants or outside specialists on assessment of personal strengths and weaknesses, developing a plan of action for getting a new job, preparation of a resume, and conducting an effective job interview. The latter is often by videotaping and critiquing a mock interview. All this advice is directed toward assisting the terminated executive to get a new job quickly. It also is directed at reducing the anger, frustration, fear, and stress of being fired, or *dehired*, to use a euphemism. Since the company pays the costs associated with such a plan and it can be structured to result in no income to the executive, it is at least of moderate importance.

Unemployment Compensation

This statutory benefit is provided to those who were terminated but not those who left voluntarily. This combination state and federal benefit is administered by the state of employment. Because of the low amounts provided, this has very low importance to the executive.

Summary of Time Off with Pay

Shown in Table 6-7 is a summary of the probable importance to the executive of each of these forms of time off with pay and their tax-effectiveness rating. Refer back to Table 6-3 for the definitions. In the "importance to executive" section, "EB" (employee benefits) and "P" (perquisites) are used when the all-employee and executive benefit coverages are different. An "✔" is used when both groups are comparable. Four are probably of high importance (i.e., employment contracts, disability protection, severance pay, and vacations).

SERVICE PROGRAMS

Companies often provide a wide range of services to the employee or executive.

TE		Benefit	Importance to Executive		
E	C		Low	Moderate	High
5	B	Holidays		✔	
5	B	Vacations		EB	P
5	B	Court Duty	✔		
5	B	Workers' Compen-sation and Disability	EB		P
5	B	Family and Medical Leave		✔	
5	B	Funeral Leave	✔		
5	B	General Leave and Sabbaticals	EB	P	
I	A	Flexible Work Schedules		✔	
*	*	Employment Contract	EB		P
5	*	Severance Pay	EB		P
I	B	Outplacement Assistance	EB	P	
I	B	Unemployment Compensation	✔		
		Summary Totals ✔ EB P	3 5 0	3 I 2	0 0 4
TE = Tax Effectivness, E = Executive, C = Company, EB= Employee Benefit, P = Perquisite					

*Depends on coverage

Table 6-7. Time off with pay summary

Assignment and Relocation Expenses

The *assignment* policy reimburses a portion of the relocation expenses of newly hired employees who must move in order to join the company. At lower levels, this may simply be the cost of travel and moving the family possessions; at the executive level, this could include guaranteeing a selling price and a loan for a new residence.

When the company wishes a current employee to relocate to another area, it is customary to reimburse the individual for a significant portion of the *relocation expense*. In addition to paying for the cost of moving the employee and family (possibly parents as well), many companies will pay all or a portion of selling costs. This would include any loss the individual might incur in selling below the appraised value of the house, travel and lodging accommodations while searching for a new home (and waiting for it to be vacated), carrying charges (e.g., mortgage payments and utilities) on the old house, and low-cost or no-cost loans until such house is sold. In addition, a flat payment (e.g., one month's pay) may be included to cover miscellaneous related expenses.When the executive must accept a higher mortgage interest on the new home, some companies will make up all or a portion of the difference for a limited period of time. An approach followed by some companies is to buy the house from the employee at the appraised price. Regardless of the approach, many companies gross up payments to cover taxes. The tax treatment of moving expenses is described in Sections 82, 132, and 217 of the IRC.

While moving expense policies apply to all employees, they usually are of greatest value to the executive due to the expense associated with moving and the extent of investment in current housing and, therefore, are of high importance.

Athletic Programs

In the spirit of providing camaraderie after work, some companies sponsor various athletic programs (e.g., basketball, golf, softball, and tennis). In addition to equipment, facilities may be on or near company grounds. Placing athletic facilities on or near an executive's residence will probably draw attention from the Internal Revenue Service (IRS) as a taxable benefit. However, when use is available in a non-discriminatory manner, it will probably not be taxable income (Section 132(j) of the IRC). It is also of low executive importance.

Attendance and Service Awards

While hourly and weekly employees might be eligible for *attendance* bonuses (for specified period of perfect attendance) or *length of service* bonuses (for each additional year of company service), executive participation is normally limited to such programs as the *service award*. For achieving milestones (normally in five-year multiples), the employee receives a pin or other item reflecting the degree of service or might select a gift from a premium catalog. In addition, 25 or more years of service usually means induction into a quarter-century club, recognized by a special dinner. Section 274(j) of the IRC reviews achievement awards, which are of low executive importance.

Clothing

Laboratory and production facilities often provide clothing or clothing allowances. Office settings rarely do, although some wish it were so. For the office, acceptable attire ranges rather significantly from the casual Friday (to full casual week) to suits and ties for men and comparable attire for women. Executives usually set the high end of the dress code and may even, in some situations, receive a clothing allowance; nonetheless, this benefit ranks low in executive importance.

Company Products

Catalogs and company stores enable employees to purchase company products at a significant discount, typically wholesale price. Selling at wholesale, the company receives revenue as if sold to a retailer, while the individual has no tax liability (Section 132(c) of the IRC). Some companies, either because of limited products or desire to provide a broader benefit, include products of other non-competitive companies.

The samples that may be given at no cost to the executive for personal use range from large-ticket items such as a car to small disposable items such as magazines or newspapers. In many such situations, the company takes the posture that it is really requiring the executive to put the product through extensive product testing and then report back any findings. Depending on the nature of company products available, a moderate importance might be possible.

Concierge Service

Buying a gift, making a dinner reservation, working with a caterer, taking a pet to the veterinarian, and getting the car serviced are duties often expected of an executive's assistant. A few companies have extended this service throughout the organization, some charging a small fee. Those working long hours or traveling extensively especially welcome a concierge service. The service may be provided by a single independent contractor or by several companies dedicated to providing such service. It could be of moderate importance for executives with little free time.

Dependent Care

Initially only childcare, this benefit has expanded to include support in caring for other employee dependents, namely, spouse and parents. Executives must often ensure that ailing parents receive proper care. The first stage of assistance is typically having someone come to their house and provide meals and housekeeping services. The next stage is providing this service in a shared living facility, sometimes called an independent living facility. In the third stage, for those still healthy enough to live on their own, meals and social events are provided in common areas. The fourth stage is full nursing service for those unable to perform one or more daily activities. Ideally, the person is able to translate smoothly from one service to another without moving. This benefit is discussed later in the home health care section.

The need for childcare has been heightened by the dramatic increase in the number of working women and single parent families. The benefit ranges from a simple referral service where recommended providers are located to a company facility (childcare) to various financial support programs. An executive perk might be a nanny provided at company expense. If financial support is provided, the company must be aware of perceived inequity by other employees. Namely, some employees are getting a benefit others are not receiving. Some have incorporated these programs into their flexible benefits programs, which will be discussed later in this chapter. Section 21 and 129 of the IRC should be useful when reviewing these programs. Executive importance ranges from low to high, depending on spouse and dependent status.

Educational Assistance

For those interested in additional education, some form of *educational assistance* is usually available. Such a program might pay 75 percent or more of tuition and related expenses. The percentage reimbursed may be based on grade: 60 percent for a C, 80 percent for a B, and 100 percent for an A. For the executive, this benefit could be combined with a fully paid sabbatical for a year to obtain an MBA or complete a Ph.D. Sometimes special programs are established in conjunction with pre-retirement counseling programs to encourage the individual to adopt new interests. Section 127 of the Internal Revenue Code (IRC) prescribes the requirements and tax treatment for educational assistance programs. See also "Scholarships" in this chapter. Importance of this benefit to executives is moderate at best.

Employee Assistance Programs

Employee assistance programs (EAPs) began by focusing on problems of substance abuse (alcohol and drugs) but have been expanded to cover virtually any problem troubling an employee, ranging from family responsibilities to marketplace issues. In addition to a doing a good deed by providing such services, companies believe that productivity is negatively affected when issues trouble employees. EAPs are intended to help. Services range from referrals to actively meeting with and trying to help the employee with his or her problem. The service may be provided on or off site. An important issue is confidentiality. If employees do not believe privacy will be respected, they are unlikely to use the service. In addition to chemical dependency and family issues, executives may find EAPs of value in addressing work stress, ranging from burnout to work load to job insecurity and, therefore, of moderate importance.

Financial Services

This is an umbrella category covering a wide variety of services companies make available. This includes auto and homeowners insurance, credit unions and loans, financial planning, legal insurance, liability insurance, pre-retirement planning, and tax assistance.

Auto and Homeowners' Insurance. For mass-merchandised insurance programs such as for automobiles and homeowners, the company often provides little more than a payroll deduction (and perhaps some office space for the administrator); in return, the employee receives a reduced rate. While this could result in an annual savings of a couple of hundred dollars, it is only of moderate interest to executives. In addition, the executive must be sure the protection is adequate. For years, most *auto insurance* protection was based on determining negligence (namely, the negligent party and the insurance company should pay the injured innocent party). Now no-fault protection is more the norm than the exception. This has eliminated a number of lawsuits where negligence was contested.

Initially, only protection against loss resulting from fire was insurable under *homeowners' insurance*. Then protection against loss caused by snow, ice, hail, and windstorm became available along with human-related events (e.g., vandalism, malicious mischief, riots, civil commotion) and man-created objects (e.g., falling aircraft and damage from other vehicles). Essentially, the homeowners' policy has become an all-risk coverage for property. However, even an apparent all-risk policy has exclusions and it is important to know what they are and whether to accept the risk of such loss or seek additional insurance to cover it. For example, if the policy value for personal property is determined inadequate, an additional personal property floater is purchased, listing additional major items (e.g., mink coat, diamond ring, or original artwork) along with insured values. Alternatively, a type of loss (e.g., flood) may be excluded and, therefore, a special add or floater purchased. Like auto insurance, homeowners insurance is of moderate interest to executives.

Credit Unions and Loans. In some companies, *credit unions* are available to cover employee needs for loans; in other instances, the company will establish a *loan policy* to cover such items as relocation (initiated by the company) and education of dependents. In addition, loans from savings and investment plans are sometimes adopted. Since it is difficult to rationalize charging less in interest than the fund managers are able to realize through investment, the interest paid may be creditable directly to the borrower's account. Depending on the amount of loan available, this may be of interest to the executive.

No-interest or low-interest loans to executives have become more common as companies require they buy and hold significant amounts of company stock. These multimillion-dollar arrangements are often specified in the employment agreement. In some instances, they may be used for other purposes such as a new home, especially where relocation is required. Carried on the company books as an asset, under some circumstances (e.g., company meeting certain financial goals) they may be forgiven. However, should the executive leave the company, repayment is required.

Its beginnings essentially date back to J. Simpson Dean, 35 T.C. 1053 (1961), when the tax court took the position that a borrower incurred no taxable income under an interest-free loan. However, the IRS consistently challenged such arrangements, attempting to either make the lender pay gift taxes or the borrower pay income tax on the value of the interest discount. For some time, the courts sided more with the lender and borrower than with the IRS; however, this changed with the 1984 Tax Reform Act. It requires that most loans in excess of $10,000 (with an interest rate lower than market rates) will require a charge of imputed income to the borrower.

Furthermore, sizable loans to executives at low or no interest often attract considerable shareholder heat. Indeed, some states require shareholder approval of a loan to a director. Usually, these loans are granted to assist the executive in purchasing company stock or financing a stock option, often after the stock price has dropped and the bank is pressuring the executive by calling unsecured demand loans—on the assumption that his or her financial position has deteriorated—or through margin calls on loans for which the stock or other securities have been pledged as collateral. Company loans may be either recourse or non-recourse. A *recourse loan* is backed by collateral (i.e., other than the stock being purchased with the loan). If the executive fails to meet the scheduled payments, the company can seize the collateral (at least to the value of the forfeited loan). In a *non-recourse loan,* the stock alone serves as collateral. The company would need to recapture the forfeited amount through other measures if the forfeited stock value were insufficient to cover the loan.

Few executives have escaped the perils of *margin calls* since buying on margin (i.e., paying only a portion of the stock's cost and borrowing the rest from the broker) is an attractive leveraging technique. By complying with Regulation T of the Federal Reserve, an executive need pay only 50 percent of the stock's cost at time of purchase. Thus, if the executive purchased $100,000 of stock, the broker would send a Regulation T call for $50,000 within five business days. However, if the executive already had $150,000 in the account, the Regulation T would simply be entered in the internal account at the brokerage firm (since the $150,000 was greater than the $125,000 needed to cover the combined investments of $100,000 and $150,000).

With Regulation T satisfied, the next requirement facing the executive is Rule 431 of the New York Stock Exchange, which requires the investor to maintain at least a 25-percent equity position (most investment firms require more). The equity position is determined by subtracting the amount owed the broker from the fair market value (FMV) of the stock and dividing the balance by the FMV. In the above example, this is $150,000 (i.e., $250,000 less $100,000) divided by $250,000, or a 60-percent equity position. In this example, when the $100,000 owed equals 75 percent of FMV, the minimum equity position of 25 percent has been reached at $133,333 (i.e., $100,000 = 0.75 FMV). Thus, when the stock value drops to $125,000, a margin call will go to the executive to deposit at least $6,250 in the account. Thus, the loan will drop to $93,750 resulting in an equity position of $31,250, or 25 percent of the $125,000. A further drop in market value to $120,000 will result in another margin call for $3,750.

If the initial $100,000 went to purchase stock A while the $150,000 was invested in stock B, the executive would not receive a margin call on A even if it went to zero, as long as the value of B was at least $133,333.

Many executives also use margin buying to shelter the payment of taxes on dividends by offsetting them with interest charges. For example, if the stock was paying a dividend equal to a 4-percent yield (i.e., $10,000 or $0.40 a share) and the margin account were charging 10 percent interest (i.e., $10,000 on the $100,000 outstanding), then the interest deduction would offset the dividend income!

While acting as banker to executives is an arguably questionable practice, it may be justified when a company pressures the executive not to sell any company stock holdings. While some companies charge as much as prime rate for loans, it may be more logical to reduce the pressure to hold stock, although this runs counter to stock-ownership guidelines. [See Chapter 8 (Long-Term Incentives).]

Other circumstances warranting a company loan range from company initiated relocation (either a "bridge" loan to cover equity needs until current residence is sold or an outright loan that otherwise would be covered by a mortgage) to personal expenses of either a routine (e.g., buy a car or finance children's education) or an emergency nature (e.g., extraordinary medical expenses).

Other issues the company must address include: Who will approve the loan (e.g., the board of directors)? What is the allowable term? How is the loan paid if the employee terminates or dies (e.g., balance forgiven, payment schedule unchanged, or payable immediately)? Is there a maximum amount available for loans? Will conditions and terms vary by individual?

Financial Planning. Although preretirement counseling often includes some financial planning, companies can develop a more comprehensive service. Such a service would focus on minimizing income taxes and maximizing both investment opportunities and estate preservation. Typically, it begins with a thorough review of the person's income, expenses, assets, and liabilities along with the individual's objectives and investment philosophy. It would also include a review of the needs of the surviving spouse and other dependents. This leads to establishing priorities and timelines with forecasted financial positions in stocks, bonds, and real estate. Performance is tracked and adjustments are made as necessary. Few have the patience, much less the knowledge necessary to undertake and complete such a process without assistance from a qualified professional. The service is expensive one-on-one but more manageable when packaged in workshops and a limited one-on-one discussion of perhaps an hour.

Today, companies have varying degrees of participation in financial counseling programs based on organization rank. Operating on the assumption that executives do not have sufficient time to focus on the long-term financial affairs of the family and that a financial planning benefit would not be taxable to the individual, many companies have implemented personalized full-service programs. However, some of these services are no longer tax deductible and those that are are limited to the amount that exceeds a stated percentage of adjusted gross income. Financial planners come in all shapes and sizes ranging from insurance agents, bankers, and stockbrokers to broad-gauge specialists. Obviously, insurance agents, bankers, and stockbrokers will be partial to their own products or at least not as knowledgeable about competing products. To avoid this drawback, many choose a broad-gauge advisor such as: a certified financial planner (designated by the Certified Financial Planners Board of Standards); a chartered financial analyst (designated by Investment Management and Research); or a personal financial specialist (designated by the American Institute of Certified Public Accountants). Each designator requires meeting experience criteria and passing an examination. Other broad-gauge advisors include CPAs and CLUs. A CPA is a *certified public accountant* and a CLU is a *chartered life underwriter*. These are only several of many possible specialty designations. Additionally, a planner who recommends stocks and bonds must register with the SEC. If the planner is not an attorney, one will be needed to set up a will and appropriate trusts. Another form of assistance comes from the *professional organizer*, who puts everything in place and sets up easy-to-maintain record systems. But the new system is not self-administering and must be kept up-to-date. Of course, for a fee someone else can do that as well.

Typically, a company selects several financial services firms, allowing the executive to choose one. However, sometimes the company will permit the executive to choose a firm not on the list. Personal chemistry is often a key determinant in the process. Regardless of choice, the company establishes a maximum amount that it is willing to reimburse (e.g., $20,000 the first year and $10,000 thereafter). The IRS stated in Revenue Ruling 73-13 that the full value of financial counseling (while a business deduction to the company) was compensation for services to the executive under Section 61 of the Internal Revenue Code. The value of the financial planning service is imputed as income to the executive and a payroll tax deduction is included. The executive can take this service, along with other non-reimbursed job expenses, as a tax deduction if it exceeds 2 percent of adjusted gross income. A number of companies gross up the tax in order to make it a tax-free perk.

At lower management levels, individuals would be eligible to attend a one or two day seminar (perhaps with spouse) to study the general nature of estate preservation techniques. Seminars often include workbooks in which to develop (in conjunction with an attorney and CPA) an individual plan, in other words, identifying location of all important papers, ensuring wills exist and are current, determining the amount of life insurance needed, and minimizing estate tax liability. In such instances, expenses might be charged off as management development and no imputed income assigned. Traditionally, computer-generated benefit statements of benefit programs are the basis for examining company coverage.

Regardless of the type of program, some companies request the executive sign a release (allowing the company to provide the financial planner with specific information about the executive's pay and benefits) and a waiver (holding the company harmless for any adverse consequences based on information received).

However, not everyone feels the need for a financial advisor; reasons include:

1. They are sufficiently knowledgeable because of their work (or extensive hobby).
2. The World Wide Web not only makes information easily available, it also makes stock transactions fast and relatively inexpensive.
3. Mutual funds make stock picking unnecessary.
4. Using an advisor still requires a lot of time, whereas doing it alone does not require a great deal more time.
5. What is saved in fees and costs can be used to invest.

Avoiding Taxes. It is important to distinguish between *tax avoidance* (the legal means by which the individual pays no more tax than is required by taking full advantage of tax law and how different items are taxed) and *tax evasion* (the illegal means by which the individual pays less tax than is required by understating income and/or overstating deductible expenses).

The importance of tax avoidance is dramatized in Table 6-8 where the pretax yield of an investment subject to income tax is equated to an investment that is not subject to federal income tax. Note that due to the ascending tax rate, it is better to avoid taxes as income increases. In this way, a smaller tax-free yield still puts the investor ahead. For example, if the effective tax rate on income was 40 percent and adjusted gross income was $500,000, after-tax income would be $300,000. Assume that of this amount, the individual has $50,000 available for investment and is looking for a 5 percent after-tax return, or $2,500. Looking across the 40 percent line and down the 5 percent column, one sees that an 8.3-percent taxable return is needed to be comparable with a 5-percent tax-free yield. (i.e., $50,000 x .08333 = $4,167; $4,167 x .60 = $2,500). However, if the individual were in a 50-percent tax bracket and was still seeking a 5-percent after-tax return on investment, a 10-percent taxable return would be required.

Personal Investing. Investors are always interested in *yields*, or returns on their investment. In the fixed-income market, investments are usually short-term (typically six months) or long-term (such as 30-year bonds). Normally, long-term rates are higher than short-term to reflect a greater degree of risk—mainly inflation. An increasing spread typically signals rapid growth, whereas an inverted spread (short-term return is higher than long-term) suggests a recession. Little or no gap between the two would signal a slowdown in the economy. Increasing interest rates slow down investment, whereas decreasing interest rates encourage investment.

Another definition of yield is the annual dividend paid on a share of stock divided by the stock price. The yield, therefore, increases only when dividends increase faster than stock price or decrease more slowly than declines in stock price. A yield rally (an increasing rate of return)

Individual Tax Rate	1%	2%	3%	4%	5%	6%	7%	8%	9%	10%
100%	00	00	00	00	00	00	00	00	00	00
90%	10.0	20.0	30.0	40.0	50.0	60.0	70.0	80.0	90.0	100.0
80%	5.0	10.0	15.0	20.0	25.0	30.0	35.0	40.0	45.0	50.0
70%	3.3	6.7	10.0	13.3	16.7	20.0	23.3	26.6	30.0	33.3
60%	2.5	5.0	8.0	10.0	12.5	15.0	17.5	20.0	22.5	25.0
50%	2.0	4.0	6.0	8.0	10.0	12.0	14.0	16.0	18.0	20.0
40%	1.8	3.3	5.0	6.7	8.3	10.0	11.7	13.3	15.0	16.7
30%	1.4	2.9	4.3	5.7	7.1	8.6	10.0	11.4	12.9	14.3
20%	1.3	2.5	3.8	5.0	6.3	7.5	8.8	10.0	11.3	12.5
10%	1.1	2.2	3.3	4.4	5.6	6.7	7.8	8.9	10.0	11.1
0%	1.0	2.0	3.0	4.0	5.0	6.0	7.0	8.0	9.0	10.0

Table 6-8. After-tax equivalents of tax-free yields at various tax brackets

may be simply the result of a falling stock price.

Those preferring the stock market over safer investments such as U.S. Treasury bonds expect to achieve a reasonable *equity premium* (historically about 6 percent) over safer investments. The premium is the sum of dividends and stock price appreciation in excess of the fixed income interest rate.

The investor in the stock market can make individual selections, put money with a stock picker, invest in a managed fund, or put money in an index fund that tracks the S&P 500, the Wilshire 5000, Russell 2000, or some other index. Mutual fund investors have the choice of going with a load or no-load fund. A *load fund* is typically sold through a bank, broker, or investment adviser. In exchange for advice and service, a commission is charged on the investment. This commission can be paid up-front (A Funds) or on an ongoing basis. B Funds have an exit fee for the first five years. C Funds charge an ongoing brokerage fee. *No-load funds* have no such charge, but they also provide no advice or service. Both charge management and administrative fees on the account while it is active. No-load funds typically do not charge exit fees. Some high-yield bond funds charge fees to avoid money managers moving cash in and out of funds. Another investment place for high net-worth executives to manage their wealth is *private banking*, typically a separate unit of a bank. For years, private banking appeared to be restricted to those with large inherited wealth who were more interested in service than in investment return (as long as it was better than cash management). Regardless of the choice, it is useful to track the equity premium and determine if charges are appropriate.

Some personal investors purchase *puts* and *calls* on stock owned to hedge losses and increase gains. A put allows the holder to *sell* stock at a stated price to the holder of the put. For example, if the stock is currently at $100, the put might be at $90. If the stock drops below $90, the put is exercised and the loss held to $10. Conversely, a call is the right to *buy* at a stated price. Let's assume $100 as in the example above. Any gain in stock price above $100 can be realized by exercising the call. Puts and calls are for short periods of time and do not have to be exercised. If not, the investor is out only the cost of the put or call. Puts and calls were reviewed in more detail in Chapter 4 (Stakeholders).

A financial planner should be helpful in determining the appropriate allocation of assets among stock (own company and others), fixed income, real estate, and cash equivalents as well as appropriate tax-avoidance vehicles.

Tax Shelters. Tax avoidance is the main attraction of *tax shelters* for many highly compensated executives. This typical shelter consists of a group of investors who have formed a partnership, thus enabling them to claim personal deductions (not available to an association or corporation) proportionate to their personal investment in the partnership.

Tax shelters were created (and are periodically massaged) by Congress to encourage investment in ventures where the risk/reward ratio is otherwise not sufficiently attractive. The 1986 Tax Reform Act removed much of the appeal of tax shelters. Contrary to popular belief, tax shelters were not designed with the sole purpose of allowing millionaires to avoid taxes. In exchange for the right to currently reduce taxable income and/or receive future income as capital gains rather than ordinary income, the individual accepts a higher risk of protecting the investment than otherwise might be the case. In real estate, it is speculation that land and property will appreciate favorably in terms of inflation. With gas and oil drilling, it is the probability of a successful strike. With equipment leasing, it is the belief that the supply of equipment will not be greater than the demand for the period of investment. Therefore, it is important that the executive identify and prioritize personal objectives regarding deferral of income, capital gains versus ordinary income, security of investment, and degree of desired liquidity.

While many shelters allow only a pro rata deduction (i.e., the later in the year the investment, the smaller the allowable deduction), others involve property that is eligible for the 10 percent investment tax credit, and thus the tax write-off may approximate the cash investment. However, the provisions of tax law generally limit the deductions under tax shelters to the amount of money "at risk" (i.e., the amount invested and/or liable to pay). Some shelters inflate the amount of deduction by adding a "non-recourse loan" (i.e., a loan for which the partners have no legal liability) to launch the venture. Thus, if five investors each put up $10,000 and a non-recourse loan of $250,000 was obtained, each would theoretically have a deduction of $60,000. Such situations must be examined very carefully because the IRS has ruled against such deductions in a number of instances.

The problem, therefore, is not finding a tax shelter but, rather, finding one which meets the investment caliber of the executive and provides an opportunity for economic value as well as tax write-offs. One of the major problems facing some executives, who have benefited from significant depreciation write-offs, is how to dispose of heavily depreciated property without massive tax liabilities. Furthermore, many tax shelter opportunities that meet the economic requirements are not timed in an effective manner for a particular executive. Unfortunately, too often executives give more consideration to purchasing a particular $50,000 car than to investing $500,000 in a specific tax shelter.

Estate Planning. A key objective in *estate planning* is not simply to minimize taxes when the executive dies, but to provide an orderly plan whereby the executive's assets are delivered to the proper individuals in the most tax effective manner, which includes minimizing the tax impact on the estate of the executive's spouse. Put in place shortly after the beginning of the twentieth century, estate taxes were intended to reduce the concentration of wealth. Effective financial planners will ensure all appropriate tax-avoidance measures are used. Perhaps one of the best measures is to take advantage of the unlimited number of individuals one can give up to $10,000 annually ($20,000 with spousal consent) for as long as one lives without any tax impact to self or recipient.

Certainly, the most basic provision is a properly executed will. A person who dies without a will is said to have died *intestate* and the appropriate state law(s) will apply. Normally, these specify a certain percentage of the estate to the children and the remainder to the spouse.

Holographic wills, or those completely handwritten by the testator, and unwritten wills, also known as *nuncupative wills,* may not conform to state laws and will not be considered "wills." Another form of will is the *living will,* which becomes active when mentally incapacitated, and specifies what type of life-sustaining treatments (if any) should be undertaken. A supplement would be executing a *health-care power of attorney*, in other words, appointing someone to make decisions on one's behalf regarding life-sustaining treatments because incapacitation prevents making such decisions oneself. It is critical that these two be carefully prepared to avoid gaps or inconsistencies.

Another key requirement of estate planning is to ensure sufficient liquidity exists, not simply to meet estate taxes but also to provide for seizing favorable investment opportunities (e.g., exercising the executive's stock options). Lump-sum payments from profit sharing and savings plans, although subject to estate taxes, will provide a form of liquidity in addition to life insurance proceeds.

Conversely, the present value of non-qualified, deferred payments to beneficiaries will be included in the estate. This will cause a significant drain on the estate without sufficient life insurance to meet the tax liability.

The 1976 Tax Reform Act had a pronounced effect on estate planning. Among other things, it established a unified estate and gift tax table. With the exception of the annual $10,000 per person exclusion ($20,000 with spousal consent), all other gifts given during the executive's lifetime will be added back into the estate for purpose of determining estate-tax liability. It should be noted both amounts are adjusted for inflation after 1998. The law also provides a lifetime exemption for gifts beyond the annual exclusion, adjusted by year. Additional changes affecting estate planning were put into law in 2001 and should be examined carefully.

A *trust* is created when an individual takes title to property and administers it for the benefit of the person creating the trust, other identified individuals, and/or the trustee. There are two types of trusts: inter vivos and testamentary. An *inter vivos trust* is created by the executive while alive; a *testamentary trust* is created by the executive's will. Inter vivos trusts may be either revocable or irrevocable; testamentary trusts are always irrevocable. The granter cannot withdraw property transferred through an irrevocable trust. Assets are distributed in accordance with the terms of the trust to beneficiaries designating the occurrence of a specified event or attainment of a point in time. Such trusts can be designed to be either short- or long-term in duration, depending on the objective in establishing the trust. One example is the *sprinkle trust*, which distributes assets from the trust at stated intervals or prescribed ages of the beneficiaries. Another example is an *educational trust,* which might be established to coincide with the completion of high school and beginning of college.

A *revocable* or living trust is a legal entity to which the executive transfers all or part of his or her assets. Although no longer in the executive's name, the assets remain under the executive's complete control since the power to add or withdraw assets and amend the conditions of the trust is retained. Some people believe the advantage of this type of trust is that beneficiaries will have immediate access to assets in accordance with the terms of the trust without going through the probate process. Others believe this is little advantage since the probate process can be short in time. However, a living trust does not reduce estate or income-tax liabilities. While the executive is alive, the IRS considers the trust non-existent since the income-producing assets are still owned by the executive.

In summary, the many aspects of financial planning are of high importance to executives and reasonably tax effective (taxable to executive but deductible above an allowance and tax deductible to the company).

Legal Assistance. Such services can be provided under an insurance contract or by direct company payment. Assistance programs take the form of either a closed panel (a specific list of attorneys) or an open panel (allowing the executive to choose an attorney). The former is an easy plan to administer for cost-control purposes, whereas the latter provides the employee more flexibility. While most plans are limited to routine work (e.g., adoptions, property closings, wills, and divorces), some offer a full range of covered services (including criminal offense). Section 120 of the Internal Revenue Code prescribes the requirements for qualified group legal services plans. Some argue that these plans give the middle class the same benefit now enjoyed by the affluent (who can afford top legal advice) and the indigent poor (who have such services provided at no cost through legal aid programs).

Executives often need someone to act on their behalf because of their unavailability or incapacitation; this can be accomplished through the *power of attorney*. The period of time may be short or open-ended. The matters affected may be narrowly defined or broadly stated. Since the power of attorney permits someone to act on one's behalf, it is important the matter be carefully thought through.

Nonetheless, the typical company does not have a qualified legal services plan for its employees, and even if such a plan existed, it would be short of the services executives might wish. While it is not uncommon for executives to draw upon inside counsel for routine matters (e.g., drafting a will or giving an opinion on a personal transaction or possible liability), more and more companies are moving away from providing comprehensive legal services, especially in the case of defense against a non-business civil lawsuit or defending against criminal prosecution. Thus, company involvement ranges from providing a list of attorneys in outside firms (with the executive being billed directly) to covering a specified dollar amount and/or list of scheduled services selected by either the company or the executive. While the company may take a business tax deduction, the executive will have an imputed income for tax purposes similar to financial planning. This can be a high importance service for executives.

Liability Insurance. Today we live in a rather litigious society. Suing for damages is a fact of life. The executive assumes both business and personal risk. Thus, business liability insurance is commonplace for corporate officers and members of the board of directors. In addition, those who have fiduciary responsibility, as defined by ERISA, are often covered for their business actions. Whether or not such protection can be purchased by the company is often a function of the state in which the company is incorporated. Where possible, it is common for the company to purchase protection, and since it is a business expense, the company takes a business deduction without creating an income liability for the executive. Should the executive be on the board of directors of own or another company, he or she should be sure that the company-provided *director liability insurance* is adequate in both amount and coverage. For example, legal fees should be reimbursed. Many executives will seek an *indemnification agreement* whereby the company agrees to reimburse the executive or director for any legal actions not covered by the director and officer liability insurance.

Because of the earnings level of the executive, many find that the liability maximums on auto and homeowners' policies are inadequate to cover bodily injury or property damage. Increasingly, they are turning to personal umbrella liability insurance, although group policies paid by the company may be available. This type of policy provides a stated maximum dollar liability beginning where the auto and homeowners' policies end. Policies in multiples of millions are not uncommon at a fraction of the cost of the basic auto and homeowners' protection. If the executive pays the premium, the company is normally able to get a lower rate by arranging for the insurance; if the company pays, it will have a tax deduction but the individual will have an imputed income probably without a tax deduction. Nonetheless, this can be a high importance executive perk.

Pre-Retirement Counseling. Preparing for retirement requires careful planning. Typically, executives and other employees nearing retirement are invited to attend seminars addressing such issues as how to utilize increased leisure time, the company benefit program upon retirement, and what the individual can expect in the way of social security and Medicare benefits. Seminars can help to estimate expenses during retirement and compare them to projected income, adjusting each for inflation and appreciation. They can then help develop strategies to reduce expenses and/or increase income, possibly deferring date of retirement until a comfortable balance is achieved. Seminars are supplemented by magazines, reports, and individual sessions with company representatives as needed. More and more companies are making such services available many years before retirement.. If one waits until a few years before retirement, it is too late. General programs such as these, although probably not taxable, are of moderate importance to executives. The more inclusive form of financial planning described earlier would include retirement planning for executives.

Tax Assistance. For many, this is an extension of financial planning and in some respects comparable to the legal services provided by some companies. Due to the low cost for most employees, this is a benefit of increasing popularity.

In addition to regularly preparing federal and other income tax returns, it is not uncommon for company advisers to give executives opinions on significant investment opportunities (e.g., tax shelters). Traditionally, company tax attorneys have provided such assistance; however, a number of executives feel uncomfortable about others in the company knowing their full financial status. Therefore, it is not uncommon for such services to be provided by an outside firm with the company and/or the executive paying the cost. Any portion paid by the company is a deductible expense, and the executive receives a like imputed income charge. All expenses related to taxes are deductible expenses for the executive if they and other described expenses exceed 2 percent of adjusted gross income. Executive interest in tax assistance is high.

Food Service

This category includes everything from vending machines with pocket lunchrooms, to full-scale cafeterias with walkthrough and table service. Typically, the company will absorb the cost of rent and related services (e.g., electricity and gas), requiring the employee to pick up all or some portion of the cost of food and its preparation. Such facilities are especially welcome when there is a lack of nearby moderate-priced facilities and on bad weather days. Many executives find cafeterias an excellent place to discuss business and/or develop personal relationships. Typically, where revenue equals or exceeds direct operating costs, there is no individual tax liability (see Section 132(e) of the IRC).

However, it is not uncommon to have an executive dining room in addition to a cafeteria on the company premises. Such facilities range from a separate room serving the same fare as the cafeteria to luxuriously appointed rooms where uniformed waiters serve dry martinis and excellent meals. In fact, the cuisine may be without equal in the city due to the impressive gourmet credentials of the chef. While such facilities are primarily used for luncheons, occasionally they are the sites for dinners. The luncheons wane in comparison to the elegant dinners, featuring delicate hors d'oeuvres, vintage wine, and fine cigars, all served by tuxedoed waiters.

The dining room or rooms are also physically placed to ensure a marvelous view, probably only matched by that of the office of the president and chairman of the board. Where there is more than one room, they may be of comparable quality in appointments or they may be structured in such a way as to indicate eligibility (e.g., corporate officers use the A room, division presidents and other key executives the B room, and the remaining executives the C room). Where rooms reflect executive level, they usually differ in size, elegance of furnishings, type of crystal and china, level of cuisine, and choice of beverages.

Another variation permitting discrimination is reserving certain tables or seats for a handful of senior officers. This may vary from a table in the executive dining room to simply a table in the cafeteria, assuring the executive of seating without having to wait in line.

In addition to their convenience, such facilities are often justified in terms of their privacy when executives meet among themselves or with important outside contacts, including customers. Executives are usually charged for a portion of the cost (either a fixed monthly charge regardless of use or on a per-use basis).

Since informal discussion of company business over lunch among company executives has a difficult time meeting IRS requirements for escaping imputed income, some companies have taken the position of scheduling regular luncheon meetings. In some instances, the company has successfully argued that the participants are not otherwise available for the meeting. Since the meal has been scheduled for the convenience of the company, there is no imputed income for the individual. Nonetheless, it is difficult to assign more than a moderate importance rating.

Home

As described in the flexible work schedule category, home is for many an extension of the work site. For those officially telecommuting, the company will usually purchase or provide some type of allowance for computer equipment. A dedicated work site, preferably a separate room, is more conducive to work-away-from-the-office.

If personal safety is a factor, the company probably also pays for the installation of an electronic security system in the executive's home. High-end security systems would include video cameras, door and window sensors, motion detectors, phone line security, and opening devices that are activated by finger or palm prints, retina scans, and voice recognition. Income may or may not be imputed depending on the specifics. Unless security is a major issue, this perk is probably of moderate importance at best.

Job Title

The job title is a very visible perquisite and entirely intrinsic compensation. Titles are often tied to salary and/or organization levels. In many instances, they have modifiers to denote corporate versus group or divisional level. While corporate officer titles require board of director approval, the approval of group or divisional titles is most likely at the discretion of the company CEO. Central approval is essential to minimize interunit inequities.

"Vice president" is a very popular title. In addition to the vertical array of assistant VP, VP, senior VP, and executive VP, these titles can be used at the corporate, group, or division levels. Given all the possible combinations, it is easy to be awash in vice presidents. To minimize confusion, no one should report to someone with the same title unless that person is in a higher corporate grouping. For example, a group vice president could not report to another group vice president but could report to a corporate group vice president.

While pay range usually goes with title, in many situations, companies use titles instead of increased pay. The result has been that in many organizations, especially those in the mature phase, growth in number of vice presidents is faster than growth in sales! The after-tax value of a job title is infinite, since there is no pay to the executive and no expense to the organization. The new hefty title may not put more groceries on the table, but for those who receive it, the basic necessities of life are already being met. The title of vice president is intended to officially recognize the importance of the individual. Unfortunately, as additional vice presidents are created, the value of the title diminishes. First to suffer are the true vice presidents. Their status is denoted by such prefixes as corporate, group, and divisional or executive, administrative, and senior. While these distinctions are helpful, much of the glitter originally part of being a vice president is gone. Nonetheless, title is a high importance factor for most executives and, like few other perks, incurs no income-tax liability nor company expense.

Matching Gifts

A very popular program with executives is the *matching gifts plan* through which a contribution made by the employee to a civic, cultural, education, or health care organization (recognized by the IRS as a 501(c)(3) tax exempt organization) is matched dollar-for-dollar by the company. For example, an executive who sends a check for $5,000 to his or her alma mater knows the company will send a matching $5,000 check. Thus, the executive gets recognition for a $10,000 contribution at a $2,500 cost (assuming a 50-percent marginal tax bracket). The company's $5,000 contribution is also tax deductible. While typically such programs are open to all employees, executives use them most because of their visibility to solicitors and their higher tax bracket. Many plans will place an annual limit per person per calendar year on the amount (e.g., $20,000) that a company will match; nonetheless, many would consider this a high importance perk since the match is not taxable income to the executive.

Scholarships

Children of employees have the opportunity to further their education at company expense through *scholarships* provided by the company. Although such programs are usually open to all employees, a high percentage of executives' children usually win. Since selection is made on the basis of competitive test scores monitored by an independent agency, this in no way implies any "hanky-panky." Rather, for whatever reason or combination of reasons, executive offspring rank high among the intellectually able. When such programs are based on eligibility, the company receives a tax deduction, and neither the executive nor the child incurs income-tax consequences if they meet the requirement of Section 117 of the IRC.

Setting up scholarships exclusively for executives' children initially looked good for the tax benefit but has since lost a significant part of its appeal. The program called for the company to make a payment to an Educational Benefit Trust (EBT). The trust in turn bestowed scholarships upon children of eligible executives. The idea was that the company could take a tax deduction, and the executive and child would escape tax consequences since scholarships are not taxable. At worst, the monies would be taxable to the child and, thereby, at much lower rates than to the executive. However, the IRS in Revenue Ruling 76-448 stated that tuition fees paid on behalf of key employees are considered income (for purposes of FICA, FUTA, and income tax) under a non-qualified, deferred compensation plan. In other words, the company could not take a tax deduction until: (a) the executive had received the "scholarship," or (b) the restrictions had lapsed and the amount was included in the executive's gross income. Thus, while some companies make educational grants to the children of their executives (with possible annual dollar limits) to cover tuition, registration fees, books, and/or room and board, for private secondary education and/or college, they are of limited tax appeal. Importance is probably moderate to the executive although appreciated if a tax-free scholarship is awarded an offspring.

Rather than company scholarships, some executives choose a different route, setting up a scholarship program in their name for children of company employees. Typically, these are funded from the executive's estate after death; however, some create scholarship funds while still serving as an executive. This puts enormous peer pressure on other executives to do something, too.

Transportation

A transportation benefit can range from simply reimbursing commuter expenses to providing access to a company jet. Some companies pay daily commuting expenses where mass transit systems (e.g., buses and trains) are available. Others facilitate car-pooling through scheduling or underwriting a portion of the expense. In some situations, company buses are available for pick up and drop off at designated locations at the company facility.

In urban areas, choice parking space is typically reserved for executives and visitors with other spots filled on a first-come, first-served basis. The company may even set aside a reserved place in the executive area for employee-of-the-month. City locations create a greater challenge with some companies providing open or covered parking, but more typically, individuals are on their own (Section 132(f) of the IRC prescribes the tax-free limitations). Parking facilities range from a designated space in the company parking lot or garage (normally very close to the office) to public parking off the premises at company expense. The first is more typical of a suburban site, the latter more representative of a metropolitan facility. Parking facilities and all-employee transportation programs (although probably tax-free) are of low interest to the executive. However, automobiles and jet aircraft are another matter.

Automobile. Use of a car (and car phone) is a rather common benefit for executives, at least for business travel (either specifically assigned or on a first-come, first-served basis). Many companies go a step further and allow personal use of company cars, which is reimbursed by a fixed monthly charge or on a mileage basis. These cars are replaced after a specified number of years and/or miles driven. The type of car (and its cost) logically lends itself to the organization level of the individual—the limousine or super-luxury car at the CEO level and a standard model at the entry level of eligibility. In many instances, the executive is provided a company-paid chauffeur for business trips.

If the executive is to avoid an imputed income, the company must assess a charge for personal use of the automobile (and phone). One approach is to maintain records of personal use and at the end of the year, impute the personal-use portion. Thus, if the total car expenses were $15,000 and two-thirds were personal use, $10,000 would be the imputed income.

Since normal commuting is not considered a business expense, where it is an issue (and the executive therefore has a tax liability), the company will impute an income either monthly or on the basis of cents per mile (perhaps factoring in an alternative form such as commuter rail cost). In such cases, the car like the airplane may be perceived as more valuable than its tax effectiveness.

Alternatively, the company could consider the entire cost personal and impute it as income. The executive would then be reimbursed for business use through the expense account. The advantage is no record keeping.

Increasingly, companies are providing chauffeured limousines under the guise of protection for the executive. This is supported by the view that the executive's well being is threatened and the chauffeur is also a bodyguard. To reinforce this view, the driver is either a former law enforcement officer or familiar with bodyguard requirements (possibly licensed to carry firearms) and is trained in defensive driving techniques such as escaping ambushes. While commuting costs are not a business expense, providing for the safety of an executive could be considered a legitimate expense. These situations would probably have to be evaluated on a case-by-case basis. A liberal auto policy may be of high value to the executive.

Jet Aircraft. Personal use of corporate aircraft has been a very popular perquisite for both business and personal use. As a business form of transportation, it affords a flexibility of scheduling not possible with commercial flights. In addition, some locations are not serviced by direct commercial flights, and use of corporate aircraft allows more efficient use of executive time. Reportedly, commercial flights only service about 10 percent of U.S. airports.

Most company aircraft are as comfortable as first-class commercial service, if not more so. Some have a galley (other than a refrigerator), and the food and beverage service is at least as good as first-class commercial.

When allowing personal use, a company must determine between company cost and fair market value. Using company cost, there is no additional expense for allowing an executive to use an empty seat on a corporate jet for personal use when the aircraft is delivering one or more executives to the same city for business purposes; the tax effectiveness is 100%. Conversely, if the executive is the only passenger, the full corporate cost could be multiples of commercial flight. Using fair market value would suggest charging the executive the equivalent of first-class commercial fare, thereby giving it a high importance to many executives.

Adopting the company cost approach would be more logical for a company that allowed personal use only in conjunction with business flights. Adopting the fair market value would seem more feasible for a company that allowed personal-use-only flights as well as hitchhiking a seat on a business flight. The company cost approach might only include operational expenses such as fuel and landing fees, on the assumption that the crew is salaried and the airplane amortization schedule is not affected.

Regardless of the method selected, you should carefully review the tax consequences.

Companies not interested in maintaining a corporate aircraft program may opt to participate in a fractional jet ownership program. For an up-front, one-time acquisition fee, a monthly maintenance fee, and an hourly fee, the company can call up a jet when needed for a specified time period (e.g., five years). The fraction of ownership selected is based on the number of hours one expects to fly. It may start as low as 1/16 and represent 50 hours.

While companies once proudly displayed their company name and/or logo on aircraft, disapproval from shareholders spotting the planes at resort communities or prominent sporting events (such as the Super Bowl) has put a damper on the practice.

The intrinsic more than the extrinsic value of company aircraft probably gives this a high executive rating.

Ships and Boats. The complement of the corporate jet is the company yacht. By necessity, this is more restricted in use than aircraft if for no other reason than the requirement of proximity to water. Determination of basis, if any, for income is the same as for corporate aircraft. Unfortunately, the 1978 Revenue Act bars company deductions for maintaining a yacht. Presumably, business entertainment on the craft (e.g., catering) would be deductible.

Cruise ship expenses for conventions, seminars, or meetings under certain circumstances may be deductible, but a significant amount of written documentation is required under Section 274(m) of the IRC. Due to all the restrictions, ships and boats are of moderate importance, at best.

Travel and Entertainment

Paying for *travel and entertainment* expenses incurred on behalf of the company due to business responsibilities is a traditional benefit. While hypothetically this is applicable at all organization levels, it has its greatest application at sales and executive levels. The IRS and Congress continue to peck away at this benefit in the belief that all executives have three-martini lunches (including an expensive, exquisite meal) and charge it off as a business expense. For the expense to be at least partially tax deductible to the corporation and not an income item for the employee, the expense must be demonstrably incurred while conducting business. Furthermore, an expense while on the road or anything in excess of $25 requires a receipt indicating: date, who was in attendance, the business purpose of the expense, the nature and amount of the expense, and where the expense was incurred. (The $25 requirement has been in effect for a number of years and, unless eventually raised, will one day require a receipt on a cup of coffee.) When the reimbursed employee owns more than 10 percent of company stock, additional documentation is needed. There may be no such thing as a free lunch, but a lunch properly documented as business-related is at least partially tax deductible if it conforms to Section 162 of the IRC. Typically, business expenses are not taxable to the individual, although non-business use is taxable. Both are tax deductible to the company. However, such expenses are limited to a 50% deduction in accord with Section 274(n) of the IRC.

Apartments or Hotel Rooms. These are often provided in a city where company offices are located. Such facilities are available for out-of-town company officials as well as key employees working at the location who after attending a late business function stay over rather than face a long commute and little sleep.

Where the use is strictly business, the company has a deductible expense and the executive avoids an imputed income charge. Some companies provide such facilities for key executives to use routinely during the week (almost a second home); in this case, the individual would probably be subject to imputed income for non-business-required layovers. Certainly, where an apartment, hotel, or house was provided as either a vacation place or a principal place of residence, the individual would have income (and the company a tax deduction). For some, the full use of a company apartment might be more attractive than relocating, especially if the executive can return to his or her home for the weekend. Thus, this perk could be of moderate importance.

Club Membership. Club memberships take different forms, ranging from simple *dining memberships* (sometimes restricted to luncheons) at facilities usually close to the office to the full-range *athletic* or *country clubs* (where indoor and/or outdoor sports as well as dining and dancing are available). While golf club memberships can have initiation fees as high as $100,000 or more and monthly dues of $1,000 and up, city clubs are available for a fraction of that expense. They may be university or athletic in name. Typically, they have restaurant facilities, overnight lodging, athletic facilities, libraries, and some recreational and entertainment activities. Many have reciprocal arrangements with other out-of-town clubs that may be used when traveling. Airline club memberships are also popular as they permit entrance to VIP lounges while in transit. The selection of club memberships that will be subsidized or fully paid by the company may be made by the executive, or by the company, or may be mutually decided. In addition, depending perhaps on organization level, a determination will be made as to how many clubs will be allowed, what portion of costs will be covered (e.g., initiation fee, annual memberships, or usage charges), and/or what annual dollar limit if any will apply. For example, the CEO may be allowed three memberships of his or her choice with a maximum annual subsidy of $20,000. The president may be allowed two memberships with an annual subsidy of $10,000, etc.

While paying all or part of the dues to an exclusive club is fairly normal, some companies go one step further: They own the club. These properties range from the simple golf club to an exclusive hunting and fishing resort available for private use as well as business entertaining. However, the Revenue Act of 1978 disallows deductions for expenses incurred in connection with the operation of these entertainment facilities. Thus, they have become a very expensive perquisite.

Where the corporation takes a tax deduction, the individual will have imputed income if such charges (i.e., initiation fees, annual membership, and monthly charges) are not directly identifiable as business expenses. Under Section 274 of the Internal Revenue Code, only that portion of dues related to business is deductible and only if that portion exceeds the non-business portion. In other words, a 51-49 business/non-business split would qualify for a 51 percent deduction, but a 49-51 split would result in zero deductions. This would necessitate that sufficient business luncheons and dinners are scheduled during the year to meet the required usage for deductibility. Properly structured, this could be a moderately important perk.

Conventions and Conferences. Oftentimes meetings are structured to allow ample time to enjoy golf, tennis, and other recreational facilities nearby. Since the individual's expenses are reimbursed by the company (for which the latter takes a business deduction) without any income liabilities, the executive is in effect receiving no-cost mini-vacations. Conventions on foreign soil are eligible for the same consideration if it is as reasonable to hold them offshore as in the United States. For some, this is added incentive to ensure multinational membership. Executive interest is probably moderate.

Credit Cards. A number of companies provide their executives with credit cards. The company not only pays the annual charge but may in fact pay the full interest charges (without attempting to separate business from personal usage). In addition, where the company is billed directly, it may be slow in requiring reimbursement from the executive for personal charges. These amounts are in effect interest-free loans; nonetheless, because of the few dollars involved, this is only of low interest.

Domestic Staff. Company provision of personal domestic staff for the executive at either no cost or reduced expense is an extension of home entertainment expenses but likely to draw attention. Newspapers and trade journals periodically identify executives who have had company workers build extensions on houses or undertake significant renovations. Such assistance may either be short-term or an ongoing service. Similarly, it may either be provided by company employees or on a contractual basis. Typically, such services trigger imputed income and are tax deductible to the company. However, the perceived value to the executive may be high due to the quality of service received and its visibility.

Expense Account. In addition to the normal travel and entertainment policy of the company, certain individuals may be given broader discretion through liberalized expense accounts. As long as the situation qualifies as a business expense and, in the view of the IRS, is not "lavish or extravagant" (Section 274(k) of the IRC), it is 50-percent tax deductible per Section 274(n) of the IRC.

A variation of this is to give the executive an expense account of a stated amount (e.g., $100,000) not subject to company review. The company considers the total amount compensation expense and the executive uses as much as possible for business-related expenses. Since the company does not reimburse the executive for expenses, the individual will itemize those non-reimbursed items on the tax form. Thus, if an executive incurred $20,000 of business expense, he or she would have a $10,000 tax deduction. A liberal expense account often receives a high rating from executives.

First-Class Travel. Another well-received perquisite is first-class travel on commercial business trips, or even business class. Certainly, it makes sense to provide such accommodations for those individuals who are entitled to use the corporate aircraft (since it approaches first-class commercial accommodations). Some companies, however, restrict usage to a certain number of air miles or time in flight before permitting such coverage. When first-class or business class accommodations are not covered on international flights, unhappy executives are sandwiched in among vacationers and small children—not the most conducive environment for getting some work done or resting prior to a meeting shortly after arrival. Not surprisingly, first class travel often scores high with executives.

Home Entertainment. A variation, or in some cases an extension, of club memberships is reimbursement for home entertainment expenses associated with business purposes. Activities can range from lawn parties to indoor formal dining with extensive catering, probably the norm rather than the exception. Such a policy may be either a simple reimbursement or a stated annual allowance. In any event, the company receives a deduction for its expenses, and the individual avoids an income liability on documented business expenses. This benefit is of moderate importance, but could be high if considerable entertainment is needed.

Personal Escort. In addition to providing first-class travel, some companies ensure that their top executives are met at the airport and have a personal escort to their hotel. Usually the executive will be checked in and out by the "host," thus saving tedious minutes in lobby lines. It is the host's responsibility to ensure that the hotel accommodations are fully satisfactory, including catering to individual whims (e.g., putting the proper brand of Scotch in the room). This fluff treatment is probably moderate in importance.

Season Tickets. Whether for sporting events or the arts (e.g., opera, ballet, and theater), season tickets are deductible under the earlier described rules of business entertainment. Therefore, in addition to providing choice locations often for hard-to-get events, this perk is very tax effective. However, sky boxes and other luxury boxes are tax deductible only to the amount of non-luxury box seats per Section 274(l) of the IRC, thereby limiting this moderate importance perk.

Spouse Travel. Because of the IRS requirement that a clear business need must exist for the spouse to accompany the executive on a business trip in order for the spouse's travel expenses not to be considered income, use of this perquisite is limited to this narrow definition. Thus, this type of perquisite is determined on a case-by-case basis. A key factor is whether or not spouses are expected to attend because of the scheduled events. Due to the business nature, this perquisite often extends down rather far in the management ranks, depending on circumstances. In many instances, some level of senior management must specifically approve the individual request and company policy may limit the number of annual trips. Companies must also determine if spousal travel is broadened to include "significant others." Also at question are same-sex partners. However, even when spouse travel expenses are considered income, they may not be considered wages; therefore, while reportable, withholding taxes may not apply. Executive interest is probably moderate.

Work Area. The office is another very visible service program or perquisite. By using different characteristics of office spaces, it is rather easy to develop a hierarchy to reflect organization status. In addition to location, an office's size, number of windows, type of furniture (including armchairs and sofas), quality of carpeting and drapes, and number and type of paintings and sculptures are all visible means of projecting the executive's importance. While there have been some questions regarding extremely expensive, original artwork, such items are normally a business expense to the company and escape tax liability to the executive.

An extension of the luxurious office is the executive washroom. It can range from a simple basin and toilet to a facility resembling a Roman bath in style, size, and opulence. Variables include tub, shower, sauna, and dressing table. Locations range from centrally located communal facilities under special lock to individual rooms located adjacent to executive offices (usually with private entrances from within the offices). Like the office furnishings, executive washrooms are tax-deductible expenses for the corporation without incurring liabilities for the executive. Lavish offices are worth at least a moderate rating.

In today's office environment, some executives no longer have the best. Instead of enclosed offices, some are losing their walls to chest-level partitions in order to promote flow and communication. And, instead of being by the windows, they are in the center of the floor (and the work flow) thereby giving this a low rating. Meanwhile, non-executives are being given more latitude to personalize their work area.

Summary of Service Programs

A summary of both the tax effectiveness and the perceived importance of service programs to executives is shown in Table 6-9. As can be seen, many of the perks are perceived as important even though they impute income that may or may not be tax deductible.

Note that in the "importance to executive" section of the table, "EB" (employee benefits) and "P" (perquisites) are used when the all-employee and executive benefit coverages are different. A ✔ is used when both groups are comparable. The "TE" section rates the tax effectiveness to employee benefits (EB) on a scale of one to five, with one being highly effective, and to perquisites (P) on a scale of A to D, with A being highly effective. (See Table 6-3.) An * indicates the rating depends on coverage.

HEALTH CARE

Certainly one of the most cost-effective benefits is reimbursement for medical expenses. It is tax deductible to the company, while the recipient has no income-tax liability. Section 105 of the IRC describes the requirements that must be met. Non-reimbursed health care expenses are deductible in accordance with Section 213 of the IRC but only if in the aggregate they exceed 7.5 percent of adjusted gross income. For executives, they are a large amount of non-deductible expenses. Therefore, company-reimbursed medical expenses (tax deductible to the company and not taxable to the individual) are of interest to the executive. The degree of interest is a function of the cost that would otherwise have to be paid by the executive.

TE		Program	Importance to Executive		
E	C		Low	Moderate	High
5	B	Assignment and Relocation Expenses		EB	P
1	B	Athletic Programs	✔		
1	B	Attendance and Service Awards	✔		
4	B	Clothing	✔		
1	B	Company Products		✔	
3	B	Dependent Care	✔		
1	B	Educational Assistance		✔	
1	B	Employee Assistance Program		✔	
		Financial Services			
1	*	• Auto and Homeowner Insurance		✔	
*	B	• Credit Unions and Loans		EB	P
3	B	• Financial Planning	EB		P
3	B	• Legal Assistance	EB		P
3	B	• Liability Insurance	EB		P
1	B	• Pre-Retirement Counseling		EB	P
3	B	• Tax Assistance		EB	P
1	B	Food Service	EB	P	
*	B	Home	EB	P	
*	A	Job Title	EB		P
1	B	Matching Gifts			✔
1	B	Scholarships		✔	
		Transportation			
*	B	• Airplanes	EB		P
5	B	• Automobiles	EB		P
	B	• Boats and Ships	EB	P	
		Travel and Entertainment			
*	B	• Apartments or Hotel Rooms	EB	P	
*	B	• Club Memberships	EB	P	
*	B	• Conventions and Conferences	EB	P	
1	B	• Credit Cards	✔		
5	B	• Domestic Staff	EB		P
1	C	• Expense Accounts		EB	P

Table 6-9. Service program summary (continued on next page)

TE		Program	Importance to Executive		
E	C		Low	Moderate	High
		Travel & Entertainment (Cont'd)			
I	B	• First-Class Travel	EB		P
I	C	• Home Entertainment	EB	P	
I	B	• Personal Escort	EB	P	
*	*	• Season Tickets	EB	P	
*	B	• Spousal Travel	EB	P	
I	B	Work Area		✔	
∂		Summary Totals			
		✔	5	6	I
		EB	18	5	0
		P	0	19	13

Table 6-9. continued

Medical

Health insurance can be significant in protecting the executive's income in times of expensive medical crises and, therefore, is of high importance. Basically, there are two types of plans: managed care and fee-for-service.

Managed Care. This has become the dominant form of health-care coverage today and includes HMOs, PPOs, and POSs. Managed care attempts to control the cost of medical expenses by controlling access of patients to specialists and negotiating the fees of health care providers (e.g., hospitals and physicians). Each person covered by a managed care organization is charged a monthly fee. The per capita charge has given these plans the name *capitation plans*.

- **Health Maintenance Organization (HMO).** An HMO typically provides covered employees (subscriber) with a list of doctors and hospitals the person may use. Normally, each patient is assigned a primary care physician who controls access to specialists. For this reason, the doctor is sometimes called a gatekeeper.

  The employer pays the HMO an agreed upon amount per employee; the employee may be required to make up the difference between that amount and the total cost. Such forms of medical care are quite attractive when the employee's residence and work site are both within easy commuting distance of the HMO center, although some are disappointed with the less personal nature of treatment than that provided by a family doctor. In addition, many executives are not eager to relinquish the ability to make a free and independent decision on the provider of needed medical services. In spite of the fact that an HMO virtually assures that needed services will be available, many executives want to be certain that a doctor or surgeon is the best in the field—not simply one capable of adequate care! While a number of very qualified surgeons are in HMOs, not all of the established top names are affiliated with such organizations.

- **Preferred Provider Organization (PPO).** The PPO is a variation of the HMO permitting patients to opt out of the prescribed list of doctors and hospitals in exchange for a greater fee and/or larger deductibles. The deductible is the amount paid by the patient before any expense coverage by the plan.

- **Point of Service Plan (POS).** The POS plan permits a patient to delay the decision of staying within the network or going outside of it until the time service is needed.
- **Fee-for-Service.** This type of medical care coverage includes Blue Cross and Blue Shield, commercial insurance, and self-insurance.

Because of a close relationship with the American Hospital Association and the American Medical Association, *Blue Cross* and *Blue Shield* respectively were able to negotiate procedural fees and hospital charges. First-dollar coverage is provided although the length of hospital stays is typically limited to control costs. Although there are a number of "Blues," they typically operate independently within a defined geographical area. Blue Cross covers hospital charges whereas Blue Shield focuses on surgical and other medical expenses.

Health care benefits provided by a *commercial insurance* company obligate the carrier to pay all covered expenses in exchange for a monthly premium. Under a self-insured plan, the company uses no outside insurer and is responsible for determining the legitimacy of claims and making payments. Since some companies find it unpalatable to personally deny a claim, they engage insurance companies for "administrative services only" to determine the appropriateness of the claim with the company then making the payment.

Insurance contracts provide coverage under either a *"comprehensive"* or a *"schedule"* plan. Comprehensive payment consists of four levels of payment: the portion paid by the employee, the portion paid by the plan, the portion in which expenses are paid by both, and the remaining portion paid in full by the plan. As an example, the employee may be liable for the first $500 of covered expenses during the year. The plan will pay the next $1,000 in full. Next, the plan will pick up 80 percent of the expense with the employee paying the remaining 20 percent, and finally, any covered expenses in excess of $5,000 will be paid in full by the plan.

Under a scheduled plan, each covered expense is identified and a maximum dollar reimbursement assigned. Typically, such plans also have an extended medical reimbursement feature that will pay a specified percentage (e.g., 80 percent) of all covered expenses beyond the schedule after an annual deductible (e.g., $500) is fully paid by the employee. Additionally, a stop-loss feature similar to a comprehensive plan is usually included. As can be seen, the two plans are highly similar. The scheduled plan will reimburse a higher percentage of medical costs in communities with lower-cost health services. Such a plan requires periodic updates to increase schedules to appropriate levels of reimbursement.

Where the company has enough employees, these plans are experience-related, which means that the premium charged by the insurance company is determined by the claims experience only of this unit. Conversely, HMOs are community-rated—meaning that premiums will be determined by the experience of the full community of users, not simply the users from a particular company. The third approach is to *pool* experience, or place a group of employees in a unit consisting of other groups; the premium is based on the experience of the entire pool.

Factors impacting on the premium charged include: (1) plan changes, (2) prices of services, (3) size of unit covered, and (4) utilization of the plan. As these increase, one can expect the premium to increase, and conversely, as these decrease, one should expect a reduction in premium. Usually a combination of different rates of increase occur among the four items.

When the insurance carrier and the employer differ significantly on the premium level for the following year, quite often they agree to write a *retrospective premium adjustment,* or "retro," into the contract. The carrier agrees to accept a lower premium; in exchange, the employer agrees to reimburse expenses at the end of the year up to a predetermined limit. Thus, the employer improves cash flow during the year in exchange for an increased level of financial risk at year-end.

Another way companies control health care expenses is by entering into a *minimum premium arrangement* with the insurance company. As the term implies, this reduces premiums to a minimum, maybe 10 percent of its former size. But, the company agrees to deposit into a bank account an amount believed sufficient in size to cover normal claim experience. The carrier agrees to pay any and all claims beyond the amount deposited by the company. The premium paid by the company is to ensure this excess protection. This approach results in savings to the company in two ways: (1) a reduction of proportionate amount (e.g., 90 percent) in premium taxes due the state and (2) significant reduction in reserves (i.e., company money held by the carrier) to cover *open and unreported claims* (commonly called "O and U"). These are claims that are incurred during the year the contract is in force but not paid until the following year (when the contract may no longer be in force) because they were either not reported or reported but not paid as of the end of the contract year.

The final step is when the company takes all financial risk for claims; in other words, it becomes *self-insured.* This may be either on a "pay-as-you-go" basis or by establishing reserves to level out payments. If the company establishes a trust in conformance with Section 501(c)(9) of the IRC, it can take a deduction for the amount contributed to the trust, or *Voluntary Employees Beneficiary Associations* (VEBAs). Additionally, earnings of the trust are not subject to taxes, thus making contributions very cost effective. While the trust is constructed to hypothetically meet all claim expenses, unusual circumstances could completely exhaust the funds before paying all claims. Rather than face this possibility, some companies purchase stop-loss protection that stipulates at what point the insurer will assume responsibility for losses.

Another manner in which companies use insurance carriers when self-insured is to purchase claim review and processing, or *administrative services only* (ASO). This approach enables a company to place a third party between itself and its employees on difficult claim reviews. It also gains the expertise of the carrier to ensure reasonable and customary amounts are being charged for services performed.

Even before an individual is hired, he or she may have received a medical benefit—the *pre-employment physical.* In addition to wanting to know the health status of potential employees, a number of companies have ongoing physical examination programs. Due to cost, such programs are often limited to multiphasic screening with emphasis on urine and blood samples. Depending on the nature of work, chest x-rays and gastrointestinal studies may also be undertaken. Additionally, the company may have a random drug testing program to determine substance abuse. When detected, the individual is typically counseled and put in a program to deal with the chemical dependency.

For individuals with specific medical problems, wallet-sized cards listing allergies, blood type, and required medications may be appropriate. For some, a bracelet or necklace identifying a particular problem (e.g., allergy to penicillin) could be very helpful in case of an accident or serious injury. Others have microfilmed their medical history highlights and carry this in their wallet.

Prescription Drugs. Prescribed medications are usually covered only while in a hospital or after satisfying the extended medical reimbursement deductible under most medical insurance programs. It is not surprising, therefore, that a number of companies have developed plans to reimburse medication expenses (normally after a modest per-prescription deductible of a few dollars)

Home Health Care. A win-win scenario for the health care provider and the patient is home health care where hospital services are provided at home rather than the hospital. The provider avoids costly hospital charges and the patient is permitted to recuperate at home. Plans may cover: equipment (e.g., beds, oxygen, and wheelchairs); nursing and therapy (e.g., infusion, physical, and speech); and service aide (e.g., assistance in bathing and cooking). Home health care may be provided directly through an independent contractor or indirectly through the health care provider. Home health care helps patients self-manage the health issue within the friendly confines of their home. The executive may find it easier to continue work responsibilities (if medically permitted) from the home than from the hospital. Home health care covers the range from recuperation to long-term care to terminal illnesses, which may require *hospice* care. In addition to providing emotional support and pain relief, assistance with household chores may also be included.

Insurance coverage can also be obtained to pay for *long-term care* in an assisted living center, nursing home, adult day care, and in-home services for self, spouse, parents, parents-in-law, and grandparents. The 1996 Health Insurance Portability and Accountability Act provided that such contracts would be viewed as accident and health plans. More specifically, paid premiums and benefits received would be considered medical care and excluded from gross income subject to Section 213 of the IRC. This section permits itemized deductions in excess of 7.5 percent of adjusted gross income.

To be eligible for favorable federal tax treatment, long-term care recipients must be unable to perform for themselves at least two of the six events of daily living for at least 90 days. They are: bathing, continence, dressing, eating, toileting, and transferring self. This applies to dying, chronically ill, and temporarily impaired individuals. While long-term protection for the executive is of some interest, more important is the peace of mind of providing such coverage for one's parents. Spending a few thousand dollars each year in premiums is worth not being hit later on with expenses of up to $100,000 a year or more. Medicare coverage is often inadequate.

Medicare. Medicare is national health insurance for those age 65 and older. In effect since 1966, it consists of Part A and Part B. Part A is focused on in-patient care (e.g., home care, hospital, and nursing home); Part B is for outpatient care. Blue Cross/Blue Shield and commercial insurance companies offer policies to supplement Medicare coverage. There are also Medicare HMOs. Given company insurance that will continue past retirement age, Medicare is of little concern to most executives. See "Retiree Medical" later in this chapter.

Adoptions

Many companies reimburse eligible adoption expenses up to a stated maximum. While this is not a medical benefit, it equates to medical coverage for childbirth expenses. Adoption-expense reimbursement levels the playing field for those unable to give birth. Section 23 of the IRC details the amount of unreimbursed adoption expenses that may receive favorable tax treatment. Given the limited expense, it is of low executive interest.

Wellness Programs

The focus of wellness programs is to keep people healthy and to prevent illness. This is a win-win scenario—the employee is healthier and the company saves money on medical expenses, disability payments, and the cost of temporary help to perform the work of the ill employee. Due to preventive emphasis, this is of moderate executive interest.

Medical Examinations. This is another part of the wellness program that may apply universally to all employees or only executives. Even when all are eligible, executives may have better programs.

Medical exams are very important to the executive since they are intended to identify correctable problems before they advance into major concerns. The exam could be given by the executive's own doctor (perhaps up to a prescribed dollar maximum), a clinic (specializing in exams), and/or the company doctor. In some instances, the results of the exam are made available to the company (as a tempering effect on manpower planning); invariably the results are given to the executive's own doctor(s).

Some examinations are performed at the employee's place of work or in his or her own community; others are coincidentally located near resort communities. If the latter, the executive can conduct his or her own cardiovascular risk analysis on the tennis court or golf course, in between examinations and tests.

Eligibility may be a function of job grade or organization rank, but the frequency and extent of examination is in some instances related to age. The value of a complete medical exam for a 25-year-old versus a 55-year-old are not the same in many eyes. Medical exams are very cost effective, as the recipient has no imputed income whereas the company has a tax deduction.

Physical Fitness Program. This is a key component of a wellness program. In some companies, fitness programs are limited to executives; other companies make them available to all employees believing that in the long run they promote good health and lower company medical costs. Physical activity may also reduce work-related stress. Thus, the fitness program does not simply promote better physical being, but also assists in shedding the tensions and pressures of work. Since unrelieved stress may lead to depression, this could truly be a perquisite intended to promote happier executives. In addition to stress management, nutrition information, smoking cessation, and weight control programs are often available.

Some companies choose to build their own facilities, while others avoid construction and related costs and join a medically oriented facility near the company site. Exercise equipment ranges from the basic treadmill, rowing machines, stationary bicycle, medicine ball, and weights to more elaborate setups with jogging tracks and courts for basketball, tennis, and volleyball.

Often under the supervision of trained company medical staff, executives are given perhaps three hourly sessions a week to work through a concentrated schedule of activity (usually during normal business hours). These sessions may lower the risk of coronary artery disease, and just as important, many participants say they feel better and more able to cope with work-related pressures and crises. Increased strength and endurance coupled with concern for proper nutrition and weight management often result in more restful sleep, higher energy levels, and a more attractive physique—all very important items to the executive. To date, physical fitness programs are tax deductible to the company and do not result in imputed income to the individual.

Dental

A shortcoming of most medical insurance plans is their limited degree of expense reimbursement for dental problems; it is not atypical for a plan to cover only repair necessitated by an accident. This void has been filled by *dental insurance.* Like medical insurance, such policies are either scheduled or comprehensive type plans. Many plans pay the full cost of normal check-ups, x-rays, and cleaning to encourage early detection of problems. Thus, early diagnosis and treatment should reduce the need for expensive restorative care. Usually covered as a separate item is orthodontia—an increasingly popular procedure. This is of moderate interest to the executive only if expenses are extensive.

Vision and Audio

There are some instances of *vision care* insurance to reimburse all or a portion of examinations and eyeglasses. *Audio care* is a similar health care item dealing with the hearing and necessary corrective devices. Neither has become very popular, perhaps due to a combination of tolerable expenses in one instance and infrequent utilization in the other. Executive interest is low.

Flexible Spending Accounts

Flexible spending accounts (FSAs) are individual employee accounts funded by pretax payroll deductions. There is no statutory limit on the total amount for medical care; however, it must be determined prior to the beginning of the year. It can be used to pay out-of-pocket expenses such as the deductible, the employee portion of co-insurance as well as expenses not covered by the medical plan. Some executives consider this of high importance, but it is more likely moderate if the medical plan is generous and has a stop-loss maximum.

Domestic Partner

While coverage for spouse and dependent children is typical in most plans, a new definition has arisen—that of domestic partner. This typically is defined as a person in a committed, exclusive relationship with the employee residing at the same address. It may be limited to a heterosexual partner or include same sex. In some areas, such coverage may be required; however, executive interest is low unless a domestic partner is present.

Supplemental Health Care Coverage

This begins where basic health care coverage stops. After the executive has been reimbursed by the basic plan covering all employees, the balance is quietly reimbursed under a supplemental plan—leaving the executive with no health care expenses. In the case of non-reimbursed, medical expenses, a deduction on personal taxes can be taken on the amount in excess of 7.5 percent of income. However, for the executive earning $100,000, this would mean the first $7,500 would not be deductible; furthermore, due to the tax bracket, the individual would also have had to earn almost twice that amount in order to pay the bills from after-tax income.

However, under Section 105(h) of the IRC, the cost of this supplemental plan while deductible by the company as a business expense is considered income to the recipient if it is provided under insurance. Under a self-insured (by the company) plan, payments received are considered income for tax purposes (unless the plan is nondiscriminatory—by definition an employee benefit, not a perquisite).

While supplemental health care coverage can be of high importance to executives, it has not received wide acceptance for a simple reason: Executives find it difficult to explain to share-holders and lower-paid employees that health care expenses are being totally reimbursed only for the top-paid executives.

In addition to full reimbursement of expenses covered under the basic health care program, the supplemental coverage could include items not covered by the basic plan. For example, massage therapy might be covered under the supposition that a relaxed executive is not only a better-functioning executive, but also a better-looking one.

Qualified-Domestic-Relations Orders

A qualified-domestic-relations order (QDRO) can be looked upon as a type of assignment benefit. It is usually an agreement between two or more parties on who will receive what benefits. While it typically includes alimony and child support, it could address a medical plan but not pension benefits, which are protected by ERISA. This is probably of low interest to most executives.

Former Employee

The Consolidated Omnibus Budget Reconciliation Act of 1985 (COBRA) requires employers to offer continued health coverage when such benefits would otherwise be terminated. Depending on the basis for termination and the nature of the benefits required, coverage may range from 18 to 36 months. Employers can require the beneficiary to pay up to 102 percent of the cost of a similar program for active employees. This is probably of moderate interest to executives.

Retiree Medical

Some companies offer the active employee medical plan to retired employees. Even though benefits are coordinated with Medicare, this can be an extremely valuable benefit especially for a person who retires prior to age 65. However, this is a very costly benefit to employers. The Financial Accounting Standards Board (FASB) issued FAS 106 "Employer's Accounting for Post Retirement Benefits Other than Pensions." It requires the company not only to recognize the current expense but also show as a liability on the balance sheet the accrued cost of retiree medical benefits for covered employees who are still working. This could result in many employers drastically reducing medical coverage for retirees at least on a prospective basis.

While health care protection and some form of company cost reimbursement is important to all employees, it can be especially attractive and of high importance to executives. Since the cost of health care can only be deducted to the extent it exceeds 7.5 percent of adjusted gross income (Section 213 of the IRC), a highly paid executive retiree could have significant out-of-pocket expenses before such amounts become tax deductible. Even then, the government pays only a portion (50 percent if the tax rate is 50 percent). It is far better to have the full amount paid by the medical plan.

Summary of Supplemental Health Care Benefits

Shown in Table 6-10 is a likely summary of the importance of health care benefits to the executive. Rather than break out the component parts of "Medical," it is listed once, since the ratings probably do not change, with the exception that prescription drugs may be of "low" importance because of the modest cost the program replaces. Medical benefits while active and after retired are very important to the executive because benefits are not taxed as income whereas expenses, if paid out-of-pocket, probably would not be tax deductible. Flexible spending accounts and supplemental health protection are also of high importance because of their tax effectiveness.

TE			Importance to Executive		
E	C	Program	Low	Moderate	High
I	B	Medical			✔
I	B	Home Health Care		✔	
I	B	Adoptions	✔		
I	B	Wellness		✔	
I	B	Dental		✔	
I	B	Vision and Audio	✔		
*	B	Flexible Spending Account			✔
*	B	Domestic Partner	✔		
*	B	Supplemental Health			✔
*	B	Qualified Domestic Relations Order	✔		
I	B	Former Employee		✔	
I	B	Retiree Medical			✔
		Summary Totals ✔ EB P	4 0 0	4 0 0	4 0 0

*Depends on coverage

Table 6-10. Health care summary

SURVIVOR PROTECTION

As the words imply, this category of benefits is intended to address the financial needs of the employee's family after the individual dies. It is designed to preserve the executive's estate assets by providing sufficient liquidity to pay the federal estate and state inheritance taxes, as well as perhaps meet longer-term income liabilities for the beneficiaries. It can be very tax effective since life insurance proceeds incur no income tax liability and the federal estate tax and state inheritance tax can be avoided with careful planning.

Most people probably buy life insurance for protection rather than investment. This is important because even policies that return a dividend to either build cash value or reduce premiums probably have a rate of return below many other investments. Also, if the face value of the contract is fixed (i.e., does not appreciate over the years in relation to some formula), it will suffer much as bonds do during periods of inflation. A $100,000 policy today is worth $50,000 seven years from now if annual inflation is 10 percent.

Types of Life Insurance

Ordinary. The most basic form of life insurance is *whole life*, in force for a person's entire life. Premiums may be paid until death (under *ordinary life policy*, also called *straight life*) or for a limited period. A limited period payment is expressed either in the number of years during which premiums are required (e.g., Twenty Payment Life denotes 20 years of premiums after which the policy is paid up) or the age at which the policy will be considered paid in full (e.g., Age 65 Life). Such policies are more common with individual than group policies.

Each year a portion of the premium is credited to a reserve created to meet the financial obligation incurred by the insurance company. The carrier invests this amount (less an amount to meet other claims), oftentimes in mortgages. Another portion is credited to a reserve for the policyholder, usually beginning several years after the policy has been purchased. This cash value is available to the policyholder during the period of insurance protection in the form of a loan against the value of the policy. The rate of interest is specified in the contract. For many, these rates are significantly below what the individual would have to pay a bank. Furthermore, there is usually no prescribed payment date, and even unpaid interest is simply added to the loan. However, when the insured dies, the cash value is not an additional amount but is included in the face amount on the policy; furthermore, the value of the outstanding loan will be subtracted from the face value of the policy at the time of the insured's death. Typically, the employee can expect to be taxed on the employer's contribution to permanent insurance unless the policy is forfeitable at time of termination.

Term. Insurance that specifies the term or period during which the value of the policy is in force is called *term insurance*. For example, Twenty-year Term means the policy is only good for the first 20 years; if the insured lives beyond that point in time, the policy has no value. The cost of term insurance is very low, especially if purchased while young (e.g., in the twenties or early thirties). However, the cost increases with age. By the time one has reached the sixties, the cost has increased very dramatically. Term insurance is pure insurance protection, paying only at time of death if the policy is still in force. There is no cash value.

Some policies are *renewable*. A renewable policy may continue for another prescribed period of time (at a higher premium) without having to undergo a medical examination. In addition, the term policy may be *convertible*, which means before its expiration, the insured may switch over to another form of insurance (e.g., whole life or endowment). Contracts with such provisions cost more than straight term since they guarantee coverage beyond the normal term even if health is poor. In addition, the payer pays a one-time conversion charge (e.g., $25 for every $100 of group term insurance converted).

Term is the typical form of insurance provided by companies to their employees. Called *group term*, it identifies a group of eligible employees and provides insurance coverage typically until (1) the employee leaves, or (2) the contract expires (traditionally the contract is renewed annually), whichever occurs first.

It is advantageous to have the definition of "group" acceptable to the IRS, because in accordance with Section 79 of the IRC, the first $50,000 of coverage incurs no income tax liability. Typically, a group plan benefits at least 70 percent of the employer's employees and at least 85 percent of all participants excluding key employees.

Shown in Table 6-11 is a worksheet indicating how this calculation is made. Note that in this example the executive is paying less than the minimum required by the IRS tax table, and there-

Analysis of group life insurance imputed income, for federal income tax purposes, for	John Jones
Age as of December 31 of taxable year	42
Employee contribution for group life insurance for taxable year	$610
Gross amount of group life insurance	$500,000
Annual exemption from gross coverage	-$50,000
Net taxable coverage	$450,000
Uniform premium rate, selected from the IRS table below for employee's age (2.04) times net taxable coverage (450) equals value of company contribution per IRS table	$918
Minus employee annual contribution	-$610
Equals imputed income subject to tax	$308

Uniform Premium Rate Table (per each $1000 of insurance)

Age Class	Annual Rate
Under 30	$0.96
30 to 34	1.08
35 to 39	1.32
40 to 44	2.04
45 to 49	3.48
50 to 54	5.76
55 to 59	9.00
60 to 64	14.04
65 to 69	25.20
70 and over	45.12

Table 6-11. Imputed income worksheet with Uniform Premium Rate Table

fore there is a tax liability on $308 of imputed income. Increase the age to 57 and the individual has a $3,440 imputed-income figure (i.e., $4,050 - $610). Assuming a 50-percent marginal tax bracket, this is a bargain since the executive would pay $1,720 tax rather than a total premium of $4,050. Actually, it is a bargain only if the executive wants the insurance; an executive who does not want it will only look at the additional $1,720 as an unnecessary tax liability.

Group Universal Life Program. A *group universal life program* (GULP) is a term policy with a cash fund that can be used to produce ordinary life insurance and/or accumulate interest tax-free. It can be paid as a death benefit or used to borrow against. The employee's payroll deduction must be adequate to cover the term insurance portion. Anything in excess of that amount goes into the cash fund where interest payments accumulate tax-free.

Endowment. An *endowment* policy is similar to term insurance in one respect, the period during which payment for death of the insured is limited. However, if death does not occur during that period, then the face value is paid to the insured, either in a lump sum or an annual annuity. Since the face value of the policy has to be paid not later than the end of the endowment period (e.g., 20 years), the premiums are higher than whole life. An endowment policy could be financed by a rollover in whole or part of a retirement plan distribution. The annuity could either be fixed or variable (fluctuating based on investment performance).

Company-Owned Life Insurance. Unlike insurance contracts where the employee is the owner and a family member the beneficiary, under a company-owned life insurance program (COLI) as the name suggests, the company is the owner. It may also be the beneficiary. Alternatively, ownership and beneficiary interests may be split between the company and the executive. Let's examine these various possibilities.

Key Employee (Key Person) Insurance. With *key employee* (also known as *key person*) *insurance*, the company is the owner *and* the beneficiary. It typically covers the loss by death of a key person, ensuring the ongoing success of the organization and either indirectly reflecting the person's value or directly providing the funds necessary to buy out the deceased's ownership in the company. Premiums are not tax deductible but proceeds are tax-free. Other than any psychic value of knowing one's life is worth several million to the company, there is no value to the executive for key person insurance.

With *key employee insurance* the company is still the owner and beneficiary. However, upon death of the executive, the proceeds are paid to the designated beneficiary. The tax treatment is the same as with key person insurance up to the point the proceeds are paid to the beneficiary. At that time, the company takes a tax deduction for the amount paid and the beneficiary has a like amount of taxable income. The amount is also most likely includable in the estate and subject to estate taxes. Because of the heavy taxes, the company may decide to gross up for taxes thereby increasing its cost net of tax deductions.

Thus, key employee life insurance takes one of three approaches: the proceeds are paid to the company (1) as recompense for the value of the deceased executive, or (2) to provide monies for a deferred compensation agreement with the executive, or (3) to provide the money needed to buy out the deceased executive's ownership in the company. The third approach is more prevalent among smaller companies and partnerships.

Under such insurance, the company has ownership rights to the policy, although it can take no tax deduction on the premiums paid [Internal Revenue Code Section 264(a)(1)]. However, the beneficiary does not have an income-tax liability on the death benefit proceeds [Section 101(a)(1) of the Code].

Provisions can be made for the executive to buy out the policy at the time of retirement: the assumption is that, by that point, the company has developed a suitable replacement and, therefore, no longer needs insurance to cover the loss. The value to the executive is that permanent insurance protection is obtained to replace the group term insurance in effect during employment. If the key employee insurance is transferred for whatever reason, it is probably best to transfer directly to the insured (perhaps for an amount equal to the cash value). Then the executive can transfer the policy to the spouse if desired. If transferred directly from the company to the spouse, the proceeds in excess of the death proceeds may be subject to income tax.

In addition, the company should structure the policy so that it can transfer coverage from executive A to another should the first leave the company. An adjustment on the premium will be required because of differences in the executives' ages and the length of time the initial policy was in effect.

A variation on the typical key employee policy is keeping the policy in force until the executive's death (even after retirement). Such a policy may be used to provide special pension payments to surviving retired executives. In structuring such a policy, the company must attempt to ensure that the proceeds are sufficient to finance the executive benefit. A key variable is life expectancy when the payments are for life rather than a prescribed period of time. Since the direct linkage of insurance proceeds to pensions would subject the executives to unfavorable tax treatment (as prefunded benefits), the life insurance and pensions must not be directly related. Nonetheless, the insurance proceeds provide the financing for the corporation to pay the pension supplements. Under such an arrangement, the company typically has heavier cash flow requirements in the early years (i.e., insurance premiums and pension supplements) than without such a plan. As with traditional key employee insurance, while the death benefit proceeds are not taxable to the company (since it is the beneficiary), neither are the premium payments tax deductible! However, interest charges are deductible (if four of the first seven years' premiums are paid in cash, not borrowed). By borrowing against the policy's increase in cash value, the company is able to lower its cash flow requirements and deduct the interest charges. Since the policy's cash values and dividends normally will exceed the after-tax cost of interest charges, the net result is a positive increase in the value of the initial company investment. This simple fact encourages the company to borrow the premium cost (after paying at least four of the first seven annual premiums) to have maximum leverage on use of corporate funds.

Split-Dollar Insurance. Split-dollar insurance is when ownership of a whole life insurance policy is split between company and executive with the face value of the policy (less the amount paid by the company, which it recaptures at time of insured's death) paid to the executive's beneficiary. Typically, the employer and the executive also split the premium. The employer premium is determined one of several ways. The most common is the *PS-58 method* with the employer's premium exceeding those shown in Table 6-12. The second most common approach is the *cash-value method* whereby the employer pays a premium equal to the increase in cash value of the policy. This is illustrated in Table 6-13. Another approach is the *level-contribution method* where the employer pays the amount in excess of a level premium paid by the employee.

The proceeds may be allocated in one of two ways. The most typical arrangement is the *endorsement* method where the company is the owner of the policy. As such, it is responsible for payment of the premiums; however, it makes a separate agreement with the executive stipulating the amount and manner in which the insured will split the premium with the company. In addition, the company allows the insured to name the beneficiary for the amount in excess of the payment to the company to recover its costs. Another approach is the *assignment* method, where the employee is the owner of the policy and an amount equal to the cumulative premiums paid by the company is assigned to it. This was attractive until the IRS Tax Reform Act of 1984 essentially killed interest-free loans. It was common for a company to agree to lend an executive annually the amount by which the cash value increased. The company in turn would agree to forward to a beneficiary designated by the insured any proceeds in excess of the loan balance at the time of the insured's death.

Age	Premium	Age	Premium
18	$1.52	50	$9.22
19	1.56	51	9.97
20	1.61	52	10.79
21	1.67	53	11.69
22	1.73	54	12.67
23	1.79	55	13.74
24	1.86	56	14.91
25	1.93	57	16.18
26	2.02	58	17.56
27	2.11	59	19.08
28	2.20	60	20.73
29	2.31	61	22.53
30	2.43	62	24.50
31	2.57	63	26.63
32	2.70	64	28.98
33	2.86	65	31.51
34	3.02	66	34.28
35	3.21	67	37.31
36	3.41	68	40.59
37	3.63	69	44.17
38	3.87	70	48.06
39	4.14	71	52.29
40	4.42	72	56.89
41	4.73	73	61.89
42	5.07	74	67.33
43	5.44	75	73.23
44	5.85	76	79.63
45	6.30	77	86.57
46	6.78	78	94.09
47	7.32	79	102.23
48	7.89	80	111.04
49	8.53		

Table 6-12. PS 58 table: annual premium per $1,000 insurance

Beginning in 2001, the IRS indicated a view that the employer and employee had two split-dollar insurance options. The owner was either the executive or the company. If it is the executive, the transaction is viewed as a loan with the executive taxed on any below market forgiven interest costs. If the company owns the policy, then the executive will be taxed each year on the difference between the face value of the policy and the amount the company would receive (at term insurance rates). The executive would also be taxed on the vested amount of the policy's cash surrender value. If the executive-owner option is not selected (and taxed accordingly), the option will revert to the company-owner.

Policy Year	Payments		End of Year		Premium
	Employer	Executive	Cash Value	Dividend	1-Year Term
1	$2,000	$24,710	$2,000	$0	$0.00
2	1,000	25,670	3,000	0	0.00
3	20,000	6,710	23,000	2,330	137.66
4	21,000	5,710	44,000	3,130	288.18
5	20,000	6,710	64,000	3,670	458.22
6	22,000	4,710	86,000	4,500	674.20
7	21,000	5,710	107,000	5,340	918.06
8	22,000	4,710	129,000	6,110	1,201.02
9	22,000	4,710	151,000	6,760	1,547.76
10	22,000	4,710	173,000	7,496	1,937.50
11	22,000	4,710	195,000	8,290	2,386.78
12	23,000	3,710	218,000	9,170	2,916.78
13	22,000	4,710	240,000	10,000	3,513.40
14	23,000	3,710	263,000	10,830	4,210.70
15	23,000	3,710	286,000	11,690	5,007.88
16	23,000	3,710	309,000	12,590	5,917.28
17	23,000	3,710	332,000	14,800	6,951.42
18	23,000	3,710	355,000	15,710	8,121.72
19	22,000	4,710	377,000	16,670	9,427.36
20	23,000	3,710	400,000	17,560	10,934.94

Table 6-13. Split-dollar insurance, $1-million policy

In addition to being a definite status symbol, a split-dollar insurance program can be of real value when there is a very large estate liability (e.g., a significant amount of deferred stock). Probably one of the greatest illustrations of need is when a company has deferred a portion of the executive's pay until after retirement and such payment is made on a scheduled basis (e.g., over 15 years). Although the beneficiary of the deferrals may be subject to the same earn-out schedule, usually the present value of all future payments will become part of the executive's estate for tax purposes. It is difficult enough to liquidate assets to pay taxes; needless to say, it is much harder to pay taxes when the assets are not available for liquidation.

Given that tax law and IRS interpretations are continuing to evolve, no attempt is made here to describe the tax consequences, since it would most assuredly be out-of-date by time of publication.

Depending on the number of executives covered, the amount of insurance, and the premium split, the company may be expending millions of dollars annually. The use of less expensive term insurance might accomplish similar objectives. One such approach is discussed next.

Retired Lives Reserve. With the *retired lives reserve* (RLR) concept, the company prefunds the executive's post-retirement life insurance by making tax-deductible contributions to a reserve fund (which in turn pays for the cost of insurance protection after retirement) to purchase a deferred life insurance policy or continue premium payments after retirement.

Normally, this approach would have a trustee own the policy and be the beneficiary of a post-65 life insurance policy on the executive. If the executive died after retirement, the trust would receive the proceeds and pay them to the beneficiary designated by the executive. If the executive died before age 65, the beneficiary would receive the life insurance proceeds directly from the carrier under the pre-65 policy. An executive who died before 65 would have no rights under the post-65 plan, and the proceeds paid to the trust from the RLR would be used to reduce the company's premium obligations for other covered executives. Proceeds paid directly to the company would be considered taxable income.

Revenue Ruling 69-382 allows deductions by the company of prefunded retirement life insurance if: (1) the reserve is solely for providing life insurance benefits to those covered, (2) the amounts in reserve are not returned to the company as long as any covered employees or retirees are alive, and (3) annual additions to the reserve are not greater than needed to meet the insurance obligations. This type of deduction was further protected by Revenue Ruling 73-599, which ruled that retired lives reserve plans are not deferred compensation plans. If they were, the company could not take deductions when paid but rather when received by the beneficiary.

The executive has no tax liability under the RLR before age 65, although the person is, of course, subject to imputed income for amounts of insurance in excess of $50,000. Furthermore, it appears that as long as the RLR is deemed to be group life insurance after retirement, the retired executive has no tax liability at that point either. Assuming the individual has success-fully assigned the policy, it may also be possible to avoid estate taxes, although under Revenue Ruling 76-490, the executive is considered to have made a gift each year of the value of the assigned group life insurance benefit.

Some argue that RLR is a more cost-effective approach than split-dollar insurance to meet similar objectives. At least the company is obtaining a tax deduction on the RLR cost, and it appears that the executive's tax liability may be more favorable than under split-dollar insurance.

However, the IRS may be concerned with the selectivity of megabuck RLR policies for exec-utives and whether such insurance is really permanent (not term) insurance. Both strike at the application of Section 79 definitions. If RLR is not Section 79, then the protection while retired may not be free of income tax consequences and the cost may not be deductible to the compa-ny until the benefits are paid.

All COLI plans are long-term commitments and reflect long-term assumptions that may or may not turn out to be true. They include no unfavorable changes in tax treatment, assumed interest rates, and mortality experience. Furthermore, COLI benefits must be compared with alternative forms of investment income available to the employer. It is important to remember that the cost of the benefit provided is the total of benefits paid plus expenses less investment return on allocated assets. Insurance does not eliminate the cost. It is simply one way of meet-ing the expenses.

Due to the complexities of insurance plan variations, the executive must examine the avail-able alternatives very carefully. Due to individual needs and circumstances, one form will be more appropriate than another. Thus, the assistance of an attorney and accountant along with an insurance expert in designing the optimal plan is critical.

Which Type Does One Choose?

Term insurance may be the only true form of life insurance. Other forms, including whole life, have some form of investment consideration in addition to insuring risk. Rather than view term and whole life as competing forms of insurance, they should be viewed as complementary—each with different characteristics that must be evaluated in terms of individual requirements.

Some advise purchase of term insurance for the amount of protection needed and investment of the difference in cost versus a whole life policy. However, when considering investing the difference between term and whole life or some other form of insurance with cash value buildups, there are a number of considerations. Is the individual willing to have no insurance beyond the period in which term insurance will expire? What is the rate of return on the alternative investment(s)? How secure is the investment? What is the risk on the rate of return? On the invested principle? Will the individual stay with the investment plan? Is the estate an issue? Does the master contract permit the employee to assign all rights of ownership to another party, thereby removing the proceeds from one's estate? The value of assignments must be examined in terms of the particulars on estate taxation. The overall importance of these various forms is probably moderate but will range from low to high given individual circumstances.

It is rather common to give each employee an insurance amount equal to two times pay. Alternatively, the contract could provide a specified amount of coverage for everyone (e.g., $50,000); however, this might mean overinsurance at the low-earnings level and significant underinsurance at the executive level. Company coverage is most probably one-year renewable term insurance purchased from a life insurance company. Being term, it has no cash surrender value and is in effect on a year-to-year contract basis with the insurance company.

Other Insurance Benefits

Survivor Benefit. A number of companies provide a *survivor benefit* in addition to—or in lieu of—the basic life insurance program. This benefit typically provides a stated percentage of the employee's earnings at the time of death (e.g., 25 percent) to the spouse (possibly higher benefits if dependent children are also involved) either for life or a stated number of years (e.g., until the deceased's 65th birthday). The amount could be constant (e.g., $10,000 a month) or adjusted based on certain milestones (e.g., $15,000 a month until children are no longer dependents, then $10,000 a month). Or it could be adjusted based on age (e.g., $12,000 a month until age 65, then $6,000 a month). Such a program might be tied to certain assumptions about social security benefits.

Sometimes such programs give executives a false sense of security, as they fail to assess the possible impact of inflation upon a constant payment. For example, inflation of 7 percent would halve the purchasing power of the payments in approximately 10 years. Thus, while such a program is very helpful, it may need to be supplemented, especially for the executive with a young spouse. It is also important to determine whether such plans permit the survivor to convert the unpaid installments into a lump sum. In addition, if the beneficiary dies before all payments had been made, the unpaid remainder would become part of the beneficiary's estate. Survivor benefits are likely also from other employee benefit plans (e.g., defined benefit and defined contribution pension plans).

In addition to any benefits provided by the employers, Social Security survivor benefits are payable to the survivor's family based on the employee's primary insurance amount (PIA) if the person was insured at time of death. In order to receive these monthly payments, beneficiaries must meet certain eligibility requirements.

Accidental Death. A number of policies include an additional benefit if death was *accidental*, on top of payment of the prescribed amount. Although some policies include such coverage only working on the job, it is more common to have 24-hour protection. Thus it would not be uncommon to have a basic coverage of two times pay plus an additional two times pay for accidental death. Due to the limited conditions under which payment will be made, this amount is not charged against the $50,000 tax-free exclusion, which will be described below and is usually paid for by the company. Even a high face value is probably only of moderate importance to an executive due to low probability.

Business Travel Accident Insurance. This kind of policy provides life insurance if the executive is killed accidentally while traveling on company business. Due to cost concerns, some plans exclude salespersons while driving in their own territory; others establish a maximum payoff for a common accident (e.g., $1 million).

Some might structure level of benefit by job category (e.g., corporate officers, $500,000; division heads, $400,000; assistant division heads, $300,000; department heads, $200,000; and all others $50,000). Others might simply use a multiple of three to five times pay, but the individual maximum (e.g., $500,000) often significantly lowers this multiple for higher-paid executives.

Some companies liberalize the business travel accident insurance for executives by lifting the individual and common accident maximum. Another approach is to include the executive's spouse (e.g., at half the executive's benefit level) when authorized to travel with the executive on company business. Another liberalization is to lift an exclusion, such as piloting private aircraft for executives who use their own planes to fly on company business. Business travel accident insurance is not subject to the $50,000 income tax-free insurance restriction. However, the earlier outlined impact of income and estate taxes (including assignment) need to be reviewed. A high face value may be of high importance to an executive who travels extensively; otherwise, it is probably of moderate importance.

Kidnap and Ransom Insurance. This is especially attractive for executives in politically volatile situations overseas. Such policies might have a face value of $5 million to $10 million, with a deductible ranging from one to 10 percent of policy value, and/or it may not include ransom payments but would cover related expenses such as negotiation costs and information leading to the apprehension of the kidnapper. Since this is typically directed at minimizing company loss, it is similar to key employee life insurance; the value to the executive is essentially intrinsic (i.e., knowledge of being sufficiently important to warrant such a policy). Needless to say, companies are reluctant to talk of such insurance policies for fear that knowledge might prompt someone to test the payout provisions. This is probably of low importance to most executives.

Supplemental Insurance. Additional insurance can be provided through a supplementary employee pay-all program. Such a plan would allow the individual to purchase insurance in specified dollar multiples (e.g., $50,000) or in multiples of pay (e.g., one, two, or three) to a stated dollar maximum (e.g., $1,000,000). The advantage of the dollar-maximum approach is that insurance protection is automatically increased with each compensation increase. This can be an important factor since it is common for such plans to have an open enrollment period at time adopted, or within a short period of employment (e.g., 30 days); after that period, enrollment or increases in dollar protection often require successfully passing a medical examination. This medical exam requirement for increased insurance can be overcome by using the multiple-of-pay approach, since the increase in protection is automatic.

Since the $50,000 tax-free insurance limitation can only be used once each year, it normally is applied to the bargain portion of the basic plan. Thus, for supplementary insurance to escape imputed income, the cost to the employee must be equal to or in excess of the Section 79 rates. Like other forms of insurance, this is probably of moderate importance to executives.

Carve-Out Insurance. Another variation of the supplemental insurance is a *carve-out* plan, where the company provides the first $50,000 of insurance at no cost and the employee pays for the remainder provided by the plan formula (either a flat amount or percentage of pay). In accordance with Section 79, there would be no tax consequences to the employee as long as the rates charged were greater than those set by the IRS.

Combination Term and Permanent Life Insurance. Often called Section 79 plans, they were designed to take advantage of the annual $50,000 benefit exclusion and Uniform Premium Table rates provided under the 1964 addition of Section 79 to the Internal Revenue Code (see Table 6-11). A popular approach was to place a Section 79 plan on top of an existing group term plan and limit participation to the top executives.

A typical Section 79 plan would call for scheduled amounts of life insurance, one part being decreasing term insurance and the other part being offsetting increases in permanent protection. The employer would pay the premium on the term portion (deductible under Section 162 of the IRC), creating imputed income to the executive in accord with the Uniform Premium Table for coverage in excess of $50,000. The executive would pay the premium on the permanent life portion; however, the company would assist in this matter by increasing salary or bonus by a comparable (or grossed-up) amount. Furthermore, as cash value started to build on the permanent insurance, offsetting the decreases in term coverage, the accumulated cash value often exceeded the actual taxes paid for imputed income. The employer received a tax deduction for group insurance premiums and compensation expense; the executive had income imputed at favorable rates on the term portion and compensation income on the other portion. This structure neatly avoided the issue of non-tax deductibility of permanent life insurance premiums, as well as reduced the amount of term coverage in later years when the Uniform Premium Table rates reflected significant increases that would otherwise result in large imputed income amounts.

The need to separate fairly the two insurance portions in order to receive the benefits of Section 79 was reinforced with Revenue Ruling 71-360. In 1979, the requirements for such plans to qualify under Section 79 were further tightened. Namely, these combination plans had to specify in writing the amount of term coverage, allow the executive to decline (or subsequently drop) the permanent insurance without any effect on the group term amount, and provide a group term benefit not less than the total death benefit less the amount of paid-up insurance.

The rules also provided that the unused portion (if any) allowable under the Uniform Premium Table for the term portion could not be used to reduce the imputed income for the permanent coverage. The effect of this requirement is to increase imputed income and reduce the attractiveness of such policies. Furthermore, the rules placed a high value on the cost of permanent insurance due to the conservative interest rate assumption of 4 percent and the Mortality Table, specified for use by the IRS. This makes it possible, especially for a senior executive after a number of years of coverage, to have the imputed income plus dividends exceed the actual premium cost! Needless to say, these changes by the IRS have significantly cooled executive interest in Section 79 plans.

Dependent Life Insurance. In addition to insuring the life of the employee, some companies provide *dependents life insurance*. Due to heavy restrictions in many states as to the amount of such coverage for spouse versus dependent child, this type of coverage is not very common.

Furthermore, the IRS will allow free coverage for spouse and dependent children only to a limited amount. Any coverage in excess of that amount and the full value of the policy will be given an imputed income value, making it still an attractive and inexpensive benefit. Nonetheless, it is at best of moderate importance.

How Much Life Insurance?

In determining how much life insurance an executive should have, the individual estimates either what is needed to replace lost future net income or what is needed to provide for survivors. Obviously, life expectancy and lifestyle are critical factors. Let's examine these two approaches.

Net Income. Under this approach, income loss is determined by taking the executive's current gross compensation (e.g., $500,000) and subtracting taxes (since life insurance proceeds are not subject to income tax), own maintenance, and investments. Assume these total $350,000, leaving a remainder of $150,000. This amount is held constant, or increased by an assumed growth in compensation, and projected for the remaining working years of the insured's life. Thus, while $3,000,000 is adequate if no compensation increases are assumed over a period of 20 additional working years, as shown in Table 6-14, almost $8.6 million is required if an annual 10 percent increase in compensation is assumed. However, as can be seen, this amount assumes

	By Year	Insurance Requirements by Year	
		0.0% Interest	10.0% Interest
None	$150,000	$8,591,251	$3,000,000
1 Year Later	165,000	8,441,251	3,135,000
2 Years Later	181,500	8,276,251	3,267,000
3 Years Later	199,650	8,094,751	3,394,056
4 Years Later	219,615	7,895,101	3,513,840
5 Years Later	241,577	7,675,486	3,623,625
6 Years Later	265,734	7,433,909	3,720,290
7 Years Later	292,308	7,168,175	3,800,030
8 Years Later	321,538	6,875,867	3,858,480
9 Years Later	353,692	6,554,329	3,890,540
10 Years Later	389,061	6,200,637	3,890,600
11 Years Later	427,968	5,811,576	3,851,730
12 Years Later	470,764	5,383,608	3,766,120
13 Years Later	517,841	4,912,844	3,624,880
14 Years Later	569,625	4,395,000	3,417,756
15 Years Later	626,587	3,825,370	3,132,925
16 Years Later	689,246	3,198,791	2,756,980
17 Years Later	758,171	2,509,545	2,274,510
18 Years Later	833,988	1,751,372	1,667,980
19 Years Later	917,386	917,386	917,386
Total	$8,591,251		

Table 6-14. Insurance required by year

no investment growth, whereas if the net investment were assumed equal to the 10 percent increase in compensation, $3,000,000 is adequate if death is assumed in the first year. Note, however, that this amount rises over the first 10 years because the decrease in number of years of payment (e.g., 5 percent when dropping from 20 to 19) is less than the increase in compensation (e.g., a constant 10 percent in this example). Thus, it is very important in estimating lost income to adequately estimate future compensation growth and assumed rate of investment on the death benefit once received. If compensation growth is underestimated and investment increase overestimated, one will be underinsured; if compensation increase is overestimated and investment growth underestimated, one will be overinsured.

While many individuals making these estimates will only project the number of years of their working life It is important to also estimate the amount of retirement income and the point in time at which it is estimated to begin. Thus, in the above example the individual might estimate that beginning in the 21st year, a pension of $200,000 will be received. This amount would be projected for the remaining lifetime (with either a constant or an increased value) and the insurance values reworked.

As Table 6-14 indicates, a net income analysis would suggest some combination of decreasing term and whole life insurance to meet the lost income needs. There are many, however, who believe that the lost net income approach results in either overinsuring or underinsuring, since the needs of the dependents are not examined. They, of course, can be factored into the analysis. It merely complicates the review.

Survivor Needs. The *survivor needs* approach estimates expenses rather than income. These needs can be identified and arranged in order of priority. First, there are settlement expenses: the amount needed to cover the decedent's expenses (e.g., burial costs, payment of outstanding loans, and probate costs) and estate taxes (especially important when large capital income programs, including non-qualified, deferred compensation, exist for the survivors). Next, there is survivor income. This can be separated into: initial adjustment period (usually several years at 75 percent or more of deceased's net annual income), the family period (e.g., until children reach age 18 or, more liberally, age 22 assuming college education), and the surviving spouse period. In addition, amounts can be established for: a mortgage fund (or a separate term insurance policy can be purchased), educational expenses of dependents, and an emergency fund to cover unexpected financial liabilities.

The ages, as well as the needs of the survivors, are critical in this analysis, as are the investment philosophy of the survivors. The more conservative, the larger the corpus or amount of money needed. In determining the needed amount at any point in time, it is helpful to remember this formula: Given the assumed rate of return, one can easily calculate the corpus by dividing the living expense by the interest rate. Thus, an annual income of $200,000 would require a $5,000,000 corpus assuming a 4-percent, tax-free return.

Expenses can essentially be separated into stable and declining needs categories. For example, settlement expenses, emergency funds, and adjustment period income are essentially stable. However, mortgage coverage and income for dependent children by definition are declining needs. Thus, one could argue for some amount of permanent life insurance and another piece of term insurance to meet the 10 to 12 times pay while the children are young (and the executive is in the mid-thirties) versus the two to four times pay immediately prior to retirement. In addition, as was done in the case of estimating income loss, some estimate of the impact of inflation on dependent needs and possible investment growth opportunities on the paid death benefit need to be taken into consideration to estimate the needed amount of insurance.

Identifying such expenses by year (including some assumption for impact of inflation) and then calculating a present value (using a reasonable but conservative investment rate assumption) makes it possible to calculate an amount, which after netting out the value of current capital investments, indicates the amount needed for life insurance. This approach assumes the last dollar has been spent the minute before all the above needs have been met. If an inheritance for children is also expected, its value must be factored in as well.

For many, this will mean purchasing whole life insurance to provide dollar protection needed for the entire life, and some form of term insurance to meet those needs that do not span the entire life (e.g., period of dependent children). For some, whole life insurance is one of the few ways in which they can actually accumulate some savings and then use this cash value to increase their net worth by borrowing against it. The reason this is attractive is that the interest rate charged is often significantly less than that available through commercial banking institutions. Thus, a person with a $1,000,000 face value policy and a cash surrender value of $500,000 would be able to increase gross earnings $5,000 a year for every 1-percentage point that interest earned exceeds interest paid. Furthermore, the level of protection remains the same at $1,000,000. This consists of $500,000 life insurance (i.e., $1,000,000 less $500,000 loan) and $500,000 in investments.

Furthermore, some borrow against the cash surrender value to pay the premiums. While there are some restrictions on how much can be borrowed for this purpose and when it can be borrowed, this feature can be very attractive. Of course, still others take the increase in cash-surrender value to purchase additional life insurance.

Obviously, the longer the executive lives and provides the needed income, the less is needed in the amount of insurance. Without adequate planning, the coverage (especially that provided by the basic company formula of a multiple of pay) either exceeds or falls short of need. This is illustrated in Figure 6-1 in a situation all too typical for many individuals—underinsured early in life and overinsured in later years.

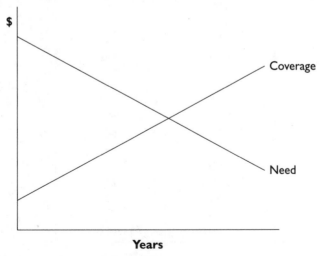

Figure 6-1. Insurance coverage vs. need by age

Design Considerations

Pay Multiple. One way companies can minimize the type of disparity created by pay multiples is by adjusting the pay multiple used to determine the amount of life insurance based on age: the highest multiple for younger employees and the lowest multiple for older employees. The example in Table 6-15 begins with a multiple of five for employees under age 25 and then decreases uniformly each year to a final value of 0.1 at age 74 (with perhaps a minimum of $5,000 of insurance). Such a plan would have to be reviewed carefully in light of the Age Discrimination in Employment Act.

An additional advantage to this type of program is that it reduces the amount of imputed income, as described earlier, in the later years when the tables are very high. Conversely, a disadvantage is that it might reduce protection faster than the executives' need and, therefore, force them to supplement this protection with additional coverage. It is also important to remember when analyzing insurance needs versus coverage that company programs are by definition only in effect during the period of employment. Thus, very attractive insurance protection at one employer may not be available at the next, and the executive must plan accordingly.

Age	Multiple	Age	Multiple
Under 25	5.00	50	2.50
26	4.90	51	2.40
27	4.80	52	2.30
28	4.70	53	2.20
29	4.60	54	2.10
30	4.50	55	2.00
31	4.40	56	1.90
32	4.30	57	1.80
33	4.20	58	1.70
34	4.10	59	1.60
35	4.00	60	1.50
36	3.90	61	1.40
37	3.80	62	1.30
38	3.70	63	1.20
39	3.60	64	1.10
40	3.50	65	1.00
41	3.40	66	0.90
42	3.30	67	0.80
43	3.20	68	0.70
44	3.10	69	0.60
45	3.00	70	0.50
46	2.90	71	0.40
47	2.80	72	0.30
48	2.70	73	0.20
49	2.60	74 and over	0.10

Table 6-15. Insurance coverage by age

Definition of Pay for Insurance Purposes. While both basic and supplementary plans were traditionally based only on salary for determining the amount of coverage, it is now rather common to use salary plus short-term incentives in determining an amount of insurance protection. This is logical where a bonus is significant and a rather stable percentage of salary; however, where the bonus can swing dramatically, it may not be attractive to the executive as he or she fluctuates between an overinsured and an underinsured position. In such situations, applying higher multiples to salary can accomplish the same degree of desired protection. To illustrate: company A allows one, two, or three times salary-plus-bonus while company B permits enrollment for one, two, three, or four times salary. Shown in Table 6-16 are salary and bonus figures for an executive and the amount of insurance protection under the two company plans.

Compensation	Year 1	Year 2	Year 3
Salary	$200,000	$210,000	$220,000
Bonus	50,000	150,000	40,000
Total	250,000	360,000	260,000
Company A			
1 times salary + bonus	$250,000	$360,000	$260,000
2 times salary + bonus	500,000	720,000	520,000
3 times salary + bonus	750,000	1,080,000	780,000
Company B			
1 times salary	$200,000	$210,000	$220,000
2 times salary	400,000	420,000	440,000
3 times salary	600,000	630,000	660,000
4 times salary	800,000	840,000	880,000

Table 6-16. Insurance for salary only vs. salary and bonus

Recognizing that protection needs depend on age of children (and their degree of financial dependency), monetary needs of spouse, and liquidity requirements for estate taxes, assume that these have not significantly changed during this three-year period. Three times salary-plus-bonus coverage under company A might mean being slightly underinsured in years one and three or, if these amounts are consistent with need, being overinsured in year two. Which of these two conditions was true would determine whether three or four times salary under company B would be more appropriate.

Premium Waiver. *Basic life insurance* may be fully paid by the company, or the employee may absorb a portion of the expense. Where the latter is true, it is common to have a waiver of premium (while continuing coverage) if the employee becomes disabled. While the company receives a deduction on its premium expense, as stated in Section 79 of the IRC, the individual receives the first $50,000 of coverage purchased by the company free of income tax liability. After that point, income is imputed in accordance with rates prescribed by the IRS. Usually, these rates are less than charged by the insurance company and, therefore, advantageous to the executive. However, the reverse may not be true if the actual premium paid is less than the IRS table. Logically, one would argue that the lower premium rates be used instead in determining the imputed income tax. However, the IRS may view this from the economic benefit perspective, rather than in terms of actual cost. This waiver feature may be of moderate interest to executives.

Conversion. Important to executives leaving the company who are not in the best of health is the *conversion privilege* that within a specified period of time, such as 30 days, allows the insured to convert the group term protection to an individual policy of permanent protection without having to pass a medical examination. Typically, companies are assessed a charge per $100 of converted coverage, in large part to offset the higher risk the carrier is assuming without receiving a higher premium. In many instances, the premium paid by the executive is higher than that charged for low-risk protection for insured persons who are in excellent health. Of low interest to executives until it happens, this option then becomes of high interest.

Assignment. Life insurance proceeds are not subject to income tax, but they are considered part of the deceased's estate and, therefore, subject to estate taxes. An exception to this is when the employee has irrevocably assigned the policy to either a trust or the individual intended to be the beneficiary. The assignee is now the owner of the policy and the beneficiary, and is responsible for paying any premiums due. Assuming such assignment meets the legal test (some argue that group term insurance can never be irrevocably assigned since it is essentially one-year term insurance) and is made at least three years prior to the executive's death, the proceeds probably will not be considered part of the estate. However, the imputed value of the insurance will be considered a gift, and while no tax payment is required at the time, it will be charged against the allowable lifetime exclusion (Revenue Ruling 79-47).

Since the IRS views any assignment made within three years of death null and void, there is a three-year period during which the benefits are at risk. One way in which a company could assist is to take out a separate three-year term assignment protection policy on the executive equal in amount to the estate taxes on the assigned policy (not the face value) plus the new policy, making the estate the beneficiary. Since the company has no rights of ownership, it could take a tax deduction; the executive probably will have a tax liability in accord with Section 79 Uniform Premium Table requirements discussed earlier in this chapter.

To meet the assignment test, all incidents of ownership must be completely relinquished. Even the ability to borrow a limited amount of money against the policy may be sufficient for the entire policy (not simply the amount available for loans) to be considered part of the estate for taxation. For those concerned about a possible subsequent divorce that might place the insurance in the wrong hands, the policy could be assigned to a trust rather than directly to the spouse. The trust in turn would name the "wife" or "husband" (whichever is appropriate) as the beneficiary, carefully avoiding a specific name.

A change in insurance carriers by the employer should not affect the assignment (Revenue Ruling 80-239) as long as the two contracts are identical in all relevant aspects. This ruling reversed a position in Revenue Ruling 79-231, which stated that such an action by the employee would begin a new three-year period before the assignment was considered effective. Overall, assignment is probably of moderate executive importance.

Form of Settlement. While the normal form of payout from the above-described policies is a lump sum amount, some policies could be structured to provide annuity payments. Annuities have a certain appeal, since they resemble the regularity of the paycheck that no longer arrives.

A prime source for the annuity is the company pension plan, which we will discuss in more detail in the next section. The important point is that the pension plan can be constructed to pay the surviving spouse an annuity if the employee died while actively employed but was eligible for retirement. In such instances, the plan will calculate a joint and survivor benefit as if the employee retired the day before death. This is more liberal coverage than prescribed in the 1974 Employee Retirement Income Security Act (ERISA). This type of benefit in the pension plan has increasing significance as the employee's creditable earnings and service accumulate; however, it is of little or no help for a younger executive.

Living Benefit. Sometimes the insured needs the proceeds from life insurance to pay large expenses. A chronically or terminally ill patient with large, non-reimbursed medical expenses for qualified, long-term care would be an example. For this reason, some plans permit a withdrawal prior to death. This is called a living benefit or *viatical* settlement. In other cases, a company specializing in such situations will buy the insurance policy of the terminally ill person. Section 101(g) of the IRC identifies a *viatical settlement provider* (VSP) as one "regularly engaged in the trade or business of purchasing or taking assignment of life insurance contracts." In return for an irrevocable assignment of the policy, the VSP returns pay amounts up to 80 percent of face value. The longer the life expectancy, the lower the payment amount. At time of death, any amount left over after meeting the assignees expenses could be paid to the estate. This is an alternative to the long-term contract described under home care in the Health Care section of this chapter and may be more attractive to the executive worried about providing financial assistance to an ailing parent. However, it is still unlikely to be of more than moderate importance.

Legacy Grant. Some make an educational or charitable organization the beneficiary of a stated dollar amount at time of the insured's death. The insured usually gets credit for the amount while living for publicity purposes. These organizations are usually very helpful in the design of such policies.

After Retirement. Typically, coverage cuts back quickly and significantly upon retirement. One way to reduce coverage is to reduce annual installments over several years until reaching a final death claim of $5000 or less within five years of retirement, regardless of the amount of protection while active. Some plans provide for one times protection until death; however, this can be a very costly benefit amount. Regardless of the plan, the executive must determine whether post-retirement insurance will be sufficient and, if not, begin to prepare well before retirement. One advantage of retiree life insurance provided by the company is that it is not subject to imputed income. Therefore, the $50,000 restraint for active employees is not an issue for retirees. Alternatively, life insurance could be provided through a retired lives reserve plan (discussed earlier in this chapter) where the funding occurs over the retiree's active period of employment.

Summary of Survivor Protection

As shown in Table 6-17, survivor protection programs and plan features overall are moderately important to the executive. High policy limits raise importance; low dollar limits lower importance. In some situations, the employee benefit protection may be adequate to meet much of the executive's needs, thereby eliminating the need for a special executive benefit add-on.

TE		Benefit	Importance to Executive		
E	C		Low	Moderate	High
		Life Insurance			
3	B	• Ordinary		✔	
1	B	• Term		✔	
3	B	• Group Universal Life		✔	
1	B	• Endowment		✔	
		• Company Owned			
1	D	- Key Person	✔		
1	B	- Split Dollar		✔	
3	B	- Retired Lives Reserve		✔	
1	B	Survivor Benefit		✔	
1	B	Accidental Death		✔	
1	B	Business Travel Accident		✔	
1	B	Kidnap and Ransom	✔		
*	*	Supplemental Life		✔	
1	B	Carve-Out Life		✔	
1	B	Combination		✔	
1	B	Dependent Life		✔	
1	B	Premium Waiver		✔	
1	B	Conversion	✔		
1	B	Assignment		✔	
1	B	Living Benefit		✔	
1	B	After Retirement	✔		
		Totals			
		✔	4	16	0
		EB	0	0	0
		P	0	0	0

*Depends on coverage

Table 6-17. Survivor protection summary

RETIREMENT

For many, age 65 is considered an appropriate age for retirement, although some retire earlier (if they have accumulated sufficient money) and others work, later either because of financial need or because they like what they do. Most give credit to Germany's Chancellor Otto von Bismarck for setting this retirement age in 1883. He did so to stop Marxists from taking over the country by promising widespread social programs. Bismarck was quite clever—he knew that few would live to that age. Nonetheless, he set the precedent not only of a retirement age but of government paying people to stop working at that age.

Whereas pension plans were once considered a gratuitous gift by the company to employees reaching an age at which they were no longer able to perform their tasks, the current thinking of many employees is that such payments are an earned right—an involuntary form of deferred compensation. Pension plans (a.k.a., "retirement plans" as the two will be used interchangeably in this review) are either defined benefit or defined contribution, or a hybrid of the two. The plan either qualifies for favorable tax treatment or it does not. A qualified, or statutory, retirement plan (indicating its status is described by tax statute) has several very attractive features. Namely, the company can make currently tax-deductible contributions to either a trust or insurance company on behalf of an active employee to ensure a pension is ready when the employee retires, but the employee has no income-tax liability until actually receiving these payments. Nor are earnings or invested funds taxable to either the company or the employee. To receive qualified-plan status, Section 401 of the Internal Revenue Code (IRC) stipulates that the plan cannot discriminate in favor of highly compensated employees. To meet this requirement, the plan must be nondiscriminatory in (a) benefits or plan contributions, (b) rights and plan features, and (c) plan changes. Plans that do not meet this requirement are called *non-qualified*, or non-statutory plans. Tax deductions for non-qualified retirement plans may only be taken at the time the individual has income and, therefore, a tax liability. The maximum tax deduction to the employer for a qualified, defined-contribution plan is 15 percent of the covered payroll. The maximum for a defined-benefit plan is dependent upon the non-funded past service liability. The maximum tax deduction, if the employer has both a qualified defined-benefit and a defined-contribution plan, is 25 percent of covered payroll.

Retirement plans that fall within the "employee benefit" category, in other words, they apply to all employees, are tax-qualified plans. Why? Because the company wants a tax deduction when it makes a plan contribution and employees do not understand why they should be taxed until they receive the plan benefits. The only way to do this is with a qualified plan. Plans that cover executives include both qualified and non-qualified, the latter beginning where the former ends. Both types will be reviewed in this chapter, because together, they constitute the executive's retirement benefit.

Accounting

The accounting requirements for pension benefits to retired employees could be a book by itself. Lack of space permits only a few highlights. Since even these may be subject to interpretation, one should definitely review the subject with inside and outside auditors.

Let's begin with Financial Accounting Standards Board (FASB) statement, FAS 35 "Accounting and Reporting by Defined Benefit plans." It dates back to 1980 and, essentially, was the first promulgation of Generally Accepted Accounting Procedures (GAAP) on the subject of pension plans. The American Institute of Certified Public Accounts (AICPA) incorporated accounting and reporting guidelines for defined-contribution plans. FAS 35 requires financial statements using accrual accounting to report net assets available for plan benefits. Records detailing activity should include: contributions, claims, distributions, participant accounts, and investments, to name a few.

The next two FASB statements that significantly affect how pension plans will be viewed by accountants are: FAS 87 "Employers' Accounting for Pensions" and FAS 88 "Employers' Accounting for Settlements and Curtailments of Defined Benefit Pension Plans and for Termination Benefits."

FAS 87 requires that the cost of the pension reflected on the balance sheet include the projected benefit obligation, factoring in such items as: discount or settlement rate, rate of salary increase, earnings on plan assets, prior service cost, and unrecognized gains and losses. Two of the measurements reflected on the balance sheet that show the funding status of defined-benefit plans are the accumulated benefit obligation (ABO) and the projected benefit obligation (PBO). The ABO shows benefits accrued to date, typically separated between vested and nonvested participants. The PBO reports the actual present value of future benefits in addition to the ABO. Comparing these two amounts with the reported fund balance indicates the amount the fund is over- or underfunded.

FAS 88 specifies the differences in accounting treatment for settlement and curtailments. Previously unrecognized gains or losses are recognized immediately under a "settlement"; however, prior service cost is not accelerated. With a "curtailment," the situations are reversed; previously unrecognized prior service cost is recognized immediately but unrecognized gains or losses are unaffected.

"Settlements" relieve the employer of the pension obligation. An example would be purchasing annuity contracts or extending lump-sum payouts in exchange for the pension obligation. "Curtailments" would reduce, but not eliminate, the pension obligation. An example would be a significant reduction in employees on the payroll.

Tax Treatment

Pensions are considered income to the executive and are tax deductible to the company. A statutory or qualified plan allows an exception to the normal rule of permitting a tax deduction only in the year in which the executive recognizes the income. The company is permitted to take a tax deduction the year it makes a contribution to the plan, even though the executive does not receive the income until a later date.

Legal Requirements

The Employee Retirement Income Security Act (ERISA) subjects all qualified pension and profit-sharing plans to requirements regarding employee eligibility and vesting, disclosure and reporting, fiduciary responsibilities, fiscal needs, funding, non-discrimination structure, and payment forms. The objective is to ensure employee rights are protected and that pension benefits will be available when they retire from the company. Companies designing special early retirement plans to avoid having to terminate excess people need to be very careful because an analysis of groups and classes may very well tilt to the higher paid, making the plan discriminatory. Section 411(d)(6) of the IRC prohibits amending a qualified pension plan to cut back or otherwise reduce accrued benefits of a plan participant. Non-qualified plans are not subject to these requirements, nor are participants protected on benefit treatment.

The federal Age Discrimination in Employment Act (ADEA) prohibits companies from forcibly retiring employees at any age, but allows an exception for executives meeting certain criteria. An executive can be forced to retire if he or she is the head of a major local or regional operation, or the head of a major department or division, *and* has a combined company pension (excluding Social Security and payments from other employers) of at least $27,000. Several states have similar laws. Such individuals, assuming they were bona fide executives at least two years immediately preceding retirement, may be retired by the company beginning at age 65 without concern for violating the terms of the act. For some, it may be easier to meet the definition of "executive" under the law than to attain the minimum pension; however, since the latter amount is not indexed, and pay (and therefore accrued pension benefits) increase each year, more and more individuals will become eligible for automatic retirement at age 65. Although there are exceptions, most companies want their executives to retire not later than age 65 (in order to open promotional opportunities), and therefore offering financial incentives through supplementary pension arrangements is a logical approach—especially if they were structured to only apply before reaching a certain age. For example, perhaps only executives retiring before age 62 would receive the supplemental pension benefits. However, the loss of 3 years of pay (and its impact on the pension benefit) would probably be greater than the supplement and, therefore, not result in a lot of retirements at or before age 62. For those who stayed on, the automatic retirement under the $27,000 ADEA requirement would probably catch them at 65.

Plan Types

As stated, retirement plans are of three types: defined benefit, defined contribution, and a hybrid, or combination of the two. The *defined-benefit plan* specifies the amount of annuity that the employee will receive after reaching a certain age and/or service requirements, and the contribution is determined annually to meet this annuity amount. The *defined-contribution plan* specifies the amount of money to be set aside each year; the value of such money at the time of retirement will be a factor of the market value of the investments made. In other words, in one case, you know how much you will get, but the ultimate cost is unknown until the assets are valued. In the other instance, you know how much is being set aside each year, but you don't know how much it will be worth when you retire.

Since the future benefit can be projected under a defined-benefit plan, one must estimate the probability of that future benefit being paid (the individual may have left the company) expressed in the present value equivalent, after factoring in investment performance. The better the performance, the lower the company contribution. Some estimate that the contribution can be reduced 4 percent for every quarter percent improvement in investment performance.

If plan benefits are related to pay received by the employee, an assumption must be made as to the level of future pay increases (this is more critical for final pay than career-earnings plans since the former affects all years of prior service). If the plan is integrated with Social Security, future increases in Social Security benefits must be estimated but only to time of estimated retirement. It is not permissible to reduce benefits after retirement because of increases in Social Security payments. In addition, assumptions must be made about how many people will leave the plan before becoming vested, when the vested employees will leave and begin drawing benefits, and how long they will live (and continue receiving benefits). Finally, any administrative expenses that will be charged to the plan must be estimated.

Qualified, defined-benefit and defined-contribution plans are of limited appeal to executives because of limits in effect to retain the tax-qualified status. First, there is a limit on the amount of compensation that may be considered for plan purposes. While this amount may be adjusted for changes in the cost of living, it is far short of what many executives are being paid in salary and annual incentives. Second, there is a maximum on the annual benefit that may be received and the annual amount that may be contributed on a combined basis by employer and employee. Third, there is an additional limit on the amount of pretax contribution that can be made and even though indexed for cost of living, it is only a fraction of the amount allowable for plan purposes as highlighted above in the first limit. Furthermore, plans must be tested to ensure they are not "top heavy" (i.e., a disproportionate benefit is given to key employees). Key employees are defined by income and/or percent of company stock owned.

Therefore, the real value of qualified, defined-benefit and defined-contribution plans to executives is not the benefits received from the qualified plan but rather the plan formula before the qualified limits are imposed. The difference between the qualified benefit and the plan formula typically will be made up by a non-qualified benefit for executives. These are called 415 plans because they refer to the limit imposed by Section 415 of the Internal Revenue Code (IRC).

Paying for the Plan

Pension plans are company-pay-all (noncontributory), employee-pay-all (contributory), or a combination of the two. Typically, defined-benefit plans are paid totally by the company, whereas defined-contribution plans could be financed any of the three ways.

The IRS has generally held that mandatory contributions by employees to defined benefit or contribution plans in total that do not exceed 6 percent of pay will not be discriminatory. Voluntary contributions in total should not exceed 10 percent of pay. Therefore, assuming both maximums were employed, employees could contribute up to 16 percent of pay. Though numbers in excess of these might be acceptable to the IRS, the burden of proof would be upon the company to demonstrate that the contributions were not so burdensome as to enable only highly compensated employees to take full advantage of the plan(s).

Integration with Social Security

Recognizing that Social Security benefits are of significantly greater value to lower-paid than higher-paid employees, companies are permitted to take this into consideration when designing their tax-qualified, defined-benefit and defined-contribution plans. The Tax Reform Act of 1986, along with supporting IRS regulations and interpretations, specify the manner in which these benefits may be "integrated" with Social Security and not discriminate in favor of highly compensated individuals. Plans must have: an integration threshold, permitted disparity, and the two-for-one restriction.

The *integration threshold* is the compensation level that separates the base from higher benefit levels or contributions. The *permitted disparity* sets the maximum difference for defined benefits (accrual rate) and defined contributions (contribution rate) between lower and higher paid. And the *two-for-one* prevents designing plans where lower-paid employees receive no benefit, since the benefits above the integration level cannot be more than twice the amount of those below that level.

Additionally, defined-benefit plans are permitted excess benefits no greater than 0.75 percent (per year of service) above that credited for earnings at or below the integration threshold or twice the lower level whichever is less. Thus, a plan crediting earnings at or below the integration level at 0.5 percent could not use a rate above the integration level of more than 1 percent (twice the lower level). However, a 1 percent rate below the integration level would permit a maximum of 1.75-percent rate above that cutoff (the 0.75-percent factor). For defined-benefit plans, the allowable difference cannot exceed 5.7 percent or twice the lower level whichever is less. A 5-percent rate for pay below the integration level could not justify more than a 10 percent rate above the level (twice the lower level), whereas a 6-percent rate would allow 11.7 percent but not higher (the 5.7-percent factor).

While one could probably justify offsetting over 80 percent of the Social Security benefit (because the employer also pays for death, disability, and spousal benefits), most choose to offset only 50 percent of the employees' primary Social Security benefit. This is easy to communicate to employees by pointing out that the company pays the same tax rate as the individual, therefore, they share costs 50-50.

While qualified plans cannot be designed to discriminate in favor of executives, too often the plans do not take full advantage of permissible provisions and in fact discriminate against highly paid individuals. A classic example is when the defined-benefit plan is not integrated with Social Security. The result is that lower-paid employees receive a higher dollar benefit than would be permissible and higher-paid employees receive a lower one.

How Big a Pension?

There are two basic approaches in determining the amount of pension to be provided: how much is needed and what is competitive? Both factors need to be evaluated and some conclusions drawn to resolve the differences. Each analysis is complicated because of various levels of earnings, years of service, and retirement ages.

How Much Pension Is Needed? While it would be nice to receive a company retirement benefit equal to last year's pay or at least equal to after-tax income, it is unlikely for pension planners to consider either seriously. Why not? There are several reasons. First, expenses during retirement are less than while working. Among those expenses that end are business-related expenses such as clothing, lunches, and transportation. In addition, payroll deductions for pension plans and other benefit programs are eliminated. Admittedly, there may be post-active expenses that need to be included, but the net effect most likely still results in a figure less than 100 percent of final pay. Another reason for targeting less than final earnings is that Social Security benefits will be paid to the retiree. However, because of the benefit level, Social Security will be a more significant factor for lower-paid than executive-level employees.

It is important to determine the appropriate percentage of final pay that should be provided from the combined Social Security and employer pension plans. Since both short- and long-term incentives are an increasing portion of total earnings as pay increases, it is not surprising that the percentage of pay replaced by pensions declines as income increases. This is because few pension plans consider long-term incentives in earnings estimates, although many now consider short-term incentives. For example, if an executive earning $1 million in salary, $2 million in annual incentives and $4 million in long-term incentives targeted the pension at 80 percent of final *annual* pay, this would be $2.4 million, or only 34 percent of *total* pay. Not that many will shed a tear for the executive receiving "only" $2.4 million in an annual pension. This simply demonstrates how the exclusion of long-term incentives can dramatically affect the percentage of total pay replaced.

Table 6-18 shows the kind of targeted income replacements that need to be developed. Note that the percentages are factors of final pay and years of service.

	Years of Service		
Final Pay	25	30	35
Under $50,000	70%	75%	80%
$50,000 - $100,000	55%	60%	65%
$100,000 - $250,000	40%	45%	50%
$500,000 - $1,000,000	25%	30%	35%
Over $1,000,000	10%	15%	20%

Table 6-18. Targeted income replacement

What Is Competitive? It is logical to determine the pension plan's competitiveness vis-à-vis the same companies that were used in evaluating current pay. By obtaining copies of competitors' pension plans and constructing model earnings examples (e.g., $25,000, $50,000, $100,000, $250,000, $500,000, and $1,000,000), one can determine competitive position at selected points along the earnings continuum. A format illustrating this kind of comparison is shown in Table 6-19 for a $250,000 executive with 30 years of service retiring at age 65. Note that the annual annuity comes from both the defined-benefit and the defined-contribution plans. Most

Company	Defined			Years of Final Pay
	Benefit	Contribution	Total	
C	$ 97,200	$154,915	$252,115	100.8
F	107,953	131,101	239,054	95.6
I	83,138	141,052	224,190	89.7
A	105,465	112,749	218,214	87.3
E	104,208	108,302	212,510	85.0
Brucell	102,155	103,379	205,534	82.2
D	103,940	83,137	187,077	74.8
G	80,350	79,522	159,872	63.9
B	57,493	59,138	116,631	46.7
H	46,805	53,996	100,801	40.3
Averages (Excluding Brucell)	98,745	91,306	190,051	76.0

Table 6-19. Annual annuity from defined-benefit and defined-contribution plans as a percentage of final pay of $250,000 with 30 years' service

companies survey these separately, never pulling them together. This is a mistake because one never sees the full pension benefit. It is against this combined benefit that one needs to measure competitiveness. Later, one can determine the relative competitiveness of the defined-benefit plan separately from the defined-contribution plan. While keeping the combined benefit in mind, there are good reasons to vary the balance of the defined-benefit and defined-contribution plans from those of the competition. Of course, since the defined-contribution plan is expressed in a lump sum, it needs to be converted to an annual equivalent. This is not that difficult with a little help from an actuary, and plan participants typically have the option to buy an annuity, so the comparison is very appropriate.

Note that in Table 6-20, both plans combine in a lump-sum form. Since many pension plans permit lump-sum payments, this is more than an academic exercise.

The primary analysis in both situations should include employer contributions only. With the defined contribution, it would be appropriate to use the maximum allowed for each plan. A separate calculation could also be prepared including the employee contribution. Actually, when reviewing with the employee, one would show three charts: employer only, employee only, and combined employer/employee. This, of course, would only be for one's own data. The inclusion of other companies allows an analysis of the competitive benefit.

As shown in Table 6-21, if we were to look at only 10, 20, and 30 years' service, for retirement ages of 55, 60, and 65, and for final year's earnings levels of $25,000, $50,000, $100,000, $250,000, $500,000, and $1,000,000, we would have 54 combinations. With the addition of

Company	Defined			Years of Final Pay
	Benefit	Contribution	Total	
C	$972,000	$1,549,153	$2,521,153	10.1
F	1,079,531	1,311,011	2,390,542	9.6
I	831,382	1,410,516	2,214,898	9.0
A	1,054,646	1,127,490	2,182,136	8.7
E	1,042,079	1,083,016	2,125,095	8.5
Brucell	1,021,553	1,033,788	2,055,341	8.2
D	1,039,400	831,367	1,870,767	7.5
G	803,504	795,221	1,598,725	6.4
B	574,932	591,384	1,166,316	4.7
H	468,051	539,959	1,008,010	4.0
Averages (Excluding Brucell)	987,453	913,063	1,900,516	7.6

Table 6-20. Lump-sum payout from defined-benefit and defined-contribution plans as a percentage of final pay of $250,000 with 30 years' service

| | Age 55 | | | Age 60 | | | Age 65 | | |
| | Years of Service | | | Years of Service | | | Years of Service | | |
Final Pay	10	20	30	10	20	30	10	20	30
$1,000,000	1	2	3	4	5	6	7	8	9
500,000	10	11	12	13	14	15	16	17	18
250,000	19	20	21	22	23	24	25	26	27
100,000	28	29	30	31	32	33	34	35	36
50,000	37	38	39	40	41	42	43	44	45
25,000	46	47	48	49	50	51	52	53	54

Table 6-21. Possible combination of age, service, and earnings

another set of retirement age or years of service, we would add 18 more combinations. With the addition of a set in both age *and* years of service, we would add 42 more models. Thus, it is easy to see the care needed in designing the matrix. It must have enough data to test the desired tilt in the plan but not so much as to be subject to analysis paralysis.

How Is It Paid Out? The normal form of payout is an annuity. Typically, these are monthly payments for a defined-benefit plan (versus a single lump-sum payment from a defined-contribution plan). Many defined-benefit plans permit conversion to a lump sum based on actuarial considerations.

Plan Payout

Payments from the plan are either in the form of an annuity for life (or a prescribed number of years) or in a lump sum. Typically, defined-benefit-plan benefits are in the form of an annuity whereas defined-contribution-plan benefits are paid in a lump sum. However, the reverse is also possible.

As for lump sums, it is important to know that while all lump-sum distributions are lump-sum payouts, not all lump-sum payouts are lump-sum distributions. Since lump-sum distributions receive favorable tax treatment (namely, they qualify for a tax-free rollover into an Individual Retirement Account (IRA) or other defined-contribution plan), it is important to know what constitutes a "lump-sum distribution." It is defined as the payment within one taxable year of the full amount the employee is eligible to receive, paid under one of the following conditions: (1) the employee is at least age 59½, (2) the employee retires or otherwise separates from employment, or (3) the employee dies. Thus, an active employee may qualify only at age 59½.

An additional complication arises if the employee is in several qualified plans and wishes to receive a lump-sum distribution from one and installment payments from another. This can be accomplished only if they are different types of plans (e.g., one is a defined-benefit and the other a defined-contribution plan). Plans that are similar will be treated as one plan for the purpose of tax distribution of payout (e.g., a profit-sharing plan and a money-purchase pension plan would probably be treated as a single plan, and it would not be possible to receive annuity payments from one and a lump-sum payment from the other). Even if they are different types of plans, it is preferable to receive payment in separate taxable years. Employers may lump sum a terminated employee's defined benefit without the person's consent only if it is below an amount set by law. The 1997 Taxpayer Relief Act set the amount at $5,000 or less.

Another point to keep in mind is that the use of unisex tables will probably penalize a male employee wishing to buy a single life annuity (say at age 65) from a defined-contribution plan and reward him for taking a lump sum under a defined-benefit plan. To illustrate: the cost of a $1,000 single life annuity might be $9,300 at 65 for a male, but a unisex table could charge $9,700. Thus, with an account balance of $9,300 in the defined-contribution plan, the male executive will not be able to buy the $1,000 annuity but only a lesser amount, using the unisex table. Conversely, taking a lump sum from the defined-benefit plan would mean receiving $9,300 under a male discount schedule versus $9,700 under a unisex schedule. The reverse would, of course, be true for a female.

Executives may find a lump-sum distribution very attractive if they either: (a) need income to start up a new venture, or (b) can afford to put it aside in an IRA and live on other income. Another alternative to the IRA is an annuity purchased from an insurance company. This becomes attractive when the lump sum is greater than the amount needed to buy an annuity equal to that available under the company plan. The degree of interest is even greater if the executive's good health lengthens the odds of reaching or exceeding normal life expectancy.

Eligibility

A retirement plan may require a minimum age (but not higher than 21) and/or years of service (not more than one or two) before becoming eligible. Once eligible, prior service is typically credited to defined-benefit plans. The reason for a minimum service is to minimize administrative record keeping for those leaving the company after only a year of employment. On the other side of the age issue, there are three retirement ages: normal, early, and late. Retirement age is more significant with a defined-benefit than with defined-contribution plans, as will be shown.

While the company may identify a normal retirement age (such as 65), it cannot legally force a person to retire at that or any other age without going counter to age discrimination laws. However, there are bona fide executive exceptions as were described earlier. It is helpful to recognize that there are really three types of employees: those who really want to work past normal retirement, those who might want to work beyond that age, and those who are going to retire at age 65 or sooner. The company either wants the employee to stay, or it is happy to see the individual leave. These combinations are shown in Table 6-22.

Situations A and F are simple because the two sides agree. In situation B, the company must ensure that performance appraisals have been carefully documented in order that the individual may exit gracefully at, if not before, age 65. The performance records help to ward off age

The Individual's Position	Company Position	
	Individual should stay	Individual should leave
Wants to stay	A	B
May want to stay	C	D
Wants to leave	E	F

Table 6-22. Company and executive positions on the retirement matrix

discrimination suits where ADEA executive exemptions are not in effect. If severance of employment is appropriate before age 65, it will be necessary to ensure an adequate severance package, such as discussed earlier.

In situation C, the company would like to convince the individual to stay. Here it is important that the intrinsic as well as extrinsic rewards to the individual are carefully laid out and described. Conversely, in situation D, the company needs to ensure that a carefully thought-out package for the executive is ready and supplemented with extensive pre-retirement counseling, thus providing the basis for the executive to voluntarily retire.

Situation E is tough because the executive wants to leave but the company wants the person to stay, probably a reflection of poor management development and succession planning. The best that can be hoped for is a very short extension of the delay in leaving (e.g., 1 year). By definition, the package has to be more attractive than in situation C simply because the executive is more inclined to leave.

Normal Retirement. Normal retirement age for most plans is 65—an age established for pensions by German Chancellor Otto von Bismarck in 1883. It is the age at which there is no reduction in the accrued defined benefit. Reductions called "discounts" are established for defined-benefit plans when the benefit will be received for a longer period and the plan has less time to fund the accrued benefit. In addition to "age only" normal retirements, there are "service only" (e.g., 20 years). However, they are more typical in the public sector than in the private sector. Some "age only" plans also establish an age and service combination rule that would qualify for a non-discounted pension. For example, a "90 combination" would mean any combination of age and years totaling 90 or more would qualify for a non-discounted pension. Examples would include age 60 with 30 years of service, age 59 with 31 years of service or age 61 with 29 years of service. Some combination plans establish a minimum age. For example, a plan with minimum age 60 would provide a non-discounted pension to anyone with a combination of 90 who was at least 60 years of age. Before 60 years of age, the pension would be discounted.

Some companies establish an earlier normal retirement age for senior executives (e.g., age 60 or 62). This is the age at which they are expected to retire. If they were not eligible to receive a non-discounted, defined-benefit pension from the qualified plan, a non-qualified plan would supplement benefits. These are identified as *Supplemental Executive Retirement Plans* (SERPs) and will be discussed later in the chapter. Early normal retirement ages for executives enable experienced, less senior executives to be promoted somewhat earlier, filling vacancies left by those departed.

Early Retirement. This is when an employee decides to retire before reaching "normal" retirement eligibility. For every year less than normal retirement, the pension benefit is reduced in three ways: (1) there is one less year of service, (2) one less year of earnings, and (3) a greater discount of the annuity. Initially, these discounts were based on the actuarial factors of age and reduced time period for benefit accrual. However, over the years, many plans have substituted less harmful discounts, in effect subsidizing early retirements. Shown in Table 6-23 are examples of an actuarial discount and two supplemental discounts, one a constant and the other weighted more favorably to late age.

Companies should note the difference between those seeking early retirement for health, family, and other reasons versus someone seeking another job (whose pay will be supplemented by the current employer's early retirement pension). The retired job seeker usually does best leav-

Retirement Age	Percentage of Accrued Benefit After Discount		
	Actual	**Constant**	**Late Age**
65	100%	100%	100%
64	94	96	99
63	88	92	97
62	82	88	94
61	76	84	90
60	70	80	85
59	64	76	79
58	58	72	72
57	52	68	64
56	46	64	55
55	40	60	45

Table 6-23. Defined-benefit discounts for early retirement

ing a company with fully vested benefits in a final pay plan and joining a company with a career earnings formula. However, if the individual has many years of life ahead, he or she should probably not leave the first employer; The combination of the heavily discounted pension from company A plus a small one from company B (due to shortness of service) may be *less* than the full pension at 65 that would have been received from company A. The graph in Figure 6-2 shows how the alternative choices can be projected to a break-even age (i.e., the life expectancy age

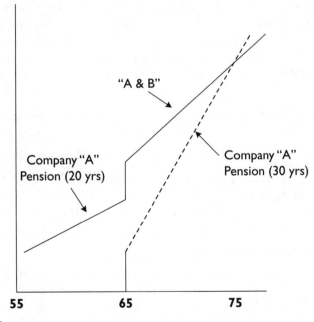

Figure 6-2. Cumulative annuity payments

beyond which it would have been advantageous to not leave company A for another job). In this illustration, joining company B at age 55 and drawing a discounted pension from company A for 20 years of service would mean greater cumulative benefits until age 75 than staying with company A and receiving a non-discounted, 30-year pension.

Furthermore, when the early retirement annuity is more generous than an actuarially determined mortality discount and/or the interest rate assumption is less than insurance companies offer, the executive may request a lump-sum payment. The lump sum can then go toward purchase of an annuity from an insurance company, beginning immediately, or be rolled over tax-free into an IRA.

Late Retirement. The definition of *late retirement* is a retirement at any point in time past "normal" retirement. Since, with the exception of certain senior executives, it is no longer legally permissible to require a person to retire when reaching normal retirement age, plans will continue to accrue benefits until the individual leaves as a late retiree. While the earnings and service credit will add to benefits, there is typically no additional percentage for late retirement to complement the discount for an early retirement. Because of mortality factors, late retirements may cost defined-benefit plans less than normal retirements.

Vesting. When individuals have earned the right to receive benefits because of the years of service, they are said to be "vested." Even though an individual may not be eligible for retirement (normal, early, or late), the person may have earned a benefit. Tax-qualified plans require that an employee's right to receive benefits (i.e., become vested) occurs after a prescribed period of time. This requirement can be met in one of two ways: the simplest is full benefits accrued after five years of service (but nothing prior). This all or nothing type is called "cliff vesting." The other way in which benefits can be vested is by using a "graduated" schedule that begins vesting 20 percent after completing three years of service with an additional 20 percent every year thereafter, reaching 100 percent after seven years. There are exceptions for multi-employer and top heavy plans. Once an employee works 1,000 hours in a year, the individual is considered to have one year's service credit. Vested benefits may be subjected to a discount schedule described in the retirement age section.

Definition of Pay

Retirement plans define earnings as salary paid during the period of employment. Many companies, if not most, also include short-term incentive pay. This was not true years ago but with incentive pay taking on greater prominence, it became necessary; otherwise, the pension would be too small. Including short-term incentives results in variable earnings year to year. This becomes important when determining the period of final years for defined-benefit plans, as will be discussed later in the chapter.

Long-term incentives are rarely included in either defined-benefit or defined-contribution plans. If they were included, pension benefits would likely be greater than final annual earnings.

Post-Retirement Adjustments

Companies sometimes increase the annuities of retirees if there has been a period of significant inflation since the date of their retirement. Typically, the adjustment is some fraction of the inflation increase similar to inflation-indexed Social Security benefits. Retirees may also receive a post-retirement increase in their annuities from a career-earnings plan if the plan were "updated" (described later in this chapter), raising the retirement amount. For example, a person whose career-earnings average was updated from $200,000 to $250,000 would receive a 20-percent increase in the monthly annuity. This increase would come from two sources. The qualified plan would pay the maximum allowable and the non-qualified, supplemental plan would make up the difference.

During times of high inflation, executives are likely to defer plans for early retirement, thereby building up additional years of credit for pension payments. This is especially true when a company does not periodically improve the annuities of retired employees. Since Social Security payments represent a greater portion of the pension of lower-paid employees, such individuals are less affected by a company's unwillingness to improve annuities of retirees than the executive whose major portion of pension is from the company plan, not Social Security.

Defined-Benefit Plans

Defined-benefit plans fall into three categories. A *career-service plan* is typically limited to hourly paid workers and negotiated by unions. Benefits accrue with length of service. For example, the benefit may equal $20 a month for every year of service. A *career-earnings plan* calculates benefits based on total earnings during employment. For example, the benefit may equal 1.4 percent per year for every $1000 in earnings over the full span of employment. A *final pay plan* is more complex than the other two, incorporating both earnings and years of service. For example, the benefit may equal 1 percent per year for every $1000 of average earned income multiplied by all years of service with the company. (Average earned income might be defined as the average of the highest-paid five of the last 10 years of employment prior to retirement.

Section 415(b) of the IRC limits the annual pension from a qualified defined-benefit pension plan to the lesser of $130,000 or 100 percent of the participant's average compensation for the highest-paid three years. The dollar limit is subject to adjustment by the IRS.

The IRC also places some restrictions on how the benefits may be funded. More specifically, Section 404 of the IRC prohibits investment of more than 10 percent of the fair market value of the plan's assets in the company's stock. This restriction applies at time of contribution. Should the company's stock outperform the rest of the portfolio, the plan's trustee may choose, but is not obligated, to sell off the appreciation. Conversely, if the portfolio outperforms the company stock and its value drops below 10 percent, the trustee may choose, but is not obligated, to purchase sufficient shares to restore its 10-percent position.

Furthermore, the IRC prohibits increasing plan benefits as a result of terminated employee non-vested forfeitures. The amount must be used to reduce employer contributions.

Career-Service Plan. Since by definition the annuity formula of a career-service plan is based solely on years of service, such plans are of no interest to highly paid executives. By excluding pay in the formula, they take on a very egalitarian appearance and not too surprisingly are typically found in group agreements such as might be seen in third-party negotiated contracts.

Career-Earnings Plan. Career-earnings plans were very common years ago; but lost their popularity during periods of inflation and significant pay increases. Therefore, most of the career-earnings plans still remaining effect "updates," bringing earlier pay years up to more recent levels. In so doing, they take on an appearance similar to final pay plans, although without the heavy cost impact of future service liability—thereby making them very attractive to financial people. For example, every several years the company might update all earnings prior to five

Year	Actual	Adjusted
20 (current)	$100,000	$100,000
19	92,500	92,500
18	87,500	87,500
17	79,500	79,500
16	72,500	72,500
15	68,500	68,500
14	65,500	68,500
13	61,000	68,500
12	56,500	68,500
11	53,000	68,500
10	50,500	68,500
9	48,000	68,500
8	45,500	68,500
7	43,500	68,500
6	41,500	68,500
5	39,500	68,500
4	37,500	68,500
3	36,000	68,500
2	34,000	68,500
1	32,500	68,500
Total (actual)	$1,145,000	
Total (adjusted)		$1,459,500
Difference		$314,500

Table 6-24. Creditable pension earnings—career vs. career updated

years ago to the five-year-ago figure. For an employee with 20 years of service now earning $100,000, this would mean updating the first 15 years of pay to that earned five years ago. Assume earnings five years ago were $68,500 and starting pay was $32,500; as shown in Table 6-24, this would translate to an increase in creditable earnings of $314,500.

Assuming a pension formula of 1.4 percent of career earnings, this $314,500 increase in creditable career earnings means an increase in the annual annuity of $4,403—from $16,030 to $20,433.

Final-Pay Plans. A final-pay plan is more popular with employees than career-service plans due to its emphasis on most recent earnings. Even updated career-earnings plans have a drawback to employees inasmuch as there is no guarantee the company will continue such actions, and without them the pension will be significantly smaller. However, corporate financial people typically prefer an updated, career-earnings plan to a final-pay plan due to the current cost impact. Under the final-pay plan, both prior and future years of service will be affected by future earnings; under the updated, career-earnings plan, only future service is affected by future earnings.

Continuing with the example above, 1 percent of the average of the highest consecutive five out of the last 10 years' earnings would generate an annual annuity of $17,280 (i.e., $432,000/5 x 0.01 x 20 = $17,280). The $432,000 is the sum of $100,000, $92,500, $87,500, $79,500, and $72,500. The highest five out of 10 is the most prevalent approach, although some plans use the highest three out of five. Anything less will have difficulties passing the IRS review for qualified-plan status. Using the average highest consecutive three out of five in our example would result in an annuity of $18,667, or 8 percent higher. Thus, since using more years in calculating the average usually drops the value, the benefit rate can be manipulated to meet a targeted payout level.

Other things being equal, the executive receiving large pay increases is more interested in reducing the number of years used in calculating the average than a person receiving more modest pay increases. Table 6-25 shows the impact of using the highest three-, five-, or 10-year earnings averages versus full career-earnings average, assuming pay increases of 5, 10, or 15 percent over 15, 25, and 35 years of service. For example, using a three-year average for a person with 25 years of service who consistently received 10 percent increases would put earnings for pension purposes at approximately 128 percent more than if a similar career average were used. The greatest variance is at the highest compound pay increase (15 percent), the most years of service (35), and the fewest number of years in the average (3). Thus, the higher the "number of years" used to define earnings, the higher the needed formula percentage and vice versa.

	Number of Years Used to Calculate Average		
	Three	**Five**	**Ten**
35 Years of Service			
15% pay increase	303%	255%	166%
10% pay increase	201	175	123
5% pay increase	94	85	65
25 Years of Service			
15% pay increase	194	159	94
10% pay increase	128	109	69
5% pay increase	61	54	37
15 Years of Service			
15% pay increase	95	72	29
10% pay increase	64	50	21
5% pay increase	31	25	12

Table 6-25. Years (service plus plan formula) and pay increase for final-pay versus career-earnings plans

Another example of the power of compounding is shown in Table 6-26. Five individuals start at $50,000 a year but receive compound average annual income of 3 percent, 6 percent, 9 percent, 12 percent, and 15 percent for 35 years. This history shows five-year intervals. The average of the final five years of pay is also shown for 5, 10, 15, 20, 25, 30, and 35 years of serv-

Final Year's Pay	Annual Compound Pay Increase (in thousands)				
Year	3%	6%	9%	12%	15%
35	$136.6	$362.5	$936.4	$2,357.1	$5,790.3
30	117.8	270.9	608.6	1,337.5	2,878.8
25	101.6	202.4	395.6	758.9	1,431.3
20	87.7	151.3	257.1	430.6	711.6
15	75.6	113.0	167.1	244.4	353.8
10	65.2	84.5	108.6	138.7	175.9
5	56.3	63.1	70.6	78.7	87.5
Average Final Five Years	3%	6%	9%	12%	15%
35	$128.9	$323.8	$794.0	$1,903.3	$4,464.3
30	111.2	241.9	516.1	1,080.0	2,219.5
25	95.8	180.8	335.4	612.8	1,103.5
20	82.7	135.1	218.0	347.7	548.7
15	71.3	100.9	141.7	197.3	272.7
10	61.5	75.4	92.1	112.0	135.6
5	53.1	56.4	59.9	63.5	67.4
% of Final Year	94%	89%	85%	81%	77%

Table 6-26. Pay progressions and final pay pension contributions (starting at $50,000 per year) Top vs. bottom: Company final year formula vs. average of five years' pay

ice. Note that as the average annual-pay rate increases, the relationship of the average final five to final year's pay decreases. To illustrate, a 3-percent compound pay increase for 35 years results in a final year's pay of $136,600 but an average final five of $128,400, or 94 percent of final year. Whereas a 15-percent compound increase for 35 years would result in a final year's pay of $5,790,300 but a final-five average of "only" $4,464,300, or 77 percent of final year's pay.

As everyone knows, in addition to the company pension, a retired employee is usually eligible for Social Security benefits. Started in the mid-1930s as a modest benefit, Social Security has been continually improved, especially in recent years, and no longer can be ignored in pension planning. Whereas a company plan of either career earnings or final pay will produce the same percentage of pay increases and years of service for both clerk and executive, when added to Social Security benefits, it produces a total retirement curve similar to the one shown in Figure 6-3. This is because the executive probably qualifies for the maximum Social Security benefit, while the clerk earns a lower benefit. Nonetheless, because the benefit represents a very significant percentage of the clerk's final year's pay and a very small portion of the executive's, we have the decreasing percentage curve shown. The X values will change depending on the increase in Social Security benefits, but the curve is likely to retain the same shape.

Given the impact of Social Security benefits, it is virtually impossible to set the company

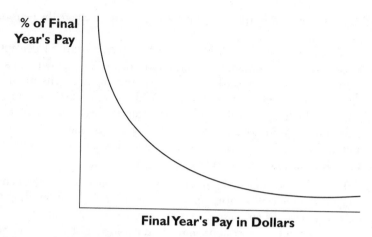

Figure 6-3. Social Security as a percentage of final pay

formula to pay off an appropriate amount at the executive level without placing the clerk's combined pension at or above the final year's pay. In addition, some portion of Social Security payments may not be subject to income tax, and thus these payments represent an even higher percentage of net than gross pay.

Therefore, many companies integrate their pension plan benefits with Social Security to try to smooth out the percentage curve. To maintain qualified-plan status, the plan must integrate in a manner acceptable to the IRS; essentially, this provides two approaches: excess and offset. Either may be used with a career-earnings or final-pay plan.

Excess Integration Method. Sometimes called a "carve-out" or "step-up" plan, the excess integration method is more common with career-average than final-pay plans. It applies one benefit rate for all earnings up to the Social Security tax base and another higher figure for earnings above the base.

Note also that while OASDI (Old Age, Survivor, and Disability Insurance) is subject to maximum taxable earnings base, the Medicare tax is not. To demonstrate the impact on the highly paid executive, look at Table 6-27. Here a 6.2-percent Social Security tax is applied to the first $80,400 of earnings whereas the 1.45-percent Medicare tax is applied to all earnings. The executive earning $100,000 pays about three times as much in Social Security as Medicare, but for the executive earning $1,000,000, those ratios are reversed.

The $80,400 maximum taxable earnings base will be out of date shortly after this book is

Income	Social Security	Medicare
$100,000	$4,985 4.98%	$1,450 1.45%
$1,000,000	$4,985 .50%	$14,500 1.45%

Table 6-27. Social Security and Medicare tax layout

published. Nonetheless, it is useful for purposes of illustrating how to calculate the pension plan benefits with an excess formula.

To illustrate the application of the excess formula, assume a plan crediting 1 percent up to the Social Security taxable base maximum and 1.5 percent on the excess. Applying this to our earlier $100,000 executive and assuming 2001 is the 20th year of work results in an annual annuity of $11,651 (i.e., $10,143 + $1,508) as shown in Table 6-28, or 11.7 percent of final year's pay. Using the same methodology but the updated earnings history of $68,500 (see Table 6-24) would result in an annuity of $15,042 or 15 percent of final year's pay.

The excess form of integration has the advantage of being relatively easy to communicate to employees; however, it has the following disadvantages:

- This form of integration does not make it clear to employees that the company's real objective is to supplement Social Security up to a certain overall benefit level.
- Although an excess plan can be structured to take into consideration adjustments in the wage base, it offers no built-in cost-containing features for legislated Social Security

Year	Earnings	Social Security Taxable Base Maximum	At 1%	Excess	At 1.5%
20	$100,000	$80,400	$804	$19,600	$294
19	92,500	76,200	762	16,300	245
18	87,500	68,400	684	19,100	287
17	79,500	65,400	654	14,100	212
16	72,500	62,700	627	9,800	147
15	68,500	61,200	612	7,300	110
14	65,500	60,600	606	4,900	74
13	61,000	57,600	576	3,400	51
12	56,500	55,500	555	1,000	15
11	53,000	53,400	530	—	—
10	50,500	51,300	505	—	—
9	48,000	48,000	480	—	—
8	45,500	45,000	450	500	7
7	43,500	43,800	435	—	—
6	41,500	42,000	415	—	—
5	39,500	39,600	395	—	—
4	37,500	37,800	375	—	—
3	36,000	35,700	357	300	—
2	34,000	32,400	324	1,600	24
1	32,500	29,700	297	2,800	42
Total Combined	$1,145,000	$1,041,700	$10,143	$100,700	$1,508

Table 6-28. Excess pension example

changes. Accordingly, major decision changes in the pension formula could be necessary each time a new Social Security law is passed.

- It is not logical to relate benefits in a retirement plan to movements in the Social Security taxable wage base, particularly when the objective is to integrate benefits from both sources to provide an appropriate amount of total retirement income.

Offset Integration Method. The second basic approach, the offset integration method, is more common with final-pay than career-earnings plans. It employs one percentage for all earnings and then another percentage (equal to or lower than the first) to the Social Security benefit. To illustrate, let's use the following formula: 1.5 percent of average earnings - 1.25 percent of primary Social Security benefits. The resulting amount will be multiplied by the years of creditable service. Assume that average earnings are equal to the highest consecutive five-year average (which in our earlier example was $86,400) and that primary Social Security equals $18,000. The annual annuity is therefore $21,420: i.e., [1.5% ($86,400) - 1.25% ($18,000)] x 20 years.

The rationale for this form of integration is that the company has contributed to the employee's Social Security benefit and it should therefore be entitled to reduce pension benefits by a portion of the Social Security benefit. With this type of plan formula, a company can develop a total retirement income objective (plan benefits plus primary Social Security) based on the employee's length of service. The offset method of integration is considered to have the following advantages:

- The offset can be designed to adjust automatically to increasing Social Security benefits; therefore, this type of integration can provide a company with some protection against spiraling benefits and costs.
- Offset integration provides a more direct approach to achieving benefit objectives (i.e., more equitable distribution of plan benefits to higher-paid employees).
- The offset approach meshes logically with benefit formulas based on earnings close to retirement. Social Security benefits are wage-indexed, and therefore an offset is a logical approach to ensure a more equitable distribution of plan benefits.

The disadvantage of offset plans is that they are not easy to communicate to employees; furthermore, pointing out that Social Security benefits reduce the company pension is a disadvantage both in fact and in the employee's mind. However, it is possible to minimize this negative aspect by using some basic algebra, if both formula values are the same (e.g., 1.5 percent - 1.5 percent). This is shown in Table 6-29.

Stated another way, using the above example, the company could say, "We will provide a pension equal to 1.5 percent (times years of service) of that portion of your final average earnings that is not 100 percent replaced by primary Social Security."

In summary, the main difference between excess and offset is that the excess integrates on the taxable earnings base, and offset integrates directly with the benefit level. For many, the offset approach is believed to be the more logical one.

Testing the Plan. Earlier, we looked at the competitive level of the combined payouts from Brucell's defined-benefit and defined-contribution plans. Now it is time to examine the competitive position of the defined-benefit plan. As shown in Table 6-30, companies are ranked by the defined benefit and Social Security expressing that total as a percentage of final pay, in this example $100,000 and 30 years service.

FAE = Final Average Earnings = $86,400

PSS = Primary Social Security = $18,000

YS = Years of Service = 20

CB = Company Benefit

CB = [1.5% FAE - 1.5% PSS] YS

CB = [1.5% (FAE - PSS)] YS

CB = [1.5% ($86,400 - $18,000)] 20

CB = [1.5% ($68,400)] 20

CB = $20,520

Table 6-29. Offset pension example

Note that Brucell currently ranks 5th; however, we can determine its new rank by substituting alternative model-plan formulas. While these calculations can be done by hand, it is far more efficient to use a computer, given the number of combinations involved. For example, in addition to testing the seven earnings examples at age 65 with 30 years, it may also be informative to test for 35 and 25 years. At age 60, earnings histories of 30, 25, and 20 might be appropriate, whereas at 55, service of 15, 20, and 25 could be appropriate. Combined, this would mean 63 worksheets before considering possible changes in the discount schedule for early retirement.

In analyzing the data, it is logical to ascertain competitive position in terms other than the simple average of the survey. Shown in Figure 6-4 is a company's non-integrated 1 percent final pay (average of highest 10 years) stated in terms of the survey's 50th, 75th, and 90th percentile (for an employee age 65 with 30 years of service). After selecting the desired competitive position, it is possible to work backward into a formula. For example, if a final pay formula (highest average five years) offset with Social Security were desired, a little trial and error with values might reveal that: 2 percent - 2 percent might equate to the 90th percentile, 1.75 percent - 1.5 percent would approximate the 75th percentile, and 1.5 percent - 1.25 percent would come closest to the 50th percentile.

Besides testing hypothetical examples, one can input actual data for key executives, thus being able to answer specific as well as general questions about the plan's competitiveness. Such an approach would also allow calculating the normal form required by ERISA (i.e., joint and survivor annuity with 50 percent of the benefit continuing to the spouse after the retiree's death), since the spouse's age could be entered into the calculations.

It should be noted that this joint and survivor form could also be included as a pre-retirement benefit. In other words, when the executive dies while actively employed but eligible for retirement, the surviving spouse will be given a benefit equal to the 50-percent survivor benefit if the employee had retired the day before his or her death. While this is a logical benefit to include in the basic plan, it should certainly be considered for executives if not adopted broadly.

A number of plans will pay a pension after a specified number of years (e.g., 10); however, this is not optimal to the executive. Rather, the company should ensure adequate long-term disability benefits and continue the employee in the pension plan (thereby accruing plan credits). Thus, when LTD benefits end at age 65 or some other age, the individual will have a reasonable pension.

Rank	Company	Company Pension	Including Social Security	% Final Pay
1	F	$43,181	$55,181	55.2
2	A	42,186	54,186	54.2
3	E	41,683	53,683	53.7
4	D	41,576	53,576	53.6
5	Brucell	40,862	52,862	52.9
6	C	38,880	50,880	50.9
7	I	33,255	45,255	45.3
8	G	32,142	44,142	44.1
9	B	22,997	34,997	35.0
10	H	18,722	30,722	30.7
Average (Excluding Brucell)		$34,958	$46,958	47.0%

Rank	Final Pay Formula	Company Pension	Including Social Security	% Final Pay
1	2% - 2%	44,640	56,640	56.6
1	2% - 1.5%	46,400	58,400	58.4
7	1.6% - 1.5%	33,480	45,480	45.5

Table 6-30. Defined benefit survey

Defined-Contribution Plans

In addition to, or in lieu of, defined-benefit plans, the company may have a defined-contribution plan. As the name suggests, the amount of the contribution not the benefit is prescribed by plan formula. The amount of benefit the plan participant receives will be based on contribution (employer and/or employee depending on plan) as well as investment gains and losses. However, qualified plans are limited by Section 415(c) of the IRC, which requires the annual addition to the individual's account be the lesser of $40,000 or 100 percent of the participant's compensation.

Forfeitures of non-vested benefits by terminating employees may, by plan design, also be allocated among plan participants. This is a key difference from defined-benefit plans where forfeitures must be used to reduce employer contributions; they cannot be used to increase benefits of plan participants. Thus, an employee in a plan that is experiencing high employee turnover may receive significantly more than the amount of the company match. This is not a required feature, and some plans take the same approach required of defined-benefit plans, namely to use the value of the forfeitures to offset the company contribution.

Employee contributions may be prohibited or permitted and if permitted, either voluntary or mandatory, and from pretax and/or after-tax pay. The advantage to employees is that, even if

Final Year's Pay

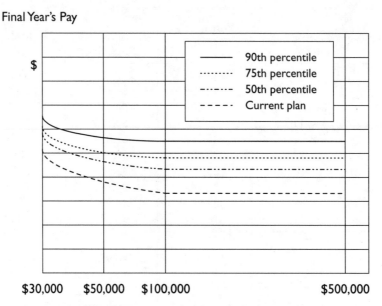

Figure 6-4. Competitive pension position (50th to 90th percentile)

their contribution is made in after-tax dollars, the tax on company contribution plus any appreciation on investments is deferred until the time of retirement. Under some conditions, it may be possible to defer tax liabilities on unrealized capital gains even further if at the time of withdrawal the amount is taken in company stock.

Unlike defined-benefit plans, defined-contribution plans are not restricted as to the amount of plan assets that can be held in company stock. By design, some defined-contribution plans are 100-percent company stock; others have varying amounts. Not atypical is that the company contribution to defined-contribution plans is in company stock while employees can usually choose what portion, if any, of their contributions will be in company stock versus alternative investment options. When individual contributions are accepted, many plans provide half a dozen or more choices, each with different reward and risk characteristics. This provides sufficient investment flexibility to participants, avoiding company liability for investment losses. The objective is to fall under the safe-harbor provision of ERISA.

In this section, we will review a number of variations of defined-contribution plans. They include: Employee Stock Ownership Plans (ESOPs), Profit-Sharing Plans, Employee Stock-Purchase Plans, Employee Stock-Option Plans, Savings Plans (a.k.a. Thrift Plan), Cash or Deferred Arrangements (CODAs), Individual Retirement Account Plans (IRAs), and Keogh Plans. We begin with ESOPs.

Employee Stock-Ownership Plans. An employee stock ownership plan (ESOP) can be viewed as a broad-based, deferred stock-award plan that meets the defined-contribution plans requirement of Section 401 of the IRC. ESOPs are either leveraged or non-leveraged. With either form, accounts for each employee are established and annually credited with the number of shares prescribed by formula.

The leveraged ESOP is one way to obtain financing for the company and pass on a portion of company ownership to employees. The company makes a contribution of company stock to an Employee Stock Ownership Trust (ESOT). The trust, in turn, uses the stock to obtain a loan, the proceeds of which it gives to the corporation. The corporation then pays off the loan through the trust and gains a tax deduction on the principal (as an employee benefit) and the interest (as a normal business expense). The amount credited to each employee's account would be in relation to his or her portion of the total payroll. For example, a person earning $100,000 would receive 1 percent of the total stock award if the total payroll were $10,000,000.

ESOPs can be very attractive to individuals who own a large portion of company stock, especially in privately held businesses. Death, disability, and retirement often create significant problems with liquidity and keeping control of the business in friendly hands. By selling stock to an ESOP, owners can get needed cash and their companies can take a tax deduction for the employee benefit. In addition, by taking out key employee insurance on majority shareholders, the trust can use the proceeds of the policy to purchase the deceased's stock from the estate. The ESOP provides liquidity and keeps control of the business in friendly hands. However, these attributes are more important for smaller organizations (than their larger counterparts) due to problems associated with determining the value of the stock and obtaining a buyer both willing to purchase at fair market value and acceptable to the other owners. These plans are also known as LESOPs (leveraged employee stock ownership plans), although the Technical Corrections Act of 1979 officially identifies them as ESOPs. A non-leveraged ESOP has no borrowings; it simply makes annual contributions to the trust that are then allocated by the above-described earnings formula to individual accounts.

For a period of time, larger companies adopted ESOPs in the form of a TRAESOP (Tax Reduction Act form of Employee Stock Ownership Plan) because of the tax credit. As the name implies, this is an ESOP provided by a tax reform act (more specifically the Tax Reform Act of 1975). The Technical Corrections Act of 1979 officially identified such plans as tax credit employee stock ownership plans. Compensation and benefit expenses usually qualify for a tax deduction, which simply means the government will underwrite a portion of the expense (i.e., the applicable tax rate). Under a tax credit, the government underwrites the full cost of the plan since the deduction is applied to taxes due rather than to company income! Needless to say, this is a more attractive form of benefit "expense" to the company—especially since it increases corporate cash flow by the amount of the expense. Unfortunately for executives, the allowable TRAESOP amounts were very meager on a per-employee basis. While all employees were to share proportionately in the amount of the credit, there was a $100,000 earnings ceiling. In other words, anyone earning above $100,000 would receive the same dollar benefit as a person earning $100,000. Furthermore, while contributions were immediately 100-percent vested, they could not be distributed before seven years, except in cases of separation from service (including disability, retirement, and death). Some companies choose to make payments only under such conditions, barring distribution to active employees. In any event, these were likely to be small accumulations except in cases of long service at high earnings for a capital-intensive company (which has a high credit and a small employee population).

The 1981 Economic Recovery Act modified and extended TRAESOPs briefly but then legislated them out of existence. The capital investment formula was replaced with a payroll-based credit of 0.5 percent for 1983 and 1984, increased to 0.75 percent for 1985 through 1987, after which TRAESOPs expired.

Profit-Sharing Plans. The typical profit-sharing plan will set aside a portion of profits for distribution to the company's employees. Profits can be defined as either before or after taxes. It may apply to the first dollar of profit or after exceeding a prescribed threshold or minimum level. Alternatively, it can be paid even if there are no profits! Although called "profit-sharing" plans, the 1986 Tax Reform Act stated that profits are not required to make a contribution. The contribution can either be by predetermined formula or determined annually in a discretionary manner. However, IRS regulation 1.401-1(b)(2) requires that the contributions be "substantial and recurring" in order to meet tax-qualified status requiring a degree of permanency. In addition, the plan cannot discriminate in favor of highly compensated individuals.

Although benefits may be paid at the end of the year, this is currently not a form of profit sharing eligible for preferential tax treatment. This form will be reviewed in the Chapter 7 (Short-Term Incentives). Benefits that are credited to an individuals account at the end of the year but not available until the attainment of a stated age or with the occurrence of a prescribed event (e.g., disability or severance of employment due to layoff, death, or retirement), are deferred, profit-sharing plans. They are eligible to be treated as tax-qualified plans under Section 401 of the IRC. This enables the company to take a tax deduction at time of contribution whereas the individual is not taxed until the later date when funds are withdrawn. If the deferred, profit-sharing plan does not meet requirements for tax qualifications, the company cannot take a tax deduction until the individual receives the benefit. If the company takes a tax deduction at time of contribution, the individual has a tax liability on income not received. This is not a good situation for the individual. Alternatively, the company has to defer the tax deduction until the monies are withdrawn years later. This is not very attractive to the company.

To be tax qualified, Section 404 of the IRC stipulates that the maximum annual tax deduction allowable to the company is 15 percent of the covered payroll. Although not required for tax qualifications, some plans permit employee contributions. Therefore, in addition to the 15-percent maximum of covered payroll, there is a 25-percent annual addition limit under Section 415 of the IRC. "Annual additions" are the sum of employer contributions, employee contributions, and reallocated forfeitures. Furthermore, it is the lesser amount of 25 percent or the dollar amount prescribed by statute, which limits its attractiveness to highly paid executives.

Allocations to individual accounts can be either a uniform amount for each or based on compensation, or compensation and years of service credit, or compensation and age. A uniform amount for everyone would give the lowest-paid employee the largest percentage of pay, whereas the highest-paid executive would receive the lowest percentage. For allocations based only on compensation, a person earning $100,000 with a covered payroll of $10 million will receive 1 percent of the profit-sharing contribution since the person's pay is 1 percent of the covered payroll. If the profit-sharing contribution were $100,000, the individual's share would be $1,000. Under a combination compensation and years-of-service plan, points are assigned by formula. Perhaps the individual is assigned one point for every $100 of earnings and two points for every year of service. In the earlier example, if the person had 10 years of service, it would result in 1,020 points ($100,000 ÷ 100) + (10 years x 2). If the total points of all employees were 105,250, each point would be worth $9.50 ($1 million divided by 105,250 points) and this person would receive $9,690.

Planners must determine the desired relationship of pay to service. In the previous formula, if it were one point for every $10 not $100 of pay, service would be much more important, relatively. Compensation and age formulas can be designed in much the same manner providing greater weight for older employees. However, such plans must be careful to ensure they do not discriminate in favor of highly compensated individuals. Since older employees are typically more highly compensated than younger employees, this could be a problem. Also, one must view the formula in light of the federal requirement of either equal costs or equal benefits, as prescribed in the Older Worker Protection Act of 1990.

While profit-sharing plans typically include all employees, there are alternatives. Highly paid employees could be excluded by title or level of pay. Alternatively, they could be included but only up to a specified earnings level.

Profit-sharing plans may pay out in stock, cash, or a combination. Those paying out solely in company stock are frequently identified as stock plans, but they are still profit-sharing plans. Plan provisions may permit loans and/or withdrawals prior to leaving the company subject to IRS regulations. However, premature distributions may be subject to a penalty tax.

Profit-sharing plans fit better in egalitarian, team-focused companies than in companies that focus on individual performance. Nonetheless, they help employees focus on improving productivity and, thereby, profits. However, company size is a factor. The ability to identify personal impact for a person in a company of 10,000 is far less than one with 100. However, even with the smaller organization, the "line of sight" between individual performance and company results is neither as straight as a laser nor crystal clear.

Savings/Thrift Plans. Section 401 of the IRC considers a tax-qualified savings or thrift plan (the two are synonymous) as a type of profit-sharing plan. However, unlike the typical profit-sharing plan, savings plans normally require an employee contribution in order to receive an employer contribution. That contribution is a percentage of the employee's contribution. The employee's contribution in the form of a payroll deduction is typically a percentage of pretax income but is made from after-tax pay.

The plan specifies the percentages of pay the employee may contribute to the plan and what portion of these contributions will be matched by the company and at what rate. A representative formula would be permitting the employee to contribute in 1 percent multiples from 1 to 15, with the company matching an equal amount for the first 5 percent. This would result in a maximum contribution of 20 percent of employee pay. A profit-sharing type feature could be added on where, depending on company profitability, an additional amount would be contributed by the company, subject to the previously described, allowable tax-qualified maximum. If possible, the individual should set aside the maximum allowable (15 percent in the above example), to capitalize on the power of tax-deferred, compound growth, which will be illustrated later. At the minimum, the individual should set aside the maximum amount on which the company matches the contribution. In the above example, that would be 5 percent.

Normally, the company contribution is in the form of company stock or dollars to purchase company stock, whereas employees normally have several choices about how their dollars will be invested (e.g., fixed income fund, common stocks excluding own company, and company stock).

Given allowable payroll deductions, company contributions, and investment alternatives one needs to decide how much to set aside and in what funds. This will result from determining the retirement income target less other sources of income. The latter consists of Social Security benefits, other company programs (e.g., defined-benefit plan), and individual investments.

The investment choices available to the employee typically permit the individual to select funds to meet conservative, moderate, or aggressive investment philosophies. While these vary by individual, they also typically vary by age. Younger employees are likely to be more aggressive, whereas older employees are more conservative, looking to minimize risk and protect funds accrued. The key factors to consider are: (1) at what point in the future is one likely to make withdrawals; (2) what is the minimum amount needed when withdrawals begin; and (3) over what period of time will the monies be needed.

Given a retirement target and time frame, one needs to balance risk versus return. The highest rate of return opportunity typically creates the greatest risk that the money will not be available. The aggressive investor accepts the higher risk for the possibility of a greater return; the conservative investor accepts a lower rate of return in exchange for assurance that the investment is protected. Bonds can run the full gamut from very conservative to very risky (e.g., high interest "junk bonds"). Many investors will seek to balance their portfolio by asset allocations that include aggressive as well as conservative investments. However, they may be weighted more in one area than another. In addition to considering the rate of return in light of investment risk, one should also consider how the likely inflation rate compares with the rate of return. If inflation is higher, the investment value will erode over time.

The serious investor will look to performance of the available possible investment alternatives and select the one or combination that best meets needs. Employing standard deviations can be useful in predicting variability around reported performance. For example, a fund with average annual return of 10 percent and a standard deviation of 20 would be expected to return between -10 percent and +30 percent, two-thirds of the time. A two standard deviation would result in a range of -30 percent to +50 percent, 95 percent of the time. Contrast that with a fund averaging 5 percent and a standard deviation of five. It would range between 0 percent and 10 percent, two thirds of the time and between -5 percent and +15 percent, 95 percent of the time. The first is more likely to be the choice of an aggressive investor; the second would be a selection by the conservative investor. Comparing standard deviations with a "risk-free" investment such as short-term treasury bills is helpful in this review as it establishes a benchmark for comparison. Assume that rate is 5 percent and a comparison of one standard deviation. On the upside, the second choice has a 5-percent advantage whereas the first is +25 percent. On the downside, the second is -5 percent and the first is -15 percent.

The chart in Table 6-31 shows the impact of a 5-percent employee contribution with a 50-percent company match for an individual currently earning $50,000. Assume the individual received 10-percent annual pay increases for 20 years and the contributions set aside grew at the annual rate of 10 percent. At the end of that time, the individual would have a fund value of $504,563, but his or her compensation would be $336,375 (i.e., $50,000 increased annually at 10 percent for 20 years). One can easily project other values based on multiples of $50,000. For example, using the same assumptions, a person currently earning $500,000 would have $5,045,630 in the plan. Part would be in the statutory plan and the balance in a non-qualified, deferred plan.

The breakdown of contributions and growth is not shown in Table 6-31, but in this situation it is:

Pay increase, percent	Annual Compound Growth		
	5%	10%	15%
30 Years			
15%	$2,436,912	$4,022,896	$7,448,824
10%	1,033,788	1,963,058	4,205,755
5%	466,219	1,083,016	2,668,999
20 Years			
15%	$539,959	$795,221	$1,227,490
10%	320,844	504,563	831,367
5%	198,997	336,122	591,384
10 Years			
15%	$95,156	$119,775	$151,709
10%	75,982	97,265	125,219
5%	61,084	79,600	104,219

Table 6-31. Effect of compound growth with savings plan

	Amount	Percent of total
Employee contributions	$143,188	28.4%
Company contributions	71,594	14.2%
Investment growth	289,781	57.4%
Total	504,563	100.0%

This example illustrates several points regarding such plans: (1) the higher the company contribution and investment rate of return, the more attractive such plans are, and (2) the projected amount at a specified date in the future looks very awesome in terms of current pay level, but it must more realistically be expressed in relation to projected pay (i.e., in this illustration $504,563 versus $336,375 or 150 percent of final pay).

In some instances, poor investment results motivated some executives to redirect their investments to some form of *guaranteed income contract* or GIC, in which an insurance company or other institution guarantees a specified rate of return for a specified number of years. However, GICs do not necessarily guarantee that the guaranteed rate will be paid if the carrier has poor financial performance as the funds are invested in the general assets of the carrier. Another group contract written by insurance carriers is the *immediate participation guarantee*, which, like the GIC, may be invested in the general assets of the carrier or placed in separate accounts. Unlike the GIC, it does not guarantee a minimum rate of return (much less the payment). Thus, the payout could be greater or less than under the GIC.

Another investment alternative to stocks are bonds. When purchasing bonds, it may be smart to buy them with different maturity dates. This approach, called "laddering," should minimize the impact of not catching a high interest rate. By smoothing out the investment period, one is dollar averaging the interest rates. As a result, one will not catch the high rate but also will not be stuck with a portfolio of low rates at a time of rising interest rates.

When considering investing in bonds, it is appropriate to consider more than rising or falling interest rates. There are a number of risks to consider: credit rating (a lower rating of the bond issue will most likely result in a lowering of its price); default (the issuer cannot make interest payments or pay principal); liquidity (issuer or market factor that makes bond easy or difficult to sell); and market (value will rise or fall with interest rates in general).

As can be seen, deciding how to invest one's money can be rather complicated. Employees logically look to the company for help in deciding where to put their money. Unfortunately, companies avoid giving advice because while not legally obligated to do so, they can be held accountable if they do give advice and the result is not what was predicted. To fill this advice void, some companies provide broad-based financial counseling with an outside vendor, whereas (as described earlier) executives look to financial planners for customized advice.

Investment advisors often suggest not more than 10 percent of the portfolio be in the company's stock. This certainly is a prudent approach to a balanced portfolio; however, the individual may regret this conservative philosophy if the company stock significantly outperforms other investment alternatives. Conversely, poor company performance will not only affect one's stock portfolio but the poor performance may lead to cutbacks and the possible loss of one's job—disastrous double whammy.

Plans that are very difficult to get money out of probably have lower levels of participation than plans with liberal withdrawal provisions. For some, *withdrawal privileges* may be as important as a higher percentage company match.

Typically, the employee has several options in taking money out. The individual who is still an employee usually can make either a partial or a full early withdrawal. As the terms imply, the difference lies in whether all or only a portion of the money is removed. The other withdrawal is the normal withdrawal that occurs when the person leaves the company, although some plans permit the individual to keep the funds in the plan until a designated date. Alternatively, the individual could roll the money over to an IRA or the defined-benefit plan of a new employer, being careful not to mingle pretax with after-tax dollars.

Depending on the objective of the plan, early withdrawals are either reasonably easy to accomplish (within the requirements prescribed by the IRC and interpreted by the IRS to avoid constructive receipt of employer contributions) or more difficult (consistent with a plan intended to be a supplement to the defined-benefit pension plan). Plan penalties set the period of suspension from the plan, the frequency at which withdrawals may be made, and in the case of partial withdrawals, the amount withdrawn. The rules may be different for partial versus full withdrawals. Withdrawals made before age 59½ (except those meeting statutory exceptions) are subject to a tax of 10 percent in addition to any income tax due.

However, many plans make an exception for *hardship withdrawals* (i.e., amounts needed to meet a financial crisis). Typically, this might include college expenses for children, purchase of a primary residence, or significant medical expenses not covered by the health care program. Under such provisions, the normal penalties for withdrawals are suspended or made less punitive.

Partial withdrawals have an advantage in that the IRS applies the familiar FIFO (first-in-first-out) accounting rule. Namely, no tax liability is incurred until the withdrawals exceed the amount of employee money invested; in other words, no taxable investment growth is acknowledged until all the nontaxable principal has been withdrawn. Meanwhile, the investment growth remains in the fund to form the basis for future growth.

Cash or Deferred-Compensation Arrangement. A cash or deferred-compensation arrangement (CODA) is often called a 401(k) plan because that is the section in the Internal Revenue
Code added in the 1978 Revenue Act where it is defined. Namely, an eligible employee may
choose to receive cash from the employer or have the employer make a comparable contribution to a qualified retirement plan. When applied to salary, it is a salary reduction plan. There
are restrictions on the amount highly compensated employees may defer and when the deferred
amounts, adjusted for investment results, may be withdrawn similar to thrift plans. Investment
opportunities often mirror those available with the after-tax savings plan.

Although a CODA could be a standalone plan, many companies combine it with their 401
defined contributions, which use after-tax contributions. Thus, the 401(k) payroll deduction
would be matched in the same manner as the after-tax savings plan deduction. Where a company has a profit-sharing plan, the employee makes similar deferrals, although typically, these
are not matched since the profit-sharing amount itself is the company contribution.

Qualified CODAs are of limited value to highly compensated executives because of their
low limit on annual deferrals. However, the amounts allowed by plan formula but in excess of
the annual limit may be deferred into a non-qualified plan. Typically, these deferrals would
either be in units (rather than actual shares of company stock, to avoid economic benefit)
and/or the equivalent of U.S. government short- or long-term debt instruments. Being non-qualified, the company cannot take a tax deduction until recognized by the executive.

IRS Revenue Ruling 98-30 permits the employer to automatically include an employee in the
401(k) plan. To be excluded, the employee must opt out by making a negative election. This action
eases administrative burden and improves the likelihood of a high level of employee participation.

Employee Stock-Purchase Plans. These plans enable an employee to purchase company stock
by authorizing payroll deductions for a stated period of time. Although not a retirement plan
per se, it is an investment opportunity to supplement other sources of retirement income.

Section 423(b)(1) through (9) of the IRC cites the nine requirements that must be met for
the plan to be tax qualified.

1. Only employees of the company and its subsidiary corporations are eligible.
2. Approval of the shareholders is required within 12 months of the date the plan is adopted
   by the granting corporation.
3. Employees owning more than 5 percent of the voting stock of the company are not eligible. See Section 424(d) for rules of stock ownership.
4. Options to purchase must be given on a nondiscriminatory basis, although it is permissible
   to exclude: (a) those with less than two years of service, (b) those working 20 hours or less
   a week, (c) those working not more than five months a year, and (d) highly compensated
   employees as defined in Section 414(q) of the IRC.
5. Participating employees must have the same rights and privileges, but the amount of stock
   available to employees may vary directly with their compensation. Furthermore, a maximum amount of stock that may be purchased by any individual can be established.
6. The purchase price cannot be less than the lower of 85 percent of fair market value (FMV)
   at (a) time of grant, or (b) time of purchase or exercise.
7. Where the grant is set at not less than 85 percent of FMV at date of exercise, the purchase
   period may run as long as five years. If the purchase price is not set in this manner, the purchase period may not exceed 27 months.

8. No employee may be granted an option that exceeds $25,000 of fair market value for each calendar year in which the option is outstanding.
9. The option is not transferable by the employee other than by will or the laws of descent and distribution, and is exercisable only by the employee during his or her lifetime.

Under such a plan, the employee agrees to purchase a specified number of shares or invest a specified number of dollars (e.g., up to 5 percent of pay) to purchase company stock on an installment basis. By terms of the agreement, the percentage discount is prescribed and may be as low as 85 percent of FMV.

Section 423(a) of the IRC describes the requirements necessary to avoid an income-tax liability when purchasing stock through a company stock-purchase plan. The employee must purchase the stock while active or within three months of termination of employment in accordance with plan terms. In addition, the employee may not dispose of the stock within two years from date of grant and one year after purchase. If these requirements are satisfied, the employee has no income at time of purchase and the gain from FMV at time of purchase to that realized upon sale will be considered long-term capital gains. If these requirements are not met, while the tax liability is still deferred until the individual sells the stock, the discount below fair market value at time of purchase is taxed as ordinary income. Any appreciation above FMV at time of purchase is subject to short- or long-term capital gains tax, depending on length of time held.

Some companies use stock-purchase plans in lieu of stock options, reserving options only for executives [see Chapter 8 (Long-Term Incentives)]. When stock options are reserved for executives and executives are also prohibited from participating in the stock-purchase plan, this may create a problem. If the stock is "flat" for several years, the stock purchase participants will realize a bigger benefit than executives. Conversely, if the stock price increases significantly over the term of the plan, the stock option is more attractive.

Employee Stock Options. A stock option is the right given by a granter (the company) to an optionee (the person) to exercise (purchase) a stated number of shares of the company common stock (the grant) at a prescribed price (grant or strike price) over a specified period of time (exercise period). Typically, time requirements are stipulated (vesting period) before the stock may be purchased. A stock option has five key dates: grant, vest, grant termination, exercise, and sale.

While more will be said about stock options in Chapter 8 (Long-Term Incentives), the focus there will be on executive stock options, which is a major portion of senior executive pay. Broad-based, stock-option plans are more of an employee benefit than an incentive. Like stock-purchase plans, they are a way of supplementing retirement income from other sources through capital accumulation of the company's stock.

A stock option that complies with the requirements of Section 422 of the IRC is called a statutory option and is eligible for preferential tax treatment.

Section 422 requires:

1. The optionee may not sell within two years from date of grant nor within one year after exercise.
2. The optionee must exercise the option not later than three months after leaving employment.
3. The plan must specify the number of shares available for grant and be approved within 12 months of date plan is adopted.

4. Grants under the plan may not be later than 10 years from adoption or approval date (whichever is sooner) of the plan.
5. The exercise period may not exceed 10 years from date of grant.
6. The grant price may not be less than the fair market value on date of grant.
7. The aggregate fair market value of the grant (i.e., grant price times number of shares exercisable in a year) may not exceed $100,000.
8. The option is not transferable by the optionee other than by will or the laws of descent and distribution, and is exercisable only by the optionee during his or her lifetime.
9. The optionee does not own more than 10 percent of the voting power of all stock outstanding.

Because of these limitations, statutory stock options have little appeal to executives. Rather, they grant nonstatutory stock options, as discussed in Chapter 8.

Stock options are typically thought of as something reserved for executives; however, they can be a broad-based method for getting stock into employees' hands. Pfizer Inc. has been granting such broad-based stock options to its employees since the early 1950s.

The number of shares granted to employees is either a constant number or a share for every prescribed increment of salary. The two are contrasted in Table 6-32, using an option price of $100 a share. Determining the number of shares-based, salary increments provides a constant percentage benefit. The same number of shares regardless of salary level provides the greatest benefit to the lowest paid. However, it also means the percentage cost of exercise is the highest at the pay level least able to afford the exercise cost. Admittedly, this becomes easier to accomplish if the exercise cost is spread over the full 10 years. However, this requires the discipline to set enough money aside annually to permit exercising the grant without immediately selling the shares.

In determining which approach to use and the number of shares or salary increments, it is important to determine how frequently options will be granted. If this is a one-time event because the company has achieved a significant milestone (e.g., 100th anniversary), the simplest approach is probably the same number of shares for everyone. Granting 100 options for a 100th

Same Number for Everyone (Example 50 shown)

Salary	Number of Shares	Exercise Cost	Cost as a % of Salary	
			1 Year	10 Years
$50,000	50	$5,000	10.0%	1.0%
$100,000	50	5,000	5.0%	0.5%
$150,000	50	5,000	3.3%	0.3%

Share for Every Increment of Salary (Example 1 for every $2,000)

Salary	Number of Shares	Exercise Cost	Cost as a % of Salary	
$50,000	25	$2,500	5.0%	0.5%
$100,000	50	5,000	5.0%	0.5%
$150,000	75	7,500	5.0%	0.5%

Table 6-32. Stock-option grant formulas compared at $100 a share

anniversary has a nice ring to it. Conversely, if grants are going to be made on a more regular basis, using the salary increment may make more sense as other retirement forms are related to pay in some form. As grant frequency increases, the number of shares granted per cycle decreases proportionately. One could grant 500 options once every 10 years or 50 options per year. Annual grants have the advantage of dollar averaging the stock price. They also better accommodate new hires.

To facilitate accumulating sufficient funds to exercise the stock option, the company may not only *offer* payroll deductions (with some type of interest factor) it may choose to *mandate* such deductions. In the earlier example, the person earning $100,000 is told he or she may receive an option up to 50 shares at $100 a share. To do so, the employee must authorize a payroll deduction of $0.20 per week for each share. At $10.40 a year, plus credited interest, the account will accumulate the required $100 before the end of the 10-year exercise period. Because of other obligations, the employee chose to authorize $8 per pay period. At $0.20 per share, this will only protect 40 shares and, therefore, he or she is given an option of 40 not 50 shares. Any withdrawals or cutbacks in the authorized deduction will result in the proportionate forfeiture of unprotected shares.

Some of the differences between a stock-purchase plan and a stock-option plan are:

- Stock-option plans allow the company to pick and choose participants, but stock-purchase plans require that essentially all employees be eligible to participate.
- Stock-option plans usually set the price as of grant date, but some stock-purchase plans set the price at time of purchase.
- Stock-option plans provide the opportunity to purchase at any point along a prescribed time period, whereas stock-purchase plans stipulate the intervals at which the stock is to be purchased.
- Stock-option plans allow the company to determine the number of shares to be optioned by individual, but stock-purchase plans require that all participants be eligible for a number determined by a common formula.

Companies that use both stock-option (perhaps for executives) and stock-purchase plans (perhaps for all other employees) find that depending on stock price movement, one is better than the other at any point in time.

Individual Retirement Account. The individual retirement account (IRA) was introduced in 1974 with the adoption of ERISA and has been modified a number of times since by tax legislation. As described in section 408 of the IRC, the IRA permits an individual to make an annual contribution of 15 percent of earned income up to a $2,000 maximum to an IRA account established with a financial institution (e.g., bank, broker, insurance company, or other investment house). The law prohibits including collectibles, life insurance, and personal property. It also prohibits transactions with the IRA's owner and spouse, parent, or children. Distributions from the IRA cannot be sooner than age 59½ without a tax penalty or begin later than age 70½ by either lump sum or life annuity equivalent. However, the IRS may permit a lowering of the minimum withdrawal based on the combined life expectancy of self and a named beneficiary. A spouse 10 or more years younger could be a big help. The amount that is tax deductible is dependent on the person's income level and above a level well below an executive's salary, no deduction is permissible. Therefore, the traditional IRA is of no value to the executive, except to ensure that children who qualify do set up IRAs, permitting the power of compounding to take effect. Babysitting and newspaper route jobs can qualify preteens to set up and contribute to their own IRA. The sooner they start, the more that will be available when they retire.

A variation on the tax deductible IRA is the *Roth IRA* (so named for the senator who sponsored the legislation). It is a nondeductible IRA, but investments accumulate tax-free and may be withdrawn at time of retirement (but not before age 59½) without being taxable. However, it too is of little interest to executives because of the low contribution limit, although it may be attractive in estate planning if, after death, the accumulated assets can be passed to heirs without incurring income taxes.

The greatest appeal of IRAs to executives is when they are set up to receive a lump-sum distribution from a qualified pension plan after the executive leaves the company. Given the alternative of immediate taxation on the lump sum in addition to a penalty tax for early withdrawal (namely less than age 59½), a tax-deferred rollover into an IRA makes a lot of sense. Defined-contribution plans usually pay out in lump sums and, therefore, are simple to rollover into an IRA. If the amount stays with the employer, the executive may find post-retirement investment choices are limited and the withdrawal schedule less than attractive. Many defined-benefit plans permit the conversion of the annuity into a lump sum that can be rolled over. However, those under a career-earnings plan with periodic updates may find it to their advantage to take the annuity and forego the IRA rollover because later updates will apply only to the annuity but not the lump sum if taken. Should the executive join a company with a defined-contribution plan accepting rollovers, the executive may choose to do so or keep it as an IRA, depending on investment alternatives.

Keogh Plans. A Keogh Plan (named after the congressman who introduced the legislation in 1962) is also called an H.R. 10 Plan (the U.S. House of Representatives number assigned to the bill). The plan permits the self-employed to participate in tax-qualified plans. In 1974, ERISA raised the yearly limits to the lesser of 15 percent of earned income or $7,500. In 1981, legislation increased the dollar maximum to $15,000. With the Tax Equity and Fiscal Responsibility Act of 1982, the maximum limits for defined-benefit and defined-contribution Keogh plans were changed to conform to those of corporate plans. Early withdrawal features are similar to IRAs.

While employed by the company, executives cannot use Keogh Plans against their company earnings, but they can use them for non-company income (e.g., director compensation if they are on other company boards). However, since many companies allow directors to defer all of their compensation, the Keogh Plan is not often used.

Simplified Employee Pensions. The simplified employee pension (SEP) was introduced with the 1978 Revenue Act and looked like a Keogh regarding annual limits but was targeted for small employers who wanted no part of complicated federal pension rules and regulations. SEPs therefore have an IRA appearance. In addition to small businesses, the self-employed could set up SEPs, thereby crossing over into Keogh land officially. The rules are similar to qualified retirement plans for eligibility, contributions, and vesting, but less complex if it is a hybrid combination of defined-contribution plans. However, there are hybrid defined-benefit/defined-contribution plans as well.

Hybrid Plans

As the name suggests, *hybrid plans* have both defined-benefit and defined-contribution features. Their emergence is in response to the need for more customized pension plan designs, addressing both employer and employee objectives. The employer seeks predictable cost, whereas the employee looks for investment opportunity and portability of benefits.

While many profit-sharing plans are self-standing, some are combined with pension plans in an either-or situation. Typically, the pension plan (defined benefit) prescribes the minimum benefit using one of the formula approaches described earlier. The profit-sharing plan stands alongside the pension plan, and the employee will receive whichever produces the greater benefit. Pension-plan liabilities are thus reduced by sustained periods of high company contributions to the profit-sharing plan. The employee still sees a very visible accumulation of assets, which form the minimum payout at time of separation from service. Furthermore, this approach combines the advantages of both while canceling several basic disadvantages. More specifically, defined-benefit plans favor older employees as plan improvements extend not only to future but also past service. Defined-contribution plans are by definition always fully funded programs that provide younger employees many years in which to build up plan values. However, withdrawal requirements exist to avoid a penalty tax.

As with either the defined-benefit or defined-contribution pension plan, the benefits from tax-qualified plans are limited by the Internal Revenue Code. However, if the benefit "lost" by the IRC restriction is made up in a non-qualified plan, the executive is very interested in plan design. To illustrate hybrid plans, let's examine cash-balance, floor-offset, and targeted benefit.

Cash-Balance. A cash-balance plan is a defined-benefit plan that looks like a defined-contribution plan. Each employee has an account that is credited with an employer contribution and a specified interest rate. The company absorbs investment gains and losses, thereby determining its contribution to the plan (as opposed to the employee's account). The employer contributions may be a flat dollar amount but more typically are a percentage of the employee's pay. This makes it look like a career-average, defined-benefit plan. It looks like a defined-contribution plan because the employee can look at any time to see what is in his or her account. Payout could be either a lump sum or an annuity.

A conversion from a defined-benefit plan to a cash-balance plan can be set up by doing a lump-sum calculation of benefits that would be paid out under the old plan. Depending on the discount rate used, the new benefit could be less than the old one. If it is less, an employee could work several extra years with essentially no increase in pension benefits until the cash-balance plan catches up with the old plan. Of course, if the person left before this happened, the individual would receive the amount from the old plan. Money in the old plan is either converted by some type of lump-sum equivalent or kept in a separate account earning interest.

Cash-balance plans typically produce greater benefits for younger employees because the flat-rate contribution is higher than would be accrued under a defined-benefit plan. Older workers lose under a conversion to a cash-balance plan. The reason is simple. Since defined benefits are a function of pay, years of service, and a discount for early retirement, a person leaving at normal retirement age probably earns half of the pension in the last five to 10 years of work. In switching to a cash-balance plan, one loses the heavy weight of those last years of earnings typically used in a final-pay formula. For that reason, many plans transition the conversion, permitting employees above a certain age and service cutoff to remain in the old plan (e.g., age 50 and 10 years). Even with this cutoff option, those ineligible (i.e., below the cutoff) may be forced to take lower future benefits.

Floor-Offset. A floor-offset plan combines a defined-benefit plan and a defined-contribution plan. The defined-benefit plan sets the minimum benefit that will be paid. If the defined-contribution plan exceeds this "floor," no payment is made from the defined-benefit plan. If it is less than the floor, the defined-benefit plan makes up the difference. This hybrid plan is attractive for those who like the defined-contribution plan but are concerned about downside risk. The defined-benefit plan provides a safety net by the "floor-offset." Some of these plans were developed by companies that had provided pension benefits through profit-sharing (defined-contribution) plans. Unfortunately, several years of bad market experience resulted in employees retiring with smaller pensions than they would have been eligible to receive years earlier. Attaching a defined-benefit plan to the bottom of the defined-contribution plans provides a floor, or stop-loss guarantee, for employees.

Pension Equity. A pension equity plan is similar to a cash-balance plan except that the benefit is expressed as a percentage of final average pay. This can be defined in the same variety of ways that final pay formulas define "final average pay." The individual is credited with an annual percentage each year and the numbers are totaled at time of retirement to determine the payment. The formula may be tilted in favor of length of service and expressed as a percentage of the average final pay. For example, the formula might call for 5 percent for each of the first 10 years of service, 10 percent for each of the next 10, and 15 percent for all years after 20. With this formula, a person with 10 years service would receive a lump-sum payment equal to 50 percent of final pay, whereas a 20-year employee would receive a lump sum equal to 150 percent of average final pay.

Profit Sharing (Age or Service Adjusted). Under a profit-sharing plan that adjusts for age or service, the employer contribution (based on employee compensation) is weighted in favor of older or longer-service employees. The rationale is that the future value of contributions by younger individuals will be greater because of the longer period for interest compounding to take place. Shown in Table 6-33 are example age-/service-adjusted, profit-sharing formulas.

One must be careful in the design of such a plan not to run afoul of age discrimination laws. Clearly, the plan is counter to "equal costs" and therefore must pass a test of "equivalent benefits."

Target Benefit. A target-benefit plan begins looking like a defined-benefit plan but ends up a defined-contribution plan. A "target" or desirable retirement benefit for a stated age and num-

Age	Years of Service	Annual Contribution As % of Pay
Up through 35	1-10	2%
36-45	11-20	4%
46-55	21-30	6%
56-Up	31-40	8%

Table 6-33. Age/service adjusted profit-sharing contributions

ber of years of service is determined. It might be stated as 1.5 percent of final average pay times years of credited service. Based on the person's life expectancy as well as actual and investment assumptions, a contribution rate is calculated to provide the targeted benefit. The rate may differ by employee. At this point, it has become a defined-benefit plan. Individual accounts are set up for each employee with various investment opportunities available. There is no guarantee the target will be met. Investment gains and losses, plus the employer contribution will determine the actual retirement benefit.

Supplemental Executive Retirement Plans

Supplemental executive retirement plans (SERPs) are pension plans that begin where the qualified plan ends. Stated another way, these are benefits in addition to the qualified, defined-benefit and defined-contribution plans. These are often called *top-hat plans* and are limited to a select group of management or highly compensated employees. The Department of Labor expanded this definition to require that such persons must be able to affect or substantially influence the design and operation of the plan, accepting attendant risks. Companies need to be certain they are in compliance with ERISA to avoid problems with the Department of Labor.

As SERPs are non-qualified, the company's tax deduction is deferred until the executive receives the benefit. However, the expense will be accrued and charged to earnings during the accrual period. There are two types of SERPs: *restorations* and *add-ons*.

Restoration Plans. These plans "restore" pension benefits that were lost when the company pension plan formula provided an amount in excess of that permitted by the IRC qualified pension plans. Restoration plans are also called 415 plans, referring to the section of the IRC that inspired them. To maintain tax-qualified status, Section 415(b) limits the annual benefit from a defined-benefit plan to $90,000 (adjusted for inflation) or 100 percent of the participant's average compensation for the highest-paid three years, whichever is less. For defined-contribution plans, Section 415(c) of the IRC limits the annual addition to the lesser of $30,000 or 25 percent of the participant's compensation. Similar restoration plans can be used when there are limits on the amount of pay that can be used in the calculation. These are also called *excess plans*, referring to the benefit in excess of the statutory limit. However, the name may imply additional and sounds similar to "excessive."

ERISA sets limits inside the qualified-plan formula and prohibits payments or set asides in excess of those amounts. Failure to do so would disqualify the plan, forcing the company either to delay taking a tax deduction or forcing individuals to incur a tax liability on amounts deferred. Because of the severity of losing the qualified plan status, companies chose instead to restore the lost benefit through a non-qualified plan. For example, if the formula for the defined-benefit plan generated a $500,000 pension but the allowable ERISA payout was $90,000, then $90,000 would be paid from the qualified plan and $410,000 from the non-qualified, restoration plan.

The same principle would apply to a defined-contribution plan. For example, assume the 401(k) Cash or Deferred Arrangement (CODA) was capped at a maximum annual amount of $10,000. An executive earning $500,000 with a plan that matched dollar for dollar on the first 5 percent set aside would be limited to a 2-percent deduction. By setting up a restoration plan, the additional 3 percent (along with a company match of 3 percent) would be a non-qualified deferral.

Some might choose to adopt alternative maximums (such as two times ERISA), although one could question whether these maximums have any meaning. The majority take the view that (1) there is a maximum of plan benefits simply through the application of the plan formula, (2) there is no reason for executives to receive less benefit in terms of the formula than anyone else, and (3) establishing a maximum within the plan requires a logic for that value. Furthermore, if the maximum is expressed in absolute dollars, the shareholders must periodically be requested to increase the amount—an act that consumes time, effort, and expense.

Add-On Plans. An add-on plan provides benefits in addition to those provided by the qualified retirement plan. Sometimes called *top-hat plans*, they are limited in application. Unlike restoration plans, which apply to all affected, "top hat" or "add-on" plans are designed to address specific issues. This may be to adequately compensate an executive who is joining the company mid-career, leaving behind the opportunity to have final pay multiplied by 30 or more years of service. This could be accomplished through either a fixed formula (e.g., double the number of years of service) or crediting the years of service with the previous employer. See earlier discussion on career change impact. In other situations, it may be to motivate an executive to leave because of faltering performance and/or a superstar replacement in the lineup; perhaps providing a full rather than 50-percent benefit to surviving spouse, eliminating the discount for early retirement, and/or increasing the benefit formula (e.g., 3 percent rather than the plan formula of 1.5 percent).

Increasing the formula for all conditions of service is less prevalent than improving the benefits for short-service executives simply because the continuity and smoothness of the annuity as a percentage of pay curve (see Figure 6-4) is disrupted. Although ERISA permits non-funded pensions for executives, it permits them for only a limited number of people, and thus those falling below this cutoff (which could include a number of very key management people) would probably have the lowest percentage of pay replacement of all employees! Thus, rather than tinker with the pension plan, the same objective can be accomplished through deferral features of long-term incentive plans. Another qualified-plan feature that results in low pensions for executives is the exclusion of annual incentive payments in the definition of earnings. Ignoring the principle of parsimony, especially in an egalitarian culture, would suggest modifying the basic formula definition rather than developing a supplemental plan. There are some who might argue a portion or all of long-term incentive payments should also be considered earnings; however, this could result in a payout in multiples of salary.

Add-on plans typically establish a target benefit that should be paid under prescribed circumstances. To the extent the qualified plan falls short of the target, it is supplemented by the non-qualified add-on.

A target plan is normally expressed as a percentage of current salary, or total direct pay of salary and short-term incentives, typically in relation to age and years of service. For example, one might conclude that the maximum target should be approximately equal to that for lower-paid employees (i.e., 75 percent) at age 65 with 30 years of service.

Next, the minimum benefit target is determined. Assume that this is set at 45 percent of calculable earnings for meeting minimum early retirement eligibility of age 55 with 10 years of service. Based on these two targets, it is possible to set up a formula for interpolation. For example, the 75 percent is based on an age and service combination of 95 whereas the minimum benefit of 45 percent equals a 65 combination. Thus, by crediting one point for every year of service and year of age over 65 and adding it to 45, the target percentage can be calculated (e.g., age 63 with 18 years equals 81; 81 − 65 = 16; 16 + 45 = 61 percent).

Another way to develop the formula is by setting up a matrix with target percentages of final pay for specific combinations of years of service and age at retirement. The simplified matrix shown in Table 6-34 suggests that 15 years of service with retirement at age 65 should be comparable in benefit to 30 years, retiring at age 55. Some may agree, others disagree; the point is simply that a matrix presentation permits examining various combinations easily and quickly, one versus the other.

Retirement Age	Years of Service	
	15	30
65	50%	75%
60	37.5%	62.5%
55	25%	50%

Table 6-34. Years of service and retirement age matrix

Other approaches to achieving the target include:

- increasing the years of service credit (e.g., 30 at 65 or actual, whichever is greater);
- crediting short service at a higher formula (e.g., first 10 years at 2 percent, next 10 years at 1.75 percent, and anything beyond at 1.5 percent);
- increasing the plan benefit by a stated amount (e.g., 50 percent); and
- lowering the discount for early retirement (e.g., no reduction at age 60 instead of 65, with discount beginning at age 60 at 4 percent per year).

All of these are ways to generate a special executive pension. While these approaches relate to the basic plan, they cannot be incorporated into the basic plan without applying to all participants.

A variation of the target approach would be an event-driven action. For example, in lieu of, or in addition to, the golden parachute payments described earlier in this chapter, a specified change of control might trigger a specified retirement benefit (e.g., non-discounted pension beginning immediately equal to 75 percent of last year's salary and annual incentive).

Typically, SERPs are non-funded liabilities that are paid out when the executive begins to draw benefits. In case of bankruptcy, the executive stands in line as a general creditor. In case of change in control, the new management may decide to cancel the obligations. For this reason, many executives want the obligation to be protected by a "rabbi trust." The benefits are still not guaranteed, but the promise to pay cannot be unilaterally turned aside. Should the executive want the benefits secured, this could be done through a secular trust where funds are set aside; however, the executive will then have an "economic benefit" tax issue. Company Owned Life Insurance (COLI), which was discussed under survivor protection, would be another approach. A variation would be to use company stock rather than cash. Stock might be set aside on an annual basis in relation to earnings and/or company performance. However, the executive would not be vested in the benefit until a prescribed age had been achieved, thereby deferring tax consequences.

Where short-service supplemental plans exist, they may be part of an *umbrella formula* that includes all payments the executive is eligible to receive. Under the umbrella might be: (1) pension benefits from the basic plan, (2) pension benefits from other employers, (3) annuity values from savings or profit-sharing plans, (4) Social Security benefits, and (5) deferred-compensation payments from the long-term incentive plan or salary.

In addition to the attractiveness of such supplements to the executive, they can also be very important to the company to: (1) attract a highly qualified, mid-career executive from another company, (2) establish a consistent approach for top people and thereby avoid a number of individual special plans, and (3) terminate an executive no longer meeting performance expectations.

In return for these special supplements, some companies require a "non-compete" agreement with the executive to ensure that he or she does not hire on with a competitor and work against the company. Similarly, such benefits would not apply to a person who, although eligible, resigned to accept other employment (even if outside industry).

SERP Swap

This is the exchange by the executive of all or a portion of non-qualified supplemental executive retirement plan (SERP) benefits for a split-dollar insurance policy with the company paying all or a portion of the premium. In essence, the executive gives up payments that would otherwise be made during his/her lifetime in exchange for more favorable estate and income taxes at time of death. This assumes payments are for a prescribed period of time. These arrangements must be carefully designed in light of accounting and tax requirements, which, due to their complexity and changing nature, are not discussed here.

Retirement Summary

As shown in Table 6-35, executives are highly interested in pension plans that meet the following requisites: they recognize at least all of annual pay (salary and short-term incentives) near retirement; and they use a liberal formula, without serious limitations, to go beyond Social Security benefits. Thus, while qualified plans may meet the annual-pay requirement, because of statutory limitations, executives need non-qualified, Supplemental Executive Retirement Plans to adequately receive benefits above Social Security. Additionally, some payouts may be eligible for long-term capital gains after ordinary income has been recognized.

For those changing companies mid-career, it is best to begin with an employer who has a generous, defined-contribution plan and end with one having a strong defined-benefit plan. The latter will use final years of pay in the formula, whereas the former provides a long period of compound growth (assuming the plan value was rolled over into some type of IRA). The reverse is also true. Starting a career with a strong defined-benefit plan means calculating benefits using the lower earnings values of early years; later, the power of compound growth to enhance the defined-contribution plan will be mitigated by a shorter time period. As a rule of thumb, it would take about 10 times one's final pay to generate an annuity equal to two-thirds annual pay for life, assuming retirement at about age 65.

Flexible Benefits

What Are They? Sometimes called "cafeteria-style" benefits, flexible-benefit plans are when a group of employee benefit plans are packaged together and the employee has a choice in the extent of participation. Such choices are typically available under stand-alone plans as well, so what sets flexible-benefit plans apart? The difference is that some benefit plans can be financed from the

TE		Program	Importance to Executive		
E	**C**	**Program**	**Low**	**Moderate**	**High**
5	B	Career Service	✔		
5	B	Career Earnings		✔	
5	B	Final Pay			✔
5	B	Excess Integration		✔	
5	B	Offset Integration			✔
5	B	Employee Stock Ownership Plan		✔	
5	B	Profit Sharing		✔	
5	B	Savings Thrift		✔	
5	B	Cash or Deferred Arrangement		✔	P
5	B	Employee Stock Purchase		✔	
5	B	Employee Stock Option		✔	
5	A	Individual Retirement Account	✔		
5	A	Keogh		✔	
5	B	Simplified Employee Pension	✔		
5	B	Cash-Balance	✔		
5	B	Floor-Offset	✔		
5	B	Pension Equity	✔		
5	B	Profit Sharing–Age/Service	✔		
5	B	Target Benefits	✔		
5	B	Limit-Restoration SERP			P
5	B	Formula-Enhanced SERP			P
5	B	Service-Credit SERP			P
		Summary Totals ✔ EB P	8 0 0	9 0 0	2 0 4

Table 6-35. Retirement summary

employee's pretax rather than after-tax dollars. Section 125 of the IRC defines and describes the benefit that meets the eligibility for pretax treatment. The Revenue Act of 1978 requires that company contributions for such programs be considered income to the highly compensated employee *unless* the plan meets nondiscriminatory standards in coverage and eligibility.

Advantages to the employee include preferential tax treatment and the ability to customize benefit coverage among the choices provided. Advantages to the employer include cost containment and providing an attractive benefit program for attracting and retaining wanted workers.

In designing a flexible-benefit plan, first set down a set of principles to guide planning and administration. They might include:

- Employees should not be permitted to opt completely out of life, medical, dental, and disability coverage—a minimum should be established.
- Employees should be permitted to choose among benefit coverage, buying additional benefits with payroll deductions (pre- or after-tax, depending on the plan selected) or receive in cash unused credits.
- The company cost for such benefits as life, medical, dental, and disability should not be increased because of adverse selection.

How Do Flexible Benefits Work? Essentially, flexible-benefit plans come in two flavors: add-on or plus-and-minus adjustments. *Add-on benefit programs* either add to existing benefits plans or existing programs are scaled back to a new minimum. Employees are then given a number of benefit dollars that they may use to purchase increased benefit coverage. Normally, such choices are already packaged (e.g., four levels of medical coverage, two levels of dental insurance, and three levels of life insurance). To minimize selecting against the plan (e.g., buying dental insurance for six months to get teeth fixed and then shifting to medical for another six months to take care of elective surgery), there are various time periods of minimum coverage (e.g., two years for dental). The *plus-and-minus* approach to customized benefit design begins with the existing benefit plans but provides opportunities for employees to reduce coverage in some areas in order to gain more in others.

The company establishes a formula for determining the number of credits each employee receives. Typically, this is based on salary. An additional factor may be added for spouse and children. The reason for the additional factor is that health care plans (medical and dental) cost more for family than single coverage. However structured, these plans are easy to install if the employee can opt for exactly the same coverage currently provided under the master plan at no additional cost to the individual.

Corporate cost-containment measures take several forms. First, a company is not compelled to introduce new programs that it partially or completely underwrites. It simply includes them under the flexible-benefits umbrella and allows employees to purchase if they wish. The second advantage is that each year the company determines what, if anything, to do with the credit-generation formula. If there is no change and benefits are rising, the employee will pay the increased costs. Alternatively, there could be some degree of sharing with the company.

Customized benefit programs are attractive to executives in that they can shed unnecessary life insurance in order to pick up additional health care coverage or place additional monies in a defined-benefit plan where the investment growth will be sheltered from taxes. The ability to make such selections was enhanced by the Miscellaneous Revenue Act of 1980. It permits the employee to make three-way trade-offs among cash, benefits, and deferred compensation. However, to avoid taxes, the program must be nondiscriminatory in nature and not simply used by executives. Because this method of flexible compensation is a cost-effective device, allowing the company to provide individuals with additional benefit coverage without incurring increased cost, not surprisingly, it has become a very popular feature of the employee benefit program.

SUMMARY AND CONCLUSIONS

Employee benefits are pay-for-membership, not pay-for-performance except to the extent they are directly related to those elements of pay that are performance-related (e.g., salary and incentives). The value to the recipient may either be current or deferred, and may be in the form of cash, stock, or other tangible goods to offset certain expenditures or provide additional income. Additional savings can be attained through group rather than individual rates and/or preferred tax treatment. The cost to the employee for employee benefits takes the form of payroll deductions, non-covered expenses, and/or additional income taxes. When the employee pays a portion of the cost of the program through a payroll deduction, the plan is said to be *contributory*; when the company requires no payroll deduction for coverage, the plan is said to be *non-contributory*.

Expenses incurred fall into four categories: (1) non-covered expenses (these are expenses outside the scope of the plan, such as cosmetic surgery in many medical plans), (2) the deductible (the amount the employee must pay before the plan will pay anything), (3) coinsurance (the plan will pay a specified percentage of covered expenses but the employee must pay the rest), and (4) full reimbursement.

Additional income-tax liabilities result from a direct compensation expense (e.g., a nonqualified, cash profit-sharing payout), an imputed income benefit (e.g., free insurance beyond $50,000), or a tax penalty (e.g., early withdrawals from an IRA). Under such conditions, the individual must *want* the benefit and be willing to pay up front, because the tax must be paid from other income rather than from the benefit itself (unless the benefit was paid in cash or something easily convertible to stock).

Normally, the company can take a tax deduction on a compensation expense at the time it becomes taxable as income to the recipient. Qualified pension and profit-sharing plans are exceptions to this basic principle. Here the company takes a deduction in advance of the time the recipient pays tax. The after-tax effectiveness for each benefit plan can be calculated (using Table 4-21 in Chapter 4) by dividing executive after-tax value by company after-tax cost.

The extent of an individual's participation in the all-employee benefit package is normally based on longevity with the company and level of salary. It is rarely related to performance. Therefore, while it is a part of executive compensation, it is merely an extension of what is in effect essentially at all salary levels. Nonetheless, to the extent enhanced by perquisites (i.e., executive benefits), several programs, especially medical and retirement can be very attractive.

A company can treat an executive in one of three ways.

- Eligible for only the same benefits as all other employees, including statutory restrictions.
- Eligible for only the same benefits as all other employees but without statutory restrictions.
- Eligible for benefits in addition to those available to all employees.

Most companies have trouble balancing the desire to do something special for their top executives with for the need to limit broader coverage for all employees. There is no easy answer to this concern. Companies with egalitarian philosophies have particular trouble justifying that some employees are "more equal" than others. Given SEC rules on disclosure, perquisites for those covered in the proxy will not be invisible. Only a few years ago, some companies sought out perks that did not have to be identified in the proxy statement. Fully reimbursed medical plans, company cars, and other perquisites became very popular. Since the SEC has lifted corporate skirts slightly with its perquisite disclosure requirements, some shy executives are blushing from the exposure. Current rules require perks exceeding $10,000 for any individual be detailed in the proxy.

In addition, it is not improbable that the IRS will compare such data with that reported by the individuals on their tax returns. Thus, executives must carefully document records, differentiating personal benefit from business use. In some instances, the cost of establishing procedures and maintaining records may exceed the cost of the perquisite, especially when the IRS and the SEC view the same event differently. For example, hitching a non-business seat on a corporate jet making a business flight may not be considered income by the IRS but is likely to be reportable as remuneration by the SEC.

When executives must pay full taxes on some perquisites, the perks lose a significant amount of their appeal. For example, if personal use of a company car results in a $5,000 tax liability, the executive must earn an additional $10,000 to pay for it (one-half paying the tax on the income, the other half paying the tax on the perquisite) assuming a 50-percent tax. It is not surprising that some companies substitute pay increases for perquisites—although the company's cost to deliver the same economic benefit to the executive is twice as much.

One approach that has some appeal is to give individual executives a perquisite allowance of a specified annual dollar amount. This could be a common percentage of pay (e.g., 5 percent). Thus, a $100,000 executive might have a $5,000 allowance, the $500,000 executive would receive $25,000 and a million-dollar executive would have $50,000 available for use. Or it could be adjusted based on salary. For example, the perquisite allowance could equal 3 percent for executives earning between $100,000 and $250,000; 4 percent for those between $250,000 and $500,000; 5 percent for those between $500,000 and $1,000,000; and 6 percent for those above $1,000,000. Additionally, the program could be divided for business-only or personal-only. While combining the two is a possibility, it would create a hybrid tax situation to the executive, who would have a tax liability on personal items but not on the business portion. Therefore, the combination approach may not be attractive. This type of program recognizes that individuals have different needs and perceived values. Therefore, rather than identifying specific programs and making participation automatic, the programs are available for use based on the individual executive's own interests. The problems with such an approach are administrative design, cost issues, and record keeping aspects.

In designing employee benefit plans and the perquisite package, it is important to link them with business strategies and desired culture. Several examples illustrate this issue. While pay-for-performance suggests minimizing pay for absence, the recognition of work and family issues suggests a careful look at employee services. Lack of sufficient health care is at the minimum a distraction from work. Survivor protection can be provided without a great deal of cost. Focusing employee attention on company financial performance suggests use of company stock to some degree in retirement programs. Another approach is to enhance company payments to thrift plans when company performance meets or exceeds certain goals. Retirement plans can also be structured to reinforce retention objectives.

Note: You should not rely on accounting, tax, SEC, or other professional service statements in this chapter. You need to seek appropriate professional counsel for such guidance. Statements made in this chapter and elsewhere are offered as being illustrative to help you frame such further investigations with the help of counsel.

Unfortunately, too many individuals concerned with executive compensation pay too little attention to employee benefits and perquisites as an important part of the total package. Executive pay is more than incentives, which takes us to the subject of the next two chapters.

Chapter 7

Short-Term Incentives

S ince salaries cannot be used effectively to adequately reward outstanding performance for short-term results (i.e., a year or less), most companies use some form of short-term incentive. A salary increase is no assurance that short-term performance levels will be maintained and salaries are rarely reduced. Short-term incentives are therefore implemented to introduce greater fluctuation in pay in recognition of performance or lack thereof. While a company may hesitate in granting a $100,000 executive a 40-percent salary increase, there is much less reticence in granting a $40,000 bonus (on the assumption that all, or a large part, will not be granted the following year if performance drops). Short-term incentives are therefore much more effective than salary for pay-for-performance objectives.

Annual incentive plans came into being early in the twentieth century, when management of companies shifted from owners to professional managers. The owners' objective was to motivate managers to act like owners (without making them owners). This was done by giving them a bonus for a portion of the financial success achieved. Bethlehem Steel was among the first with such a plan.

While salary actions are typically based on individual performance and long-term incentives on corporate performance, short-term incentives often include both. They may also include "groups." The number of groups will vary by organization and company size. Groups may be defined vertically and/or horizontally. The vertical definition is by organization level as one descends down through the company (e.g., corporate, sector, group, division, department, and section). The horizontal definition (sometimes combination horizontal and vertical) consists of groups, sometimes called *teams*, made up of people from various parts of the organization. Teams may be defined as ad hoc or long-standing as well as project versus process. Since executives typically are not paid on the basis of teams, that definition of group is not included in this section. However, groups that are defined vertically descending down through the organization are included because an "executive" usually heads each one.

Short-term incentive plans range from highly individualistic rewards for individual accomplishment to sophisticated profit-sharing plans, with emphasis on corporate, group, and/or division performance and little variance for individual recognition. The main drawback of the profit-sharing model is that it will overpay the marginal performer in good years and underpay the outstanding performer in poor years.

Furthermore, a low-salary/high-bonus mix will overpay mediocre performers in good years and risk losing top-quality executives in poor years. Conversely, a high-salary-low-bonus combination will reinforce mediocre performance in poor years by overpaying the marginal performers, while underpaying the outstanding performers. Therefore, the incentive plan design must be consistent with the message. One cannot emphasize the importance of individual contribution if the plan excludes any individual performance factors.

Thus, incentives are the visible reward (for successful performance) and punishment (for less than outstanding accomplishment). Unfortunately, some companies are more interested in form than substance; however, more and more companies are prepared to measure performance and pay for the degree of accomplishment. This is more difficult with discretionary plans than those with prescribed formulas, as will be discussed later in the chapter.

Importance by Type of Company

Short-term incentives are not of equal importance to all companies. Not-for-profits have a difficult time convincing the Internal Revenue Service (IRS) that a short-term incentive plan is consistent with a non-profit tax status. If this cannot be done, the short-term incentive is not simply of "low" importance, it is non-existent, as shown in Table 7-1. This creates definite difficulties in overcoming the traditional executive view of short-term incentives to attract (high), retain (moderate), and motivate (high). However, individuals may be attracted to not-for-profits for altruistic motives, such as giving back to a defined cause or community. Intrinsic reward rather than extrinsic pay is their driver.

The for-profits line up much better with those executives interested in extrinsic compensation. However, companies in the early stages of market development have to overcome their cash shortages and appeal in other ways (e.g., with long-term incentives). Note again in Table 7-1 that privately held companies have a somewhat higher emphasis on short-term incentives in the early stages of market development than their publicly held counterparts because of greater limits on long-term incentives (namely, no publicly traded stock).

	Market Stage			
	Threshold	**Growth**	**Maturity**	**Decline**
For-Profits • Publicly traded • Privately held	Low Moderate	Moderate High	High High	Moderate Moderate
Not-for-profits	Low	Low	Low	Low

Table 7-1. Possible relative importance of short-term incentives

Eligibility

Eligibility for short-term incentives is normally determined by one of the six methods described in Chapter 5 (Salary): key position, salary, job grade, job title, reporting relationship (organization level), or a combination of two or more methods.

Key Position. The *key position* approach examines each job to determine if it should be included in the incentive plan. Administratively, this has two drawbacks. First, it is possible that two jobs in the same salary grade will be treated differently—one eligible for bonus, the other not. Normally, this would require discounting the salary structure for the bonus-eligible by at least a portion of the bonus—usually the normal or minimum award. Second, it will be necessary to review the list of eligibility on almost an annual basis for appropriate additions and deletions. This approach is generally more prevalent among small than among large organizations. When used it typically results in fewer staff jobs being eligible for bonuses (than when using salary or job grade), thus making it more difficult to move individuals internally.

Salary. Using *salary* to identify eligibility is much simpler, once the appropriate salary level is identified; however, it must be adjusted annually because short-term incentives are typically expressed as a percentage of salary.

Job Grade. The use of *job grade* to determine short-term incentive eligibility is probably the most common approach among larger corporations. The rationale is simple: the value of the job to the organization has already been determined when each job was placed in a job grade (and given a minimum and maximum range). The approach is superior to use of salary in that it relates to the job, not to the person's earnings. However, it does place pressure on the compensation program to upgrade positions into the eligible group. It can also cause administrative problems since discounting salary to accommodate a bonus can create a situation where the maximum salary for the first bonus-eligible grade may be less than the grade immediately below it, as shown in Figure 7-1.

Job Title. Eligibility could be determined by *job title* (e.g., vice presidents and above). The problem with this approach is that the lowest-level vice president may have less responsibility than the highest-level director. It also raises the issue of organizational comparisons. For example, are divisional vice presidents as important as corporate vice presidents? Or even, are vice presidents in one division as important as vice presidents in another? However, for division-only plans such vertical and horizontal organizational comparisons may not be important.

Reporting Relationship. Using reporting relationship to determine eligibility (e.g., the top three organization levels in the company) poses the problem of "executive assistants" and "assistants to" who meet the definition but are of less importance than many jobs lower in the organization. For this reason, reporting relationship is rarely the sole criterion for participating in short-term incentive plans.

Combinations. Because each of the five approaches has one or more disadvantages or shortcomings, the best approach may be a *combination* of two or more definitions. For example, combining organization level and job grade, such as anyone in Grade X within the top three levels of the organization, takes pressure off both job re-grading and otherwise including "assistants" and "assistants to."

There are no inviolate rules about how far down in the organization short-term incentive plans should go. Historically, they included only the first several levels of management.

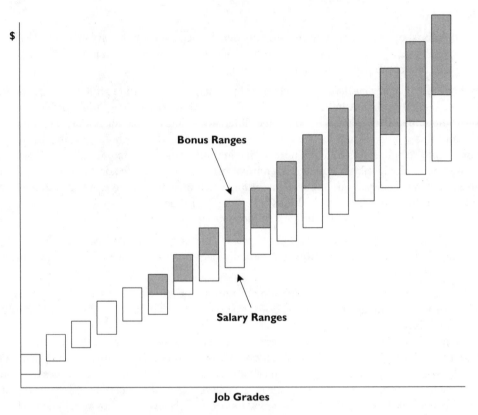

Figure 7-1. Salary and bonus ranges

However, over the years, the move has been to include more and more individuals in a short-term incentive plan wherever possible. In some organizations, this means not only all individuals exempt from overtime requirements but all individuals in the company! While some of the material in this chapter could be considered for broad-based, short-term incentive plans, the emphasis is on plans for those in the upper levels of the organization—the executives! When executives are involved in short-term incentive plans (and it is logical to reward them for short-term success), target amounts must be carefully examined in relation to potential payouts under long-term incentives. If short-term incentives are financially more attractive, executives might not adequately focus on long-term issues.

The percentage of employees included in the short-term incentive plan depends on the specific characteristics of the company, but it usually ranges from around 1 percent to 5 percent. On one end of the scale is the highly profitable, heavily capitalized, high-tech, decentralized company in the maturity phase. In such a company, 3 percent or more of the total employee population may be affected. On the other end of the scale is the labor-intensive, low-tech, strongly centralized company in the threshold stage. In such a company, less than 1 percent may be affected. The specific combination of these factors, as shown in Table 7-2, has a strong impact on the percentage of eligible employees in a specific company.

Low Percent	High Percent
Labor-intensive	Capital-intensive
Low technology	High technology
Centralized management	Decentralized management
Threshold stage	Maturity stage

Table 7-2. Percentage of employee population eligible for short-term incentives

Once an incentive plan is established, requests to expand eligibility will begin within a very short time. Therefore, plan designers need not only a strong rationale for eligibility when the plan is introduced but also must consider how eligibility will be expanded and over what period of time. Alternatively, planners can develop a firm basis for the demarcation. Unfortunately, a clear line between eligibility and ineligibility is rare. There is almost invariably a gray area. Yet, for the employees, the situation is simple—they are either bonus-eligible or not.

The status associated with being in the bonus plan is sufficient reason for employees to lobby for expansion. A significant compensation difference between the lowest-paid and the highest-paid bonus candidates compounds the problem.

I will return later to the subject of eligibility when I discuss awards, but first it is necessary to highlight some accounting, tax, and Securities and Exchange Commission (SEC) considerations.

Accounting, Tax, and SEC Implications

The accounting rules for short-term incentives are basically simple and straightforward. The cost is an expense and taken as a charge to earnings in the income statement (typically identified as "selling, general, and administrative expenses").

Unlike employee benefits and perquisites (see Chapter 6), taxation is rather simple. The payment is 100-percent taxable as income to the executive and 100-percent tax deductible to the company. For those items that are paid in subsequent years, an accrual is established to retire a liability charge on the balance sheet since the company cannot take a tax deduction until the executive has taxable income. An exception to this rule is that if payment is made within 75 days of the close of a calendar year, it may be charged to the previous year for tax purposes. This is one reason why companies hurry to ensure they pay year-end bonuses within the prescribed window.

While there is no federal law requiring shareholder approval of the incentive plan, some states have requirements for companies incorporated under their laws. Similarly, the stock exchange on which the company stock is listed may have such a requirement.

The reader is again reminded not to rely on accounting, tax, or SEC statements in this chapter. One needs to seek appropriate professional counsel for such guidance. Statements made in this chapter and elsewhere are offered as being illustrative to help frame such further investigations by the reader with counsel.

Plan Types

Essentially, short-term incentive plans come in three varieties: payout based on group performance, individual performance, or a combination of the two. One of these variations can form the basis for individual payment and/or determining a fund from which individual payment would be made. All will be reviewed later in this chapter.

AWARD SIZE

Award size can be expressed in relation to the amount of incentive needed to be competitive on total annual pay in the marketplace. This is illustrated in Figure 7-2. The examples range from no risk (all salary) to high risk (low salary). The amount of incentive (shaded area, Figure 7-2) needed to bring the individual's pay to the competitive level is called the *target award*. The difference between the competitive annual level and the person's salary is the risk level, often called the *downside risk*. The amount of incentive available above the target amount is called the *upside opportunity*. Typically, this increases at least proportionately with the amount of the risk.

Salary-only plans are no-risk plans, as are those with some incentive opportunity above salary but only for superior performance. Some describe bonus as a payment for performance above expectations. This would be consistent with the "no-risk" profiled in Figure 7-2. However, in this section "bonus" and "annual incentive" will be used interchangeably.

One would expect to find no-risk plans in government agencies, while low-risk plans might be logical in heavily regulated industries and high-risk plans would be found in a very competitive industry. One might also expect risk to increase as individual performance becomes dominant and decrease as group performance becomes a factor. In other words, risk varies directly with importance of individual performance.

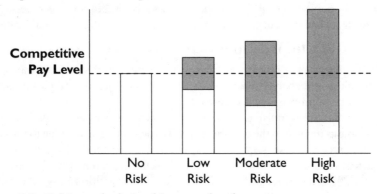

Figure 7-2. Risk/reward relationship to market data

Target Awards

In addition to determining the appropriate *risk/reward relationship,* planners need to determine the *probability level,* in other words, the probability of hitting the targeted performance level. Some plans set the target performance level at 50-50; i.e., there is an equal chance of either achieving or failing to meet the target. Other plans set a *stretch target* with perhaps a 40-percent probability of attaining the target and a 60-percent chance of failing.

Threshold and Maximum Awards

Some plans set the two outer limits (threshold and maximum) by determining the probability of achieving the award level. For example, some might set the threshold at a point where the probability of achievement is 90 percent, and conversely, the probability of attaining the maximum performance level is 10 percent. Some plans strive for this symmetry or reciprocal rela-

Maximum	Probability of Achieving Payment as percent of normal award	10-20% 150-200%
Threshold	Probability of Achieving Payment as percent of normal award	80-90% 10-20%

Table 7-3. Probability and payments at threshold and maximum levels

tionship as shown in Table 7-3. Others find it too difficult or subjective to determine the probability and simply set the award size as a percentage of a normal award, stipulating they will not pay less than 10 percent of the normal award nor more than double.

Performance/Payment Relationship

Following the *progressivity principle* described in Chapter 5 (Salary), one would expect the highest short-term incentive both in absolute and relative (to salary) terms to be at the highest job level (typically the Chair/CEO). At that level, the normal award may be 100 percent of salary with a threshold of 20 percent and a maximum at 200 percent.

The performance-target relationship can be expressed in a chart such as shown in Figure 7-3. In this example, the payment line is linear. It could be curvilinear with either an increasing or decreasing rate of growth from threshold to target and/or target to maximum. In addition, the threshold and maximum could be higher or lower in relation to the target awards. No payment is made below threshold performance unless there is either a *carry forward* from previous years or an allowance for *discretionary payments*.

A multiple-goal bonus can be developed using the same approach. Shown in Table 7-4 is a matrix for two performance variables. For example, if performance were at target for objective A but at threshold for objective B, payout would be at 60 percent. This is the average of 100 percent (target and 20 percent (threshold) for single measurement plans.

FORM AND TIMING OF AWARDS

It is difficult to discuss the last two sub-elements separately. The form of the bonus is cash

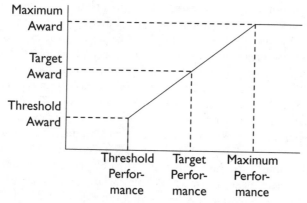

Figure 7-3. Threshold, target, and maximum bonus opportunities

Objective A Performance	Objective B Performance		
	Threshold	Target	Maximum
Maximum	100%	150%	200%
Target	60%	100%	150%
Threshold	10%	20%	100%

Table 7-4. Multiple performance bonus opportunities

and/or stock and the timing is current and/or deferred. If the individual leaves during the year in which earned, the amount is typically forfeited. The same applies to leaving before deferral payment dates. However, most companies will prorate the amount in case of disability or death.

The matrix in Table 7-5 shows the nine possible combinations of form and timing, ranging from an immediate lump-sum cash settlement to a combination of cash and stock, one part paid immediately and the remainder in deferred installments.

	Forms		
Timing	Cash	Stock	Combination
Current	1	4	7
Deferred	2	5	8
Combination	3	6	9

Table 7-5. Form vs. timing of short-term incentives

Certainly the current cash payment (#1) has the greatest impact on the lower-level executive. Even though a third or more of the award may be lost in taxes, the balance still represents a significant increase in the recipient's income. Due to family obligations (e.g., mortgages and college tuition), this time-form combination is probably most popular with persons in their thirties and forties. Companies that pay within 75 days of the close of their fiscal year usually can take a tax deduction in that year rather than when paid.

If the award is all in stock (#4), the recipient may have difficulty paying taxes without selling some of the stock, thereby partially defeating the objective of giving the executive an investment in the future growth of the organization. For this reason, a combination (#7) form of stock and a sufficient amount of cash to pay taxes on the total award is a logical approach. For many, this would argue for half the value in stock and the other half in cash (to meet tax liabilities).

Deferred cash (#2), deferred stock (#5), and a combination of the two (#8) could be the result of voluntary deferral, mandatory deferral, or a combination of the two. For example, the company may mandate that the portion of the award not tax deductible to the company under Section 162(m) of the IRC be deferred until leaving. Mandatory deferrals are typically unpopular with executives, who believe they must earn the bonus twice—first by performance and secondly, by remaining to collect it. Some plans make deferrals more palatable by crediting some form of appreciation. The issue of deferred compensation was reviewed in some detail in Chapter 3.

A combination of current and deferred cash (#3), current and deferred stock (#6), and a combination of current and deferred cash along with current and deferred stock (#9) address both current and future income needs. Again, the deferrals could be voluntary, mandatory, or a combination of the two.

In addition, use of company stock need not be restricted to those on the corporate staff. Using stock for divisional awards reinforces identification with corporate success, not simply divisional performance.

Companies that pay a large amount of the award in company stock must realize that they are placing heavy liquidity pressures on the individual unless the person is free to sell a portion of the amount. For companies that pay the total award in stock, tax requirements create a significant concern for recipients. Companies that pay half in cash and half in stock and also discourage employees from selling the stock portion, in effect, create a salary reduction plan with a heavy shift to deferred income.

Paying all or a portion of the award in stock also poses problems for corporate officers due to the requirements of Section 16(b) of the Securities Exchange Act. It stipulates that any profit made by an officer or director of a company by purchasing shares of the company within six months of selling similar shares must be returned to the company.

In general, the SEC does not consider payment of stock under an incentive program as a purchase. However, subsequent sale by the executive is considered a sale under the definitions of the act. This becomes important where the company also has a stock option or other long-term incentive plan using company stock.

Whether the individual receives the award in cash or something other than cash (e.g., company stock), the tax treatment is the same: income tax on the value of the award on the date when received. (See Chapter 3 for more on deferred income.)

The individual award must relate to individual performance—especially for the better performer. When the award does not appear to adequately reflect performance, the plan is in trouble. In other words, if a plan gives essentially the same award to both the marginal and the outstanding performer, two things happen. The marginal performer is no longer attentive to requests to improve performance; the outstanding performer will either lower future performance to meet the award level (by increasing off-the-job activities for either intrinsic or extrinsic compensation) or be receptive to job offers from other companies. Most companies would find these two results undesirable.

WHAT SHOULD BE MEASURED?

The factors selected for measurement must support the company's business strategy. (Chapter 2 focused on performance measurements both organizationally and individually.) As one drills down into the organization, a clear *line-of-sight* must be maintained between performance measurements and business objectives. In addition, performance targets throughout the organization should be of *equal stretch* or difficulty. The measurements and how they relate to business objectives must be clearly communicated to all bonus candidates and to shareholders.

Organizational Performance

The organization level of the individual significantly affects the determination of what to measure. For example, the CEO and other top corporate officers would be measured on company-wide performance and to some extent on individual performance objectives. This is illustrated in

Eligibility Level	Performance Measurements			
	Company-Wide	Group	Sub-Group	Individual
Corporate	90%	—	—	10%
Group	30%	60%	—	10%
Sub-Group	—	30%	60%	10%

Table 7-6. Performance measurements by organizational level

Table 7-6. Moving down to the next organization level, one would identify appropriate group measurements; however, many will argue that a portion of the award should include company-wide performance, thereby reinforcing an all-for-one team approach.

The same rationale applies in moving down to the next organization level. Here the decision may be to not include a company-wide factor as the individual has far less impact (being an additional level lower in the organization). Also, including a company-wide measurement would further dilute the weighting of group, sub-group, and individual. Nonetheless, those wanting to reinforce importance of the company will add a company value (perhaps 10 percent) proportionately reducing group and sub-group.

Individual Performance

It has often been said that what gets measured gets attention. When measurements set the level of pay, they get a lot of attention. Because of the short time frame (a year or less) and the inclusion of an individual performance component, short-term incentives more than any of the other four pay elements focus the individual on what has to be done. It is, therefore, critical that the measurements be selected carefully and that they support the achievement of the business plan. Furthermore, objectives should not only be attainable, they should be limited in number. Too many objectives dilute focus.

As stated in Chapter 2, performance should not be judged by financial measurements alone. While they may be easy to attain, financial measurements focus on past performance and do little to illustrate how value is created.

SETTING THE TARGET

In setting the goal, planners have several choices. One choice is to examine historical results, namely, last year's and maybe several years before it. This is called the *look-back* approach. Another choice is to essentially build a goal from the bottom up much like zero based budgeting establishes a budget beginning with zero. This is called the *look-forward* approach. A third choice is to use the data from a given peer group. This is called the *look-around* approach.

Historical (Look-Back) Approach

The historical approach often uses a fixed-percentage increase to establish the following year's target [e.g., a 15-percent increase over previous year's earnings per share (EPS)]. This has the benefit of simplicity but most assuredly will either be too generous or too conservative depending on the circumstances. Namely, it can be affected by acquisitions and divestitures, as well as

On increase in SPS of	Resulting Bonus at 95% x E Salary		On increase in EPS of
20% & Above ——→	50.0 - -Maximum- -	50.0% ◄———	20% & Above
19	45.0	45.0	19
18	40.0	40.0	18
17	35.0	35.0	17
16	30.0	30.0	16
15	25.0	25.0	15
14	22.5	22.5	14
13	20.0	20.0	13
12	17.5	17.5	12
11	15.0	15.0	11
10 ——————→	12.5 - - -Target - - -	12.5 ◄———————	10
9	10.0	10.0	9
8	7.5	7.5	8
7	5.0	5.0	7
6 ——————→	2.5- - Threshold - -	2.5 ◄———————	6
5 & Less	0.0	0.0	5 & Less

SPS = Dollar Sales Per Share of Stock Outstanding
EPS = Dollar Earnings Per Share of Stock Outstanding

Table 7-7. Look-back annual incentive formula (increase over previous year in sales and earnings)

a change in accounting. Recalculating both periods on a comparable basis can offset this impact, however, the results are artificial. Using the formula in Table 7-7, the bonus calculation is shown in Table 7-8. In this example, the threshold payment is 5 percent (for a 6-percent increase in both factors over the previous year). The target award is set at 25 percent for a 10-percent increase in both measurements and the maximum award is 100 percent of salary for an increase of 20 percent or more in both measurements. Note that the unadjusted financial results would result in no bonus. However, by recalculating for the ongoing business a payment is made.

The advantage to this approach is that it focuses on continuous improvement and avoids gamesmanship of managers low balling targets for high payouts. The disadvantage is that it is not sensitive to outside factors.

Business Plan (Look-Forward) Approach

The look-forward requires setting targets each year based on an assessment of threats and opportunities to the company. This approach allows individuals to *lowball* or *sandbag*, in other words, underestimate realistic targets enabling large incentive awards. Offsetting this risk requires outside assessment of the appropriateness of the considerations and the results. The advantage of the approach is that it permits building in aggressive goals or stretch targets. However, these targets must be accurate or the payout will either be too generous or too low. A representative formula is shown in Table 7-9. Note the target award is set for 50 percent of salary (if both performance targets are met). Threshold is 10 percent of salary for 96 percent of both

Actual Results			
Company Results	**Previous Year**	**Last Year**	**% Change**
Sales Per Share	$20.48	$21.49	4.9%
Earnings Per Share*	2.13	2.41	13.2%

Incentive Plan Formula	
Sales Per Share	4.9% Inc = 0
Earnings Per Share	4.9% Inc = 0
Total	0% of Salary

Recalculated for Ongoing Businesses			
Company Results	**Previous Year**	**Last Year**	**% Change**
Sales Per Share	$17.49	$20.43	16.8%
Earnings Per Share*	2.60	3.06	17.7%

Incentive Plan Formula	
Sales Per Share	16.8% Inc = 34.0
Earnings Per Share	16.8% Inc = 34.0
Total	68% of Salary

*Cannot exceed increase in sales per share

Table 7-8. Look-back possible incentive payouts

target achievements and maximum payout is 100 percent of salary if 125 percent or more of both performance targets is achieved.

Again, if actual results were the basis for payment, the executive would receive nothing as shown in Table 7-10. However, if recalculated for ongoing business, the payout would be 62.4 percent of salary.

Peer Comparison (Look-Around) Approach

The peer comparison approach can stand alone or be a tag-on to performance targets set by historical or business plan approaches. The comparison can be set up using a specific list of companies that in composite (rather than individually) represent one's own company. For example, if 90 percent of company sales were in over-the-counter (OTC) products and 10 percent in prescription drugs, it is unlikely to find a lot of companies with that same makeup. Instead, nine over-the-counter healthcare companies and one ethical pharmaceutical company may in aggregate represent the company makeup. Some companies find it too difficult to set up peer groups, as the composition of these groups frequently changes, due to acquisitions and mergers, and instead opt for a broad composite, such as the S&P 500. Comparisons can be expressed either in percentiles or as a percentage of the average.

Percent of SPS Target Achieved	Resulting Bonus as % of Salary		Percent of EPS Target Achieved
125%	→50.0% – – Maximum – –	50.0% ←	125%
124	49.0	49.0	124
123	48.0	48.0	123
122	47.0	47.0	122
121	46.0	46.0	121
120	45.0	45.0	120
119	44.0	44.0	119
118	43.0	43.0	118
117	42.0	42.0	117
116	41.0	41.0	116
115	40.0	40.0	115
114	39.0	39.0	114
113	38.0	38.0	113
112	37.0	37.0	112
111	36.0	36.0	111
110	35.0	35.0	110
109	34.0	34.0	109
108	33.0	33.0	108
107	32.0	32.0	107
106	31.0	31.0	106
105	30.0	30.0	105
104	29.0	29.0	104
103	28.0	28.0	103
102	27.0	27.0	102
101	26.0	26.0	101
100	→25.0 – – –Target – – –	25.0 ←	100
99	20.0	20.0	99
98	15.0	15.0	98
97	10.0	10.0	97
96	→5.0 – – –Threshold – – –	5.0 ←	96
95	—	—	95

SPS = Dollar Sales Per Share of Stock Outstanding
EPS = Dollar Earnings Per Share of Stock Outstanding

Table 7-9. Look-forward annual incentive formula (percent of target achieved in sales and earnings)

An example of a *standalone target* would be a plan that paid out X percent of the excess shareholder value (if any) created above the average for the index. Say that the percent is 10 and the average shareholder return for the identified index was 10 percent for the year and the company's was 15 percent. If the 15 percent represented an increase in stock value of $150 million, the 5 per-

Actual Results			
Company Results	**Previous Year**	**Last Year**	**% Change**
Sales Per Share	$22.53	$21.49	95.4%
Earnings Per Share*	2.34	2.41	103.0%

Incentive Plan Formula	
Sales Per Share	95.4% of Target = 0%
Earnings Per Share	95.4% of Target = 0
Total	0% of Salary

Recalculated for Ongoing Businesses			
Company Results	**Previous Year**	**Last Year**	**% Change**
Sales Per Share	$19.24	$20.43	106.2%
Earnings Per Share*	2.86	3.06	107.0%

Incentive Plan Formula	
Sales Per Share	106.2% of Target = 31.2%
Earnings Per Share	106.2% of Target = 31.2%
Total	62.4% of Salary

*Cannot exceed increase in sales per share

Table 7-10. Look-forward possible incentive payouts

cent "better than average" would equal $5 million (i.e., 10 percent of $150 million minus $100 million). This $5-million fund could be awarded in cash and/or stock. An industry percentile formula could be constructed in either an absolute or a relative format. An example of an absolute formula would be: no payout below the 50th percentile and $100,000 for every point above. Thus, at the 75th percentile, the fund would be $2.5 million [i.e., $100,000 (75 - 50)]. An example of a relative formula would be one that had no payout below the 50th percentile but 2.5 percent of the aggregated salaries of bonus candidates above that level. Thus, at the 75th percentile, this would be a fund equal to 62.5 percent [i.e., 2.5% (75-50)] of the aggregate bonus-candidate salaries. If the latter were $100 million, this would mean a bonus fund of $62.5 million.

An example of an add-on approach is shown in Table 7-11. Note that the threshold payment is 20 percent of the normal award if the peer group's EPS is 120 percent of the company's, and the maximum payment is double the target if the peer performance is 75 percent of the company's.

Shown in Table 7-12 is another example of bonus adjustment based on corporate performance versus a peer group. Note that if percentage change in EPS were the same as the peer group, the CEO would receive 100 percent of this performance-based bonus. However, if the compa-

Percentage That Peer EPS Is of Our EPS	Percentage of Annual Award
More than 120%	0
120	20% Threshold
115	40
110	60
105	80
100	100 Target
95	120
90	140
85	180
75 or less	200 Maximum

Table 7-11. Annual incentive adjusted for peer performance

ny EPS increase were 10 percent better than the peer group, then the CEO bonus would be increased by 10 percent (i.e., 10 x 1%). Conversely, if the peer group was 20 percent better than the company, the CEO's bonus would be reduced to 60 percent of its performance based amount [i.e., 100 - (20 x 2)]. The amounts for the chief operating officer (COO), chief financial officer (CFO), and chief legal officer would be adjusted in a similar manner.

Shareholders like the penalty aspect of this type of formula, if outperformed by the peer group. However, they do not like paying a substantial award in a year when the company outperformed the peers but had a bad year, although not as bad as its peers. The other downside is the often difficult job of getting good peer data.

INDIVIDUAL AWARDS VS. AGGREGATE TOTALS

Companies need to decide if the plan should be driven from the top down or built from the bottom up. A *top-down plan* begins with a determination of how much to pay in aggregate and then proceeds to determine individual awards. A *bottom-up plan* begins with individual award determinations summing them to an aggregate total.

Title	Average EPS Growth Equal to Peer Group	Amount Adjusted for Every 1%		
		Below Peer Average	Above Peer Average	Maximum Total
CEO	100%	2.0	1.0	200%
COO	80	1.6	0.8	160
CFO	60	1.2	0.6	120
CLO	50	1.0	0.5	100

Table 7-12. Adjusted bonus based on peer EPS performance

Top-down plans begin with a fund. It may be determined by formula, by judgment (discretion), or be a combination of the two. A formula driven fund is typically found in larger organizations with some history in determining fund size. Discretionary funding is more typical of smaller organizations and/or those with little history in fund determination.

Bottom-up plans typically begin with individual performance, although they may be based solely on organizational performance (corporate, group, and subgroup as appropriate). Tables 7-7 through 7-10 are examples of plans based on organizational performance.

Actually, there are more than simply these two approaches; combining variables will achieve 12 possible scenarios. In other words, there are four funding possibilities: none, discretionary, formula, and some combination of discretionary and formula. Similarly, there are three individual award possibilities: discretionary, formula, and a combination of the two. These combinations are illustrated in Table 7-13.

	Individual Award Determination		
Funding	**Discretionary**	**Formula**	**Combination**
None	A	B	C
Discretionary	D	E	F
Formula	G	H	I
Combination	J	K	L

Table 7-13. Funding and individual formula awards

Non-Funded Plans

Discretionary Individual Awards (A). This combination works best with small organizations. The CEO looks at the performance of each individual and determines what is believed to be an appropriate bonus.

Formula Individual Awards (B). This is a very common approach. It is plan "A" advanced to the stage where size necessitates a more formal approach to determining the size of the individual awards. Shown in Table 7-14 is an example of such an individual formula-determined approach.

Here target payouts (identified as the normal award) are tied to the business-plan objective and are structured to vary with degree of target attained. Note the drop-off in salary percentage below target is greater than the increase above target. Payout is a percentage of salary with both a minimum and maximum established and incremental in distribution. In this case, the business plan calls for an operating income of $45 million.

Another example of an individual formula plan is shown in Table 7-15. Note that the CEO has less incentive opportunity than the COO and executive vice president (EVP). This is unlikely unless there were another incentive piece for the CEO (such as increase in shareholder value).

Combination Formula and Discretionary Individual Awards (C). This is a "B" type plan that includes a subjective measurement, such as degree of difficulty or other considerations, which typically are used to increase the amount determined by the formula portion of the individual award. The discretionary aspect might also apply to qualitative goals.

Operating Income	Percent of Salary			
	CEO	COO	EVP	
$75 mil and up	200%	160%	120%	**Maximum**
75	180	144	108	
70	160	128	96	
60	140	112	84	
50	120	96	72	
45	100	80	60	**Target**
40	70	56	42	
35	40	32	24	**Threshold**
30 and below	0	0	0	

Table 7-14. Individual formula award based on operating income

Diluted EPS	Percent of Salary			
	CEO	COO	EVP	
$0.75	100%	120%	120%	**Maximum**
0.70	90	108	108	
0.65	80	96	96	
0.60	70	84	84	
0.55	60	72	72	
0.50	50	60	60	**Target**
0.48	40	48	48	
0.46	30	36	36	
0.43	20	24	24	
0.40	10	12	12	**Threshold**
0.30 and below	0	0	0	

Table 7-15. Individual formula award based on diluted EPS

Earlier, the issue of *stretch targets* was reviewed. The important point is that a greater reward should be given for meeting a stretch goal than a normal goal. Furthermore, stretch goals should have comparable levels of difficulty to ensure a level playing field. A discretionary facet of the individual award determination coupled with an objective portion meets this goal.

Discretionary, Funded Plans

Discretionary Individual Awards (D). The discretionary funding decision may be determined before or after individual awards have been calculated and summed. Typically, discretionary funding limits rather than increases the individual award total. It is a combination willingness and ability-to-pay. This approach works best where the CEO is intimately involved in the individual award determinations, thereby exercising control with no need for a formal fund formula, using instead the total amount that can be spent as an informal guideline. This approach is more typical of small organizations than large ones.

Formula Individual Awards (E). Although this approach may include a guideline fund determined at the outset, it is more likely established after the sum of the individual awards has been calculated. The discretionary calculation could be used to reduce the total awards, but since they are formula driven, it is more likely they would be increased because of a belief in the hard work and effort expended. This is similar to a "B" plan with a discretionary overview on the total to be paid.

The individual formula could be a percentage of the discretionary fund, a stated dollar amount, or some combination of the two. Another variation is to give the individual the percentage of the fund that was equal to his/her annual pay in relation to the company payroll.

Combination Discretionary and Formula Individual Awards (F). This is very similar to a "C" combination with the discretionary funding decision made at either the outset or after the individual awards have been summed to determine if the total is appropriate. A *negative discretion* formula used by some to comply with tax requirements would be an example. The individual formula sets the maximum, which is then reduced by discretion of the compensation committee to comply with Section 162(m) of the IRC (described in Chapter 4) to an amount deemed appropriate. That law states the company is barred from taking more than a $1-million tax deduction for any of the named executives in the proxy unless it is a performance-based plan approved by shareholders. Since such plans may not permit any positive discretion in determining pay amounts, it opened the door for negative discretion formulas. Many look like the shareholder protection formulas that will be described later.

Formula Funded Plans

Discretionary Individual Awards (G). The formula for determining fund size is typically a percentage of profits and is usually found in smaller companies. Discretionary determination of each individual's performance is made and summed. If the total exceeds the fund available, the awards are adjusted downward. An example of this is shown in Table 7-16. In this situation, a total of $950,000 is available for discretionary awards.

Formula Individual Awards (H). This is clearly the most quantitative of the 12 possibilities. A formula is used to determine the available fund and the fund is allocated by formula to the participants. Possible formulas include: the same dollar amount for everyone (unlikely for an executive plan); a percentage equal to each person's percent of total salaries of all bonus candidates; or a percentage of the fund based on organizational responsibilities. An example of the latter is shown in Table 7-17. This type is most likely in mid-size companies. The fund itself might have

Bonus Fund:
100% first $100,000 (and 50% of remainder) of 60% Pre-Tax Income

Example:

Pre-Tax Income	=	$3,000,000	
		$3,000,000 x 60% =	$1,800,000
		$1,800,000 - $100,000 =	$1,700,000
	=	$1,700,000 x 50% =	$ 850,000
Fund	=	$850,000 + $100,000 =	$ 950,000

Table 7-16. Formula-funded discretionary award example

Position	Percent of the Fund
CEO	30%
COO	20
CFO	10
VPs (8)	5
Total	**100%**

Table 7-17. Fund distribution by responsibility level

been generated by a percentage of net income, the most common being the *profit-sharing plan.*

Another example is shown in Table 7-18. Note that the formula is similar to that shown for discretionary awards within a funded plan (Table 7-16). In this example, a total of 10,000 points are available for distribution. The total is deliberately set high enough to avoid changing the formula every several years. Note also a maximum per point has been established to prevent wind falling. In this example, a participant with 100 points would receive a bonus of $350,000 (i.e., 100 x $3,500).

Combination Discretionary and Formula Individual Awards (I). This is similar to "H" except the formula allocations are less than 100 percent of the fund (e.g., 90 percent), thereby allowing the remaining portion (e.g., 10 percent of the fund) to be used to increase some awards and/or to give awards to some not in the formula plan.

Combination Formula and Discretionary, Funded Plans

Discretionary Individual Awards (J). This is the same as the discretionary individual award determination/formula funded plan except a discretionary component has been added to the fund determination. This discretion could be either positive (increase the amount) or negative (decrease the amount). Companies would have to have very good reason to increase the amount having established a formula. However, negative discretion may be well received by the shareholders. For example, management may have decided that for whatever reason (e.g., unforeseen good news for company and /or bad news for competitors), financial performance reflects something of a windfall and therefore discretion is applied to bring the fund back to a more appro-

---

Bonus Fund:
100% first $10 million (and 50% of remainder) of 60% Pre-Tax Income

Participants:
Each executive receives a number of "points"
Each "point" equals .01% of the fund—maximum $5,000 per point

Example:

Pre-Tax Income	= $100,000,000		
	$100,000,000 × 60%	=	$60,000,000
	$60,000,000 - $10,000,000	=	$50,000,000
	$50,000,000 × 50%	=	$25,000,000
Fund	= $10,000,000 + $25,000,000	=	$35,000,000
Point	= $35,000,000 × .01%	=	$3,500

Participant with 1 "point" would receive $3,500
Participant with 10 "points" would receive $35,000
Participant with 100 "points" would receive $350,000

Table 7-18. Formula funded and formula individual award example

priate amount. Even lacking such unforeseen events, the formula (unless periodically adjusted) will likely continue to generate ever-higher amounts as the company grows.

Formula Individual Awards (K). This is a formula individual award determination/formula funded plan with some discretion on the size of the bonus fund or a combination discretionary/ formula funded plan with discretionary individual award determination with the individual's awards determined by formula not discretion. This is probably a top-down, bottom-up, top-down with the last an allowable adjustment based on a discretionary adjustment to the total fund.

Combination Discretionary and Formula Individual Awards (L). This is a combination discretionary/formula funded plan with formula individual award determination with discretion added to individual awards determination or a combination discretionary/formula award determination formula funded plan with discretion also included in fund determination. It is the most sophisticated of the combinations, requiring independent judgment both on funding and individual award determination. Negative discretion could be applied to both the overall fund and to individual awards.

Other Fund Types

Deductible vs. Non-Deductible Fund Formulas. One of the main problems in constructing the formula is generating an adequate amount. It is here that the very common deductible or threshold approach (e.g., X percent of net income minus Y percent of common stock equity) results in a very steep trend line. After a few years, the formula often generates an embarrassingly high amount because of corporate financial growth (factors in the formula often move faster than the number and base earnings of the bonus candidates). When the formula generates more than is allocated, a decision must be made (assuming the plan permits) whether to return to net income or carryover a portion to the next year. The rationale for the *carryover provision* is to offset extraordinary circumstances (a real concern if the formula is especially "tight"); the danger is that such an approach may result in paying out almost as much in mediocre years as in outstanding periods—giving confusing signals to both executives and shareholders.

Conversely, such deductible formulas cause problems if the company has a loss year. The issue is not with the bonus that year, for obviously there is no bonus (assuming no carryover from previous years). However, since a loss reduces the company's net worth, it thereby lowers the deductible the following year. Thus, the company pays out a greater-than-planned portion of earnings during profitable years following loss years. To illustrate, assume the formula is 10 percent of the amount by which net income exceeds 6 percent of shareholder equity. At the end of the first year, shareholder equity is $100 million, net income is $7 million, and the bonus fund equals $100,000. The second year, the company experiences a $1 million loss, thereby reducing shareholder equity to $99 million, and the bonus fund is, of course, zero. The third year, the company returns to its profitable ways with an $8.5 million net earnings figure. Assuming no dividends paid during the period (simply to uncomplicate the example), net worth is now $107.5 million and the bonus fund equals $205,000 (i.e., 10 percent of the amount that $8.5 million exceeds 6 percent of $107.5 million). This is $6,000 more than if the previous year had been a no-earnings-no-loss year. Even more dramatically, if the company had a 10-percent increase in both the second ($7.7 million) and third ($8.5 million) year, the bonus fund for year two would have been about $124,000, but the bonus fund the third year (because net worth would be $118.2 million not $107.5) would be $141,000—$64,000 less than the $205,000.

Some will argue that it is more difficult to show such a turnaround after a loss year; be that true or not, this type of formula encourages a cyclical earnings pattern rather than steady growth. It is certainly to management's advantage to ensure that all costs that can be taken are taken in a year that earnings will not exceed 10 percent of shareholder equity.

For this reason, the *limitation* or tandem type formula seems more appropriate (e.g., a percentage of net income, or X percent of net income minus Y percent of common stock equity, whichever is lower). As shown in Figure 7-4, a limitation formula protects against payout at low net-income levels and tempers runaway conditions at high-net income levels. Since companies in the mature stage are less likely to generate fluctuations of the magnitude of a threshold or growth company, developing a bonus fund is less risky.

Economic Profit Plans. One popular deductible formula is the *economic profit formula* that allows deductions for the use of capital (usually both long-term debt and equity). Economic profit is not new. Economists dating back to Adam Smith have contended that in order for business to be successful it must produce a competitive return on its capital, or economic profit. Some refer to these plans as *Economic Value Added* (EVA). (EVA® is a registered trademark of Stern Stewart & Co.) General Motors was one of the first to use this type of plan. *Economic profit* equals *income* less the *cost of capital*. Therefore, one must define three items: profit, capital, and cost of capital. *Profit* probably should be operating income (which excludes interest expense, depreciation, and amortization of goodwill) less taxes. Some refer to this as NOPAT (Net Operating Profit After Taxes). *Capital* is the sum of debt and shareholders' equity. The *cost of capital* is what borrowers are charging directly (debt) or indirectly (shareholder expected return). Cost of capital could be a blended rate (i.e., one rate that includes both debtor and

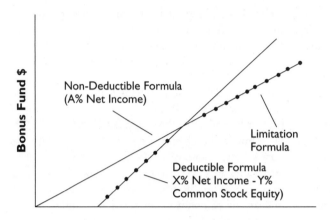

Figure 7-4. Bonus fund formulas (deductible—non-deductible—limitation)

shareholder) or separate calculations for each. To illustrate, assume a company has debt of $60 million and shareholders' equity of $20 million. Assume borrowing costs are 8 percent and expected shareholder minimum return is 12 percent (risk free government security of 6 percent plus a 6-percent equity-risk premium). The cost of capital would be $7.2 million (i.e., $60 million x 0.08 + $20 million x 0.12). If profit is defined as net operating income after taxes and that figure were $10 million, then the economic profit would be $2.8 million (i.e., $10 million – $7.2 million). Obviously, one improves economic profit (EP) by increasing operating income and/or reducing the amount and/or cost of capital.

The above is a very simple example. The formula can be far more exacting. However, as the formula becomes more detailed in an attempt to be a more valid measurement, it becomes more complicated and difficult to understand. If the bonus candidates do not understand the program, it is unlikely to drive their behavior, regardless of its precise accuracy and relevance. In addition, EP is not a substitute for business strategy; rather it should support the business strategy. Furthermore, some choose to use multiple-year periods thereby converting the original short-term bonuses into long-term incentives.

Economic profit formulas will expose companies that are growing profits in absolute amounts while doing so at an increasing cost of capital and thereby destroying, not creating additional capital. One could say this results in *Economic Value Lost* (EVL). Companies with little capital and high growth rates may not be as interested in economic profit formulas as those with a large infrastructure of buildings, equipment, and inventory but more modest growth rates. Stated another way, economic profit formulas may be more appropriate for companies in the later stages of the market cycle than those in the earlier stages.

Selecting the most appropriate formula is very important. For example, using a deductible formula in regard to return on capital can encourage management to avoid making full use of its borrowing capacity. If the bonus fund were generated by a formula taking 8 percent of net income in excess of 10 percent on capital, any investment return of less than 10 percent (after taxes) would lower executive bonuses. For example, it might be attractive from a shareholder viewpoint to borrow at 9 percent pretax (4.5 percent after-tax assuming a 50-percent tax rate) and get an 18 percent pretax (9 percent after-tax) return, but since this action would reduce the bonus fund, it is financially unattractive to management.

In any event, fund formulas need to be reviewed on a regular basis to ensure they are consistent with current company conditions. One reason many plans developed 10 or more years ago are generating excessive amounts today is that corporate growth has outdated them. This is especially true for deductible plans.

Shareholder Protection Plans. Shareholder protection plans are formula-driven plans that ensure the shareholder that no monies will be paid to executives until certain financial targets have been met. Many companies adopted these plans years ago and have not modified them. Where these formulas are used, they often begin with a percentage of profits (either pretax or after tax) and proceed to make some consideration for shareholders' equity or provide for a dividend of a minimum amount. Examples are shown in Table 7-19.

1. 12½ percent of consolidated net income less 6 percent of the average common stock equity less the amount of current dividends for the year.

2. 10 percent of net income after deducting 5 percent of average capital in business.

3. 6 percent of profits after taxes that are in excess of 6 percent of capital.

4. 8 percent of the first $5 million net income plus 10 percent of the next $5 million plus 1 percent of the remainder after net income has been reduced by the larger of: (a) 6 percent of average net capital, (b) dividends on preferred stock plus $2.50 per share of common stock.

5. 6 percent of net earnings before taxes and percentage compensation or 8 percent of earnings after taxes and percentage compensation.

6. 6 percent of net earnings before taxes, after deducting 10 percent of capital employed.

7. 10 percent of the excess after dividend requirements of preferred stock plus 5½ percent of the total stated value of common stock plus 5½ percent of the surplus.

8. 12½ percent of the amount by which net income exceeds 6 percent of stockholders' equity.

9. 15 percent of net income (plus minority interest in net income less variable compensation and interest on long-term debt) less 7 percent of invested capital.

10. 20 percent of bonus net income (net income less 6 percent of capital stock and surplus for current and preceding years plus provision for the bonus fund).

11. The amount by which net earnings before taxes plus 10 percent of invested capital exceed $10 million.

12. 12 percent of net earnings after deducting 6 percent of net capital.

13. 3 percent of the amount by which net income exceeds 6 percent of capital investment

14. 2½ percent of the total combined salaries of plan participants multiplied by the percentage points that consolidated income exceeds 35 percent of capital employed—to a maximum of 35 percent of total combined salaries of plan participants.

15. 3 percent of the first $15 million net income plus 5 percent of net income exceeding $15 million.

Table 7-19. Shareholder protection formulas (continued on next page)

16. 6 percent of net income, maximum equal to 25 percent of aggregate paid dividends on common stock.
17. 6 percent of the amount by which consolidated pretax earnings exceed 10 percent of shareholder's equity.
18. 6 percent of net income in excess of 6 percent of return on equity (ROE).

Table 7-19. Continued

The formula should articulate the basic objectives of the company. Is there a minimum rate to be provided for shareholder return? Is there a minimum increase (dollar or percentage) in earnings before any bonus can be paid? The minimum-increase-in-earnings approach promotes identification with the shareholder but does so at the risk of allowing tax policy to have a significant impact on the bonus fund. Will the impact of extraordinary items be removed from formula values? If so, within the Financial Accounting Standards Board (FASB) requirements, who will make the decision?

The formal plan (including the fund formula) should be as broad as possible to allow the executive compensation committee to make specific determinations within the plan parameters.

Developing the Fund Formula. Once the basic objectives have been identified, determining the number of bonus participants and the size of the bonus fund will set formula values. The approximate amount of bonus dollars needed in a good year depends on overall profitability, requirements for capital expenditures, and the stability of profits. Certainly, formula figures will be lower if profits are high or stable, or if capital requirements are low. As these change negatively, formula percentages will need to rise to allow for an adequate fund.

To quickly estimate the needed amount, multiply the percentage of bonus candidates times the percentage of their salaries to be paid in incentives to determine the percentage of payroll. The latter multiplied by the payroll indicates approximate dollars. For example, if 20 percent of the monthly paid employees will be eligible, and the awards will average 10 percent of their salary, then the bonus fund will need approximately $4 million for a $200 million payroll. This is only an approximation, however, and it will err consistently on the *low* side because the candidates are paid more than the total group average. This can be easily adjusted if one knows the average salary of candidates versus the total payroll. Thus, if the candidates average approximately $100,000 in salary versus $50,000 for all monthly paid (twice the average), then the needed fund is $8 million (i.e., $4 million x 2).

To build the formula, determine how much bonus should be generated under moderate, successful, and very successful financial conditions. Often these are called *threshold*, *target* and *maximum*. By summing the desired bonus amounts for each candidate under the three conditions, it is possible to determine how much total bonus is needed. Normally, this is adjusted upward by another 10 to 20 percent (better to err on the high side than the low). Once the amount needed has been calculated, trial and error with various formulas will find the one that best meets the requirements.

Testing the Fund Formula. To set up a formula-driven fund, calculate a target bonus for everyone and sum the totals. As most formula plans are a percentage of something, one can solve for the unknown X.

For example, a company may choose to use a certain percentage of net income for normal awards. If last year's net income was $10,000,000 and the sum of normal bonuses is $1,000,000, then the bonus fund percentage should be 10 percent.

Next, one needs to determine what is the minimum or *threshold* amount that would be paid to individuals. Typically, this is 10 percent to 20 percent of the normal award. Thus, if the normal award for a particular job is $50,000 and the threshold was set at 20 percent of the normal award, the threshold amount would be $10,000. The threshold is the lowest payment above zero and is often described in terms of probability of achievement. For example, some might set the probability of achieving the threshold at 80 percent and therefore set the threshold payout at 20 percent of the normal award. Others might set the probability of achievement at 90 percent and therefore the threshold payout at 10 percent of the normal award.

The formula is then further tested to see if it is appropriate at individual threshold performance. If the sum of threshold performance awards were $100,000, it would suggest that net income could be as low as $1,000,000 and still payout $100,000. Upon review, the chief financial officer might indicate that there should be no payout at $1,000,000 of net income but could agree with $200,000 at $2,000,000 net income, thus suggesting the threshold level be set at 20 percent of normal award (e.g., $200,000 ÷ $1,000,000 normal award).

The same approach can be used to set the *maximum* payout. If the threshold payment was set at 80-percent probability, one might set the maximum performance level at 20-percent probability and a payment double the normal award. This would suggest a payout of $2,000,000 (e.g., $1,000,000 normal award x 2) or a net income of at least $20,000,000 (e.g. $2,000,000 = 10% of $20,000,000).

Target vs. No-Target, Funded Plans. Fund formulas can be structured around a target, but they do not have to be. If a target is established, it normally equates to budgeted financial performance. This type of plan is sometimes called a *target plan*. It may also be referred to as a *performance-sharing* or *goal-sharing plan*. (This should not be confused with *gain sharing* where payment is based on sharing a reduction in expenses with employees. Gain sharing plans are typically unique to a particular location and include all employees, although executives at the site may be excluded.) A target plan may or may not stipulate a maximum payout (typically 150 percent or 200 percent of target) and a minimum or threshold below which there will be no payment. Target plans are structured a number of different ways: looking at past performance, looking forward to expected performance, and looking around to seeing what peer companies are doing. When one includes whether or not the formula will use a threshold, or deductible, there are four possible combinations, as shown in Table 7-20.

1. **No Deductible/No Target (A).** This type of plan typically uses a formula to set aside a portion of earnings. It is a non-qualified version of a profit-sharing plan.
2. **No Deductible/Target Plan (B).** This is a simple refinement of the no deductible/no target

	No Target	Target
No Deductible	A	B
Deductible	C	D

Table 7-20. Target and deductible combination plan

plan. Based on history and/or future expectations a targeted or expected level of payout is determined. This is helpful in communicating the value of the plan to participants.

3. **Deductible/No Target Plans (C).** The two types of plans in this category are shareholder protection and economic profit plans. Both were reviewed earlier.

4. **Deductible/Target Plan (D).** Similar to the no-deductible/target plan an expected level of payout is set but in this case in relation to the net of the deductible. An example of such a plan would be to combine Table 7-21 with a shareholder protection formula so that payments would be made only to the extent financial results exceeded the protection formula (e.g., 6 percent of shareholder equity). With an economic profit approach, only financial results in excess of the cost of capital would permit bonus payments.

Compound Growth in EPS Over Period	% of Normal Award Payable				
15% and up	100%	125%	150%	175%	200%
13.0% - 14.9%	75%	100%	125%	150%	175%
11.0% - 12.9%	50%	75%	100%	125%	150%
9.0% - 10.9%	25%	50%	75%	100%	125%
Below 9%	0%	25%	50%	75%	100%
Average Return on Capital	Below 10%	10.0%-11.9%	12.0%-13.9%	14.0%-15.9%	16% and Up

Table 7-21. Award table based on EPS and return on capital

Fund Formula Considerations. Where two factors (e.g., growth in EPS and return on capital) are prime objectives, building a matrix can help determine payment level at any combination of performance, as shown in Table 7-21. For example, if the compound growth in EPS were 11.5 percent and the average rate of return on capital for the same period were 14.5 percent, the normal award would be increased by 25 percent. All combinations in the matrix must be tested in advance to ensure that payout level is logical given other possibilities. In addition, the matrix can be expanded if a third factor is considered essential. For example, to better relate to shareholder objectives, perhaps the matrix could include the compound annual change in stock price. Thus, if the stock in our example decreased an average of 4.6 percent over the period, then the normal award would be 119.25 percent of normal award (i.e., 125% x 95.4%).

In addition, formulas that do not take into consideration growth relative to the industry can be either too generous or too conservative. Consider the situation of a company with a consistent 10-percent growth in net earnings over five years while its industry has shown 5, 7.5, 10, 12.5, and 15 percent growth rates. One could argue that a plan with a constant percentage of net earnings set aside for a bonus fund would under reward executives during the early years and over-compensate during the later years.

This scenario encourages many companies to adjust the bonus fund relative to the performance of others in the industry. For example, the EPS of the company could be compared to a select group of companies. The fund would be adjusted to the extent it was above or below

EPS As Percent Of Industry Average	Adjustment To Bonus Fund
150%	200%
140	180
130	160
120	140
110	120
100	100
90	80
80	60
70	40
60	20
50	0

Table 7-22. Bonus fund vs. industry average EPS

the average of this group, as shown in Table 7-22. Thus, if the company EPS were 120 percent of the industry average, the bonus fund would increase by 40 percent.

Unfortunately, this approach is cleaner in concept than in fact simply because of differences in weight of product mix even among companies that are supposedly comparable. Which companies to include and how to weight them are questions sufficiently open to debate in most cases. Therefore, when the analysis does not generate the amount management thinks appropriate, they will apply pressure to modify the basis of comparison.

Carryover Provisions. Sometimes companies will find that the performance is not sufficient to generate an incentive fund. This always creates a problem because invariably there are individuals who should receive an award because of their performance. Some companies will simply shrug their shoulders and indicate "that's the way cookie crumbles." Others concerned about losing top performers but not wanting to violate the terms of the plan will look to something else such as a special stock option grant (covered in the long-term incentive chapter). Others will make an exception to the plan and award some discretionary payments. The problem with this approach is that the company has lost credibility. Individuals will in the future also look for the company to provide money even if the fund does not.

An alternative sought by others is to ensure the bonus formula is sufficiently liberal that there are always monies left unused. By terms of the plan, this amount would be carried over to the next bonus period thus avoiding the problem of what to do if the next year's performance generated no bonus pool. The carryover amount could be used to reward the outstanding individuals. Such plan provisions typically apply for only one year. Two successive years of poor performance creates a problem in the second year. However, by that time some drastic changes will be needed anyway.

Divisional Funds. From one main corporate fund, divisional funds may be generated by either quantitative formula or qualitative judgment. Unless, in fact, the division is a wholly integrated operation, it is unlikely that the same formula used for the corporate fund can be applied at the divisional level. Even if it could, the number of participating executives (and their level of pay) often does not relate in a consistent fashion to the profit level, thus making a common formula ineffective. More commonly, reference is made to the degree of success in attaining divisional goals.

Assessing Divisional Performance. Self-standing division formulas are much more likely to be present in non-related, multi-industry companies when the corporation's role is essentially one of providing capital. In such a situation, it is not unrealistic to have separate bonus plans for each unit based on percentage of profits above a stated return on investment. As the investment in the unit increases, so does the income needed in order to generate a bonus fund.

The basis for judging divisional performance under a corporate fund can range from use of a single factor (such as return on investment for a profit-making unit) to a number of financial and non-financial factors. In addition, bookkeeping calculations can be made to adjust financial performance. For example, divisional profits may be reduced by a corporate charge for use of capital. This is similar to the economic profit approach described earlier. This could be a simple charge on all capital or a higher charge beyond a certain amount. In the first instances, if the company charges 7.5 percent, a division with $100 million of assets would have profits reduced by $7.5 million; in the second approach the same division would be assessed $7.3 million if the charge were 7 percent on the first $90 million and 10 percent of anything above. Both require determining a minimum percentage to ensure divisions recognize the cost of capital and don't simply rush to increase profit without regard to capital costs. The second formula requires determining the desired capital base [to ensure the division is not undercapitalized, the formula can be changed to charge only above a specified amount (e.g., $90 million)]. This determination should be made on a division-by-division basis. For those who find this too cumbersome, an interim step such as a charge on excess inventories can have a similar effect, although more narrowly defined (in this case keep inventories down).

Performance Factors. While the use of only one factor to determine performance is certainly simpler, it provides no reinforcement of other performance factors. Regardless of the number of factors, ideally, performance should be quantifiable in accordance with a previously agreed-to measuring basis and the various scores connected to specific levels of performance. In addition, the unit being rated should have access to the data throughout the year, not simply at year-end.

Any payment in relation to profit budget (the amount of profit management hopes to make for a stated period) places an emphasis on accurate forecasts. If top management imposes such a relationship, it is outside the unit's control; if the unit develops it, it encourages conservative estimates. In addition, a unit may increase its own profitability (and bonus fund) by taking actions not in the best interest of the company (or even the unit in the long run).

We can argue that forecasts and performance can always be adjusted for factors outside the unit's control. Conceptually this is logical; unfortunately, it is often difficult to quantify, much less identify, uncontrollable factors.

Not to take into account extraordinary circumstances (e.g., to say, "Let the chips fall where they may") is to either over-reward mediocre performance or under-reward outstanding accomplishments. Some try to rationalize having it both ways (i.e., cutting back when outside events would generate too much bonus, but identifying with shareholders when results are negated by outside events). In such situations, it could be said that the decision-makers are consistent in their inconsistency (i.e., they keep bonus amounts down). For many, a more rational approach is to consider the impact of extraordinary items, within FASB rules, in determining the bonus fund. Clearly, if managers are unprepared or unwilling to make adjustments, they place an unrealistic burden on the efficacy of the bonus formula. Conversely, they must resist pressure to make adjustments when bonuses are legitimately low due to less than optimal performance without outside factors.

Identify Divisional Goals. In order to establish a quantitative reference, the first step is to identify the division's goals—both quantitative and qualitative. Quantitative goals are most directly applicable to marketing and production operations, whereas qualitative goals are more compatible with the staff functions of legal, finance, and personnel. Actually, however, there is crossover; the quantitative and qualitative goals are present in all functions although admittedly to different degrees. Quantitative goals are measured by "how much"; qualitative goals by "how well." (Chapter 2 includes a review of performance measurements.)

Each division's goals are listed under the two categories, quantitative and qualitative. Before proceeding any further, there must be an understanding between division manager and company president concerning the value of attaining those goals. Many corporations bypass this step and it is here that they can get into real trouble. One division manager may be the optimistic type, setting very difficult objectives within an almost-impossible-to-meet timetable; another may know how to play the game, setting goals that, although impressively stated and possibly many in number, are rather easy to attain. The president has two alternatives: either readjust all goals to a reasonable level or, following the concept of mutual agreement, leave the goals unchanged but readjust the normal fund for each division up or down in relation to the difficulty of its objectives.

One of the more difficult tasks is to allocate divisional funds from a short-term incentive plan. In spite of all the formulas developed (including performance relative to others in the industry), a subjective judgment must be made about the degree of difficulty that tempered performance outcome. However hard it may be to make that assessment, the likelihood of inequity in the treatment of two divisions is much less than if no tempering judgment is applied.

Furthermore, it is important that divisions understand that divisional targets have equal stretch and degree of difficulty even though the targets are different. Otherwise, very profitable divisions, even though falling below their target, will expect a large payout because their absolute level of achievement exceeds other divisions.

Having weighted the sum total of the division's goals and objectives against a normal fund, the next step is to relate the value of each of the objectives. The simplest technique is to begin by assigning each objective an equal value and then adjusting plus or minus. To make this work quantitatively, assume a total value of 100. If the division has five goals, each begins with an arbitrary value of 20. This value is adjusted by reference of one to another, after the ranking of the five in order of importance. There is nothing magical here. It is merely a trial-and-error method of structuring the basis for determining the subsequent size of the divisional fund at the end of the year.

Measure Performance. Having weighted each goal one to another, the next step is to determine how to quantitatively measure attainment of the objective. Two philosophies emerge. The first states bonus should only be paid for outstanding performance (described as attainment of the specified objective; less means no bonus). This binary approach of either "hit" or "miss" makes a bonus program simple to administer, but top management will have a hard time calling a very near miss a zero. In addition, while such a program adequately differentiates in pay between outstanding and less-than-outstanding performers, one must question whether or not it adequately differentiates between poor and adequate performers.

The second approach states that there are degrees of success and failure, and bonuses should be structured accordingly. This second view requires the outlining and subsequent weighting of each defined goal. Assume that one of five goals for a division is to increase net earnings from 15 percent to 18 percent. This goal was given a weighting of 30, instead of an unweighted 20 (i.e., a total of 100 divided by 5 goals), as shown in Table 7-23. With 18 percent being the normal target, it is possible to build values above and below this number to reflect easy or difficult targets. Note that it is even possible to relate attainment in fractions of a point, if such were desirable (e.g., attainment of net earnings in the amount of 18.5 percent would translate to 32.5 points).

Percent	Points
21.0 and up	45
20.0	40
19.0	35
18.0	30
17.0	25
16.0	20
15.0 and lower	15

Table 7-23. Point schedule vs. EPS attainment

An important point is that although numbers may be used to determine the size of the division fund by the measurement of goals and objectives, it is imperative to realize that this is not a magic numbers show. The weighting scale, especially in the measurement of qualitative goals, is only as good as the judgment of evaluator.

Other Ways of Allocating Funds.

Corporate versus Own Unit. Another basic approach to allocating funds is shown in Table 7-24. In addition to the handful of top executives (whose fund is determined only by corporate success), there are three types of divisions: support staff (e.g., finance, legal, personnel), cost centers (e.g., production), and profit centers (e.g., sales/marketing). In this example, two-thirds

	Performance Basis, %	
	Corporate	**Own Unit**
CEO/president and staff VPs	100	—
Support staff	67	33
Cost centers	50	50
Profit centers	33	67

Table 7-24. Corporate vs. unit performance allocations

of the normal fund for support staff is based on corporate success and one-third on the attainment of their objectives; for cost centers, the split is 50-50 between corporate success and divisional success; profit centers have two-thirds of their normal fund determined by their own success or failure and one-third by corporate success.

The rationale behind this approach is that top executives are defined as those people who cross divisional lines in their responsibilities and strive for optimization of corporate success. The objectives of the support staff also cross divisional lines, and their success or failure has a definite effect on corporate success (almost always in minimization of expenses or the optimization of output for the same level of expenses). Cost centers can be quantitatively judged on their failure or success in attaining assigned budgets. Profit centers can most assuredly be judged against sales and profit attainment, but to remind them of their membership on the corporate team, a portion of their normal bonus is predicated on corporate success. Paying division heads strictly on the basis of their own accomplishments (such as ROI, sales, and/or profits) is consistent when divisions are completely autonomous and the transfer of top managers between divisions is not a factor.

By Responsibility. A variation on this same theme would move the support staff in with top executives, making both completely reliant on corporate profits, and keep profit centers unchanged (2 parts division and 1 part corporate), relating the cost centers on a prorated basis to the profit centers they serve. An example of the latter would be the case where a production division's total output was split: 50-percent chemical business, 35-percent pharmaceutical business, and 15-percent agricultural business. These same percentages would make up the total of its normal award (excluding the corporate one-third). Thus, if its normal award were $1,500,000 with $1,000,000 being for division attainment, $500,000 would depend on the chemical business meeting its profit objectives, $350,000 on the pharmaceutical, and $150,000 on the agricultural. Obviously, these figures could be adjusted upward or downward, depending on the degree of success or failure of each of the businesses in meeting its profit objectives.

By Organizational Level. Another variation on this approach is to separate the organization in terms of level of unit (e.g., corporate, group, division, and individual) and determine the effect that each will have on a particular job. As in Table 7-25, the CEO/president and staff vice presidents would have their entire bonuses generated by corporate performance. A group president, on the other hand, might have half of bonus contingent on group performance and the other half on corporate (to ensure corporate visibility). A division president within the group might have half of bonus at risk with division performance and the remainder split between cor-

	Corporate	Group	Division	Individual
CEO/president and staff VPs	100	—	—	—
Operating group VPs	50	50	—	—
Division president	25	25	50	—
Division VP	—	—	50	50

Table 7-25. Allocation of bonuses: corporate, group, division, and individual

porate and group achievement. Finally, a division vice president could have half of bonus based on divisional performance and the remainder on individual achievements.

The manner in which divisional and corporate portions are structured will reinforce a particular behavior. For example, placing the entire payout on divisional performance (ignoring group and corporate) will encourage a division manager to take actions that are self-benefiting regardless of long- or short-term impact on the rest of the organization. In this illustration, the division head realizes that half of bonus will come from outside the division. Thus, the person must be responsive to actions beneficial to the group and corporation as well as the executive's own division.

Impact of Minimum Performance on Divisional Funds. However the guideline bonus fund is generated, the plus and minus variations from desired payout must be in the desired relationship. To illustrate: Employing the concept advanced in the earlier discussion on fund formulas, assume it is desirable to pay nothing below a minimum growth rate. Thus, we could express actual growth (e.g., income before corporate allocation) in terms of expected minimum to determine a divisional bonus relationship, as in Table 7-26. Note the problem with a projected loss situation.

Division	Minimum	Actual	Relationship
A	$10,000,000	$9,000,000	0.90
B	-2,000,000	2,000,000	Infinity
C	16,000,000	20,000,000	1.25
D	15,000,000	16,000,000	1.07

Table 7-26. Performance vs. target for four divisions

However, by introducing targeted growth, we can express the relationship of actual to targeted versus minimum in a manner that cancels out the problems of negative values. Note that the formulas will always generate a positive number as long as target is greater than minimum (a logical requirement) and actual is greater than minimum (when it is less, there is no bonus pool).

$$\text{Relative performance} = \frac{\text{Actual - minimum}}{\text{Target - minimum}}$$

Continuing our example, we will use "income before corporate allocation"; however, this approach can be employed for any quantifiable measurement (e.g., pretax dollar profit, pretax profit percentage, return on investment, net dollar profit, or net dollar percentage). As shown in Table 7-27, actual performance for both division B and division C exceeded their respective minimums by $4 million. However, division B had the higher percentage using the above formula because its relative growth was higher. Division A was actually a minus .5 [(9 - 10) ÷ (12 - 10)]; however, all minus values would be expressed as a zero.

The importance of accurate minimum and target values is demonstrated by the following example. Shown in Table 7-28 are three divisions with a common minimum but varying targets. Given three different actual performance levels, note the differences, recognizing that if all three should have had the same target (e.g., $20 million), then division A is being overrated and divi-

Division	Minimum	Target	Actual	Performance
A	$10,000,000	$12,000,000	$9,000,000	0.00
B	-2,000,000	000	2,000,000	2.00
C	16,000,000	20,000,000	20,000,000	1.00
D	15,000,000	18,000,000	16,000,000	0.33

Table 7-27. Relative performance vs. target for four divisions

Division	Minimum	Target	Performance Rating by Sales Attainment $19,000,000	$20,000,000	$21,000,000
A	$16,000,000	$19,000,000	1.00	1.33	1.67
B	16,000,000	20,000,000	0.75	1.00	1.25
C	16,000,000	21,000,000	0.60	0.80	1.00
Averages			**0.78**	**1.04**	**1.31**

Table 7-28. Performance rating by sales attainment for three divisions

sion C underrated. Note further that the impact of erring on the low side is more dramatic than erring on the high side (e.g., at $21 million, the A division received 34 percentage points more than it should have, whereas division C received 20 percentage points less than it should have).

The same types of problems occur with misjudging the "minimum." Thus, this approach requires a high degree of confidence in being able to equitably set "minimum" and "target" for each division. Furthermore, the rating relationship generated must adequately reflect the bonus position. In the example in Table 7-29, assume that the minimums and targets are accurately reflected as shown; further assume that all divisions have a guideline normal bonus of $1,000,000. Given the results, does Table 7-29 appear to be appropriate for the performance generated? To the extent that Table 7-29 is not considered to be an equitable balance, an additional factor(s) must be introduced to adjust the funds. Or, an alternative formula(s) must be developed.

Some plans require that whatever has been generated, and allocated, must be distributed. However, it is believed that a much more logical approach is simply to use the fund as the max-

Division	Minimum	Target	Bonus Pool by Attainment $19,000,000	$20,000,000	$21,000,000
A	$16,000,000	$19,000,000	$1,000,000	$1,330,000	$1,670,000
B	16,000,000	20,000,000	750,000	1,000,000	1,250,000
C	16,000,000	21,000,000	600,000	800,000	1,000,000

Table 7-29. Bonus pool by sales attainment for three divisions

imum limit. Furthermore, as indicated earlier, in a number of instances, the plan formula provides that the unused amount may be carried over—in many cases, indefinitely. Some form of *carryover* is often needed to provide for the contingency that the company formula produces an insufficient amount to compensate divisions with outstanding years.

When companies do not permit a carryover of unused funds, divisions will apply greater pressure to adjust targets during or after the year based on those factors that they consider beyond their control (e.g., late release of new product). While there may be sufficient justification for such actions, management must be careful to avoid charges of simply changing the targets to ensure an adequate payout. Some might logically ask why the payout targets for the professional manager should be lowered when the owner-manager does not have the same opportunity.

Structuring the Individual Payouts Example. Regardless of the specific nature of the deviation from the basic approach of two or more funds providing the total award, it is important to describe how this interaction is done statistically. An example has to be constructed for this purpose. The fictitious Brucell Corporation has 35 salary grades and all persons in grade 20 and up are eligible for bonuses.

In setting up the individual award schedule, the objective is, if possible, to incorporate annual incentive guidelines without affecting the compensation midpoints used for grading positions. Otherwise, jobs would have to be re-graded. Steps to take include:

- *Midpoint total compensation* should equal *salary range midpoint* plus *target bonus*. This remains the value for market pricing the position (e.g., for grade 35, the total compensation midpoint $1,390.9, shown in Table 7-30, is the same as the salary midpoint shown in Chapter 5 in Table 5-4).
- *Minimum* and *maximum salary* is constructed around the salary midpoint to give the same spread as current schedule (for grade 35, this is 8.6 percent of $1,095.2 or 18.9 percent maximum over minimum).
- *Midpoint total compensation* is salary midpoint plus bonus midpoint [for grade 35, this is $1,095.2 + ($591.5 ÷ 2) = $1,390.9].
- *Maximum total compensation* is salary maximum plus bonus maximum for grade 35, this is $1,189.6 + $591.5 = $1,781.1), the same as Table 5-4 total maximum.

Bonus percentages are calculated by first determining the maximum for each grade. This is determined by dividing the bonus dollar maximum by the salary maximum (for grade 35, this is $591.5 ÷ $1,189.6 = 49.7%). For aesthetic purposes, we'll round this to 50 percent, which is divided by six to get guidelines for ratings 1, 2, 3, 4, and 5 (i.e., 8.3%, 16.7%, 25.0%, 33.3%, and 41.7% for grade 35). Table 7-31 reflects these calculations for all 35 grades and includes the previously described threshold (marginal), target (good), and maximum (outstanding) payout levels.

If a more aggressive incentive schedule (such as the one shown in Table 7-32, which cuts off a grade 20) were desired, the schedules would need to be significantly reworked, namely, by calculating new lower minimums and maximums. This can be illustrated by simply looking at the current minimum salary for grade 35 (i.e., $1,000,700) and applying the 200-percent maximum from Table 7-32. The result would be $3,002,100 total pay or $1,221,000 (i.e., $3,002,100 - $1,781,100) more than the current schedule's maximum. Similarly, the new midpoint would be $610,500 greater than the current total compensation midpoint (i.e., $2,001,400 -$1,390,900). To have the same maximum total compensation with these more aggressive bonus

Grade	Salary					Bonus	Total Compensation	
	Minimum	Lower 1/3	Upper 1/3	Maximum	Midpoint	Maximum	Midpoint	Maximum
35	$1,000.7	$1,063.7	$1,126.6	$1,189.6	$1,095.2	$591.5	$1,390.9	$1,781.1
34	884.1	942.5	1,000.9	1,058.3	971.7	505.4	1,224.4	1,564.7
33	785.2	837.4	889.5	941.7	863.5	440.3	1,083.6	1,382.0
32	695.5	743.9	792.4	840.8	768.2	376.3	956.3	1,271.1
31	617.5	660.7	703.8	747.0	682.3	327.5	846.0	1,074.5
30	548.7	588.9	629.0	669.2	609.0	280.1	749.0	949.3
29	489.1	526.6	564.0	601.5	545.3	239.8	665.2	841.3
28	486.8	470.4	504.0	537.6	487.2	209.4	591.9	747.0
27	391.4	422.8	454.3	485.7	438.6	179.7	528.4	665.4
26	350.8	380.1	409.5	438.8	394.8	154.0	471.8	592.8
25	315.9	342.4	369.0	395.5	355.7	135.2	423.3	530.7
24	285.1	310.1	335.0	360.0	322.6	116.1	380.6	476.1
23	257.1	280.5	303.9	327.3	292.2	99.4	341.9	426.7
22	233.0	255.1	277.1	299.2	266.1	85.2	308.7	384.4
21	210.6	231.4	252.2	273.0	241.8	72.4	278.0	345.4
20	189.7	208.5	227.2	246.0	217.9	63.3	249.5	309.3
19	172.3	190.0	207.6	225.3	198.8	53.8	225.7	279.1
18	156.0	172.6	189.3	205.9	181.0	45.3	203.6	251.2
17	142.2	157.9	173.5	189.2	165.7	38.2	184.8	227.4
16	128.9	144.3	158.8	173.2	151.6	33.3	168.2	206.5
15	118.9	132.6	146.2	159.9	139.4	28.0	153.4	187.9
14	108.6	121.6	134.6	147.6	128.1	23.0	139.6	170.6
13	99.8	111.7	123.6	135.5	117.7	20.1	127.7	155.6
12	92.3	103.7	115.0	126.4	109.4	16.5	117.6	142.9
11	84.3	95.1	106.0	116.8	100.6	13.1	107.1	129.9
10	78.0	88.4	98.7	109.1	83.6	10.3	98.7	119.4
9	72.1	82.0	91.8	101.7	86.9	7.8	90.8	109.5
8	66.8	76.2	85.7	95.1	81.0	5.7	83.8	100.8
7	62.2	71.1	80.0	88.9	75.6	4.5	77.8	93.4
6	58.0	66.2	74.5	82.7	70.4	4.3	72.5	87.0
5	54.2	61.9	69.7	77.4	65.8	3.8	67.7	81.2
4	50.4	57.6	64.8	72.0	61.2	3.6	63.0	75.6
3	47.0	53.7	60.5	67.2	57.1	3.4	58.8	70.6
2	43.6	49.8	56.0	62.2	52.9	3.2	54.5	65.4
1	40.6	46.4	52.2	58.0	49.3	3.0	50.8	61.0

Table 7-30. Salary schedule discounted for annual incentive (in thousands)

guidelines would require a maximum salary of $593,700 (total compensation maximum of $1,781,100 = 3x, x = $593,700). However, this creates an impossible situation since retaining the existing total compensation midpoint of $1,390,500 would require a salary midpoint of $695,250 (i.e., $695,250 + 100% of $695,250), or $101,550 more than the $593,700 maximum.

Since the midpoint was the basis in setting a competitive pay structure, it should be retained, and a new salary schedule should be built around the revised midpoints. The results would be reduced minimums and maximums as well as narrower ranges (i.e., less spread between minimums and maximums).

Brucell has devised a grid to adjust the normal bonus (a 3 rating) up or down for a division based on profit success. This grid, based on Tables 7-30 and 7-31, is shown in Table 7-33.

Grade	0 Un-acceptable	1 Marginal	2 Acceptable	3 Good	4 Very Good	5 Superior	6 Out-standing
35	0	8.3%	16.7%	25.0%	33.3%	41.7%	50.0%
34	0	8.0	16.0	24.0	32.0	40.0	48.0
33	0	7.7	15.3	23.0	30.6	38.3	46.0
32	0	7.5	15.0	22.5	30.0	37.5	45.6
31	0	7.3	14.7	22.0	29.3	36.7	44.0
30	0	7.0	14.0	21.0	28.0	35.0	42.0
29	0	6.7	13.3	20.0	26.3	33.3	40.0
28	0	6.5	13.0	19.5	26.0	32.5	39.0
27	0	6.3	12.7	19.0	25.3	31.7	38.0
26	0	6.0	12.0	18.0	24.0	30.0	36.0
25	0	5.7	11.3	17.0	22.7	28.3	34.0
24	0	5.3	10.6	16.0	21.3	26.7	32.0
23	0	5.0	10.0	15.0	20.0	25.0	30.0
22	0	4.8	9.7	14.5	19.3	24.2	29.0
21	0	4.7	9.3	14.0	18.7	23.3	28.0
20	0	4.3	8.7	13.0	17.3	21.7	26.0
19	0	4.0	8.0	12.0	16.0	20.0	24.0
18	0	3.7	7.3	11.0	14.7	18.3	22.0
17	0	3.3	6.7	10.0	13.3	16.7	20.0
16	0	3.2	6.3	9.5	12.7	15.8	19.0
15	0	3.0	6.0	9.0	12.0	15.0	18.0
14	0	2.7	5.3	8.0	10.7	13.3	16.0
13	0	2.3	4.7	7.0	9.3	11.7	14.0
12	0	2.2	4.3	6.5	8.7	10.8	13.0
11	0	2.0	4.0	6.0	8.0	10.0	12.0
10	0	1.7	3.3	5.0	6.7	8.3	10.0
9	0	1.3	2.7	4.0	5.3	6.7	8.0
8	0	1.0	2.0	3.0	4.0	5.0	6.0
7	0	0.8	1.7	2.5	3.3	4.2	5.0
6	0	0.8	1.7	2.5	3.3	4.2	5.0
5	0	0.8	1.7	2.5	3.3	4.2	5.0
4	0	0.8	1.7	2.5	3.3	4.2	5.0
3	0	0.8	1.7	2.5	3.3	4.2	5.0
2	0	0.8	1.7	2.5	3.3	4.2	5.0
1	0	0.8	1.7	2.5	3.3	4.2	5.0

Table 7-31. Annual incentive awards as percent of salary

It is used for corporate profit goals as well as division goals, where appropriate. As can be seen, this is an abbreviated schedule showing only every fifth grade. However, the reader can easily interpolate to determine the factors for missing salary grades.

Division A attains 105 percent of its profit goal while the corporation only meets 98 percent of its profit objectives. Query: What is the total fund available for division A? Since in this plan three parts of the fund are based on division success and one part on corporate success, it

Grade	0 Un-acceptable	1 Marginal	2 Acceptable	3 Good	4 Very Good	5 Superior	6 Out standing
35	0	33.0%	67.0%	100.0%	133.0%	167.0%	200.0%
34	0	32.0	63.0	95.0	127.0	158.0	190.0
33	0	30.0	60.0	90.0	120.0	150.0	180.0
32	0	28.0	57.0	85.0	113.0	142.0	170.0
31	0	27.0	53.0	80.0	107.0	133.0	160.0
30	0	25.0	50.0	75.0	100.0	125.0	150.0
29	0	23.0	47.0	70.0	93.0	117.0	140.0
28	0	22.0	43.0	65.0	87.0	108.0	130.0
27	0	20.0	40.0	60.0	80.0	100.0	120.0
26	0	18.0	37.0	55.0	73.0	92.0	110.0
25	0	17.0	33.0	50.0	67.0	83.0	100.0
24	0	15.0	30.0	45.0	60.0	75.0	90.0
23	0	13.0	27.0	40.0	53.0	67.0	80.0
22	0	12.0	23.0	35.0	47.0	58.0	70.0
21	0	10.0	20.0	30.0	40.0	50.0	60.0
20	0	8.0	17.0	25.0	33.0	42.0	50.0

Table 7-32. Aggressive annual incentive awards as percent of salary

Salary Grade	Midpoint	Minus Per 1 Percent	Bonus Target Percent	Plus Per 1 Percent	Maximum Bonus Percent
35	$1,095,200	2.50	25.0	1.25	37.5
30	609,000	2.00	21.0	1.00	31.0
25	355,700	1.50	17.0	0.75	24.5
20	217,900	1.00	13.0	0.50	18.0

Table 7-33. Bonus percentages adjustments by corporate performance

is necessary first to determine the weighted average guideline percentage. This is done for each job incumbent in each salary grade. An example would be a person in grade 30 in division A. Adjust the bonus target percentage of 21 by 5 points (i.e., 5 x 1.00) to 26 since the division did 105 percent of target. It is then given a weight of 3 for a total of 78 (i.e., 26 x 3). Next, reduce the bonus target percentage of 21 by 4 (i.e., 2 x 2.00) to 17 since the corporation only did 98 percent of its objective. It is then given a weight of 1 for a total of 17 (i.e., 17 x 1). Total the two and divide the sum by 4 (i.e., 78 + 17 = 95, 95/4) to equal 23.75 percent.

In a similar fashion, the guideline percentage was weighted out for every person in division A, as shown in Table 7-34. The bonus percentage was then multiplied by the total salaries in that grade and totaled, resulting in a sum of $249,572 available to that division for bonus distribution.

In many instances, this type of divisional calculation is a preliminary rather than final step. If there is a corporate formula that generates a total fund from which corporate and divisional

Salary Grade	Employees	Average Salary	Guide Percent	Guide Bonus
30	1	$600,000	23.75%	$142,500
26	1	400,000	20.00	80,000
25	1	350,000	19.06	66,710
22	2	260,000	16.35	85,020
20	3	220,000	14.37	94,842
Total	**8**			**$249,572**

Table 7-34. Guideline bonus example, one division

awards are to be made, then preliminary divisional calculations have to be summed and related to the available pool on a proportionate basis, as shown in Table 7-35. In this example, division A's available pool has been reduced 4.8 percent from $249,572 to $237,631 because the total available for divisional awards is only $702,634 versus $737,938 projected (sum of the preliminary awards). If the total available were higher than the aggregate preliminary awards, then each divisional final bonus would be proportionately higher.

Division	Preliminary Amount	Percent Total	Total Available	Final Bonus
A	$249,572	33.82	$702,634	$237,631
B	167,198	22.66	702,634	159,217
C	123,470	16.73	702,634	117,551
D	197,698	26.79	702,634	188,235
Total	**$737,938**	**100.00**		**$702,634**

Table 7-35. Guideline bonus example, four divisions

A variation on this method of determining divisional awards is to express the performance evaluation in terms of an interim score and later convert this score to a bonus percentage. This can be illustrated with a multi-goal requirement.

Goals By Organizational Level Example. Assume that the corporate goal is to increase net earnings by 10 percent, the group goal is to improve net income before allocation by 12 percent, and the divisional goal is to increase income before corporate allocation by 15 percent. Rating scales such as the ones in Table 7-36 might be developed.

Note that in these evaluation grids there is equal reward or penalty for a percentage point; the earlier grid penalized below-goal achievement more severely than it rewarded overachievement. The former is more consistent with a company that has discounted its salary line by some portion of bonus and therefore has to be more tolerant of below-expected performance

Evaluation	Corporation Increase in Net Earnings	Group A Increase in Income before Allocation	Division A Increase in Income before Allocation
6	13.0% and Up	16.5% and Up	21.0% and Up
5	12.0	15.0	19.0
4	11.0	13.5	17.0
3	10.0	12.0	15.0
2	9.0	10.5	13.0
1	8.0	9.0	11.0
0	Below	Below	Below

Table 7-36. Evaluation schedule for corporation, group, and division

in allowing some bonus; the latter approach is appropriate for a company that has a competitive salary (without discount) and is therefore prepared to cut back sharply on below-target performance. Note also that the progression on the division performance table is more dramatic than the corporate (even though both are arithmetic constants).

Given the high percentage income expectations, it appears that Division A is in an earlier stage of development than the corporation, although new products and/or significant price increases might be accounting for the difference.

A totally different situation is shown in Table 7-37. Here's a division that is obviously in trouble since its objective is to just break even. Note that the objective is expressed in absolute rather than relative terms (i.e., dollar amount of profit or loss rather than percent change).

In addition to Table 7-36, let's assume that division A has several other objectives: sales, return on capital, and affirmative action achievement. The first two are financial; the last is a non-financial EEO goal. Shown in Table 7-38 are possibilities for each.

Income before Allocation, Millions	Evaluation
$1.5	6
1.0	5
0.5	4
0.0	3
-0.5	2
-1.0	1
More	0

Table 7-37. Additional example of a divisional performance schedule

Performance	Increase in Net Sales	Return on Capital	Percentage Point Increase in Parity Goal
6	21.0% and Up	19.0% and Up	9.0 and Up
5	19.0	18.0	8.0
4	17.0	17.0	7.0
3	15.0	16.0	6.0
2	13.0	15.0	5.0
1	11.0	14.0	4.0
0	Below	Below	Below

Table 7-38. Multiple performance criteria for one division

Another variation would be to have one financial objective top-line focused (increase in net sales), with another three bottom-line focused (return on capital, income before allocation, and increase in net earnings). In this instance, the goals might be weighted in the following manner: income before allocation (40 percent), increase in net sales (30 percent), return on capital (10 percent), and increase in parity goal (20 percent).

The attractiveness of the above-described goals is their quantitative nature. Sometimes the non-financial goals are more qualitative in nature, possibly including manpower planning and development, efficacy of long-range planning, and organizational effectiveness. In most instances, these and other worthy goals are not included simply because it becomes too difficult to agree on the levels of performance and how to measure them.

Returning to our Table 7-36 example, after the conclusion of the year, the results are tallied and reveal:

Corporate earnings increase	11.5%
Group A income increase	12.0%

Division A

Increase in income before allocation	17.5%
Increase in net sales	16.3%
Return on capital	17.0%
Percentage point increase in parity goal	8.8%

The next step is to identify the performance for each goal. Notice that most require interpolation between values. Thus, an 11.5-percent increase in corporate earnings is a 4.5 rating. In a similar manner the performance ratings for each of the other objectives may be calculated, resulting in the following:

	Performance Rating
Corporate earnings increase	4.50
Group A income increase	3.00

Division A

Increase in income before allocation	4.25
Increase in net sales	3.65
Return on capital	4.00
Percentage point increase in parity goal	5.80

Determining the overall divisional performance is a matter of adjusting these scores by their respective weights and dividing by 100.

$$\frac{4.25(40) + 3.65(30) + 4.0(10) + 5.8(20)}{100} = 4.4$$

Calculate the combined rating by weighting the corporate, group, and division performance ratings in a similar manner.

$$\frac{4.5(25) + 3.0(25) + 4.4(50)}{100} = 4.1$$

To use this rating to determine the bonus fund, a bonus table similar to the one in Table 7-31 (shown earlier) must be established. As can be seen, bonus percentages are established by grade for each level of performance. The amount of reward should be proportionate to the degree of risk; therefore, bonus percentages increase as one moves upward through the salary structure. By many standards, this would be considered a relatively modest level of payout at the upper end of the structure. Certainly, this would be true in the absence of long-term incentives. In this particular example, bonus eligibility begins with grade 20.

Since the combined weighted performance rating in our example is 4.1, it is necessary to interpolate 10 percent of the difference between columns 4 and 5. To generate a guideline bonus total, multiply the appropriate percentage for each grade by the average salary and the number of employees, as shown in Table 7-39. This is called a *performance-adjusted, sum-of-the-targets* approach.

It can be argued that bonus, like salary, should vary not only with performance but also with position in range; otherwise, the company runs the risk of losing an outstanding individual who is low in range, while proportionately overpaying a person high in range. Addressing this objective requires adding the dimension of position in range to the bonus guidelines in a

Salary Grade	Employees	Average Salary	Guide Percent	Guide Bonus
30	1	$600,000	28.7%	$172,200
26	1	400,000	24.6	98,400
25	1	350,000	23.3	81,550
22	2	250,000	19.8	99,000
20	3	210,000	17.7	111,510
Total	**8**			**$562,660**

Table 7-39. Evaluated performance and bonus example, one division

Performance	Position in Salary Range Grade 30				
	Below Minimum	**Lower 1/3**	**Middle 1/3**	**Upper 1/3**	**Above Maximum**
6	63.00%	52.50%	42.00%	32.50%	21.00%
5	52.50	44.75	35.00	26.25	17.50
4	42.00	35.00	28.00	21.00	14.00
3	31.50	26.25	21.00	15.75	10.50
2	21.00	17.50	14.00	10.50	7.00
1	10.50	8.75	7.00	5.25	3.50
0	0.00	0.00	0.00	0.00	0.00

Table 7-40. Bonus guidelines for grade 30 by position in range

manner similar to the rework of grade 30 shown in Table 7-40. Note that the values in Table 7-31 are equal to those in the middle one-third in Table 7-40.

Following the same method of interpolation as in the previous example would result in the values shown in Table 7-41 for a 4.1 rating, depending on the position of the individual within the salary range. Thus, if the individual were in the lower one-third, a guideline percentage of 35.98 percent would be applied to the individual's salary (i.e., 44.75 - 35.00 ÷ 35.00 = 9.75; 9.75 x .1 = .975; 35.0 + .98 = 35.98). Using the salary schedule in Table 7-30, this would mean a salary somewhere between $548,700 and $669,200, or a bonus value ranging from $191,422 to $240,778 for an individual in grade 30. Such an approach translates not only to higher bonus percentages for those low in range but also to higher bonus dollars (e.g., compare $197,422 and $240,778 in this example with $172,200 in Table 7-39).

Below Minimum	**Lower 1/3**	**Middle 1/3**	**Upper 1/3**	**Above Maximum**
44.05%	35.98%	28.70%	21.53%	14.35%

Table 7-41. Interpolated bonus guidelines using position in range

While such an approach is more logical, it is also more cumbersome, and for this reason, many do not see it as administratively practical.

Division and Individual Performance. In many instances, the division president receives a fund to be allocated that has already been reduced by the president's own award (normally the guideline amount). Typically, he or she does not have carte blanche on the distribution but must submit a list of proposals for review and approval by either the CEO or the compensation committee of the board of directors.

To illustrate using the example in Table 7-39, the division president who is a grade 30 would receive $177,200. The remaining $390,460 (i.e. $562,660 - $172,200) is available for distribution among the remaining seven employees. If the seven bonus candidates all performed at exactly the same level of proficiency in relation to their assigned targets (e.g., 4.1 rating), then each would get the bonus percentage used in generating the fund (e.g., the grade 26 would receive an amount equal to 24.6 percent of salary). Since this is highly unlikely, the amounts should be plus or minus from the guideline percentage depending on the level of performance attained. Some would be inclined to reserve half of the guideline amount of $390,460 or $195,230 for sharing in division performance. The remaining $195,230 would be allocated based on individual achievement. For several, this might mean no bonus, for others a significant amount. Table 7-42 shows how this 50-percent division and 50-percent employee performance approach might be utilized. Note that the performance rating is used to look up the appropriate bonus percentage for that grade (see Table 7-31), but only half is used (since one-half has already been set aside for division performance). The sum of these bonuses is $198,215 or $2,985 more than allowable (i.e., $198,215 - $195,230). Therefore, the awards are proportionately reduced by the ratio of $195,230 to $198,215, or 0.9849. Adding the individually adjusted bonus to the division bonus produces the total for each person. These could be rounded to the nearest $100, if deemed appropriate to finalize the calculation as long as the division total does not exceed $390,460.

Grade	Emp.	Salary	Perf.	Individual Bonus		Division Bonus	Total Bonus
				Unadjust.	Adjusted		
26	AB	$400,000	4	$48,000	$47,277	$49,200	$96,477
25	BC	350,000	5	49,525	48,779	40,775	89,544
22	CD	270,000	2	13,095	12,898	24,750	37,648
22	DE	230,000	5	27,830	27,412	24,750	52,162
20	EF	220,000	6	28,600	28,169	18,585	46,754
20	FG	210,000	4	18,165	17,891	18,585	36,476
20	GH	200,000	3	13,000	12,804	18,585	31,389
Totals				$198,215	$195,230	$195,230	$390,460
Variance				$6,365	—	—	—

Table 7-42. Bonus by individual based on own and division performance

Individual Performance Only. If the executive's bonus is determined totally on individual performance, the calculations are similar to those in Table 7-43. Note also that performance in this instance is expressed to the nearest tenth of a percent. Using the individual's grade and performance rating, the appropriate interpolation is made within the figures on Table 7-31. This amount multiplied by the salary generates an unadjusted bonus. The sum of the latter is $28,310 over the allowable divisional total (i.e., $418,770 – $390,460) so each award is proportionately reduced by the ratio that $390,460 is to $418,770, or 0.932. These figures are reported in the adjusted column, and if desired, they may be rounded. Alternatively, rather than

Grade	Emp.	Salary	Perf.	Bonus		
				Percent	Unadjust.	Adjusted
26	AB	$400,000	4.2	25.2%	$100,800	$93,986
25	BC	350,000	5.3	30.0	105,000	97,902
22	CD	270,000	2.5	12.1	32,670	30,461
22	DE	230,000	5.1	24.7	56,810	52,969
20	EF	220,000	6.0	26.0	57,720	53,818
20	FG	210,000	4.1	17.7	37,170	34,657
20	GH	200,000	3.3	14.3	28,600	26,667
Totals					$418,770	$390,460

Table 7-43. Bonus by individual based only on individual performance

reduce each by the same percentage, individual adjustments could be effected as long as the total does not exceed the control total.

The essential difference between the combination division-individual approach and the individual-performance-only approach is that the first smoothes out bonus variations (at the expense of holding back on the outstanding performer and being somewhat generous with the marginal performer). The attractiveness of the combination approach is that it rewards group achievement (the one-for-all philosophy). This is critical if teamwork is needed and to discourage individual performance gains at the expense of the unit.

Midpoint vs. Actual Pay. A variation on both of these examples is to use the bonus percentage against the midpoint of the range rather than the individual's actual salary. The former emphasizes the importance of structure and will result in a greater award for an individual below midpoint and less for a person above midpoint than using actual salary. Tying bonuses to the midpoint emphasizes competitive levels of pay; basing the bonus on actual salary emphasizes the importance of current salary. The latter is an advantage to those better performers who have been in the grade longer and are therefore above the midpoint, but it is a disadvantage to better performers who are low in range because of brevity of service.

Bonus as a Percent of CEO's Award. Another variation on determining the individual award, particularly at the corporate level, is to do it strictly by a formula set for that year. Assume there are seven top corporate officers and that the normal compensation relationship among the seven (based on compensation midpoints) is as shown in Table 7-44.

Based on targeted net income of $100 million (an increase of $10 million over the previous year), a formula is set for the CEO that is expected to generate a $60,000 bonus.

$$\text{Bonus} = 0.0002 \text{ (net income)}$$
$$+ 0.004 \text{ (net income minus previous year's net income)}$$

The president's award would be set equal to 75 percent of the CEO's (unless there was a spe-

	Compensation Midpoint Ratio	Incentive Bonus Basis	
		Corporate	Group
CEO	100	100%	—
President	75	100	—
VP, Group A	60	50	50%
VP, Group B	50	50	50
VP Finance	40	100	—
VP Legal	35	100	—
VP HR	30	100	—

Table 7-44. Incentive compensation vs. midpoints for seven officers

cific reason to make it different). The staff vice presidents would also have percentages comparable to the pay relationship as shown above unless a specific need for a different relationship were important. If so, that would be reflected in an adjusted percentage.

The bonuses for the group vice presidents would be determined half by corporate and half by their own group performance. Thus, the VP of group A would not have 60 percent of the CEO's bonus for corporate, but rather 30 percent (i.e., 60 percent x 50 percent). Furthermore, since budgeted income for group A is $70 million (an increase of $5 million over previous year), the following formula might be appropriate:

$$\text{Group bonus } 0.00015 \text{ (group net income)}$$
$$+ 0.0015 \text{ (increase in group net income)}$$

Assuming the corporate and group targets were met, the bonus would be:

CEO Bonus = $60,000

Group A VP Bonus:
Corporate Portion = 0.30 ($60,000) = $18,000
Group Portion = 0.00015 ($70,000,000) + 0.0015 ($5,000,000) = $18,000
Total Bonus = $36,000, or 60% of CEO Bonus

Note that in the above example the group VP would have received a greater or smaller group portion depending on group performance. To the extent group performance was better than budgeted, the VP would have a bonus higher than 60 percent of the CEO's; to the extent group A's performance was less than budgeted, the VP's bonus would have been less than 60 percent of the CEO's incentive payment.

A comparable calculation can be made for the other group VP; note that the bonus percentages will have to be different from the other group VP in order to attain the desired relationship to CEO pay since group B's targeted income is $30 million (an increase of $5 million). Perhaps 0.00025 of sales while retaining the 0.0015 of increased net income would be justifiable. This would be a targeted bonus of $15,000 that, when added to the $15,000 for corporate (i.e.,

$60,000 x 0.5 x 0.5), would yield a total of $30,000 or 50 percent of the CEO's bonus.

If "income before allocation" is deemed more appropriate for determining a group performance incentive, comparable values can be determined in a similar manner through a series of trial-and-error calculations until acceptable formulas are developed.

It is imperative that such formulas be reexamined each year to ensure that values are still appropriate. In most cases, it will be necessary to make at least minor adjustments in the formula values. Such minor annual adjustments preclude major problems in future years.

Some companies are reluctant to give large bonuses for fear of poor shareholder relations. These companies are misdirecting their apprehension; the focus of concern should not be the size of the bonus but rather the relationship to performance and the amount of the total compensation package! As a matter of fact, it is in the shareholder's best interest that a large segment of top management's total compensation be in bonus incentives structured to reward success and penalize failures. How often would a corporation reduce the salary of one of its managers if the division did not meet its objectives?

Year-to-Year Pay Comparison. To illustrate that raising or lowering performance level can have an impact on total compensation, let's continue our example for the executive in grade 25. Table 7-43 showed that the executive received a $97,902 bonus for a 5.3 rating; assuming the same rating was used for salary purposes, the $350,000 salary (which was in the middle one-third) was probably increased 11 percent, or $38,500, using the earlier described performance matrix (Table 5-25 in Chapter 5). Thus, the individual received $486,402 (i.e., $97,902 + $350,000 + $38,500). Now let's examine the dollar impact of varying levels of performance the following year on current compensation using Tables 5-25 and 7-31. Table 7-45 shows the salary increases and bonus amounts for different levels of performance. Salary increases are for the middle one-third, on the assumption the structure increased sufficiently for the individual to retain the position; if not and the executive is now in the upper one-third, the salary range maximum of $395,500 (shown in Table 7-30) would limit many of the salary increases. Bonus calculations are based on current salary.

Performance	Salary			Bonus	Total	Variance	
	Increase	After Increase				Amount	Percent
6	$50,505	$439,005	$132,090	$571,180	$86,473	17.8%
5	42,735	431,235	109,942	541,181	56,474	11.7
4	34,965	423,465	88,190	511,655	26,948	5.6
3	27,195	415,695	66,045	481,740	-2,967	-0.6
2	19,425	407,925	43,900	451,825	-32,882	-6.8
1	11,655	400,155	22,145	422,300	-62,409	-12.9
0	0	388,500	0	388,500	-96.207	-19.8
Current		$388,500	$96,207	$484,707	—	—

Table 7-45. Individual bonus examples based on different performance ratings

Note that because the individual had such a high rating (and resulting high bonus) last year, anything less than a 4 will result in a decrease in total compensation (even though there will be a salary increase). Conversely, if last year's performance rating (and bonus) had been lower, there would still have been a possibility for less compensation (for a significantly lower performance rating) but the upside potential would have been proportionately greater. This specific example can be broadened to a full test of the "stretch" by examining all performance possibilities (current versus previous year) for the highest grade (e.g., 35) and the lowest (e.g., 20). Shown in Table 7-46 are the results of such a test. Note that there are 49 (last year versus current year performance) combinations, although pragmatists would challenge the likelihood of dramatic changes (e.g., 6 last year and 0 this year). However, even an examination limited to plus or minus one level of performance (e.g., 4 last year could be 3, 4, or 5 this year), shown in the banded area, results in appreciable change in rate of movement. For example, in grade 20 a person with a 3 rating last year would receive 2.2, 7.0, or 11.8 percent, depending on whether this year's rating was 2, 3, or 4.

In comparing the results from the two grids, it is also apparent that there is considerably more upside and downside risk in compensation at grade 35 than at grade 20, although repeating the same performance would generate about the same increase. For example, while a 3 last year would receive 7 percent if a 3 again this year in both schedules, the impact of being a 6 this year would be a 21.6-percent increase in grade 20 versus a 35.1-percent adjustment in grade 35.

Change in Total Compensation, Grade 35

Last Year's Performance	This Year's Performance						
	0	1	2	3	4	5	6
6	(34.6)	(26.1)	(18.3)	(10.4)	(2.6)	5.2	13.1
5	(31.0)	(22.1)	(13.8)	(5.5)	2.7	11.0	19.3
2	(26.8)	(17.3)	(8.6)	0.2	9.0	17.8	26.6
3	(21.9)	(11.7)	(2.4)	7.0	16.4	25.7	35.1
2	(16.0)	(5.1)	5.0	15.1	25.3	35.2	45.3
1	(8.8)	3.0	13.9	24.9	35.8	46.8	57.7
0	0.0	10.0	25.0	37.0	49.0	61.0	73.0

Change in Total Compensation, Grade 20

Last Year's Performance	This Year's Performance						
	0	1	2	3	4	5	6
6	(14.4)	(9.0)	(4.4)	0.0	4.7	9.3	13.8
5	(13.1)	(7.6)	(2.9)	1.7	6.3	11.0	15.6
2	(10.9)	(5.3)	(0.4)	4.3	9.0	13.8	18.5
3	(8.5)	(2.8)	2.2	7.0	11.8	16.8	21.6
2	(6.0)	(0.7)	5.0	10.0	15.0	20.0	25.0
1	(3.1)	3.0	8.2	13.4	17.2	23.7	28.9
0	0.0	6.3	11.7	17.0	22.3	27.8	33.3

Table 7-46. Compensation comparison using current year and last year performance

Stated another way, there is a greater proportional reward for improving performance in the upper grades as well as a more dramatic drop in pay for not maintaining performance levels.

The amount of impact a lower performance rating has on total compensation is a function of salary and bonus guidelines. The more spread in both for differences in performance, the greater the downside risk for reduced compensation if performance drops off.

The Balanced Scorecard. Typically, plans will use only financial measurements. As described in Chapter 2, while financial measurements dominate the landscape, there are other factors that can be used. Sometimes, they are even better than financial measurements. Robert Kaplan and David Norton addressed the need for multiple measures in what they called the *Balanced Scorecard*. It defines four areas of measurement: financial, customer, internal business processes, and learning and growth.

Striking a balance between short- and long-term performance periods, financial and non-financial factors, and internal and external factors is key. All are linked to the company vision, mission, and strategies. The process distinguishes between outcome measures (lag indicators) and performance drivers (lead indicators). The former reports degree of actual success; the latter suggest degree of potential future achievement.

Each to some extent relates to each of the six possible strategies identified in Chapter 1, namely: product/service innovation, employee intimacy, customer satisfaction, shareholder return, operational optimization, and community partnership.

The financial goals include internal and external measurements. The customer perspective includes acquisition, satisfaction, retention as well as measures of responsiveness in meeting and anticipating their needs. Internal processes are linked to financial and customer measures through productivity and innovation. Learning and growth are linked to the other three by addressing the identified gap between what is needed and the current organizational capabilities.

For each of the four areas of measurement, Table 7-47 shows examples of measurements appropriate to the six business strategies.

However, the balanced scorecard should support and not substitute for management. Furthermore, not only should the goals be quantifiable, they should be consistent with the dominant focus of the business strategy. In addition, it is important not to overload the scorecard with too many goals or ones the participants cannot impact.

OTHER BONUSES

In addition to annual incentive awards, some companies have additional bonuses. These include: special accomplishment awards, executive succession awards, hiring bonuses, leave bonuses, retention awards, transaction awards, and transition awards. Let's examine each briefly.

Special Accomplishment Award

This award has the avowed purpose of recognizing any singularly notable accomplishment that contributes to the successful conduct of the business. The emphasis on accomplishment distinguishes such programs from suggestion system programs, where a recommendation on a product or process improvement is submitted and payment given in relation to some formula related to cost savings (e.g., 15 percent of the first year's net labor and material savings).

Typically, the special accomplishment award program has a number of levels. It may range from a token recognition award, often paid in non-monetary gifts such as dinners, theater tick-

Strategy	Financial	Customer	Internal/ External	Learning & Growth
Product/ Service Innovation	Percent of sales from new products	Anticipate new needs	Defect-free product/service	Identify market changes
Employee Intimacy	No loss of top performers	Helpful employees	Employee attitude surveys	Train for new skills
Customer Satisfaction	No product returns	Customer retention	Facilitate getting new customers	Provide decision-making information
Shareholder Return	Economic profit gains	Increased market share	Reduce cost of sales	Align incentive with performance
Operational Optimization	Reduction in cost of production	On time delivery	Shorten time to market	Provide new technology
Community Partnership	No EPA violations	Disposable discards	Environment friendly processes	Conserve environment

Table 7-47. Alignment of balanced scorecard with strategy

ets, and merchandise (perhaps with a maximum of $500), to the chairman's award for a major research discovery or outstanding financial contribution to the corporation (with perhaps a minimum value of $25,000). In between are various levels of departmental and divisional awards, all with different levels of accomplishment and payouts.

One problem with such programs is defining the level of contribution necessary to qualify for an award. In addition, financial controls and feedback procedures have to be established to ensure interunit equity.

Companies with such programs must ensure that they are not used to compensate for poorly performing short-term incentive programs. Normally, such misuse occurs only with programs that are approved within a division. A review of the number and size of awards by organization level, coupled with special attention to individuals repeating as recipients, should indicate degree of misuse. Because of their low dollar amounts (except for a research discovery), these awards are of little value to executives.

Executive Succession Award

Occasionally, a special bonus perhaps equal to salary is given to a CEO for effecting a smooth transition with the successor.

Hiring Bonus

A hiring bonus (typically for executive talent) is used to induce an individual to leave his of her current employer and join the hiring company. It may also be called a *front-end bonus*, *acceptance bonus*, or *sign-on bonus*. The amount is at least the cash equivalent of unvested payments left behind. It may also include a present-value estimate of future forfeited benefits as well as something extra to close the deal. This bonus can be very attractive and lucrative to highly placed executives. The award may be paid in installments and subject to repayment if the executive leaves before a specified period.

Leave Bonus

This is actually separation pay and is covered in some detail in Chapter 6 (Employee Benefits and Perquisites). In addition to a formal policy and an employment agreement, some companies find it so important to remove an executive quickly and without legal problems that a "sweetener" is added, occasionally exceeding the annual output of sugar-producing countries. It is sometimes called the *golden boot*.

Retention Award

In addition to or in lieu of deferred compensation, an executive may also receive an award (one-time or annually) that will be paid if he or she is on the payroll at a prescribed point in time. It looks a lot like a mandatory deferral of current pay except the award is usually in addition to current pay.

Transaction Award

A payment to executives who have successfully divested a portion of the business or integrated an acquisition is often called a transaction award. It can be expressed as a percentage of salary or in terms of the size of the business affected or stock price after the transaction

Transition Award

A transition award is generally used to retain an individual until a particular event has transpired. It may take the form of an executive succession award or a transaction bonus. Alternatively, it could be awarded to a key contributor whose presence is needed to close a business. Typically, the amount is expressed in terms of a portion of salary.

APPROVAL OF PAYMENTS

If a fund formula is used, it is typical to have the chief financial officer attest to the amount generated. The same would be true for financial performance targets (e.g., ROA). The compensation committee of the board of directors might take responsibility to approve the sum of all proposed awards (within an authorized fund if there is one) or simply the awards for the CEO and other executives named in the proxy, delegating responsibility for other payments to the CEO and his or her subordinates.

BENEFIT PLAN IMPACT

Over the years, more and more companies have included annual incentive payments as compensation for many benefit plans. The most significant is for pension plans. Most surveys show a majority of companies will include annual incentives in pension plan calculations, both defined benefit and defined contribution. Less popular is its inclusion in survivor benefit and other plans

SUMMARY AND CONCLUSIONS

Short-term incentives are an expense and therefore a charge to the company's income statement for the period in which earned. They are also tax deductible to the company and taxable as income to the executive. Proxy treatment is equally simple: they are reported for the year in which they were earned.

Although all companies provide salary and benefits (and possibly some perquisites), not all provide short-term incentive opportunities. By definition, results have to be measurable within a short period (e.g., one year). It cannot be assumed that simply because a company produces an annual earnings statement it needs a variable compensation plan tied to the results. The annual model cycle in an industry (e.g., automobiles) is a classic situation arguing for an annual incentive plan. However, to the extent eligibility goes beyond those making the decisions impacting on results, the plan shifts to a profit-sharing plan.

To be cost effective, performance must be commensurate with incentive. By definition, overpaying those whose performance has slipped narrows the pay difference between barely acceptable and outstanding performance. Unfortunately, some managers expect the bonus system to automatically preclude this from happening. They have confused the ends with the means. The incentive plan is merely a pay delivery system; it has no native intelligence. Certainly, it is unrealistic to assume that in developing an incentive plan, all possible conditions can be examined and factored into the formula.

To the extent the incentive plan correlates positively with performance, it will be possible to retain aggressive, results-oriented individuals—as well as attract new ones to the company. These are people who are more concerned with self-actualization and ego reinforcement than security. The mere existence of an incentive plan will not assure their presence; it is, however, the payoff that will determine their interest in remaining with the company.

Low bonus potential in problem divisions may also be a significant retardant in getting highly qualified executives to accept a transfer from a profitable division.

Some companies rely strongly on the noncommittal or "golden gut" approach of, "Just do a good job and we'll take care of you." Unfortunately, it is very difficult for an executive to identify strongly with this type of organization inasmuch as specific objective results related to bonus payment are nonexistent.

Companies with divisional allocations should be careful not to overpay profitable divisions and underpay unprofitable ones. Is it logical to pay a highly profitable division more than an unprofitable one if the former is losing market share while the latter is achieving a miraculous turnaround? In many cases, relative performance is more important than absolute. In addition, how much of the credit for success or failure should go to the present management team? Were they the decision-makers or were they simply in the chairs at the time the results were measured? Consider the executive who never held an assignment for more than three years, and in each instance, the unit showed marvelous results (only to sink to lower depths after the individual's departure). Was the executive the solution or part of the problem?

Consider the division president who agrees to an unrealistic increase in employee wages to settle a union contract and avoid a loss in sales. This action may place undue pressure on other units of the company regarding the size of their settlements or increases to non-organized employees. In addition, one must ask whether it is possible to pass these increased costs along in the way of price increases.

Because they can go up and down within a year's time, short-term incentive programs, more so than any other compensation element, provide the vehicle for reinforcing desirable performance and penalizing undesirable results. Unfortunately, because of design flaws and management reticence in administration, the degree of success in meeting this objective is more apparent than real. Conversely, it is not logical to adopt a short-term incentive plan where key decisions are few, results cannot be judged for years, only a handful of executives make the decisions (except perhaps for an active committee system), and a comfortable environment exists in which inadequate performance is seldom penalized.

Many plans fail because of poor performance appraisals and inadequate financial controls. However, the surest way to ensure plan failure is to have those responsible for administration not prepared to penalize failure (rewarding success is a problem only relative to rewarding mediocrity). The CEO and compensation committee must firmly believe in the incentive principle and be prepared to make it work. Lacking this conviction and resolve, the best plan is doomed to failure.

Because of the complexities of corporate responsibilities today, the authoritarian CEO is an anachronism; most decisions are reached by consensus among management committees. Given this climate, it is unrealistic to assume the CEOs will make unpopular decisions re-grading subordinate pay increases. Need for objectivity seems to increase with the distance from the rater and ratee! Most executives find it difficult to be objective with their own subordinates but fully expect them in turn to pay their subordinates in relation to attainment of objectives. Many a well-designed incentive plan has failed simply because it has not recognized this basic truth.

Companies with bonus plans generally are reported to be paying 20 percent or more for comparable positions than non-bonus-paying companies. For some companies, these additions to the executive payroll are cost effective; for others they are additional expenses that have little to do with pay-for-performance. The hypothesis that companies with incentives outperform those without has been challenged by many. It is possible to construct a study to prove that non-bonus companies outperform bonus companies. Nonetheless, others will argue that companies should not abandon pay-for-performance because of problems in performance measurement, but rather should work to improve the performance criteria.

One should be careful to avoid making the plan overly complex. A simple plan is probably easier to communicate and understand. An example of a simple but effective incentive plan was implemented hundreds of years ago. Typically, workers would add sand to the floor of a room when they were decorating the walls, gradually almost filling the room so they could work on the ceiling. To motivate a speedy removal of the sand, the owner announced at the end of the job that he had planted a number of pieces of gold at the bottom, near the floor, which were rewards for those who found them. Such a plan, however, will only work once. Next time the workers will begin searching the sand the morning after the job has begun, thinking the owner planted the gold overnight. Fortunately, well thought-out incentive plans are likely to last much longer. However, they too must be updated.

Note: You should not rely on accounting, tax, SEC, or other professional service statements in this chapter. You need to seek appropriate professional counsel for such guidance. Statements made in this chapter and elsewhere are offered as being illustrative to help you frame such further investigations with the help of counsel.

In the next chapter, we'll review incentives with a measurement period in excess of one year, appropriately identified as long-term incentive plans.

Chapter 8

Long-Term Incentives

The essential difference between long-term and short-term incentives is the length of the performance period; while short-term incentives are typically one year, long-term are multiyear in nature. Some would further break up long-term incentives into a mid-term (e.g., three to five years such as restricted stock and performance unit plans) and a long-term (e.g., more than five years such as stock options and SARs). However, this chapter will combine these latter two categories under "long-term incentives."

IMPORTANCE OF TYPE OF COMPANY

The type of company definitely affects the importance of long-term incentives within the company. While very important in for-profit companies, they are virtually nonexistent in not-for-profits. In the for-profit sector, publicly traded companies with publicly traded stock are at an advantage over privately held stock companies. This is due mainly to the more restricted market for securities. Shown in Table 8-1 is a variation of Table 1-16 (Chapter 1) and Tables 6-1 and 6-2 (Chapter 6). Publicly traded for-profit companies (unlike privately held or not-for-profits) place high emphasis on long-term incentives in the threshold and growth stages.

Plans use either a form of stock and/or cash. Stock plans may consist of publicly traded, privately traded, or not traded (i.e., formula calculated). Each can consist of full value or appreciation only. The full value may or may not require an investment on purchase by the executive. The possibilities are illustrated in Figure 8-1.

Long-term plans typically require some form of discounting to give them a present value and thereby permit valuation versus salary and short-term incentives.

All payouts are subject to ordinary income tax except where a cost basis has been established either through investment or making a Section 83(b) election to be taxed currently on a

	Market Stage			
	Threshold	**Growth**	**Maturity**	**Decline**
For-Profits • Publicly traded • Privately held	 High Moderate	 High Moderate	 Moderate Moderate	 Low Low
Not-for-profits	Low	Low	Low	Low

Table 8-1. Possible relative importance of long-term incentives under varying circumstances

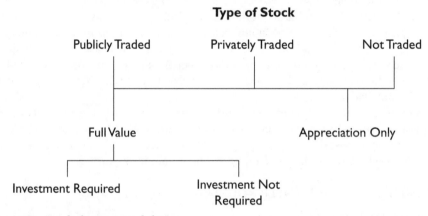

Type of Stock

Figure 8-1. Stock design possibilities

no investment plan when receipt is deferred to a future date. The company will of course receive a tax deduction on the same date the individual is taxed at ordinary income tax rates. The company has no tax deduction if the individual is taxed at long-term capital gains rate.

This chapter will describe the various types of plans available as well as their likely accounting and tax treatment. Design objectives are also reviewed since certain plans are more or less attractive depending on the objectives.

ELIGIBILITY

As with short-term incentive plans, eligibility may be determined using key position, salary, job grade, title, reporting relationship, or some combination of these methods. Typically, the degree of organization penetration from the CEO down is not as extensive as with short-term incentive plans if the eligibility basis is tied to those who have an impact on the long-term success of the organization. This criterion would relate to a *time-span measurement* of decisions and actions. Namely, what is the length or span of time that must pass before measuring the appropriateness of the decision/action? Typically, this correlates rather well with organization level since the longer-term, larger-risk decisions are handled at the top of the organization. For example, a decision to build a multimillion-dollar plant will not only take several years to complete but even longer before it returns the cost of investment. Conversely, the time lapse to determine whether a porter has satisfactorily cleaned an office is virtually at time the task was completed. In between these two extremes lie the other organizational jobs.

If the driving reason for eligibility is an egalitarian view that all employees should participate in the long-term plan (the time-span measurement would determine only the extent of participation), then eligibility might extend all the way down the organization. We saw in Chapter 6 that the most prevalent form of such broad-based plans is the stock option.

While methods for determining eligibility are similar to those discussed in Chapter 7, it could be argued that only those executives whose performance period exceeds a year (because it takes longer to determine the impact of their decisions) should be included in long-term incentives.

However, there are other reasons to include people in long-term incentive plans. Retention is one such reason. The multiyear nature of the plan, typically with multiyear earn-out periods before the recipient is eligible or vested in any benefits, make long-term incentives one of the more viable retention pay elements. Another reason for including individuals in long-term incentive plans when company stock is used is to promote ownership in the company. This should also be an incentive to do what one can do to increase the price of the stock. Such an objective also puts stock in friendly hands.

This is not to say that a portion of an executive's total compensation cannot consist partly of short-term incentives, but rather that a significant portion should be based on the longer time span for adequate assessment, especially for chief executive officers and other highly placed individuals whose decisions impact longer time frames in the future.

ACCOUNTING, TAX, AND SEC IMPLICATIONS

The accounting rules for long-term incentive plans are not as simple as with short-term incentives. At least two exceptions exist to the rule that compensation is a charge to earnings. As was discussed in Chapter 4, companies may decide to use the Accounting Principles Board's APB 25, which requires no charge to earnings for employee stock options whose number of shares and price are both known at grant date and the price (cost to executive) is equal to fair market value. Additionally, when the number of shares and the price per share is known at time of grant of a restricted stock award, the charge to earnings will be accrued over the earn-out period based on the price at time of award, not at time of payment.

As for taxation, the basic rule still applies. Namely, compensation is taxed as ordinary income when received and the company has a like-amount tax deduction in that same year. However, there are two basic exceptions: exercise gain on statutory stock options and long-term capital gains (when stock has been held for the required length of time). There is neither income recognition nor a company tax deduction on the difference between grant price and fair market value at time of the exercise of a statutory stock option. Considerable time will be spent reviewing this feature later in the chapter. However, such gains are considered tax preference income and are taken into account when calculating an alternative minimum tax. Secondly, companies receive no tax deduction on income gains to the executive taxed as long-term. This will also be reviewed in detail later in the chapter.

The Internal Revenue Code (IRC) not only requires shareholder approval of statutory stock-option plans, it also requires shareholder approval of long-term incentive plans affecting the CEO and other four named executives in the proxy to avoid the limit of a $1-million compensation tax deduction on total pay for each. This is detailed in Section 162(m) of the IRC and was discussed in Chapter 4

The Securities and Exchange Commission (SEC) defines insiders (those with information not available to the public that could affect the price of the stock), conditions under which they may buy and sell company stock, and what reports they must make regarding purchases, sales, and holdings. Additionally, the SEC details the manner in which long-term incentive plans must be reported for the five named executives in the proxy.

The reader is again reminded not to rely on accounting, tax, or SEC statements in this chapter. One needs to seek appropriate professional counsel for such guidance. Statements made in this chapter and elsewhere are offered as being illustrative to help frame such further investigations by the reader with counsel.

PLAN TYPES

Like their short-term cousins, long-term incentives are either dependent upon stock price (market-based) or independent of stock price (non-market based). This section will deal with both type plans. However, due to their nature, there are considerably more variations within each category than can be described in detail within the confines of this chapter. Nonetheless, the chapter should provide sufficient detail to enable the reader to create his or her own program. We begin with market-based plans.

PUBLICLY TRADED STOCK PLANS

Market-based plans typically use common stock, which is traded on one or more stock exchanges. Plans either deal with an option to buy or an outright grant of stock (thereby requiring no financing by the executive. The stock may be received either in the form of actual stock certificates or credited electronically to an account in the executive's name. This is sometimes called a *book-entry form*. We begin this section by reviewing the most popular form of market-based plans, the stock option.

Stock Options

A stock option is the right (but not requirement) given to a person (optionee) by a company (grantor or optioner) to purchase (exercise) a stipulated quantity (number) of shares of the company's stock at a stated cost (grant or strike price) over a prescribed period of time (exercise period) in accordance with stated eligibility periods (vesting requirements). Thus, there are five key dates in a stock option: date of grant; date to exercise or purchase; date option expires; date of actual exercise; and date of sale. Each of these will be examined further.

The use of stock options dates back to the 1920s or earlier. Some were granted at fair market value, and others were discounted. However, the length of the option period was typically three to five years. Little more information is available prior to the Securities Exchange Act of 1934 because of limited reporting requirements. However, in the early 1920s, the Internal Revenue Service (IRS) reportedly ruled that the spread between fair market value and exercise cost on the date of purchase constituted income to the employee. Then, in the late 1930s, the IRS focused on intent. If compensation were not the intent of added value, the spread at time of exercise would not be considered taxable income. This is similar to compensatory versus non-compensatory plans described by APB 25 in 1972. It also laid the seed for tax-qualified stock options, introduced with the 1950 Revenue Act. This legislation may have been aided by the reversal in the IRS's position in the mid 1940s, when it went back to its position of the 1920s, eliminating the question of intent.

Stock options are either statutory (qualified) or non-statutory, referring to the Internal Revenue Code (IRC). Those options that comply with Section 422 of the IRC are said to be statutory options and, therefore, qualified for favorable tax treatment. Namely, optionees are not taxed at time of grant or at time of exercise but only at time of sale. If held long enough, the entire spread between exercise cost and selling price could be treated as long-term capital gains. The company has no tax deduction on long-term capital gains,. However, if the optionee does not meet the required holding period before sale of a statutory option, the difference between purchase cost and selling price will be considered ordinary income. This is called a *disqualifying disposition.*

Options are non-goal-oriented plans (i.e., the company does not prescribe certain goals that must be achieved in order to receive payment). This is, however, a two-edged sword: market swings (probably more dependent upon investor view of equities in general than this stock in particular) may make the option very lucrative or literally worthless. For example, a rise in interest rates usually means falling stock prices as investors shift from the stock to the bond market.

Some believe that options only motivate recipients to increase the price of the stock, rather than improve company performance, which in turn should result in a higher price. Cynics argue that improved performance leading to higher stock price is about as successful as pushing on a string. Similarly, it is much easier to pull that string (and pull the stock price down) by announcing glum news, since the stock price is essentially future earnings discounted to a present value. With the stock exchange, SEC, IRS, and the Financial Accounting Standards Board (FASB) monitoring activities, stock price manipulation is virtually impossible without some form of legal action falling on the company

Many believe the market to be a good indicator of coming recession or recovery, namely that the market will drop prior to a recession. As the recession continues, stock prices increase in anticipation of a recovery. Once the recovery has been assured, the stock is vulnerable to dropping off again. This lag between economic performance and stock prices is important to understand when using company stock. Unfortunately, it is easier to understand than to utilize due to the uncertainty of predicting economic conditions, except on a historical basis at which time it is too late.

The consideration of downside risk is also important in stock option plans. The executive is placed in a precarious position when having to borrow to exercise the stock option if the intent is to hold it for some time. Consider this illustration: The individual borrows $100,000 at 10-percent interest to exercise a 1,000-share option at $100. If the market price were currently $160, there would be a paper profit (and tax-preference income, if a qualified option of $60,000). Will the dividend be sufficient to cover interest costs? If the stock starts to slide, concern sets in. With each drop, the bank becomes more vocal about additional collateral. Obviously, if the price drops below $100, the executive has a paper loss. To the extent this necessitates sale of the stock, the executive may have lost money at some point above $100 a share (based on the manner in which the gain at exercise was taxed versus the loss realized).

While there is no federal governmental requirement that shareholders approve a non-qualified stock option plan, it may be a requirement of the state in which the company is incorporated or the exchange on which the company's stock is listed. Furthermore, the SEC may not consider exempt a grant of stock options under a plan not approved by shareholders, and therefore, shareholder approval of stock-option plans is the rule, rather than the exception. Most shareholders want management to grant them the right to approve option and other stock-based compensation plans because of their dilution potential. In addition, shareholders must approve Section 422 stock-option plans for them to retain their tax status and Section 162(m) also requires shareholder approval for the tax deduction.

An additional question is whether or not to register the stock. In those companies that do not undertake the expense of registration, the executive must make an investment representation before exercising the option. The negative aspect of such a representation is that the executive cannot sell the stock for two years without incurring a high penalty discount on the value. Not many executives find this restriction an attractive motivational compensation technique.

If there is a stock split, the company adjusts the option accordingly. For example, an option for 1000 shares at $100 a share pre split is adjusted to an option for 2000 shares at $50 a share following a two-for-one stock split. In each situation, the cost to exercise the full option is $100,000.

If one company acquires or merges with another in a stock transaction, it is appropriate to restate the option price for purchase of the acquiring company in relation to their respective prices. This is called a rollover or a *re-denominated type stock option*. For example, assume company B's stock was selling at $100 and the executive had an option on 100,000 shares at $60 a share when it was acquired by company A. Accounting treatment depends on how the redenominated stock option is calculated. The Emerging Issues Task Force issued EITF 90-9, which states that no compensation expense is required because there is no new measurement date if: (1) the option spread is not greater, (2) the ratio of exercise price to market price is not reduced, and (3) the option and vesting terms remain the same.

The ratio of company B to company stock is .67 (i.e., $100 divided by $150). By adjusting the number of option shares by this ratio, the grant is restated at 66,666 shares. To determine the option price, one would determine the ratio of company B option price to fair market value. In this case, it would be .6 (i.e., .6 times $150). The total option spread of the redenominated option is $39,999 (i.e., $150 - $90 times 66,666 shares). This is not greater than the option on company B stock, which is $40,000 (i.e., $100 - $60 times 100,000 shares) and therefore meets the first EITF 90 test. The ratio of exercise price to market price for company B stock and company A stock are each 60%. Therefore the ratio of exercise price to market price has not been reduced and the second EITF 90 test has been met. Since the option and vesting terms remain the same, the third EITF 90 test has been met.

Alternatively, a part of the business could be spun off to shareholders. Spinoffs were covered in Chapter 1. Options could exist for both the former company and the spinoff. These are called *split type options* as the executive has a stock option in both companies. For example, if the company stock were considered to be worth $100 a share before the spin-off and $80 afterward (with the spin-off worth $20 a share), existing parent company options would be re-priced at 80 percent of value for 80 percent of the number of shares, with the unused 20 percent creating new subsidiary options, assuming a 3 to 1 stock exchange. If not, the previously described three-part test of EITF 90-9 would have to be met. They may operate independent of each other or be part of a single option or stapled option. Both stapled and independent stock option grants are subject to EITF 90-9. Alternatively, the spinoff executives might receive a concentrated stock option, namely all the options would be on the spinoff stock consistent with EITF-90.

Dividends are payable only on shares of issued stock. Therefore, shares under option do not receive dividends (of course they could receive dividend equivalents). The receipt of a stock-option grant is not a taxable event (at least in the U.S.); however, the exercise or purchase of stock under an option does have tax consequences (as will be discussed later). However, as of 1991, the grant date (not the exercise or purchase date) is considered a purchase under Rule 16(b) for purposes of the six-month test on "insiders." An insider is defined by the Securities and Exchange Act as any person who owns 10 percent or more of any class of stock in a publicly held company or is an officer or director of the company. In 1996, the SEC went one step further and eliminated the requirement that either the option or its shares had to be held for at least six months if a qualified transaction, thereby significantly broadening their 1991 ruling.

The long standing *APB 25*, issued by the Accounting Principles Board (APB) in 1972, established the *Measurement Date Principle*. It states that expense should be determined for stock-based plans on the first date the number of shares and the price paid by the recipient is known. Stock-option plans that state at time of grant the number of shares and a price equal to the fair market value (FMV) on that date incur no charge to earnings since the "bargain" is zero. However, when the number of shares or the price per share is not known at date of grant, there is a charge when both are known. For example, if the period under which options granted become exercisable is tied to some financial measurement (such as stock price or earnings per share), the company will have to take a charge to earnings for the difference between fair market value and option price when exercisable.

The FASB issued Financial Accounting Standard *(FAS) 123* in 1995, permitting companies to make a choice between APB 25 or a present value pricing model such as Black-Scholes to measure the compensation expense for stock plans. If APB 25 were used, the FAS 123 calculations would have to be reported in a footnote. Studies have reported that if the cost of stock options were charged to the earning statements rather than simply reported as a footnote, earnings would be significantly reduced for those with high use of stock options. In addition, a significant portion of cash would be used (negative cash flow) if some form of cash payment replaced the options. Whatever approach is adopted, it must be used for all employee stock plans. Once adopted, the company is expected to continue to use the method selected.

Optionee Eligibility

Executives. Who should receive a stock option? Typically, options are given to the CEO and other highly positioned executives. Beyond that, as with short-term incentive plans, candidates may be determined by base salary, job title, job grade (or job evaluation points), organization level, a banding of comparable level positions, or on a job-by-job selection basis. The degree of organization penetration from the CEO down is normally not as deep as with short-term incentives (except for previously described broad-based plans), although the extent of coverage is a function of corporate objectives. Very limited participation corresponds to the view that only a limited few can have sufficient impact on corporate earnings.

Rather broad coverage is consistent with a desire to place a large number of executives and managers "at risk" with stock price and thus more closely associated with other shareholders.

Admittedly, individuals further down in the organization may not have the same impact on corporate performance, but they may be more interested in effecting economies and improving performance if they are part owners. The price for broader coverage is greater dilution to shareholder equity since more shares must be placed under option. (Broad-based plans were reviewed in Chapter 5.)

If the company has a broad-based stock-option plan (extending eligibility to many if not virtually all employees in the organization), it must determine whether or not those executives selected for key grants should be included. The argument for inclusion of executives is that a broad-based plan is by definition an all-employee program. The argument for exclusion is that executives have their own plan and therefore should not be greedy. In addition, exclusion permits shares that would have been granted to executives to be available for the all-employee grant).

Other Eligible Employees. Additionally, companies might make a grant to new hires as a hiring incentive, perhaps to offset in part forfeited future compensation from previous employment. Stock-option grants may also be made to an employee for an outstanding contribution and/or future potential. Shown in Table 8-2 is a possible array of performance and future potential ratings. In this example, the two ratings are added together for a combined score. For exam-

Performance Rating

Numeric	Verbal	Description
4	Outstanding	Significantly surpassed or Surpassed over major obstacles
3	Superior	Surpassed over obstacles or Achieved over major obstacles
2	Very Good	Surpassed or Achieved over obstacles Almost achieved over major obstacles
1	Good	Achieved or Almost achieved over obstacles or Partially achieved over major obstacles
0	Acceptable	Partially achieved Little accomplishment over major obstacles
0	Marginal	Little accomplished Nothing accomplished over major obstacles
0	Unacceptable	Nothing accomplished

Promotability Rating

2	Excellent	Likely for more than one promotion
1	Good	Likely for at least one promotion soon

Table 8-2. Performance and promotability ratings

ple, a "very good" performance (value of 2) and an "excellent" promotability assessment (value of 2) would be added together for a rating of 4. These will be used later when we review size of the stock-option grant.

The problem with a promotability factor is that the chairman/CEO has no further promotion possibilities. Some companies address this issue by assessing whether—or implying that—their CEO could run a much larger, complex organization. Hmm, is this a message for executive recruiters?

Many companies do not grant options to those close to normal retirement age, although this may be counter to age discrimination laws. It would be better to make the grant but limit the exercise period after retirement. On the other hand, a few plans will permit the optionee to exercise after retirement to the full term of the grant, thereby removing another barrier to retirement. Some may want to limit such an extended exercise on the condition the individual does not engage in competition with the company, act contrary to any written agreement, or act in a way that the company reasonably determines to be materially harmful to it. Those who argue that the option is in part a reward for past efforts (especially a factor in determining number of shares) question even the 10-year limit on the option. Why not 15, 20, or more years?

Non-Employees. In addition to employees, companies can make grants to non-employees. However, these can only be non-statutory type grants. The most common group included are non-management members of the board of directors. A few companies have also made stock-option grants to suppliers, such as consultants. Some innovative companies may also include major customers, bonding them further to the organization.

Grant Transfer. Many options do not permit transferring or pledging ownership to anyone else. However, some companies (in their grant) give the optionee the right to transfer a non-statutory option, while living, to a family member. Some executives find it advantageous to pay a gift tax on the option before it has increased in value enough to draw an estate tax at time of death. However, the transfer does not also transfer income-tax liability to the new optionee during the executive's lifetime. Several issues need to be addressed. First, is the gift complete for taxation purposes when transferred or when vested? Secondly, what is the basis for valuing the transfer, spread between fair market value and option price, or some type of present-value modeling? The IRS has ruled on both of these issues. Revenue Ruling 98-21 states that a gift is not complete until the option is vested. Revenue Ruling 98-24 adds that a pricing model such as Black-Scholes should be used in determining the value of a vested option that has been transferred.

Table 8-3 illustrates who has a taxable event (and when) with a transferred stock option Recall that there is an annual $10,000 exclusion ($20,000 if joint with spouse). Amounts exceeding the annual exclusion would apply to the annual lifetime exclusion maximum. Gifts in excess of this amount would draw gift tax in the year in which the gift was made.

Frequency of Grants

Multiyear vs. Annual. It used to be common practice to grant options every three to five years; however, *annual grants* are now by far the most common action. Fewer shares on a more frequent basis minimizes the impact of rising compensation and swings in the price of the stock, as well as the visibility of large grants to insiders. If options are not granted on an annual basis, the company will need a mechanism for interim (off year) grants to new hires and the recently promoted.

	Is Event Taxable at Time of:			
	Grant	**Gift**	**Exercise**	**Sale**
Transferor				
Gift Tax	No	Yes	No	No
Estate Tax	No	No	No	No
Income Tax	No	No	Yes	No
Transferee				
Gift Tax	No	No	No	No
Estate Tax	No	No	No	No
Income Tax	No	No	No	Yes

Table 8-3. Type and timing of transferred stock option taxation

Catch-ups with Multi-year Grant Periods. When interim or catch-up grants are made between normal grant dates the regular stock-option-grant guidelines are adjusted by: the estimated future market value, the previous grant (number of shares and option price), the extent of lapsed time since the regular grant, and the current option price. These requirements are expressed in the formula shown in Table 8-4.

Assume the company has a three-year grant cycle. One year after the stock-option grant, one individual was promoted after receiving a grant of 8,000 shares. In addition, one person was hired into a grade that last year, during the major grant, called for a normal award of 10,000 shares with the stock price at $100. The stock is currently at $110, and the growth rate is anticipated to be 10 percent a year (or $133 a share two years hence at the time of the next major grant). The known values are shown in Table 8-5. Rounding the results would suggest granting 9,613 shares to the new hire and an additional 1923 shares to the recently promoted individual.

However, the formulas in Table 8-5 erroneously equate a straight-line relationship between

$$RT\,[NS_g(FMV - OP_m)] - [NS_m(FMV - OP_m)] = NS_c\,(FMV_f - OP_c)$$

RT = percentage of time remaining before next major grant
NS_g = number shares granted this grade in last major grant
NS_m = number shares granted this person in major grant
NS_c = number shares to be granted this person in catch-up
FMV = estimated fair market value of stock at time of next major grant
OP_m = option price of last major grant
OP_c = option price of catch-up grant

Table 8-4. Formula for interim of catch-up stock option

	New Hire	Promoted
RT	0.67	0.67
NSg	10,000	10,000
NSm	0	8,000
NSc	?	?
FMVf	$133	$133
OPm	$100	$100
OPc	$110	$110

Promotion
0.67 [10,000 (133 - 100) - 8,000 (133 - 100)] = NSc ($133 - $110)
                                        NSc = 1,923 shares

New Hire
0.67 [10,000 (133 - 100) - 0 (133 - 100)] = NSc ($133 - $110)
                                        NSc = 9,613 shares

Table 8-5. Example of stock-option catch-up grant

time and an increasing stock value effected by compound growth; nonetheless, this is not a serious flaw given the fact that the solved unknown is most likely to be rounded and otherwise adjusted by management judgment. In addition, formulas can be developed to use present value, if that is deemed appropriate. Regardless of the approach, the basic logic is give options to recent hires and promotions that equate to the major grant optionees *only for the remaining time until the next grant.* Using the above approach (or for that matter, any time-adjusted formula), the catch-up grant will be too generous vis-à-vis the previous major grant if the stock price is greater than assumed; conversely, it will be too low if growth in the stock price is less than assumed. In our example, the issue is plus or minus the assumed $133.

The problems of catch-up grants are essentially eliminated with the use of annual grants. In addition to responding to organizational changes, they allow for fine tuning with regard to the stock price—a form of dollar-value averaging. They also permit a form of deferred compensation similar to the cash award that has to be earned out over five years. By establishing a one-year waiting period, and then a maximum exercise of 25 percent of the total option in each of the succeeding four years, the recipient has a layered series of parts of five different options after five years. Furthermore, the executive will *never* be able to exercise all the outstanding options if terminating employment, except as permitted under the plan for retirement, disability, and death.

Exercise Period

Waiting Period. The stock-option grant specifies a beginning date (typically the date of the grant) and an end date (when the right to purchase the shares expires). Within this period (typically 10 years), there is a date when first eligible to purchase (typically called the *waiting period*) before any shares may be exercised. The grant will also specify the maximum number of shares that may be exercised on or after that date.

While most plans have a fixed exercise period (e.g., 10 years), some use a failure to meet stated financial targets or stock prices at prescribed dates during the exercise period to automatically cancel the option. This is one way to minimize, if not completely avoid, underwater stock options (i.e., the option price is above the market price). Some refer to this as a *truncated stock option* for its shortened period of exercisability.

Vesting. Many plans have a one-year waiting period after which all shares granted might be exercised. Others have additional eligibility requirements (typically called a *vesting* period). One form is the *cliff vest*, which sets a waiting period before which no shares are exercisable, and after which all shares are exercisable. A typical example would be five years on a ten-year option. Another version is the *installment vest*. A typical approach would be to vest 20 percent of the shares after one year, 40 percent after two years, 60 percent after three years, 80 percent after four years, and 100 percent after five years. Such vesting schedules are designed to penalize optionees who leave shortly after receiving a stock option since they will have to forfeit the unvested portion. However, they are not as severe in penalizing as the five-year or longer cliff vest. While many plans vest only in full years, some vest over shorter time periods (e.g., days, months, or quarter years).

If the option is intended as a form of "golden handcuff," then a long vesting period is appropriate. It could also be combined with an additional forfeiture clause such as the requirement that the optionee sell the stock back to the company at exercise price if the individual left before a stated period after exercising the option (e.g., five years). This is sometimes called a *clawback option*, which will be discussed in more detail later.

A variation of the cliff or installment vesting schedule is a *performance vest*. It prescribes the conditions under which an option will vest. An example of such a vesting requirement would be a grant of 10,000 shares at $100 a share that will vest 20 percent a year for every year that earnings per share increases by at least 10 percent over the previous year. A similar approach would be where the option would vest at 20 percent a year for every year the stock price increased 10 percent over the previous year-end close. When the option is not exercisable unless the performance criteria have been met, it is sometimes identified as a *performance requirement vest* or an earn-it or lose-it option. This is illustrated in Table 8-6. With this grant, if the stock price reaches $120, the executive can exercise 20 percent of the grant, locking in a tax base for later appreciation or wait until the price appreciates further before taking action. These are *forward vesting* grants and require a charge to earnings on the spread between fair market value and option price when exercisable under variable-based compensation accounting.

Another variation is the *backward vest*, where a stock option vests 100 percent on the earlier of a prescribed vesting date (e.g., eight years on a ten-year grant) or when the company stock trades at or above a specified dollar amount on average for a prescribed period of time

Option Price	Percent of Grant Vested	Stock Price is at or Above
$100	20	$120
	40	140
	60	160
	80	180
	100	200

Table 8-6. Performance required vesting

(e.g., 20 consecutive trading days). This is called by some a *performance accelerated stock option plan* (PAYSOP). The performance feature could be expressed in multiple terms. For example, if the stock option were granted at $100 (equal to fair market value), the option might fully vest in four years, or vest 50 percent when the stock reaches $125 and 100 percent when it reaches $150, if either are sooner than four years. Some performance vest options may use multiple performance measurements. For example, in addition to trading at or above $150 for 20 consecutive trading days, total shareholder return since date of grant must be at or above the average of a defined peer group of companies. This enhanced performance-vesting schedule rewards the optionee for a significant increase in stock price sooner. It is typically called *performance-accelerated vesting* and should avoid an earnings charge if properly structured.

Another situation in which the grant might be 100-percent exercisable sooner than the prescribed vesting schedule is at time the company is bought, or at least a stated portion of shares (perhaps 20 percent of the total outstanding) are owned by one individual or company. Called a *change-of-control vest* provision, it is common for it to be written into the option grant. Conversely, if a business unit is sold, rather than have the option cease on date of sale, extending the exercisable date for one year gives an individual a little more leeway in their financial planning.

Effect of Terminating Employment. Should the individual terminate employment, many plans provide a very limited exercise window (e.g. 90 days). In cases where the individual is quitting or being terminated for cause, the option may logically cease on date of termination. Periods of six months to one year, on the other hand, are not uncommon after termination due to disability or death. On the other hand, many non-qualified plans simply use IRS rules for qualified plans, namely, 90 days from date of termination except for disability (one year) or death where it runs the term of the option.

If disability status does not constitute termination of employment, eligibility continues until service ends, at which time the exercise eligibility will continue for one year unless the individual has retired. In this case, retirement provisions will apply.

As for death, some plans distinguish between death while an active employee or as a retiree. With both, the grant may be fully vested, but the while-active exercise period may only extend for a year whereas the while-retired would extend for the full term of the grant. A few companies may also take a more liberal view for retirement, allowing the option to run to its normal expiration. Additionally, some companies waive vesting provisions, making the full grant exercisable in exchange for an agreement that the individual will not engage in competition with the company or act in a way that is reasonably determined as materially harmful to the company. A range of possible exercise periods is shown in Table 8-7.

Stock Price. Option price is set in one of three ways: equal to market value, below market value, or above market value. Still the most frequently used approach is to set grant price equal to *fair market value* (FMV) at the time of the stock-option grant. Typically, this is calculated as being equal to the average of high and low prices for the grant date. Another approach would be to set the price equal to the closing price of the stock on the date of grant.

Market Value. Pricing an option equal to fair market value is a popular approach because there is no compensation charge under APB 25 if the number of shares under option are also known at time of grant.

	Time to Exercise (in months)		
	Modest	**Reasonable**	**Liberal**
Disability			
• But still on payroll (STD)	FT	FT	FT
• Off the payroll (LTD)	3	12	60
Death			
• While on payroll	3	12	FT
• While retired			
- retired	12	60	12
- other	3	6	FT
Retirement	12	60	FT
Termination			
• Involuntary			
- For cause	0	0	0
- Other	1	3	6
• Voluntary			
- Company concurrence	1	6	12
- Solely individual initiative	0	1	3

FT = Full Term

*All time periods assume such time shall available to exercise. If less time exists, that would control.

Table 8-7. Permitted exercise period for change in status condition

Below Market Value. For grants priced below market value, the price is either determined at date of grant or calculated during the term of the grant in accordance with a prescribed formula. An example of the first would be an option price set at $85 at time of grant when the fair market value equals $100. This makes it look like a stock purchase plan defined by Section 423 of the IRC (see Chapter 6).

This type of discount is used when a company wants an option to have immediate value. Discounts, which are calculated during the term of the option, use a formula prescribed in the grant. As an example, a $100 option price might be reduced by $1 for every increase in fair market value over $100. Thus, if the FMV was $150 five years into the grant period, the option could be exercised at a cost of $50 per share. If the FMV were $200 or greater, there would be no cost to exercise the shares, making it look like a stock award. This is sometimes referred to as a *yo-yo option* due to its up and down adjustments. Discounted stock options will require a charge to earnings amortized over the grant period. However, if the IRS considers the discount too deep, it may deem it a stock award, not an option to buy. Even a 50-percent discount may raise questions. If deemed an award and not an option, it may be taxed when the vesting requirement had been met even if not exercised.

Another variation to the discounted option is the *purchased option*, where the optionee pays the company on date of grant an amount equal to a desired discount. For example, to receive a

15-percent discount on stock price, the optionee pays the company an amount equal to the discount for the optioned shares. Assume a grant is made when the FMV is $100 a share. For a 15-percent discount, the grant requires the optionee to pay the company $15 for every share under option. The price and number of shares granted are both known on date of the grant, and there is no real discount since the combination of the $85 option price and $15 payment by the optionee equals FMV. Therefore, there is no charge to earnings.

Above Market Value. Setting the option price above the FMV on date of grant is done either with preset prices at specified dates (sometimes called a *premium option*) but more correctly identified as a *fixed price premium option* (FIPPO) or by a prescribed formula tracking percentage change in the consumer price index (CPI), the Dow Jones Industrial Average, or some other readily available index. Not surprisingly, these are often called *index options* but are more correctly defined as a *variable price premium option* (VAPPO). Both FIPPOs and VAPPOs are premium options.

Under a FIPPO option, prices are set for specified future dates. This can range from a one-time adjustment (e.g., price of $105 when at time of grant the fair market value is $100) to the far more difficult performance hurdle when grant prices are increased annually (e.g., by $5 a year for each of the 10 years). And although the future prices of the grant are known, some argue that since it is unknown at what price the option will be exercised, the option is not eligible for fixed accounting. Similarly, with a VAPPO option, since the future prices are unknown at time of grant, there will be a charge to earnings under variable-based accounting. In both situations the company can take a tax deduction on the spread between fair market value and option price at time of exercise since the optionee has a like amount of taxable income.

As a rough rule of thumb, option pricing models typically value a premium priced option at about half that of a fixed fair market price grant—less for an aggressive premium and more for a conservative one. To illustrate using the values in Table 8-8, if after four years the fair market value of the stock is $174.90 a share (a 15-percent compound growth), but the grant price of two shares was indexed at 10 percent, the gain would only be $28.49 (i.e., $174.90 minus $146.41), or $56.98. Compare this with the $74.90 gain over a $100 fixed-price stock option. Conversely, if the grant were indexed at 5 percent the premium-priced option would be worth

| Year | Compound Growth Rate | | |
	5%	10%	15%
1	$105.00	$110.00	$115.00
2	110.25	121.00	132.25
3	115.76	133.10	152.09
4	121.55	146.41	174.90
5	127.63	161.05	201.14
6	134.11	177.16	231.31
7	140.71	194.87	266.00
8	147.75	214.36	305.90
9	155.13	235.79	351.79
10	162.89	259.37	404.56

Table 8-8. Compound growth rate comparisons

$53.35 (i.e., $174.90 - $121.55), or $106.70 for the two shares. This is $31.80 more than one fixed price option at $100 a share (i.e., $106.70 - $74.90).

Stock Split. When a company makes a stock split, option prices must reflect the action. For example, a two-for-one should halve the price because the number of shares will be doubled. The net effect is that the cost to exercise the total option is the same.

Number of Shares. While broad-based stock option plans (see Chapter 5) may grant the same number of shares to all candidates, key person grants typically give the most shares to the chair/CEO and then proportionately reduce the number as the program cascades down through the organization. Determining the number of shares to give under option to each executive defines the absolute amount of opportunity for appreciation for that executive and the amount relative to other executives. The most shares are given to the CEO, while executives at lower levels of management get successively smaller numbers of shares. Classically, the CEO receives not only more shares than the next job down but also a greater award *relative to compensation.*

Methodology. Essentially, six possible methods may be used to determine the number of shares: exercise cost, historical value, future value, present value, stated number of shares, and stated percentage of total shares.

The *exercise cost method*, sometimes called *investment cost*, has historically been the most prevalent method, although its popularity is decreasing for reasons that will be reviewed. The number of shares granted multiplied by the price per share equals the exercise cost (or investment cost). If an option for 10,000 shares were granted at an option price of $100 a share, the cost would be $1 million. Since the size of the grant is relative to pay, the cost method requires assigning a value to pay to determine the size of the grant. More specifically, *pay* times *multiple* divided by *stock price* equals the *number of shares to be granted.*

It is rather easy to determine a competitive multiple for a CEO using proxy data from comparison companies. Multiply the number of shares granted by the grant price and divide by the CEO's salary—all three are reported in the proxy. The result is the *stock-option multiple.* Additional surveys and studies are available from consultants and others reporting multiples at various pay levels. The old rule of thumb was that the cost to exercise the annual grant should be equal to the CEO's salary. However, today it is not unusual to see exercise costs exceeding five times salary-plus-bonus.

Logically, the multiple for salary is higher than that for salary-plus-bonus (proportionate to the ratio of salary alone to salary-plus-bonus). When using such data, it is useful to know whether the average represented is the mean or the median; the former is often easier to calculate, but it is subject to influence by a limited number of very high or low values.

Logically, reported multiples are subject to pressure to decrease during periods of falling stock prices and to increase during periods of rising prices. Furthermore, higher multiples are more typical of mature companies than of their growth counterparts (i.e., the lower the presumed potential for increase, the higher the multiple).

In addition, an attempt should be made to separate companies relying solely on stock options from those who combine stock options with other forms of long-term incentive compensation. Presumably, the multiples for the first would be higher than the second. If the two were combined in a survey, the data would lead a company using only stock options to grant fewer shares than competitively appropriate. Conversely, the company using other plans as well would likely grant more options than competitively suggested.

Having identified an appropriate multiple for the CEO (and perhaps other key executives) based on survey data, the next step would be to determine how far down in the organization to go and what the multiple should be at that level. Using the 35-grade compensation structure identified in Chapter 7,the Brucell Company has determined 4.3 as the appropriate annual multiple for its CEO (grade 35) and that the options will extend down through grade 11 of the organization. Table 8-9 shows these multiples along with interpolations for other grades. It also expresses the multiples in relation to the salary-plus-bonus midpoint for comparison purposes with surveys that report data in that manner. It would be a simple process to convert these multiples to less frequent grant cycles. For example, if grants were to be made every other year, one could simply double the multiples. Those wishing a more sophisticated analysis might include a factor for the additional year wait.

The next step is to determine the number of shares, or *stock option targets,* to be granted using these assigned multiples. Based on a current market price of $105, the number of shares or the CEO (grade 35) would be 44,851 shares (i.e., 1,095,200 x 4.3 ÷ $105). Following the same methodology for all 25 grades (and rounding to the nearest 100) results in the numbers

Grade	Salary Midpoint	Multiple	Salary plus Bonus Midpoint	Multiple
35	$1,095.2	4.3	$1,390.9	2.2
34	971.7	4.0	1,224.4	2.1
33	863.5	3.8	1,083.6	2.6
32	768.2	3.6	956.3	1.9
31	682.3	3.3	846.0	1.8
30	609.0	3.1	749.0	1.7
29	545.3	2.9	665.2	1.6
28	487.2	2.7	591.9	1.5
27	438.6	2.6	528.4	1.4
26	394.8	2.5	471.8	1.4
25	355.7	2.4	423.3	1.4
24	322.6	2.3	380.6	1.3
23	292.2	2.2	341.9	1.3
22	266.1	2.1	308.7	1.3
21	241.8	2.0	278.0	1.2
20	217.9	1.8	249.5	1.1
19	198.8	1.6	225.7	1.0
18	181.0	1.4	203.6	0.9
17	165.7	1.2	184.8	0.8
16	151.6	1.0	168.2	0.7
15	139.4	0.8	153.4	0.6
14	128.1	0.6	139.6	0.5
13	117.7	0.4	127.7	0.4
12	109.4	0.3	117.6	0.3
11	100.6	0.2	107.1	0.2

Table 8-9. Stock-option multiples for annual grants

shown in column 3 in Table 8-10. It could remain a one-column chart, perhaps adding a zero or no-option column for those not performing satisfactory and/or about to leave the company.

The next possible enhancement would be to build a range around the targeted rating (i.e., column 3 number). This could be accomplished by adding columns 2 and 4. A further refinement would be to add column 6, now resulting in a schedule of columns 0,2,3,4, and 6. For more reference points, add columns 1 and 5 resulting in the full table shown in Table 8-10. A further step would be permitting the grantor to select a number between, rather than precisely under, the column headers based on performance (and possible promotability factors). This seven column chart can either key to a performance-only rating such as reported in Table 5-21 in Chapter 5 or a combination performance/promotability rating as shown earlier in Table 8-2. On the other hand, a very simple guideline could be constructed around the normal award (i.e., a "3" rating). Executives considered immediately promotable would have their multiple adjusted by 1.25 (providing a 25-percent premium). Conversely, executives considered either at their peak or no more than long-term promotion candidates would be adjusted by a 0.75 factor (a 25-percent reduction).

Grade	Number of Shares by Rating						
	0	1	2	3	4	5	6
35	0	18,000	36,000	45,000	54,000	72,000	90,000
34	0	15,000	30,000	37,500	45,000	60,000	75,000
33	0	12,500	25,000	31,250	37,500	50,000	62,500
32	0	10,500	21,000	26,250	31,500	42,000	52,000
31	0	8,700	17,400	21,750	26,100	34,800	43,500
30	0	7,200	14,400	18,000	21,600	28,800	36,000
29	0	6,000	12,000	15,000	18,000	24,000	30,000
28	0	5,000	10,000	12,500	15,000	20,000	25,000
27	0	4,400	8,800	11,000	13,200	18,600	22,000
26	0	3,800	7,600	9,500	11,400	15,200	19,000
25	0	3,300	6,600	8,250	9,900	13,200	16,500
24	0	2,900	5,800	7,250	8,700	11,600	14,500
23	0	2,500	5,000	6,250	7,500	10,000	12,500
22	0	2,200	4,400	5,500	6,600	8,800	11,000
21	0	1,900	3,800	4,650	5,700	7,600	6,500
20	0	1,500	3,200	3,950	4,800	6,400	8,000
19	0	1,300	2,600	3,250	3,900	5,200	6,500
18	0	1,000	2,000	2,500	3,000	4,000	5,000
17	0	900	1,800	2,250	2,700	3,600	4,500
16	0	700	1,400	1,750	2,100	2,800	3,500
15	0	500	1,000	1,250	1,500	2,000	2,500
14	0	400	800	1,000	1,200	1,600	2,000
13	0	300	600	750	900	1,200	1,500
12	0	200	400	500	600	800	1,000
11	0	100	200	250	300	400	500

Table 8-10. Stock option targets by rating

If unit heads are permitted to recommend the size of a stock-option grant for their subordinates, they should have a total pool to work with. Such an approach permits the management compensation committee to adjust the control totals up or down for division to reflect unit performance. This is illustrated in Table 8-11.

Employee	Grade	Award Range			Proposed
		Minimum	Normal	Maximum	
AB	26	0	9,500	19,000	10,000
BC	25	0	8,250	16,500	8,000
CD	22	0	5,500	11,000	6,000
DE	22	0	5,500	11,000	5,000
EF	20	0	3,950	8,000	3,600
FG	20	0	3,950	8,000	3,200
GH	20	0	3,950	8,000	4,800
Total			40,600	81,500	40,600

Variance to control total = 0

Table 8-11. Award range by individual example, shares of stock

Using a sum of the normal awards to construct a division total, the unit head could then work out the appropriate awards, using the range (except when a zero award was appropriate). The guidelines could be very specific (such as shown in Table 8-10) or in an open range from zero to a maximum with the normal or target award in the middle (as shown in Table 8-11).

This approach functions much in the same way as a salary range; therefore, the width is a function of the degree of deviation management wishes to make at a given salary level. Recognize that the greater the spread, the greater the overlap in ranges above and below the one being examined. Thus, it is more likely for a department head to get an award equal to or greater than the supervisor with a ±100-percent spread than a ±25-percent spread.

One should be cautious about using multiples without ensuring they are reasonably current since the curve will drift up and down in response to market value of the stock. To illustrate: a CEO earning $500,000 in salary-plus-bonus might receive $4.5 million worth of stock under option if the stock were selling at $100 (i.e., 4,500 shares), but it is unlikely a successor would receive 9,000 shares if the stock dropped to $50! Conversely, the successor would be happy to receive 4,500 shares even though the price, now having doubled to $200 a share, makes the award worth $9 million and a considerably higher multiple than originally intended. It is this very movement of stock prices that causes the most problems with the multiple approach.

The advantages of the exercise cost method are its ease of use and ease of getting competitive market data. The disadvantages include problems in adjusting during rising and falling stock prices, ignoring growth potential differences from one company to another, and difficulty in comparing company value with other present or future value compensation programs.

Historical value is the second possible method for determining the number of shares to grant. Easier than predicting what an option might be worth is examining on a retrospective basis what previous options have been worth. This is especially important in studies of competitive total compensation packages. Unfortunately, even here there is considerable debate as to the correct approach. The possibilities include: (1) total gain between selling price and option price and (2) spread between option price and fair market value on date of exercise.

The more troublesome of these two approaches is the first, utilizing total gain between selling price and option price. The complications of tracking options over varying time intervals and attempting to relate their gain to a specified time frame are awesome, but more important, it may be inappropriate. Once the executive has received the stock, when to sell is the individual's decision (except for the six-month limitation imposed on insiders); thus, the person is like any other stockholder in the company. In retrospect, the decision to sell may run the gamut from propitious to disastrous. Nonetheless, the selling decision is not a function of the executive compensation program.

Admittedly, using the spread between fair market value and option price on date of exercise as the basis for measurement has the logic of being consistent with tax rules. Unfortunately, the problem of using total gain is also a factor here. Since the date of exercise (within certain limitations of the grant) is at the discretion of the executive, it too is a market investment decision (similar to selling). In retrospect, the amount of the gain may either be overstated or minuscule in relation to the total gain (if any) realized at time of sale. The argument for using this approach is threefold: (1) the appreciation is real, (2) it is directly a function of the form of compensation, and (3) presumably, the executive is exercising at the point in time believed to be most advantageous.

Future value is a third possible approach. It simply calculates the spread between options granted and the fair market value at the end of a prescribed period. The advantages include a look forward rather than a look-back factor and the ability to differentiate on grant potential. The disadvantages include being more difficult and complex to calculate as well as more difficult to find market data.

Using Table 8-12, one can approximate the future value of a stock option. For example, if an option granted at $100 a share is estimated to grow at 10 percent a year, it should be worth $33 a share after three years (i.e., $133-100). This is useful when comparing the option to another long-term plan that is expected to run three years (e.g., a performance unit or share plan as will be described later in this chapter). Sometimes the *Rule of 72* is helpful. As a rough guide, a value will double when *interest times years equals* 72. For example, if one wanted to double one's investment in eight years, one would need a 9-percent annual compound growth rate.

Present value is the fourth method for determining the number of shares to grant. Essentially, it takes the future value described above and discounts it to its present-day value. This method is replacing the cost method for a simple reason: the desire to put a current value on the total pay package. The value of salary, employee benefits, perquisites, and short-term incentives are rather easy to determine. However, the unknown future value of stock options (and other forms of long-term incentives) is a problem. By discounting the estimated future value to present day, one can present a total pay picture. Present-value methodology is also useful when attempting to compare and contrast stock options with alternative forms of long-term incentives such as those reviewed later in this chapter.

Some argue that an option given at 100 percent of FMV by definition has no value. On the surface, this may seem valid, but it is simply not logical. Since the option is a contract to purchase in the future a stated number of shares of stock at today's price, its present value is a function of future stock price. It is without value only if the future market price is equal to or less than the current price.

Compound Growth Rate	Increased Percentage Value at the End of Specified Years (nearest 1%)									
	1	2	3	4	5	6	7	8	9	10
1%	1	2	3	4	5	6	7	8	9	11
2	2	4	6	8	10	13	15	17	20	22
3	3	6	9	13	16	19	23	27	30	34
4	4	8	12	17	22	27	32	37	42	48
5	5	10	16	22	28	34	41	48	55	63
6	6	12	19	26	34	42	50	59	69	79
7	7	14	23	31	40	50	61	72	84	97
8	8	17	26	36	47	59	71	85	100	116
9	9	19	30	41	54	68	83	99	117	137
10	10	21	33	46	61	77	95	114	136	159
11	11	23	37	52	69	87	108	130	156	184
12	12	25	40	57	76	97	121	148	177	211
13	13	28	44	63	84	108	135	166	200	239
14	14	30	48	69	93	119	150	185	225	271
15	15	32	52	75	101	131	166	206	252	305
16	16	35	56	81	110	144	183	228	280	341
17	17	37	60	87	119	157	200	251	311	381
18	18	39	64	94	129	170	219	276	344	427
19	19	42	69	101	139	184	238	302	379	469
20	20	44	73	107	149	199	258	330	416	519
21	21	46	77	114	159	214	280	359	456	573
22	22	49	82	122	170	230	302	391	499	630
23	23	51	86	129	182	246	326	424	544	693
24	24	54	91	136	193	264	351	459	593	759
25	25	56	95	144	205	281	377	496	645	831

Table 8-12. Effect of compound growth rate

The *Black-Scholes Model* is the most widely used model for estimating the present value of stock options granted by a company to its employees. In 1973, Fischer Black and Myron Scholes developed the formula at the University of Chicago. It includes: option price, price of an underlying security, stock-price volatility, risk-free rate of return, dividend yield, and expected term of the option grant. This is shown in Table 8-13, Designed to value shorter-term, freely traded options, typically of about six months, one could argue that it may not be appropriate for estimating the value of a 10-year option that is not freely traded or even transferable.

Other things being equal, the Black-Scholes (and other pricing models) will place a greater value on a higher-priced stock option. For example, a stock option priced at $81 a share may be said to be worth $32.69. Because of a significant decline in the price of its stock the following year, the company issues an option at $63 a share, which is given a valuation of $22.32 a share. This is illustrated in Table 8-14. Is there anyone who does not believe the $63 option is more valuable to the optionee than the $81 option?

Some have argued that option recipients place a much smaller value on the option than does the Black-Scholes formula. A few have gone further, indicating that if the Black-Scholes value is $33 on a $100 option, the more likely true value is a third ($11) or maybe half ($16.50)

$$c = Se^{-q(T-t)}Nd_1 - Xe^{-r(T-t)}Nd_2$$

c = Call option value
S = Stock price (current)
e = 2.71828 (exponential constant)
q = Expected dividend yield
T-t = Time to expiration
N_{dx} = From standard normal distribution probability
      that random draw is less than dx
X = Exercise or strike price of the option
r = Risk-free rate of return expectation

Table 8-13. Black-Scholes Formula for a call option

	Last Year	This Year
Term	10 Years	10 Years
Strike Price	$81.00	$63.00
Market Price	$81.00	$63.00
Volatility	26%	31%
Risk-Free Rate	6,526%	5,487%
Dividend Yield	1.83%	2.7%
Valuation (Per Option)	$32.69	$22.32

Table 8-14. Stock option valuation

that amount. It could be argued, therefore, that options "cost" the company more than the value assigned them by the optionee. In any event, is the option really a cost to the company or a transfer of value from the shareholder? If it is a transfer, why should it be taken as a charge to earnings as recommended by FAS 123?

The *binomial model* is quite similar to the Black-Scholes since it includes the market price of stock on the date of grant, the exercise price of the option, the expiration date of the option, the dividend yield of the stock, the volatility of the stock, and the risk-free interest rate.

Another variation is the *minimum option value method*. It calculates the present value as being equal to the current fair market value of the stock price discounted by a risk-free rate of return for the full period of the option's term as well as the expected dividends over the same period (discounted in the same manner as the market value of the stock). Essentially, it is the Black-Scholes with zero volatility.

Another model is the *capital assets pricing model*. However, it is not really a valuation model but rather a method to derive a growth rate and discount rate to be used in a "growth model" option valuation method. It may be the most widely used model to estimate the cost of equity. It is the result of an expected return on a risk-free asset plus stock price volatility in relation to the equity market times an expected risk premium.

Regardless of the methodology chosen, it is important to recognize the probable impact of increases or decreases in option-pricing variables. These are shown in Table 8-15. Only two (the option exercise price and the dividend yield) have an inverse relationship to the option value. Namely, if they go down, the option value goes up; the reverse is also true. For the other four, the relationship is direct. Namely, if the value increases, so does the option value; if it decreases, so does the option value.

Option Pricing Variables	Impact on Value of Option Based on Direction of Change
1. Option Exercise Price	Inverse
2. Length of Stock Option Term	Direct
3. Stock Price Market Value	Direct
4. Stock Volatility	Direct
5. Dividend Yield	Inverse
6. Risk-Free Rate of Return	Direct

Table 8-15. Impact of pricing variable on option value

The *stated number of shares* is often the result of earlier use of exercise-cost, future-value, or present-value methodology. Unfortunately, unless the stock price moves at a progression similar to the other four elements, it will result in either over or undervaluing this portion of the pay program.

The *stated percentage of total shares*, as indicated earlier in this book, is a typical approach for companies in the threshold stage, especially pre-IPO (Initial Public Offering). However, as the company matures it will shift to one of the other approaches described.

Updating guidelines is important. If the guidelines are not periodically adjusted, over time their value relationship to other pay elements will change as a result of stock price movement relative to increases in the other pay elements. This changed relationship may be desirable, but it should be planned and not the result of lack of review. Given the likelihood that stock price changes over time will not be a smooth progression, it would probably be inappropriate to change the guidelines based on annual stock-price changes. However, it might be very appropriate to adjust them annually, based on a trailing average of say three to five years, thereby smoothing out annual swings. Yearly averages based on daily prices would be better than simply taking a year-ending number.

Other Considerations. Having decided on an appropriate methodology to determine the number of shares to be granted for the normal stock-option grant, next consider other aspects of the grant. These include: performance and index options; in-lieu-of options; share-deposit options; dividend rights; mega-grants; cancel-and-reissue grants; and option reloads. Let's take a look starting with the performance and index grants.

If the stock option is tied to either a *performance* or *index,* as described earlier, it would be

Year	Fixed Cost	Variable Cost Based on Appreciation	
		5%	10%
10	$100.00	$162.84	$259.37
9	100.00	155.13	235.80
8	100.00	147.75	214.36
7	100.00	140.71	194.87
6	100.00	134.01	177.16
5	100.00	137.63	161.05
4	100.00	121.55	146.40
3	100.00	115.76	131.10
2	100.00	110.25	121.00
1	100.00	105.00	110.00
0	100.00	100.00	100.00

Table 8-16. Comparisons of fixed vs. variable option prices

logical to grant more shares than one would with a simple market-value grant, as the former have higher exercise costs and therefore less appreciation opportunity per share. This is illustrated in Table 8-16 where a grant at market value (i.e., $100 in this example) is contrasted to grants with 5-percent and 10-percent appreciation rates (either as the result of preset or indexed values). Look what happens after seven years if the stock is trading at $200 a share. An executive with an option on 10,000 shares at $100 a share has a paper profit of $1,000,000 [i.e., ($200 - $100) x 10,000]. An optionee holding 10,000 at $140.71 a share would have a paper profit of $592,900 [i.e., {$200 - $140.71) x 10,000], or $407,000, less than the person with a grant at $100 a share. For a paper profit of $1,000,000, the second optionee would have to have an option on 16,866 shares [i.e., $1,000,000 ÷ ($200 - $140.71)]. The third optionee is in an even worse position, having a paper profit of only $51,300 [i.e., ($200 - $194.87) x 10,000]. For a paper profit of $1,000,000, the third optionee would need a grant of 194,932 shares [i.e., $1,000,000 ÷ ($200 - $194.87)]. Thus in determining how many additional shares to grant, one must make an assumption on the break-even point in the future. For example, in year 10, if the price is $250 a share, 10,000 options at $100 would have an appreciation of $1,500,000 [i.e., ($250 – $100)x10,000], whereas the second optionee with a grant of 16,866 shares would have a paper profit of $1,470,041 [i.e., ($250 - $162.84) x 16,866 shares]. The third optionee would have no gain since the option cost ($259.37) is greater than the market value ($250).

The point is simple: if market value increases faster than option cost, the option will have value; the amount of value is dependent upon the degree of spread between the two growth rates. If market value increases more slowly than option price, there will be no appreciation gain.

One solution is to increase the number of shares covered by the option by the same percentage as the increase in option price. Thus, in year 10, the 10,000 share option would have increased to 16,284 (5-percent increase) or 25,937 (10-percent increase). The extent the option was worth anything would still be a result of how much market price exceeded option price.

Another type of performance stock option is where the option price and number of shares are unchanged. However, the option is not exercisable unless certain prescribed financial targets have been met (e.g., a compound 15-percent increase in EPS beginning after year three of the grant). A variation of this would be to introduce step targets (e.g., 25 percent of the option for a compound 15-percent increase, 50 percent for 15 percent, 75 percent for 17.5 percent, and 100 percent for 20 percent or more).

The same type of analysis can be done for the more conservative one-time, premium-adjustment grant. For example, if the premium were $5 for all years on a grant with fair market value of $100 on grant date, the adjustment would be far less dramatic. In our example, it would require 10,526 shares to equate to the $200 price with a $1,000,000 paper gain after seven years [i.e., $1,000,000 divided by ($200-$105)]. If the balance point is a $250 share price, it would require 10,345 shares with a $1,500,000 paper gain after 10 years [i.e., $1,500,000 divided by ($250-$105)].

In-lieu-of options are in addition to normal stock-option grants. The company decides to permit executives to elect to forego a salary increase, receiving instead a stock option, probably a 10-year grant priced at current market value. A simple approach would be to equate the present value of a salary adjustment with the present value of a 10-year, non-discounted stock option. It could be argued that the lost value of a salary increase to a 25-year-old is substantially greater than for a 55-year-old, assuming both stay to age 65—perhaps a low probability with the 25-year-old. In Table 8-17, the value of $1 received at four different ages (25, 35, 45, and 55) is extended to age 65 and then discounted back to the respective age.

Discount Rate	Discount from One at Age 65 to...			
	Age 25	Age 35	Age 45	Age 55
1%	$26.87	$22.26	$16.39	$9.05
2	18.12	16.56	13.46	8.20
3	12.26	12.36	11.07	7.44
4	8.33	9.25	9.13	6.76
5	5.68	6.94	7.54	6.14
6	3.89	5.22	6.24	5.58
7	2.56	3.94	5.17	5.08
8	1.84	2.98	4.29	4.63
9	1.27	2.27	3.57	4.22
10	.88	1.72	2.97	3.86

Table 8-17. Discount value in dollars based on time and interest rate

For example, a $1 increase in salary received at age 25 would result in $40 at the end of a 40-year period if no interest is paid on the $1 over the 40 years (i.e., one dollar a year). This $40 would have a present value of $5.68 if a 5-percent discount rate were assumed.

Table 8-18 expresses the present value in percentage terms. The example of a $1 increase at age 25 over a 40-year period assuming a 5-percent discount would result in the same $5.68 shown in Table 8-17 (i.e., 40 years times 0.142 = $5.68).

Discount Rate	Discount from One at Age 65 to...			
	Age 25	Age 35	Age 45	Age 55
1%	.672	.742	.820	.905
2	.453	.552	.673	.820
3	.307	.412	.554	.744
4	.208	.308	.456	.676
5	.142	.231	.377	.614
6	.097	.174	.312	.558
7	.067	.131	.258	.508
8	.046	.099	.215	.463
9	.032	.075	.178	.422
10	.022	.057	.149	.386

Table 8-18. Discount value in percentage based on time and interest rate

If, however, the $1 set aside does appreciate, then it is obviously worth more than a $1 years later. Table 8-19 shows the power of compound growth shown earlier in Table 8-12. Thus, $1 set aside and allowed to grow at a rate of 10 percent a year would be worth $45.26 forty years later. Using Table 8-18, we know that the present value of $45.26 received 40 years in the future (age 25 to 65) at 10 percent is the equivalent of $1 (i.e., $45.26 times 0.022 = $1).

Share-deposit options are another form of add-on stock options that some companies may consider appropriate, matching by prescribed formula the number of stock options that will be granted if the executive turns over to the company shares of stock already owned. Say the formula is two options for every share deposited. Assume also the FMV is $100 a share. The executive turns over 1,000 shares (worth $100,000) and receives an option for 2,000 shares with an exercise cost of $200,000. For the executive to recover the $100,000 worth of deposited stock, the price has to increase 50 percent to $150 a share. At that time, the paper gain will be equal to $100,000. As one might suspect, there are a host of design alternatives available regarding conditions (if any) under which the executive would be given back the deposited shares.

Dividend rights might be attached to non-statutory stock options, permitting the optionee to receive an amount equal to the dividend for each share while under option. These could be paid in cash at time of dividend payment or deferred (with a value equal to units of the stock) and paid at time the option is exercised. For example, a grant of 10,000 options carrying dividend rights will receive 100 additional units if a dividend of $1 a share is declared and the stock price is $100 a share (i.e., 10,000 times $1 divided by $100). If the full option is exercised a year later when the stock is selling at $110, the 100 units will be worth $11,000 (i.e., 100 times $110). Another variation would be to grant them as freestanding equivalents not attached to any form of stock, payable for a stated period of time. Alternatively, the right could be for paid in cash for each unexercised share—in this case $10,000 (i.e., 10,000 x $1).

A variation to the annual grant is the *mega-grant*, typically a pull forward of future grants. For example, a company with a practice of annual grants might believe the stock is due to

	Years			
Growth Rate	**10**	**20**	**30**	**40**
1%	$1.11	$1.22	$1.34	$1.49
2	1.22	1.49	1.81	2.21
3	1.34	1.81	2.43	3.26
4	1.48	2.19	3.24	4.80
5	1.63	2.65	4.32	7.04
6	1.79	3.21	5.74	10.29
7	1.97	3.87	7.61	14.97
8	2.16	4.66	10.06	21.73
9	2.37	5.60	13.27	31.41
10	2.59	6.73	17.45	45.26
11	2.84	8.06	22.89	65.00
12	3.11	9.65	29.96	93.05
13	3.40	11.52	39.12	132.78
14	3.71	13.74	50.95	188.88
15	4.05	16.37	66.21	267.86
16	4.41	19.46	85.85	378.72
17	4.81	23.11	111.07	533.87
18	5.23	27.39	143.37	750.38
19	5.70	32.43	184.68	1,051.67
20	6.19	38.34	237.38	1,469.77

Table 8-19. Compound growth in dollars for selected years

increase dramatically over the next several years. Therefore, rather than grant the CEO 45,000 shares (see Table 8-10) with additional grants each year thereafter, the decision might be to grant 135,000 shares (i.e., three times the 45,000) and not make another grant until three years from now. A more aggressive action would be to grant 225,0000 shares and make no additional grants for another five years. A range of three to five times annual grant is representative. The greater the pull-forward, the greater the potential opportunity, but the risk is also greater that there will not be a lower price opportunity in the future.

Some companies choose to make mega-grants without considering them pull-forwards of future grants. One rationale would be because a number of earlier grants are "underwater" (i.e., the option price is above the market price).

A *cancel-and-reissue,* or *re-pricing,* is another action focused on negating the underwater stock option. Rather than grant an additional option, the company acts to cancel outstanding underwater options and replace them with new grants at the current lower prices. In a true reissue, one expects the original expiration date to be in effect. A more liberal approach would be to restart the clock on a new 10-year period. The number of shares could be the same or reduced by some formula to an equivalency value based on the lower price. In other words, the present value at time of the original grant could be revisited using current price and remaining option period.

Another more liberal approach would argue for a higher number of shares (even assuming the same dollar per share increase over the coming 10 years) than was projected when the earlier option was extended. The increase would be based on recouping of lost time. For example, if an option was extended at $50 a share five years ago and the market price is currently $25, it might be decided to give twice as many shares since there are only five years left on the option.

The arguments for re-pricing include:

- They are of little if any incentive value to the optionee since they are below current market price.
- Re-priced options increase the hold on executives otherwise likely to be lured away by other employment opportunities.
- If fewer replacement options are granted, it will reduce the number of shares outstanding.

The disadvantages of re-pricing include:

- They remove or significantly reduce the downside risk that is supposed to balance upside potential in incentive pay, actually rewarding optionees for lower prices.
- They protect the optionees, but not the shareholders, from paper losses.
- They create a precedent for future bear markets (i.e., how does one not repeat the action under similar circumstances?)
- They decrease corporate cash flow and increase EPS dilution because the proceeds, being less, buy back fewer shares.
- Investors will not support the action and may sue if the plan does not specifically permit re-pricing.
- Employees not similarly protected in savings plans, stock purchase plans, and other benefit plans will view this as a double standard.
- Those who exercised options before the drop in market price will seek something to offset their paper losses.
- The public will view the action as one of excessive executive greed.
- "Pooling of interest" accounting may be delayed for two years since the SEC considers re-priced stock options as "tainted." However, with the elimination of pooling in 2001 by FASB, this is no longer a concern.
- FASB views each re-pricing as a new option, requiring an earnings charge for the difference in option prices. If the company re-prices an option within six months of canceling an outstanding underwater grant, the company must recognize an expense for the difference in price up to the number of shares of the cancelled grant. If the company guaranteed to offset any appreciation in stock price between market price on date of cancellation and new grant, it should be treated as an SAR for that period. This 2000 ruling (FASB Interpretation No. 44) slowed, but did not stop, re-pricings since companies could avoid an earnings charge by simply separating the dates of the cancelled and replacement option by more than six months.

Re-pricing may be more palatable if:

Top executives are excluded.
- Performance hurdles or future higher prices are included.
- Exchanged shares are economically equivalent, thereby resulting in fewer shares under option.

• The plan is approved by shareholders in advance of the action only if stock drops below a stated percentage of affected options (e.g., 50 percent for prescribed sustained period of time such as 90 days) and the plan is good for a stated period of time (e.g., five years). Companies may be required to include on the proxy a shareholder request that shareholders approve re-pricings prior to such an action. Many, however, find it more palatable to avoid re-pricing. Instead, they simply grant additional options at the lower price or even establish a phantom plan not using company stock.

In deciding whether or not one has a re-pricing issue, it is helpful to look at outstanding options in relation to current stock price. In Table 8-20, we see the 10 years of outstanding grants. If the current stock price were at $100, even though one grant is slightly below market value, one would not consider re-pricing. But what if the fair market value were $50? In this case, five grants are below market value. A generous approach would be to re-price all those above $50; a more conservative approach would be to simply re-price those that lost more than 50 percent of their market share. In this situation, only the $105 option would be re-priced.

Year	Under $25	$25-50	$50-75	$75-100	$100-125	$125 Up
1	$18.50					
2	$21.25					
3		$28.25				
4			$50.25			
5			$56.50			
6		$36.00				
7			$57.50			
8		$45.50				
9				$78.70		
10					$105.00	
Total	2	3	3	1	1	

Table 8-20. History of outstanding stock option prices

Alternatives to repricing include (1) do nothing on the belief that the stock price will rise in time for the option to have value; (2) give an additional stock option or restricted stock grant; or (3) buy out the underwater option with a restricted stock award. Doing nothing is a very reasonable approach if the option is not significantly underwater and/or there are a number of years remaining on the grant. Giving an additional stock option will avoid an earnings charge as long as it is a standalone grant or, if it isn't, does not expire for at least six months after the market price returns to the price of the original option. The latter is called a *collared stock option*. Buying out the original grant with a restricted award based on a present value model, such as Black-Scholes will result in an earnings charge but, as will be seen later when reviewing restricted stock awards, the charge will be fixed using current price over the term of the award. The advantage of a restricted stock award is its retention feature: if the person leaves before the restrictions lapse, the award is forfeited.

Option reload, sometimes called a *replacement* or *restoration* option, gives the optionee a new stock option after an existing option has been exercised, typically by tendering or attesting to the ownership of company stock. Option reloads act like a stop-gain order, capturing profits on the full-value grant and receiving a new option on the equivalent of shares tendered. The new options are granted at current FMV and typically run for the remaining term of the option exercised, while carrying the vesting requirements from the original grant date. This addresses the disadvantage identified in Table 8-22 (i.e., the "lost" 625 shares). This is highlighted in Table 8-21. Note that the two disadvantages identified in the stock-for-stock exercise in Table 8-22 have been eliminated. More specifically, the number of shares "at work" is unchanged (i.e., it is again 1,625), and ownership of stock is promoted two ways. First, the optionee needs to own stock and use it to exercise the grant and second, early exercise is encouraged as it will mean a longer exercise period for the second grant.

- Optionee has 625 options
- Option price is $160 per share
- Cost to exercise is $100,000
- Grant expires date of original grant
- Optionee owns 1,000 shares
- Current market price of the stock is $160
- Current market value of shares owned is $160,000 (1,000 × $160)
- Number shares "at work" is 1,625

Table 8-21. Example shown effect of a reload option after exercising 1,000 shares by tendering stock

Should the terms of the option be amended to add a reload feature, both FASB and the SEC will regard the "reload" as a new grant, not a continuation of the underlying grant In this situation FASB ruled that variable award accounting rules apply and that a charge to earnings must be taken for the difference in price. However, in 2000, FASB also stated that variable accounting was not required if the reload provision was part of the original grant. The plan must also consider shares tendered as available for future grants; otherwise, the optioned shares will be counted twice, more quickly depleting those authorized by shareholders and requiring a quicker return for many shares than would have been anticipated.

Some will argue that reloads do not contribute to increased dilution. This is technically correct; the number of shares in the market (375 in the example) plus the number in the reload grant (625 in this example) are equal to the total of the original option (1,000 in this example). However, missed in this argument is that without the reload, the dilution would have been decreased by the number of shares tendered. In our example, of the 1,000 shares under option, only 375 were used, thereby decreasing the dilution by 625 shares.

The "reload" may be attached to both statutory and non-statutory options when granted but only to non-statutory retroactively. Reloading a statutory grant will make it a non-statutory option.

Typically a "reload" is done only once. When multiple reloads are permitted, they often require a minimum appreciation in price appreciation and/or length of time to lapse before they can be triggered (e.g., six months or more).

Assumptions
- Optionee has 1,000 stock options
- Option price is $100 per share
- Cost to exercise options is $100,000 (1,000 × $100)
- Optionee owns 625 shares of stock
- Current market price of the stock is $160.00
- Current market value of shares already owned is $100,000 (625 × $160)

Option Exercise
- Optionee gives the company 625 shares
- Company gives the optionee back two stock certificates
  - One for 625 shares
  - One for 375 shares
- Advantages
  - Optionee has been able to exercise 1,000 stock options without using any cash
  - The transaction involving the 625 shares is a non-taxable event at the time it takes place; the 375 shares are taxable income.
- Disadvantages
  - Before exercise optionee had 1,625 shares "at work" in the market (625 owned and an option for 1,000 shares) but after exercise optionee has only 1,000 shares (all owned).
  - Does not encourage ownership of stock by employees

Table 8-22. Example of a stock-for-stock exercise

Another feature is that a company may require the optionee to hold the stock obtained on a reload until leaving the company or for a prescribed time period (e.g., 10 years), whichever occurs first. Some may require the optionee to have met any established stock ownership guidelines in order to "reload" an option, and/or the reload feature may expire at time of termination.

Reasons for using "reloads" include:

- They encourage stock ownership, if the reload requires tendering stock owned.
- Downside risk is reduced by in-the-money exercise to get the "reload."
- Dilution is reduced if tendered shares are not available for future grants.
- After-tax effectiveness is enhanced with exercise-and-hold strategy if there is a significant difference between the ordinary and long-term capital gains tax rates.

Reasons against using "reloads":

- Little or no spread between ordinary and long-term capital gains taxes would discourage the ownership required to tender stock.
- Stock ownership is not encouraged if optionee can get the reload by using cash to exercise the option. Shareholders are likely to vote against a plan permitting reloads.
- The SEC requires proxy disclosure, giving the appearance of an additional grant.
- Reloads increase administrative work.

- Additional communication work is required to ensure optionees as well as shareholders understand how they work.
- The FASB and the SEC require disclosure.
- Dilution is not reduced if tendered shares are available for future grants.

Stock Split. When a company makes a stock split, it must adjust the number of shares under option accordingly. For example, if it is a two-for-one split, then the number of shares under option should be doubled and their price halved. The net effect is that the cost to exercise the total option is the same.

Exercising the Option

Methods. If the terms of the option are met, the optionee has a unilateral right (but not a commitment) to buy the stock at the price stipulated. The exercise (or purchase) may be accomplished in one of several ways as long as they are permitted by the plan. These include: paying cash, tendering company stock, and/or simultaneously buying and selling the stock (called a *cashless exercise*).

Cash Exercise. If cash is used, it may come from the sale of company stock (using the after tax proceeds) or from other sources. Once "exercised," the stock is transferred to the optionee, who then decides whether to keep all, sell all, or sell enough to pay the taxes (assuming a non-statutory option).

Companies can use the stock option exercise proceeds (plus the cash flow from any tax deductions) to buy back a portion of the shares issued with the exercise of the option. The greater the difference between market value at time of exercise and grant cost, the smaller the percentage that may be bought back. For example, if 4,000 shares of an option priced at $100 a share are exercised when the fair market value is $200 a share, the company has received $400,000 from the optionee and could buy 2000 shares. However, if the company has a tax deduction on the $100 spread (and the corporate tax rate is 35 percent), then it has an additional $140,000 to buy back an additional 700 shares. As a net result, shares outstanding are increased by 1,300 shares, not the 4,000 exercised. However, if the fair market value were $400, then (using the same methodology) the company would be able to buy back only 2,050 shares, resulting in an increase in number of shares outstanding of 1,950 shares.

Should the company decide to give the executive a loan to exercise a stock option, it is important to determine whether it will be recourse or non-recourse. An interest-free loan may not be used to exercise a statutory option. A *recourse loan* will carry with it the right for the lender to not only recapture the stock exercised but also lay claim to other assets of the borrower until the full value of the outstanding loan is satisfied. A *non-recourse loan* entitles the borrower only to recapture the stock received from exercising the stock option.

According to the Emerging Issues Task Force (EITF Issue 95-16) fixed date accounting is permitted for both recourse and non-recourse loans if the interest rate is not variable and the loan is not prepayable. Under fixed date accounting, the grant price at time of purchase and the interest cost for the period of the loan are subtracted from the fair market value of the stock on the date of exercise. This amount is expensed over the period of the loan. If variable accounting is required, the loan amount plus the interest paid will be subtracted from the fair market value of the stock purchased on the date the loan is paid. If fixed accounting is permitted, the income charge is determined on the date the loan is given (not when paid).

For a brief period several companies permitted cancel-and-forgive exercises also called *rescissions*, before the regulatory agencies made it very unattractive to the company. This policy permitted the executive to undo an exercised stock option if the market value subsequently dropped significantly below the grant price. In essence the company would give the executive back the exercise dollars and reinstate the stock option under its original terms. It also cancelled a loan if one was granted to exercise the stock option. Some also called this the *disappearing stock option exercise.*

Tendering Company Stock. Rather than sell company stock and have to pay taxes, it is more advantageous to tender (i.e., turn over to the company shares of company stock owned) or attest (i.e., confirm in writing the number or shares owned whose value without reduction for taxes is sufficient to exercise the stock option). This is called a *stock-for-stock exchange,* or *stock swap,* enabling the optionee to defer tax on the value of shares tendered until they are actually sold. This form of payment may also be used to exercise a statutory option, however both the shares tendered and new shares must meet the one year and two year requirements of statutory options to avoid a disqualifying disposition.

A stock-for-stock exchange allows a company to help the executive avoid financing problems. Specifically, it permits the optionee to use stock already owned to meet a portion of the exercise cost. This is illustrated in Table 8-22. Assume the executive owns 625 shares of company stock and decides to exercise an option for 1,000 shares at $100 a share. The cost to exercise is therefore $100,000. Assume, further, the fair market value (FMV) is $160 a share at time of exercise. By transferring to the company the 625 shares already owned (purchased at $30 per share), the executive meets the exercise requirement.

The executive would receive two certificates, one for 625 (replacing the one transferred to the company) and another for 375. Since the first was a tax-free exchange, the 375-share certification is considered compensation in the amount of $60,000 (375 shares x $160 FMV). This amount is the same as if the executive simply exercised the option with a check for the amount of $100,000. In other words, the difference between option price of $100 and FMV of $160 multiplied by 1,000 shares, or $60,000. The cost basis for the 625 shares remains $30 a share; the cost basis for the 375 shares is $160 per share (after paying the taxes).

Had the individual sold the 625 shares in order to obtain funds to exercise the option, the taxable income would have been $81,250 [i.e., ($160 – 30) x 625]. Had the sale qualified for long-term capital gains, and if that tax were 20 percent, the tax could have been as high as $16,250 (i.e., 20 percent of $81,250). Therefore, the additional cash needed to exercise the option would have been $35,000 since the net proceeds from stock sale would be only $65,000 (i.e., $81,250 – $16,250). Individuals may also wish to have sufficient shares withheld to meet the tax-withholding requirements of the exercise.

The IRS stated in Revenue Ruling 80-244 that an employee could deliver stock owned as payment for exercising a non-qualified stock option without incurring a taxable event on the unrealized appreciation of shares delivered. It separated the exercise into two actions. First was the delivery of owned shares in a tax-free exchange. The second was receipt of new shares at a cost basis of zero, representing the spread between exercise cost and the FMV of delivered shares owned. Since tax withholding is required on this spread, many choose to satisfy the withholding requirement by reducing the number of new shares. In 1999, the FASB stated that companies that withheld in excess of the minimum required must take a compensation expense for the amount of the excess.

At about the same time, the SEC amended Rule 16b-3, enabling insiders to engage in such transactions and also stated that shareholder approval of such a feature was not necessary. As a result, a number of companies not only incorporated this method of exercising stock options in their subsequent grants but also amended outstanding options to permit payment with company stock. However, companies had to be careful to ensure that such stock received was not "tainted" in the eyes of the SEC, as this would preclude "pooling-of-interest" accounting—a concern that disappeared in 2001 when FASB eliminated "pooling."

Tendering stock to exercise an outstanding stock option and then immediately retendering the shares received, continuing this virtual simultaneous exchange of shares received in ever-increasing amounts to exercise remaining shares is called *pyramiding*. It would be possible to exercise the option by tendering one share and then engage in the rapid-fire pyramid until the entire option was exercised. Since the tendered stock has not been owned for at least six months, the company is subject to recognize a charge to earnings on appreciation. Furthermore, such an action would be precluded for 16(b) executives.

Shown in Table 8-23 is an example of a stock-for-stock exercise combined with a "reload" grant. The two disadvantages shown in Table 8-22 have been negated, namely, "shares at work"

Assumptions
- Optionee has 1,000 stock options
- Option price is $100 per share
- Cost to exercise options is $100,000 (1,000 × $100)
- Optionee *owns* 625 shares of stock
- Current market price of the stock is $160
- Current market value of shares already owned is $100,000 (625 × $160)

Exercise of the Stock Option
- Optionee gives the company 625 shares
- Company gives the optionee back two stock certificates
  - one for 625 shares
  - one for 375 shares
- Company also gives the employee a new stock option grant on 625 shares at the current market price of $100 per share

Advantages
- Both *before exercise* and *after exercise* the optionee has 1,625 shares "at work" in the market
- Encourages early exercise of valuable options *and* the retention of shares because shares will be needed for subsequent reload exercises
- Employee has been able to exercise 1,000 stock options without using any cash
- The entire transaction is a non-taxable event at the time it takes place

Disadvantages
- Use will result in larger number of stock option grants reported in the company's annual report and proxy statement
- Use will more quickly deplete shares available for use, both requiring a quicker return to shareholders unless tendered shares are available for reuse

---

Table 8-23. Example of a stock-for-stock provision with a reload feature

and ownership issues. However, two new potential disadvantages have been added, namely, proxy disclosure and shares available for use.

Shown in Table 8-24, the before- and after-exercise positions of an optionee with and without a "reload" grant are highlighted

Before Exercise	Share Status	After Exercise	
		Without Reload	With Reload
625	Shares Owned	1,000	1,000
1,000	Under Option	—	625
1,625	Total at Work	1,000	1,625

Table 8-24. Before-and-after stock option exercise look

Cashless Exercise. If the optionee wishes simply to receive the after-tax appreciation in stock price over option price, the cashless exercise is the most efficient method. As the words imply, the optionee does not have to put up the cash to exercise the option but instead borrows the needed monies from a broker to exercise the options and then has the broker sell those shares.

Cashless exercises became possible in late 1987 when the Federal Reserve Board amended Regulation T, permitting brokers to loan money using unexercised stock options as collateral. Prior to this change, the broker could use as collateral only stock or other assets already owned by the buyer.

If the executive chooses not to borrow money from the broker to exercise the option but merely receives the appreciation (less tax withholding) in cash or shares of stock, the transaction is sometimes called an *immaculate exercise* (perhaps because it is so clean). However, since it functions as an SAR, companies must be very careful they do not lose grant date accounting. The presumption that executives will choose this exercise method rather than cash, cashless (with broker loan) or stock-for-stock must be overcome; otherwise grants may be subject to variable accounting like SARs.

In 1991, the Securities and Exchange Commission significantly reduced the requirements and restraints of the "short swing" insider trading rules under Section 16 of the Securities Exchange Act of 1934. This section applies to insiders, defined as officers, directors, and those owning 10 percent or more of publicly traded companies. It defined the purchase date of a stock option as the date on which it was granted, not the date on which it was exercised, thereby making it possible to exercise and sell the option on the same date without violating six month, short-swing rules. The action steps and their sequence are described in Table 8-25. In many cases, steps 7 and 8 are electronic rather than paper transactions.

Tax Liability Deferral

The exercise of a non-statutory (i.e., non-qualified) stock option triggers a taxable event regardless of whether the cost obligation is satisfied by cash or with stock. However, *tax-liability deferral* is possible if elected at least six months prior to exercise of the option.

As shown in Table 8-26, the optionee holds a stock option for 1,000 shares at a grant price

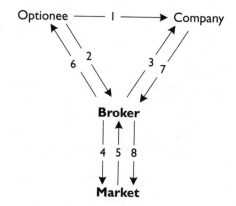

1. Optionee notifies company to exercise the option and send stock to broker.
2. Optionee borrows money from broker to cover exercise cost and tells broker to sell the shares being exercised paying company the option price
3. Broker sends check to company (for option price and withholding).
4. Broker sells stock.
5. Proceeds of sale sent to broker.
6. Broker sends check to optionee for balance (less commission and loan interest)
7. Company sends stock certificate to broker.
8. Broker sends stock certificate to buyer

Table 8-25. Cashless exercise

of $100 a share—total exercise cost is $100,000. The optionee owns 625 shares of company stock worth $100,000 at current market value of $160 a share. The executive tenders or attests to the ownership of the 625 shares needed to exercise the full grant and, to avoid potential constructive receipt issues, selects an exercise date more than six months in the future. In addition, the optionee selects a subsequent future date when the shares should be delivered (and the taxable event recognized). Assume at that time the FMV is $210 a share, thus resulting in income of $41,250 (i.e., $110 appreciation on 375 shares).

Key points to remember in designing this feature include: use mature shares (i.e., those held for more than six months) to avoid variable accounting and an earnings charge; use unfunded share units rather than actual shares to avoid current taxation issues; and be certain exercise action is set for a date more than six months in the future while an active employee.

Permission to elect a deferral could be accomplished by permitting the action in the stock plan and/or by establishing an unfunded, executive-deferral plan that permits the deferral of stock-option exercise gains. While it may be best to do both, certainly the appropriate deferred-compensation plan should be in place. Nonetheless, the gain at time of exercise is probably subject to FICA, FUTA, and most importantly (because of no earnings cutoff) Medicare (IRC Section 3121).

With the six-month advance notice requirement, the transaction probably avoids SEC Section 16 issues. However, some may argue that the spread at time of deferral should be taken as a charge to earnings. This is questionable if only mature shares are used to exercise the grant and the deferred shares from the exercise are converted to units and paid in actual shares at some future date (such

Assumptions
- Optionee has 1,000 stock options.
- Option price is $100 per share.
- Cost to exercise options is $100,000 (1,000 × $100).
- Optionee advises company wishes to exercise option seven months from today and receives the stock two years after that date.
- Optionee owns 625 shares of stock.
- Market price of the stock is $160 at time of exercise.
- Market value of shares already owned is $100,000 (625 × $160).

Option Exercise
- Optionee exercises on prescribed date attesting to ownership of 625 shares valued at $100,000 (625 × $160).
- Company recognizes event and sets up deferral account for 375 share units.

Shares Delivered
- As requested, two years after exercise optionee receives the 375 shares (recognized at time of execise) plus an additional 25 shares (reflecting dividends) are given to optionee.
- Stock price is now $210 per share.
- Fair market value of gain is $44,000 [400 shares × $110 appreciation ($210 - 100 exercise cost)].

Advantages of Deferred Stock Tax Liability Include:
- Optionee has the benefit of ownership without taxation during the deferral period.
- Ordinary income tax may be lower at time of payment.
- Company's delayed tax deduction may be for greater amount.

Disadvantages of Deferred Stock Tax Liability Include:
- Optionee will pay ordinary income (not long-term capital gains) on the appreciation from date of exercise.
- Ordinary income tax may be higher than at time of exercise.
- Company's tax deduction is delayed and may be less (due to lower stock price and/or lower corporate tax rate).

Table 8-26. Example of tax deferral on option exercise

as retirement or other termination). The Emerging Issues Task Force stated in EITF Issue No. 97-5 that making an election at least six months before exercise to defer the option gain will not involve additional company expense. A new measurement date is not required unless the deferral is converted into something other than company stock, then it is treated as if it were a cash SAR.

These three methods (cash, stock-for-stock, and cashless) are compared and contrasted in Table 8-27. In this example, the current stock price is $160 a share and the option price is $100 a share. One can see that before the exercise, the optionee had 1,625 shares "at work" (625 owned and 1,000 under option).

After paying the $100,000 in cash, the optionee would still have 1,625 shares "at work"—all owned. In the stock-for-stock transaction, the 625 shares tendered (worth $100,000) would have exercised the full 1,000 shares under option. The executive would receive back the original 625 shares with their original cost basis and another certificate for 375 shares, representing

Executive Stock Status After Exercising the Option

		Exercise Methods		
Before Exercise	Share Status	Cash	Stock	Cashless
625	Shares Owned	1,625	1,000	625
1,000	Under Option	—	—	—
1,625	Total at Work	1,625	1,000	625

Executive and Company Cash Status After Exercising the Option

	Executive	($100,000)	—	$60,000
	Company	$100,000	—	$100,000
Increase in Outstanding Shares		625	375	1,000

Table 8-27. Contrasting the exercise methods

the appreciation (1,000 shares at $160 - 625 shares tendered at $160 a share or $60,000 ÷ FMV of $160 a share = 375 shares). In both the cash and the cashless exercise, the company received $100,000 cash, whereas the executive was out $100,000 in the first situation but up $60,000 (375 shares at $160) in the second. All of these numbers are before taxable income considerations on the exercise to the optionee or before tax deductions to the company. With the cash exercise, the company has an additional 625 shares outstanding, 375 more with the stock-for-stock exercise, and 1,000 additional shares with the cashless exercise.

Another device is the *cash supplement*. It provides the executive with cash equal to some percentage of the spread between option price and fair market value. If the objective were to ensure that the executive does not have to sell stock to meet tax liability, it would be logical to give an amount comparable to the spread (on the assumption the individual is in a 50-percent marginal tax bracket). Needless to say, this can be rather expensive to a company with extensive use of options, especially when the spread becomes appreciable.

A variation of the cash supplement is a *buy-back* program in which the company buys back a portion of the exercised option, lessening the executive's financing requirements and the dilution of equity to the company. Thus, an executive who exercised an option to buy 1,000 shares at $100 a share when the market value was $160 would have to dig up $100,000 to exercise the option plus an additional $30,000 (assuming a 50-percent tax rate) to meet the tax bill. If the buy-back were designed to simply provide sufficient cash to meet the tax liability, the company would buy back 188 shares at $160 a share (i.e. $30,000 ÷ 160). Such plans have to be examined very carefully for 16b-3 executives.

Forfeitures

Options that lapse (i.e., the period of exercisability is exceeded) are considered voluntary forfeitures. The typical reason is that the option price is "under water" (i.e., the option price is greater than the fair market value at time the option expires). Typically, these unexercised options are returned to the pool available for grant.

The other type of forfeiture is the involuntary. The most common type relate to a *clawback* clause in stock options or stock-award plans. It would require that all profits received by the executive within a stated period of time (e.g., one year) be returned to the company if during that period, the individual violated a non-compete clause or engaged in acts deemed to be injurious to the company.

Selling the Stock

Stock received may be held, passing from generation to generation, or more likely, the optionee will sell at some point in time. This sale is a disposition, and if the acquired stock was under a statutory grant, the sale is either a qualifying or disqualifying disposition.

A *qualifying disposition* means the stock has been held the prescribed period of time. If this time period is equal to or greater than the long-term capital gains (LTCG) tax-holding period, the favorable spread will be taxed to the individual at the favorable long-term rate, but the company has no tax deduction. However, if the statutory holding period has not been met, the sale is a *disqualifying disposition*. The gain is taxed as ordinary income and the company has a tax deduction of like amount.

Obviously, if the form of exercise is a cashless exercise, the disposition occurred at time of exercise.

Companies wanting the executive to retain stock acquired may either motivate them to hold on to the stock or put restrictions in place that must be met before the stock could be sold. An example of an incentive to hold would be to award restricted shares in some formula (e.g., one for every 10 shares acquired). Restrictions would lapse after a stated number of years or after a stated number of shares had been acquired. Restrictions on sale without company approval could be attached either to time requirements or stated level of share ownership.

History of Statutory Stock Options

The first stock option form receiving favorable tax treatment was the "restricted" option as defined in Section 424 of the Internal Revenue Code. It came into being with the Revenue Act of 1950 and lasted until the Revenue Act of 1964, when it was replaced by the "qualified" option. The "qualified" option lasted until the Tax Reform Act of 1976 legislated it out of existence (the burial was on May 21, 1981). However, it also was subjected to heavy attack by changes in the 1969 Tax Reform Act. Like Lazarus, the qualified stock option returned to the world of the living in the form of the "Incentive Stock Option" with the 1981 Economic Recovery Act.

The essential features of the early restricted option in the *Revenue Act of 1950* included: (1) an option price as low as 85 percent of market value at time of grant, (2) capital gains treatment on the difference between market value at time of sale and option price for stock held more than *six months* after exercise and more than two years after date of grant, (3) a period as long as *10 years* during which the grant could be exercised, and (4) *no restriction* as to which sequence options need be exercised in.

The Revenue Act of 1964 introduced a new form of statutory option (i.e., "qualified"), while terminating the restricted form. Like the restricted option, the qualified imposed no tax liability on the holder at either time of grant or time of exercise. However, (1) the grant could not be for less than *100 percent* of market value at time of grant, (2) the option period could not exceed *five years*, (3) an option could not be exercised while the holder had an earlier-granted, qualified option outstanding at a higher price, and (4) capital gains treatment was available only if the stock was held for more than *three years*. If the stock was not held for more than three years, the executive was considered to have made a disqualifying disposition and the spread at exercise was taxable in the year of sale. At that point, the company took a like amount of deduction for tax purposes.

Thus, while the qualified option was not as attractive as its predecessor, it was still more palatable than anything else, given (1) a rather favorable growth in stock prices and (2) marginal tax rates as high as 70 percent (91 percent before the 1964 Revenue Act).

The 1969 Tax Reform Act took three further swings at the attractiveness of the qualified option. First, it lowered the maximum marginal tax rate from 70 percent to 50 percent on earned income (namely, payment arising out of employment), thereby making cash more attractive.

Second, the long-term capital gains tax maximum of 25 percent was increased to one-half the ordinary income tax rate (maximum 70 percent) except for the first $50,000, which was still subject to a 25 percent rate. Thus, the tax spread between salary and bonus versus stock option was reduced from a difference of 45 percentage points (70 percent versus 25 percent) to a difference of 15 percentage points (50 percent versus 35 percent).

Third, it introduced a new form of tax—an alternative minimum tax (AMT) that would apply to certain items (i.e., preference income). This tax preference income (TPI) would be taxed at the rate of 10 percent above a $30,000 exclusion. However, this exclusion was further increased by the amount of tax liability for the current and up to seven prior years. The spread between market value and option price on the date a qualified option was exercised met the definition of tax preference income (unless sold within the same tax year), as did one-half of the long-term capital gains at time of sale.

Assume the executive exercised the option, and the "spread" equaled $50,000. Further, assume that the individual paid $22,000 in federal taxes. Since the $30,000 exclusion plus the tax liability exceeded the TPI, there was no tax liability. However, any TPI over the $30,000 exclusion reduced dollar-for-dollar earned income subject to the 50- percent maximum tax, thus making it subject to a possible 20-point increase in taxes.

In spite of prophecies that the qualified option was dead, it continued to be a viable part of the compensation program—especially for those under the 50-percent maximum tax bracket—primarily because the stock market continued to produce profits.

However, a later downturn in the stock market was coupled with the 1976 Tax Reform Act, which legislated the qualified stock option out of existence on May 20, 1981. Any qualified stock options that were not exercised by that date were taxed as non-qualified stock options. Furthermore, it made use of such options less attractive during their remaining life by (1) eliminating the $30,000 annual TPI exemption, (2) increasing the AMT to 15 percent, and (3) lowering the overall TPI exemption to the greater of $10,000 or one-half of the regular income tax for the current year (the carryover of unused previous year's credit was eliminated).

The Conference Report accompanying the 1976 Tax Reform Act requested the IRS to develop and promulgate rules that would govern an individual's election to have the option valued at time of grant rather than exercise and sale. In addition to the option price and length of the option, some estimation of future earnings of the company was to be considered. To date, the IRS has been reluctant to take this action, perhaps since the future aspects of the company's success make it unlikely that the value will be "readily ascertainable" as required in Section 83(3).

The 1978 Revenue Act reduced the portion of long-term gains subject to taxes from half to

40 percent, thus effectively lowering the maximum capital gains tax from 35 percent (i.e., 50 percent of income x 70 percent tax rate) to 28 percent (i.e., 40 percent of income x 70 percent tax rate). In addition, the untaxed portion of capital gains income was no longer subject to the 15-percent preference tax. In addition, the reclassification of $1 of personal service income as ordinary income for every $1 of untaxed capital gain income was eliminated. However, these two tax features still applied to the difference between fair market value and option price at time of exercise for TPI purposes.

Each of these legislated changes made nonqualified stock options comparatively more attractive. In the eyes of many, the official death of the qualified option on May 21, 1981, was more a "mercy killing" than a vicious act. The period of mourning was brief as the 1981 Recovery Act (ERTA) restored the statutory stock option with the following requirements:

1. The optionee may not sell the acquired shares sooner than two years from date of grant nor within one year after exercise.
2. The optionee must be an employee and must exercise the option not later than three months after leaving employment, one year for disability, or to term for death.
3. The plan must specify the employees or class eligible, the number of shares available for grant, and be approved by shareholders within 12 months of date plan is adopted.
4. Grants under the plan may not be later than 10 years from adoption or approval date of the plan (whichever is sooner).
5. The exercise period may not exceed 10 years from date of grant (five years if the optionee holds more than 10 percent of voting power of stock outstanding).
6. The grant price may not be less than the fair market value on date of grant (110 percent if a 10 percent shareholder).
7. The values of the grant (i.e., grant price x number of shares first exercisable in a year) may not exceed $100,000 per person, with limited carryover to subsequent years.
8. The option is not transferable by the optionee other than by will or the laws of descent and distribution, and is exercisable only by the optionee during his or her lifetime.

ERTA also lowered the long-term capital gains tax to 20 percent and the maximum income tax to 50 percent. The 1986 Tax Reform Act lowered the maximum income tax to 28 percent but eliminated the favorable long-term capital gains tax. The Omnibus Budget Reconciliation Act (OBRA) of 1993 created a new top marginal tax of 36 percent but restored a long-term capital gains tax of 28 percent. The 1997 Tax Payer Relief Act lowered long-term capital gains rate to 20 percent for those assets held 18 months or longer while retaining a 28 percent rate for those held more than 12 months, but less than 18 months. A year later the 20 percent applied to assets held more than 12 months.

Comparison of Statutory Stock Options

A comparison of the new statutory stock options that resulted from the 1950 Revenue Act, the 1964 Revenue Act, and the 1981 Economic Recovery Act are shown in Table 8-28.

A Closer Look at Accounting and Tax Treatment of Stock Options

Statutory Option. The various actions of grant, vest, exercise, and sale of a statutory stock option are examined in Table 8-29. In this example, the one-year vesting requirement combined with retaining the purchased stock for an additional year meets the "two years from date of grant

	1950 Revenue Act	1964 Revenue Act	1981 ERTA
Option Name	Restricted	Qualified	ISO
Option Price	85% FMV	100% FMV	100% FMV
Exercise Period	10 Years	5 Years	10 Years
LTCG • After Grant • After Exercise	2 Years 6 Months	— 3 Years	2 Years 1 Year
Eligibility	—	—	Employee
Exercisability • Termination • Disability • Death	— — —	— — —	3 Months 1 Year Term
Grant Exercise Cost	—	—	$100k/Year
Restrictions	—	Exercise Sequence	Not Transferable

Table 8-28. Statutory stock option comparison

	Grant	Vest	Exercise	Sell
Time Lapse	Today	One Year	Five Years	Eight Years
Stock Price • Fair Market Value • Option Price	$100 $100	$110 $100	$160 $100	$210 $100
Individual • Ordinary Income • Long-Term Capital Gains	— —	— —	— —	— $110
Company • Tax Deduction • Expense	— —	— —	— —	— —

Table 8-29. Statutory stock option

and one year after exercise" described as an earlier requirement of Section 422 stock options. However, the $60 paper profit at time of exercise, while not considered ordinary income, is subject to the alternative minimum tax described earlier. Since the sale occurred three years after the purchase date, the $110 gain is all treated as long-term capital gains. The company has no tax deduction (there was no ordinary income) nor (in accordance with APB 25) does it have any expense, and it does have positive cash flow ($100 in this example). Had the optionee not met the more than two years from grant and more than one year after exercise requirements at time of sale, the optionee would have lost qualified status. The optionee would have had ordinary income on the spread between FMV and option price and the company a like tax deduction. This is the previously described disqualifying disposition.

Executives must be careful not to trigger a *wash-sale* transaction. This would occur if the individual acquired stock through the exercise of an option within 30 days before or after selling any stock of the same company at a loss. The IRS would deny recognition of the loss but will include the amount of the loss in determining the FMV of the stock acquired under exercise. However, the SEC ruled the grant date not the exercise date is the purchase date making it easier to avoid wash-sale problems.

Non-Statutory Stock Option. By definition, this is a stock option that fails to meet all the requirements of a statutory option and therefore is more flexible on grant size, ability to exercise, length of grant, and holding period. Like the statutory option, there is no tax liability at time of grant; however, at time of exercise, the spread between market value and option price is taxed income. Since it is taxed as income, the TPI does not apply at time of exercise although the gain at time of sale (assuming long-term capital gains treatment) will be subject to the alternative minimum tax without adverse maximum tax consequences. The holding period to achieve long-term capital gains is the same as for other holdings (i.e., currently more than one year).

Companies find the non-statutory option more tax effective since it has a deduction at time of the optionee's exercise. The only way for a company to receive a similar deduction under the statutory option is if the optionee sells the stock short of the holding requirement. This premature sale is called a disqualifying disposition and allows the company to take a tax deduction equal to the spread between market value at date of exercise and option price.

The most common form of non-statutory options is a non-discounted, 10-year grant, probably due to a carryover of the former SEC rules that an option for insiders could neither be discounted nor exceed 10 years in duration in order to be an exempt transaction at time of grant (i.e., neither a purchase nor a sale). With the lifting of the SEC no-discount rules, some nonqualified options were discounted. Using the same format shown in the previous section for statutory plans, let's review what happens with a non-statutory grant. We'll start with a *non-discounted stock option* with the same price and action dates used for the statutory grant. These are shown in Table 8-30. The only difference, albeit a significant one, is that at time of exercise, the optionee has an ordinary income-tax liability on $60. There is no earnings charge because the number of shares and price are both known at grant date, and there is no discount from fair market value on grant date. The company has a $60 tax deduction.

A *discounted, non-statutory stock option* is illustrated in Table 8-31. Everything is the same as the example in Table 8-29 except the option price is set at $10 below the fair market value of $100 at time of grant. Because of this discount, the company will have to take a charge to earnings for the $10, accruing it over the period of option until time of vesting. The individual has an additional $10 of taxable income at time of exercise and the company has $70 as a tax deduction.

A *premium-priced, non-statutory stock option* with the price (e.g., $105) set at date of grant is illustrated in Table 8-32. As the number of shares and price are both known at time of grant and that price is not less than fair market value at time of grant, there is no charge to earnings.

Time Lapse	Grant	Vest	Exercise	Sell
	Today	One Year	Five Years	Eight Years
Stock Price • Fair Market Value • Option Price	$100 $100	$110 $100	$160 $100	$210 $100
Individual • Ordinary Income • Long-term Capital Gains	— —	— —	$60 —	— $50
Company • Tax Deduction • Expense	— —	— —	$60 —	— —

Table 8-30. Non-statutory, non-discounted stock option

Time Lapse	Grant	Vest	Exercise	Sell
	Today	One Year	Five Years	Eight Years
Stock Price • Fair Market Value • Option Price	$100 $90	$110 $90	$160 $90	$210 $90
Individual • Ordinary Income • Long-term Capital Gains	— —	— —	$70 —	— $50
Company • Tax Deduction • Expense*	— ⟶	— $10	$70 —	— —

*Accrued until fully vested

Table 8-31. Non-statutory, discounted stock option

The spread between fair market value and option cost at time of exercise ($55) is income to the individual with a like amount as tax deduction to the company. Having met the holding requirements for long-term capital gains, the individual has a favorable tax rate on $50 of income.

A *multiple-priced premium non-statutory stock option* with the future prices fixed at the date of grant is illustrated in Table 8-33. Although the number of shares is known at the time of grant, the price at which it will be exercised is not known, therefore variable accounting and a charge to earnings of $35 at the time of exercise is in effect. The spread between fair market value and option price at time of exercise ($35) is income to the individual with a like amount as tax deduction to the company. Three years later, having met the holding requirements for long-term capital gains, the individual has a favorable tax rate on $50 of income (i.e., $210 - $160).

Time Lapse	Grant Today	Vest One Year	Exercise Five Years	Sell Eight Years
Stock Price • Fair Market Value • Option Price	$100 $105	$110 $105	$160 $105	$210 $105
Individual • Ordinary Income • Long-Term Capital Gains	— —	— —	$55 —	— $50
Company • Tax Deduction • Expense	— —	— —	$55 —	— —

Table 8-32. Non-statutory, single-priced premium stock option

Time Lapse	Grant Today	Vest One Year	Exercise Five Years	Sell Eight Years
Stock Price • Fair Market Value • Option Price	$100 $100	$110 $105	$160 $125	$210 $125
Individual • Ordinary Income • Long-term Capital Gains	— —	— —	$35 —	— $50
Company • Tax Deduction • Expense*	— ———————————→	— 	$35 $35	— —

*Accrued over period of exercise

Table 8-33. Non-statutory, multiple-priced premium stock option

In Table 8-34, we have a *non-statutory, index stock option*. In this example, the option prices are the same as shown for a multiple-priced premium option in Table 8-33 except those future prices were not known at time of grant, only the method for determining those prices over the period of the grant. Like the multiple-priced premium option, the company must accrue a charge to earnings over the option period for the $35 bargain cost at time of exercise. All other aspects are the same as the single premium priced option.

A *performance vest, non-statutory stock option* is highlighted in Table 8-35. In this example, it is similar to a non-discounted option as shown in Table 8-30. The only difference is vesting is dependent on attaining prescribed financial goals (e.g., stock price or earnings per share). In

Time Lapse	Grant	Vest	Exercise	Sell
	Today	One Year	Five Years	Eight Years
Stock Price				
• Fair Market Value	$100	$110	$160	$210
• Option Price	$100	$105	$125	$125
Individual				
• Ordinary Income	—	—	$35	—
• Long-term Capital Gains	—	—	—	$50
Company				
• Tax Deduction	—	—	$35	—
• Expense*	———————————————→		$35	—

*Accrued over period of exercise

Table 8-34. Non-statutory, index-priced option

Time Lapse	Grant	Vest	Exercise	Sell
	Today	One Year	Five Years	Eight Years
Stock Price				
• Fair Market Value	$100	$110	$160	$210
• Option Price	$100	$100	$100	$100
Individual				
• Ordinary Income	—	—	$60	—
• Long-term Capital Gains	—	—	—	$50
Company				
• Tax Deduction	—	—	$60	—
• Expense*	——————————→	$10	—	—

*Accrued until fully vested

Table 8-35. Non-statutory, performance-vested option

this example, that goal was met after one year. Since the number of shares is not known at time of grant (and the option cannot be exercised if they are not met), the company must take a charge to earnings for the appreciation at time the vesting requirements have been met.

A *non-statutory performance-accelerated stock option* is highlighted in Table 8-36. This example is similar to that shown in Table 8-35 except that the grant is not dependent on attaining prescribed financial goals. The option is exercisable on the earliest of the vesting date of the financial goals. Since the number of shares and the price of the option are known on date of grant and there is no discount from fair market value, there is no charge to the earnings statement.

	Grant	Vest	Exercise	Sell
Time Lapse	Today	One Year	Five Years	Eight Years
Stock Price • Fair Market Value • Option Price	$100 $100	$110 $100	$160 $100	$210 $100
Individual • Ordinary Income • Long-term Capital Gains	— —	— —	$60 —	— $50
Company • Tax Deduction • Expense	— —	— —	$60 —	— —

Table 8-36. Non-statutory performance-accelerated stock option

Why Stock Options?

For years, stock options have been one of the more acceptable forms of incentive compensation to shareholders because (1) the executive must put up some of his or her own money, (2) the value, like the shareholder's, is at risk with the price of the company stock, and (3) assuming no discount, there is no charge to corporate earnings. Options are a form of profit sharing that link the professional manager's financial success to that of the shareholder.

While such programs have been widely used in many companies, there are organizations where they are not available as a compensation device because the company stock is not publicly traded.

However, for those who are about to make an Initial Public Offering (IPO), moving the company from a privately held to a publicly traded company, there is a high degree of interest in large stock-option grants. Historically, stock prices increase dramatically in the days and weeks preceding an IPO. Ideally, key employees will have options at lower prices; however, such grants must be made with care. The SEC is likely to scrutinize grants made below the IPO offering price to determine if such options were really granted at "true" fair market value (FMV). If not, they are deemed to be "cheap stock," therefore requiring the company to take a charge to earnings for the difference between the option price and the deemed FMV of the stock on the grant date.

As stated in Chapter 1, stock options are extensively used in the initial threshold, or start-up, stage because of a lack of cash and the potential for long-term appreciation in stock price. As shown in Table 8-37, there are significant differences between threshold and later stages of the market cycle in terms of: reason for, eligibility, dilution, vesting, price, re-pricing, and definition of stock owned.

Since a company does not pay federal income tax on any profits it may realize in selling its own stock, stock options are expensive to the company in direct proportion to the realized value the executive receives in appreciation. Heavy use of stock options in such situations results in a significant loss of income to the company. For example, assume an individual receives an option of 1,000 shares at $100 a share. The individual exercises the option when it is selling at

Item	Threshold	Vest
Reason	Retention	Performance
Eligibility	Extensive	Selective
Dilution	High	Moderate
Vesting	Four-Five Years	One-Three Years
Price	FMV	Performance
Reprice (How?)	Share-for-Share ↑ Common ↓	Unlikely Prorated
Ownership Definition	Stock Held + Unexercised Option	Stock Held

Table 8-37. Variances in stock options by market stage

$160 a share. The executive has a tax liability on $60,000 (i.e., 1,000 shares x $60). Similarly, the company has a tax deduction of $60,000 or a reduction in taxes of $24,000 (assuming a 40-percent rate is in effect). If par value of the stock is $1, par value of $1,000 is added to the par value account for the additional 1,000 shares now outstanding, and $99,000 (i.e., $100,000 - $1,000) is added to the capital surplus account (also called the additional paid-in capital account) resulting from the savings in taxes, for a total increased retained earnings of $123,000. However, had the company sold the stock at $160, capital surplus would have been increased by $159,000 (i.e., $160,000 - $1,000). Thus, the option has "cost" the company $26,000 (i.e., $159,000 - $123,000) or the portion of the $36,000 gain not reimbursed (i.e., $60,000 less a $24,000 reduction in taxes).

Another way to evaluate the cost of stock options is to determine the extent of dilution to equity. A popular method for calculating this is the *treasury method*. This assumes that the proceeds from the stock option plus any tax benefit received are used to purchase shares of the company stock on the open market. Dilution is therefore a function of spread of market value over option price. For example, using the same 1,000 shares described above at an option price of $100, the company received $100,000 from the executive plus $24,000 (assuming a 40 percent tax rate) in tax benefits from the $160 market price. This $124,000 can be used to purchase 775 shares at $160 a share. Thus, the dilution of equity is 225 shares. The Financial Accounting Standards Board (which replaced the Accounting Principles Board in 1973) allegedly was considering excluding the tax benefit (since there is no charge to earnings under stock options) in a clarification to APB Opinion No. 15 (which deals with earnings-per-share calculations). However, FASB Interpretation No. 128, "Earnings per Share," reaffirmed the use of the tax benefit in calculating diluted EPS.

Stock Appreciation Rights

The *stock appreciation right*, or SAR, is another feature many companies used in conjunction with a non-statutory option. (Attaching an SAR to a statutory option would automatically make it a non-statutory option). The SAR permits the optionee to receive the appreciation of FMV over option price in stock and/or cash *without providing funds* to pay the option price.'

Type of SAR

The SAR may be granted in parallel (independent), in tandem (dependent), or on top of (additive) a stock option. A *tandem grant* would mean the exercise of one would proportionately reduce the other. If an individual received a stock option for 10,000 shares, exercising 4,000 options under a tandem grant would leave 6,000 options and SARs. A *parallel grant* would mean the two are independent of each other. Under a *parallel grant,* 6,000 options and 10,000 SARs would remain. Under an *additive grant,* the exercise of 4,000 options would automatically result in the additional payment of 4,000 SARs (typically in cash to meet tax withholding requirements). A *limited SAR* (LSAR) is one that is in effect only under specified circumstances. An example of a common LSAR would be as part of a golden parachute (either single or double trigger). When activated, it would immediately convert all of the stock option gains to cash SAR payouts.

SARs can also be freestanding, namely, not connected in anyway to a stock option. *Self-standing,* or *freestanding,* SARs are really phantom awards, since there is no accompanying stock option. Such a plan must be designed carefully to avoid an IRS ruling of constructive receipt due to lack of alternative right. An important point to remember in structuring a plan to avoid constructive receipt is the basic principle that if income is available only if the individual forfeits a valuable right, then income is subject to a substantial limitation and not constructively received. In Revenue Ruling 80-300, the IRS, applying this logic, indicated that since the exercise of the SAR would mean the loss of valuable right (namely, the chance for further appreciation in the market price), the gain should not be recognized as income until the rights are exercised. Thus, the normal tax treatment of an SAR is to tax when exercised and the company has a tax deduction in the same amount.

As for the SEC, the grant of an SAR is not considered a purchase. Rather, at the time of exercise, the stock received is considered to be a purchase and the six-month rule is invoked. Initially, the SEC viewed the receipt of cash in lieu of stock as a simultaneous purchase and sale and therefore a prohibited transaction with all gains forfeitable to the company. After further reflection, the SEC agreed to permit the payment in cash provided certain rules were met. These include:

1. The SAR must be administered by a disinterested board of directors or by a committee of three or more disinterested persons.
2. The SAR cannot be exercisable for the first six months.
3. The SAR can be exercisable only between the third and twelfth business days following the release of quarterly company earnings data.

The SEC requires that SARs in tandem with stock options be excluded from the remuneration table and instead be reported separately and preferably in the stock option table. Freestanding SARs require separate disclosure, again preferably in a separate table. This table should show the number of SARs granted during the period, exercised during the period, and outstanding at the end of the period. Furthermore, the amounts received as a result of the exercise of such rights should be reported along with the value of unrealized gains from rights outstanding at the end of the reporting period.

As for accounting treatment, the SAR is considered income because the number of shares (or amount of cash) is not known at time of grant. The expense will be equal to the spread between FMV and underlying option price divided by the number of optioned shares exercised, accrued over the period from grant to date of exercise.

Eligibility. While it might be nice to extend SARs to all with options (and thereby minimize the amount of new stock issues), the existence of APB 25 and the required charge to the earnings statement makes it prohibitively expensive. The individual can achieve the same net gain through a "cashless exercise" (described earlier without the earnings charge to the company) and therefore are no longer popular.

Frequency. The SAR could either be attached to the stock option at time of its grant or later. Typically, most companies are premature in assignment (as well as too liberal in eligibility). Rather than automatically attaching SARs at time of grant, it is more rational to monitor the performance of outstanding options before making a decision. For example, after five years (on a 10-year option), it is logical to ascertain whether there is sufficient spread to obviate the need for SARs (i.e., whether fair market value is significantly above option price) except perhaps for insiders with financing difficulties. If not, perhaps 25 percent of the option should have an SAR attached (at a price equal to the original grant). The following year the review is made again. If the stock market is still sluggish, the SAR could cover another 25 percent of the grant.

The advantage of waiting is that the impact upon the earnings statement is more closely monitored (APB 25 again) and statements are issued only on a need basis. Accounting regulations require quarterly determination and accrual of compensation-expense liability based on change in the market price of the stock. Therefore, sharp rises or drops in company stock price can have a significant effect on earnings if the company uses SARs extensively.

FASB Interpretation No. 31 requires that when stock or cash is available under payout, it will be assumed to be stock unless there is a reasonable basis for assuming otherwise. A resolution by the compensation committee to make SAR settlements in cash would presumably meet this reasonable basis. If the executive had a choice, it would probably be necessary to assume a stock settlement. However, if the executive decided to exercise the stock option rather than take the SAR, the accruals established as a charge to earnings logically would be eliminated since the SAR liability has been removed. The advantage of paying the 16(b) executive (defined as an insider by the SEC) in cash rather than stock is that the individual has no downside risk during the six-month period following exercise. However, cash settlements of SARs are not as attractive to the company since they result in negative cash flow (versus the positive cash flow resulting from the tax benefit if stock is issued). FASB Interpretation No. 128 later ruled the determination is made each period based on available facts.

Exercise Period. Probably the most common approach is to make the SAR exercisable at the same time(s) as the underlying stock option.

Some plans put limitations on this tandem option-SAR arrangement by requiring that a minimum percentage of the option must be exercised for the full stock—thereby putting a portion of the executive's potential growth at risk with this investment (exercise price). This approach could be very unattractive to 16(b) executives due to financing problems.

Other plans allow recipients to exercise the SAR only within prescribed time periods (i.e., windows) each year. Such periods may be limited, such as the 10 days following quarterly earnings statements, and may apply to 16(b) executives and others, for stock as well as cash settlements. It would not be surprising if a few companies decided to handle the exercise of the stock option in the same manner.

In addition, companies need to decide whether or not to keep the SAR open after death or other termination. If so, they may want to limit the number of shares (i.e., the spread) available on date of termination (rather than allow continued recognition of market growth) or valuable at time of exercise, whichever is less.

Stock Price. The underlying stock price is determined in any one of the previously described methods.

Number of Shares. Normally, the number of SARs is equal to the number of shares under option; however, one variation would be to attach SARs to only half the stock options and require that a stock option be exercised with every SAR. Plans may allow for issuance only at time of option grant or, as is more logical, anytime during the life of an outstanding option, since this more carefully limits the charge to earnings problem. The SAR may be eligible for the full market gain over the option price or artificially limited (e.g., no more than a 25-percent increase); this will minimize the exercise of SARs when larger gains are attainable by exercising the accompanying option. The settlement in some plans permits only stock, whereas others allow a combination of stock and/or cash settlements. Some plans provide for a supplementary cash payment to cover the estimated tax liability; such provisions are more logical when settlement is in stock, as the executive will not be forced to sell stock in order to meet tax obligations. This could be accomplished by giving an SAR payable in cash in addition to stock received in exercising the option.

Exercising the SAR. Table 8-38 illustrates a typical SAR in *tandem* with a stock option, namely, the exercise of one cancels the other. Assume the executive was granted an option of 1,000 shares at $100 a share with SARs attached to all shares. Several years later the stock is selling at $160, and the executive, rather than seek financing, wishes to exercise the 1,000 shares as appreciation rights. The 1,000 shares have an aggregate option price of $100,000 and a fair market value of $160,000. The $60,000 difference divided by the market price of $160 a share

---

Assumptions
- Optionee has 1,000 stock options and an SAR on each option
- Option price is $100 per share
- Cost to exercise options is $100,000 (1,000 × $100)
- Current market price of the stock is $160

Option Exercise
- Optionee exercises the SARs (forfeiting the underlying options)
- Company gives the optionee back a stock certificate for 375 shares

Advantages
- Optionee has been able to exercise 1,000 stock options without using any cash

Disadvantages
- Before exercise optionee had 1,625 shares "at work" in the market (625 owned and an option for 1,000 shares) but after exercise optionee has only 1,000 shares (all owned)
- Does not encourage ownership of stock by employees
- The $60,000 SAR is a charge to company earnings.

Table 8-38. SAR exercise example

would mean the executive would receive 375 shares of stock worth $60,0000 or any combination of stock and cash totaling $60,000 (if permitted by the plan and in conformance with SEC requirements). The corporation would have a deduction for $60,000 and the executive would have a tax liability for a comparable amount of income. The company would also have a $60,000 charge to earnings. If the plan permitted, (1) 375 shares, not 1,000, would have been charged against any plan maximum in effect per participant, and (2) 625 shares, the difference between 1,000 and 375, would have been returned to the plan for future grants. Note that the executive ends in the same position (an additional 375 shares) as if a stock-for-stock exercise had been done (see Table 8-22). However, the company has a $60,000 charge to earnings it did not have with the stock-for-stock exercise.

A Closer Look at Accounting and Tax Treatment of SARs

Using the earlier example of SARs attached to a grant of 1,000 options at $100 a share, exercised as SARs when the price is $160 a share will result in taxable income to the individual of $60 a share, the company having a like deduction in taxes. The company will also have accrued a charge to earnings up to the time of exercise, resulting in a charge to earnings of $60 a share, spread over the five-year period. This is illustrated in Table 8-39.

	Grant	**Vest**	**Exercise**	**Sell**
Time Lapse	Today	One Year	Five Years	Eight Years
Stock Price • Fair Market Value • Option Price	$100 $100	$110 $100	$160 $100	$210 $100
Individual • Ordinary Income • Long-term Capital Gains	— —	— —	$60 —	— $50
Company • Tax Deduction • Expense*	— 	— 	$60 → $60	— —

*Accrued over period of exercise

Table 8-39. Stock appreciation right

Why SARs? SARs are most attractive in times of high interest rates and low stock price appreciation and were created at a time when insiders had to wait six months after exercising an option before they could sell the acquired stock. When the SEC decided that the grant date, not the exercise date, constituted the purchase date, executives had to wait only six months after grant to exercise and sell the stock without having a short-swing profit problem. Since virtually no grants were exercisable sooner than one year after grant, SARs were no longer needed.

The popularity of SARs has waned with the spread of "stock-for-stock" and "cashless exercises" of stock options, since the executive ends up with the same number of shares (or cash equivalent) that would have been received through exercise of the SARs as illustrated earlier. While all three transactions bring a tax deduction to the company, the SAR results in a charge to corporate earnings whereas the "stock-for-stock exchange" and "cashless exercise" do not. Since there is no difference in result to the executive, there are limited applications for SARs. Typically, they are now used in two situations. The first is when the country in which the optionee resides imposes onerous taxes (typically at time of grant) and/or prohibits holding the security of a foreign country (or perhaps using foreign currency to purchase those shares). The second situation is when there is a change-of-control of the company (see Chapter 6 discussion on employment agreements). A typical clause would be the 100-percent vesting and automatic payout of the stock option appreciation in the form of SARs.

Stock-Purchase Plans

While stock options promote ownership among key employees, excessive use will dilute shareholder equity. An alternative form of promoting ownership is the executive stock-purchase plan. The key difference between the option and the purchase plan is that the latter has a much more limited period in which the executive decides whether or not to buy the stock. While the stock option may allow up to 10 years, the purchase plan typically allows a month or two.

The executive stock-purchase plan should not be confused with the tax qualified purchase plans described in Chapter 6 (Employee Benefits).Those plans require nearly all employees to participate and allow up to five years for the individual to purchase stock as low as 85 percent of market value (determined either at time of offer or time of purchase, depending on the structure of the plan). Such plans are developed in accordance with Section 423 of the Internal Revenue Code and must be nondiscriminatory in participation. Executive stock-purchase plans are much more flexible in design and limited in participation. Executive plans can be described in terms of the basis for determining cost of the shares and the basis for payment. Since each can be either fixed or variable in nature, four possible combinations result: (1) fixed cost and fixed basis for payment; (2) fixed cost and variable basis for payment; (3) variable cost and fixed basis for payment, and (4) variable cost and variable basis for payment.

Fixed Cost and Fixed Basis for Payment (FCFBP). The cost might either be at or below market value of the stock at the time the offer is made; the basis for payment is a specified yearly schedule which will pay for the stock over a stated period of years or in a lump sum payment at the end of a defined period. Such arrangements are attractive because typically the company gives the executive a low-interest or no-interest loan to purchase the stock (see Chapter 6). Ideally, the executive's annual bonus is sufficient to meet the loan repayment amount. However, since the bonus is of course taxable, this would suggest that a $100,000 bonus is necessary to retire $50,000 of the loan in a given year (assuming a 50-percent marginal tax rate). In addition, it may be appropriate to structure the loan so that after a period of years, the executive can cancel the loan balance by returning to the company the number of shares whose market value equals the loan balance plus any unpaid interest. Should the executive leave the company, typically, such loans are required to be paid in full immediately (although a forgiveness clause might be structured in the event of the executive's death). The company may also choose to forgive the interest if the stock acquired is retained for a specified period of time.

Since the executive will have income at time of purchase equal to the difference between purchase price and fair market value, it is desirable from the executive's point of view to immediately purchase all the shares (when this difference is little or nothing) through a loan arrangement. However, the company must be careful to ensure that the Federal Reserve margin requirements are followed when shares are used as collateral.

If the purchase price is discounted, the stock is typically given to the executive with a number of restrictions regarding disposition. The discount may be a stated percentage (e.g., 50 percent) or a stated value (e.g., par or book value). Discounted stock-purchase plans are designed to ease financing (by lowering the cost) and minimize the negative impact of a subsequent drop in market price (by setting the purchase price significantly below market value).

Restrictions are placed on the executive to minimize temptations to sell the stock prematurely for a quick profit. Restrictions also affect tax treatment since the company deduction and executive's income are both deferred until the restrictions lapse, assuming the restrictions satisfy the "risk of forfeiture" requirement of the IRS to avoid current taxation. Such restrictions lapse in installments (e.g., 10 percent a year for 10 years) or a cliff all-or-nothing (e.g., 100 percent after five years but zero vesting before then). While the restrictions are in effect, the shares of stock affected generate dividends, which are taxable to the individual but probably tax deductible to the company. The company must recognize the discount value as a charge to the earnings statement.

Shown in Table 8-40 is an example of a FCFBP plan. The stock is offered at a 10-percent discount with a five-year cliff vest. Since the stock is under restriction and must be sold back to the company at $90 a share if the executive leaves before the stock is vested, there is no income recognition by the individual until the vesting date (or termination date, if sooner). Similarly, the company has no tax deduction until that date. However, the company must begin to accrue a charge to earnings of $10 over the five-year period or $2 a year in accordance with the Measurement Date Principle. At the time the stock vests, it is selling at $160 a share. The individual has $70 of income and the company a like deduction. Two years later, the executive sells the stock and qualifies for long-term capital gains treatment on the $50 spread between current price of $210 and the cost adjusted price of $160.

	Purchase	**Vest**	**Sell**
Time Lapse	Today	Five Years	Seven Years
Stock Price • Fair Market Value • Option Price	$100 $90	$160 $90	$210 $160
Individual • Ordinary Income • Long-term Capital Gains	— —	$70 —	— $50
Company • Tax Deduction • Expense*	— ———————▶	$70 $10	— —

*Accrued over period of exercise

Table 8-40. Fixed cost and fixed basis for payment

Another variation of this type of plan is when the stock purchased is convertible into common stock. The stock purchased is a class B non-voting stock without dividends. Offered at a discount from the fair market value of class A common stock, it is typically convertible on a one-to-one basis from class B to class A stock. This type of plan is often called a *junior stock plan*. There is no tax impact to the executive at time of grant, although a Section 83(b) election could be made, thereby permitting long-term capital gains if held more than a year after converting to class A common stock. The company has a tax deduction on any ordinary income but not on long-term capital gains. The company will incur a charge to earnings, but since the price and number of shares are known at time of purchase opportunity (grant date), the charge will be based on discount value at that time, accrued over the vesting period. Unless the company had already set up class B stock, it would have to amend its certificate of incorporation and request shareholder approval. Companies anticipating a significant increase in stock price but wanting to help their executives avoid financing problems were attracted to junior stock plans. However, when FASB indicated the difference between fair market value of junior stock and company common stock would be a charge to earnings (FASB Interpretation No. 38), junior stock lost much of its appeal. Furthermore, the executive had no market to sell the stock if the conversion opportunity did not materialize.

Let's look at how this might work. Our executive receives an option to purchase a stated number of shares of class B stock (e.g., 1,000 shares) at a stated price, either equal to common stock (e.g., $100 a share) or reflecting a bargain price (e.g., 75 percent of common stock price). Since it is non-voting, it has no right to receive dividends and is restricted (i.e., convertible to class A common stock only under certain conditions). In the latter situation, the price is set by an independent financial organization. The option period is brief (e.g., 90 days). The purchase is payable either in cash, through a secured low-interest recourse loan from the company (repayable from bonus checks), or by tendering company stock owned by the individual.

Within 30 days of the transfer of stock, the recipient makes a Section 83 election recognizing any spread between purchase price and fair value (FV) as income. Thus, if the FV of the class B stock were $90 and the purchase price $75, the individual would have $15,000 of ordinary income on 1,000 shares at time of purchase. The cost basis would now be $90, and any further gain realized at sale (more than one year later) would be eligible for long-term capital gains tax treatment. The class B stock is convertible into the company's class A common stock after a prescribed number of years of continuous service (e.g., five years), either all at once or in annual installments (e.g., 20 percent a year). Additionally, the company may prescribe that a stated cumulative earnings per share target (e.g., 15 percent per year) be attained at the end of the period. If these restrictions are not met, the company buys back the non-voting stock at the original purchase price ($75 in this example), and the individual is out the tax paid. If the restrictions have been met, the conversion to class A common stock is effected. At time of conversion, the class A common stock is selling at $115, but the cost basis for selling the class A common stock remains at $90. Assuming it was sold two years later when the stock was at $130, there would be a long-term capital gains tax on the $40 (i.e., $130 - $90).

The advantage to the executive is long-term capital gains tax treatment on the appreciation in class A common stock over the FV of the class B stock at time of purchase. However, the company incurs a charge to earnings for the difference between the Fair Market Value of the class A common stock (at the date of the grant) and the purchase price of the junior stock ($25 per share in this example) but only a tax deduction for the ordinary income segment ($15 per share in this example). Furthermore, the junior stock will be considered as shares outstanding for the purpose of determining earnings per share.

Discounted and non-discounted junior stock plans are compared with three types of stock options [incentive stock options (ISOs), non-discounted, and discounted non-qualified stock options] in Table 8-41. The non-discounted junior stock and non-qualified stock option provide the same net income to the executive, which is less than both an ISO and a discounted stock option. However, the discounted junior stock provides greater income than the other four, but it also provides the lowest amount of cash flow to the company.

Another form of fixed cost and fixed basis for payment is the *debenture*. The company typically sells this debt security with a fixed interest rate to an individual. That individual could be an executive but it has limited appeal for those wanting an equity position in the company unless it contains a convertible feature. If it were convertible into company common stock, the instrument would stipulate the conversion rate (i.e., number of shares in relation to each $1,000 of note face value). Under APB 25, the issue would be valued on the difference between current market value and that permitted under the conversion formula. There is no expense charge at

	Common			Junior Stock	
		NOSO			
	ISO	Discount	No Discount	Discount	No Discount
Individual					
Option Price	$100.00	$75.00	$100.00	$75.00	$100.00
Exercise	105.00	105.00	105.00	90.00	105.00
Convert	—	—	—	115.00	115.00
Sale	$130.00	$130.00	$130.00	$130.00	$130.00
Income					
LT Capital Gains	$30.00	$25.00	$25.00	$40.00	$25.00
Ordinary	—	30.00	5.00	15.00	5.00
Total	$30.00	$55.00	$30.00	55.00	30.00
Taxes					
LT Capital Gains [1]	$6.00	$5.00	$5.00	$8.00	$5.00
Ordinary [2]	—	15.00	2.50	7.50	2.50
Total	$6.00	$20.00	$7.50	$15.50	$7.50
Net Income	$24.00	$35.00	$22.50	$39.50	$22.50
Company					
Tax Deduction	0	$30.00	$5.00	$15.00	$5.00
Earnings Charge	0	25.00	0	15.00	0
Cash Flow [3]	$100.00	$87.00	$102.00	$81.00	$102.00

[1]Assumes 20% rate   [2]Assumes 50% rate   [3]Assumes 40% rate

Table 8-41. Comparison of junior stock-purchase plans with stock option plans

time of conversion. For tax purposes, the difference between market value and cost at time of purchase would be ordinary income, and subsequent gains after conversion would be subject to long-term capital gains at time of sale.

The instrument may also require meeting certain financial objectives over a prescribed period of time before permitting the conversion (e.g., a minimum compound 10-percent EPS increase over a five year period). Such a requirement would make the convertible debenture a fixed-cost-and-variable-basis-for-payment type of plan. This will be reviewed next.

Fixed Cost and Variable Basis for Payment (FCVBP). Given an amortization schedule to retire a loan, a company may establish a formula indicating the portion of annual payment that may be canceled by corporate performance. These loan forgiveness amounts are charged to company earnings, reported as income to the executive, and taken as a company tax deduction.

As an example, the schedule may call for an annual $10,000 payment over five years toward retiring the loan on the purchase of 500 shares. However, this amount would be reduced by $1,000 for every 1-percent increase in EPS above 10 percent. Thus, a 15-percent increase in EPS in one year would reduce the payment to $5,000, with the other $5,000 being "forgiven." This is illustrated in Table 8-42 where the purchase price was halved, thereby effectively reducing the purchase price to $50 a share. In this example, the vesting schedule is 20 percent a year, so the $60 gain in relation to market price would be recognized as income for one-fifth of the shares, or 100 (i.e., 20 percent of the 500 purchased). Since the price of the stock for payment purposes was unknown at time of purchase, it probably is subject to variable base accounting and a $60 charge to earnings is taken after the first year on 100 shares. The next year, a similar calculation is made and the expense trued up over the two-year period. After seven years, the executive sells these 100 shares at $210 a share and receives long-term capital gains treatment on $100 (i.e., $210 - $110).

In addition, or in lieu of, the performance variable, a time-in-job factor could be designed. For example, $1,000 might be forgiven each year for each year of service since receiving the

	Purchase	**Vest**	**Sell**
Time Lapse	Today	One Year	Seven Years
Stock Price • Fair Market Value • Purchase Price	$100 $100	$110 $50	$210 $110
Individual • Ordinary Income • Long-term Capital Gains	* —	$60 —	— $50
Company • Tax Deduction • Expense*	— ————————→	$60 $60	— —

*Accrued over period of exercise

Table 8-42. Fixed cost and variable basis for payment

stock. Thus, $9,000 would be required after the first year, $8,000 after the second, and so on. This accelerated "earn out" makes staying with the company very attractive to the executive.

Variable Cost and Fixed Basis for Payment (VCFBP). Rather than set purchase price at the time of purchase, it is possible to determine in advance the cost of the shares to be purchased that year. The amount of annual discount is taken as a charge to company earnings, reported as income to the executive, and identified as a company tax deduction.

For example, the formula might set the cost to 50 percent of market value each year for five years. If 500 shares of stock were involved, installment-vested over five years, this would mean that the value of 100 shares would be determined each year in relation to the then-current market value. This is illustrated with the example in Table 8-43, where after the first year, the stock is selling at $110 a share, and therefore the executive's cost is $55. This $55 profit is income to the individual, a tax deduction to the company, and a charge to the income statement.

	Purchase	**Vest**	**Sell**
Time Lapse	Today	One Year	Seven Years
Stock Price • Fair Market Value • Purchase Price	$100 —	$110 $55	$210 $110
Individual • Ordinary Income • Long-term Capital Gains	— —	$55 —	— $100
Company • Tax Deduction • Expense	— —	$55 $55	— —

Table 8-43. Variable cost and fixed cost for payment

Alternatively, or on the assumption that price should really be a function of earnings, the formula could use some multiple assigned to EPS. For example, if the formula called for a multiple of 20, the cost for year one would be $60 for each share (or $6,000 for 100 shares) if the EPS were $3.00, whereas it would be $66 per share in year two, or $6,600 for 100 shares if the EPS were $3.30.

Another variation is to use company performance to set the discount through a formula, as shown in Table 8-44. Assume the executive agreed to purchase $500,000 of stock over five years. After the first year, the EPS was at 11 percent; therefore, the executive only paid $40,000 [i.e. $100,000 x (100% - 60%)].

Variable Cost and Variable Basis for Payment (VCVBP). This is simply a combination of two variable formulas, one determining the cost and the other determining the extent of forgiveness. By definition, it is not only the most complicated combination but also the most subject to dramatic swings in the amount of value delivered to the executive.

EPS	Discount
15%	100%
14	90
13	80
12	70
11	60
10	50
9	40
8	30
7	20
6	10
5 & lower	0

Table 8-44. Stock purchase price based on company performance

Stock Awards

Essentially, a stock award is a stock purchase with a 100-percent discount. It too can either be given immediately or restricted, with ownership deferred to a future date(s) with much the same treatment as outlined for stock purchases. Some companies choose to use *stock units* rather than stock awards. A stock unit is the right to receive a share of company stock at a specified time in the future. Typically, this is to simplify SEC reporting and avoid possible insider trade violations.

Awards that are paid immediately could be in recognition of a special accomplishment, a feature of the annual incentive plan, or part of a package designed to attract an executive to the company. If the award is deferred to a future date, this decision could be by individual choice or plan design. The process for an individual successfully deferring compensation without triggering either constructive receipt or economic benefit was reviewed in Chapter 3. This section covers plan-designed deferrals that are under some form of restriction (typically, the person must still be employed when the restrictions lapse).

A *restricted stock award* is structured around a conditional transfer of company stock to the executive. While the individual is prevented from assigning, transferring, or selling the stock without a tax liability, the executive has the right to vote the stock, receive dividends, and even possess the stock certificate (although it is noted on its face as being restricted in sale). The restrictions lapse over time, either on a set schedule or one accelerated by the attainment of prescribed financial goals. Lengthy periods of restriction (such as retirement) are sometimes called *career-restricted stock*. If the individual terminates employment before the restrictions lapse, the stock is forfeited. However, the company may choose to waive the forfeiture requirements. Typically, this would be because of disability, retirement, or death. Restricted stock awards may be especially attractive in a number of situations. Included among these are:

- A front-end bonus to hire a top executive without distorting the compensation program.
- A privately held company interested in tying payment to book value, thus avoiding the market swings of publicly traded stock.
- A company in the mature phase with reduced opportunities for growth in market value of company stock.

- A form of golden handcuffs to retain key talent.

Restricted stock can be attractive to the company for the reasons cited above, in addition to locking in the charge to earnings over the earn-out period, based on price at beginning of period if the number of shares and price are known at that time. While there is dilution, it is less than that of stock options, since more option shares are required to deliver comparable value.

Shareholders, however, are less than enthusiastic about giving stock away to executives when they have to buy it.

There are three ways to restrict stock: (1) vested solely on remaining with the company to a specified date; (2) number (1) with earlier payment if prescribed performance requirements have been met; and (3) performance-only vesting.

Performance can be defined by an internal financial measurement such as ROE, ROI, ROA, or EPS. Alternatively, it can be based on stock price. An example of the latter would be a plan that would award a stated number of shares contingent upon company stock trading at or above a stated price, reflecting a premium over current price (e.g., $150 with current price at $100), for a specified number of consecutive trading days (e.g., 20), within a specified period (e.g., three years).

In planning restricted stock awards, remember two measurements: how many shares and when the shares are received. This results in four possible combinations:

1. *Fixed number of shares to be received at a prescribed date.* Since they lack a performance feature, shareholders do not like these plans, even though they may be used to attract a talented person to the company and/or lock in a person who otherwise might leave.
2. *Fixed number of shares to be received at a variable date.* The award typically has a target date but could be received earlier or later, depending when and if performance factors are met.
3. *Variable number of shares to be received at a prescribed date.* This is frequently described as the traditional *performance-share* plan.
4. *Variable number of shares to be received at variable dates.* This type of plan establishes performance factors for both amount and date.

Fixed Number of Shares and Fixed Date. Let's assume eligible executives are given stock awards every three years that vest after three years in accordance with the schedule in Table 8-45. Using Table 5-4, let's assume the CEO is in grade 35 with a current salary of $1 million.

Grade	Award Multiple	Shares of Stock
35	1.5	15,000
34	1.4	14,000
33	1.3	13,000
32	1.2	12,000
31	1.1	11,000
30	1.0	10,000
29	0.9	9,000
28	0.8	8,000
27	0.7	7,000
26	0.6	6,000
25	0.5	5,000

Table 8-45. Stock award multiple by grade example

Using the Table 8-42 value of 1.5 would require a restricted stock award worth $1.5 million. If the stock were currently selling at $100 a share, the CEO would receive 15,000 shares (i.e., $1.5 million ÷ $100). The tax and accounting treatment is shown in Table 8-46.

Time Lapse	Award	Vest	Sell
	Today	Three Years	Five Years
Stock Price			
• Fair Market Value	$100	$130	$160
• Share Price	—	—	$130
Individual			
• Ordinary Income	—	$130	—
• Long-term Capital Gains	—	—	$30
Company			
• Tax Deduction	—	$130	—
• Expense*	——————————→	$100	—

*Accrued over period of vesting

Table 8-46. Cliff vesting on three-year restricted stock

If the restrictions are only contingent upon continued employment, it is logical to assume the charge to earnings is based on the value at time of grant. At that date, both the price and number of shares are known and must conform to the Measurement Date Principle of APB 25. In this example, the charge would be $100 for each share spread over the three-year vesting period. The individual has no income liability until the shares vest after the third year. Since the stock is selling at $130 a share, the person has income of $130 on each share and the company has a like tax deduction. The company also has a tax deduction for dividends paid on restricted stock. When the individual sells the stock two years later, assumedly having met long-term capital gains (LTCG) holding requirements, the $30 gain (i.e., $160 - $130) for each share would be at the LTCG rate.

As was discussed in Chapter 3, the individual can elect to pay the tax on the value of the restricted property at time of award (i.e., $100 not later than 30 days after date of transfer) rather than waiting for the restriction to lapse. This is a *Section 83(b) election*, referring to the section in the Internal Revenue Code (IRC). Doing so makes the cost basis for later LTCG $100, and the LTCG tax payable on a $60 gain ($160 - $100). The downside of this action is that if the individual does not satisfy the vesting requirement and therefore does not receive the stock, the person forfeits the tax amount, as it cannot be claimed as a tax deduction. Needless to say, one must be very confident of receiving the stock and that the value of the stock at that time will be greater than today. This is illustrated in Table 8-47.

A variation of the above would be for one-third of the shares to vest each year. The accounting treatment would be the same, since the expense is known at time of award. This is unaffected by any change in stock price at the time the vesting lapses. However, the tax treatment would change. Namely, the recipient would be taxed on the value of one-third of the shares

Time Lapse	Award	Vest	Sell
	Today	Three Years	Five Years
Stock Price • Fair Market Value • Share Price	$100 —	$130 —	$160 $100
Individual • Ordinary Income • Long-term Capital Gains	$100 —	— —	— $60
Company • Tax Deduction • Expense	$100 $100	— —	— —

Table 8-47. Section 83(b) election on three-year cliff vesting stock

freed from restriction and the company would have a like tax deduction.

Another variation would be *career-restricted stock,* which would not have restrictions removed until retirement. Termination prior to that date would result in forfeiture of the shares. In the meantime, the individual would receive dividends and credit for the shares against any ownership guidelines.

Fixed Number of Shares and Variable Date. Using the same example in the previous section, we can introduce a performance factor as to when (possibly if) the executive will receive the shares. These plans go by either of two names: *performance-accelerated, restricted stock plans* (PARSAPs), or *time-accelerated restricted stock plans* (TARSAPs). The more generous approach would be to allow the executive to receive stock sooner than the specified date if certain company financial goals have been met. Instead of cliff vesting after three years, let's assume 100-percent vesting in at *least* seven years—sooner if prescribed financial targets have been met. There are numerous ways to structure such an early earn-out. Among the choices are:

- Which performance measures to use: earnings per share, stock price, return on investment, return on assets, and return on total capital, to mention a few.
- When to measure: prescribed date(s) and/or over a stated period of time (e.g., seven days).
- How much stock to release from restriction: all or a stated portion.

As an example, a plan may lift restrictions on the first date after three years that the stock trades at a price equal to 150 percent of current value for a consecutive period of seven days. Another example would begin in the second year. At that time, the plan will remove restrictions on 25 percent of the shares if return on total capital exceeds 20 percent for the year.

As there is a predetermined date when vesting will occur (in this example, seven years) and the number of shares under restriction are known at time of award, the plan qualifies under the Measurement Date Principle of APB 25, which locks in the charge to earnings at time of award and accrues over the earn-out period. The recipient of course does not have a tax liability until the restrictions lapse, at which time the company also has a tax deduction. This is illustrated in

	Award	Payment Vests	Stock Sold
Time Lapse	Today	Five Years	Two Years Later
Stock Price • Fair Market Value • Share Price	$100 0	$150 0	$200 —
Individual • Ordinary Income • Long-term Capital Gains	0 —	$150 —	— $50
Company • Tax Deduction • Expense*	0 ———————→	$150 $150	— —

*Accrued over period to vest date

Table. 8-48. PARSAP/TARSAP example

Table 8-48, where the payment vests after three years because the $150 stock-price target has been achieved. The $150 expense charge is accrued after three years.

If the plan is structured to have not only an early vesting feature, but also a minimum performance to receive the stock, the plan will not qualify for locking in the stock price at time of award. Rather, the plan must accrue the expense over the period, based on the stock price in effect over the period, truing up the cost when restrictions lapse. An example of this type of plan would be one that lifts stock restrictions the first date after three years that the stock trades at a price equal to 150 percent of present value. If this target is not reached, the restrictions will lapse on the first date after seven years that the stock is at or above 125 percent of present value for a consecutive period of seven days. If this does not occur within 10 years, the stock is forfeited. Since there is a downside risk with such plans, usually more stock is awarded. Illustrated in Table 8-49 is an example of such an award. Here, the performance target is *not* met, and therefore *no* award is given. (N.A. means not applicable.)

Another form of the restricted award is *career stock*. These are shares the individual cannot sell while with the company. Only after leaving are the shares released from restriction. As the termination date is unknown, the plan falls under variable accounting for determining the charge to earnings. The plan has to be carefully crafted to avoid constructive receipt to the individual. However, it may be advantageous to the executive in order to pay taxes at time of award (since receipt is virtually guaranteed) and thereby establish a cost basis for long-term capital gains.

Variable Number Shares and Fixed Date. Instead of varying the date restrictions lapse based on company performance, some plans set the payout date, but the number of shares to be awarded is determined by company performance. These are typically called *performance-share plans*, although the case could be made to use the same name for variable-date plans, too. Performance-share plans were introduced in the early 1970s to offset a prolonged period of flat stock prices and therefore little appreciation in stock options. To illustrate how they work, assume the same

	Award	Payment Vests	Stock Sold
Time Lapse	Today	?	
Stock Price • Fair Market Value • Share Price	$100 0	N.A. N.A.	
Individual • Ordinary Income • Long-term Capital Gains	$100 —	— —	— —
Company • Tax Deduction • Expense*	— —	0 0	— —

Table 8-49. Performance restricted award example

15,000 shares highlighted in Table 8-45 were awarded, also with a three-year cliff vest. A full conversion of Table 8-47 is shown in Table 8-50 to show the other job grades.

Now, however the number of shares to be received is a function of the compound growth in earnings per share (EPS) over the three-year period. Only if EPS were 12 percent of higher would the full 15,000 shares be released. Below 8 percent, no shares would be released. To reflect both upside potential and downside risk, it would be more logical to adjust the schedule to pay out the 15,000 shares at target. This could be done by either awarding 30,000 shares and using the unadjusted schedule in Table 8-51, or awarding 15,000 shares using the adjusted percent-release column, namely, doubling the percentages. Thus, the percentage at 16 percent or higher would be 200 percent (or 30,000 shares if 15,000 were targeted).

Another variation would be to allow for interpolation of EPS in setting award size. An example of this is shown in Table 8-52.

Grade	Award Multiple	Shares of Stock
40	1.5	15,000
39	1.4	14,000
38	1.3	13,000
37	1.2	12,000
36	1.1	11,000
35	1.0	10,000
34	0.9	9,000
33	0.8	8,000
32	0.7	7,000
31	0.6	6,000
30	0.5	5,000

Table 8-50. Example of performance-share by grade

Compound Growth in EPS Over Period, Percent		Percent of Restricted Award Released	
		Unadjusted	Adjusted
Maximum	16.0 or higher	100%	200%
	12.0-15.9	75%	150%
Target	10.0-11.9	50%	100%
Threshold	8.0-9.9	25%	50%
	below 6.0	0%	6%

Table 8-51. Restricted-stock award based on EPS

Compound Average Percent Increase in EPS of Three Years	Percent of Stock to Be Paid
15.0 or more	200
14.0	180
13.0	160
12.0	140
11.0	120
10.0	100
9.0	80
8.0	60
7.0	40
6.0	20
Under 6.0	0

Table 8-52. Example of performance-share corporate formula

Further, assume that after an analysis of competitive pay and desired position, the decision-makers (i.e., the compensation committee) believe Table 8-52 is an appropriate after-tax position for executives.

To achieve the net-tax position, we can either double the number of shares of stock or leave the shares as stated but award an equal cash bonus (assuming a 50-percent tax rate). The former is appropriate if the executives have sufficient means to pay the tax liability without selling stock (e.g., large short-term incentive payments); the latter is more logical in the absence of such liquidity, as it precludes short-swing trade problems with the insiders, who might be forced to sell stock to meet their tax obligations.

The tax treatment is the same as illustrated in Table 8-47, but the accounting is different. Since the number of shares to be given when restrictions lapse is unknown at time of award, variable accounting is required. Namely, the annual accrual must reflect not only the initial stock price but also any changes. If at the end of three years the stock price is $130, then $130

	Plan	Payment Vests	Stock Sold
Time Lapse	Today	Three Years	Five Years
Stock Price • Fair Market Value • Share Price	$100 0	$130 0	$150 0
Individual • Ordinary Income • Long-term Capital Gains	0 0	$130 0	0 $20
Company • Tax Deduction • Expense*	0 ———————→	$130 $130	0 0

*Accrued over period to vest date

Table 8-53. Variable number shares at fixed rate

must have been charged to the income statement over the three-year period. This is illustrated in Table 8-53.

Another way to incorporate company performance in the value of the award is not to vary the number of shares but rather establish a variable cash bonus. This also addresses the recipient liquidity problem, since the full market value of the stock received will be considered income (assuming a Section 83(b) election were not made). Table 8-54 illustrates how such a bonus might be constructed. Note that the table is similar to Table 8-51. However, it illustrates several design variables, namely, smaller incremental steps above 50 percent and a zero award at a slightly higher EPS growth (i.e., 7 percent). Note also a more aggressive high-end EPS requirement (i.e., 22 percent or higher) to receive the maximum payout. This type of program would require determining how much one is willing to pay in stock-plus-cash at target, threshold, and maximum. If for example, target were set at 10 percent to 12.9 percent of compound growth in EPS, the stock portion would be two-thirds of the total and cash one-third, since cash

Compound Growth in EPS Over Period, Percent		Percent of FMV of Stock Paid in Cash
Maximum	22 or higher 19.0-21.9 16.0-18.9 13.0-15.9	100% 87.5% 75% 62.5%
Target	10.0-12.9	50%
Threshold	7.0-9.9 below 7	25% 0%

Table 8-54. Contingent cash bonus based on company performance

is fifty percent of stock value. This would suggest a stock award of 10,000 shares rather than the 15,000 in the earlier example.

Another variation would be to use both Table 8-51 and Table 8-53, although it would be logical that the EPS factors be the same for both the number of shares and the amount of the cash award. This is illustrated in Table 8-55. Assume that it is a cliff-vested plan and that we set the target at $1.5 million, half in stock (7,500 valued at $100 a share) and $750,000 in cash. If after three years, the compound growth rate were 23 percent, the executive would receive 15,000 shares (7,500 x 200 percent) worth $1.95 million (because the FMV of the stock price was at $130 a share) and a cash award of $1.95 million (i.e., 15,000 shares x $130). Thus, the total award would be $3.9 million. The company would have accrued this amount over the three-year period and taken a tax deduction in that amount after the third year, since the individual would have a like amount as income. The cash bonus is probably sufficient to pay the tax liability without having to sell any of the stock. Note that if the cash bonus is set in terms of FMV at time of award, it may not be sufficient to meet tax liabilities. By the time restrictions are lifted, the FMV has probably increased! Conversely, the cash bonus may be more than required if FMV has decreased.

Compound Growth in EPS Over Period, Percent		Percent of...	
		Restricted Stock Released	Stock Value Paid in Cash
Maximum	22.0 or higher	200.0	200.0
	19.0-21.9	175.0	175.0
	16.0-18.9	150.0	150.0
	13.0-15.9	125.0	125.0
Target	10.0-12.9	100.0	100.0
Threshold	7.0-9.9	50.0	50.0
	below 7.0	0	0

Table 8-55. Contingent stock and cash award based on company performance

After the third year, a new table would be devised for another three-year period. At such time, the list of candidates would again be reviewed. Some companies freeze the list for each three-year period, thus precluding any additions. Others make additions (usually as a result of replacing a terminated executive) but are careful to stay within a control total number of shares.

In establishing the multiple-year target, one must be careful not to fall into a mathematical logic trap if a multiple-year base is used. For example, a 15-percent annual compound growth in EPS is equivalent to a 23-percent increase over a two-year base and a 31-percent increase over a three-year base (assuming annual 15-percent increases). As in Table 8-56, the average of the first two years is $107.50. Although the third year amount of $132.25 is 15 percent larger than the previous year's $115.00, it is 23 percent greater than $107.50. A similar calculation can be performed using a three-year average for base.

Initially, companies established the payout only after the third year, with no payments after the first and second. Needless to say, this caused significant blips in earnings for top people. The

Year	First Year Average	Second Year Average	Third Year Average
1	$100.00	—	—
2	115.00	$107.50	—
3	132.25	123.51	$115.75

Table 8-56. Establishing multiple-year base

first refinement was to make prorated payments after the first and second years. Normally, this meant a simple one-third of the payment after the first year, but in the second year, it was necessary to first calculate two-thirds of the earned award and then subtract the actual first year payout. A similar calculation was then made in the third year by calculating the three-year award and netting out the amounts paid for the first and second.

To illustrate, assume the company increase in EPS after the first year was 10 percent: the CEO would received 2,500 shares (one-third of 7,500). After the second year, the company EPS experienced an 8-percent increase, or a compound average of 9 percent. The calculation for the second-year award for the CEO would be 2,500 shares (i.e., two-thirds of 3,750 - the 2,500 received after year one, or a zero award). After the third year, the EPS increase was 13 percent, or a compound average for the three-year period of 10.3 percent. Thus, the third-year award for the CEO would be 5,000 shares (i.e., 7,500 - the 2,500 already received).

The above prorating approach results in a payout very similar to a short-term annual incentive and, without additional controls, could result in a greater-than-desired payout (e.g., significantly better EPS growth in the first year than subsequent years). Therefore, few companies have retained such a feature

What a number of companies have done is establish consecutive three-year plans with a potential payout each year as one of the three plans matures. Installing consecutive three-year plans requires one-year and two-year phase-in plans for each. After the second year, each payment is for a three-year period. Unless there is a need for a significant increase in compensation, this approach also allows a gradual buildup in compensation as well; one-third of the increase the first year, two-thirds after the second, and only after the third year is the full increase in effect. For companies that are fully competitive and merely changing emphasis within the elements, this allows a three-year wind-down of other elements.

Additional advantages of such an approach include: (1) annual adjustments for candidates rather than several years of waiting, (2) increased retention factor since portions of two awards (i.e., a one-third and a two-thirds) are always outstanding, (3) a smoothing of payout from one year to the next, and (4) the unlikelihood of business journals adding these annual payments to salary and short-term incentive payments in reporting annual compensation (since they are attributable to three years' performance). The impact of the annual payout of multiyear performance versus the single-year payout is demonstrated in Table 8-57. After six years, both plans have paid out the same amount, but the impact on total pay during each of the last six years is quite different. Unfortunately, this type of stock-award plan results in a double whammy to the earnings statement under APB 25. First, the probable number of shares of stock (at initial market value) that will have to be paid must be amortized. Second, the increase or

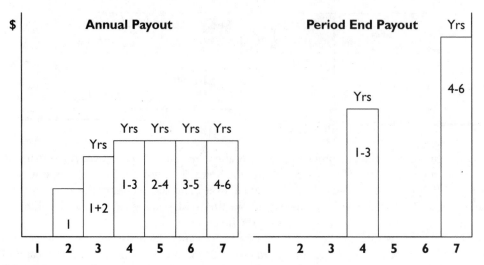

Table 8-57. Annual vs. periodic payout under multiyear plans

decrease in stock price also has to be included in the estimated cost of the plan. Thus, if the stock price doubles during the period, the impact on the earnings statement will be twice as large as was intended when the award period began.

Regardless of when payment is made, the annual payout requires the ability to quantify objectives with varying degrees of plus-and-minus performance over several years. Not surprisingly, most plans provide some form of adjustment in objectives while the plan is operating. While this is necessary to offset interim changes in accounting and tax treatment, it will be tempting to adjust for business conditions, too—and possibly defeat the purpose of the plan. Indeed, some critics claim that a good incentive plan is invariably adjusted after a bad financial year.

While it is logical to adjust targets when conditions outside the executive's control dictate, it is important to resist changing simply because of the manifestation of normal business risks. The rationale for mid-course change is that if such factors had been known at the beginning of the period, the goal would have been appropriately modified. Thus, mid-course corrections require separating impacting factors from actual performance—a measurement more conceptually understandable than practically administered in many situations. Furthermore, it is important to remember that the true entrepreneur has no one changing his or her goals and profit targets—that individual is stuck with making the best of a bad situation. Some argue that it should not be any different for the professional manager.

For those concerned about altering goals during the period, it is logical to keep the plan cycle as short as possible. By definition, the further out in time the plan, the more suspect the conclusions. Therefore, a three-year plan is less likely to need change than a five-year program. Even so, setting targets as short as three years may be hazardous in cyclical industries.

An alternative to company EPS targets would be to set company growth (measured in terms of EPS, or some other financial factor) in relation to other key companies within the same industry as shown in Table 8-58. On the other hand, the award could be split so that half was dependent upon company performance and the other half on performance relative to identified

Percent of Industry Average	Percent of Stock to Be Paid
150	200
140	180
130	160
120	140
110	120
100	100
90	80
80	60
70	40
60	20
Under 60	0

Table 8-58. Performance-share payout vs. industry performance

key companies. The advantage of using relative performance only is that it avoids the problem of setting specific targets for each plan.

Percentile rankings may replace percentage of industry average in the calculation. Thus, in Table 8-52 the value of 200 percent would equate to the 100 percentile. Each subsequent line would be reduced by 20; thus, at the 50th percentile, 100 percent of the stock award would be paid. The methodology for calculating percentile rankings is shown in Table 8-59.

1. Array the values being measured low to high.
2. Determine own company numerical rank position.
3. Subtract one from one rank position and one from the total number of values.
4. Divide adjusted rank by adjusted total.
5. Subtract result from 1 to get percentile.

Thus, if own company is ranked third among nine other companies (10 counting oneself), then: 3 - 1 = 2 and 10 - 1 = 9. Therefore, 2 ÷ 9 = .222 and 1 - .222 = .778 or the seventy-eighth percentile.

Table 8-59. Calculating percentile rankings

It is easy to set up a table using two financial measurements and pay in relation to peer performance. The schedule in Table 8-60 measures both earnings per share (EPS) and total shareholder value (namely, stock price plus reinvested dividends) in percentile terms relative to the peer group.

This table is set up by determining how much to pay at threshold, target, and maximum. If that is determined to be 2,500, 10,000, and 20,000 shares respectively, one needs only to interpolate the other values. As the number of shares to be awarded and their value are both unknown at time the plan begins, the company must begin an accrual, adjusting each year based on performance for the plan period. After the third year, the accrual would be adjusted to

Percentile EPS	Shares of Company Stock				
81-100	10,000	12,500	15,000	17,500	20,000
61-80	7,500	10,000	12,500	15,000	17,500
41-60	5,000	7,500	10,000	12,500	15,000
21-40	2,500	5,000	7,500	10,000	12,500
0-20	—	2,500	5,000	7,500	10,000
	Total Shareholder Value Percentile				
	0-20	21-40	41-60	61-80	81-100

Table 8-60. Three-year, peer-rated, two-dimensional, performance-share plan, year 3

equate the value actually paid. For example, if after the first year, the company was in the sixty-seventh percentile on both scales, one third of the 15,000 shares in the table at the current price of $110 would be expensed, or $550,000. After year two, the calculation is made again and the percentile ranking is seventy-eighth on EPS, but fifty-sixth on shareholder value. The table indicates the performance is headed for a 12,500-share payout. The current stock price is $120 a share. Therefore, the estimated payout would be 8,375 shares (i.e., two-thirds of 12,500), or a cost of $1,005,000. (i.e., 8,375 x $120). Since $550,000 was accrued after year one, year two needs to reflect a charge of $455,000 (i.e., $1,005,000 - $550,000). The third year ends with the company in the 70th percentile for EPS and the 67th percentile for total shareholder value, or a payout of 15,000 shares. At the time, the stock is trading at $130 a share for a total value of $1,950,000. Since the total accrual for the first two years is $1,005,000, the company must take a charge in the third year for $945,000 (i.e., $1,950,000 - $1,005,000).

Rather than wait for the end of the third year before paying anything, it would probably be appropriate to set up a one-year and two-year plan to phase into the full three-year cycle. These are shown in Table 8-61 and Table 8-62.

Percentile EPS	Shares of Company Stock				
81-100	6,667	8,334	10,000	11,667	13,334
61-80	5,000	6,667	8,334	10,000	11,667
41-60	3,334	5,000	6,667	8,334	10,000
21-40	1,667	3,334	5,000	6,667	8,334
0-20	—	1,667	3,334	5,000	6,667
	Total Shareholder Value Percentile				
	0-20	21-40	41-60	61-80	81-100

Table 8-61. Indexed, peer-rated, two-dimensional, performance-share plan, year 2

Variable Number Shares at Variable Dates. Essentially, this is nothing more than a combination of the last two general category plans, putting both number of shares and when received as variables. Needless to say, it is the most complicated version as well.

An example is shown in Table 8-63. Here the amount of payment (if any) is dependent on

Percentile EPS	Shares of Company Stock				
81-100	3,334	4,167	5,000	5,833	6,667
61-80	2,500	3,334	4,167	5,000	5,833
41-60	1,667	2,500	3,334	4,167	5,000
21-40	833	1,667	2,500	3,334	4,167
0-20	—	833	1,667	2,500	3,334
	Total Shareholder Value Percentile				
	0-20	21-40	41-60	61-80	81-100

Table 8-62. Indexed, peer-rated, two-dimensional, performance-share plan, year 1

Compound EPS Growth	Number Shares Awarded Based on Consecutive Years Performance			
	2	3	4	5
18% and up	20,000	30,000	40,000	50,000
16.0-17.9	15,000	20,000	30,000	40,000
14.0-15.9	7,500	12,500	17,500	25,000
12.0-13.9	5,000	7,500	10,000	12,500
10.0-11.9	2,500	5,000	7,500	10,000
8.0-9.9	—	2,500	5,000	7,500
Below 8.0	—	—	—	—

Table 8-63. Variable number of shares and variable date payment

the cumulative, average compound growth in EPS. For example, if the EPS averaged 18.5 percent for two years, the executive would receive 20,000 shares of company stock at that time. The third year was not as good, and the average for the three-year period declined to 17.5 percent. This would call for 20,000 shares, but since the executive already received 20,000 shares, no additional shares would be awarded. The following year, the compound average for the four-year period was 16.2 percent, calling for an award of 30,000 shares. Since 20,000 had already been awarded, the executive would be given an additional 10,000 shares. After the fifth year, the EPS average for the five years was 15.8 percent, which would require a 25,000-share payout. Since the executive already received 30,000, the person was overpaid. If the plan paid out only after the fifth year, there would have been no payment after years 2-4, but then it would have been a variable-number/fixed-date plan.

Tracking Stock. Sometimes called *letter stock* or *target stock*, this is stock of the parent company that is linked (or tracks) the performance of a business unit within the company. The belief behind the concept is that the business unit's financial performance will be reflected in its own stock price. If the letter stock is publicly traded, then APB 25 will be used; if not, it will be treated as cash compensation for accounting purposes.

Letter stock is often considered an alternative to a spin-off of a subsidiary or created at time of acquisition of a business, thereby permitting the acquired's shareholders to still be tied to the financial performance of its company. This was behind the creation of tracking stock by General Motors in 1984, when it acquired Electronic Data Systems (resulting in the issuance of General Motors class E stock). A year later, it created class H for its Hughes Electronic subsidiary. Some dubbed these *alphabet stock*, or simply letter stock.

Tracking stock is also used for stock awards and stock options for a unit's key executives. While this hypothetically is a stronger pay-for-performance plan than use of the general company stock, the stock issued is still of the parent company, not the business unit. Therefore, its value can be significantly affected by overall company performance, namely, how other business units fared. Additionally, tracking stock may create internal problems in deciding on cost allocations and transfer pricing decisions.

Market Value Design Issues

Objectives. The objectives of the ideal plan are fairly simple. The perfect plan:

1. Identifies with the shareholder
2. Coordinates with individual performance
3. Correlates with group performance
4. Correlates with corporate performance
5. Is easily understood by all
6. Requires no special target setting
7. Ties the high performer to the company
8. Has no earnings charge
9. Has no dilution to shareholder equity
10. Is tax deductible to the company
11. Is not taxable to the individual
12. If taxable, is tax deductible to individual
13. Requires no investment by the individual
14. Has no downside risk for the individual

When considering the objectives of the long-term incentive plan, first determine the two or three most important objectives and then identify the performance measurements best suited to those objectives.

Performance Measurements. Performance can be measured using internal measurements (financial and other), market value of company stock, or some combination. Additionally, they may relate to peer performance rather than individual company results. As indicated earlier in this chapter, the value of stock options is a direct result of market price (less the cost of purchase).

Performance-share plans have value based on stock price and the attainment of financial goals. Performance-unit and other cash plans have their value determined solely by financial performance. Many of these measurements are similar to those described in Chapter 7 (Short-Term Incentives)except that they are evaluated over a longer period of time, typically the compound average over the performance period or the period-ending value. Earnings per share, return on equity, and total shareholder return are among the most frequently used measurements. A representative list might include the following (see Chapter 2 for definitions):

- Cash flow
- Earnings
- Earnings per share
- Economic profit
- Equity growth
- Market share
- Net-worth growth
- Operating income
- Return on assets
- Return on equity
- Return on invested capital
- Return on sales
- Revenue
- Total shareholder return

Like short-term incentives, long-term incentives typically set a threshold, target, and maximum objectives. *Target* is the expected performance outcome for fully satisfactory performance. Although there may be some difficulty in meeting target, it is believed to be fully attainable. *Threshold* is the first payment above zero. While it is the minimum performance expectation, it is not considered a satisfactory result. *Maximum* is the performance beyond which it is believed there was something working positively outside of the recipient's control.

These objectives are often expressed as a probable degree of difficulty. In other words, what is the probability of hitting the threshold, target, and maximum? For the target value, it may range from a 50-50 probability to a 40-60 probability, with the latter being the more aggressive approach. The threshold probability may range from 80-20 to 90-10 and the maximum probability from 10-90 to 20-80. Some plans use reciprocals to set the threshold and maximum (e.g., 90-10 and 10-90, or 80-20 and 20-80). If the degree of difficulty cannot be quantified and explained to participants, reciprocals are more easily accepted than other values.

If peer group measurements are included, they could be any from the above list, but the two most prevalent are total shareholder return and earnings per share. However, market indicators are usually included only in corporate-level plans. If the plan is not at the corporate level, it means the removal of market value indicators. If non-financial targets are included, likely candidates would be customer satisfaction, product quality, and project results.

If internal measurements are set, they too will likely have a target, threshold, and maximum.

Eligibility. Stock-option plans typically extend further down in the organization than other forms of long-term compensation. Indeed, some plans include everyone in the organization. The idea is to promote ownership and a closer relationship to shareholders. Although this can create significant dilution issues, there is no charge to earnings. Any of the other plans would be prohibitively expensive for such broad-based coverage because they would require a charge to the earnings statement. The more expensive the form of long-term compensation, the more limited the eligibility.

The problem with any eligibility definition is the pressure it puts on the cutoff. If *salary* determines eligibility (e.g., $100,000), it will be unlikely to find anyone earning between

$95,000 and $99,999. If *grade* is the determining factor (e.g., grade 25), don't be surprised to find there are no jobs in the next lowest grade (e.g., grade 24). If it is *job title* (e.g., vice president), stand back for the flood of re-titling requests. If it is *organization level* (e.g., first three levels in the organization), how does one resolve the inequity of including a third level "assistant to" and excluding a fourth level "general manager"?

One definition that might not create as much internal pressure is *elected corporate officer*, if such status limits the individual in buying and selling company stock. It is a great ego boost to be an elected corporate officer, but it comes with heavy restrictions that can be costly, not simply cumbersome.

One possible way to minimize pressures is to pick a *combination* that seems appropriate (e.g., a vice president in grade 25 or higher who is in the first three levels of management). Another alternative is to make the determination totally *discretionary,* alleviating many of these pressures. However, this approach introduces the issues of comparability, ensuring a level playing field, and including all the right jobs.

Another consideration is how to handle promotions and demotions. Prorating is a good solution, since it diminishes problems of over and under compensation in the interim until an adjustment can be made. persons promoted should be put into the higher schedule at the time of their promotion. The portion of time in the higher grade would determine the portion of the difference between the two payments for the period in question. In Table 8-64, a person is promoted January 1st after year 3 from a grade 31 to a 33. Fractional years can be determined using similar methodology

For Plan Period	Years in Grade		Target Payment		
	31	33	31	33	Prorated
1-4	3	1	6,000	8,000	6,500
2-5	2	2	6,000	8,000	7,000
3-6	1	3	6,000	8,000	7,500
4-7	0	4		8,000	8,000

Table 8-64. Prorating a promotion

While uncommon, the ability to demote an executive should exist, within the limits of the law and a contractual commitment. If a company chooses to take such an action, any outstanding incentive pay could also be prorated.

In a similar manner, a new hire would be granted a prorated award. In the above example, assume the person was hired directly into grade 33, essentially joining the company at the end of year three. The respective target would be 2,000 (¼ of 8,000).

Plan Period. Most stock options are for 10 years since that is the maximum permitted for statutory stock options, and non-qualified options are often granted at the same time. Those who take a charge to earnings for stock options might opt for a shorter period (e.g., five or seven years). Stock appreciation rights—where they are still granted—are typically for the same period of the underlying stock option, or more commonly, for the option they are replacing (typically, in international situations because of local tax-law restrictions on company stock).

Stock-award plans are usually half the duration of options or less. Performance-share and unit plans (as well as percentage-cash plans) are typically three to five years in length. A capital-intensive company might opt for the longer period to allow time to achieve return on investment. A company in a less-than-stable industry might opt for a short period. A restricted stock award with no performance requirements is probably three to five years in duration. A performance-based, restricted award (i.e., the earlier described PARSAPS and TARSAPS) are often five-year or seven-year awards, with opportunity to receive as early as two years if stated performance requirements are met.

Award Size. The size of the long-term incentive award is based on marketplace and internal relationships. The mantra is: *externally competitive and internally equitable.* The stock option section looked at different ways of valuing the stock option competitively and then developing an internal structure. The same is true with other long-term incentive plans. First, determine how much of the executive's pay should consist of long-term incentives versus salary and annual incentives. Next, determine the proportion of each incentive plan to total long-term compensation. It is a rare company that has only one form of long-term incentive.

In determining award size when two or more plans are in place, make a distinction between *tandem* and *independent* awards. With tandem awards, there are two plans and the recipient chooses which to participate in. With independent plans, the recipient may participate in both. Tandem plans lower the downside risk associated with independent plans. A stock award will always be more valuable than a stock option Both have the same appreciation opportunity; however, the stock award also has the underlying value of the stock. Therefore, options are usually awarded in multiples of stock awards. The value of a stock option is typically set at about one-third the current value of the stock, or a three-to-one ratio. Their comparable values are both functions of future value. In Table 8-65, assume a 50-percent increase in value yielding a three-to-one ratio. Below 50 percent, the stock award is more valuable. Above 50 percent, the option is more valuable. In this example, the current stock and option prices are both $100 and values are expressed in thousands of dollars.

Number Shares Stock		Change in Stock Price			
Award	Option	-50%	0	50%	100%
0	30,000	—	—	$1,500	$3,000
5,000	15,000	$250	$500	1,500	2,500
10,000	0	500	1,000	1,500	2,000

Table 8-65. Comparison of stock option and stock award value

The above works well if the target is a 50-percent increase in stock price over the plan period. A more modest increase (e.g., 25 percent) would require an increase in options from the three-to-one ratio to perhaps five-to-one. Conversely, a more dramatic price increase would require fewer shares (e.g., two for one with a 100-percent increase).

The simplest way to determine the appropriate size of long-term incentives is to create a survey or chart of current compensation levels in a peer group of companies. Published reports in business magazines and proxy information are great sources of data for creating the survey. From this data, select a target for own company's CEO. Next, determine a target for the lowest eligible level that is appreciable but does not significantly disrupt the pay curve relative to the level one below. This should ensure a relatively seamless transition into long-term incentive eligibility. With these targets set, connect the dots and calculate the target values for all jobs between the two. Next, build threshold and maximum values around each target. At the CEO level, it would not be unreasonable for target to equal two times salary, a threshold at 25 percent, and a maximum at four times salary. At the lowest eligible level, these values might be 5 percent (threshold), 25 percent (target), and 50 percent (maximum) of salary. Percentages greater than these will cause an appreciable disruption in the total pay level of the organization, unless offset by larger annual incentives for levels ineligible for the long-term plan.

Once a plan is designed, it may require a phase-in period to get it up and running. This usually requires an additional short-term plan. A few good candidates are performance-share, performance unit, or similar plans. Since the regular plan makes no payment until after the end of the performance period, no payment will be received for the first three to five years (depending on the length of the plan period). The phase-in plan must address the issue of no payments during this interim.

Shown in Table 8-66 is a phase-in to a four-year plan. It phases in with a one-year, two-year, and three-year plan, at which point the regular plan's payouts kick in. After the phase-in period, a new four-year plan begins each year so that four plans are operating at any given time. As one plan matures, it is replaced by another and each of the other three plans advance a year in maturity

Plan Years	Years Paid	Percent of Four Year Plan Paid This Year						
		2	3	4	5	6	7	8
1	1	25%						
1-2	2	—	50%					
1-3	3	—	—	75%				
1-4	4	—	—	—	100%			
2-5	4	—	—	—	—	100%		
3-6	4	—	—	—	—	—	100%	
4-7	4	—	—	—	—	—	—	100%

Table 8-66. Portion of four-year plan paid during phase-in

If the four-year plan pays out at the end of each year based on that year's performance, it most likely will pay out more than if it paid out only at the end of the four-year period. If annual payments are to be made, overpayments will be minimized if the payment is based on plan-to-date performance less amounts paid. Thus, at the end of year two, the two-year performance would be calculated and the first year's payment subtracted to determine second-year payout.

Grant Frequency. The most common practice in both stock options and performance share/unit (and similar plans) is an annual grant. This dollar averages the highs and lows of the stock price. An added advantage of annual grants is the resulting overlap. With a four-year performance-share plan, there are four unvested plans at work. With a 10-year stock option, there are 10 years of options outstanding at any time. This annual overlap is a positive factor in retaining executives (assuming the stock will have value at the end of the vest period.)

A calculation to determine the annualized number of shares for companies that do not grant annually is to divide the total number of shares used over a period of time by the number of years. This is referred to as the *average annual run total*. When it is divided by the total shares outstanding, the resulting number is the *average annual run rate*.

Vesting. Stock options are typically *installment vested* at the rate of 20 percent to 25 percent a year (making the grant fully exercisable after four or five years). Some use the all-or-nothing *cliff vest* (e.g., 100 percent vested after four years). As described in the stock options section some grants are not exercisable until certain price or performance requirements have been met. Most other forms of long-term incentive are typically cliff-vested. A participant in a four-year performance-share plan has no rights to any payments until after the fourth year.

That raises the question of what to do, if anything, in cases of *death, disability, retirement, or change of control*. Most plans provide some form of liberalized vesting. For more detail, see the stock option section of this chapter. Many plans make the non-vested option exercisable for a stated period of time. The same would also be true for a restricted stock award. However, it is more difficult with performance share/unit and similar plans. Namely, the full value has not been calculated because the performance period is not completed. In such situations, it is rather common to prorate the benefit. For individuals who do not work a full year, it would be appropriate to prorate, counting a fraction of a month as a full month in cases of death, disability, retirement, or change of control.

Shown in Table 8-67 is an example of how an individual in a four-year plan would be treated if payment were prorated. The percentage shown is the value determined at the end of time period, based on the percentage of the plan period the executive was employed.

	Employed				After Retirement				
Years	**1**	**2**	**3**	**4**	**5**	**6**	**7**	**8**	**9**
1-4	✔	✔	✔	✔	100%				
2-5		✔	✔	✔	✔	75%			
3-6			✔	✔	✔	✔	50%		
4-7				✔	✔	✔	✔	25%	
5-8					✔	✔	✔	✔	0%

Table 8-67. Prorating payments after retirement

Other possible actions are: full payment for the period, prorating in a discretionary manner, or complete forfeiture. The latter is not only the harshest, under the circumstances, it seems the most unjust. Voluntary and involuntary "for cause" terminations would receive only vested benefits: no prorating of non-vested benefits. Other involuntary terminations might be eligible for prorating.

Shares Required. Given the type of long-term incentive plans and the number of eligible candidates and possible award sizes, one can estimate how many shares will be needed. Typically, plans span a 10-year period and must receive shareholder approval.

Historically, shareholders deemed appropriate a stated percentage of outstanding shares each year for executive stock plans. For years, many institutions used the *five & ten formula* in deciding whether or not to vote in favor of a stock-plan proposal. The idea was that a request for anything up to 5 percent was reasonable, between 5 percent and 10 percent *might* be reasonable, and anything above 10 percent was unreasonable. However, those benchmarks have significantly eroded over time. Startup companies, high technology organizations, and those with broad-based stock option plans going well down into the organization will require higher numbers. How a company might analyze the stock situation is shown in Table 8-68.

Shares Authorized		1,000,000,000	
Shares Outstanding		325,000,000	
Shares Available for Grant		20,000,000	
Currently Available Awaiting Shareholder Approval	5,000,000 15,000,000		
Options Outstanding		10,235,000	
Percent Shares Outstanding			3.1%
Total Options Available and Outstanding		30,235,000	
Percent Shares Outstanding			9.9%

Table 8-68. Review of authorized, outstanding, and available stock

In this example, the company is awaiting shareholder approval on a proposal for an additional 15 million shares, or 4.6 percent of shares outstanding. The authorized shares are included in this review in case the company is considering a stock split. It has enough for a two-for-one split and is just short of that needed for a three-for-one split (i.e., 325,000,000 + 20,000,000 + 10,235,000 = 355,235,000), since the 1,065,705 required (i.e., 355,235,000 x 3) exceeds the 1 billion shares authorized.

Let's take the analysis one step further. In Table 8-69, the company has estimated the number of shares it will need for the next five years, based on its stock-option plan and a performance-share plan. The performance-share plan is shown at maximum value number to be safe. Target would be one half that amount.

	Stock Options	**Performance Share**	**Total**
Year 1	1,500,000	1,000,000	2,500,000
Year 2	1,500,000	1,000,000	2,500,000
Year 3	1,500,000	1,000,000	2,500,000
Year 4	1,500,000	1,000,000	2,500,000
Year 4	1,500,000	1,000,000	2,500,000
Total	7,500,000	5,000,000	12,500,000

Table 8-69. Estimated number of shares needed for plans

The 12.5 million shares is well within the 15 million shares requested, so the company will not have to return to the shareholders for at least five years, longer if the performance-share plan pays out below the maximum. This example assumes a static number of participants and awards for each of the five years. A more detailed examination would estimate changes in the number of eligible candidates and their awards by year.

Dilution is always a shareholder concern. An increase in the number of shares outstanding dilutes earnings per share and may therefore impact stock price. In the Table 8-68 example, the current dilution is 3.1 percent, but the total dilution is 9.9 percent. Some call this additional 6.8 percent the *overhang* or *future overhang*. Others refer to the 9.9 percent as the *total potential overhang* or *total future overhang*. Under FAS 128, *EPS* (earnings per share) is simply earnings divided by shares outstanding. *Diluted EPS* is also calculated using FAS 128 earnings per share (replacing APB Opinion 15).

This standard requires the treasury stock method to determine the increased number of shares in the denominator resulting from outstanding options that are "in the money" (i.e., market price exceeds option price). More specifically, the cost to exercise in-the-money options is used to buy back as many shares as possible, based on current market price. Using the data in Table 8-68, assume the average option price is $60 a share (and all of the 10,235,000 options outstanding are in the money). Further assume current fair market value of $100. The calculation would be as follows:

10,235,000 x $60 = $614,100,000
$614,100,000 ÷ $100 = 6,141,000 shares
10,235,000 - 6,141,000 = 4,094,000 shares added to the denominator

Some believe it appropriate to go beyond the FAS 128 requirement and use the cash value of any tax deductions as well. For example, were all the stock options non-qualified, there would be a tax deduction of $409,400,000 (i.e., $40 x 10,235,000 shares). If the corporate tax rate were 35 percent, this would generate an additional cash flow of $143,290,000 (i.e., .35 x $409,400,000). At a cost of $100 a share, the company could buy back an additional 1,432,900 shares, reducing the increase in the denominator to 2,661,100 (i.e., 4,094,000 - 1,432,900).

A more appropriate way to measure dilution may be to assume the option price (i.e., strike price) and the tax value of the deduction (if any) is used to repurchase shares on the market. In this way, only the incremental number or shares (i.e., those not repurchased) dilute outstanding shares. Some companies do exactly this, as there is no associated expense; however, the company does lose the positive cash flow of the option proceeds and tax deductions.

Market capitalization, or *market cap* for short, is nothing more than current stock price multiplied by the number of shares outstanding. In Table 8-68, assuming $100 a share, the market cap is 32.5 billion. By any standards, this is a large cap, if not a mega cap. Although definitions vary, market cap can be broken into parts: *micro-cap* (under $100,000 million), *small-cap* (between $100 million and 1 billion), *mid-cap* (between $1 billion and $10 billion), *large-cap* (between $10 billion and $100 billion), and *mega-cap* (above $100 billion).

The Formal Stock Plan. A formal stock plan consists of two slightly different documents. The first is a document typically prepared for shareholder approval and referred to here as the formal plan or the shareholder plan. It authorizes management to use company stock as a form of compensation within the limits prescribed by the plan. Various overseers may mandate such a document including the SEC, the state in which incorporated, and/or the listing stock exchange. It may also be needed to take advantage of the tax deduction requirements of Section 162(m) or 412 of the Internal Revenue Code (IRC). The second document is created for the executive and is referred to here as the executive plan. This document is typically approved by the compensation committee of the board and specifies the terms and conditions of the stock award/option. Each is a formal contract: one with shareholders and the other with the executive. Let's examine the contents of both, as well as some design considerations.

Purpose. The formal plan will typically state its purpose as being to effectively attract, retain, and compensate key employees to ensure company success and provide a reasonable return on shareholder investment. The executive plan (typically in the form of a letter) may repeat this and go further. If it includes a stock option, the letter will indicate the opportunity to share in the future growth of the stock price (hopefully, the result of the collective efforts of key employees). If it includes a time-based stock award, the letter will talk of the value of providing future pay (with the hidden message that the executive must stay around to cash in). If it includes a performance-based stock award, the nature of such performance will be described (e.g., financial or shareholder).

Definitions. Both documents will identify and describe key words used in each plan. The shareholder plan will be broader in scope since it covers all plans. However, it will not go in-depth into any one plan like the executive plan, which will be more detailed in nature and may include material covered in this chapter.

Administration. The formal plan will identify the respective responsibilities of the board of directors and its compensation committee in setting up rules and administering the plan. It may define the composition of the compensation committee, indicating the minimum (and perhaps maximum number of members) and their relationship to the company (e.g., disinterested, non-management members). [This will be reviewed in more detail in Chapter 10 (The Board of Directors).] The executive plan will contain much of the same material, but again go further, indicating the respective responsibilities of others as delegated by the compensation committee. For example, the CFO may be responsible for collecting and summarizing peer company data, if that is included in the basis of payment. The chief legal officer would be responsible for signing off on executive agreements. The chief human resources officer may be responsible for summarizing and presenting the outcomes and proposals to the compensation committee.

Participation. The formal plan will set a wide parameter on the definition of who is eligible. This may include all employees, outside directors, and sometimes even suppliers such as consultants in lieu of cash. The document may also state who is not eligible. The executive plan will likely describe eligibility in more specific terms such as salary, job grade, organization level, or title.

The shareholder plan may identify sub-plans (typically located outside of the United States) that are subject to the same terms and conditions of the shareholder-plan except to the extent adjustments are necessary to conform to local law and regulations. The executive letter would refer to one of the sub-plans only if it covered the executive.

The formal plan may also permit, limit, or prohibit awards and options due to leave of absence, disability, or death. For example, the plan may limit transfers only at time of death in accordance with estate provisions, or it may permit a more liberal definition and include transfers while alive.

The executive letter will specifically indicate what happens under each of these situations, being no more liberal than the shareholder-approved plan and possibly more restrictive.

Both plans may state under what conditions (if any) it will permit the compensation committee to require the surrender of an option/award in order to receive a new one (e.g., re-pricing).

Number of Shares. The shareholder plan will state the maximum number of shares that are available for use. This may be in addition to unused shares from another still-active plan. A plan that automatically replenishes used shares from an authorized total is called an *evergreen plan*. The formula could be stated in absolute numbers (i.e., always X million shares), in relative terms (e.g., Y percent of shares issued and outstanding), or a combination of the two (either expressed as the higher or lower of the alternative formulas). A variation would be to include a performance factor calling for an up or down adjustment based on either an absolute or relative measurement. An absolute measure might be 15-percent ROE; a relative measure might refer to a peer group (e.g., total shareholder return for preceding year in excess of identified group of companies).

Since options require two to four times as much stock as stock awards, many plans do not set inside limits on stock awards. However, some shareholder groups will extract a promise from management to establish a specific inside limit in exchange for a favorable vote from the institution. The executive plan will detail the number of shares (and other particulars) in the grant/award letter, specific to each individual.

The shareholder plan will stipulate whether or not shares granted/awarded that went unused because of forfeiture or lapse of time can be reused in a future grant/award. If this is permitted, requests for more shares are less frequent. The executive plan may be silent on this point, as it does not directly affect the executive.

Terms of the Plan. The shareholder plan will state the date beyond which no shares may be awarded from the plan. An exception is the evergreen plan, which typically has no expiration date. If one or more amendments have been made to the plan, there may be more than one date. If there are outstanding plans, expiration dates will be cited for each, referring back to the shareholder-approved date. The executive grant/award letter will stipulate only the date at which the option/award will lapse.

Type of Stock Plan. The shareholder-approved plan will indicate what forms of stock compensation may be used. Almost all will include stock options. If so, it will state how the option price will be determined (often in terms of "not less than X," leaving complete flexibility for any figure above that amount). The plan will also set a minimum exercise period. It may permit the grant of statutory options, allowing the administering authority to take the necessary actions for the grant to qualify for statutory treatment. Not uncommon would be the authorization to use stock to pay awards from non-stock plans (e.g., performance-unit or salary-percentage plans).

The shareholder plan may also identify only those stock awards permitted (e.g., stock appreciation rights, performance-share plans, restricted stock, and stock purchases) or, conversely, only those excluded (e.g., restricted stock with no performance feature). The advantage of the exclusion approach is that it allows for innovation in new plans without the need to return for shareholder approval. Needless to say, management would like the plan defined as broadly as possible. Such broad-based plans are often called *omnibus plans*.

The executive letter will describe the specific plan along with all the terms and conditions.

Re-capitalization. The shareholder-approved plan will describe what will happen should the number of shares outstanding change as the result of re-capitalization, liquidation, stock split, or stock dividend.

The executive letter would probably repeat the same.

Amendment and Revocation. Typically, the shareholder-approved plan will give the board of directors the right to take any action it deems appropriate to alter, amend, or revoke the plan. However, the board may not reduce the rights of outstanding options/awards (without shareholder approval) or change shares that may be issued. The executive letter—if it says anything—would probably repeat the same.

Dividends. In addition to paying dividends on stock issued (including those under restrictions), dividends are sometimes paid on stock under option or performance plans where shares or their equivalent have not been issued. Typically, these are called *dividend equivalents*. It is also possible to grant *freestanding* or *stand-alone* dividend equivalents, namely, dividends not associated with another plan. These would be covered, if applicable, in both the shareholder plan and the executive plan.

Communication. The specific terms and conditions of each plan are detailed in a formal plan for shareholders and a letter to the executive. To the executive, it is useful to include an historical as well as future look at the total compensation package. More will be said of this in Chapters 9 and 10, but let's look at how the long-term incentive portion might be set up. Shown in Table 8-70 is an example of what an individual's stock option and performance-share report might look like.

In this example, we see the total number of option shares still outstanding, when they become exercisable, and at what price. We also see the performance-share plan schedule and the 15,000 shares paid out in year five (this year).

Stock Options

Grant Year	Option Price	Number Shares Vested at Year End				
		Year 4	Year 5	Year 6	Year 7	Total
1	$57.50	15,000				15,000
2	45.50	15,000	15,000			30,000
3	78.50	—	15,000	15,000		30,000
4	105.00	—	—	15,000	15,000	30,000
	Total	30,000	30,000	30,000	15,000	105,000

Performance Share Awards

Plan Period	Share Schedule			Paid Out in First Quarter of...			
	Threshold	Target	Maximum	Year 5	Year 6	Year 7	Year 8
1-4	1,000	10,000	25,000	15,000			
2-5	1,000	10,000	25,000		✔		
3-6	1,000	10,000	25,000			✔	
4-7	1,000	10,000	25,000				✔

Table 8-70. Long-term incentives worksheet for Ms. Jolly Goodshow

Shown in Table 8-71 is an example of a letter the Chairman of the Compensation Committee might send to Ms. Jolly Goodshow, informing her of the year five payout from the performance-share plan.

RE: Performance Share Plan

Ms. Jolly Goodshow:

As you know, you were included in the Performance Share Plan for the four-year period ending last December. The Compensation Committee has determined the Company achieved 120% of its earnings per share target. The Committee then certified that based on the approved schedule, you are to be awarded 15,000 shares.

As of yesterday, the determination date of the award, your award was valued at $165,000. By earlier correspondence, you were advised of the tax withholding and issuance requirements. Your shares will be distributed to you six months from today due to a six-month holding requirement under SEC section 16.

The value of the award is not considered as earnings for the purposes of the Company Retirement Plan and its related supplemental plan. Nor is the value of the vested shares considered earnings for the purposes of the Company Savings Plan.

For your reference, attached is a copy of the original letter explaining the terms of your performance share plan. Since this is a copy of the original letter, the stated number of shares has not been adjusted for last year's stock split.

I.M. Right
Chair
Compensation Committee

Table 8-71. Sample performance-share plan letter

Stock Ownership

Not only do many long-term incentive plans pay in relation to stock performance, more and more companies are expecting their CEO and other top executives to hold on to the stock received through stock options and stock awards. These expectations range from verbal encouragement to firm requirements.

What Are the Program Objectives? Defining clear objectives will help delineate the program. In identifying objectives, ask questions such as, "Do we want to more closely align senior management with the shareholders? To what extent should the executive portfolio be in company stock? To what extent will executives be permitted to cash out gains in stock options and stock awards?"

In establishing the objectives, keep in mind that many things outside of management's control can and will affect the price of stock in both a positive and negative manner. In addition, since executives, especially new hires, will not view stock-ownership guidelines as a plus, develop a strategy to address this concern. A longer phase-in period or assistance in obtaining the stock may help. Chapter 9 will review objectives in more detail.

Do not confuse stock options with stock ownership. The first is an opportunity to acquire stock at favorable prices, but if cashed out, there is no increase in stock ownership. This does not mean, however, that those holding options are not interested in the stock price. They are as long as they hold the option. Stock options are also more likely to motivate than stock awards because they are leveraged and have less downside risk.

The downside of stock-ownership guidelines is that once implemented, they de facto endorse diversification of the executive's portfolio unless stated as minimums and periodically increased. Some argue for a range of ownership with an aggressive high-end number. For example, instead of a guideline that is five times salary for the CEO, it might be expressed as a minimum of five times salary with a target of 15 times salary and no maximum.

Who Is Affected? Guidelines are directed at those executives with the strongest influence on stock price. For that reason, they usually apply to the CEO and other very senior executives. When ownership guidelines go further down in the organization, the objective is to create a closer connection between individual assets and company stock performance.

How Are Guidelines Determined? The guideline is typically expressed as a multiple of pay; however, some choose to specify a number of shares or a percentage of a transaction (such as stock option exercises).

When pay is the basis, the multiple may be assigned to job grade, organization level, or pay directly. Regardless of the base, this method is called the *multiple approach*.

Multiple Approach. A multiplier is applied to pay (either salary or salary–plus-bonus) and the product divided by the price of the stock. If the multiplier is 4 (i.e., 400 percent) and pay is $500,000, the product is $2 million. If the stock price were $100, the guideline would be 20,000 shares (i.e., $2 million ÷ $100).

The multiple is often assigned to the salary, although some companies combine salary and bonus. If the latter were used, one would expect a lower multiple. For example, a multiplier of 800 percent on salary would be the equivalent of a multiplier of 400 percent on salary–plus-bonus if bonus were equal to salary, but 600 percent if bonus were half the amount of salary. This illustrates the importance of the definition of pay as well as the relative size of the pay component. In addition, since salary is much more constant that total annual pay (i.e., salary plus bonus), movements in stock price are more likely to have a more negative impact on a salary-only formula. This is based on the supposition that bonus may vary more in line with stock price than salary.

Not surprisingly, ownership targets are often highest for CEOs who have held the position longest. Not only are they increased from time to time, they may also depend on time in position. An example would be 100 percent for every year. In our example, the CEO would only need to have 20,000 shares after one year in position, increasing annually. After 10 years in the position (assuming no change in salary or stock price), the CEO would need 200,000 shares to stay within guidelines.

Even if the share requirement is not time adjusted, they are likely to increase periodically. Oftentimes, this occurs when the company asks shareholders for more shares in the stock plan. It's a trade off, "Give us more shares and I promise we will own more shares."

In addition to comparing stock ownership targets to stock owned for the CEO and the other four top paid executives in the proxy, it is useful to compare the shares owned to total shares outstanding. Why? The higher the percentage the executives own, the greater their tie to other shareholders. On the other hand, differences in these ratios between companies are often the result of stage in market cycle. One would expect top management of threshold companies and recent IPOs to own a larger percentage than those of large mature organizations.

The assigned multiple approach also works well below the CEO level and can be based on organization level, job grade, or pay itself.

By *organization level*, the multiplier might be 800 percent of salary for the CEO, 700 percent for the next level (perhaps an executive vice president), and so on down the organization. By *job grade*, it might be 800 percent for grade 35, 700 percent for grade 34, etc. By *pay*, it might be 800 percent for $2 million and up (salary–plus-bonus), 700 percent for $1.8 million to $2 million, 600 percent for $1.6 million to $1.8 million, etc.

Specified Number of Shares. Again there are three approaches: organization level, job grade, and pay itself. For organization level, the CEO might be required to own 100,000 shares, the executive vice president, 80,000 shares, and so on. Using job grades, one might set 100,000 shares as the requirement for grade 35, 95,000 shares for grade 34, 90,000 shares for grade 33, etc. Using pay directly might result in a requirement of owning 100,000 shares for a salary of $1 million and higher; 75,000 shares for a salary between $750,000 and $1 million, 50,000 shares for a salary between $500,000 and $750,000; and 25,000 shares for a salary between $250,000 and $500,000.

Using a set number of shares has the advantage of cushioning the executive in times of rising or falling stock prices, which is not true of the multiple approach. Falling stock prices would force the executive to buy and hold more stock, which could cause a significant financing problem. Needless to say, guidelines will be sorely tested in a long-term bear market. Expressing the guidelines as a percentage of the last three or more years of options granted might minimize the impact of sharp increases or decreases in stock price. In any event, the guideline will require periodic updating to avoid losing its value over time as pay increases. When and how much to adjust the number of shares is a major problem with this type of approach.

Stock Acquired. Rather than set an overall target, this approach does it transaction by transaction on either stock received through awards or through exercising stock options. An example would be to require the executive to hold those shares remaining after taxes have been paid. A variation would be to require the executive to own a number of shares equivalent to the average number of stock options granted (not exercised) over a stated period of time (e.g., three years). Another variation would be to limit the executive to exercising options only after the paper gain of options outstanding exceeded the ownership guideline. Thus, if the guideline were 800 percent of salary and salary was $1 million, then the executive could exercise those options over $8 million of paper profit. However, this approach always leaves options that cannot be exercised. One way to avoid this and still achieve an ownership target is to require that all exercised options be converted to restricted shares of stock. The restrictions will lapse in installments over a period of years in accordance with the ownership guideline target.

What Is the Definition of Shares Owned? The broader the definition of shares owned, the easier to meet the stated target. The most stringent is the straightforward shares owned outright. The first liberalization of this definition would be to count share-equivalent of the executive's own contributions to the 401(k) plan invested in company stock. Some go one step further and include the value of the company contributions made to the executive's account in company stock. Some go so far as to include the "paper gain" in unexercised stock options, either vested or both vested and unvested. The impact of this is illustrated in Table 8-72.

Salary = $1 million	Cumulative Totals	
	Share Value	Percent Salary
Shares Owned Outright	$2,000,000	200%
$500,000 Executive Contributions in Company 401(k) Plan	2,500,000	250%
$500,000 of Company Match in Company 401(k) Plan	3,000,000	300%
$2 million "Paper Gain" in Vested Unexercised Stock Options	5,000,000	500%
$3 million "Paper Gain" in Non-vested Unexercised Stock Options	8,000,000	800%

Table 8-72. Definition differences of shares owned

This illustrates the importance of the definition of "shares owned." Depending on the definition used, the executive has anywhere between two to eight times salary (i.e., 200,000 to 800,000 shares) in company stock. Therefore, one would expect that a more liberal definition of stock owned to require a higher number of shares be held.

However, when individuals cash out stock options without retaining any shares (sometimes called *flipping*) there is no increase in the number of shares owned, and, depending on the definition of shares owned, the number may actually have decreased. One way to determine how aggressively executives have cashed in their stock options is to look up the total number of shares exercised, say over the last five years, and compare that to stock currently held. Or, even better, if records are available, how many shares were owned 10 years ago? Table 8-73 compares the transactions of three individuals.

Here we see that each owned 5,000 shares five years ago, and each exercised options on 200,000 shares in the five-year period. "Person C" apparently kept most, if not all, of the shares exercised after paying taxes. "Person A" essentially cashed out the grants, and "Person B" made some progress toward whatever target he or she was assigned. Even if the records for five years earlier are unavailable, one can still see the differences in the exercise strategies of the three by simply comparing the shares currently owned with those exercised over the past five years. "Person A" only owns 5 percent of shares exercised, whereas "Person C" owns 50 percent. It is not difficult to see who is trying to build stock ownership.

Guidelines or Requirements? Ownership objectives can be met in one of three ways (or any combination thereof): encouraged by the company, rewarded through plan design, and/or man-

	Shares Owned		Shares Exercised in Last Five Years
	Five Years Ago	Now	
Person A	5,000	10,000	200,000
Person B	5,000	25,000	200,000
Person C	5,000	100,000	200,000

Table 8-73. Shares exercised vs. owned

dated by the company. The first is one of objective-by-leadership; typically, the CEO takes an aggressive personal ownership in company stock and asks other senior executives to join in. The second is through a number of stock-plans features described earlier including option reloads, additional share awards for exercised options held for a stated period, share deposit options, cancellation of non-recourse loans, and other devices. The third is more straightforward. Individuals are given a number of years (typically five) to attain the stated number of shares. Barring unusual circumstances, the person may be denied new options until the requirement is met.

In meeting guidelines, progress is typically tracked annually, as illustrated in Table 8-74. Note that the executive is still 5,000 shares below the target, although ownership has increased by 6,000 shares the past year.

Number of Shares Owned, Year End	
Last December 31st Year Previous	75,000 69,000
Current Target Total Number of Shares @ $100 a Share:	80,000
In Relation to Target Below Target Above Target	5,000 —

Table 8-74. Stock ownership status report

What Is Communicated? In addition to communicating stock ownership objectives to both shareholders and executives, the guidelines must also be clearly stated. Who is affected? How are the guidelines determined? What is the definition of shares owned? Are they guidelines or requirements? And what happens if they are not met?

PRIVATELY HELD STOCK

As indicated in the introduction of this chapter, company stock can be issued two different ways. It could be publicly traded on a stock exchange or it could be privately held by the owners of the company. The last major section dealt with publicly trade stock. With respect to compensation plans, *virtually anything that can be done with publicly traded stock can also be done with privately held stock.* The major difference between the two is that while price quotes are available almost daily for publicly traded stock, the price—or estimated value—of privately held stock is more difficult and costly to attain. The value of a share of publicly traded stock can be found simply by looking to the financial section of any major newspaper. However, to determine the value of privately held stock, a company has to hire outside financial specialists to review company books and determine an appropriate value. This expense thus limits the use of stock plans commonly employed by publicly traded companies.

PHANTOM STOCK PLANS

Plans that do not permit the recipient to own publicly traded or privately held stock are called phantom plans because the "stock" does not really exist. Such plans may also be called *shadow* or *pretend* stock plans. There are two types of phantom plans: market-value-based and non-market-based plans.

Market-Value-Based Stock Plans

These plans are a form of incentive pay that uses company stock (typically publicly traded) as the basis for measurement but not necessarily the form of payment. There are three types: dividend equivalents, appreciation rights, and full value units. Sometimes payment is in stock if it is available, but usually payments are in cash. These plans are typical of countries where individuals cannot own foreign company stock and/or the taxing of such stocks and options is prohibitive.

Dividend Equivalents. The recipient is awarded a dividend equivalent equal to a stated number of shares of company stock. The executive does not receive the stock but will receive each year an amount (typically in cash) equal to the dividend paid. Thus, an executive who received 10,000 shares/units with dividends equaling $1 each would receive $10,000 for the year. The following year, if the executive received an additional 10,000 units and the dividend was increased to $1.10, payment would total $22,000. Such grants may be in effect for long periods of time, e.g., until death or age 85 whichever comes *last.* Since the employee has income, the company has a deduction and an ongoing charge to the income statement. The early death of an executive could cause considerable cash liquidity problems for the estate if payments continue, because estate taxation requires including in the estate payments to be received in the future.

Appreciation Rights. These operate exactly like the SARs described earlier in the chapter except they are not attached to actual shares of company stock. A stated number of phantom stock units at a prescribed price are given to the executive with a specified date of valuation. Thus, at valuation date, the executive receives the difference between fair market value and price at time of grant, typically in cash. The company has a tax deduction at time of payment and the executive has a comparable amount of income. The company has to amortize the compensation liability.

A variation on the appreciation from fair market value at time of grant is a discount, which can be prescribed at time of grant or by formula and calculated at time of valuation. If the discount were 100 percent, it would be a *full-value unit* as described below and would be similar to a deferred-stock bonus (especially if payment were in the form of company stock).

Full Value Units. This approach differs from appreciation rights only in that appreciation is from first dollar to fair market value at date of valuation. In other words, the price at time of grant is zero rather than current fair market value.

Non-Market-Based Stock Plans

In general, anything that market-based plans can do non-market plans can also do. While most common in privately held companies, under certain circumstances, they are useful for publicly traded companies as well. In addition, non-market plans probably have the most attractive and certainly the simplest payout—cash.

The formula for these plans is not tied to company stock in any way. Instead, it specifies the amount of cash that will be paid with the achievement of defined objectives (note that performance-unit plans, paying in cash, not stock, would meet this description). The award can be paid immediately or deferred over a period of time. The company has a deduction at the time of payment equal to the amount the executive has earned in the way of income. The earnings statement is charged with accrued expense over the performance period.

However, the strength of these plans is their weakness. With cash payments, there are no opportunities for long-term capital gains tax treatment. Also, although they are not likely to go "underwater" or remain flat for prolonged periods like market-based stock plans, so too, they are not capable of rising dramatically in times of a bullish stock market. These characteristics make such plans almost a form of guaranteed-payout profit sharing. Of course, establishing a minimum growth target before payment thwarts this problem.

Non-market-based plans are sometimes called *employer stock plans* because they have no market-value stock component. Sometimes, publicly traded companies use them instead of stock. When prices are languishing on the stock market, an internal valuation might be more beneficial because of languishing stock price. Publicly traded companies also use them for strategic business units (SBUs) that do not have their own stock. However, they are most common with privately held companies where they are an attractive alternative to diluting ownership.

Measurements Used. Lacking a market measurement, non-market-based plans rely on internal financial measurements. Probably the most common is *book value*, or shareholder equity (i.e., assets minus liabilities) divided by shares outstanding. Another form of phantom stock is the earlier described *tracking stock*. In a private company, it could be at any level—company wide or by division. In a public company, it typically would be found in an SBU. The measurement could be a financial one that would relate to that unit (e.g., gross margin or EBITDA). The phantom stock issued could be full value units or appreciation. Other possibilities include those described in Chapter 2 (Performance Measurements). These include: budget attainment, cash flow, earnings, earnings per share, economic profit, equity growth, market share, net-worth growth, return on assets, return on equity, return on invested capital, return on net assets, return on sales, revenue and total shareholder return. Variable accounting rules are in effect to determine charge to earnings and the company will have a tax deduction when the individual receives the income.

Dividend Equivalents. A privately held company may also use phantom stock to pay dividends of some form of interest. This is advantageous in closely held organizations where the owners do not wish to dilute ownership. Alternatively, the dividends could be paid on stock actually awarded.

Appreciation Rights. An appreciation right on the phantom stock of privately held companies or SBUs would use some measuring device other than market value. Many plans are constructed around book value. Unlike company stock, which can bounce up and down under the influence of macroeconomic issues rather than company performance, book value usually has a nice steady progress. (However, it is affected by acquisitions and divestitures.) Book-value plans have been used primarily by privately held companies, although publicly held companies may also adopt them when stock performance is lackluster. Simply stated, such a plan allows executives an opportunity to benefit from appreciation in book rather than market value.

Another variation deals with earnings per share; such plans are likely to use a moving multiyear average (or total) to avoid small annual swings. Still another variation for those in mining or drilling might relate to established reserves; certainly, this would place a significant emphasis on new discoveries.

Full Value Units. The 100-percent discount of full value units may be accomplished by allowing the executive to purchase stock at its current book value (e.g., repaying the loan with dividends received). Alternatively, the stock might be awarded outright. Using the example shown in Table 8-75, assume an executive received 10,000 book value units at $25 a share. If the plan specified that payment could also include dividends, the executive would have received almost enough (i.e., $23.90 a share) in dividends after 10 years to cover the $25 initial stock price. The stock would be worth $648,600 (i.e., 10,000 shares at $64.86 a share).

		Allocation of EPS		
	EPS	Dividend	Retained	Book Value
Base		—	—	$25.00
1	$4.00	$1.50	$2.50	27.50
2	4.40	1.65	2.75	30.25
3	4.84	1.81	3.03	33.28
4	5.32	2.00	3.32	36.60
5	5.86	2.20	3.66	40.26
6	6.44	2.41	4.03	44.29
7	7.09	2.66	4.43	48.72
8	7.79	2.92	4.87	53.59
9	8.57	3.21	5.36	58.95
10	9.43	3.54	5.89	64.86
Total	$63.74	$23.90	$39.84	
Appreciation				$39.84

Table 8-75. Example of book value stock purchase

If the executive were simply given appreciation units, no investment would be required and the executive would have $398,400 from appreciation. If dividend equivalents were also a feature, the executive would receive an additional $239,000 during the 10 years. Both would be ordinary income with the company receiving a like tax deduction when paid; however, expense would have been accrued over the 10-year period.

Typically, the executive must sell the stock back to the company when employment is terminated. In case of death, disability, or retirement, the stock would be bought back at current book value. However, with voluntary terminations some form of penalty may exist (e.g., buyback at original book or forfeiture of all gains for the previous five years).

Rather than award the book-value stock outright, the executive might be given the option to purchase. A variation to book value would be book-value-plus-dividends-paid. The advantage of this approach is that a change in the level of earnings retained has no impact on the valuation. Remember period-ending book value is by definition equal to book value at beginning of period plus earnings per share less dividends paid.

Following the same example repeated in Table 8-76, the executive would be offered an option to buy at $25. If the executive exercises the option five years later, the gain would either be $15.26 (i.e., $40.26 - $25) or $24.42 (i.e., $49.42 - $25) per share, depending on which definition of book value was used for purposes of the option.

		Allocation of EPS		Book Value	Book Value Plus Dividend
	EPS	Dividend	Retained		
Base		—	—	$25.00	$25.00
I	$4.00	$1.50	$2.50	27.50	29.00
2	4.40	1.65	2.75	30.25	33.40
3	4.84	1.81	3.03	33.28	38.24
4	5.32	2.00	3.32	36.60	43.56
5	5.86	2.20	3.66	40.26	49.42
6	6.44	2.41	4.03	44.29	55.86
7	7.09	2.66	4.43	48.72	62.95
8	7.79	2.92	4.87	53.59	70.74
9	8.57	3.21	5.36	58.95	79.31
10	9.43	3.54	5.89	64.86	88.74
Total	$63.74	$23.90	$39.84		
Appreciation				$39.84	$63.74

Table 8-76. Example of book value stock option

At time of exercise, the executive would have income in the amount of $152,600 or $244,200 (again depending on the definition), assuming 10,000 shares were purchased. There would be no tax event if constructive receipt were avoided. Assume the individual retires five years after when the book values are $64.84 and $88.74, or $648,400 and $887,400, respectively, for 10,000 shares. The difference of $495,800 and $643,200, respectively, could qualify for long-term capital gains taxation.

The company would have a tax deduction and charge to earnings equal to the amount the executive received as ordinary income, but not on any long-term capital gains. The total increase at retirement, either $495,800 or $643,200, would have been charged to earnings, and the company would have a like tax deduction assuming no long-term capital gains tax availability. The lack of long-term capital gains would greatly reduce the attractiveness to executives of this type of plan. One would have to wonder why anyone would purchase phantom stock unless it could qualify for long-term capital gains.

However, privately held companies must be very careful in setting up such plans if they may at some point go public through an initial public offering (IPO). Plan design should ensure that accounting and tax issues do not complicate such a transaction. Lacking an ownership interest, management cannot buy out owners because they have no real stock.

Except for acquisitions, spin-offs, changes in accounting procedure, or other unusual events that could affect book value (all of which can be netted out), the appreciation of this type of value is a direct function of corporate financial success and not subject to external factors. Thus, the executive with book-value units in a publicly traded company is not concerned with the stock market assessment of corporate performance. As long as shareholder equity is increasing on a per-share basis, the potential value of the non-market incentive is also increasing. Not surprisingly, the executive's degree of interest in book-value options is almost directly inversely related to the direction of movement in common stock: great interest in times of bear markets, little interest during bull markets.

While book value has been used here to illustrate non-market type plans, a number of other measurements are available. Let's take a look at several variations using earnings per share (EPS): performance-cash plans, performance-unit plans, and performance-percentage plans.

Rather than set the schedule in shares of stock, *performance-cash plans* use the current value of the stock to develop a dollar or cash figure. In Table 8-77, the performance shares in the earlier example (Table 8-40) have been converted using $100 a share.

The dollar allocation is adjusted by company performance as shown in Table 8-78. Note that this is a version of Table 8-45. Thus, if the corporate three-year average EPS were 16 percent, instead of 30,000 shares, the payment would be $3,000,000 (i.e., $1,500,000 x 2). This amount would either be paid in cash, stock, or a combination. If paid in stock, the difference would inversely reflect the change in stock price. That is to say, if the price of the stock dou-

Grade	Award Multiple	Shares of Stock	Cash Value
35	1.5	15,000	$1,500,000
34	1.4	14,000	1,400,000
33	1.3	13,000	1,300,000
32	1.2	12,000	1,200,000
31	1.1	11,000	1,100,000
30	1.0	10,000	1,000,000
29	0.9	9,000	900,000
28	0.8	8,000	800,000
27	0.7	7,000	700,000
26	0.6	6,000	600,000
25	0.5	5,000	500,000

Table 8-77. Performance-share converted to performance-cash plan

Percent Growth in EPS Over Period	Percent Cash Award Paid
15% or higher	200%
12.0%-14.9%	150%
10.0%-11.9%	100%
8.0%-9.9%	50%
below 8.0%	0%

Table 8-78. Percent cash award based on EPS

bled, one would receive half the number of shares that would have been given if it were a performance-share plan. Namely, had this been a performance-share plan (again referring to Table 8-52), the executive would have received 30,000 shares (i.e., 15,000 x 2) worth $600,000 (i.e., 30,000 shares x $200). With these same numbers, under the performance-cash plan the individual would have received 15,000 shares (i.e., $3,000,000 ÷ $200).

Since the plan is insulated from market factors, it will exactly equal the dollar value believed appropriate at a prescribed level of performance. While the expected dollar allocation must be amortized, there is no adjustment for movement in company stock since its market value has no impact on the dollar value of the award.

It is a simple step to convert from a performance-cash to a *performance-unit plan*—simply remove the dollar signs and the values become units. As illustrated in Table 8-79, each unit is worth a dollar.

Grade	Cash Value	Performance Units
35	$1,500,000	1,500,000
34	1,400,000	1,400,000
33	1,300,000	1,300,000
32	1,200,000	1,200,000
31	1,100,000	1,100,000
30	1,000,000	1,000,000
29	900,000	900,000
28	800,000	800,000
27	700,000	700,000
26	600,000	600,000
25	500,000	500,000

Table 8-79. Performance cash converted to performance units

Why make this conversion? Because it means never having to redo the plan if one decides at a future date to increase the payout. To increase payouts by 10 percent, one would have to restate the payments in Table 8-77. Namely, $1,500,00 would become $1,650,000, $1,400,000 would become $1,540,000, etc. However, if the plan were in units, the number of units would not be changed, only the unit value, which would now become $1.10. It is easy to see that a performance-unit plan can easily and quickly be adjusted on a frequent basis to maintain the desired relationship to salary and annual incentives. Again, the payout can be in cash, stock (valued at time of payout), or some combination. Accounting and tax treatment are the same as performance-cash plans.

There are four possible variations of performance-unit plans:

1. Fixed number of units and fixed price per unit
2. Fixed number of units and variable price per unit
3. Variable number of units and fixed price per unit
4. Variable number of units and variable price per unit

The "fixed number of units and fixed price per unit" is illustrated in Table 8-79.

Alternatively, the unit value may vary based on performance in relation to predetermined financial targets. This is illustrated in Table 8-81. This is the second type of performance unit plan: fixed number of units but with a variable price per unit.

Another variation is to hold the unit value constant (e.g., at $1 per unit) and adjust the number of units each year. This is an example of the third type of performance-unit plan: variable number of units with a fixed price per unit. However, in this case, it would probably be simpler to use the straight performance-cash plan. Why go through the extra step of converting back to cash if the unit value does not vary?

The fourth type of performance-unit plan is where both the number of units and the price per unit are variable. An example would be to take Table 8-80 and add another performance factor, varying the number of units based on performance attained. This is illustrated in Table 8-81.

Compound Increase in Return on Equity	Unit Value
20% or more	$2.00
19	1.90
18	1.80
17	1.70
16	1.60
15	1.50
14	1.40
13	1.30
12	1.20
11	1.10
10	1.00
9	.75
8	.50
7	.25
6	0

Table 8-80. Unit value set by performance

Compound Increase in Shareholder Value	Number of Units	Compound Increase in Return on Equity	Unit Value
20% or more	2,000,000	20% or more	$2.00
19	1,900,000	19	1.90
18	1,800,000	18	1.80
17	1,700,000	17	1.70
16	1,600,000	16	1.60
15	1,500,000	15	1.50
14	1,350,000	14	1.40
13	1,200,000	13	1.30
12	1,050,000	12	1.20
11	900,000	11	1.10
10	700,000	10	1.00
9	500,000	9	.75
8	300,000	8	.50
7	100,000	7	.25
6 or less	0	6 or less	0

Table 8-81. Number of units and unit value set by performance

Thus, if the compound increase in shareholder value was 17 percent and the compound increase in ROE was 14 percent, the recipient would receive 1,700,000 units valued at $1.40 each, or $2,380,000.

Conversely, a performance-share plan could be converted into a performance-unit plan, using the number of shares in Table 8-50 (again valued at $100 a share). The result is seen in Table 8-82.

Because performance-share-plan costs have two variables (level of performance achieved and price of stock at time of payout), the performance-unit plan quickly followed the perform-

Grade	Performance Shares	Performance Units
35	15,000	1,500,000
34	14,000	1,400,000
33	13,000	1,300,000
32	12,000	1,200,000
31	11,000	1,100,000
30	10,000	1,000,000
29	9,000	900,000
28	8,000	800,000
27	7,000	700,000
26	6,000	600,000
25	5,000	500,000

Table 8-82. Performance shares converted to performance units

ance-share plan in the early 1970s, following the issuance of APB 25. Performance-unit plans only have one variable—performance. Price of company stock is not a factor.

Another variation is the *performance-cash-percentage* plan. Here, rather than express the payout in cash or in units, the payout is typically expressed as a percentage of salary, although it could be of salary-plus-annual incentive. An example is illustrated in Table 8-83.

Grade	Percentage of Salary Paid Versus Three Year Compound EPS				
	Below 8	8.0-9.9	10.0-11.9	12.0-14.9	15.0 and up
35	0	75	150	225	300
34	0	70	140	210	280
33	0	65	130	195	260
32	0	60	120	180	240
31	0	55	110	165	220
30	0	50	100	150	200
29	0	45	90	135	180
28	0	40	80	120	160
27	0	35	70	105	140
26	0	30	60	90	120
25	0	25	50	75	100

Table 8-83. Performance cash percentage plan

Barring a desire to change the relationship of the long-term plan to salary (or salary-plus-annual incentives if included in the formula), there is no need to change the percentages annually. When salary is increased, the long-term payout will bear a constant relationship.

All four of these plans have the same tax and accounting treatment as illustrated in Table 8-84. Note the absence of stock-price reference, since it is not a factor in the payment.

The advantages of cash plans are:

- The executive has no financing issue, no money at risk, and a tax liability only when the cash is received.
- The company has a tax deduction, and the earnings charge is solely on performance; company stock value has no impact.

The disadvantages include:

- The executive has no opportunity to share in the increase in stock price nor is there an opportunity for favorable long-term capital gains tax treatment.
- The company has a charge to earnings and the tax deduction is deferred to a future date.

COMBINATION PLANS

The various plans described may be used in combination with each other. Indeed, it is commonplace for companies to use two or more of the plans for their executives.

While many company plans provide two or more forms of long-term incentives, all eligible employees may not use all plans, and some plans may not be used by anyone. Those that are used may be separated by organization levels (e.g., performance-unit plan for the top 20 exec-

Time Lapse	Plan Start	Payment Vest
	Now	Three Years
Stock Market		
• Fair Market	—	$150,000
• Option Cost	—	—
Individual		
• Ordinary Income	0	$150,000
• Long-term Capital Gains	0	0
Company		
• Tax Deduction	0	$150,000
• Expense*		→ 150,000

*Accrued over period to vest date

Table 8-84. Performance plans without stock

utives and stock options for the next 100 key people).

By developing combination plans, it is possible to neutralize some of the individual plan disadvantages. A good example of this is the development of the performance-unit plan with an attached stock option, which neutralized the impact of the unknown stock price of the classic performance-share plan. A stock award coupled with sufficient cash to cover tax liabilities makes sense, especially to those with short-swing profit problems. In addition, putting the executive at risk with company stock can be coupled with a non-market plan to provide some protection. The most typical combination is a stock-option plan and a stock-award or cash plan. The stock option is the more highly leveraged of the two, typically because about three options are equated to one share of full value stock using Black-Scholes or other present-value methods. However, the option is worthless if market value does not go above option price. A stock award, on the other hand, has value even though the stock price declines, assuming it does not go all the way to zero. Stock awards in such combinations may be performance-based, time-based, or a combination. Cash plans, of course, are unaffected by stock market changes.

Plans may be either independent (self-standing) or dependent (tandem). Independent plan combinations are, as the word suggests, independent of each other. What happens with one has no effect on the other plan. Under the dependent plan, the action taken with one plan will typically reduce benefits under the other plan.

Under an independent plan, if the executive receives 18,000 options and 6,000 awards, he or she would be entitled to both. However, if the person were given the same in the form of a dependent plan, the choice to exercise 6,000 stock options would result in the forfeit of 2,000 restricted stock awards. Dependent plans need to be carefully structured to avoid both constructive receipt and economic benefit as described in Chapter 3.

Market Value Combination

For years, stock options were essentially the only form of long-term incentive compensation for many companies. Executives found that when price-earnings multiples increased, the levels of compensation were significant—creating more than one multi-millionaire. Conversely, when the multiples dropped, increases in EPS were meaningless in terms of stock prices, as many options went underwater. This volatility caused many companies in the early 1970s to cut back on the use of options and introduce an additional form of compensation such as the perform-ance-share or performance-unit plan (which is not affected by the market price of stock).

It is possible to compare and contrast the degree of downside risk with upside growth potential for each type of plan. Shown in Figure 8-2 is a comparison of 10,000 shares under a stock option of $50 a share, a performance-share plan of 5,000 shares at $100 a share, and a per-formance-unit plan of $500,000. Note that all three will generate $500,000 if the stock price rises to $100 share—not an unrealistic assumption about seven years out, assuming no change in price-earnings multiple and a constant increase in earnings per share of 10 percent. However, everyone is familiar with the problems in assuming such a constant relationship. As shown in Figure 8-2, the stock option is the most highly leveraged form—worthless below $50 a share and worth $1 million at $150 a share [10,000 ($150 - $50)]. Conversely, the performance unit has no leverage; the number of shares awarded is adjusted inversely in relation to market direc-tion. The performance-share plan is between the two.

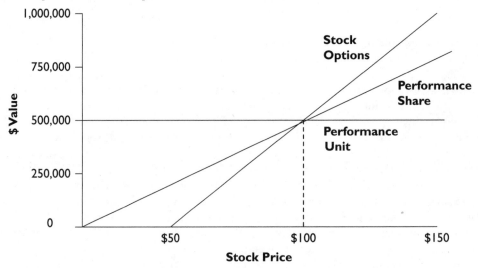

Figure 8-2. Value comparison of stock option, performance share, and performance unit

Combining plans essentially eliminates the negative aspects. For example, by targeting the performance-unit fund at $500,000 for 100-percent attainment of objectives and giving the indi-vidual an option for 10,000 shares at $50, we have: (1) avoided accrual for increases beyond $50 a share, and (2) given the executive the opportunity to participate in the growth of com-pany stock price. Following this approach, the chart values would be additive. In other words, assuming 100 percent attainment of target and stock price at $100, the performance-unit plan would generate $500,000, and the stock-option gain would be $500,000. This is the equivalent of having given the executive 10,000 performance shares; however, in this case the charge to earnings is one-half that required by the performance-share plan (i.e., $500,000 not $1 million).

Stock Price Change	Old Plan Option of 6,000	New Plan Option of 3,000	Award of 1,000	Total	Variance
100%	$600	$300	$200	$500	$100
50%	300	150	150	300	0
25%	150	75	125	200	(50)
0%	0	0	100	100	(100)
-25%	0	0	75	75	(75)
-50%	0	0	50	50	(50)

Table 8-85. Plan comparisons (option only vs. option and performance shares) dollars in thousands

Shown in Table 8-85 is a stock-option-only (old plan) vs. a combination stock option and performance-share plan (new plan). Note that the stock options were halved and the remaining half was put into performance shares. Remember the guideline of one stock award for every three shares of stock option? A price of $100 a share was used in the example. Note that if the stock price were to double, the old plan is better. At a 50-percent increase, the two are comparable and below that, the new plan is better. This assumes the stock award and stock option are for comparable periods. If not, the calculations have to be adjusted. Additionally, if the award is at "target" but a maximum award of twice as much is possible, this should also be calculated.

One could also create a dependent market-based plan. For example, one could grant a number of restricted shares of stock along with a stock option. The award might be at time of stock-option grant or at time of stock-option exercise. Restrictions would lapse in accordance with a stated retention period before the exercised options could be sold. Often times, this is called an *exercise-and-hold option*, or a *combination option and award*. This is illustrated in Table 8-86. The objective of this type of combination plan is, of course, to motivate the executive to exercise (buy) and not sell the stock. The cost to the company is additional expense and increased dilution.

Some companies granted both qualified and non-qualified stock options to executives. If each option were self-standing (i.e., not affected by the other), it would be a *parallel stock-option grant*. If the exercise of one reduced the number of shares exercisable under the other, it would be a *tandem stock-option grant*.

To illustrate, the executive might receive 5,000 shares of a non-qualified option for 10 years and 5,000 shares of a qualified grant for five years—each at the same price. This would be a parallel grant. If, however, the individual received a grant of 10,000 each but the exercise of one would proportionately reduce the other, this would be a tandem grant. Thus, exercising 2,000 shares as a qualified grant would lower the maximum available under each grant to 8,000 shares.

Just as companies were warming to this approach, Revenue Ruling 73-26 rendered it useless. It stated that whenever the action on a non-statutory option affects the exercise rights of a qualified grant, that qualified grant becomes a non-qualified option for all purposes (except remaining in effect for exercise sequence issues). Pay planners giveth and the IRS taketh away! The incentive stock option introduced the $100,000 per year maximum, which would have made tandems of little value even if allowed.

Assumptions
- Optionee receives 1,000 options at $100 a share.
- Options vest at the rate of 20 percent a year, fully vested after five years.
- At time of exercise optionee will receive one restricted share of stock for every ten options exercised.

Actions
- Two years after the grant optionee exercises 400 shares and receives 40 shares of stock, restricted for five years.
- Three years after exercise the optionee sells 200 shares at $125 a share, thereby reducing the number of restricted shares to 20.
- Five years after the grant, having held the 200 exercised shares, the optionee receives the 20 shares, no longer with restrictions. The optionee also exercises the remaining 600 options and receives 60 new restricted shares, again restricted for a five-year period. The fair market value is now $175.
- The company has a charge to earnings for the restricted stock under variable accounting of $3,500 (20 X $175) over the five-year period plus an accrual begun on $10,500 (60 x $175).

Table 8-86. Exercise-and-hold example

For companies that have both stock options and qualified, stock-purchase plans, it is not illogical to preclude the executive from participating in the first while in the second. After the individual exercises all the options, they expire, or the executive voluntarily surrenders the grants, the person is again eligible for the stock-purchase plan. Such an action is plausible if the stock has been underwater for a time; conversely, it would not seem as logical if the company stock were experiencing strong growth, since the spread under the option would probably exceed the 15 percent discount under the stock-purchase plan. More likely is granting a stock option at time of purchasing shares in a non-statutory purchase plan. Typical would be granting an option on more than one share at fair market value for every share acquired under the purchase plan. Such options might have a cliff vesting of five years and would be forfeited as shares acquired under the purchase plan were sold prior to exercising the stock option.

Non-Market Value Combination Plans

This is an example of one type of combination plan that could be set up, in this case for a newly formed joint venture (JV), which will be staffed with key people from the two organizations.

The plan consists of restricted phantom partnership units, namely Full Value Units (FVUs), Appreciation Units (AUs), and Option Units (OUs). As shown in Table 8-87, if the joint venture "goes public," stock options will be granted as well. They will be comparable in number to those OUs remaining unexercised and will be in tandem with the OUs, namely, to the extent one is exercised, a comparable number will be forfeited under the other. Each participant in the incentive plan will be given a no-interest loan to cover the cost of exercising any option plus the tax liability for a period one month beyond that necessary to obtain long-term capital gains (e.g., 13 months).

The OUs are not exercisable until the completion of the fifth full fiscal year. If it is not possible to structure the OU in such a way for the individual to obtain long-term capital gains tax

Level	FVU	AU	OU
President	25,000	25,000	50,000
Executive VP	20,000	20,000	40,000
Senior VP	10,000	10,000	20,000
VP	6,000	6,000	12,000
Sr Director	3,000	3,000	6,000
Director	1,500	1,500	3,000

Table 8-87. Non-market value combination plan

treatment, then the number of OU units will be increased by 50 percent and the total added as AUs. Thus, a person eligible for 1,500 FVUs, 1,500 AUs, and 3,000 OUs will instead have 1,500 FVUs, 4,500 OUs, and 6,000 AUs. If the company "goes public," the individual would then receive 3,000 options at fair market value and for every share exercised would forfeit 1.5 AUs. Designated key employees will retain parent company existing stock options but will not participate in new grants of former company; the no-interest loan will not apply to these options.

Each phantom unit will be valued at $10 at time of startup. For plan purposes, partnership capital at time of formation shall be divided by an appropriate number of units to equal the $10 value. At the conclusion of each subsequent year, accumulated partnership profits before distribution shall be reduced by the statutory corporate tax rate in effect that year to calculate annualized profit for plan purposes. The remainder shall be divided by the total number of units identified at time of formation to calculate the new unit value or UV. This process is analogous to a corporation's book value per share before payment of dividends.

As an example, if partnership capital at time of formation equaled $200 million, 20 million units would be deemed to exist at $10 per unit. One year later, accumulated profits before distribution equaled $10 million; assuming a 40-percent company "tax rate" were in effect, this would be reduced to $6 million, which divided by 20 million units would equal $0.30, thereby increasing the unit value to $10.30. Thus, each FVU would be worth $10.30 and each AU and OU would be worth $0.30.

The plan runs for 10 years. There are no payments until termination of employment unless the compensation committee deems it appropriate. Barring such action, no payments from the plan will be made within the first five years. However, employees terminated by the company (except for cause) would be 100-percent vested in the unit value of the most recently completed fiscal year. Termination after five, but before 10, years will result in use of a $10 unit value in case of quit. Termination before five years or any time due to unlawful or improper actions would result in no payment. Termination for any other reason would result in use of the phantom partnership unit value of the most recent complete fiscal year. If termination occurs after the 10-year period, the full partnership unit value at the end of the tenth year plus a form of annual interest approved by the compensation committee from that date to time of receipt of monies will be paid.

Individual agreements would be prepared for each participating employee covering the terms and conditions of this plan.

Market Value and Non-Market Value Combinations

A good reason to use two or more plans is to offset the disadvantages of each plan while still having the benefit of their respective advantages. Here's an illustration of how a combination market and non-market plan might be structured. Let's go back to our previous book market plan example. The company's current book value is $25 a share, and it is assumed earnings will increase at a compound growth rate of 10 percent a year for the next 10 years. Further, assume that the company plans on maintaining a dividend policy equaling 37.5 percent of earnings per share. The estimates of EPS, dividends, retained earnings, and book value for the time period are reported in Table 8-88. Note that the common share stock price has also been increased on the same progression (retaining its 10 times price-earnings multiple).

		Allocation of EPS			Book Value Plus Dividend	Common Stock Price
	EPS	Dividend	Retained	Book Value		
Base		—	—	$25.00	$25.00	$36.00
1	$4.00	$1.50	2.50	27.50	29.00	40.00
2	4.40	1.65	2.75	30.25	33.40	44.00
3	4.84	1.81	3.03	33.28	38.24	48.40
4	5.32	2.00	3.32	36.60	43.56	53.20
5	5.86	2.20	3.66	40.26	49.42	58.60
6	6.44	2.41	4.03	44.29	55.86	64.40
7	7.09	2.66	4.43	48.72	62.95	70.90
8	7.79	2.92	4.87	53.59	70.74	77.90
9	8.57	3.21	5.36	58.95	79.31	85.70
10	9.43	3.54	3.89	64.84	88.74	94.30
Total	**$63.74**	**$23.90**	**$39.84**			
Appreciation				**$39.84**	**$63.74**	**$58.30**

Table 8-88. Ten-year projection of book value and stock price

Assume that it is decided that the executive should receive an award whose estimated appreciation 10 years hence should be worth $500,000. If a non-qualified, market-value option were to be given, it would probably be for about 22,400 shares [i.e., $500,000 ÷ ($58.30 - $36)]. However, the same value could be extended by giving appreciation rights on about 33,700 shares of book value [i.e., $500,000 ÷ ($39.84 - $25)], or 12,900 shares of book value plus dividends [i.e., $500,000 ÷ ($63.74 - $25)]. The advantage of excluding dividends from the calculation is that any change in the dividend payout has an adverse effect on the increase in book value plus dividends.

Rather than simply use one of the three approaches, a combination plan can be set up using either a tandem or parallel approach as shown in Table 8-89. Under the parallel approach, each action is self-standing and unaffected by any other actions. Although any desired relationship can be set, a logical choice might be that half of the estimated $500,000 value should be attained from the market price and the other half from book value. Thus, the number of shares available

	Number of Shares		
	Market Value	Nonmarket Value Appreciation	
	Options	Book Value	Book Value Plus Dividends
Independent	22,400	33,700	12,900
Combination Parallel			
A	11,200	16,850	
B	11,200		6,450
Tandem			
A	22,400	33,700	
B	22,400		12,900

Table 8-89. Book value vs. market value stock option comparison

for an independent or separate action is reduced by half as shown on the grid. Under the A plan, the executive would receive 11,200 option shares for common stock at $36 a share and appreciation on 16,850 shares of book value at $25. Under the B plan, the executive would receive 6,450 appreciation units on book value (defined to include dividends) plus an 11,200-share non-qualified, market-value option.

Under the tandem approach, the same number of shares is given under both market-value and non-market-value options that would have been given if it were the only plan. However, as the individual exercises options under one plan, a comparable number are forfeited under the other plan. For example, in plan A, the executive would receive 22,400 shares of common stock at $36 a share and 33,700 book-value appreciation units at $25 a share. Assume that the executive exercised 3,400 shares of the market-value stock two years later. Not only would that reduce the maximum remaining number of shares under the market value option to 19,000, it would also reduce the number of book-value appreciation units by 5,116 (leaving 28,584). This was determined in the following manner: since 3,400 is 15.18 percent of 22,400 then 15.18 percent of 33,700 results in 5,116. Namely, for every share of common stock exercised, book-value appreciation units will be reduced by almost a share-and-a-half. Conversely, for every three shares of book-value appreciation units chosen, the common stock option will be reduced by approximately two shares.

Plan B under the tandem approach functions the same way. The only difference is that a different definition has been constructed for value (i.e., book value plus dividends).

Thus, the tandem approach is a hybrid of independent and parallel plans in that it allows the recipient to choose how to exercise the option. Note that if all the options under the market-value plan are exercised, it is the same as if the executive received only a market value option; the same is true of completely exercising the non-market-value option. Exercising half of each has the same effect as the parallel option. Policy has no impact on the calculation. Under the straight book-value approach, an increase in dividend payout has an adverse effect on the increase in book value.

| | Number of Shares Awarded | | |
| | | Nonmarket Value | |
	Market Value	Book Value	Book Value Plus Dividends
Independent	8,500	12,500	12,900
Combination			
Parallel			
A	4,250	6,250	
B	4,250		3,700
Tandem			
A	8,500	12,500	
B	8,500		7,800

Table 8-90. Book value vs. market value restricted stock award comparison

A similar approach can be employed with stock awards. Using a phantom common stock restricted award coupled with the book-value plan (see Table 8-89), the executive could receive the same number of shares in the above example, either tandem or parallel, assuming payout was on total value. Assuming the same anticipated stock values 10 years hence, the number of restricted shares to be awarded if payout was on total value (not simply appreciation) are shown in Table 8-90. This is based on the same $500,000 target ÷ $58.30 future market value on about 8,500 shares. Book value would require about 12,500 shares ($500,000 ÷ $39.84) and book-plus-dividends about 7,800 shares ($500,000 ÷ $63.74).

Cash awards (non-market) can also be combined with market awards. For example, performance-unit plans can be used in combination with stock options to net the executive the same income possibilities at a lower cost to the corporation but with the same deduction. Here's how it works. Instead of giving our grade 35 executive 15,000 performance shares, the executive will receive $1.5 million cash if performance target is met and a stock option for 15,000 shares at current fair market value of $100 a share. Three years later when the performance target has been met, the executive receives $1.5 million cash and has appreciation of $300,000 on the stock options because the stock price is now $120 a share. The $300,000 is the equivalent of 2,500 shares at $120 per share. If the executive had been under a performance-share plan receiving 15,000 shares valued at $120 per share, the award would be worth the same $1.8 million.

However, since gain to the executive of a stock-option plan is not charged to earnings, the company has charged a total of $1.5 million (all under the performance-unit plan) or $300,000 less than the $1.8 million it would have charged under a performance-share plan. Note that it would be of no value to add appreciation rights to the stock-option plan as the appreciation would have to be charged to the earnings statement—thus having the same effect as a performance-share plan.

Designing combination plans, more than any other reason, popularized the use of present-value methodology with stock options. How else could one do tradeoffs in increasing or decreasing the number of shares under a stock option with various types of stock-award plans?

Another consideration when designing combination plans is the vesting requirement. For example, if the company has both a stock option and a performance-share plan (both of which are granted annually), and the performance-share plan has a four-year vest, would not four-year cliff vesting of the stock option also be appropriate?

When designing combination plans, the advantages of one should offset the disadvantages of another. There is virtually no limit to the combinations. However, one must be careful in not making the plan so difficult and complex that few if any understand it.

SUMMARY AND CONCLUSIONS

Long-term incentive plans are designed to reward executives for long-term results. However, their nature is by definition a large part of their problem—predicting performance expectations for several years in the future. The difficulty of setting such targets is a function of the degree of cyclical fluctuation within the particular industry. In some, such as chemicals and paper, production capacity within the industry is a very significant factor in defining probable success.

As illustrated in this chapter, there is little difference in tax treatment of the basic forms of long-term incentives. Essentially, they are tax deductible to the company and subject to tax for the executive. All plans that payout in company stock offer the subsequent opportunity for long-term capital gains tax treatment (beginning from the income level previously recognized for tax purposes). All dividends paid on company stock are non-deductible to the company and subject to ordinary income tax to the executive, except for dividends under restricted stock, which are treated as compensation.

As a basic rule, all compensation paid will be a charge to earnings at time of payment, accrued over the performance period, and all stock issued is a dilution. In addition, not only is all stock issued a dilution to earnings but also all "in the money" outstanding stock options and unvested stock awards must be used to calculate diluted earnings per share. There are two exceptions. First, assuming APB 25 is used, there is no charge to earnings for stock options issued at fair market value at time of grant with number of shares known. Second, the amount accrued over time as a charge to earnings for restricted stock is based on the price at time of award if measurement date principle has been met. All other payments over time are accrued for expense at the end of the period.

Stock acquired by the executive's exercise of a stock option will be construed to be a purchase under SEC Rule 16(b)3 at time of grant (not exercise). When acquisition is not subject to the executive's control and discretion, it will probably be an exempt transaction for the purpose of short-swing profit situations.

The SEC requires disclosure of the long-term incentive plans in the company proxy statement. The requirements are a combination of reporting plan schedules, grants made and payments received. One will want to examine these requirements carefully.

Incentive plans cannot be developed and turned over to accountants on the assumption that they will be self-monitoring. Adjustments are often required during the incentive period, not to mention the time and effort required at the close of the period to determine the extent to which performance was positively or negatively affected by factors outside the executives' control. In some plans, such action is needed to adjust individual payments; in all plans, it is a requirement for setting future targets—even the stock-option grant must make some assumptions about the future.

In smaller organizations, the contact between the CEO and key executives is on a daily basis; in larger organizations, the contact may be almost as frequent, but the additional layers of management with their own needs and perceptions cannot be given the same degree of personal involvement. Thus, it is necessary that a more formal basis of identifying objectives and evaluating performance be adopted. For some, this is the long-term incentive plan. By specifying the basis for payment, all key executives are included to determine how such performance (and payment) can be maximized. However, this means that individuals may be encouraged to take actions that are not in the best interests of the company. For example, a plan based on return on assets might encourage an enterprising executive to sell some assets (and lease them back) to improve performance.

However, if real growth rather than current dollars were the basis for payment, it would be difficult for some companies to show a positive growth rate. These are companies far into the maturity stage, if not already in the decline phase, which are essentially liquidating themselves by paying out dividends that should be reinvested in the business. Others with a strong cash position might find the best investment alternative is to buy back some of their stock. This will strengthen earnings per share (EPS), but it has not brought in new earnings. Performance-share and performance unit plans would bring additional attention to paying executives for apparently riding the corporation to its final internment. Performance unit and performance share plans work better in non-cyclical industries than in those with periodic ups and downs, since the latter require continually adjusting targets that in retrospect are either too liberal or too restrictive. Companies in such industries would probably be better off either using market-value stock options or book-value plans.

Some will argue that long-term incentive plans do not provide incentive to executives to work harder or smarter. Assuming this is true, it still seems logical to pay them in relation to key measurements of corporate success. Simply paying a salary or a short-term incentive based on current earnings is insufficient for a CEO because a longer-term pay delivery system is needed for a significant part of such an executive's earnings. How else can shareholders be assured that the CEO is focusing on strategies to optimally position the company in the next five to ten years?

Some companies discourage executives from selling stock they have acquired through exercising options, SARs, or receiving stock awards. The normal message is that such plans were approved by shareholders to promote a common interest in the company's growth. A measurement of confidence in this growth is expressed through holding rather than selling stock.

In determining which type of long-term incentive plan to use, it is necessary to sort through the company's priorities. Stock options are structured to maximize compensation in terms of rising stock-market prices. Phantom plans are designed to reward for improvement in corporate financial performance regardless of market valuation of company performance. Performance-share plans are designed to reward executives for both improvement in corporate financial performance and stock price. Essentially, they are all group rather than individually oriented. The extent of participation is a function of organization level rather than individual performance.

Note: You should not rely on accounting, tax, SEC, or other professional service statements in this chapter. You need to seek appropriate professional counsel for such guidance. Statements made in this chapter and elsewhere are offered as being illustrative to help you frame such further investigations with the help of counsel.

More will be said about design issues in the next chapter—Design and Communication Considerations.

Chapter 9

Design and Communication Considerations

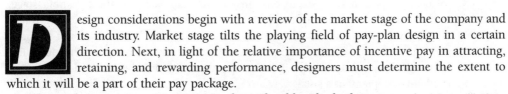esign considerations begin with a review of the market stage of the company and its industry. Market stage tilts the playing field of pay-plan design in a certain direction. Next, in light of the relative importance of incentive pay in attracting, retaining, and rewarding performance, designers must determine the extent to which it will be a part of their pay package.

The total executive compensation package should embody the company's vision, mission, objectives, goals, and strategies. More specifically, the pay delivery system should be aligned with goals and objectives. The framework or skeleton for this system consists of those compensation objectives appropriate to the organization. In designing a pay plan, the characteristics of each pay element will determine its importance relative to the other elements, to the marketplace, and to company goals and objectives. Let's begin with a short review of the five elements of compensation.

COMPENSATION CONSIDERATIONS

Salary

The salary element will be most important in not-for-profits because of statutory limits on incentives. At the other end of the spectrum, for-profits with publicly traded stock tend to place the lowest emphasis on the salary element. It serves primarily to determine eligibility for the other pay elements.

Market stage also influences the salary element. In the early or threshold stages, cash is scarce, and therefore salaries are de-emphasized. However, they take on more importance in later stages.

	Market Stage			
	Threshold	**Growth**	**Maturity**	**Decline**
For-Profits • Publicly traded • Privately held	 Low Moderate	 Moderate High	 High High	 High High
Not-for-profits	Moderate	Moderate	Moderate	Moderate

Table 9-1. Probable relative importance of salary in different market stages

The specific characteristics of each organization will dictate how important salary is in attracting, retaining, and motivating key employees. In other words, salary is typically an important tool in attracting a person to an organization; however, in a threshold for-profit company, it is probably de-emphasized because of the shortage of cash and the availability of incentives.

Table 9-1 illustrates the distinctions of the salary element in for-profits versus not-for-profits companies.

Employee Benefits

In the absence of meaningful incentives, not-for-profits place "high" importance on employee benefits, as shown in Table 9-2. Indeed, the presence of a medical plan, time-off with pay, and some type of pension plan may be even more important than salary in the threshold stage. Nonetheless, the relative importance of employee benefits in most companies is low (attract), moderate (retain), and low (motivate). These ratings make it more difficult for the not-for-profits to attract, retain, and motivate executives. However, such ratings are oversimplifications. For some people, employee benefits are very important. An example would be a second-career executive who needed to supplement a small pension.

	Market Stage			
	Threshold	**Growth**	**Maturity**	**Decline**
For-Profits • Publicly traded • Privately held	 Low Low	 Moderate Moderate	 Moderate Moderate	 High High
Not-for-profits	High	High	High	High

Table 9-2. Probable relative importance of employee benefits in different market stages

Perquisites

The perquisite essentially begins where employee benefits end. As defined earlier, there are two types: restorative and additive. The first "restores" something taken away by statutory limitations (typically pension payments); the second is something that is in addition to the existing benefit.

As shown in Table 9-3, perquisites, like employee benefits, are typically of high importance in the not-for-profit compensation program, especially business-related perks such as a very nice office or a car. A special supplemental pension plan would be very attractive to a second

	Market Stage			
	Threshold	**Growth**	**Maturity**	**Decline**
For-Profits • Publicly traded • Privately held	Low Low	Low Moderate	Moderate High	High High
Not-for-profits	High	High	High	High

Table 9-3. Probable relative important of perquisites in different market stages

career executive. As with employee benefits, perquisites are not particularly effective at attracting, retaining, or motivating key employees. Nonetheless, they may be sufficient for some.

In for-profits, perks are typically of low to moderate importance in the early stages of the market cycle, although privately held companies may place a slightly higher importance on them because of their low visibility and the absence of publicly traded stock.

Short-Term Incentives

Not-for-profits may have a difficult time satisfying the Internal Revenue Service (IRS) that a short-term incentive plan is consistent with a non-profit tax status. Therefore, the short-term incentive is not simply of "low" importance, it is usually nonexistent, as shown in Table 9-4. (Not-for-profits might approach the pay-for-performance of short-term incentives with a substitute form of lump-sum merits for executives. These can take on the appearance of incentives without running into difficulties with overseeing agencies.) Since these incentives are an important part of the package for many executives, not-for-profits have a distinct disadvantage in attracting, retaining, and motivating. However, individuals may be attracted to not-for-profits for more altruistic motives, namely, giving back to a defined community than for the pay. Intrinsic rather than extrinsic reward is their driver.

	Market Stage			
	Threshold	**Growth**	**Maturity**	**Decline**
For-Profits • Publicly traded • Privately held	Low Moderate	Moderate High	High High	Moderate Moderate
Not-for-profits	Low	Low	Low	Low

Table 9-4. Probable relative importance of short-term incentives in different market stages

Conversely, the for-profits line up much better with those executives interested in extrinsic compensation. However, companies in the early stages of market development have to overcome cash shortages and appeal in other ways (e.g., with long-term incentives). Note again in Table 9-4 that privately held companies have somewhat higher emphasis on short-term incentives in the early stages of market development because of greater limits on long-term incentives (namely, no publicly traded stock).

Long-Term Incentives

Although shown as a "low" in Table 9-5, long-term incentives are essentially nonexistent in not-for-profit companies for the same reasons explained above for short-term incentives. Privately held companies are somewhat better off. They do have stock but lack the public trading forum, thereby restricting the use of tax-advantaged stock plans. This is not so, of course, with the publicly traded for-profits. For them, stock options are the major compensation device in the early stages of market development because of their accounting and tax treatment. Other forms of stock plans take on importance beginning with the later stages of the "growth" phase.

	Market Stage			
	Threshold	**Growth**	**Maturity**	**Decline**
For-Profits • Publicly traded • Privately held	High Moderate	High Moderate	Moderate Moderate	Low Low
Not-for-profits	Low	Low	Low	Low

Table 9-5. Probable relative importance of long-term incentives in different market stages

EXECUTIVE COMPENSATION PHILOSOPHY

There are four steps leading to the development of a compensation strategy:

1. Verbalization of the significance of the market stage.
2. Importance of the attract/retrain/motivate objectives.
3. Determining the degree of risk to be built into the system.
4. Combining the above three into a compensation design template.

Market Stage Significance

The first step in developing a compensation philosophy begins with the market cycle. Shown in Table 9-6 is the same table described in Chapter 1 (Table 1-15). This table is for a publicly traded company.

Examples of how this table is converted into compensation design statements include:

- **Threshold.** "Given the importance of using cash to market the business and the desire to focus everyone on the possibility of significant success, the heavy emphasis is on long-term incentives and, more specifically, stock options. The other four elements will be increased only to the extent absolutely necessary."
- **Growth.** "As the company is more established and enjoying increasing success, salaries and employee benefits should be competitive to similar companies. Given that the long-term picture looks good, long-term incentives should continue to receive top attention. Stock options are still dominant, although various types of performance-based stock awards should be adopted where appropriate. Short-term incentives need to be structured to reward both individual and unit performance."
- **Maturity.** "Given that our new products are essentially extensions of existing products it is important that we place high emphasis on short-term incentives (both individual and

Compensation Element	Emphasis by Market Stage			
	Threshold	**Growth**	**Maturity**	**Decline**
Salary	Low	Moderate	High	High
Employee Benefits	Low	Moderate	Moderate	High
Perquisites	Low	Low	Moderate	High
Short-Term Incentives	Low	Moderate	High	Moderate
Long-Term Incentives	High	High	Moderate	Low

Table 9-6. Compensation elements versus market stage

group) in order to maximize sales as well as reduce costs."
- **Decline.** "Our shrinking revenue means it is essential to reduce fixed payroll costs (salary, employee benefits, and perquisites) and increase the emphasis on short-term incentives with a primary focus on reducing costs. Long-term incentives should be shifted to internal measurements, since the company stock price will return little if any appreciation."
- **Turnaround.** "Because it is important to return the business to a growth stage (given our new products), it is essential we place high emphasis on both short- and long-term incentives. The former will be focused on both individual and group success; the latter will be a combination of stock options and performance stock awards."

Attract/Retain/Motivate Significance

Within the context of the market stage, one has next to look to the respective importance of the attract/retain/motivate objectives. Table 9-7 was described in Chapter 4 (Table 4-1).

Examples of how this table is converted into compensation design statements include:

- **Attract.** "Our short-term incentives will be featured in attracting the top talent we need. This will include bonuses to compensate for any unvested compensation from current employer but with clawback features should the person leave us within five years. The short-term incentive will also calculate at least half of the bonus opportunity based on individual performance."

Compensation Element	Impact on Individual Executive		
	Attract	**Retain**	**Motivate**
Salary	High	High	Moderate
Employee Benefits	Low	Moderate	Low
Perquisites	Low	Moderate	Low
Short-Term Incentives	High	Moderate	High
Long-Term Incentives	Moderate	High	Moderate

Table 9-7. Impact of five compensation elements on executives

- **Retain.** "Our long-term incentive plan will consist of annual stock-option grants with five year cliff-vesting and annual grants of five year performance-share plans."
- **Motivate.** "In addition to annual incentives based on group performance, and long-term incentives based on corporate performance, the annual incentive offers an opportunity to earn at least half of the award based on individual performance."

Degree of Risk Significance

Next, determine the degree of risk to build the pay program. The normal rule is the higher the risk, the greater the reward for success. This is illustrated in Table 9-8.

Compensation Element	Emphasis on Compensation		
	Degree of Risk		
	Low	Moderate	High
Salary	High	Moderate	Low
Employee Benefits	High	Moderate	Low
Perquisites	High	Moderate	Low
Short-Term Incentives	Low	Moderate	High
Long-Term Incentives	Low	Moderate	High

Table 9-8. Importance of degree of risk on compensation elements

Examples of how this table is converted into compensation design statements include:

- **Low Risk.** "Total compensation will be in the 60th percentile of defined competition, as will annual cash compensation, but salaries will be at least equal to the 60th percentile. Long-term incentives will be at the 40th percentile or less."
- **Moderate Risk.** "Total compensation as well as each of the five elements will be positioned at the 50th percentile of defined competition."
- **High Risk.** "Total compensation will be at the 60th percentile of defined competition. Salary, employee benefits, and perquisites will be at the 40th percentile, and both short- and long-term incentives will be at the 75th percentile."

One would expect that an increase in risk would result in an increase in the use of incentives. Certainly, this is desirable from the shareholders' viewpoint. To the extent this is not true, it might suggest management has had a very strong say in plan design. After all, they would like high pay associated with low risk.

Compensation Design Template

Having considered the characteristics of the five pay elements within the context of type of company, market stage, and executive attributes, one needs to describe the compensation strategy that will be consistent with these parameters and meet specific company goals. A rather simplistic template is shown in Table 9-9. Create a personalized template by filling in the blanks with the degree of importance, the specific percentile, and the types of programs as appropriate.

---

1. Salaries are of _____ importance and will be positioned at the _____ percentile of the _____ market. It will be of _____ importance in our pay-for-performance program.

2. Employee benefits are of _____ importance. Our major emphasis will be on the _____ categories. More specifically, we will position our _____, _____, and _____at the _____ percentile of the _____ market.

3. Perquisites are of _____ importance. Our major emphasis will be in the _____ category using _____, _____, and _____. Our competitive position on these is targeted at the _____ percentile of the _____ market.

4. Short-term incentives are of _____ importance because _____. [If incentives are used then additional clarifications are required indicating percentile ratings at threshold, target, and maximum, thereby defining downside risk and upside potential. Individual versus group and company performance also need to be identified.]

5. Long-term incentives are of _____ importance because _____. [If long-term incentives are used then additional clarifications are needed starting with the specific types of long-term incentives that will be used and the importance of company and peer company performance. Present values for future value plans need to be defined in competitive terms.]

Table 9-9. Statements of compensation strategy

Not shown, but a worthwhile addition, would be the rationale for the values and plans selected. To illustrate, three different versions of long-term incentive positions are offered in Table 9-10.

A more detailed statement of compensation philosophy is shown in Table 9-11. It is from a publicly traded company in the growth stage, wishing to ensure it pays for individual, group, and corporate performance (with a high risk/high reward profile) as well as maximize the probability of attracting, motivating, and retaining top performers.

A Not-for-Profit Company ... Long-term incentives are of no value to us as they are unavailable because of our private not-for-profit status.

A For Profit Publicly Traded Company ... Long-term incentives are of high importance to us because we are in the growth phase; they are consistent with the long development period before our products reach the market; and we believe they can be structured to reward executives for long-term company financial performance and shareholder value. For that reason, we use both market value stock options and performance share plans tied to outperforming companies in our industry in earnings per share and shareholder value.

A For-Profit Privately Held Company ... Long-term incentives are of moderate importance as we are in the maturity phase of our cycle and our decision is not to further diffuse the ownership of the company. Increasing retained earnings is important and, therefore, a phantom stock plan based on book value shares is used for key executives.

Table 9-10. Long-term incentive strategy statements

1. Total compensation will be at the 60th percentile of the defined competition. Salary, employee benefits and perquisites will be at the 40th percentile and both short- and long-term incentives will be at the 75th percentile.

2. Although annual compensation (salary plus short-term incentives) is set at the 50th percentile, stretch targets are set at the 60th percentile with the increase being solely in the short-term incentive plan.

    Up-front bonuses will be paid to offset unvested losses of outstanding talent for leaving their current employer to join us. Such awards will contain a clawback feature (return of the amount to the company if the individual voluntarily leaves within five years of joining us).

3. In response to identification with shareholder interests and their cost effectiveness (a tax deduction but no charge to earnings) annual non-statutory stock option grants (with five-year cliff vests) are given to the top 5% of the employee population (the executives). Gains of exercises received within one year of departure are forfeited to the company unless waived by company action.

4. The top 1% of the population are annually put into a five-year performance unit plan with payment based on performance relative to our 10 company peer groups over the five-year period in terms of earnings per share and total shareholder value.

5. Annual incentives are based on corporate, group, and individual performance. Corporate performance is based on an economic profit formula; group performance is based on EBITDA for the unit; and individual performance is based on at least five (but no more than 10) measurable objectives.
    - The mix will be 80% corporate/20% individual for the CEO (Chief Executive Officer), CFO (Chief Financial Officer), CHRO (Chief Human Resource Officer), and CLO (Chief Legal Officer).
    - The mix will be one-third each for corporate, group, and individual for all other executives.

6. The company will review the structure of the pay at least semi-annually program to determine what changes if any are needed, bringing them in the way of proposals to the board of directors.

Table 9-11. Sample compensation philosophy

INCENTIVE PAY CONSIDERATIONS

As pointed out earlier, it is very difficult, if not impossible, to structure incentive pay plans in not-for-profits. However, even companies without the legal limitations should examine the issue carefully. Whether incentive pay is included in the package should be a function of objectives and ability, not availability. When incentives are included, they play a major role in the executive pay package.

Do You Really Want Incentives?

Designing short- and long-term incentive plans takes a lot of time and effort. A company must not only be willing to put in the time and effort but also believe performance can be expressed quantitatively. This is easy for financial data. For qualitative goals (such as designing and implementing a new executive compensation plan), it is more difficult. It is fairly easy to determine if timetables are set and deadlines met. It is more difficult to assess how well it was done. Performance goals set at the beginning of the year need to be updated during the year and factored into the incentive plan. Goal setting will be more difficult as individuals learn to "lowball" their targets, making it easier to receive incentive pay. The importance of factors outside the executive's control need to be assessed and a determination made as to whether or not such factors should affect the incentive payout.

Incentives must not only help the organization achieve its mission and vision, they must be consistent with the culture of the organization. In addition, the relative importance of short- and long-term incentives must be consistent with the product lifecycle. It would be inconsistent to put strong emphasis on long-term incentives when the lifecycle is a year or less, and the reverse would also be true.

For short-term incentives, designers must weight the importance of individual contributions versus group performance. Individual plans have a number of advantages. They include: alignment between group objectives and individual performance; a defined link between performance and pay; and a "performance-counts" culture. Disadvantages could include: too much emphasis on individual outcomes; an invalid and/or unreliable measurement system; and difficulties in accurately budgeting payouts.

Advantages of Incentive Pay. The overriding advantage of incentive pay is that it meets the objective of pay-for-performance. In other words, payment will be in direct relation to attainment of identified objectives. When these objectives are financial, it lowers pay for poor financial performance and raises it for good financial performance. The absence of incentive pay is the most costly to the organization for poor performers (because of fixed pay) and the least expensive for good performers (again because of fixed pay).

Disadvantages of Incentive Pay. Designing and maintaining an effective plan is time consuming. Additionally, plan designers run the risk of not effectively focusing efforts on appropriate objectives, using the wrong measurements, or running counter to the desired corporate culture.

Below is a brief list of some common arguments against incentive pay plans, followed by counter arguments.

- Incentives discourage teamwork and cooperation. (This can be minimized by establishing shared goals/objectives.)
- Incentives do not make high performers work harder. (No one suggests they will work harder; incentives simply ensure they put their efforts where they are needed.)
- Incentives punish those who do not meet their objectives/goals. (Underperformers still have their salary, assuming their performance is not so bad as to result in termination. Therefore, they are not punished, they are simply not rewarded for not meeting expectations.)
- Incentives create risk-aversion mindset. (It requires a real effort on the part of raters and ratees to ensure the goals and objectives have sufficient stretch.)

After this introspective analysis, if the negatives outweigh the positives, one is probably better off working simply with salary, employee benefits, and perquisites. If not, it is time to determine what plans are most appropriate.

The Ideal Plan

Having reviewed the five compensation elements in some detail in the previous chapters, and examined one's willingness to use incentive pay, it's time to see what forms of these elements are most important in the design of the executive compensation package. This requires identifying the objectives one wishes to accomplish. The ideal plan is rather easy to describe, as shown in Table 9-12.

---

  1. Identifies with the shareholder.

  2. Correlates with individual performance.

  3. Correlates with group performance.

  4. Correlates with corporate performance.

  5. Is easily understood by all.

  6. Requires no special target setting.

  7. Ties the high performer to the company.

  8. Has no earnings charge.

  9. Has no dilution to shareholder equity.

10. Is tax deductible to the company.

11. Is not taxable to the individual.

12. If taxable, is tax deductible to individual.

13. Requires no investment by the individual.

14. Individual has no downside risk.

Table 9-12. The ideal compensation plan

What Objectives Are Important?

Unfortunately, no plan or combination will meet all of the above objectives. If it did, this book would be considerably shorter. Therefore, one needs to examine the possible plan components to determine the extent to which they match up with the above objectives. Some will be more important (e.g., identifies with shareholders) and some will be less (e.g., charge to earnings). Shown in Table 9-13 is a three-factor rating scale for each of the 14 ideal plan objectives.

COMPARING PLAN POSSIBILITIES WITH DESIRED OBJECTIVES

Creating a Matrix

One might set up a matrix with each of the 14 objectives on one axis and the various plan possibilities for each of the five pay elements on the other axis. Admittedly, this would be a very extensive matrix. In Chapter 6 (Employee Benefits and Perquisites), over 100 possibilities were identified. The value of a complete matrix is that it creates an array of each plan's score for each of the 14 elements, thereby, providing a basis for identifying those plans and plan variations to review more thoroughly. Before proceeding, review the definitions and values in Table 9-13. Some are subject to interpretation; others are subject to law and/or regulations.

1. Identifies with the shareholder

1.0 Payment is in stock based on increase in shareholder value (i.e., stock price plus dividends).

0.5 Payment is in stock but only partly based on increase in shareholder value.

0.0 Payment not based on shareholder value.

2. Correlates with individual performance

1.0 Income increases and decreases in direct relation to performance.

0.5 Income may increase with performance but does not decrease with performance or linkage is weak.

0.0 Income not affected by performance.

3. Correlates with group performance

1.0 Income increases and decreases in direct relation to performance.

0.5 Linkage between payout and performance is modest.

0.0 Income not affected by performance.

4. Correlates with corporate performance

1.0 Income increases and decreases in direct relation to performance.

0.5 Linkage between payout and performance is modest.

0.0 Income not affected by performance.

5. Is easily understood by all

1.0 Exact payout can be determined using several known factors.

0.5 Payout can be determined but methodology complicated.

0.0 Basis of payout at best only known generally.

6. Requires no special target setting

1.0 No target setting required.

0.5 Go and no-go target required.

0.0 Multiple targets or hurdle factors required.

7. Ties the high performer to the company

1.0 Long-term golden handcuff (three years or more)

0.5 Short-term handcuff (1-2 years)

0.0 No handcuff—immediately vested

8. Has no earnings charge

1.0 No charge required.

0.5 Charge of known (or maximum) amount.

0.0 Earnings charge of open-ended liability.

9. Has no dilution to shareholder equity

1.0 No dilution.

0.5 Partially dilutive.

0.0 Full payment is dilutive.

10. Is tax deductible to the company

1.0 Is 100% tax deductible.

Table 9-13. Ideal plan objective weightings (Continued on next page)

0.5 Is partially tax deductible.
0.0 No part is tax deductible.

11. **Is not taxable to the individual**
1.0 Nothing is taxable.
0.5 Is partially taxable or taxable at favorable rate.
0.0 Is 100% taxable as ordinary income.

12. **If taxable, is tax deductible to the individual**
1.0 Is 100% tax deductible to the individual.
0.5 Is partially tax deductible.
0.0 No part is tax deductible.

13. **Requires no investment by the individual**
1.0 No investment required.
0.5 Investment requirement less than FMV.
0.0 Full FMV investment required.

14. **Individual has no downside risk**
1.0 No downside risk.
0.5 Some downside risk.
0.0 Significant downside risk.

Table 9-13. Continued

A Tale of Two Companies

The appropriate pay plan will differ from one company to the next, depending on the objectives selected as most important. This is illustrated in Table 9-14 where Company A and Company B have selected completely different objectives. With Company A, the appropriate plan would be non-qualified stock options. With Company B, a performance unit plan would be logical. All four plans shown in Table 9-14 were discussed in detail in Chapter 7 (Long-Term Incentives). Let's review the basis for the scores.

Company A

1. **Identifies with the Shareholder.** Both the incentive stock option (ISO) and non-qualified stock option (NQ) receive a "1" because full value is based on shareholder-value increases. The performance-share-plan (PSP) value is partly based on changes in stock price but also based on degree of attaining prescribed financial targets. The performance-unit plan (PUP) is a cash-based PSP. Stock price has no impact.

6. **Requires No Special Target Setting:** Stock options require no target setting (only the number of shares to be granted), whereas PSPs and PUPs require internal targets to determine unit of payment.

8. **Has No Earnings Charge.** By definition, an ISO requires no earnings charge. If the non-qualified stock option (NQ) is "plain vanilla" (i.e., stock price is equal to FMV at time of grant) and number of shares under option is also known on that date, there is no earnings charge under APB No. 25. The PSP has a charge to earnings because the payout is stated in number of shares and that liability is open-ended (because of stock price variability) whereas PUPs' liability is a factor only of financial performance.

Selected Objective	Stock Option		Performance	
	ISO	NQ	Share	Unit
Company A				
1. Identifies with the Shareholder	1.0	1.0	0.5	0.0
6. Requires no Special Target Setting	1.0	1.0	0.0	0.0
8. Has no Earnings Charge	1.0	1.0	0.0	0.5
10. Tax Deductible for Company	0.0	1.0	1.0	1.0
11. Is not Taxable to Individual	0.5	0.0	0.0	0.0
Total	**3.5**	**4.0**	**1.5**	**1.5**
Company B				
4. Correlates with Corporate Performance	0.5	0.5	1.0	1.0
7. Ties High Performer to Company	0.5	0.5	1.0	1.0
9. Has No Dilution to Shareholder Equity	0.0	0.0	0.5	1.0
13. Requires No Individual Investment	0.5	0.5	1.0	1.0
14. No Downside Risk to Individual	0.0	0.0	0.5	1.0
Total	**1.5**	**1.5**	**4.0**	**5.0**

Table 9-14. Selected objectives vs. stock options and performance plans

10. **Is Tax Deductible to Company.** Unless the optionee does not meet the holding requirements (i.e., makes a disqualifying disposition), there is no tax deduction with an ISO.
Conversely, with the NQSO, the full value of the gain is tax deductible. With the PSP and
PUP the total of the payout is the deductible.
11. **Is Not Taxable to Individual.** Stock (under a NQ or PSP) or cash (under a PUP) is 100-
percent taxable as ordinary income when received. With an ISO (assuming holding
requirements are met), there is no tax upon receipt (except for possible alternative minimum tax) and long-term capital gains tax will apply to gain at time of sale.

Company B

4. **Correlates with Corporate Performance.** With stock options, the linkage between stock

price and corporate performance is not as direct as many would like, whereas with PUPs, payout is based solely on attainment of corporate performance. PSPs are a combination of corporate performance and stock price.

7. **Ties High Performer to Company.** Stock options that may be fully exercisable in one or two years have some retention value, although it is stronger if vesting occurs after five years. PSPs and PUPs typically are three- to five-year plans with annual startups, so unvested benefits exist in any given year.

9. **Has No Dilution to Shareholder Equity.** Since the full payment is in company stock, usually one needs more options than share awards to achieve comparable values. Therefore, options receive the lowest score while PSPs are somewhat better only because they require fewer shares to deliver comparable value. PUPs, of course, have no dilution if paid in cash.

13. **Requires No Individual Investment.** Both stock options require financing the cost of the underlying stock, although the optionee can avoid this if he or she has no need to hold the stock. PSPs and PUPs require no investment at all.

14. **Individual Has No Downside Risk to Individual.** Both stock options have the downside risk of losing all value. They are worth nothing "underwater" and may be worth little after taxes in the absence of sufficient appreciation. With a PSP, there is some downside risk since payment is in company stock (but there was no investment), whereas with a PUP, there is no downside risk since payment is in cash.

Weighted vs. Unweighted Objectives

A variation to the unweighted identification of important objectives shown in Table 9-14 would be to give them importance weightings. Actually, Table 9-14 reflects a binary weighting of one or zero with only those objectives listed being given a one. This two-point scale could be expanded to a rating scale of zero to five. The higher the scale, the more calibration required in setting the relative ratings of the 14 objectives. Look what would happen with even a three scale rating system with a "2" as very important, a "1" for important, and "0" for not important. For Company A, if we give objective 11 a rating of "2", and the other four listed all "1" (the other nine objectives obviously received a "0"), ISOs and NQs would have each received a score of 2.0. This suggests that ISOs be used to the maximum permitted by law and then supplemented with NQs.

This is a scaled down illustration, but it should provide a basis for constructing one's own table of objectives, weighting their relative importance, and rating their strength against specific plans.

Division vs. Corporate Incentives

Designers must also consider the impact of the interaction among division and corporate short-term and long-term plans. Shown in Table 9-15 are nine possible combinations. An individual-performance factor has been left out here, but it could be included, at least for short-term incentives.

Each of these combinations has certain consequences. An organization with incentive plans only at the division level ("1") has questionable reinforcement of corporate results. A short-term division plan and a long-term corporate plan ("2") is probably the most common combination. It encourages short-term divisional success, while reinforcing corporate results. A "3" is a bridge plan. It has a divisional short-term plan and combines a divisional long-term with a corporate long-term plan. A "4" is the reciprocal of "2" and will encourage long-term divisional decreas-

Short-Term Incentives	Long-Term Incentives		
	Divisional	**Corporate**	**Both**
Division	1	2	3
Corporate	4	5	6
Both	7	8	9

Table 9-15. Divisional and corporate short and long-term incentive plans

es such as research and development investment, assuming other divisions can maximize revenues and minimize expenses. Having all plans at the corporate level ("5") places all the emphasis on corporate results. The disadvantage is that there is no incentive to achieve divisional objectives. A "6" is like a "3" except the short-term weighting has shifted from division to corporate and suggests there are problems with measuring short-term divisional results. A "7" is dominantly weighted with the division and might be found in a portfolio organization with self-standing businesses that provide little corporate synergy. An "8" recognizes the importance of the standalone division but also focuses significant attention on corporate performance, both short and long-term. Having short- and long-term plans at both the division and corporate levels ("9") is a balanced approach but also the most difficult to design and communicate, since payout is based on four different plans.

WHAT OTHER CONSIDERATIONS SHOULD BE ADDRESSED?

Given the general parameters determined by the review of plans against prioritized objectives, it's time to focus on other issues. Some are more important than others, based on the established plan parameters. They are clustered into the following categories:

- What are we attempting to accomplish?
- How will we structure the package?
- Why do we want to make these changes?
- Who will be eligible and who will be involved in the design?
- When should we undertake the review?

What Are We Attempting to Accomplish?

1. What type of culture is one trying to establish, or maintain if already established? A culture that believes superstars are more important than a cohesive organization will single out such individuals for significant incentive opportunities and perquisites. The egalitarian organization will minimize special treatment and special incentives. To the extent possible, everyone will be in the same program, but executives will receive greater pay through such programs for their additional responsibilities. The egalitarian organization is also more concerned with the gap between highest and lowest paid.

2. Is teamwork a critical aspect of the desired culture or are individual contributions more valued? Teamwork is reinforced through group incentives and threatened by individual incentives. Meanwhile, strong individual contributors may be dissatisfied with group incentives. It is possible, of course, to have both at the same or different levels, such as an individual and team annual incentive at the SBU level. Another example would be an individual annual incentive and a long-term group incentive at the SBU or corporate level. At the corporate level, even long-term incentives can be individual although it is more difficult to structure.

3. Before beginning to structure a new or revised executive compensation plan resulting from a merger or acquisition, what does one have to do? During a merger or acquisition, a number of areas need to be explored. Data must be gathered and analyzed before recommendations can be made. A good place to start is with organization charts showing the names and titles of the executives of both companies before and after the acquisition or merger. With an acquisition, the changes will be predominantly with the acquired company. In a merger, one would expect both organizations to be affected. Examine current salary and descriptions, as well as recent and pending payouts of short-term and long-term incentive plans. What type of stock options are outstanding? How many total shares have been granted but not exercised? How many are vested? When do the unvested vest? How many shares are available for grant? What stock-award plans are in place? What non-market plans are being used? Deferred compensation arrangements should be reviewed. Who is included? What are the deferral formulas? How has it been deferred? What are the commitments for future deferrals? How is this being handled for pension plan purposes? What is on the balance sheet? Copies of all employment contracts need to be obtained and reviewed (including most importantly change of control contracts). Special benefits for each executive need to be identified and tax treatment determined.

The above is intended to be a representative not exhaustive list of the type of information gathering that must occur. Next, one must determine what will be allowed to continue and what must change. This is a function of the desired culture one wishes to reinforce.

4. How important are cultural differences in acquisitions and mergers? They are critical to future success. Too often, in spite of the financial advantages, two organizations cannot work with each other because of basic deep-seated differences. It may be as simple as dress code and as complex as how individuals are viewed and treated. Nevertheless, even small differences should be addressed if both groups are expected to work closely with each other. Although some companies try to combine the best from each and form a new culture, it may be more appropriate to start over from the top. Identify those values and characteristics present in the two organizations that one wants to maintain in a new culture. It is critical the leadership be clear on these values and that the pay delivery system reinforce them.

5. How does one know if one's company has been *acquired* or really merged with another organization, since some companies avoid using the "A" (i.e. acquisition) word? Do not simply pay attention to the rhetoric. Look at what is happening. Some of the key signposts include: Is one company's name more prominent than the other post merger? Where is the corporate headquarters? Does one company's shareholder gain a greater portion of new shares outstanding? Which company has more directors on the new board? How are the chairman, CEO, and COO's responsibilities divided? Which company provided these executives? Under a merger, one would expect a balance in the above criteria. In an acquisition, they will lean significantly to one side. One can also watch the stock market to see how investors view the transaction. Whose stock went up and whose went down? Keep in mind, however, that the acquiring company's stock price does not always increase. Sometimes, it is the acquired that increases.

6. What will the replacement needs be for senior executives in the next 5 to 10 years? If the company is shifting into the upper portion of a mature stage, it may have few replacement needs other than for retirement. An emerging company, however, will be faced with significant growth in management positions. These two situations face significantly different needs. Merit pay will have to be adequate for most of the people and promotional adjustments will offset modest merit increases. Perhaps as much as two-thirds of top executives' salary today has come through prior promotional adjustments (taking new jobs) and only one-third for merit (job performance). Fast trackers expect to double their pay every 5 years—a virtual impossibility without significant promotional adjustments, and/or double digit merit increases caused by a high rate of inflation.

7. Is a particular type of executive needed? A high-risk situation within the company will need someone with special talents. It would be difficult to bring in this high-risk seeker without affording the opportunity to earn a very high bonus (based on degree of success). The individual willing to accept high risk is also likely to seek high rewards; since salary alone is unlikely to meet this expectation, the company needs some type of performance-related payoff.

8. To what extent is it desirable to lock the executive in golden handcuffs through restricted pay devices? While many consider this a practical solution to retaining executives, it is necessary to understand that golden handcuffs have varying strengths. They are most effective with the least attractive (to other companies), low-mobility (unlikely to change jobs) executive. In other words, a forfeited value can always be offset by another company if the executive is that good, thereby locking in only the less-than-outstanding performers. However, one can at least make it very expensive for the new employer to buy out all the forfeited pay.

9. What should happen if the short-term incentive formula says there are no dollars available but there were some outstanding contributions? One view says no bonus dollars, no payout for anyone. The countering view is that outstanding contributors need to be rewarded; otherwise, they will leave or at least be demotivated. One can meet this requirement by amending the formula to allow for a carry forward of unused money, thereby having some dollars available even if the fund that year is zero. Another solution is to agree to have a discretionary bonus pool of a stated amount (perhaps 5 percent to 10 percent) of target award. Alternatively, one could compete in an entirely different manner, such as granting stock options to the outstanding performers.

10. What is the desired relationship between individual, unit, and corporate performance? For the CEO, it probably is simply corporate performance. For the business head, it is probably both corporate and own business performance. Decide if they should be equally weighted. If not, is it 2 to 1, 3 to 1, 4 to 1, or some other ratio? Which receives the dominant weighting? For the next layer down, is it individual plus unit and corporate? What are the respective weightings? The advantage of multiple performance considerations is reinforcement of the "line of sight" with corporate performance.

11. What is the significance of risk in structuring the incentive plan? The higher the risk, the greater the expected reward for achieving the goal. In other words, the more risk built into the plan, the greater the reward should be for meeting or exceeding expectations. This is consistent with an investor who will accept a low rate of return for a federal government security but expect a return in multiples of that for a high-risk "junk" bond.

12. In looking to competitive pay practices and levels of pay what companies should be surveyed? In addition to those within one's industry(s), one might include companies that would be included in a search for an executive replacement. For example, in determining what companies to survey for the head of human resources one might look to companies outside of own industry with similar cultures and where human resources responsibilities were comparable.

How Will We Structure the Package?

This section addresses some of the most commonly asked questions when designing pay programs. Because some of the answers to these questions are a function of company specifics, my answers will at least guide the planner in the appropriate direction.

1. How does one determine the respective emphasis of short- versus long-term incentives at a given level in the organization? Long-term incentives should have the greatest relative weighting at the CEO level and the lowest weight at the entry level. The decisions affecting long-term success or failure of the organization correlate rather well with organization hierarchy. Conversely, salaries have the lowest relative weight at the CEO level because of the weightings of incentive pay. An example of the type of relationship that might be sought is shown in Table 9-16.

Organizational Level	Salary	STI	LTI	Total
CEO	20%	20%	60%	100%
Next Down	30	20	50	100
Next Down	40	20	40	100
Next Down	50	20	30	100
Next Down	60	20	20	100

Table 9-16. Compensation relationships by organization level

2. If the pay package is to be redesigned with more emphasis on incentive pay, how does one proceed? It is appropriate to view the percentage of total pay for each of the five elements at the representative levels in the organization and then determine what it will be after the changes have been effected. An abbreviated schedule is shown in Table 9-17 for the chief executive officer, the executive vice president, and the vice presidents.

In this example, the salary portion is reduced dramatically. It may not be possible to achieve the new relationship by simply freezing salary unless a significant total pay increase is also warranted. The higher incentive payout on an unreduced salary will dramatically increase total pay. One needs to know whether the 100 percent figure is to be set equal to the current total dollar payout or a different amount. It is then a relatively easy process to determine the dollar amount for each element.

3. Are the payoffs from short- and long-term incentives in reasonable relationship to each other? Too much emphasis on short-term profit results will do little to encourage the executive to look at the long-term impact of current decisions. Conversely, too much emphasis on long-

Pay Element	CEO		EVP		VP	
	Old	New	Old	New	Old	New
Salary	40%	20%	50%	30%	60%	40%
Employee Benefits	15	15	16	15	17	15
Perquisites	5	5	4	5	3	5
Short-Term Incentives	20	20	15	20	10	20
Long-Term Incentives	20	40	15	30	10	20
Total	100%	100%	100%	100%	100%	100%

Table 9-17. Before and after compensation element weightings

term results may mean underpaying the individual for current performance and thus increasing market vulnerability (i.e., losing the executive to another firm).

4. Is upside financial opportunity appropriately balanced with downside financial risk? The answer to this question is a function of who is asking the question? The executive prefers a significant upside opportunity but would prefer no downside risk, arguing that loss of job is sufficient risk for not meeting performance targets. The shareholder, on the other hand, would like the two more in balance with personal financial risk in owning stock.

5. Is the CEO prepared to make pay differences among those reporting to him or her? A CEO who believes it appropriate to pay two group vice presidents the same salary even though they have significant differences in level of sales and profits may be unlikely to accept an incentive plan that will result in a different payout for each.

6. What portion of the executive pay (at varying levels) should be at risk with the stock market (and thereby closely associated with shareholder interest)? Incentive plans dealing with company stock (especially options) are very popular devices with the board of directors. The board can more easily sell a plan to shareholders that directly links the professional manager's financial success to their own. However, when the market softened, stock options were sometimes shored up with appreciation rights and performance-share plans. Worse, at least in the eyes of the shareholders, is a cancel of outstanding, high-priced options and a reissue at current lower prices. Thus, while there still may be identification with the shareholder, this significantly lowers the degree of risk.

To the extent stock options are employed, the company is saying that it wishes its key employees to share in its growth. Conversely, they are also saying we aren't prepared to give anything if the stock does not appreciate! When the stock does not appreciate and the company has utilized only stock options, it scurries for alternative programs, especially if the lack of stock growth is inconsistent with corporate performance.

Although use of company stock (especially options) has a high degree of identification with the shareholder, a more basic issue is the extent to which the incentive plan is a risk-reward vehicle. Shareholders seem to accept high payouts for very exceptional performance, but they also expect the payout to drop in some relationship with less-than-outstanding achievement.

Plans that have little variance in payout for varying levels of financial success, especially marginal levels, may be subject to significant shareholder criticism.

7. Is the shareholder's return on investment consistent in terms of increases in compensation and benefits of top management? A corporate objective could be that dividend increases will not be less than pay increases for corporate officers, or more conservatively, they will be at least equal to dividends plus appreciation in stock price. Granted, such an approach sounds good, but it creates significant problems in application. For example, is stock price measured at beginning and end of year, or is it averaged per quarter, per month, or per day? Also, how do you calculate a percentage increase in dividends if the previous period had a zero payout? If dividends rose 7 percent in each of the last two years, how do you ensure that average executive pay, which was 50-percent higher than last year, but only 10-percent higher than two years ago, is understood by shareholders? The problems of application may make this approach inappropriate, but do preclude its consideration.

8. Given the financing and earnings-per-share (EPS) objectives, how much additional stock is it appropriate to issue? Certainly, the greatest diluter of EPS is the option, and the smallest is the stock bonus, among stock-based awards. However, the option does aid the financing objective (albeit at a lower price than market), whereas the stock award returns no capital (other than the tax deduction).

9. Given the financing and earnings-per-share (EPS) objectives, how much stock is the company prepared to offer executives over the short and long term? If significant stock is available, it allows considerable flexibility in incentive design; however, if the amount is limited, this impacts upon the type of plan and number of participants. For example, stock options require more stock than stock awards, since the value of the former is only through appreciation.

10. What is an acceptable discount price from market value for company stock before alternative forms of non-equity debt financing become attractive? This question strikes directly at the stock-option program. Some delude themselves into thinking that there is no cost for such a program since the company receives capital. However, the cost to the company can be measured in terms of (a) dilution and (b) the dollar gap between fair market value and option price. The former depresses EPS, and the latter is an indication of lost opportunity in corporate refinancing.

11. What is the role of the top executive group? Is it actively involved in planning and decision issues, or is it a resource generation and allocation vehicle for its captive companies? The former describes a company where divisional results are strongly influenced by corporate officers, and therefore divisional funds must be strongly influenced by corporate results. The latter describes a situation more conducive to separate divisional or group incentive plans, with little if any adjustment for corporate performance.

12. What is the desired relationship of total pay and the relative emphasis of components to the defined executive labor market? Because it is often difficult to obtain data on long-term incentive plans in a compensation survey, it is possible to be fully competitive on salary and short-term incentives, yet either be significantly overgenerous or undercompetitive on total compensation, depending upon the magnitude of long-term incentive programs. Undercompetitiveness is likely to show up before over generosity: underpaid people are more likely to leave than are those who are overpaid.

13. Will significant increases in total pay for top executives be desirable in terms of employee relations? What pressure at the bargaining table or non-organized dissatisfaction will occur if top management is receiving pay increases in multiples of others? Is it of concern that the hourly employee may receive a 5 percent adjustment while senior managers get 15 percent to 20 percent?

14. What is the relationship between pay increases for corporate officers and those for outside directors of the board? Is it logical that pay of corporate officers increases annually, while that of directors is adjusted only every several years and then by a comparatively modest amount? Most organizations state that the pay of their employees is in relation to their responsibilities. Does this apply to outside directors as well? If not, why not? Isn't their responsibility increasing at least at the same rate as that of the senior corporate officers? In recent years, there has been increasing emphasis on the role of the director in setting corporate policy. Board membership is no longer simply a prestigious honor; failing to properly discharge the fiduciary role can result in litigation.

15. Is management prepared to estimate the cost to the company of the incentive plan versus the value to the individual? Whereas one is forced to do this with cash awards, many shy away from attempting a similar analysis for other forms—especially stock options. Yet, if options are to be used, it seems logical to make such an attempt. Just as performance-share values can be established based upon a stated compound growth in earnings per share, so too can stock options be valued after factoring in the assigned price-earnings multiple. Granted, the control of this multiple is outside management's hands, especially in the two-tier market compounded by the bull and bear cycles; nonetheless, management must still make an attempt to estimate both the future and present value if the option is to be part of the executive compensation package. Ootherwise, how can it be compared to alternative forms of compensation?

16. How does one determine what factors to measure? Both the short and long-term incentive plan should focus on measuring factors that are linked to core competency performance. Core competencies, of course, are those inherent organizational strengths that give a company a unique competitive advantage. These strengths need to be maximized and appropriately rewarded for successes and penalized for underperformance.

17. How many factors should be measured? There needs to be a balance between enough factors to accurately describe performance but not so many as to make it difficult to remember what is important. There is no easy answer. As a general rule, measure a handful at most. If reasonably balanced using only two or three is even better. One solution would be to use one or two for short-term incentive plans, and a different one or two for long-term incentive plans.

18. Should one include the cost of capital in the design of the incentive plan? If not included, a company is paying twice for the cost of capital—first to the lender and the second time to the executive.

19. What should be the basis for setting goals? Create a basis for setting goals by looking back (historical performance), looking forward (projected performance), or looking around (peer performance). In addition to any combination of these, one needs to determine if the way in which performance is achieved is important. This addresses the values or culture of the organization.

20. Is there a link between degree of difficulty in meeting a target and the payout? If so, how does one quantify it? There is a link and it can be expressed at three different points when designing an incentive plan. They are threshold (minimum payment above zero), target, and maximum. As the probability of attainment decreases, the possible payment increases. Target is typically viewed as a 50-50 probability of achievement for a company believed to be competitive on total pay. For one discounting its salary and placing more emphasis on incentives, the probability of achieving the target should be enhanced and, therefore, lowered. An organization paying above market salaries would reverse this scenario.

The maximum (above which nothing would be paid) is often set at a 20-80 probability. That is to say, there is only one chance in five that it will be reached. A 10-90 would be a somewhat higher, less attainable target, whereas a 25-75 would be somewhat lower. The threshold is often the reciprocal of the maximum. Namely, if the maximum is 20-80, the threshold might be 80-20—four chances in five that it will at least be met. Other possibilities would be a probability of 90-10 or 75-25.

21. To what extent is the company willing to define performance objectives and evaluate the degree of achievement? Most will agree that evaluating performance is rather difficult; however, after-the-fact assessment of performance is still considerably easier than defining in advance proper corporate and individual goals. The need for accuracy in defining an appropriate target and measuring the extent of attainment is basic to all incentive plans, although perhaps to different degrees.

The incentive impact must be tempered to the extent these factors are not definable or measurable and/or are subject to considerable fluctuation by factors outside the incentive recipient's control.

22. What happens when there is a change in measured factors during the year? Or something happens outside the executive's control to dramatically affect one or more of the factors being measured? It would be very unusual to have everything go as was planned at the beginning of the year. But should changing conditions, which may lower payout, be officially reflected in the pay plan? This is where the purist and pragmatist take different paths. The pragmatist says, "Of course one must reflect the changes, otherwise individuals will be demotivated and may leave." The purist says, "No, because that will open the expectation that future plans will always be changed if something bad happens." A middle ground position might be to set annual goals with an understanding that they will be reviewed at mid-year. However, adjustments should not be made simply to favor executives. If mid-year reviews address unexpected shortfalls, the same consideration should also be given to unexpected windfalls.

23. To what extent will individual executive achievement in meeting the corporate objective(s) be recognized? Since most agree that pay will not motivate unless there is some identifiable linkage between degree of successful individual performance and extent of reward, structuring the magnitude of the reward requires a direct link with ability to measure performance. This question leads to other questions. Is it appropriate to identify five to 20 people within the corporation to participate in an incentive pay program? Or is it more desirable to have an egalitarian approach with participation defined in terms of a smooth line directly correlating with organizational structure?

24. To what degree will "performance" relate to objective factors? It is virtually impossible to build an incentive plan (short of straight profit sharing) that is self-administering. Therefore, one must determine how performance factors will be measured and the validity of the selected measuring sticks. For example, plans based on EPS will encourage a move to long-term debt (even though this might cause later difficulties in a recession). Conversely, plans using ROA are subject to swings in inventories and accounts receivable (usually financed by short-term borrowing). In other instances, one will attempt to objectively evaluate subjective factors. Under such conditions, remember that the measurements used should not be more sophisticated than the ability of the rater to measure.

25. What effect does performance volatility have on the relationship of salary and short- and long-term incentives? Many argue that the more volatile company performance is, the more risk should be built into incentive pay; however, this creates publicity during big payout periods and unhappy executives during low payout periods. For this reason, many companies increase salary and lower incentives in volatile earnings situations—thereby smoothing out the earnings swings of executives. Companies with smaller fluctuations put more at risk and allow the executive to participate in company success or lack thereof.

A related question is: Are these relationships based on competitive data and/or value assessments about what is right with the company?

26. Is the CEO prepared to make unpopular decisions regarding objective achievement? An incentive plan that requires appraisal of goal achievement in terms of modifiers can be completely inconsistent with a CEO that operates within an environment of participative management. Modifying goals or adjustments results in subjective terms and often requires making unpopular decisions.

27. Is the company prepared to define and evaluate individual or unit performance for incentive-plan purposes? It is contradictory to talk about incentive plans based on performance and then to be fuzzy about what constitutes performance. Furthermore, most studies reveal that individual performance plans are more effective in behavior modification than group plans, yet most executive incentive plans are based on group performance (e.g., corporation, group, or division)—not individual.

28. Will individual performance be assessed for the purpose of adjusting group unit performance? Most plans that pay individuals in relation to corporate performance will not attempt to adjust for individual performance. However, the next allocation of units (or bonus range) will probably be adjusted in relation to how the individual performed. Unfortunately, this will probably underreward the individual at one time and overcompensate at another.

29. Should the short- and long-term incentive plans be based on unit or corporate performance? In answering this question, be careful not to set up plans that can lead to inappropriate strategies and actions. For example, it is common to base short-term incentives on unit success and long-term incentives on company success. However, this could encourage a person in the unit plan to maximize short-term results (including cutting advertising, training, and research expenses) to achieve profit goals, thereby putting long-term unit success at risk. One way to minimize this would be to add a long-term unit plan to the other two plans.

30. Are two or more divisions essentially in competition for the same sales dollar? In such situations, it is not uncommon to find these units competing more avidly against each other than the rest of the market. Developing separate divisional funds with little or no group or corporate identification will simply reinforce such behavior.

31. If corporate staff functions are to be included, what will be the basis for the evaluation? Some plans restrict eligibility to those with bottom-line accountability and thereby cause varying levels of participation. Such an approach is based on a position-by-position analysis to determine eligibility. Those not eligible are either on a straight salary or qualify for a short-term incentive plan.

32. Are the goals of top executives quantifiable in terms of performance and time span needed to measure degree of success? To what extent are they shared with others? The ideal plan would have a payout scale for each objective determined at time of closure. Thus, one goal might be adequately assessed after three years and constitute a value of zero to $50,000, while another might not be ascertainable for five years with a range from zero to $75,000.

While not all objectives have the same time frame or end on the same date, few designers are prepared to develop a payout scale on this basis.

33. What is the long-range planning period? It is logical to tie the long-range incentive plan to the same cycle management uses for the planning and review process. In the absence of mitigating circumstances, one would not expect a five-year performance-measuring period for incentive plans in a company with three-year forecasts and appraisals.

34. Is management interested in influencing factors not in the incentive formula (e.g., strategy planning and certain policy issues)? To the extent management does have such interests, it logically should adjust the formula-suggested awards by the assessed impact of these other factors. To fail to do so is to diminish the degree of impact on non-incentive factors.

35. What financial measurements should be included in the incentive plan? Financial performance that tracks with key business strategies should be identified and measured. Typically, these are stated in the form of returns or some form of investment. But financial performance is not the only key to success. There are others and they should be included in the incentive plan.

36. What is the appropriate time period for short-term and long-term incentive plans? The typical short-term plan is one year; it is tied to the financials of the company's fiscal year. Long-term plans are typically 10 years for stock options (following the maximum permitted for tax-qualified plans) and three to five years for performance plans. Whether or not these are appropriate for a particular company is another question. What length of time is necessary to determine whether a decision today was good, bad, or indifferent? What is the cycle time of one's industry? Answers to these questions should weigh heavily in determining the period of time for incentive plans.

37. What is the desired relationship of salary to annual and long-term incentives at different levels of performance attainment? Shown in Table 9-18 is a possible relationship among these three factors. At target, they contribute equally; at maximum, annual and long-term, they are two and four times salary, respectively, placing significantly more emphasis on long-term. If each incentive payout were double salary, the percentages would be 20 percent, 40 percent, and 40 percent. Note what happens below threshold.

38. How much will the plan cost under different scenarios and is that cost acceptable? It would be appropriate to take the data shown in Table 9-17 for each executive and profile the

Performance Attainment	Incentives			Total
	Salary	Annual	Long-Term	
At Maximum	$1,000,000	$2,000,000	$4,000,000	$7,000,000
	14%	29%	57%	
At 3rd Quartile	$1,000,000	$1,500,000	$2,000,000	$4,500,000
	22%	33%	44%	
At Target	$1,000,000	$1,000,000	$1,000,000	$3,000,000
	33%	33%	33%	
At 1st Quartile	$1,000,000	$500,000	$500,000	$2,000,000
	50%	25%	25%	
Below Threshold	$1,000,000	0	0	$1,000,000
	100%			

Table 9-18. Salary/incentive pay relationships

aggregate costs against performance. By expressing these costs in relation to such values as earnings per share or economic profit, one can determine if the value created is in excess of the pan costs and, if so, by how much.

Why Do We Want to Make These Changes?

1. How much of the reason for adopting an incentive plan is to be in vogue and how much is to truly pay in relation to performance? One approach will require significant effort to design a meaningful plan, the other is much easier, since the plan is more pro forma.

2. How important are tax avoidance and minimization? If these are basic concerns, one must be prepared for major revisions in executive pay on almost a regular basis. It will take a constant effort of altering form and timing to optimize this approach. These major changes (rather than oblique movements) will make any type of continuity highly unlikely.

3. To what extent are shareholder relations a concern? With many companies, holdings have shifted from individual investors to large institutions that have greater impact on stock price (by buying or selling in large blocks of shares). If this is a concern, any of the following actions should be considered: limit perquisites and other special pay arrangements not directly related to performance; separate salary from incentive pay (especially in cyclical performing companies); report the bonus in the year immediately following (delaying an additional year might result in big bonuses being reported after a poor financial year); and ensure the short-term incentive fund formula, while adequate, does not generate excessive amounts (especially in poorer-performance years). Some institutional investors have become more critical of executive compensation plans and pay levels that appear unwarranted in terms of corporate performance.

4. Since shareholders want executive pay tied to stock price (and dividends), in addition to stock payment selected (e.g., options and awards), what other considerations are appropriate? Rules that encourage early acquisition of stock (e.g., reload or restoration options), and holding of acquired stock (e.g., stock ownership guidelines), are worth consideration.

5. Is divestment of unprofitable operations a significant requirement in attempting to shift back to a more attractive position in the market life cycle? Rather than simply condition an incentive payment on sales per se, a market-related incentive plan, paying for every full point increase in the company stock, might be feasible. For example, if the stock were selling at $25, it might be appropriate to pay a bonus of $25,000 for every point above that five years hence. A non-market plan (e.g., book value) would be troublesome in structure if the sale of assets actually reduced book value per share.

6. Is the company in an industry that is recession-resistant? Earnings are more predictable in these industries, and short- and long-range incentive formulas are easier to construct. If a company is subject to recessionary pressures, not only is care needed in developing incentive formulas due to cyclical swings in profits, but stock options become even more unpredictable (assuming the price-earnings multiple remains constant). Optionees are likely to relive the pauper to prince, or prince to pauper tale.

7. What is the likelihood of wage controls being again imposed? This scenario would suggest wider salary ranges (in case structural adjustments are suddenly limited, although the company might be permitted to operate an existing program) and documented administrative procedures within a written plan. For many companies, the period between 1971-1974 is a departure point for the next go-around (whenever it happens).

8. Do the incentive plans reward desired outcomes or is there an inconsistency between expectations and the reward delivery system? This is probably *the* major problem with incentive plans. They become structured to pay in relation to an *undesired* outcome. Sometimes, this is the result of a poorly thought out plan. In other instances, it may be the result of an out-of-date plan (e.g., one that was tied to specific targeted goals but is now out of date because the goals and/or their relative importance has changed).

It may take some work, but the problem is not difficult to resolve. Identify, describe, and weight the importance of the desired goals including threshold (minimum expectations) and reasonable maximums. Then incorporate these into the incentive plan design.

9. Is the pay program reinforcing the desired corporate culture? If not, is a change needed? The pay program is a major lever in reinforcing desired culture or how the organization will deal with customers, employees, shareholders, and other interested parties. Incentive programs can be especially important when a significant change in culture is expected. Transformational leadership needs a pay program that will reward expected behavior and penalize inappropriate actions.

10. Are the respective weightings of the pay elements still consistent with where the company wants to be in the market life cycle? If not, is a change needed? Many overlook the market-cycle impact when reviewing the makeup of their pay program. Often, designers align the program only to where the company currently is in the cycle, overlooking where it wants to be. Those in the threshold stage should be looking at what their plans should be in the growth cycle, and plan for the phase-in. Those in the maturity and decline stages are looking at how to shift back into the growth phase, either with their current organization or a redefined package of products and services. Those in the growth phase wish to maximize their position, but they are also probably looking for threshold opportunities to create new markets.

Who Will Be Eligible and Who Will Be Involved in the Design?

1. How important is the clarity of the eligibility definition? As soon as the level of eligibility is defined (by job level, salary range, or position-by-position inspection), pressure will develop to include those just below the cutoff. This factor probably more than any other causes a good plan to go bad, as those brought in by pushing the lower limit do not have the degree of impact intended in the plan. For this reason, some argue such plans should not be tied to salary levels or job grades because it places additional pressure on increases and upgrading. Admittedly, it does, but it also allows the needed review of total pay.

2. Have key players been involved in identifying the objectives of the executive pay program? Including key players in the process is a critical requirement to ensure accuracy, completeness, and support. Who are the key players? One way to identify them and weigh their input is to start with 10 points (or 100 if there are numerous individuals). Beginning with the chairman and CEO, not only identify the individuals but give them power ratings. For example, if the board of directors and CEO are about equal, and the four executive vice presidents are each about a third as important, the weightings would be: board of directors (three points), CEO (three points), and each EVP (one point). In this situation, each member of the board of directors would be polled and a composite rating created.

3. Is the organization still run by its founder or an heir? A founder or one who has taken an organization through periods of major growth is not likely to be interested in diffusing ownership (through stock-based plans) or extending liberal incentive plans. For some, the organization is an instrument of power and position within the community; having attained it, the individual may not be inclined to adopt programs that may diffuse this position.

4. What is the best use of a consultant? To answer this question, one needs to examine the characteristics of the consultant that may be lacking internally.

The consultant should possess complete objectivity in applying technical knowledge and combine efforts with those of company planners to design an appropriate program. Another factor is the amount of time involved, which might not be available internally. The consultant will solve that problem—for a price.

Some use consultants to do their thinking in identifying desired objectives. Shouldn't this be the responsibility of the board of directors with input from general management? A good consultant is the one who is helpful in providing a process to facilitate thinking and shorten the time commitment of the board and the compensation committee.

Some might also choose to let the consultant take over the administrative role, but is this really the best use of resources? Help in setting up the process clearly is. But doing all the work?

An independent view is appropriate given the corporate governance responsibilities of the board and its compensation committee. How much help is required in structuring a new plan depends on all these considerations.

5. How does one choose the best consultant? First, one needs to decide on the role of the consultant. Next, identify at least several major well-known consulting firms, as well as several other capable but lesser known consultants. The human resource department, the legal division, and the outside auditor should be able to help.

Next, one might want to send out a request-for-proposal (RFP) to those identified, indicating what is wanted. Several internal resources, including the purchasing function, should be helpful in structuring the RFP. Review those that have been returned and select at least two. Three or more would be better, time permitting. Invite them in and have them make a presentation before the compensation committee. Based on the consultant that appears to best meet the requirements (including timing and cost), make a selection. In addition, determine exactly *who* will be the consultant. The person making the presentation is not always the on-site consultant; request that whoever will do the work not only be at the presentation but lead it as well.

6. Should the board of directors have its own consultant? The board of directors clearly should have a consultant able to provide an objective view independent of an internally driven proposal. Does that mean there are two consultants (one for the board and one for management) or is there one consultant with two clients? The first is clearly doable, although probably more expensive and vulnerable to one-ups-manship. It is also likely to take longer because proposals have to be reviewed by both consultants.

Assuming a consultant has the ability to keep both customers in perspective, hiring one is the better answer; however, it may be more difficult to find someone acceptable to both management and the board of directors, especially since the consultant should be answerable only to the board of directors.

7. Will the customer be involved in assessing performance? A decade or two back, this question would be summarily dismissed as ludicrous, other than to the extent that the consumer's assessment is measured in revenue. Now, companies are looking for ways for customers to rate performance. Questionnaires are included with the product and/or a telephone call or personal visit. However, this measurement is more likely included in a short- rather than long-term incentive plan.

When Should We Undertake the Review?

1. How much time can pass before one should review the structure of the executive pay package? At most, one year. An annual review process will capture opportunities that a failure to would have missed. Annual reviews are also generally associated with moderate change. Less frequent reviews suggest more dramatic change. In addition, the need for significant changes in design will be better anticipated with annual reviews than less frequent ones.

Obviously, any change significantly affecting the company would also trigger a review (e.g., acquisition, merger, sudden shift in market stages, or a new CEO, to name a few). In rapidly changing times, more frequent than annual review is appropriate.

2. Is it understood that the incentive plan will have to be reviewed annually in terms of appropriateness to industry, company, management, tax, accounting, and Securities and Exchange Commission (SEC) issues? Unfortunately, the view of almost everyone is that after sweating through the installation of a new pay program, they can forget about it for at least several years. The result is that, after such a time span, the plan requires major surgery and continuity is significantly jolted.

Fund formulas should be reviewed periodically. Old and outdated formulas will typically provide greater funds than required because they were established when earnings were lower. One test of efficacy is ascertaining whether the same amount of discipline is exerted as when the formula was last modified. A related question is whether the budgeted targets have similar stretch to earlier goals.

Conversely, financial performance will be more positive under historical-cost accounting than if those figures were adjusted for inflation and present-day cost of replacing assets. Therefore, formula-based historical-cost accounting to generate short- or long-term incentive payouts should be examined very carefully before being modified.

Parenthetically, it should be noted that while most plans can deal with the results associated with FIFO (first in, first out), LIFO (last in, first out), and NIFO (next in, first out), no one has been able to develop a meaningful incentive plan when FISH is employed (i.e., first in, still here).

This list of questions is intended to be representative (not exhaustive) and hopefully helpful in stimulating thinking of additional considerations that must be addressed.

STRUCTURING PAY RELATIONSHIPS

The next step is to determine how the total pay package is to be broken down. Assume that based on survey data and internal considerations, it is determined that the CEO's total pay should be $5 million (if performance targets are met), and that salary will be set at $1 million [an amount that maximizes use of the 162(m) million dollar cap for non-performance pay]. It is further decided that the annual incentive target should be equal to salary, but that long-term incentives should be half of the $5 million. These amounts (along with employee benefit and perquisite allocations) are shown in Table 9-19. Also shown are the decisions on the target short- and long-term incentive opportunities at lower income levels. These amounts are incorporated into the design of the plans. To place short- and long-term incentives on a comparable plane, the long-term values are expressed in present-value amounts.

Pay Elements	Income Targets Below the CEO				CEO
Salary	$75.0	$137.5	$200.0	$300.0	$1,000.0
Employee Benefits	15.0	27.5	40.0	60.0	200.0
Perquisites	—	2.5	10.0	40.0	300.0
Short-Term Incentives	8.0	32.5	80.0	180.0	1,000.0
Long-Term Incentives	2.0	50.0	170.0	420.0	2,500.0
Total	$100.0	$100.0	$500.0	$1,000.0	$5,000.0

Table 9-19. Possible compensation distribution in dollars (in thousands)

As shown in Table 9-20, it is a simple matter to convert these dollars into a percentage of salary in order to structure target payments. For example, at the million-dollar salary level, the annual incentive target will be 100 percent of salary. The next decision will be to set the threshold percentage (perhaps 20 percent of salary) and the maximum payout (perhaps 200 percent of salary). The same process would be followed at lower income levels.

Lastly, one can profile the five elements as a percentage of total pay, as shown in Table 9-21. Thus, at the $5 million total-pay level, short-term incentives are expected to make up 20 percent.

Pay Element	Income Targets Below the CEO				CEO
Salary	100.0%	100.0%	100.0%	100.0%	100.0%
Employee Benefits	20.0	20.0	20.0	20.0	20.0
Perquisites	—	1.8	5.0	13.3	30.0
Short-Term Incentives	10.7	23.6	40.0	60.0	100.0
Long-Term Incentives	2.7	36.4	85.0	140.0	250.0
Total Percentage	133.4%	181.8	250.0%	333.3%	500.0%
Total Dollars	$100.0	$250.0	$500.0	$1,000.0	$3,000.0

Table 9-20. Percentage relationship of elements to salary

	Total Compensation				
Pay Element	**$100.0**	**$250.0**	**$500.0**	**$1,000.0**	**$5,000.0**
Salary	75.0%	55.0%	40.0%	30.0%	20.0%
Employee Benefits	15.0	11.0	8.0	6.0	4.0
Perquisites	---	1.0	2.0	4.0	6.0
Short-Term Incentives	8.0	13.0	16.0	18.0	20.0
Long-Term Incentives	2.0	20.0	34.0	42.0	50.0
Total	100.0%	100.0%	100.0%	100.0%	100.0%

Table 9-21. Possible compensation distribution as a percentage of total compensation

DISCLOSURES AND COMMUNICATION CONSIDERATIONS

Many people think they are communicating when in fact they are simply disclosing. *Disclosure* is a one-way message; *communication* requires an indication by the receiver that the message is understood. If not understood, there is an interchange between sender and receiver until the message *is* understood. Too many people are satisfied in simply sending what they believe either meets their obligation and/or is sufficiently clear as to require no further effort. At the minimum the sender should indicate to the receiver willingness to meet and discuss if there are any questions.

Having designed the pay delivery system it is critical that the approvers of the plan (typically the board of directors and perhaps its compensation committee) clearly understand how it works and what it will cost with varying levels of performance. This objective will be discussed in the next chapter. Once the plan is approved, it must be clearly understood by the eligible candidates. How can a plan motivate performance if the individual does not clearly understand what is expected?

Guidelines for developing a strong communication process can be put in the context of what, who, how, why, when, and where.

- *What* information is being communicated? Is it past, present, and/or future? Does it deal with plan changes or simply an update status report?
- *Who* is to receive the information? Is this going to the executives, other employees, shareholders, customers, suppliers, or the community? Or is it intended for the Financial Accounting Standards Board, IRS, SEC, or an institutional shareholder service?
- *How* is the information to be conveyed? Will it be face-to-face; via image or voice response; or report format and/or interactive modeling?
- *Why* is the information being provided? Is it legally required or a voluntary action? Is it to show results or possible outcomes?
- *When* is the information to be given? Automatically upon attainment of a date or event or in response to a request?
- *Where* is the information provided? Is it at a meeting or a location (physical or web site)?

Required vs. Voluntary Disclosure

The previously discussed Section 16 of the Securities Exchange Commission rules outlines what the executive must disclose to the SEC on Forms 3, 4, and 5, and what the company must disclose to shareholders in the proxy statement. Additionally, there are a set of benefit-plan disclosure requirements indicating what benefit-plan information must be sent to employees. Much of this pertains to pensions and comes from the Employee Retirement Income Security Act (ERISA), although there are other requirements as well. Suffice it to say that the legal requirements be carefully reviewed, especially since they change from time to time.

Having ensured that legal disclosure requirements are met, the company needs to determine what additional information it will provide, when, to whom, and in what level of detail. The basic reason for additional disclosure is to make certain the executive understands the plan. This is especially important if the individual needs to make a decision at some point (e.g., exercise a stock option).

Why Bother With Voluntary Disclosure Programs?

First and foremost how can one expect the pay delivery system to channel and maximize individual effort without clearly disclosing what will be rewarded? Clearly communicating all relevant plans so that eligible candidates understand them usually involves greater detail than that required by the SEC and other overseers. Having justified this level of disclosure, many companies find it insufficient, pointing out the need to calibrate different performance levels and their payment amounts.

Clearly, describing the pay delivery system is also essential when trust is low. In this situation, it is not an end but a means to build trust. Recipients will be watching carefully for consistency between words and actions. Trust of superiors is typically based on a combination of personal characteristics (e.g., integrity, openness, and consistency) with performance and professional competence. When trust is low, a simple assurance by the superior is not sufficient to convince an executive of something he or she does not believe. The *perception* of reality is more important than reality itself. This is especially troublesome in light of evidence that most employees underestimate the contribution of others (at comparable organizational levels), while overestimating the level of other's pay. A completely open pay communication system might eliminate the same misconceptions. However, the more open the system, the more likely supervisors are to minimize pay differentials for variances in performance, since they would have to defend deviations. Thus, one must question whether open pay systems and pay-for-performance are complementary or conflicting objectives.

Determining What to Communicate

Executives want to know how the pay program works. The honor of being singled out to participate in the incentive program or receive a particular perquisite is not enough. The executive is not inclined, as in years past, to simply trust the company; the individual wants to understand the basic features of the plan. This may be due to prior failures on the part of a plan to deliver when the executive performed well, but more likely, it is simply a desire to minimize efforts expended in non-productive areas.

Nonetheless, the executive must receive enough information to believe the compensation program to be a logical system that pays in relation to performance. If pay is to have any motivational aspects, the executive must perceive a definite link between performance and pay. However, to the extent that this communication becomes specific about the pay of others, it can become a demotivating factor. This is simply because the executive typically has a higher regard usually for his or her own level of contribution than for that of others in the peer group.

Therefore, it is logical for an executive to know the amount that can be expected in compensation for doing a commendable or outstanding job, especially in incentive pay. This is much easier when the incentive plan is formalized than when subjective judgement is an important factor. Whether or not the individual should know his or her own salary range is a matter of debate, but certainly the process should be carefully explained. For some people, the belief that the pay delivery system is logical and systematic is sufficient.

Structuring the Disclosure. Written materials and oral presentations of the plan should be structured in layers. The first layer can probably be done on one sheet of paper. It answers the basic questions of what, why, how, when, where, who, and cost. For each of the seven questions, a second layer is provided with additional information. The third layer is more extensive in detail and may actually consist of the plan documents. Thus, every question is answered in a specific manner using levels one, two, and three, as needed. Even if levels two and three are not pursued by the executive, they will be helpful in briefing the plan administrators.

Having gotten through the explanation of the plan, one next moves on to a personal description. This focuses on *three* time frames: past, present, and future. Shown in Table 9-22 is a total compensation report for Ms. Jolly Goodshow, a hypothetical executive with Brucell. In this example, year five is the current year and years one to four are previous years. Note in the "annual compensation," pay elements have been displayed both in W-2 and proxy format. The difference is with incentives, which for proxy purposes are shown for the year earned. For W-2 purposes, incentives are reported in the year paid, which is typically after the year in which earned. Since year five is still underway, the annual incentive and performance-share amounts are unknown. The stock option table shows the number of shares granted and remaining under option by year of grant and grant price. It also shows the number of shares vested at the end of each year. Currently, 30,000 shares are vested, but after the end of the current year (year five) an additional 30,000 shares will vest. The performance-share schedule shows the various four-year plan periods, the payout schedule, and when paid. Note that the first plan period was paid out in the first quarter of the current year—an amount of 15,000 shares. Payouts remain to be determined for the next three years.

Annual Compensation

	Year Earned (Proxy)		Year Paid (W2)	
	Year 4	Year 5	Year 4	Year 5
Salary	$375.0	$400.0	$375.0	$400.0
Annual Incentives	175.0	NA	150.0	175.0
Performance Shares	165.0	NA	—	165.0
Total	**$715.0**	**NA**	**$525.0**	**$740.0**

Stock Options

Grant Year	Option Price	Number of Shares Vested at Year End				
		Year 4	Year 5	Year 6	Year 7	Total
1	$57.50	15,000				15,000
2	45.50	15,000	15,000			30,000
3	78.50	—	15,000	15,000		30,000
4	105.00	—	—	15,000	15,000	30,000
	Total	**30,000**	**30,000**	**30,000**	**15,000**	**105,000**

Performance Share Awards

Plan Period	Share Schedule			Paid Out in First Quarter of ...			
	Threshold	Target	Maximum	Year 5	Year 6	Year 7	Year 8
1-4	1,000	10,000	25,000	15,000			
2-4	1,000	10,000	25,000		✔		
3-6	1,000	10,000	25,000			✔	
4-7	1,000	10,000	25,000				✔

Table 9-22. Total compensation report example

Showing the Effect of Performance on Future Pay. Shown in Table 9-23 are the resulting actions of different performance ratings for two years. Namely, each of the five possible ratings are modeled for each of year one's ratings. To illustrate, in year one a performance rating of "5" would result in an annual pay increase of 25 percent for our executive, currently earning a $400,000 salary and an annual incentive of $175,000. The following year, compensation actions range from a 5.7-percent increase to a 24.9-percent decrease, depending on the performance rating. At the other extreme, if the executive were given a "1" rating this year, it would result in a decrease of 13.3 percent. The following year, pay actions would range from a 47.9-percent increase to a 2.0-percent increase, depending on performance rating. This two-year table clearly illustrates the upside potential as well as the downside risk of the plan. Schedules such as these can be very powerful in clearly communicating the pay opportunities at different levels of performance.

Rating	Possible Compensation Next Year			% Increase	Rating	Possible Compensation Two Years from Now			% Increase
	Salary	Incentive	Total			Salary	Incentive	Total	
5	$438.8	$280.0	$718.8	25.0%	5	$452.4	$307.2	$759.6	5.7%
					4	452.4	254.5	706.9	-1.7%
					3	452.4	206.2	658.6	-8.4%
					2	452.4	153.6	606.0	-15.7%
					1	438.8	100.9	539.7	-24.9%
4	$438.8	$232.0.8	$670.8	16.7%	5	$452.4	$307.2	$759.6	13.2%
					4	452.4	254.5	706.9	5.4%
					3	452.4	206.2	658.6	-1.8%
					2	452.4	153.6	606.0	-9.7%
					1	438.8	100.9	539.7	-19.5%
3	$430.1	$188.0	$618.1	7.5%	5	$452.4	$301.1	$753.5	21.9%
					4	452.4	249.5	701.9	13.5%
					3	452.4	202.2	654.6	5.9%
					2	448.6	150.5	599.1	-3.1%
					1	431.0	98.9	530.0	-14.3%
2	$419.3	$140.0	$559.3	-2.7%	5	$452.4	$293.5	$745.9	33.4%
					4	452.4	243.5	695.6	24.4%
					3	449.9	197.1	646.9	15.7%
					2	438.7	146.8	585.4	4.7%
					1	423.7	96.4	520.1	-7.0%
1	$406.3	$92.0	$498.3	-13.3%	5	$452.4	$284.4	$736.8	47.9%
					4	449.0	235.6	684.6	37.4%
					3	437.8	191.0	628.7	26.2%
					2	426.6	142.2	568.8	14.2%
					1	414.5	93.4	508.0	2.0%

Rating Definitions: 5 - Outstanding; 4 - Superior; 3 - Good; 2 - Satisfactory; 1 - Marginal

Table 9-23. Possible future salary and annual incentive payout

A long-term plan reflecting various performance levels for the following year might be presented in the manner illustrated in Table 9-24.

The Effect of a Pay Increase on Employee Benefits. Communicating a salary increase is rather simple and straightforward, the individual is told he or she received an increase of $X, or Y percent, effective Z date. Companies stopping here lose a great opportunity to show the multiplied effect of a salary increase, namely, the flow-through to increased benefit coverage. Shown in Table 9-25 is a worksheet for the Brucell Company. For illustration purposes, a 40-year-old receiving a $1,000 annual increase is shown. Space is provided for the person to fill in own pay increase and years to retirement. Additionally, the increased annual benefit cost is also shown. While providing such a worksheet is helpful, the complete statement is better. The statement can stand alone, or accompany a personalized benefit statement, showing the values received or due from various company benefit plans during active service and at time of disability, death, or retirement.

Performance Rating	Incentive			
	Salary	Annual	Long-Term	Total
5	$439	$280	$439	$1,158
4	439	232	329	1,000
3	430	188	215	833
2	410	140	105	664
1	406	92	0	498

Table 9-24. Possible total payments by performance (in thousands)

When Should One Communicate the Pay Program? The company should send a report to the executive *annually* on the current compensation package, such as illustrated in Table 9-22. This annual report should include at least the following year's range of total pay possibilities such as reported in Tables 9-23 and 9-24. Additionally, whenever there is a plan change, the pay-out possibilities should be illustrated and compared to that of previous plans. The differences should be clearly explained. For example, a company deciding to move from stock-options-only to a combination stock-option and performance-share plan should provide a side-by-side comparison and explain why the change was made. In Table 9-26, Brucell determined by present-value methodology that three of its options were equivalent to one outright share of stock.It therefore moved from an all-option program to half option and half performance share. The rationale was to take some of the uncertainties of the stock market out of the long-term incentive plan. The old plan called for 60,000 stock options; the new plan stipulates 30,000 options and a targeted performance share award of 10,000 shares. Note that with a 50-percent stock-price increase, the two plans pay out the same. Above that, the stock-option plan is more attractive; below that, the combination plan is better.

To avoid issues with disgruntled executives, it is often prudent to find out how they view proposed changes before revising the plan. Shown in Table 9-27 is a questionnaire that Brucell used before making the plan change. Note that the first question distinguishes between stock options and stock awards. Question 2A distinguishes between a simple stock award and a performance-share award. Question 2B distinguishes between a "plain vanilla" stock option and a performance-based stock option. Question 3 permits the responder to weight the answers to 2A and 2B.

SUMMARY AND CONCLUSIONS

The two key requirements for an effective pay delivery system are design and communication. A good design ensures that the system will do what it is intended to do, namely, reward executives for achieving selected objectives to lead the organization to success. Effective communication ensures that executives (and all other stakeholders) clearly understand how the pay delivery system works and what awards are available for stated levels of performance. Both of these requirements must be done well. Failure to do so will most assuredly result in an ineffective executive compensation program.

		Example	You	Your Factor
Increase in Annual Salary		$1,000	$	
Increased Benefit Coverage	**Multiplier**			
Basic Life Insurance	2	$2,000		
Supplemental Life Insurance[1]	0-3	3,000		
Business Travel [2]	6	6,000		
Disability–Short-term [3]	0.5	500		
Disability–Long-term [4] Year to 65 [25] x .5	12.5	6,250		
Savings and Investment Plan Year to 65 [25] x .125	3.125	$3,125		

Contribution	Mutiple	Contribution	Mutiple
10%	.125	5%	.075
9%	.115	4%	.060
8%	.105	3%	.045
7%	.095	2%	.030
6%	.085		

Retirement Plan[5] Years to 65 [25] x .014	.35		
Life Expectancy Factor	15		
Retirement Factor	[52.5]	$52,200	

[1] Depends on coverage elected. Example employee has three times salary and is not affected by $500,000 maximum.

[2] Amount six times salary (maximum benefit of $250,000). Essentially individual earning $41,667 per year or less will have an increase.

[3] May be eligible for more but assumes long-term disability applies after six months.

[4] Includes Social Security benefit to a maximum annual benefit of $36,000 (pay $72,000 or less).

[5] Your benefits may be greater than this if the integrated formula is applicable.

Table 9-25. Employee benefit pay increase worksheet (continued on next page)

Some of the issues addressed in this chapter were: On whose performance will the short- and long-term incentives be based? What financial and other measurements will be used? What is the relationship among corporate, unit, and individual? Will the performance of other companies be a factor? Who will set the targets? Who will do the ratings?

The type of review highlighted in this chapter is both difficult to perform and critical to the successful construction of an effective pay delivery system. In an executive pay program, designers must consider a number of factors. A partial listing of those reviewed in this book include:

- *Performance.* What performance measurements should be the basis for payment? How do these relate to the goals and objectives of the business plan? How long is the measurement period? Will performance of other companies be a consideration? Should performance tar-

Increased Benefit Cost Per Year	Example	You
Basic Life Insurance, $1.80 per $1,000	$3.60	$
Supplemental Life Insurance Under 35 - $2.40 per $1,000 35-39 - 3.00 40-44 - 4.20 45-49 - 9.00 50-54 - 9.00 55-59 - 12.00 60-64 - 18.00	12.60	
Business Travel	0	0
Disability - Short-term	0	0
Disability - Long-term Increase in compensation over $18,000 bu less than $72,000 x .005.	5.00	
Savings and investment plan increase 1,000 x 10% contribution free	100.0	
Retirement Plan	0	0
Total Annual Employee Cost	$121.20	

Table 9-25. Continued

| Stock Price Change | Old | New | | | |
	Stock Options Only	Stock Options	Performance Shares	Total	New Versus Old
100%	$6,000	$3,000	2,000	$5,000	($1,000)
50%	3,000	1,500	1,500	3,000	—
25%	1,500	750	1,250	2,000	500
0%	0	0	1,000	1,000	1,000
-25%	0	0	750	750	750
-50%	0	0	500	500	500

Table 9-26. Comparison of old and new stock plans (in thousands)

gets be set? If so how, and will minimums and maximums also be established? What should payout be at different organization levels?

- *Eligibility.* What is the basis for eligibility? What happens if the executive leaves before payout of incentives?
- *Ownership.* How important is it for executives to own stock? How much? Are these

---

1. If you had a choice of receiving one share of Brucell stock at no cost (except for taxes) or an option for ten years to purchase three shares at today's market price, which would you choose?
   A. The One Share
   B. The Option on Three Shares
   C. Some Combination of the two

2. If you chose:

   A. The one share. Would you prefer one share regardless of company or stock price performance or a formula which would give you two shares if certain performance criteria were met, but no shares if they were not met?
      (1) The One Share
      (2) The Variable Plan

   B. The option on three shares. Would you prefer the same three-share option or one that might deliver six shares if company or stock price performance objectives were met, but if not met all options would be below water (i.e., option price would be greater than market price)?
      (1) The Option on Three Shares
      (2) The Possibility of Six Shares

   C. Some combination of the two. Would you prefer:
      (1) Equal weighting of A and B
      (2) More weighting on A than on B
      (3) More weighting on B than on A

Table 9-27. Stock plan questionnaire

guidelines or requirements? How will the company enforce them? What amount of investment, if any, should executives be required to make?

- *Accounting.* How important is minimizing (or completely avoiding) a charge to earnings? How important is minimizing or completely avoiding dilution of stock ownership?

- *SEC.* If a publicly traded company, who will be responsible for insider reporting requirements to the SEC?

- *Taxation.* How important are current deductions versus those deferred to a future date? How important is providing long-term capital gains to the executive? How important is it to avoid or minimize alternative minimum tax issues? Is tax position clear or is a private letter ruling from the IRS needed?

The problem in developing an incentive program is certainly not the lack of alternatives. Rather, the difficulty involves how to narrow the possibilities to find the the best fit. Given financial performance as the criteria for incentives, one can select from: profits before taxes, profits after taxes, return on investment, return on equity, return on capital employed, and earnings per share. These measurements can be expressed in absolutes or as relative amounts of change. They can be based on corporate, and in many instances, group or divisional results. Too many executive compensation programs are extensions of previous company programs, or faddish adaptations of another company's plan. Lacking is a basic examination of how the program should be structured given individual and corporate objectives versus the impact of federal pay policy (e.g., taxation) and perception of the public (including shareholders).

The company must sort through these factors and array them in importance. Different businesses, like different industries in different stages in their market cycle, have different needs. For example, the late-threshold-early-growth-stage company has a strong capital need for future growth. Therefore, these companies should not place great emphasis on current profits because of the need to reinvest to promote future growth.

Examining the needs and impacting factors carefully will not guarantee success, but ignoring them completely will almost certainly guarantee failure. Since recognizing failure is easier than quantifying success, a failing design will lead to either continually tinkering with the plan or abandoning it in complete disgust.

The keys to success are alignment and communication. The pay delivery system must be closely aligned with the vision, mission, objectives, and goals of the organization. In other words, performance measurements must clearly and consistently be tied to achieving these goals. In addition, performance expectations and the pay delivery system must be clearly communicated to the beneficiaries and the administrators.

Note: You are again reminded not to rely on accounting, tax, SEC, or other professional service statements in this chapter. You need to seek appropriate professional counsel for such guidance. Statements made in this chapter and elsewhere are offered as being illustrative to help frame such further investigations by the reader with counsel.

Having reviewed design and communication considerations, let's move to review the role of the board of directors and its compensation committee in the process.

Chapter 10

The Board of Directors

T he shareholders entrust the board of directors to represent their interests. They do so by electing individuals each year to serve on the board of directors. What once was an honorific position is today one of great importance and responsibility.

As far back as 1919, the view of the courts has been that, "a business corporation is organized and carried on primarily for the profit of the shareholders" (Dodge versus Ford Motor Company).

During the 1930s the Securities Act and Securities Exchange Act were passed, setting down disclosure requirements for companies offering to sell securities. Rules and responsibilities for board directors were also proscribed. Stockholder power was further enhanced in 1942 when the Securities and Exchange Commission (SEC) adopted a rule requiring companies to bring shareholder resolutions to a vote by all shareholders. However, SEC Rule 141-8(c)(7) has allowed companies to exclude from the proxy and shareholder vote those proposals that deal, "with a matter relating to the conduct of the ordinary business operations" of the company. The SEC determines on a case-by-case basis if a specific shareholder resolution is excludible or includible. Shareholders may submit proposals outside of this rule but would have to incur the cost of preparing a proxy statement and soliciting votes.

With the increasing financial resources of pension plans, institutional shareholders have been gaining an increasing portion of the stock market. Institutional shareholders with large blocks of stock have become a powerful voice in determining what companies should and should not do. They are also very influential in determining who will serve as directors. Once content to simply disagree by selling their stock, many shareholders today push the issue of corporate governance to the forefront of the board agenda and the shareholder meeting.

At the turn of the century, corporate governance evolved with the passage from privately held companies to publicly held companies. This shift grew out of the need for private companies to "go public" in order to raise needed capital through the issuance of company stock. Funds from the sale of stock were a debt-free solution to capital needs.

A number of organizations have identified what they believe to be appropriate corporate governance principles. Among the most notable are: The Business Roundtable, the California Public Employees' Retirement System (CalPERS), the National Association of Corporate Directors (NACD), and Teachers Insurance Annuity Association-College Retirement Equities Fund (TIAA-CREF).

THE BOARD OF DIRECTORS

Major responsibilities of the board of directors include hiring the chief executive officer (CEO), approving an annual business plan, and adopting a long-term strategy. The board must also monitor the CEO's progress and performance within the framework of the approved actions. Traditionally, the CEO's performance assessment is converted to an approved compensation package (normally, through an annual review). However, recent tax-law changes, specifically, Section 162(m) (the million-dollar limit on company tax deductions for non-performance-based pay of the five named executives in the proxy), have forced CEO pay issues to shift to a committee of the board, typically, named the compensation committee or executive compensation committee. Before exploring the role of this committee, let's take a look at the board itself.

Responsibilities of the Board of Directors

In addition to hiring and firing the CEO, and approving annual and long-term plans, a representative list of responsibilities might include:

1. Adopt or amend company by-laws
2. Approve (subject to shareholder approval):
   - Amendments to the certificate of incorporation
   - A merger with one or more companies
   - Sales, lease, or exchange of most if not all company's assets
   - Dissolution or revocation of dissolution of corporation
   - The number of shares of company stock authorized for issuance
   - Plans using company stock for compensation
3. Approve strategic direction of the company, monitor its performance, and take action as appropriate
4. Determine the size of the board and appointment of directors between shareholder meeting dates
5. Determine what board committees should exist, their responsibilities, the directors assigned to those committees, and periodically review committee reports
6. Set compensation forms and amounts for the directors
7. Elect and remove corporate officers
8. Declare dividends and fix record and payment dates
9. Set date, time, and place of board meetings for the year
10. With regard to the annual shareholder meeting:
    - Set date, time and place
    - Propose candidates for board of director positions
    - Propose approval of company outside auditor

- Approve company position with regard to shareholder proposals
- Approve proxy materials (including SEC registration statements and other filings)
11. Call special meetings of the board and of shareholders as needed
12. Authorize the issuance of stock and debentures within shareholder-approved plan
13. Take such action as may be required by applicable law or regulation
14. Take whatever other action is consistent and appropriate with corporate governance responsibilities

Table 10-1 is a chart depicting respective responsibilities of the shareholders, the board of directors, and board committees. The three most common committees are audit, compensation, and governance. Several other committees found in some companies are also shown. Not listed is the compensation committee since a considerable portion of this chapter will be devoted to its role.

The board must decide not only what committees to have but also the extent of their responsibility. Will they be authorized to act on behalf of the board, or will they merely be asked to recommend action to be taken by the board? State law must be reviewed to ensure the extent of authority delegated is legally permissible. Ultimate responsibility for any board matter rests with the board not its committees. In conflict with this position is Section 162(m) of the Internal Revenue Code (IRC). This section stipulates the provisions for tax-deductible pay for the named executives in the proxy. To be tax deductible (beyond the $1 million limit in the law) the per-

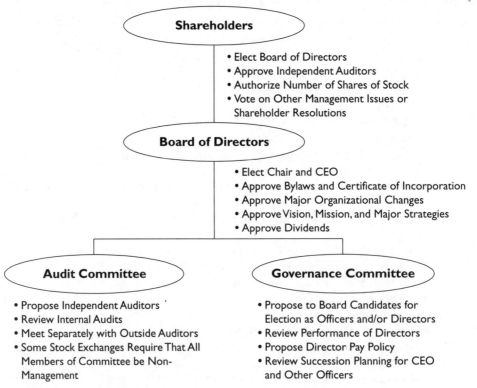

Table 10-1. Shareholders, the board of directors, and its essential non-compensation committees

formance goals for these executives must be made by an independent committee of the board consisting of two or more outside directors of the board. Such goals must be set down in writing not later than 90 days after the beginning of the performance period. This will be discussed in more detail later in the chapter when the compensation committee is reviewed.

Each committee needs to decide when and how frequently to meet. The "when" is usually on the date of the board meeting. This minimizes travel. The "how frequently" depends on the nature of regular duties versus special assignments. The former would probably suggest two to five times a year.

Other possible committees:

- **Executive committee.** Several directors authorized by the board to act on their behalf to the extent legally permitted
- **Finance committee.** Responsible for approving capital budgets and proposing dividend action, sometimes combined with audit committee
- **Pension committee.** Approves fund managers, sets financial expectations, and reviews results
- **Strategic planning committee.** Responsible for proposing specific plans, reviewing results versus plans, and reporting appropriate action directly to the board

Chairman of the Board

The vast majority of companies elect the CEO as the chairman of the board. This, however, may not occur simultaneously. If the individual is new to the company, the board may want his or her full attention focused on being the top executive. This gives the CEO time to adjust to one job before taking on another. Later, the chairman title is added. In the interim, one of the outside directors serves as chair. Rather than separate CEO and chair, some identify a *lead director*. The lead director would be the contact for agenda topics and other requests by outside directors. He or she would also step in when the chair was unavailable to run the board meeting or when the outside directors wanted to meet without the management directors (possibly to talk of firing the CEO).

Director Liability

Directors have an ongoing, everyday obligation to oversee the company's compliance with legal requirements. Shareholders are likely to initiate action when they believe directors have not acted in their best interests. Director actions will be examined in terms of federal and state laws and regulations, as well as common law principles.

Directors are expected to exercise *prudent judgment,* acting in good faith on an informed basis only after obtaining material facts. It is further expected directors will call on legal and other experts in evaluating alternative actions. Assuming directors have exercised care in selecting such experts, their information, evaluations, and advice is assumed reliable.

Directors must act without *conflict of interest,* keeping in mind the best interests of the shareholder and the company. Possible conflict should be disclosed to other directors. The board minutes should record such disclosures and inform shareholders. It is further expected that directors will respect the confidentiality of discussions until they are disclosed by the company and will not act upon such confidential information to benefit self, friends, or family.

If the directors have acted in this manner, the *business judgment rule* says they should not be held liable for mistakes or decisions that did not turn out as expected. Therefore, directors must ensure an appropriate compliance reporting system exists for their review.

It will be virtually impossible to find individuals willing to serve as directors without a reasonable liability insurance policy in place. In addition to covering damages, it should also cover the reimbursement of legal fees.

Directors facing the burden of paying legal and related expenses will want the company to advance them payments for such costs; the company will want the director to sign a written promise to reimburse the company if indemnification is later denied. However, directors might seek the further comfort of an *indemnification agreement* whereby the company agrees to reimburse the director for any legal actions not covered by the liability insurance.

Advisory Board

Some companies find it advantageous to form advisory boards. The most typical reason for their formulation is high-level expertise and/or excellent contacts. CEOs can easily access professional opinions on new ventures or markets, receive assistance in developing needed core competencies, and/or reach high-level decision-makers. Advisory board members often find such service more attractive than regular board service. It requires less of a time commitment and may incur no financial liability (if the advisory board is not a legal entity).

The CEO must determine needs before reaching out to recruit directors. The first director brought in should be of sufficient "star quality" to attract others to the board. Individuals must clearly know what is expected of them and what they will get in return for their services.

Board Meetings

The key questions about board meetings are: How many? Where? When? What will be discussed at each? Who gets invited?

There should be a sufficient number of meetings to discharge the governance role of the board. Each board has to sort through this issue on its own. Some boards will meet every month, some only once a quarter, and others will fall somewhere in between. Common practice would be eight to ten meetings a year.

Meetings are typically held at company headquarters for the convenience of the CEO and other members of management. However, it is not unusual to have at least one meeting a year at an offsite location to review the strategic direction of the company.

When during the month meetings will be scheduled is a function of what will be discussed. A number of boards meet during the second or third week after the close of a financial quarter to review the results before issuing a public statement. More frequent meetings often take place at a regular time so directors can lock in their calendars. Thus, for example, meetings might be the second Thursday of every month, or at least every month following a financial quarter.

It is also helpful to standardize the meeting agenda so directors know what they can expect. An abbreviated example is shown in Table 10-2. Lunch may either precede or follow the meeting.

In addition to the directors, the board may allow specified members of management who are not board members (e.g., chief legal officer and chief human resources officer) sit with them (but usually not at the table itself). This provides directors an opportunity to evaluate such individuals based on their behavior. Others prefer that only directors be in attendance. Those having business with the board enter only when their agenda item is called and leave when finished. Where people sit ranges from assigned seats (based on various criteria) to open seating.

A. Minutes from last meeting

B. Standing Committee Reports
  1. Audit Committee
  2. Compensation Committee
  3. Governance Committee

C. Special Committee Reports

D. CEO's Report
  1. Management Committee Report
  2. Financial Report
  3. Items of Interest Since Last Meeting

E. Report from One of the Businesses

F. Other Matters

G. Date and Agenda For Next Meeting

Table 10-2. Sample board of directors agenda

Board Book

In addition to providing directors with a copy of the board meeting agenda in advance of the meeting, it is appropriate they receive copies of material to be discussed. This material should be in their hands at least a week before the meeting, providing them an opportunity to read it and note their questions. Ideally, the questions should be called in and answered prior to the meeting. This provides the maximum amount of time at the meeting for discussion. Fact gathering should be prior to, not at, the meeting.

The book will contain minutes of the previous board meeting as well as the minutes of the board and management committees that have met since the last meeting. The book might also include reports from the various operating and staff divisions describing their activities since the last meeting. If there are any resolutions to be approved by the board, they would be included along with reasons for such action.

Obviously a significant portion of the book will be focused on the financial performance of the company and its various operating units. This will include an income statement and perhaps a cash flow statement and balance sheet. In addition to product category financials, this should include narrative descriptions of the "why" as well as financial information about the industry and key competitors, including acquisitions, divestitures, and mergers.

The narrative should also include comments on the present and possible future of economic conditions affecting the company by analysts and other experts. This information is critical in putting in perspective the company's performance, enabling the director to better question (if appropriate) current and future performance.

Size of the Board

The number of directors is typically about 12, fewer for small companies and a little more for larger organizations. One way to determine how many directors are appropriate is to determine the number of board committees and multiply it by three. (This is based on the belief that three directors is a representative and workable number.) This permits committees to meet concurrently, perhaps before the board meeting, without anyone having to choose which meeting to attend. Thus, if the board had three committees (e.g., audit, compensation, and governance), it would need nine directors.

Most of these directors would be *outside directors* (i.e., they do not work for the company), distinguishing them from *inside directors* (also called management directors since they work for the company). Typically, at least the CEO sits on the board as an insider. Others may include the COO (chief operating officer) and perhaps the CFO (chief financial officer).

Outside directors are either dependent or independent. An *independent director* is one without a professional, financial, or family relationship to the company or CEO or other key officers other than being a member of the board of directors. Some go beyond this and require the individual not have been an executive officer or significant customer or vendor to the company for a period of several years. Additionally, the director's other activities and relationships should not affect his or her independent thinking and action. Review the definitions not only of the SEC but also of institutional shareholder groups and the appropriate stock exchange to determine whether or not the company is in compliance. An outside director who does not meet the independent qualifications is often called an *affiliated director*.

Good governance would suggest that independent directors should comprise at least a majority of the board, in addition to being the only ones to serve as committee members. Some institutional shareholders will seek a substantial majority, which could be at least two thirds of the total number of directors.

The size of the board or number of members should be in balance. It must be large enough to meet the requirements of diversity and small enough to promote good discussion. At the minimum, there need to be enough directors to staff the committees.

Composition of the Board

Having decided how many outside directors to have, what should be their qualifications? The most common is an active or retired CEO from another company. Academicians, attorneys, bankers, and retired government officials account for most of the rest. The board should reflect diversity of backgrounds, experiences, gender, and ethnicity. However, expertise important to the company must be represented on the board.

Some CEOs may like directors who sit on a number of boards or who have a lot of demands on their time so they won't be as active on this board. Others look for celebrity or "trophy directors" (those with recognized star-name status) to add prestige to the board. Good CEOs move beyond both of these approaches.

Some companies require the CEO to leave the board at retirement. Others permit the CEO to stand for election, believing his or her experience could be valuable. Those who prefer the retired CEO to leave the board reason that the new CEO will be in an awkward position, especially if it is necessary to change some of the predecessor policies.

Director Time

For many companies, board meetings last half a day with committee meetings typically held just before the board meeting. This enables committees to report to the board in a timely fashion. However, when adding up preparation time, travel time, and committee meetings, it is not uncommon to find directors spending over 150 hours a year for board-related work. A large portion of board time deals with company strategies and financial management. (Replacing a CEO or setting pay based on evaluation of performance may not take as much time as the other items, but it is certainly as important.)

Limits on Outside Director Activities

Given the amount of time that may be required to effectively discharge corporate governance responsibilities, directors may voluntarily limit (or be requested to limit) the number of other boards they serve on. The CEO may be limited to one or two additional boards. Other members of management may be limited to one. Directors on more than a handful of boards not only have a difficult time meeting obligations, they may also find institutional shareholder groups pressuring them to limit such activities.

Shareholders scrutinize not only the number of boards a director serves on but also *which* boards. Of special interest is when CEOs serve on each others' boards, or worse, when they serve on each others' compensation committee.

Directors who serve as a consultant or service provider to the company will not only find they are limited as to committee assignments but they are also likely to draw institutional shareholder attention.

Election Term

Annual elections of the entire board of directors used to be the general rule. Each director would serve one year and be up for re-election the next. However, when corporate raiders rose to prominence in the 1980s, a number of companies adopted *staggered* or *classified boards*.

These are boards with staggered terms; typically, only one-third of the directors are up for election each year. Companies defend the practice as reinforcing continuity; critics say it makes it more difficult to hold the board accountable, and it is an entrenchment vehicle. Companies argue that classified boards put them in a better negotiating position during a takeover because the takeover company cannot immediately replace the entire board.

Even when a shareholder resolution against a classified or staggered board receives a majority of the stock voted, some companies take the position that it is a non-binding resolution. Unless a supermajority (75 percent) is acquired, it is insufficient to amend the company's article of incorporation. In order to thwart this approach, some shareholders are introducing *binding resolutions*, which bind the corporation to act on the voting results.

Cumulative voting is one way to offset the classified board. The number of votes a shareholder has is determined by multiplying the number of shares owned by the number of directors being elected. Under cumulative voting, it is easier to seat a director if the number of slots up for election is large rather than small. For example, a shareholder with 10,000 shares would have 50,000 votes under cumulative voting if five directors were up for election versus 20,000 votes if only two were up for election. All 50,000 votes could be cast for one person.

Length of Board Service

A significant majority of companies put an *age limit* on board eligibility, typically age 70. At that age, the individual must leave the board. A small minority of companies imposes *term limits*. A term limit is usually set somewhere around 15 years (e.g., no more than five terms of three years each). Proponents of both approaches argue that long tenure results in director complacency.

While these practices remove directors who have "burned out," they also remove productive directors. Term limits and mandatory retirement age policies exist because few boards appraise directors individually.

An alternative approach would be to require each director to submit a letter of resignation to the chairman after every five-year period of board service (or after every term for those with classified boards) and annually after age 70. These letters would be submitted to the full board for a secret ballot to decide whether or not to accept the resignation.

Resignations

Directors are expected to offer their resignation if their status has changed since the time of election. For example, a retiring CEO might also be expected to resign from the board. Another change that might trigger a resignation is a personal relocation a significant distance from board meeting sites, requiring considerable time and expense to attend meetings.

Director Performance Appraisal

While most boards have a formal process for appraising the performance of the CEO, few have a similar process to evaluate individual directors. For that reason, more and more companies are rethinking the age and term limit issues.

Of those who do individual director appraisals, many use the less sensitive self-assessment rather than the more obtrusive peer review. Self-assessments are intended to improve performance without threatening the body of directors. But are self-assessments valid? Do poorer performing directors rate themselves lower than outstanding directors? Is perceived self-importance on one hand, or modesty on the other, dramatically affecting the results?

Critics of individual review point out that the board should be evaluated as a whole (for this is how its impact is felt) rather than its parts. However, lacking an individual review process, power shifts to the CEO to decide whom he or she wants on the board. Some suggest the CEO should have a heavy vote, and a supermajority vote by the full board be required to remove a director from standing for election. Staggered boards also make it more difficult to remove a newly elected non-performing director.

The reason typically given for not doing individual reviews is that it is counterproductive to bonding and taking unpopular stands to ensure all major issues are discussed. However, a number of boards evaluate their own overall performance, providing opportunities for the group to improve.

With or without a formal appraisal, each director is expected to attend each board and committee meeting fully prepared on all issues. Each director should be knowledgeable of issues facing the company, constructively confronting proposed actions, and be available outside of these meetings to advise management.

Effective boards receive adequate information in time for review prior to the meeting and thoroughly discuss issues during the meeting before taking action. Boards that do not perform well typically suffer from one or more of the following problems: The CEO is domineering; some directors are either not qualified or not performing to potential; some directors are disruptive at meetings; needed information is either not available or not timely; and information is voluminous and requires extensive time to evaluate. The board may also suffer from too many directors, too many inside directors, pervasive distrust, and a lack of open and honest communication.

CEO Performance

Evaluating CEO performance is a two-step process. First, identify performance expectations; then tie them to annual and long-term incentive plans. (Expectations such as succession plans, access to management, and positive board relationships might also be added.)

The expected performance of the CEO will begin with, and be defined by, the business plan. The CEO develops this plan—the result of the strategic thinking process outlined in Chapter 1. What is the company's vision? What is its mission? What are the objectives and goals that will enable fulfillment of the vision? What are the threats and opportunities facing the organization? What are the major strategies the company needs to undertake to address the resulting issues?

Directors will evaluate the plan, helping the CEO consider strategies from different perspectives. Once the board approves a plan, it will expect periodic progress reports from the CEO.

The second step is to evaluate performance in terms of the expectations laid out in the business plan. Pay actions will be based on these assessments. CEOs must know which objectives will be evaluated, and the board must ensure consistency with approved plans. The board should also articulate how it expects these objectives to be accomplished. Accomplishments should embody honest and ethical behavior. Furthermore, the CEO must convince those in the company (and on the board) of his or her full commitment to achieving the vision. More will be said on this subject later in the chapter when the role of the compensation committee is reviewed.

If performance does not meet board expectations, especially over several consecutive years, the CEO may be fired. Boards are more likely now to take such action than in the past. The main reason is that institutional shareholders have become big players, with the power to sell large blocks of shares and thereby depress stock prices. Boards tend to pay attention to these shareholder groups. Some groups even seek representation on the board to ensure their voice is heard. Some have suggested that more CEOs get fired for "how" they did their job than for the financial numbers they produced. Directors who were brought in by the CEO are not as likely to pull the trigger as someone who was on the board before the CEO arrived. Objectivity is somewhat easier when there is no sense of obligation.

If a board faces the challenge of firing the CEO, it must next find a replacement. It may be a good idea to have one or two directors who are capable of stepping in, at least on a temporary basis, if not as a long-term successor.

Before starting the recruiting process, the board must be clear on exactly what it wants the new CEO to do. This sets the basis for determining if there is an internal candidate. If not several executive search firms have an excellent track record and will be of enormous help to the board. Qualified candidates should be interviewed (either by the governance committee, or a special committee of the board). Differences and issues must be clearly identified and resolved before proceeding to due diligence on the person.

The candidate will likely engage an attorney to help work out the terms of the offer. How much will the new company award for unvested money left behind? How much for the expected growth on those amounts until retirement? And how much for packages that would have been received had the individual remained with current employer? Given the risk of moving, it is likely the candidate will want an employment contract in addition to a change-in-control agreement. The individual will recognize that he or she loses a significant amount of bargaining power after accepting the offer. It is therefore important that the board not only have an excellent compensation planner to review the proposal but also to help negotiate. An attorney representing the board would also be appropriate.

It is critical that the new CEO spend time individually with each board member to understand his or her perspective, as well as particular strengths and interests. As stated earlier, the new CEO may not immediately get the chairman title. In this case, the interim chair will be mentor, helping the CEO succeed not only in the job but also with the board, and positioning the person to later move into the chair position.

Delegation of Authority

The board determines how it will delegate authority to board committees. This is done by approving a resolution specifically naming the committee and stating its responsibility. In other words, on what actions does the committee have final say and what needs to be proposed to the board for action? An abbreviated example is shown in Table 10-3.

It is hereby resolved that in accord with Section 15 of the Company Bylaws that an Executive Compensation Committee of the Board of Directors is established and further

RESOLVED, that Committee shall not consist of less than three members meeting appropriate statutory and regulatory requirements as independent and disinterested persons; and further

RESOLVED, that said committee shall review and approve objectives of the executive compensation program; and further

RESOLVED, that performance goals for the CEO approved by the Board be the basis for a performance evaluation; and appropriate pay action; and further

RESOLVED, that said Committee shall determine the particulars of the executive compensation program and the eligibility for participation, and further

RESOLVED, that said Committee shall review and approve contractual agreements for those in the executive compensation program; and further

RESOLVED, that said Committee will review competitive pay practice and peer company performance in approving components of the compensation program as well as specific pay actions for certain executives; and further

RESOLVED, that said Committee may engage services of others to assist them in the performance of their duties; and further

RESOLVED, that said Committee is to prepare a report to shareholders in accord with the Securities and Exchange Commission rules and respond to shareholder questions; and further

RESOLVED, that the Committee is to file a copy of its meeting minutes with the Board and respond to questions and requests from the Board.

Table 10-3. Board resolution of executive compensation committee responsibilities

The Compensation Committee

The establishment of a committee of the board of directors responsible for the pay of corporate officers and employee directors has become commonplace. In addition to approving the design and mix of compensation programs, it is also responsible for approving payments. Thus, it is accountable not simply for the form in which the corporate officers are paid but also the level of payment. To ensure comparable treatment, the committee would also review for information purposes pay increases of other non-officer executives within the company who are at a comparable pay level.

Probably the greatest obstacle facing the committee is simply "getting up to speed" with the forms of compensation and their relationship to specific accounting, tax, and company situations. Unfortunately, too few committee members are well schooled in executive pay programs before joining the committee; some can't tell the difference between a stock option and a stock award. The task is difficult enough given the myriad pay delivery forms, and it is unduly complicated by media messages promising 101 ways to reward executives effectively. Too often, these are shallow gimmicks rather than creative new techniques, and the committee members must see through these messages.

Committee Role

Because of their fiduciary role to the shareholder, it is logical to expect members of the compensation committee to be performance-oriented in direction but cautious in specific plan design. A plan that is similar to those of other companies (especially in the same industry) is more likely to be acceptable than an innovative creation. However, the plan may not be right for this company.

In large part, this conservative approach is attributable to a lack of knowledge by which to adequately judge the efficacy of a new approach. It is much easier to rely on the judgments of other boards: "If they have it and apparently it is not causing problems, then it is probably right for us, too." This is not to imply that compensation committees are unique in this respect. It is not uncommon for some executives to be more risk-taking in their rhetoric than in their actions. The committee needs to be sure that the proposed plan is appropriate

In addition to having to absorb a significant amount of compensation design and basic accounting and tax considerations, the compensation committee must also be able to see those areas likely to be applicable as well as those which are inappropriate. Having discarded the latter, the committee must focus on determining the appropriate program(s) for this company's elected officers. It must be conscious of relative pay levels within the total compensation mix, as well as aware that to the extent salaries are high, any incentive payment may be superfluous.

Thus, it is critical for the compensation committee to have sufficient knowledge of company objectives and compensation design to be able to judge the efficacy of a specific proposal. It is just as important to ask whether this is the optimum solution, as to ask whether the proposed course of action itself needs some modification. In other words, before being certain that the specific plan has no inconsistencies or inaccuracies, be certain that a more desirable plan has not been overlooked or incorrectly discarded! This can only be accomplished by reviewing all the forms of executive pay design and deciding why each is appropriate or inappropriate for this company. It is insufficient to test the efficacy of a proposal simply on the basis of whether or not it appears to reflect good staff work. In a number of situations, these committees are initiating their own studies and proposals instead of passively awaiting a proposal from management. Many suffer from a plethora of reports and recommendations to digest, and from little staff support to ensure efficacious analysis.

On the one hand, the pay package must be attractive and competitive; on the other hand, the committee must ensure that the compensation package is not considered by shareholders to be a waste of corporate assets. If the latter is the case, a lawsuit may very well follow. Just because several companies in desperate need of a particular CEO have offered a multi-million-dollar bonus is no rationale for increasing the pay of several vulnerable people by several hundred thousand dollars.

In order to meet its social responsibilities and shareholder obligations, the committee should ensure that its pay delivery system for top managers is consistent with expected short- and long-term results. This is the optimum. The minimum is to ascertain that pay is not inconsistent with company goals. Between these two is the "no-man's-land" into which the majority of pay systems fall. Many a compensation committee has heard the plea to change the plan because, "it isn't paying anything." This may be the best indication that it is a good plan. It may not be paying because performance is not adequate. However, few resist the temptation to change the goals or the plan in order to make an adequate payout. In these situations, performance becomes a secondary consideration.

With the selected plan or combination of plans in hand, and the defined level of pay for officers under specific conditions of company performance decided, it is necessary for the plans to be formally drafted by counsel and submitted to the full board for approval. In almost every case, the plan would also be submitted to shareholders after board approval, although awards instead could be made contingent on shareholder acceptance. A company may choose one form over another simply because of the low profile it may get in the proxy statement. For many years, stock options were much less visible than stock awards in isolating individual gains. Now, present-value calculations and exercise gains receive significant attention.

The compensation committee would also determine how much should be paid from the sum of previous carry-forwards and current year performance. It would also typically authorize the amount to be carried forward to the next year. This could simply be the total available less this year's awards; however, apart from a reserve to cover warranted bonuses in consecutive lean years, it would be reduced.

Typically, the committee makes performance decisions on the CEO and other executives named in the proxy (and perhaps other selected executives. This would occur after reviewing the actions for individuals in the next lower organizational level, perhaps decided by a separate committee, for informational purposes. When determining the form in which to distribute the award, the executive's stated preference should be considered. However, it is also important to examine company needs. If the company is in a cash bind, it should lean toward distribution in the form of company stock; if there were a concern about equity dilution, then distribution would be in cash. If both are true, a combination award (perhaps with deferred payment) will be made to lessen the impact on dilution and cash flow.

After making the awards, the committee is responsible for monitoring plan performance and acting upon salary recommendations for officers. Some committees want not only to be responsible for the pay of corporate officers but also to be fully appraised of succession plans. Thus, the committee has a basis for judging the depth of management talent or lack thereof. It is also helpful in understanding differences in recommended pay increases (one person may be on the inside track and the other an outside shot, at best). Some request that management succession plans be in writing and reviewed at least annually.

Administration of the actual pay program will focus on all five components of the officers' pay package, including their relative mix. It is therefore assumed the committee will be responsible not only for approving any recommendations on salary increases but also the units of participation under both the short- and long-term incentive plans. This committee would also determine modifications to basic employee benefit plans (such as allowing an unfunded plan to restore benefits curtailed by the maximums of the Employee Retirement Income Security Act) and eligibility for specific perquisites

Action Responsibilities

Logically, the various actions should be identified, the basis on which a decision is to be made should be stated, and the responsibility for proposing and approving various actions should be indicated. Table 10-4 shows how the five compensation elements might be handled by a company with two compensation committees: an executive compensation committee for elected corporate officers consisting solely of non-employee directors and an employee compensation committee consisting of the CEO, COO, and vice president of human resources for all others.

For Salary

Action	Basis	Proposed by	Approved by
Obtain competitive data	Comparable size/ industry	Director, Compensation and Benefits Division VP HR	Executive Compensation Committee (corporate officers) Director, Compensation and Benefits (all others)
Approve job gradings	Competitive data Internal equity	CEO (corporate officers) Director, Compensation and Benefits (others above $100,000) Division HR VP (those below $100,000)	Executive Compensation Committee Employee Compensation Committee Director, Compensation and Benefits
Approve salary structure and guidelines	Competitive data	CEO Director, Compensation and Benefits	Executive Compensation Committee (corporate officers) Employee Compensation Committee (all others)
Allocate divisional salary budgets	Compa-ratio Unit performance	Director, Compensation and Benefits	Employee Compensation Committee
Approve salary changes	Unit and individual performance	Immediate Supervisor ↓ Division President Employee Compensation Committee	Executive Compensation Committee (corporate officers) Employee Compensation Committee (except corporate officers)

For Employee Benefits

Action	Basis	Proposed by	Approved by
Obtain competitive data	Comparable size/ industry	Director, Compensation and Benefits	Employee Compensation Committee
Amend pension plan	Competitive data Employee attitude surveys	VP HR/Finance ↓ Employee Compensation Committee	Board of Directors

Table 10-4. Action responsibilities (continued on next page)

For Perquisites

Action	Basis	Proposed by	Approved by
Establish/amend other plans	Competitive data Employee attitude surveys	Director, Compensation and Benefits	Executive Compensation Committee (over $25,000 per year) VP HR
Obtain competitive data	Comparable size/ industry	Director, Compensation and Benefits	Executive Compensation Committee (corporate officers) Employee compensation committee (all others)
Establish/amend plan	Competitive data Internal equity	CEO ↓ Employee Compensation Committee Director, compensation and Benefits	CEO Employee Compensation Committee Director, compensation and Benefits
Give to individual	Job grade Salary level Organizational level	CEO Director, Compensation and Benefits	Executive Compensation Committee (for CEO) Executive Compensation Committee (corporate officers) Employee Compensation Committee (all others)

For Short-Term Incentives

Action	Basis	Proposed by	Approved by
Obtain competitive data	Comparable size/ industry	Director, Compensation and Benefits	Employee Compensation Committee
Amend plan	Competitive data Company performance	VP, HR/Finance ↓ Employee Compensation Committee ↓ Executive Compensation Committee ↓ Board of Directors	Shareholders
Establish targets	Competitive data Company short- range forecasts	CEO ↓ Executive Compensation Committee	Board of Directors

Table 10-4. Action responsibilities (continued)

For Short-Term Incentives (continued)

Action	Basis	Proposed by	Approved by
Allocate divisional funds	Unit and corporate performance	CEO	Executive Compensation Committee
Grant individual awards	Individual performance	CEO ↓ Division President ↓ Director, Compensation and Benefits Immediate Supervisor	Executive Compensation Committee (for CEO) Executive Compensation Committee (other corporate officers) Employee Compensation Committee (others above $100,000) Division President (others)

For Long-Term Incentives

Action	Basis	Proposed by	Approved by
Obtain competitive data	Comparable size/ industry	Director, Compensation and Benefits	Employee compensation committee
Amend plan	Competitive data Company performance	VP HR/Finance ↓ Employee Compensation Committee ↓ Executive Compensation Committee Board of Directors	Shareholders
Establish targets	Competitive data Company long-range forecasts	CEO ↓ Executive Compensation Committee	Board of Directors
Determine eligibility	Job grade Salary level Organizational level	Director, Compensation and Benefits	Executive Compensation Committee (corporate officers) Employee Compensation Committee (non-officers)
Grant individual awards	Corporate performance Unit performance and potential	CEO Division President ↓ Director, Compensation and Benefits	Executive Compensation Committee (corporate officers) Employee Compensation Committee

Table 10-4. Continued

Committee Responsibilities

It would be appropriate for the compensation committee to commit to writing what it believes to be its responsibilities and then have these approved by the board of directors. A representative list might include:

1. Clarify in writing the responsibilities delegated by the board and gaining board approval of the write-up.
2. Review and approve executive compensation objectives and pay philosophy.
3. Review specific goals for the CEO and subsequent performance in relation to goals.
4. Review and determine eligibility for participation in the executive compensation program and specific awards for participants.
5. Review and approve contractual agreements for those in the executive compensation program.
6. Review competitive pay practices and performance of peer companies in approving the design and specific pay levels for executives.
7. Determine what compensation actions will be reviewed for information only, which reviews will result in actions (e.g., all corporate officers except those approved by the board of directors), and which will be proposed for action by the board of directors.
8. Engage experts in the executive compensation field as necessary.
9. Prepare the compensation committee report for the proxy statement.
10. Respond to requests by the CEO and the board.

In discharging its responsibilities, the compensation committee should always require that material be received in sufficient time for committee members to review prior to the meeting. This should include the ability to call in their questions. Time at the meeting is best used for discussion rather than information gathering. The committee should refuse to consider proposals received without adequate lead-time (except in rare emergency situations). The committee should indicate format requirements to management to minimize confusion and delays. The committee should also hold management responsible not only for raising issues but also for offering possible solutions (with costs and rationale). However, the committee should not be expected to research and resolve all issues raised by management.

At the meeting, directors should discuss issues fully and, where appropriate, introduce and consider advice from specialists in reaching a decision. Decisions should be the result of the careful examination of sufficient information, and not the result of limited time.

Pay Philosophy

Logically, the compensation committee should have a stated pay philosophy. To create one, look at the philosophy of the rest of the organization. It would be odd to pay the non-officer group at the median of defined industry competition but pay officers at the 75th percentile. This is not to say the pay philosophy has to be the same, but certainly there should be a quantifiable reason for degree of difference. On possible rationalization for the situation described above could be if the non-officer group, while adequate, was not considered likely to provide officer replacements. These therefore would have to come from outside the company at significant increases in pay above the community median.

Pay vs. Performance

Pay for executives in general and the CEO in particular are usually viewed in absolute dollars and not in relation to performance. However, a CEO paid a fraction of the pay of a counterpart may be overpaid in relation to performance. Conversely, a CEO paid several times that of a counterpart may be underpaid in relation to performance. Take the example of two CEOs each working for a comparably sized company in the same industry. One is paid $10 million and the other $1 million. Before concluding the first is overpaid and the latter perhaps underpaid, add that the first company has had compound EPS increases of 30 percent for the last three years and tripled total shareholder return whereas the second CEO's company has had negative growth in EPS and halved total shareholder return in the last three years. Still believe the first is overpaid and the second underpaid?

The relationship of pay to company performance is shown in Table 10-5.

		Company Performance		
		Poor	**Average**	**Good**
Pay	**High**	High Risk of Shareholder Wrath	Review Calibration	Correct
	Average	Review Calibration	Correct	Review Calibration
	Low	Correct	Review Calibration	High Risk of Losing Executive

Table 10-5. Company performance vs. executive pay relationship

In this nine-cell matrix, there are three situations where pay and company performance are correctly aligned; four situations where the calibration needs to be reviewed; and two that are definitely out of balance. High pay combined with low company performance will draw criticism from shareholders (and perhaps employees); low pay in relation to good performance suggests the company is at risk of losing the executive unless there are mitigating circumstances (e.g., the executive is a major shareholder and does not need additional pay).

Furthermore, it is important to view executive pay (especially for the CEO) in relation to others in own peer group. Performance should not simply be company financials but also *total shareholder return* (TSR), which is stock price plus reinvested dividends. This becomes especially critical when comparing executive pay with that for non-U.S. companies. Critics are quick to point out that after adjusting for size of company and financial performance, U.S. executives are paid much more than their non-U.S. counterparts. They fail to mention that U.S. shareholders of these same companies have done significantly better than their overseas counterparts. In many of these situations, overseas executives are not given stock options, the very form of executive pay that has accounted for most of the rise in U.S. executive pay. Some argue that paying a CEO 1 percent to 2 percent of what he or she created in increased total shareholder value is a good bargain for the shareholders.

Competitive Data

It would be appropriate for the compensation committee to request an analysis of competitive position of pay for at least the CEO and four other executives named in the proxy. Shown in Table 10-6 is how this summary of might look for the chairman/CEO (from Chapter 4).

	Brucell	**Survey**	**$**	**%**
Salary	$1,016.7	$872.4	$144.3	16.5%
Short-Term Incentives	1,925.0	932.7	992.3	106.4
Long-Term Incentives	1,790.4	2,015.1	(224.7)	(12.6)
Benefits	862.1	986.2	(124.1)	(12.6)
Perquisites	180.5	238.2	(58.1)	(32.1)
Total	**$5,774.7**	**$5,044.6**	**$729.8**	**14.5%**

Table 10-6. Competitive pay position of Brucell CEO

Shown in Table 10-7 is a company-by-company breakdown of the same data for salary and incentives, ranked by salary-plus-annual incentives.

Rank	Company	Salary	Bonus	Salary & Bonus	% Chg From Last Year	Present Value of LTRC	Total	% Chg From Last Year
1	D	$945.5	$1,413.0	$2,358.5	8.9	$1,892.1	$4,250.6	11.6
2	H	1,102.1	1,162.0	2,264.1	12.7	703.1	2,977.2	9.1
3	B	866.3	820.0	1,686.3	19.9	1,067.1	2,753.4	12.5
5	I	984.0	865.0	1,849.0	9.4	2,316.2	4,165.2	19.2
6	K	541.7	1,000.0	1,541.7	14.6	4,613.6	6,155.3	27.8
7	E	950.0	959.6	1,909.6	11.2	2,517.7	4,427.3	14.3
8	A	1,112.5	1,112.5	2,225.0	2.5	1,329.0	3,554.0	11.1
9	J	920.0	586.7	1,506.7	12.6	783.0	2,289.2	4.6
10	G	800.0	731.3	1,531.3	4.7	2,874.9	4,406.2	13.4
11	C	794.3	800.0	1,594.3	6.5	2,054.2	3,648.5	7.2
12	F	580.1	800.0	1,380.1	15.7	1,382.9	2,763.0	6.9
	Averages	**$872.4**	**$932.7**	**$1,805.1**	**11.9**	**$2,015.1**	**$3,472.0**	**17.8%**
4	**Brucell**	**$1,016.7**	**$1,925.0**	**$2,941.7**	**17.7**	**$1,790.4**	**$4,732.1**	**18.2%**

Table 10-7. Company-by-company pay data

While each of these two analyses suggests Brucell's CEO is overpaid, such a conclusion should be withheld until Brucell's financial and shareholder return performance has been compared with the survey group.

Review of Job Grades

The compensation committee should assign job grades for the CEO and other corporate officers. This process was described in Chapter 5 (Salary). In assigning grades, proposals with supporting documentation are brought forth by management for committee action. Decisions would be based on a combination of external parity and internal equity.

As part of this decision process, the committee must determine not simply the total annual compensation structure, but what portion will be salary and what portion short-term incentive. What relationship will each of the three have to the marketplace? At what percentile ranking?

Setting the Pay Relationship

In designing annual and long-term incentive plans, one needs to determine not only the payout at target but also the prescribed minimum and maximum.

In structuring the annual and long-term plans, it is necessary to determine the relationship of each to salary and the percentage all three constitute of total compensation. Shown in Table 10-8 is an example where the three are expected to contribute equally at target, but at maximum, annual and long-term are two and four times salary, respectively, placing significantly more emphasis on long-term. Where they both double salary, the percentages would be salary (20 percent), annual incentive (40 percent), and long-term incentive (40 percent). Note what happens below threshold. This is the same as Table 9-18 in Chapter 9.

	Salary	Annual	Long-Term	A) Total
At Maximum	$1,000,000 14%	$2,000,000 29%	$4,000,000 57%	$7,000,000
At 3rd Quartile	$1,000,000 22%	$1,500,000 33%	$2,000,000 44%	$4,500,000
At Target (2nd Quartile)	$1,000,000 33%	$1,000,000 33%	$1,000,000 33%	$3,000,000
1st Quartile	$1,000,000 50%	$500,000 25%	$500,000 25%	$2,000,000
Below Threshold	$1,000,000 100%	0	0	$1,000,000

Table 10-8. Pay relationship

Approving Plans

The advantages and disadvantages of each specific plan must be reviewed in terms of anticipated performance and level of payment over the prescribed time period. Only by simulating results and examining payment will it be possible for the compensation committee to judge the efficacy of the proposals. It would also be logical to have the consultant attend every annual shareholder meeting, not just when a plan change is proposed—both to provide expert answers to shareholder questions and to get first-hand impressions of shareholder pay concerns.

Approving Payouts

Management would submit for approval a schedule of payouts, including calculations of performance factors in accordance with the plan. Management would attest to the accuracy, enabling the committee to accept the validity of the information. The committee would then discuss and approve the payouts. Payment would be reported to the board. Depending on board policy, the report may simply be accepted or the matter reviewed and discussed. In any event, action must be in accordance with Section 162(m) of the Internal Revenue Code (IRC) if the company wishes to get a tax deduction for payments in excess of $1 million for the proxy-named executives. This means the board cannot overturn the committee's actions, although it should be informed of the committee's decisions.

Unreasonable Compensation

A major concern of the compensation committee should be whether or not the pay of executives will be viewed as reasonable. Have the executives really earned their pay? To date, the courts have been reluctant to substitute their judgment for that of the board of directors or its appropriate committee. Attention has primarily focused on whether or not there has been an abuse of fiduciary trust, lack of good faith, or outright fraud.

However, when the courts have been required to determine whether or not compensation is reasonable, they have examined the specific facts about the company and the executive. Listed in Table 10-9 are situations that tend to either support compensation as being reasonable or suggest that it is not.

It is difficult to generalize, since each case will be judged on its special merits. However, the likelihood of a favorable ruling is enhanced if more facts fall to the right side than the left in the following listing. Nonetheless, the matter should be reviewed with counsel.

In addition to a shareholder suit, the committee has to be aware of potential tax problems. If the IRS rules a portion of the compensation to be unreasonable, that portion cannot be claimed as a business expense. This risk has prompted some companies to establish a repayment provision in the executive's contract requiring that the individual repay the company for that portion of compensation ruled to be unreasonable. However, such an agreement may give the IRS additional reason to examine the level of compensation on the presumption that it wouldn't exist unless there was possible cause for a case of unreasonable compensation.

If the company is challenged to demonstrate that a reasonable relationship exists between the value of pay versus the value of the service provided by the executive, it may be helpful to point to total compensation, not simply salary and bonus. If employee benefits and perquisites were significantly less liberal than for comparable companies, it would be logical to include these costs in a total compensation review. Otherwise, a company with competitive total compensation but almost all its pay in salaries and bonuses may find it difficult to demonstrate a competitive position.

Fortunately, the IRS appears to include in its deliberations (when determining reasonableness) what other employers in like businesses of comparable magnitude are paying their executives. Thus, all could be overpaying (underpaying would be unlikely), and there may be no problem. Apparently, this is the same basis the courts are using to determine reasonableness in a tax case; as indicated, they have been chary of looking behind the decision of level of pay in a corporate law case.

	May be unreasonable	**May be reasonable**
Company	Privately held Family-controlled Small company No or low dividends	Publicly held Diffuse ownership Large company Attractive dividends
Executive	Little experience Light work schedule Either significant increase in pay or no change for years Pay significantly higher than for other companies or data not available Pay set near end of year (when profits can be more exactly measured) Pay of shareholder-owners higher than comparable non-shareholder employees Has significant holdings of company stock	Extensive experience Works long hours Increase in pay consistent with growth of company, increase in responsibility, or back pay for lean years Pay is basically consistent with comparably sized companies in comparable industries Basis for pay clearly set at beginning of year Pay of shareholder-owners comparable to or lower than others in firm with similar responsibilities Non-stockholder or one with insignificant percentage of ownership

Table 10-9. Unreasonable compensation checklist

Shareholder Questions

Although questions from shareholders could come at any time during the year (especially after something has been reported in the press), they are most likely at the company shareholder meeting.

No longer are compensation levels or programs subject solely to scorn by a professional shareholder at the annual meeting. The audience may include retired employees, union representatives, legislative aides, institutional investors, and government officials. In most instances, management still has sufficient control of proxies to ensure the outcome on key issues (e.g., new compensation plans); however, it must be prepared to hear dissenting views from other shareholders. The earlier reticence of the shareholder to express concern has faded. Many companies attempt to identify likely questions prior to the meeting and then research the appropriate response. Regardless of how much time is spent on this process, invariably there will be unexpected questions. Nonetheless, the process is still worthwhile as it stimulates thinking.

A starting point is the proxy statement.

- Any significant changes in the compensation and incentive tables from the previous year?
- Anything in the compensation committee report likely to raise questions? Any descriptive changes regarding pay elsewhere in the proxy?

Examples that could be drawn from this review might include:

- Is the CEO on the compensation committee of any member of the company's compensation committee?
- What were the performance objectives for the CEO along with their weighting and rating?
- What was the increase in the CEO's total pay for the last year versus the increase in shareholder value?
- What perquisites did the top five receive and what was the cost for each?
- Are the companies used for pay comparisons the same as in the proxy stock chart? If not, why not?

Issue Management

Executive pay is from time to time a hot topic, either in a general sense or for a particular company, when CEO pay and company performance seem to have little relationship. Rather than wait for a challenge from one or more stakeholders, or the business press, it would make sense for the committee to identify the issue. They could then frame it, prepare appropriate responses, and identify the company spokespersons and their respective audiences. The outline might look something like that shown in Table 10-10.

---

1. What is the issue?
2. What is the background?
   - Company and industry performance
   - Economic indicators
   - Pay actions
3. What has and is likely to happen?
   - FASB/IRS/SEC
   - Possible legislation
   - Industry association
4. What is our response?
   - Initiate debate or wait to respond?
   - Script or bullet point?
   - Internal or external use?
5. Who are our spokespersons?
   - CEO?
   - Executive Compensation Committee Chair?
   - Chief Legal Officer?
   - Chief Financial Officer?
   - Chief Human Resource Officer?
   - Chief Public Relations Officer?

Table 10-10. Issue management outline (Continued on next page)

6. Who is our audience?
   - Business press?
   - General interest press?
   - Shareholders?
   - Professional shareholder groups?
   - Third-party commentators?
   - Our executives?
   - Our other employees?

Table 10-10. Continued

Items 5 and 6 could be combined with one list on the X-axis and the other on the Y-axis. This would enable an identification of what spokespersons are responsible for what audience, thereby preparing a targeted strategy. Here are four possible issues:

1. The issue of "how much" pay should be positioned in terms of "for what performance." A better situation exists if one is able to relate executive pay to relative performance than if one must justify the absolute level of pay.
2. Is the relationship between short-term and long-term incentives appropriate for the company? Are the right measurements being used? What is the importance of internal financial performance versus external stock price changes?
3. How much subjectivity is applied in making performance awards and/or payouts? Who decides and on what basis? Where formulas are used, how often are they reviewed for appropriateness?
4. Is upside potential appropriately balanced by downside risk in the incentive plan? Are the thresholds, targets, and maximums appropriate?

Some of this material could also be covered in preparation for the annual shareholder meeting.

Composition of the Committee

Depending upon the makeup of the particular board, the compensation committee could consist of former government officials, bankers, lawyers, academicians, or executives of other firms. Some people are critical of companies whose board membership consists of retired members of management and those considered to be suppliers of contractual services (e.g., bankers, outside counsel, and management consultants). The retired executive may have fraternal ties to existing management, having hired and trained them. The presence of suppliers on the board may give a false signal to others that this company is "tied up" with a supplier. Such individuals cannot be considered true outside directors, i.e., individuals independent of management. Furthermore, Section 162(m) of the IRC imposes even stricter requirements. It stipulates the conditions under which pay in excess of $1 million for any of the proxy-named executives may be tax deductible to the company. In addition to excluding anyone receiving fees from the company for any professional services, and current employees of the company, it also excludes former officers of the company, as well as any former employee receiving compensation for prior services (except for statutory benefit plans).

Knowledge of executive compensation programs is obviously extremely helpful in serving on a compensation committee. When attempting to sort out the pros and cons of various plans, one must understand the terminology. For example, what are the advantages of a performance-unit plan coupled with non-qualified stock options over a non-market, book-value and market-value tandem stock option? This is one reason having a compensation committee consisting mostly of executives from other companies makes a lot of sense. They are more likely to be knowledgeable about a wider range of forms of compensation than those not exposed to executive pay plans. However, boards should be careful in appointing members to the committee to avoid *interlocking relationships*, namely, where CEOs sit on each other's compensation committees.

Another excellent candidate for the compensation committee is the professional director (i.e., someone whose only employment is serving on a number of boards), usually a retired executive. This may become a very attractive second career for those who wish to take early retirement within their own firms, especially if shrinking inside-board sizes preclude being elected while working.

However, from the viewpoint of knowledge, the best candidate is an executive compensation consultant or similar individual in the employ of another company. Either of these individuals would be a candidate where eligibility for the committee required simply that candidates be "disinterested parties" and not necessarily members of the board of directors. Where a company is using several consultants, it may find the industry expert more appealing, not only to bring another dimension but also to avoid potential conflict-of-interest charges.

Because experience is important, it may be unwise to rotate members of the committee too early. Perhaps rotation of one person every several years would allow the committee to retain the needed expertise.

Committee Chair

The responsibility of the chair is to prepare the agenda for each meeting (ensuring members have meeting materials in sufficient time to review prior to the meeting), preside at each meeting, and ensure committee actions are reported in meeting minutes and later implemented.

Before preparing a monthly meeting agenda, the chair should establish a key event timetable similar to the one in Table 10-11 for the year. In this illustration, salary actions are effected on a common date (April 1st) rather than distributed throughout the year; short-term and long-term incentive awards are also reviewed in March. However, benefit and perquisite actions are effected the first of the year. As the year progresses, this timetable is adjusted to reflect the additions of other committee or management requests.

The committee's task is not an easy one; it must balance financial expectations of management with degree of difficulty in goal attainment and cost to shareholders. In many instances, simply quantifying corporate strategy and goals in a manner that will allow structuring a short- or long-term incentive plan is a challenge in itself. Add to this the need to relate to pay levels of officers of other companies after adjusting for profit performance, and it is easy to see the responsibility is more easily defined than accomplished.

A logical requirement is an annual report reflecting pay levels for a specified list of companies. This could be prepared either by an internal staff or by an outside consultant. Using this data, the committee could ascertain what level of adjustment is appropriate for the affected group. This in turn might be reviewed with an outside consultant for reasonableness.

	Division Head	Director, Comp & Benefits	VP Hr	Employee Comp Cmte	Executive Comp Cmte	Board of Directors	Share-holders
January							
Allocate divisional salary budgets				✔			
Allocate short-term incentive funds to division					✔		
Allocate long-term incentive funds to division	✔			✔	✔		
Review individual performance							
February							
Establish short-term incentive targets					✔	✔	
Establish long-term incentive targets					✔	✔	
March							
Approve salary changes				✔	✔		
Approve short-term incentive awards	✔			✔	✔		
Approve long-term incentive awards				✔	✔		
Identify competitors				✔	✔		
April							
Amend short-term incentive plan							✔
Amend long-term incentive plan							✔
May							
Obtain competitive data		✔					
June							
Obtain competitive data		✔					
July							
Analyze competitive data		✔					

Table 10-11. Timetable for compensation actions (Continued on next page)

	Division Head	Director, Comp & Benefits	VP Hr	Employee Comp Cmte	Executive Comp Cmte	Board of Directors	Share-holders
August							
Approve job gradings		✔					
Analyze competitive benefit data		✔					
September							
Approve job gradings				✔	✔		
October							
Amend short-term incentive plan				✔			
Amend long-term incentive plan				✔			
November							
Amend pension plan				✔			
Amend other benefit plans			✔	✔			
Approve perquisite plans				✔	✔		
Determine perquisite eligibility				✔	✔		
Determine long-term incentive plan eligibility				✔			
December							
Amend pension plan						✔	
Amend short-term incentive plan						✔	
Amend long-term incentive plan						✔	
Approve perquisite plans						✔	
Approve salary structure and guidelines				✔			

Table 10-11. Continued

Committee Secretary

Rather than appoint one of the committee members as secretary, it might be appropriate to select the head of human resources (since it is expected that person will be in attendance at virtually every meeting anyway). An alternative would be to appoint someone from the general counsel's staff, such as the attorney responsible for SEC matters.

In addition to ensuring the meeting minutes are prepared and distributed in a timely manner, the secretary should see to other requests by the chair and committee members. This ranges from ensuring a meeting place with appropriate support materials, beverages, and food to compiling and distributing agenda materials in accordance with the chair's request. By ensuring these are distributed in advance, committee members have an opportunity to call in and ask questions prior to the meeting, thereby reserving meeting time for discussion rather than fact-finding.

Committee Meetings

While meetings could be scheduled for anytime during the year, it is common practice to schedule meetings to immediately precede board meetings. This not only minimizes scheduling problems, it also ensures timely reporting to the board of committee actions. For many, the meeting would be scheduled for the morning the board is to meet. However, committee members arriving the night before might use the opportunity to informally discuss the meeting agenda over dinner.

Meeting Agenda. The chair may wish to begin and end each meeting in executive session with only members of the committee present. This allows them to express any comments or concerns. When not in executive session, in addition to the committee secretary, it is common to extend an invitation to the board chairman and CEO.

Committee members should be able to rely on information presented. Namely, it should be complete and not misleading or biased. Therefore, it is important that the credentials of the presenter be reviewed and any relationships with management revealed. Sufficient time must be permitted to thoroughly review the material. It may be appropriate to schedule two meetings— one for discussion and the next for voting. An example agenda is shown in Table 10-12.

A. Minutes from last meeting

B. Standing Reports
    1. Organization Changes
    2. Stock Option Exercise/Stock Sales of Insiders

C. Special Reports

D. Response to Committee Requests

E. Management Requests

F. Date and Agenda For Next Meeting

Table 10-12. Sample compensation committee agenda

Meeting Minutes. The secretary of the committee will be asked to take minutes of the meeting. An example is shown in Table 10-13. The secretary would be expected to forward the minutes, a copy of the agenda for the following meeting, and any supporting documents to the committee in advance of the next meeting. Because of travel plans and other commitments by the committee members, it is helpful to send the materials at least 10 to 14 days before the next meeting, providing them sufficient time to work a review of the material into their own calendars.

Brucell's
Executive Compensation Committee Meeting
for
October 15, 2000 Meeting

1. The meeting at the Company's New York City headquarters was called to order by Committee Chair, Ms. Right, at 7:00 am.

2. In attendance were Committee members Ms. Right (Chair), Mr. Ready, and Mr. Able. There being no items for executive session of the Committee, it invited the following guests to join the meeting: Ms. Reals (Chair and CEO), Mr. Brett (Vice President of Human Resources), and Mr. Evans of the Evans compensation consulting firm. Mr. Brett served as secretary for the meeting.

3. The minutes of the September 17, 2000 meeting were approved by the Committee as amended.

4. The Chair asked for standing Committee reports. Ms. Reals reported there were no organization changes to report and Mr. Brett indicated there were no stock option exercise or sales by insiders since the last meeting.

5. Ms. Reals reviewed the proposed change in the annual incentive plan that had been sent to the Committee on October 1st. The change would permit recipients an opportunity to defer (not later than the day before the beginning of the bonus period) up to 50% of any award they may receive. Executives would be permitted to choose between units of company stock or 30 year Treasury bills. Mr. Evans supported the proposal as being competitive with peer company practice. After discussion the proposal was approved.

6. The Committee agreed its next meeting would be October 31, 2000 at 7:00 am at the Company's New York headquarters to discuss a management proposal for change in control contracts.

7. There being no further discussion the non-Committee attendees were excused and the Committee went into executive session.

8. The meeting was adjourned at 9:00 am.

Table 10-13. Executive compensation committee meeting minutes example

Report to the Board. The committee secretary may be asked to script a presentation by the committee chair to the board of directors reporting on the committee meeting. This request is more likely to come from a new chair and/or one not well versed in executive compensation. An example is shown in Table 10-14.

Committee Report to Shareholders. Each year, the compensation committee of a publicly traded company is required to publish a report in the shareholder proxy. Among the requirements is whether or not the compensation of the named executive officers is in compliance with Section 162(m) of the Internal Revenue Code. It should also indicate the pay philosophy in general and how the CEO pay was determined in particular. The SEC warns committees not to use boiler-plate language but rather to personalize and customize the report to the company in question.

The Committee met this morning and I'd like to report to you our actions.

1. As you know this is the time of year when we review salaries and annual incentive awards for the elected corporate officers, based on their performance in relation to their objectives (and the performance of the company).

2. Given the Section 162m cap of $1 million tax deduction for proxy named executives and the fact our CEO is currently receiving a $1 million salary the committee is proposing no change in the salary.

3. As for the annual incentive, the Board will recall that our CEO Ms. Real's goals for this past year were approved by the Board at the beginning of the year.

4. Ms. Reals did a self-evaluation of each of these as did the committee independently. You can see (show slide) the results of these evaluations.

	Own	Committee
A. Achieve or exceed operating Gross		
• Increase in cash flow of 20%		
- 31% achieved	6	6
• Increase in Economic Profit of 15%		
- 12% achieved	5	3
B. Implement performance based culture		
• New pay plans in place	6	5
C. Adopt best-in-class governance practice	5	5
Average	**5.8**	**4.8**

As you can see our CEO has a slightly higher self-assessment (5.8) than that of the Committee (4.8). Before going further I'd like to walk the board through the rationale for our ratings and that of the self-appraisal. You have in front of you a copy of each. Let's take them point by point. (Each rating is reviewed and a consensus rating by the full Board if obtained.)

5. Based on your overall evaluation of a 5.1 you can see by the chart attached to the performance ratings this would call for an award of $1,100,000 or 110% of salary. This is within the allowable of the shareholder approved negative discretion formula.

6. These proposals have been reviewed by our consultant Mr. Evans who is with us. Would you like to make any comments?

(Consultant's comments)

7. May I have a motion from a member of the Executive Compensation Committee for the CEO's proposed incentive award of $1,100,000. Is there a second? Discussion? All members of the committee in favor? Opposed? Motion is _____.

8. (After reaching agreement on the award) I'd like to bring in our CEO now so we can advise her of her incentive award and thank her for her contributions.

Table 10-14. Sample scripted compensation committee report to the board (Continued on next page

> (CEO enters - thanked - told new pay)
> 9. I'd like to turn the meeting over to the CEO who will walk you through a similar process for her direct reports.
>
> (CEO makes presentation; Executive Compensation Committee takes action on proposals)
> 1.0.Executive Compensation Committee portion of meeting ends and consultant exits the meeting.

Table 10-14. Continued

The members of the committee are to be named at the end of the report. A very brief sample is shown in Table 10-15. One is cautioned to develop such a report carefully, ensuring it meets disclosure requirements. It should be specific to the company and more detailed than shown here.

> The Executive Compensation Committee (hereinafter called the "Committee") during the past fiscal year consisted of Mr. Able, Mr. Ready, and Ms. Right, all of whom were non-employee independent members of the Board of Directors of the Company. The Committee is responsible for approving compensation philosophy, policies and pay for the Company's executive officers, including those named in the Summary Compensation Table.
>
> **Compensation Philosophy and Policies**
>
> The Company's executive compensation policies are designed to enable the attraction, motivation, and retention of talented performers focused on the success of the business. A significant portion of pay is in the form of incentives rewarding financial success and creation of shareholder values.
>
> The Company's Chief Executive Officer's (CEO) pay is determined in relation to competitive levels in the marketplace with the emphasis on performance versus predetermined standards. These include increases in revenue, earnings per share, cash flow, and shareholder value. Additionally, the Committee includes as expected performance qualitative factors including succession planning, individual development actions, and a positive work environment conducive to employee commitment. With regard to each of these factors the company exercises its judgement; however, in no instance will the Chief Executive Officer (or any other named executive) receive annual pay (excluding any income from exercising and/or selling stock received by options granted by the Committee) in an amount exceeding 1% of net revenue.
>
> The pay program consists of salary, employee benefits, perquisites (executive benefits), short-term incentives and long-term incentives.
>
> **Salary**
>
> This is the base portion of the pay program since the other four elements are tied to it in some manner. Since salary is rarely reduced it is not an effective element in the pay-for-performance program. Nonetheless it is important it be set after due consideration of the marketplace and the importance of the other elements. The CEO received no salary increase

Table 10-15. Sample executive compensation committee report (Continued on next page) this past year as it is believed her salary is still competitive and appropriate in relation to the other elements.

Employee Benefits and Perquisites

As one would expect, the CEO (and other named executive officers) participate in the Company employee benefit programs. However, because of the tax limitations placed on the defined contribution and defined benefit retirement plans they are unable to receive the full benefits accorded by formula and available to all other employees. For that reason the Company has set up unfunded deferred compensation plans to provide these otherwise lost benefits. Being unfunded they are accorded no special status and are similar to obligations to other Company general creditors.

Additionally, the Company pays the annual cost of financial planning services for the named executives. For the CEO this was $20,000 and for the other four named executives totaled $55,000. It is believed this perquisite or executive benefit is very cost-effective as it ensures individuals comply with tax and other legal requirements. It also frees up their time for company business.

Short-Term Incentives

As stated earlier the annual incentive plan is based on performance versus prescribed standards set in writing early in the year. For each named executive officer there is a target (or expected performance level) as well as a threshold performance level (below which no bonus is paid) and a maximum performance (above which no further bonus payment is made). For the CEO these percentages were 10% of salary (threshold), 100% of salary (target), and 200% of salary (maximum). Based on an evaluation of performance the Committee awarded a bonus of 110% of salary or $1.1 million. The bonus targets for the other four named executives range from 60% to 75%.

Long-Term Incentives

The long-term incentive plan consists solely of stock options for the CEO and the other named executive officers. It should be noted that from time to time the Company gives stock options to all employees of the Company.

The Committee believes it appropriate that the long-term incentive represent a target opportunity for the CEO of 200% of salary. This is because it is believed that the CEO's focus on the Company's long-term success should be twice as important as annual results with its target of 100% of salary. Using a present-value formula the Committee concluded it needed to grant 60,000 shares at the then market price of $100 a share and it did so.

Accounting and Taxes

The above described pay elements are all considered compensation and charged against the income statement when paid (except the short-term incentive award, which is charged to the year for which earned since it is paid within 75 days of the end of that year). Also, stock options, which are granted at fair market value in accord with APB 25 are not charged against the income statement. However, in accord with FAS 123 the present value of such grants is reported in a footnote in the Company's Annual Financial Report.

Table 10-15. Continued

> Additionally, the Committee has been advised that the Company is in compliance with the requirements of Section 162(m) of the Internal Revenue Code, which limits the tax deduction to $1 million each for the named executive officers unless amounts in excess meet the performance based requirements of this section of the Code. The stock option plan has been approved by shareholders as has the 1% of net revenue limitation on cash payments.
> Ms. Right (Chair)
> Mr. Able
> Mr. Ready

Table 10-15. Concluded

Use of Consultants

To assist the committee in sorting through these issues, many companies turn to outside consultants. This is not a slap at the competency of the inside executive pay planners but a reference to fiduciary trust. It seems a little less than an "arms-length" transaction to have the inside executive pay planner (who is in the reporting chain to the CEO) advise the compensation committee on the appropriate form and level of pay of the CEO. It would be unlikely that many CEOs would advance a negative report. One answer is to have the pay planner report directly to the committee, although the career possibilities of such an individual would be questionable. The other alternative is to utilize an outside consultant.

Consulting firms range from boutique specialists to broad-based global organizations. Some have star or celebrity practice leaders, whose names are widely known because of their frequent appearance in the business press. Some are very pro-management, others more skeptical of the size of executive pay packages.

This raises the question: Who should engage the consultant? Should it be management, the committee, or both?

Reporting Relationship. Historically, the consultant has been engaged by management to support the validity of its request. Needless to say, this puts enormous pressure on the consultant to agree with management. If management engages an executive pay expert (assuming there is not sufficient confidence in the company's executive compensation expert), the compensation committee may wish to have its own consultant review the proposal and comment on the points of concern. These would be forwarded to management for review and comment. The reply (including any modifications to the proposal) would be forwarded to the committee's consultant for review. By the time the committee would meet on the subject, the points of agreement would be described and the points of difference clarified, with alternative proposals for consideration. The two-consultant process is obviously going to be more expensive than the use of one. If only one consultant is hired, the committee should take control of the process (from selection to defined role and project cost), with cooperation of management. However, if management takes a strong hand in the process, there may be a temptation to bury opinions not supporting management's position. The committee must remember its fiduciary responsibility. The committee might like to receive in writing from its advisor concurrence on proposed actions for its own record.

Which Consultant? Rather than immediately sign up a consultant, it would seem appropriate to do a little market research. Some consulting firms have broad-gauge management views: "We can tackle anything." Others are more specialized in nature, ranging from total compensation planning to only executive pay design. Each has their advantages and disadvantages. Broad-gauge management consulting firms are more likely to design a program related to the company's short- and long-term needs; however, the extent to which such plans reflect a creative approach will be a function of the degree of executive compensation knowledge, or lack thereof, of the compensation consultant assigned. On the other hand, a top-notch pay planner from a more specialized firm will be more likely to custom-tailor a plan. However, the individual may not have sufficient broad-gauge management background to have accurately assessed corporate needs.

Few committees seem to approach the problem objectively. Rather than identify one firm, several should be selected and asked for an RFP (request for proposal). Provide each candidate sufficient data to allow an accurate assessment—what, when, and how much. Does the firm have the necessary expertise? Ask for references. A partial list of questions to ask is shown in Table 10-16.

- What is the firm's reputation? Is it trustworthy? Will it honor commitments?
- Who will be the lead consultant? Do celebrity consultants come in to sell the client and then turn over to juniors?
- What are the qualifications of those who will do the work?
- Is there a mutually clear understanding of what is expected when and from whom?
- Is there good chemistry between committee, management, staff, and the consultant?
- Will they be expected to help put in the plan, even administer it, or will they leave once it is adopted?
- What is the estimated cost for the project? How will potential cost overruns be handled? In what detail will fees and costs be presented and when?
- Does the firm have any ties to management or members of the Board (including committee members)?
- Will the firm conduct an analysis after project completion of project quality?

Table 10-16. Questions to ask a potential consultant

Each proposal should be analyzed to determine if the problem has been accurately defined as well as whether the approach suggested is feasible. A cost-benefit analysis of the proposal should be prepared, including such items as consultant charges, company time, disruption, and program cost.

In looking at consultants, one should also attempt to identify the loud proponents of a specific form of plan. If Ms. X is recognized as a performance share advocate, the company should be more interested in how she will justify that type of plan within the company than surprised that she recommends such a program. She has a solution in search of a problem. Unfortunately, unless the problem meets the definition, the misapplied solution subsequently becomes part of the problem.

During the research phase, it is also necessary to identify the real reason (not the obvious avowed response to fiduciary trust) for engaging a consultant. Possible reasons include:

- **Image.** Engaging an individual and/or firm well recognized for preeminence in the area of executive compensation design is an overt signal to the outside world that this committee is "doing right"—excellence by inference. With "so-and-so" as the consultant, one must conclude the company has an effective pay delivery system.
- **Buffer.** Employing a consultant prepared to support the position of the committee gives validity to the program if challenged by a shareholder.
- **Magician.** Belief that the individual engaged will bring forth powers of alchemy. With a wave of the person's wand, the laborious design process will be circumvented by the materialization of a simple, easy-to-understand, and easy-to-operate plan that will be perceived as equitable by all parties concerned. Committees with this approach probably still believe in the tooth fairy.
- **Resources.** Limited time frame and/or lack of executive compensation plan design within the company could necessitate going to a consultant who can provide the know-how and sufficient resources to accomplish the job quickly.

Consultant Alternatives. It would be logical to engage an executive compensation specialist as a consultant to the compensation committee. The chosen specialist should be neither an employee nor engaged in consulting assignments with the company, thus avoiding potential conflict-of-interest situations. The individual could be employed to review the quality of recommendations and/or to develop specific recommendations based on committee objectives.

An extension of this would be to appoint the consultant as a permanent member of the committee, with the written agreement that the person will not work for management. As indicated earlier, an executive compensation expert in the employ of another company outside the industry might also be a candidate for membership in the compensation committee. Even combining these two sources, there are many more opportunities than there are knowledgeable individuals.

On the other hand, some companies look to the auditing firm to comment on the appropriateness of the design of a pay package and its level of payment. This is a logical extension of what they may later have to comment on anyway; the reasonableness issue is one that will have to be addressed with the IRS if not with shareholders. The auditing firm has an advantage over another consulting firm in that it already knows the company rather well.

Company Compensation Expert

Even if management consultants are employed, it is critical that a large company have an internal executive compensation expert. To be successful, the individual must have sufficient rapport with counterparts in other companies to be able to obtain needed data. In addition, the person must be articulate in oral and written communication, analytical but practical, and emphatic but independent. Ideally, the individual should also be sufficiently versed in all forms of executive pay to provide another dimension to material advanced by the external consultant.

The companies with top-flight executive compensation pay planners appear to have a distinct advantage. Since the supply is significantly less than the increasing demand, it is predicted that a two-tier market in levels of pay will emerge, separating the "pros" from the "adequates." Internal relationships will be reassessed, and many will see that an additional increase in pay for such a person is extremely cost-effective given the total executive payroll. It is also less than might be incurred in consulting fees.

Directors' Pay

Pay Philosophy

Typically, all directors are paid the same (assuming same committees and attendance). However, one could argue that the same pay is valid only if one accepts that all outside directors are of equal ability when assigned comparable responsibilities (i.e., all committees are equally important), and that they are equally proficient in discharging these responsibilities. That assumes a lot of equality! Why then are they all paid the same? Essentially, boards are reticent about making the evaluations necessary to pay for performance. Modest remuneration of equal amounts for all was certainly appropriate when board membership was more honorary than risk-oriented. The $20 gold piece at the director's place was probably a reasonable compensation level given the responsibilities. Some might argue that restoring this practice (given the premium prices for mint-condition, turn of the century $20 gold pieces) might be reasonable in today's times as well. However, in today's situation, treating all the same is not automatically synonymous with treating everyone equitably.

Larger companies (measured in revenue) tend to pay more than smaller companies. With larger companies, the percentage of total pay in the form of equity payments (stock awards and/or stock options) will be greater and the percentage in meeting fees will be smaller—the one offsetting the other.

Recognizing that surveys exist to identify the competitive levels of directors' fees, few examine the level of remuneration in terms of what consultants would receive for a half-day or day of work, estimate the hourly rate (i.e., total fees and attendance) and compare it to the billing rates of senior management consultants, attorneys, or accountants. Perhaps one can adjust this in some relation to value received; however, the degree of responsibility of the individuals is different. Few would argue that advisers should be paid as much as those responsible for the decisions.

Some have argued that the responsibility of the board is easily as much as that of the CEO, and therefore, the pay of the directors should be proportionate to the CEO in terms of amount of time. Thus, if the CEO is paid $1 million based on 260 working days in the year, an outside director should receive approximately $4,000 for every day spent on board work. Twenty-five days of board and committee meetings with preparation and follow-up time would suggest directors receive $100,000 a year.

Few companies pay directors this much due in large part to a slowness in recognizing that the role of the director has changed significantly in the last few years. Those who do pay handsomely recognize that board membership is no longer an honorary function. Board work is much more demanding due to social responsibility and other issues. Directors are liable to lawsuits in instances where it appears that they have not prudently governed the business. Even where director and officer liability insurance would reimburse losses, few like the thought of the annoyance of a legal action and the public embarrassment of being charged with negligence. As indicated earlier, an up-front sign-up bonus similar to that used in professional sports may become necessary, especially for troubled companies. Board members may also seek a change-of-control contract, especially if such contracts exist for senior executives. The formula for cash awards would be tied to board retainer (and possibly meeting fees), or some period of W-2 earnings. Definitions of single versus double trigger contracts would mirror those of executives, too. This was discussed in Chapter 6.

Annual Retainer and Meeting Fees

Probably the most prevalent method of paying board members is a combination of annual retainer and meeting fee. Other arrangements could simply be one or the other. Companies that have retainer and attendance fees for the full board acknowledge an ongoing responsibility and away-from-the-site work. They also recognize a need to attend meetings in order to discharge these responsibilities. Those with only a retainer are implying that regardless of attendance, the director is responsible for board actions; those with only an attendance fee are requiring the director to appear and make his or her position known. The retainer-only approach is similar to the salary element for executives; those with a meeting-fee only have an attendance (not to be confused with a performance) bonus. However, when the practice is not consistent with the philosophy, obviously the practice should be changed. For example, a company might conclude that the ongoing responsibility and attendance are of about equal value. Assuming 12 board meetings a year, the attendance fee should logically be 1/12 of the annual retainer. Typically, the size of such payment is related to size of organization, with the multi-billion-dollar companies paying significantly more than those a fraction their size.

In addition to the normal director's compensation for serving on the board, most companies pay extra for serving on board committees. In some instances, they pay the traditional retainer plus a per-meeting fee. In other cases, they pay only a fee for meetings attended or simply a retainer with no meeting fees. Some companies provide a separate annual retainer for the chairman of each committee in recognition of organizational responsibilities (e.g., developing agendas, meeting with management, coordinating staff work, and reviewing recommendations), in addition to or in lieu of annual retainers for other committee members. Some pay each committee chair the same dollar retainer; others differentiate based on perceived importance and/or amount of work.

Some elect not to pay a meeting fee if held on the same day as the board meeting. This suggests payment is for the inconvenience of meeting rather than the committee importance. In such situations, committees may decide to hold some meetings by telephone at a different date in order to be paid for their services—an example of how a poorly designed program can modify behavior. Some consider it inappropriate to pay directors for telephone meetings and/or actions taken by written consent.

Probably the most prevalent practice is for a company to pay the same fee for attending a committee meeting as a board meeting. This may be appropriate, but the company should examine the relationship. For those who conclude that much of the critical work is done in committee and that the board meetings are more perfunctory, the decision could be to have committee fees higher than board attendance fees. Conversely, if the board is the focal point and the committees are more information gathering in nature, perhaps board fees should be higher. The important point is that the impact of each should be assessed in setting the fee structure. A related issue is what to pay for visits to company sites.

Few companies pay management directors a board retainer or fee for attending meetings; however, with the exception of the CEO, many probably consider the elevation to the board as an increase in responsibilities that should result in a higher job grade and higher pay.

In addition to a retainer and meeting fees, some directors receive additional compensation from the company for their specialized services (e.g., investment banker or attorney). As indicated earlier, most identify these individuals as *affiliated, non-management directors.*

The problem with flat retainers and meeting fees is the assumption that not only are relative responsibilities the same but that each director is performing equally well. This takes us back to the issue of performance appraisal of directors discussed earlier.

Some directors are interested in deferring part or all of their retainer and/or meeting fees. Such deferrals may be at a specified rate of interest, tied to a special financial vehicle (e.g., 6-month Treasury bills or the prime interest rate), and/or tied to company stock performance. As explained in Chapter 3, this type of decision is a wager by the individual on the probable tax rate, amount of inflation, and lack of attractiveness of alternative forms of investment. Another alternative is investment in the Keogh plan described in Chapter 6.

Annual and Long-Term Incentives

Since pay-for-performance is unlikely to be found in the board retainer and/or meeting fee program, one needs to look elsewhere. Short-term incentives are inappropriate since they would have directors focusing on annual rather than long-term results. That leaves the long-term incentives, which by definition are more consistent with the role and responsibility of directors. It makes sense to tie director pay to the value of company stock, thereby tying the director more closely to other shareholders and the interest in creating shareholder value. To avoid potential problems with the SEC, it makes sense to set in advance the date and number of shares each director will receive.

It is not surprising, therefore, that many companies use stock options and/or stock awards to pay their outside directors. Some use stock options to supplement directors' pay, either making it a part of the annual compensation with annual 10-year, non-qualified grants, or using them as a front-end, one time incentive to get a new director on the board. Some choose to pay the equivalent of retainers all in company common stock. This may be a problem for those intending to supplement their income with board fees (e.g., university professors and former government officials). Others may pay part in cash and part in stock, probably with the view that the cash will meet tax requirements without having to sell any stock. Alternatively, it may be required to be deposited in an unfunded, deferred account until leaving board service. Rather than use actual stock, many companies use stock units when deferrals are involved. No stock is issued, only a promise that the company will pay a number of shares of stock equal to the number of units at the end of the deferral period. Typically, the units would also be credited with dividend equivalents during the period of deferral.

It has been argued that directors will increase their identification with the shareholder if given stock awards and/or stock options. These could either be real or phantom plans. Essentially, any plan described earlier for executives could be developed for non-employee directors. However, a key planning consideration is the limited period many will serve as directors. Thus, a 10-year, non-qualified stock may not be as attractive as stock awards. However, a stock-purchase plan, where the corporation matches director purchases in whole or in part, may be very attractive. An additional advantage of stock-based compensation is that it avoids the embarrassment of listing in the proxy directors with only a token number of shares of stock (e.g., 100).

Some companies have also adopted *stock ownership guidelines* much like those described earlier for executives. The requirement may either be a stated number of shares or the value of shares as a stated multiple of the annual retainer. It is important to ensure it is not so high as to create financial hardship.

Benefit Coverage

For tax purposes, outside directors are not "employees" of the company, but rather self-employed individuals. Thus, including them under company benefit plans is more difficult. For example, they cannot be included under qualified, defined-benefit or contribution plans, since such benefits can only apply to employees. An identical plan paralleling the benefits can be established; however, this could require compliance with ERISA and careful design to ensure the income was not taxed until received. However, Keogh plans enable directors to set aside a portion of their retainer and fees.

Let's examine the various benefit categories for possible coverage. If a director under the retainer-only program misses a meeting, one could argue that he or she is receiving *time off with pay*, although that was not the intent. More likely, the individual does not receive pay for time worked while preparing for board meetings. One might also argue that the director has an employment contract for the length of elected service albeit a short one when each director is elected annually, and only slightly better with staggered boards (e.g., each serving a three-year period).

Under *service programs*, it is common to include outside directors in the matching gifts program, a director and officer liability insurance plan, as well as to reimburse them for business travel expenses. Some outside directors are also entitled to personal use of company aircraft, testing of company products, access to club memberships, personal umbrella liability coverage, legal service, tax preparation, and/or financial counseling. Certainly, the most tax effective is the title, member of the board of directors.

Since most directors are covered under some other *healthcare plan*, nothing additional is typically provided. *Survivor protection* is usually limited to business travel accident. However, some companies provide life insurance to their non-employee directors either at no or reduced cost. The amount may be a flat amount (e.g., $100,000) or a multiple of earnings (although this means coverage is a function of number of meetings attended where per-meeting fees exist). Remember that the $50,000 life insurance exclusion applies only to employees; also, the less favorable PS 58 rates (not the Uniform Premium Rate table) are applicable beginning with the first dollar of coverage. Since the amount of imputed income increases significantly with age, it would be appropriate to allow directors to opt out of the program when such protection is no longer needed.

The final category is the *retirement* benefit. For a period of time, a number of companies established and maintained a pension plan for outside directors. Not atypical was a plan that would pay an amount equal to the annual retainer for the number of years equal to board service. These virtually disappeared when they came under shareholder attack as promoting tenure rather than performance.

However, directors typically are permitted to defer a portion or all of their retainer and meeting fees. In some cases, when stock is used, the deferral may be mandatory. Deferrals are more attractive to those currently receiving a significant level of pay (e.g., CEOs of other companies) than those with less hefty income levels (e.g., educators). The manner in which the deferral is credited with some form of interest varies significantly. As stated earlier, it is important to carefully structure such deferrals to avoid constructive receipt and economic benefit issues.

Since director compensation is self-employment income, it is subject to social security taxes in the year received. Until recently, the director receiving social security benefits might also be subject to an earnings test for level of benefits. However, since 2000, there is no longer an earnings test for an individual age 65 or older.

Responsibility for Action

A separate issue is who is responsible for pay decisions with respect to outside directors. It is not uncommon for the corporate secretary to draw together data on competitive practice, and present it to the CEO, who will analyze it and make a recommendation to the full board. Logically, the non-employee directors would abstain from voting. The role of the company pay planner in this process is a function of his or her credibility.

Others believe it more appropriate for the corporate governance committee to review the matter and bring a proposal to the full board for consideration.

It is interesting that while most companies annually review the pay package of their executives, it seems that few do it as frequently for the pay of outside directors. Objectivity notwithstanding, it is difficult for some directors to understand why they should approve annual pay actions for the senior management when their compensation has been the same for several years. Furthermore, in addition to varying the compensation package (depending on the role played and the number of committees involved), it may be necessary to have a front-end, one-time recruiting cash payment or (more appropriately) stock award for troubled companies.

SUMMARY AND CONCLUSIONS

It is simple logic that the attainment of desired financial and social objectives would be maximized if capable people are in the positions of authority and rewarded in proportion to their success. By definition, this also means being punished for degree of failure by the amount of pay withheld. Obviously, there is a point at which failure is handled by dismissal, but a successful pay delivery system reinforces desired performance as well. Boards and their directors are stepping up to this responsibility.

More and more compensation committees have taken responsibility for initiating studies of executive pay delivery systems, rather than simply reviewing and approving those prepared by consultants and compensation staff at the request of senior management.

Compensation committees define their role as taking the corporate objectives established by the board and relating them to a pay delivery system that will reward in proportion to accomplishment. In addition, they attempt to determine the extent to which performance is being measured and the basis for salary actions and incentive awards—not simply for corporate officers but also for other key members of management. Good compensation committees recognize the need to be competitive; however, they temper the input of firms that offer multi-million-dollar packages in a desperate attempt to buy the management needed to "turn a company around."

Probably most important of all, boards and their compensation committees are realizing that executive pay programs are a means to an end and not an end unto themselves. They are sometimes complicated and too often don't work well, but they are the best technique available for ensuring that shareholder interests are placed in proper focus.

Note: You are again reminded not to rely on accounting, tax, SEC, or other professional service statements in this chapter. You need to seek appropriate professional counsel for such guidance. Statements made in this chapter and elsewhere are offered as being illustrative to help frame such further investigations by the reader with counsel.

And now we proceed tothe final chapter, which summarizes some of the concepts covered in this book and provides an historical perspective on executive compensation.

Chapter 11

Summary

This book has identified and defined the basic elements of the executive compensation package. It has described their key features and the various forms each might take in a current or deferred manner. Additionally, it identified the various stakeholders and rulemakers and assessed their perspectives. It has examined various design considerations as well as the role of, and pay for, the board of directors and its compensation committee. Communication and disclosure aspects have been highlighted throughout. It has also discussed how accounting, tax, and Securities and Exchange Commission (SEC) issues impact compensation plans. Additionally, tax tables have been developed to allow the reader to see the impact of subsequent changes.

The objective in all this has been to give the reader a frame of reference for subsequently discussing any element or segment in comparison with the total package. While the emphasis has been on concepts and approaches rather than specific solutions, it has been liberally supported with figures and tables for those interested in a more detailed analysis. Where specifics were added, you should remember that items such as accounting, legal requirements, and tax treatment are subject to change, and that such change may significantly alter the attractiveness of a specific alternative. In any event, although this material reflects the author's understanding, you should not rely on the material should without verification by the company's own accounting, tax, and legal experts.

REMINDERS AND CAUTIONS

It is important to remember that while the ideal of an effective compensation program is to attract, retain, and motivate, at the very least, it should not repel, encourage turnover, or demotivate. Not all plans will create positive results, but they should, at the minimum, avoid negative responses. In earlier days, the executive owned the business, much as he or she does now for threshold companies. However, executives of companies in growth, mature, and declining market stages are essentially professional managers. Their individual stock holdings are usually well under 1 percent of outstanding shares—far short of enabling direct control. Their risks, like their rewards, are different.

The Ideal Pay Plan

The plan for an individual company can only be structured by reviewing the specific objectives of that company, assessing their priority and degree of importance, and creating a delivery system that facilitates their attainment in a cost-effective manner. Too often, the right decision is made at the wrong time (e.g., give more stock options because the stock is performing well, or adopt a non-market plan because the stock price is low). In other instances, priorities are confused (e.g., placing tax effectiveness ahead of individual needs and corporate objectives). Table 11-1 recaps the characteristics of the ideal pay plan reviewed earlier.

1. Identifies with the shareholder.
2. Correlates with individual and unit performance.
3. Correlates with group performance
4. Correlates with corporate performance
5. Is easily understood by all.
6. Requires no special target setting.
7. Ties the high performer to the company.
8. Has no earnings charge.
9. Has no dilution to shareholder equity.
10. Is tax deductible to the company?
11. Is not taxable to the individual.
12. If taxable, is deductible to the individual
13. Requires no investment by the individual.
14. Individual has no downside risk.

Table 11-1. The ideal pay plan

There is *no* plan that meets *all* of these objectives. Therefore, the best way to develop the incentive plan is for the CEO and others responsible for pay determinations is to identify and weight the various objectives (as described in Chapter 9). Unfortunately, the temptation is strong to immediately look at several alternative plans. Even with alternative plans, it is still imperative to examine them in terms of their strengths and weaknesses before moving beyond the conceptual stage. For example, stock options are positive vehicles for raising capital but significantly affect the dilution of shareholder equity.

Design Cautions

The compensation program, when properly structured and controlled, is probably the most potent weapon the chief executive officer has in is or her arsenal of reward –and punishment devices. Compensation is highly effective at motivating individual executives to higher levels of performance. Optimum usage of this arsenal, therefore, calls for plus-and-minus deviations to the individual's package in direct relation to performance. Table 11-2 highlights some precautions.

Companies can reconcile the difference between what they say and what they do with regard to pay for performance. If companies are unwilling or unable to take valid measurements,

1. Measuring too few factors is as bad as measuring too many. The first means not all major goals are addressed; the second is difficult not only to communicate, but to remember.
2. Measuring only the easy-to-measure factors probably means overlooking more important but difficult-to-measure factors.
3. Measuring only outcomes and not behavior may result in optimizing results but in a way inconsistent with desired culture.
4. When measuring behavior it must be consistent with the desired culture. This is critical in organizations undergoing transformation
5. A balance must be struck between individual and group incentives. Too much on individual will undermine teamwork. The reverse may make it difficult for the individual to believe his or her output will have any real impact.
6. If performance measurements are not championed by top management they are likely to be ineffective.
7. The payout should be consistent with the degree of difficulty otherwise individuals will be either over or under compensated for performance.
8. Short-term incentives in the absence of long-term incentives will lead to short-term thinking.
9. Incentives not understood clearly do little if anything to incent desired behavior/outcomes.
10. Incentive plans that are not continually reviewed to ensure a link with corporate and divisional objectives/goals will over time be totally ineffective.

Table 11-2. Design cautions

they would do better to honestly admit that performance is only marginally important than to claim they want to pay for performance, but no one has developed the right pay system for them. In many instances, companies need to challenge their human resource groups to develop effective training programs to assist in managing performance appraisal. Invariably, the executive receives a very impressive manual explaining in detail how much to award for a certain level of performance. This is where most companies and compensation plans fail. It is one thing to say the company has a performance management program; it is something quite different to train managers so that they can apply the system effectively! Chances for success are improved when the CEO uses the performance program to manage the business.

Some companies are apparently guided by the philosophy, "Let's adopt the plan that gives the best payout." In this case, "best" is defined as biggest rather than most cost-effective given corporate performance. These companies might be typified by frequent, very radical departures in plan programs (e.g., stock options one year, performance shares the next, stock appreciation rights the year after, etc.). Others simply add new programs on top of existing plans, increasing the probability of excessive compensation. A study of such compensation for top corporate officers would result in little correlation to performance in return on equity, earnings per share, or other indicators of corporate success. This is especially true when a large portion of total compensation is in salary and benefits, but even multiyear incentive plans that smooth out annual fluctuations, and emphasis on stock market-related awards, will do little to promote a higher correlation.

It is difficult to believe a company is really interested in the incentive aspect of short- and long-range compensation programs when it continually adjusts targets after the fact, apparently in order to ensure adequate payout for executives. Such situations have made cynics out of many who believe the prime objective of such plans is to have a structure that will obfuscate, hide, and serve as the scapegoat for huge incentive awards. Conversely, those who believe that the perfect executive incentive plan is "just around the corner" are about as optimistic as those who describe a recession as a short interval of below-average economic expansion. Fortunately, SEC disclosure requirements for executive pay are putting it in the spotlight, subject to shareholder scrutiny. The only way to justify the level of executive pay is in terms of what other companies are paying for comparable responsibilities. Some, however, argue that this approach is a never-ending spiral of pay adjustments as companies chase each other's pay actions. They find it difficult to believe that a corporate executive should be paid more than the president of the United States or amounts in excess of 100 times that of the lowest paid worker in the organization. For years, executives have contributed to the pressure to increase their pay. They approved the extra layers of management that resulted in the compression of pay (i.e., decreasing absolute and relative differentials in pay between organizational levels. Later, after removing many of those layers, there is little sympathy among the pubic and politicians for executive pay problems. Some have suggested that the pay of every executive be viewed as a corporate asset: Is the shareholder receiving at least as high a return as on net assets? This negative view frustrates executives, especially since they are more concerned with the relative (i.e., in relation to pay of other executives) than the absolute level of pay. Furthermore, some try to argue that their predecessors fared better. Such arguments are a function of marginal tax brackets and stock market performance.

While most companies review programs in terms of competitiveness, some are reluctant to adopt any programs that are not consistent with a majority of the companies studied. Adopting such a policy results in a paradox—programs completely justifiable in terms of the business world but probably inappropriate for a specific company. Too often, the average is simply a measure of a central tendency that describes few if any real situations.

Conversely, resistance to change, that natural enemy of progress, and fear of accepting a plan that may be less than perfect, have resulted in many corporations doing less than they should in structuring their executive compensation program. Interestingly enough, this often results in staying with an old, outdated, but familiar program rather than developing an improved compensation plan.

The person charged with the responsibility of developing and maintaining the compensation package, especially at the executive level, must not only be a good administrator but also a creative, analytical person able to assess and respond to the needs of the corporation and its individuals. Although a number of statistical techniques are available for use in establishing and monitoring a program, the pay planner must be able to adapt conceptually to a profession that is more art than science, responding to changes in accounting, tax, and SEC requirements. Compensation programs are only as good as the judgment of those involved in their construction and maintenance. Consistency is pertinent only to the extent that deviations are not in fact justifiable. The program must be flexible and responsive to the corporation's need; it should bring order to the system, but not inflexible discipline.

The importance of a systematic, logical, and orderly review process cannot be emphasized too strongly. Conversely, it is critical to keep the analysis phase in perspective. It is easy to become inundated with data or, even worse, subject the data to measurement far more sophisticated than required. This analysis-paralysis can mesmerize. The planners become ruled by the data rather than using it as the basis for making decisions on executive pay.

The responsibility of senior management is to assess competitive strengths and weaknesses, and then develop and execute the strategy that will best utilize available corporate assets. The board of directors and its compensation committee should ensure that the compensation program rewards goals and objectives appropriately.

Good and No-So-Good Pay Practices

The interest in executive compensation does not give signs of dissipating. Designers, approvers, and recipients of executive pay must not only be aware of the stakeholder issues, but be responsive to them, fully explaining actions which appear to be counter to their views. Influences on executive pay probably will be in response to bad practices, with good practices serving as the model for action. Executive compensation practices that may be perceived as good or not-so-good (even bad) are highlighted in Table 11-3.

Good Practices	No-So-Good Practices
1. Pay for performance	1. Pay for existence
2. Include all employees in incentive plan	2. Limit incentive plans to executives
3. Base pay on stock	3. Base pay on cash
4. Establish stock ownership guidelines	4. Consider stock as cash compensation and no policy encouraging stock ownership
5. Base pay on performance	5. Base pay on surveys
6. Use same employment guarantee for all	6. Give employment contracts to executives only
7. New plans modify and/or replace outdated plans	7. New plans are added on top of old plans
8. Realistic severance pay plans for all	8. Unnecessary rich change-of-control contracts
9. Issuing stock options on a regular basis	9. Instituting cancel-and-reissue stock options
10. Linking shareholder and executive with stock price performance	10. Paying solely on internally established financial goals
11. Request shareholder approval of tightly targeted designed plans	11. Instituting omnibus plans permitting virtually any type program
12. Request shareholder approval of shares when needed	12. Adopt evergreen plans that automatically replace stock used
13. Reload options using only mature stock	13. Reload options using cash
14. Performance based restricted stock awards	14. Non-performance restricted stock awards

Table 11-3. Good and not-so-good executive pay practices

Possible Threats to Executive Pay

Some might argue that the best of the good practices would include performance-based stock options and awards, combined with stock ownership requirements. Possible threats resulting from such pay abuses are identified in Table 11-4.

- Accounting changes, especially for stock options
- Board/compensation committee requirements
- Employee alienation
- Executive greed
- Public populism
- Securities and Exchange Commission actions
  - Expanded disclosure rules
  - Tighter limits on stock purchases/sales
- Stock market declines
- Tax policy
  - Higher taxes (money and capital gains)
  - Loss of business deductions to company
  - Expanded definition of income

Table 11-4. Possible threats to executive pay

Ellig's Laws

There are always obstacles on the path to the ideal plan; some are so consistent and so predictable that the author has set them down, somewhat tongue-in-cheek, as "Ellig's Laws":

1. Treating everyone the same is inconsistent with treating each individual equitably.
2. Individuals believe that others in similar positions work less and are paid more.
3. Appearance is at least as important as reality (e.g., pronouncements are often accepted as performance).
4. Performance ratings will always support the recommended pay action.
5. The highest performance ratings will go to the immediate subordinates of the manager.
6. Complete flexibility usually results in less rather than greater use of discretion.
7. An action correcting an inequity results in creating a new inequity.
8. Formal procedures and programs apply to those one level below the executive making the pronouncement.
9. A decision is difficult to modify even though the parameters have changed, because the action is not examined in terms of the changing situation.
10. An arithmetic increase in the number of people involved results in a geometric increase in the time required to reach agreement.
11. Time is our most valuable resource; once spent, it can never be regained. How it is spent is a significant factor in our happiness and effectiveness.
12. Outcome is the sum of small details.
13. It is easier to be successful than to continue being successful.
14. One's level of success is the sum of one's own performance and the performance of those being managed.
15. It is easier to pull individuals to a desired outcome than to push them.

16. Change is the one constant in life.
17. Change is exciting when *we* are doing it; it is threatening when it is done to us.
18. Everyone is entitled to an opinion; no one is entitled to be wrong with the facts.
19. One can afford to lose many skirmishes, a few battles, but no wars.
20. In life, every absolute is relative.
21. Strive for perfection, and you will achieve excellence.

HISTORICAL LOOK BACK

The philosopher Toynbee cautioned that he who has not learned from the past is likely to make the same mistakes. Therefore, the early stages of the 21st Century, is an appropriate time to look back and see how executive pay evolved. Table 11-5 shows highlights of executive pay developments during the 20th century.

This listing of events while extensive is most assuredly incomplete as many other "firsts" occurred during this century. Unfortunately I can only report what has been provided in various public records. I hope to to be able to include additional items in the next edition.

1900-1909

1902	Annual executive cash bonus plan (Bethlehem Steel)
1903	Non-restricted stock awards (DuPont)
1904	Executive stock purchase plan (DuPont)
1906	Dividend equivalents (DuPont)
1909	U.S. President pay set at $75,000

1910-1919

1918	Bonus awards (General Motors)

1920-1929

1924	Economic value plan (General Motors)
1925	Financial planning for officers (General Electric)
1929	Million dollar annual pay (Bethlehem Steel)

1930-1939

1931	Performance stock award plan (Gillette)
1932	Dividend Equivalents on outstanding options (Bethlehem Steel)
1934	Stock appreciation rights (Marshall Field)
1935	SEC publishes insider stock transactions
1937	Shareholder protection formula (General Electric)
	NAM does executive pay survey
	Federal Trade Commission pay study
1938	McGraw-Hill publishes book on executive pay
	Underwater stock options repriced (Pan Am Air)

1940-1949

1940	*Manual of Job Evaluation* published (Benge, Burk & Hay)
	Five year grant term on stock options (General Electric)

Table 11-5. Selected highlights of executive pay developments

1941	Executive medical exams (General Electric)
1942	Mandatory deferral of pay portion (General Electric)
1943	*A Theory of Human Motivation* published (Maslow)
1944	Special vacation plan (DuPont)
1945	Stock option grant based on job grade (General Electric)
1946	Installment vesting of stock option (General Electric)
1947	Stock option grant based on pay level (Pfizer)
1948	Consultant does executive pay survey (McKinsey)
1949	U.S. President pay set at $100,000

1950-1959

1950	AMA begins executive pay studies
1951	Single regression analysis of pay (AMA
1952	Broad-based statutory stock options (Pfizer)
1953	Multiple regression analysis of pay (General Foods)
	Business use of company airplanes (General Electric)
1954	Management by objectives introduced (Drucker)
1955	Split dollar insurance for executives (General Electric)
	World at Work begins as Midwest Compensation Association in Columbus, Ohio
	Wage and Salary Administration published (Belcher)
1956	Tax preparation for officers (General Electric)
1957	Apartment for executives (General Electric)
1958	Club membership for executives (General Electric)

1960-1969

1960	Premium for taking bonus in stock (General Mills)
1965	Half price stock purchase paid back at variable interest (ITT)
1966	Return of non-statutory options (Northrop)
1967	Single trigger change of control vesting (Conoco)
1969	U.S. President pay set at $200,000
	Exercise cost used to set option grants (Xerox)
	SARs granted in tandem with stock options (Xerox)

1970-1979

1970	Variable price (yo-yo) stock options (3M)
	Executive sabbatical (Xerox)
	Executive business travel accident insurance (American Express)
1971	Fixed price discounted stock option (Digital)
	Performance share plan (CBS)
1972	APB25 (Accounting Principles Board)
	Cancel-and-reissue underwater stock options (Pfizer)
	Tandem book value and common stock purchase (Citicorp)
	Indexed stock option (Heinz)

Table 11-5. Continued

Performance unit plan (Heinz)
SARs granted in parallel with stock options (General Electric)
Stock option grant based on targeted gain (American Express)
Stock-for-stock exercise of stock options (American Express)

1973   Omnibus stock plan approved by shareholders (Pfizer)
Present value created for stock options (Black & Scholes)
Tandem market value and book value options (Citicorp)
Executive supplemental health insurance (General Electric)

1974   Appreciation units on book value plans (ITT)
Million dollar bonus (Revlon)
Performance based stock options (Corning Glass)
Mega stock option grant (Gulf Oil)
Tandem stock option and phantom stock (General Electric)

1975   Clawback stock options (IBM)
Convertible debentures (Westinghouse)
Restricted stock awards (Harris Bank)

1976   Dividend equivalents on restricted stock (Xerox)
Tandem stock options and performance units (Xerox)
SARs in tandem with performance units (Xerox)
Executive perquisite allowance (Hewitt)

1977   Performance accelerated stock option vesting (Maryland National Bank)

1978   Stock-for-tax withholding (Citicorp)

1979   All 25 executives in *Business Week* above $1,000,000 in total pay
Single trigger change-of-control contract (Bendix)

1980-1989

1982   PARSAP/TARSAP (Gerber)
Stock Option performance forgiven loan (Digital Research)

1983   Stock awards for outside board of directors (Dart Kraft)
All 25 executives in *Business Week* above $1,000,000 annual pay

1984   Letter or tracking stock (General Motors)
Evergreen stock plan (Citicorp)
Takeover poison pill (Crown-Zellerbach)

1985   Stock option in lieu of cash (International Multi-Foods)
Deferral of stock option exercise gain (E.F. Hutton)
Junior stock plan (E.W. Scripps)
Charitable bequest executive life insurance (Westinghouse)

1987   Stock award for holding exercised options (St. Paul Co.)

1988   Unbundled stock units (Pfizer)
Reload stock options (Norwest)
Director pension plan (Pfizer)
Stock options in lieu of salary increase (General Mills)

Table 11-5. Continued

1989	Fixed price increase stock options (Disney)
	Stock Ownership Guidelines for executives (Warner-Lambert)
	Stern Stewart launches EVA®
1990-1999	
1990	Additional stock options for shares in escrow (General Mills)
	Stock ownership guidelines for directors (Campbell Soup)
1991	Fifteen year grant term on stock options (Chiquita)
1992	Balanced scorecard (Kaplan and Norton)
	Mega restricted stock award (Coca-Cola)
1994	Performance threshold stock options (Bristol Myers Squibb)
	162(m) negative discretion formula (General Electric)
1995	CEO granted retention bonus (Gillette)
	Director pension plan terminated (Pfizer)
	Deferral of stock option gain (Pepsi)
	FAS 123 (Financial Accounting Standards Board)
	Transfer of stock option exercise rights (Warner Communications)
	Choice of stock options or performance unit plan (Pepsi)
1996	Cash to exercise options in event of COC (Apache Corp)
	Succession success bonus to outgoing CEO (Perkin-Elmer)
1997	Performance accelerated mega grants (Hercules)
	Cash to defray option exercise taxes (Barnett-Banks)
1998	Loans based on meeting stock ownership targets (St. Paul Co.)
	Portion of expected cash bonuses replaced by stock options (Monsanto)
	Outside directors may elect to take restricted stock rather than cash (Pioneer Hi-Bred)
	Performance incentive added to Evergreen plan (Dell Computer)
	Mandatory deferrals based on stock ownership targets (Wellman)
	Acquisition completion bonus (Nipsco Industries)
	Bonus payouts converted to discounted stock options (Dell)
	1999 Discount options of mutual fund (Reliance)
	Divestiture transaction bonus (Mallinckrodt)
	Breach of contract covenant (Compaq)
	Performance based split-dollar insurance (Western Resources)
	Optionee able to cancel exercised stock option (Medscape)
2000-	
2000	Guaranteed stock option value (Amazon.com)
	Performance forgiveness loans to buy stock (Union Pacific)
	Underwater stock options exchanged for stock awards (Genesis Health Ventures)
	U.S. President pay set at $400,000

Table 11-5. Concluded

THE FUTURE

One can only wonder what a book like this one closing out the twenty-first century one hundred years from now will report. In spite of the full and rich history of executive pay in the twentieth century, it is unlikely to be of any real value in attempting to predict what will happen over the full period of the twenty-first century. However, it is fascinating to contemplate recognizing that executive pay changes will be shaped by a number of factors, namely significant world events, interest rates, stock prices, income tax rates, accounting rates, SEC requirements, and mergers and acquisitions to name a few.

It is hard to imagine executive pay continuing to significantly outpace that of persons at lower organizational levels for any appreciable time in the future. There are various actions that stakeholders and regulators can take to take some of the helium out of the pay balloon.

Institutional investors may move their focus from the "how" to the "how much" CEOs and others are paid although that is not likely if they believe the "how" is aligned with shareholder interest. Employees if shareholders may express their concern through resolutions, although that is more likely to result in a public relations issue than a change in practice. Customers and suppliers are unlikely to have much impact. But as for the community regulators, while the SEC has made publicly-traded companies reveal details of the pay package for the CEO and other top four executives that does not mean there may not be additional future actions. And the FASB is likely to continue its assault on stock options as well as tightening up on new forms of pay created by ingenious pay planners. Also, it is not out of the realm of possibility that Federal legislators concerned over what they consider to be excessive levels of executive pay take action to raise personal income taxes, further lower the limits on deductible pay by the corporation or more drastically attempt some type of controls on top pay.

You are again reminded not to rely on accounting, tax, SEC, or other professional service statements in this chapter. You need to seek appropriate professional counsel for such guidance. Statements made in this chapter and elsewhere are offered as being illustrative to help frame such further investigations by the reader with counsel.

For those who consider the foregoing too time-consuming and are looking for a simple, albeit sophisticated-appearing, manner of setting pay levels for executives, I offer the formula in Figure 11-1. It reads: Compensation of the executive is a function of job value between the limits of zero and infinity (no need to arbitrarily limit the earning potential) times the hat size of the executive (rough indicator of cerebral capacity) times his or her weight (should be prepared to reward a heavyweight) times size of mouth divided by shoe size (indicating ability to put foot in mouth) times speed in running the 100-meter dash (need for a fast-tracker) is a function of the individual's degree of willingness between the limits of zero (no) and one (yes) to fight a tiger barehanded (degree of risk taking).

$$C_E \longrightarrow {}_0f^{\infty} \, JV \, [H_E \cdot W_E] \cdot \left[\frac{M_E}{S_E}\right] \cdot 100 \, MD \, {}_0f^{1} \, FT$$

Figure 11-1. The secret formula

Wouldn't it be great if it were that simple? Unfortunately designing pay programs is more an art than a science, and there are only imperfect solutions for an imperfect world—qué será será.

Appendix A

Selected Laws

The information in this appendix is intended to be illustrative and should not be relied upon as necessarily complete or accurate. Nonetheless, it should be helpful as a starting point for specific inquires with appropriate counsel.

1798 Revenue Act
  - Federal property and estate tax enacted
  - Repealed in 1805

1861 Revenue Act
  - First federal income tax established to help finance the Civil War–a flat tax of 3% on annual income in excess of $800
  - Repealed in 1872

1890 Sherman Anti-Trust Act
  - Protects the public from corporate monopoly abuse

1894 Revenue Act
  - Federal income tax restored (held unconstitutional by Supreme Court in 1895)

1909 Tariff Act
  - Company profits in excess of $5,000 taxed at 1 percent

1913 Underwood-Simmons Tariff Bill
  - Graduated tax: 1% on income over $20,000; increased at 1% multiples to a maximum of 6% for income in excess of $500,000
  - Estate tax enacted

1914 Clayton Act
  - Prohibits individual from serving as an officer or director of a competing firm

1917 Revenue Act
- Maximum income tax rate of 77% established on income over $200,000

1920 Revenue Act
- Top tax rate cut to 50% on income over $200,000

1921 Revenue Act
- Introduction of capital gains tax

1926 Mellon Plan
- Top tax reduced again to 25% (from 50%)
- Earned income treated more favorably than unearned

1932 Revenue Act
- Maximum income tax rate of 77% restored on income over $200,000

1933 Glass-Steagall Act
- Prohibits underwriting of stocks or bonds by banks

1933 Securities Act
- Requires the registration with the Securities Exchange Commission (SEC) of every offer and sale of a company security. Offerings not made to the public (private offerings) and certain other transactions are exempt from the requirements.
- Rule 144 of the Act requires an executive to hold non-registered shares (restricted stock) for two years before selling to the public subject to certain requirements to avoid legislative violations.

1934 Securities Exchange Act
- Section 16 defines those who have information not available to the public as insiders; defines short-swing situations (purchase and sale within a six-month period) whereby profits must be returned to the company and disclosure requirements for changes in stock ownership and amount of stock owned.
- Section 16 also prescribed insider filing requirements: Form 3 for beneficial ownership upon attaining insider status and Form 4 for monthly changes in beneficial ownership

1935 Federal Insurance Contribution Act (Social Security)
- Old Age, Survivors and Disability Insurance (OASDI) established

1938 Fair Labor Standards Act (FLSA)
- Established minimum pay of 40¢ per hour
- Established employee categories that were exempt from overtime pay
- Those that were not exempt were entitled to time and a half for all hours worked over 40 in the week

1942 Stabilization Act
- Froze wages and salaries but permitted increases in fringe benefits

1943 Current Tax Payment Act
- Income tax withholding instituted

1944 Victory Tax
- Capital gains tax of 25% but top income tax rate raised to 91%

1947 Labor Management Relations Act
- Covered collective bargaining of multi-employee pension plans

1950 Defense Production Act
- Established Wage Stabilization Board with orders to curtail pay increases and permit reasonable increases in fringe benefits

1950 Revenue Act
- Introduces the first statutory stock options, the "restricted stock option"

1954 Internal Revenue Act
- Major rewrite of the Internal Revenue Code replacing 1939 IRC

1958 Federal Welfare and Pensions Disclosure Act
- Requires participants be provided with information upon request on pensions and welfare plans as well as file an annual report to the government

1962 Self-Employed Individuals Tax Retirement Act
- Established Keogh (a.k.a. HR-10) retirement plans for self-employed

1963 Equal Pay Act
- Requires men and women performing work requiring equal effort responsibility and skill to be paid equally
- Codified the benefit principle of equal costs or equal benefits

1964 Revenue Act
- Maximum tax rate reduced to 77% (was 91%)
- Established nondiscriminatory eligibility, benefits, and contributions of pension plans
- Replaced restricted stock options with qualified options (Section 422)
- Introduced statutory employee stock purchase plans (Section 423)

1964 Civil Rights Act
- Title VII prohibits pay and other employment actions based on race, color, sex, religion, and national origin
- Equal Employment Opportunity Commission charged with compliance

1965 Tax Reform Act
- Maximum tax rate lowered to 70% (was 77%)

1965 Social Security Act
- Established Medicare and Medicaid

1967 Age Discrimination in Employment Act
- Prohibits employment discrimination between ages 40 and 65

1969 Tax Reform Act
- Lowered ordinary income maximum tax to 50% (was 70%) but raised long-term capital gain (LTCG) tax to 35% on earned income (was 25%)
- Required restricted stock to be taxed upon receipt if not subject to a substantial risk of forfeiture (Section 83)
- Introduced 10% alternative minimum tax on tax preference income (TPI)
- Considers spread an exercise of qualified stock options subject to alternative minimum tax (AMT)

1970 Economic Stabilization Act
- Gave President authority to establish wage and price controls
- President Nixon used this in 1971–74 and President Carter in 1978

1973 Health Maintenance Organization Act
- Required employers to offer qualified HMOs to employees

1974 Employee Retirement Income Security Act (ERISA)
- Covered employee eligibility and vesting, financial responsibility, fiscal responsibility, form of payment, funding and reporting as well as more extensive disclosure of employer pension plans than in the Welfare and Pensions Disclosure Act
- Established individual retirement accounts (IRA) for those not covered by company pension

1975 Tax Reduction Act
- Introduced Tax Reduction Act Employee Stock Ownership Plan (TRAESOP)

1976 Tax Reform Act
- Eliminated qualified stock options and broadened eligibility requirements in employee stock purchase plans
- Modified TRAESOP allowable credit
- Increased the holding period for capital gains
- Raised the tax on preference income to 15% (was 10%)
- Liberalized tax treatment of deferred payouts
- Introduced favorable tax treatment for legal services plans

1978 Age Discrimination in Employment Act (ADEA)
- Raised the protected age to 70 (was 65) except for exemptions

1978 Revenue Act
- Lowered LTCG to 28% but deductible portion of long-term capital gains subject to alternative minimum tax
- Continued favorable tax treatment of deferred compensation
- Added section 401(k)—cash or deferred compensation (CODA)
- Shifted from investment to payroll-based employee stock ownership plan (PAYSOP)
- Introduced non-taxability of educational assistance
- Disallowed tax deductions on recreation facilities
- Introduced simplified employee pension (SEP)
- Eliminated discriminatory self-insured medical plans
- Introduced "cafeteria benefit plans" (Section 125)

1979 Technical Corrections Act
- Creates tax credit employee stock ownership plans
- Identifies TRAESOPs as tax credit ESOPs as opposed to leveraged ESOPs

1980 Miscellaneous Revenue Act
- Permits employee to make three-way tradeoff among cash, benefits, and deferred compensation

1980 Multiemployer Pension Plan Amendments Act
- Permits Secretary of Labor to treat severance as welfare not pension plan

1981 Economic Recovery Act (ERTA)
- Introduced incentive stock options (ISOs)
- Provides tax incentives for child and dependent care benefit (Section 129)
- Lowered LTCG to 20% and lowered max tax to 50%
- Extended IRAs to all workers as well as increased ceiling to $2,000; Keogh Plan maximum increased to $15,000
- TRAESOPs replaced by payroll-based credits through 1987

1982 Tax Equity and Fiscal Responsibility Act (TEFRA)
- Company and individual pension plan parity established
- Lowers maximum pensions permitted under Section 415
- Added new top heavy rules in qualified pension plans (Section 416)
- ISOs subject to alternative minimum tax as gain at exercise considered tax preference income

1983 Social Security Act Amendment
- FICA tax on deferred compensation due at the latter of when services performed or when the compensation is no longer subject to the substantial risk of forfeiture.
- Phased in age 66 and 67 retirement ages

1983 Technical Corrections Act
- Pyramiding stock-for-stock exercise of ISOs will result in taxable disqualifying disposition.

1984 Deficit Reduction Act (DEFRA)
- Revised qualified retirement estate-tax exclusions, distribution rules and top-heavy rules
- Prevented most taxable benefits from being included in Section 125 flexible benefit plans
- Lowered holding period for long-term capital gains to six months.

1984 Tax Reform Act
- Essentially killed interest-free loans
- Made changes in IRAs and ESOPs
- 20% excise tax on excess golden parachute payment to executive and loss of company tax deduction if in excess of stated allowable

1984 Retirement Equity Act
- Pre-retirement survivors annuity of qualified pension plan required under joint and survivor rules
- "Qualified domestic relations order" established

1985 Consolidated Omnibus Budget Reconciliation Act (COBRA)
- Assures unemployed individuals access to health insurance for a specified time period

1986 Omnibus Budget Reconciliation Act (OBRA)
- Further tightened defined benefit funding standards and placed additional restrictions on plan terminations

1986 Age Discrimination Act
- Eliminated mandatory retirement at any age except for occupational and executive

exemptions
- Pension credit after normal retirement required

1986   Immigration Reform and Control Act
- Illegal aliens can not be hired; employers required to verify new hires are not illegals

1986   Tax Reform Act
- Lowered max tax to 28% but eliminated favorable taxation of long-term capital gains
- Alternative minimum tax (AMT) increased to 21%
- Eliminated exercise sequence rule for Incentive Stock Options
- $100,000 ISO limit on amount exercisable in a given year (was $100,000 calendar year limit)
- Lowered ten year vesting to five years for qualified single-employer plans
- "Highly compensated employee" defined
- Phased out capital gains treatment in lump sum distributions
- Limited 401(k) plan contributions to $7,000 per year (CPI adjusted)
- Introduced 15% tax on tax qualified pension payouts
- Modified integration rules of company pension plans and social security
- Froze Section 415 limit on payment
- Made IRAs less attractive to some
- Limited favorable tax treatment of lump sum distributions
- Repealed PAYSOP
- Established non-discrimination rules for healthcare and other qualified welfare plans

1988   Insider Trading and Security Fraud Enforcement Act
- Penalties increased if trading on insider information

1988   Technical and Miscellaneous Revenue Act
- Alternative minimum tax on disqualifying dispositions is voided only if disposition is in year of exercise
- Single premium life insurance contracts made less attractive with definition of taxable withdrawals

1989   Deficit Reduction Reconciliation Act
- Modified Medicaid reimbursement

1989   Omnibus Budget Reconciliation Act (OBRA)
- Adds COBRA clarification
- Added transitional rule for Medicare maximum taxable earnings

1989   Worker Adjustment and Retraining Notification Act (WARN)
- Requires employers with 100 or more workers to give at least 60 days advance notice of a plant closing or mass layoff

1990   Omnibus Budget Reconciliation Act (OBRA)
- Increased maximum marginal income tax to 31% (was 28%)
- Increased alternative minimum tax (AMT) to 24% (was 21%)
- Expanded Medicaid coverage

1990   Older Workers Protection Act
- Seemingly restores "equal benefit or equal cost" payment in age-based employee ben-

efit differences
- Waivers and releases must be voluntary

1990 Americans with Disabilities Act
- Provides employment protection to physically and mentally impaired individuals

1991 FDIC Improvement Act
- Directors required to defend pay practices of executive officers to federal regulatory agencies as well as stockholders

1991 Civil Right Restoration Act
- Permits recovery of up to $300,000 in legal fees and punitive damages in addition to back wages in discrimination cases

1991 Securities Exchange Act
- Introduced the mandatory filing of Form 5 within 45 days of the close of the fiscal year to report any stock transactions not reported during the year on Forms 3 and 4 (e.g., company stock in qualified pension plans).

1992 Unemployment Compensation Amendment Act
- Imposed mandatory 20% withholding on non-IRA rollover and lump sum distributions
- Liberalized rollover rules between plans and IRAs

1992 Pension Portability Act
- Permits direct transfers to IRA of lump sum pension payout

1993 Family and Medical Leave Act
- Required employers with more than 50 employees to give up to 12 weeks of unpaid leave to care for a newborn child or medical emergency of a family member
- Also required continuation of medical coverage while on leave

1993 Revenue Reconciliation Act, also called the Omnibus Budget Reconciliation Act (OBRA)
- Corporate tax rate set at 35%
- Created new top marginal tax rate of 36% as well as 10% surtax on income over $50,000 resulting in 39.6% max tax on income over $250,000 for single filer
- Capital gains tax set at 28%
- Introduced Section 162(m) limiting pay deductions to $1 million for proxy named executives unless linked to performance
- Removed limit on Medicare taxable earnings (was $135,000)
- Raised the alternative minimum tax to 28%
- Established limit of $150,000 credible earnings for pension calculations
- Taxable portion of Social Security benefit increased to 85% (was 50%) for upper income recipients
- Tax withholding on bonuses increased to 28 percent (was 20 percent)
- Tax deductability of business meals and entertainment reduced to 50 percent (was 80 percent)

1994 Retirement Protection Act

- Administrative changes on cash-out values, mortality table, and under funded plans

1995   Consolidated Omnibus Budget Reconciliation Act (COBRA)
- Required continuation of medical expense coverage for terminated employees and certain dependents

1996   Family and Medical Leave Act of 1996 (FMLA)
- Up to twelve weeks unpaid leave per year for specified personal problems

1996   Health Insurance Portability and Accountability Act
- Eliminates eligibility discrimination of health related factors
- Liberalizes coverage of pre-existing conditions
- Provides favorable tax treatment for qualified long-term care
- Introduces medical savings accounts
- Loan interest resulting from borrowing to buy corporate-owned life insurance no longer tax deductible
- Added COBRA clarifications

1996   Source Tax
- Prohibits states from taxing much of the Income earned by individuals while working in that state but having since moved elsewhere (affects pension payments and other deferred compensation)

1996   Taxpayer Bill of Rights also called Small Business Job Protection Act
- Introduces Savings Incentive Match Plan for Employees (SIMPLE) for small businesses
- Excludes from income accelerated death benefits from life insurance contracts for terminally ill
- Eliminates in year 2000 the combined limitations on defined benefit and defined contribution plans
- Added safe harbor for early distribution of 401(k) moneys due to need

1997   Taxpayer Relief Act
- Lowered LTCG to 20% if held 18 months, otherwise 28% (or less for lower brackets) for 12 to 18 months. Also lowered rate to 18% if acquired after 2000 and held for more than five years
- AMT set at 26 percent for income up to $175,000 and 28 percent above that level
- Eliminated 15% excise tax on excess distributions from qualified retirement plans and increased cash-out limit to $5,000
- Company tax deduction limited on corporate-owned life insurance (COLI)
- Introduction of a nondeductible education IRA and a nondeductible (Roth) IRA permitting contributions (reduced by other IRA) below prescribed earnings level
- Increased child tax credit
- Estate tax exemption increased

1998   IRS Restructuring and Reform Act
- Lowered the LTCG holding period to twelve months retroactive to January 1, 1998

1999   Gramm-Leach-Bliley Act
- Repealed 1933 Glass-Steagall Act

- Banks allowed to sell insurance and stocks; insurance companies permitted entry to banks

2000 Senior Citizens Freedom to Work Act
- Eliminates earnings test requirement to receive Social Security payments if age 65 or older

2000 Worker Economic Opportunity Act
- Stock options with purchase price of at least 85% FMV excluded from overtime calculations

2000 Electronic Signatures in Global and National Commerce Act
- Electronic signatures legally binding for e-commerce transactions

2001 Economic Growth and Tax Reconciliation Act
- Multi year phase in of tax cuts including repeal of estate tax in 2010
- Expanded retirement plan contribution limit
- All provisions rescinded in 2011 unless reenacted by Congress

Source: United States Code

Appendix B

Selected Internal Revenue Code Sections

This listing is intended to include what some would consider the more commonly identified sections of the Internal Revenue Code as would pertain to aspects of executive compensation and therefore does not include all applicable sections of the IRC. Again, the reader is reminded the material is not intended to give advice but rather to be helpful in the assistance of forming questions for review with appropriate counsel.

Partners and Partnerships

Regulated Investment Companies and Real Estate Investment Trusts

Gain Or Loss on Disposition of Property

Capital Gains and Losses

Tax Treatment of S Corporations and Their Shareholders

Estate and Gift Taxes

Employment Taxes

Qualified Pensions Etc. Plans . . . . Sections 4971-4980

Golden Parachute Payments . . . . Section 4999

Information and Returns

Source: United States Code

Appendix C

Selected Revenue Rulings

These revenue rulings are intended to be illustrative rather than the basis for forming definitive tax positions. Such matters should be taken up with appropriate counsel.

Deferred Compensation
- ***Rev.Rul. 60-31*** Stated that an unsecured promise by the company to make a payment to a person in the future will not result in currently taxable income even absent a risk of forfeiture of such payment.
- ***Rev.Rul. 68-454*** Disallows deferred compensation by certain officer-employees under certain circumstances
- ***Rev.Rul. 69-145*** Compensation could be recognized for pension plans if all employees were eligible to defer compensation.
- ***Rev.Rul. 69-650*** Indicated that a decision by December 31 is required in connection with compensation to be earned during the following year. This is the *year-before-the-year principle.*
- ***Rev.Rul. 70-435*** The mere promise to pay does not trigger an income tax liability to the recipient as long as such promise does not include earnings and funds that put the recipient ahead of general creditors.
- ***Rev.Rul. 72-25*** Combined with Rev.Rul. 68-99 suggests the company can fund a deferred compensation obligation without triggering an income liability to the employee if the company owns all policy rights.
- ***Rev.Rul 73-599*** Retired lives reserves plans are not deferred compensation plans.
- ***Rev.Rul. 79-328*** Combined with Rev.Rul. 77-25 and 78-263 deal with when payments may be excluded from FICA taxes.

- ***Rev.Rul. 80-300*** Forfeiture of possible future appreciation can be a sufficient risk of forfeiture to avoid constructive receipt.
- ***Rev.Rul. 80-350*** Voluntary versus mandatory employee contributions to defined contribution plan are described.
- ***Rev.Rul. 80-359*** Expands on Rev.Rul. 68-454 and suggests that deferred compensation can be considered pay for benefit purposes if all employees are eligible to defer compensation.
- ***Rev.Rul 98-30*** Employers permitted to automatically enroll employees in the plan while allowing employees to opt out of the plan.

Executive Benefits
- ***Rev.Rul. 73-13*** The full value of financial services provided to an executive by the company are income to the individual and tax deductible to the company.
- ***Rev.Rul. 76-448*** Tuition fees paid on the behalf of key employees are considered income when paid.

Stock Options and Stock Appreciation Rights (SARs)
- ***Rev.Rul. 67-257*** Requires companies to withhold on the spread between option price and fair market value on date of exercise of a non-statutory stock option.
- ***Rev.Rul. 71-40*** Statutory stock options may be exercised with employer provided loans.
- ***Rev.Rul. 71-52*** Income received as a result of a disqualifying disposition of a qualified stock option is not considered wages for purposes of tax withholding.
- ***Rev.Rul. 73-26*** Statutory stock options lose their tax-qualified status if part of tandem stock option.
- ***Rev.Rul. 76-83*** In a community property state a stock option may be split between employee and spouse after divorce without risking nontransferability issues.
- ***Rev.Rul. 78-359*** Income received from stock option and SAR exercises are considered "personal service income" and therefore subject to the 50% maximum marginal tax rate.
- ***Rev.Rul. 80-244*** Permits an employee to tender stock already owned as payment for exercising a non-qualified stock option without incurring a taxable event that date on the unrealized appreciation on the shares delivered.
- ***Rev.Rul. 80-300*** SAR taxed when exercised, not before.
- ***Rev.Rul. 82-121*** Tandem SAR/stock options with the exercise of one canceling the other avoid constructive receipt.
- ***Rev.Rul. 98-21*** The gift value of a transferred stock option occurs when the option is vested.
- ***Rev.Rul. 98-24*** An option pricing model (such as Black-Scholes) should be used to determine the fair value of a transferred stock option.

Survivor Benefits
- ***Rev.Rul. 55-713*** Premium payments by the employer does not trigger taxable income to the employee.
- ***Rev.Rul. 64-328*** Amends Rev.Rul. 55-713 requiring a determination of economic benefit in accord with the amount of one-year term insurance rates.
- ***Rev.Rul. 66-110*** When published one-year term life insurance rates are lower than the PS 58 rates sited in Rev.Rul. 64-328 the lower rates may be used to determine the economic benefit.

- *Rev.Rul 67-154* Stated that the term life insurance company one-year rates could only apply to all-risk applicants.
- *Rev.Rul. 69-382* Allows deductions by the company of prefunded life insurance under certain conditions.
- *Rev.Rul. 71-360* Need to separate term from permanent life insurance to use Section 79 of IRC.
- *Rev.Rul. 73-599* retired lives reserves plans plans are not deferred compensation plans.
- *Rev.Rul. 76-490* The executive is considered to have made a gift of the value of an assigned group life insurance benefit.
- *Rev.Rul. 79-47* The imputed value of assigned life insurance is considered a gift and will be charged against the lifetime allowable exclusion.
- *Rev.Rul. 79-231* If the employer changes insurance carriers, a three-year period must be completed before the change of an assigned policy becomes effective.
- *Rev.Rul. 80-239* Assignment of life insurance is not affected by an employer changing insurance carriers. This was a reversal of Rev.Rul. 79-231.
- *Rev.Rul. 81-198* Transfer of ownership rights of a split-dollar insurance policy to a third person triggers a gift tax equal to the terminal value plus unearned premiums less the employer's dollar rights to the policy. Annual gift tax is based on the executive's economic benefit increase plus premiums paid.
- *Rev.Rul. 86-109* Compensation paid to the estate of a deceased employee for services performed is not considered income for tax purposes and therefore not subject to tax withholding. However, FICA will apply for payments in same year as death.

Source: U.S. Internal Revenue Service

Appendix D

Selected SEC Actions

This listing of relatively recent SEC actions is intended to be representative rather than exhaustive. Anyone seeking information on SEC actions should seek appropriate legal counsel.

1976 Revised rules for use of Form S-8 increasing the administrative requirements on companies and its officers for the offer or sale of company securities in benefit and compensation programs.

Rule 16(b)-3 amended to exempt exercise of stock appreciation rights.

1977 Clarified treatment of stock appreciation rights (SARs) for insiders.

Value of perquisites for senior officers should be disclosed in the company proxy statement.

1978 Expanded reporting requirements for highest paid five (was three) executive officers.

1980 Exempts as a sale tendered in a stock-for-stock exercise of a stock option.

1986 Permits shares from a stock award or stock option to be used to meet tax withholding requirements, however, this must be an irrevocable decision at least six months prior to the event.

1987 Proxy disclosure rules changed to no longer require disclosure of stock sales acquired through option exercises.

1990 Shareholders allowed to vote on golden parachute proposals.

1991 Stock options are considered to be acquired when granted not when exercised for Section 16 purposes, thereby permitting the immediate sale of the share.

The grant of a stock option is a reportable event.

1992 Relaxed rules enabling investors to more easily interact with each other on governance initiatives.

1993 Made extensive changes in the disclosure requirements of executive pay in company proxy statements. This included: persons reported; tabular requirements; a compensation committee report and a stock performance graph.

Issued clarifications of previous year disclosure requirements including: who was to be included as a named executive and the inclusion of the Compensation Committee's pay philosophy and the applicability of Section 162(m).

1994 Six month advance notice no longer required to have shares withheld to meet income tax withholding requirements.

Stock options may be transferred without losing their Rule 16(b)-3 exemption status.

1996 Transactions (rather than shareholder approval) will obtain exemption status from Rule 16(b)-3 short-swing profit recovery rules under certain prescribed situations. It eliminated the requirements that either the option or its shares and to be held for at least six months if a qualified transaction, thereby significantly broadening their 1991 ruling on stock option purchases.

1998 Permits shareholder vote on repricing of stock options.

1999 Approved New York Stock Exchange removal of shareholder approval requirement for broadly based employee stock plans.

2000 Executives not barred from buying or selling their stock regardless of what information they possessed if such transactions were formally contemplated before the inside information was available to the insider.

Source: U.S. Securities and Exchange Commission

Appendix E

Selected Accounting Interpretations

These interpretations are intended to be illustrative rather than the basis for forming definitive accounting positions. Such matters should be taken up with appropriate professionals.

American Institute for Certified Public Accountants (AICPA) 1939-1959

- *Bulletin No 43* "Compensation Involved in Stock Options and Stock Purchase Plans" (1951). Following the newly authorized restricted stock options under the 1950 Revenue Act, this action made it an exception to the basic rule that the company must expense the full value of a compensation item, be it cash or stock over the performance period.

Accounting Principles Board (APB) 1959-1973)

- *APB 12 "Deferred Compensation Contracts" (1967).* Accrual of non-ERISA plans require amortization of prior service costs following the terms of the plan.
- *APB 15 "Earnings per Share" (1969).* Described three types of earnings per share: primary (included outstanding stock options and other stock based awards); simple (no stock awards included); and fully diluted (included forms of convertible securities). Stock based awards and other convertible securities had to exceed to a 3% materiality threshold before the dilution had to be included.
- *APB 16 "Conditions of Pooling of Interest Methods of Accounting for Combination" (1970).* If the acquisition is deemed a purchase then Goodwill will be charged with the amount paid in excess of the net asset fair market value. If the acquisition meets the rules for pooling, then the historical cost basis is retained and the financials of the companies merged. Unless otherwise detailed acquisitions are considered to be purchases.
- *APB 25 "Accounting for Stock Issued to Employees" (1972).* Established the Measurement Date Principle, namely that the compensatory value of stock is measured on the first date on which both the number of shares and the price is known. If this is known

at date of grant the accounting is set or fixed at that date; if not known to a later date then variable accounting is in effect.

Financial Accounting Standards Board (FASB) 1973 to Present

Standards

- **FAS 5 "Accounting for Contingencies" (1975).** Pertains to when golden parachutes, deferred compensation, and similar arrangements are disclosed.
- **FAS 8 "Accounting for the Translation of Foreign Currency Transactions and Foreign Currency Financial Statements" (1975).** Required that the cost of inventory be based on historical rather than current rates of exchange.
- **FAS 43 (1980) "Accounting for Compensated Absences."** Employee compensation for future absences must be recognized as an accrued liability when estimable payments are vested and payment is probable.
- **FAS 87 "Employers' Accounting for Pensions" (1985).** Following accrual of pension costs using benefit formula, the balance sheet is required to reflect the unfunded accumulated pension obligation.
- **FAS 88 "Employers' Accounting for Settlements and Curtailments of Defined Benefit Pension Plans and for Termination Benefits" (1986).** Accelerated recognition is required of unrecognized gains and losses, as well as prior service obligations. The expense of contractual termination benefits must be taken when the triggering event occurs; for special termination benefits the expense must be taken when the offer is accepted.
- **FAS 91 "Accounting for Nonrefundable Fees and Costs Associated with Originating or Acquiring Loans and Initial Direct Costs of Leases" (1986).** Indicates that interest received from loans to employees is income; non-interest loans are to have an imputed interest calculated. If loan proceeds are less than the amount of the loan the difference is a compensation expense.
- **FAS 106 "Employers' Accounting for Post-retirement Benefits Other than Pensions" (1990).** Required employers to accrue retiree healthcare and other non-pension benefits over the working lives of the employees
- **FAS 109 "Accounting for Income Taxes" (1992).** A deferred tax asset resulting from compensation expense prior to the issuance of shares of stock is reversed when the shares are issued.
- **FAS 112 "Employers' Accounting for Post-employment (but pre-retirement) Benefits" (1992).** Required employers to accrue estimated future severance pay and disability payments
- **FAS 123 "Accounting for Stock-based Compensation" (1995).** Company provided a choice of either reflecting a present value charge to the financial statements with a formula such as Black-Scholes or continuing to use APB 25 but reflecting impact of the present value on net income and earnings per share in financial footnotes.
- **FAS 128 "Earnings per Share" (1997).** Replacing APB 15, it requires the disclosure of Basic EPS (which excludes dilutive effect of stock options and wards) and Diluted EPS (which includes their dilutive effect and eliminates the 3% materiality threshold).
- **FAS 132 "Employers' Disclosures about Pensions and Other Post-retirement Benefits" (1998).** An amendment to FAS 87, 88, and 106 this statement standardized the disclosure requirements.

- **FAS 133 "Accounting for Derivative Instruments and Hedging Activities" (!998).** States that stock-based compensation covered by FAS 123 are not considered derivatives under FAS 133.

Interpretations

- **FAS Interpretation 28 "Accounting for Stock Appreciation Rights and Other Variable Stock Option or Award Plans" (1978).** This is an interpretation of APB 25 stating that if both the number of shares and the price to be paid per share are not known at time of grant then changes in the market value of the stock must be accrued until known.
- **FAS Interpretation 31 (1980) "Treatment of Stock Compensation Plans in EPS Computations."** This addressed concerns regarding certain type stock options and stock appreciation rights raised in FAS Interpretation 28, as well as expanding on the treasury stock method.
- **FAS Interpretation 38 "Determining the Measurement Date for Stock Option, Purchase, and Award Plans Involving Junior Stock" (1984).** Determined variable accounting for such plans was in effect and the cost would be determined on the first date the number of regular shares of common stock will be received in exchange for the junior stock and the price per share of the stock is known.
- **FAS Interpretation 44 "Accounting for Certain Transactions Involving Stock Compensation—An Interpretation of APB Opinion No. 25" (2000).** This interpretation of APB 25 reviewed stock award grants to non-employee directors, modifications of existing awards and repricing of stock options.

Emerging Issues Task Force (ETIF) Issue Numbers

- **84-13 "Purchase of Stock Options and Stock Appreciation Rights in a Leverage Buyout."** Expensing of payments to acquire stock options and SARs is required.
- **84-18 "Stock Option Pyramiding."** Holding period of at least six months required before tendering shares to exercise a stock option can avoid variable accounting.
- **84-34 "Permanent Discount Restricted Stock Purchase Plan."** Company right-of-first-refusal to buy back shares at current market value less the amount of the discount, is probably a grant-date compensatory plan.
- **85-1 "Classifying Notes Received for Capital Stock."** Notes received should probably be a reduction in shareholder equity.
- **85-11 "Use of an Employee Stock Ownership Plan in a Leveraged Buyout."** Agreed with relevance to AICPA Statement of Position 76-3.
- **85-45 "Business Combinations: Settlement of Stock Options and Awards."** Acquired company must expense cost of options and awards if part of acquisition plan.
- **86-27 "Measurement of Excess Contributions to a Defined Contribution Plan or Employee Stock Ownership Plan."** Accounting treatment of the stock and its dividends are described.
- **87-6 "Adjustments Relating to Stock Compensation Plans."** This covered: changes to TRA 1986 stock options; tax-offset cash bonus plans; stock option shares used to meet tax withholding requirements; and attestation of mature stock owned for stock-for-stock exercises.
- **87-23 "Book Value Stock Purchase Plans."** Described treatment of the transaction when employees sell their ESOP shares back to the company.

- **87-33** *"Stock Compensation Issues Related to Market Decline."* Described fixed and variable accounting treatment of stock options and stock awards that are modified or cancelled in exchange for new shares.
- **88-6 "Book Value Stock Plans in an Initial Public Offering."** Described when fixed and variable plan accounting is required.
- **88-23** *"Lump Sum Payments under Union Contracts."* Described when a portion of the lump sum may be deferred and amortized.
- **88-27** *"Effect of Unallocated Shares in an Employee Stock Ownership Plan on Accounting for Business Combinations."* Described when unallocated ESOP shares are not considered tainted for pooling-of-interests accounting.
- **89-8** *"Expense Recognition for Employee Stock Ownership Plans."* Described when shares-allocated method must be used.
- **89-10** *"Sponsor's Recognition of Employee Stock Ownership Plan Debt."* Debt is to be recorded as a liability.
- **89-11** *"Sponsor's Balance Sheet Classification of Convertible Preferred Stock with a Put Option Held by an Employee Stock Ownership Plan."* Described when such arrangements should not be considered equity.
- **89-12** *"Earnings per Share Issues Related to Convertible Preferred Stock Held by an Employee Stock Ownership Plan."* Described how the numerator is adjusted for EPS calculations.
- **90-7** *"Accounting for a Reload Option."* No change in accounting if shares are at current market price, the total number of shares does not exceed original grant (excluding mature shares tendered) and other terms are unchanged.
- **90-9** *"Change to Fixed Employee Stock Option Plans as a Result of Equity Restructuring."* Defined when option changes do not result in a new measurement date.
- **92-3** *"Earnings Per Share Treatment of Tax Benefits for Dividends on Unallocated Stock Held by an Employee Stock Ownership Plan."* Indicated no EPS adjustment for such dividends charged to retained earnings.
- **94-3** *"Liability Recognition for Certain Employee Termination Benefits and Other Costs to Exit an Activity (including Certain Costs Incurred in a Restructuring)."* Defined when termination payments are to be expensed in the period the plan is approved.
- **94-6** *"Accounting for the Buyout of Compensatory Stock Options."* Defined the amount that should be recognized as compensation expense when the company buys out stock options.
- **95-16** *"Accounting for Stock Compensation Arrangements with Employer Loan Features under APB Opinion No. 25."* Defined accounting treatment for both recourse and nonrecourse loans used with stock options.
- **96-5** *"Recognition of Liabilities for Contracted Termination Benefits or Changing Benefit Plan Assumptions in Anticipation of a Business Combination."* Indicated that such contingent liabilities would not be recognized until a merger agreement was signed.
- **96-13** *"Accounting for Derivative Financial Instruments Indexed to, and Potentially Settled in, a Company's Own Stock."* Described measurements and balance sheet accounting for such contracts.
- **96-18** *"Accounting for Equity Instruments That Are Issued to Other Than Employees for*

Acquiring, or in Conjunction with Selling Goods or Services." Measurement date should be the earlier of performance commitment or date when performance is complete.

- 97-5 "*Accounting for Delayed Receipt of Option Shares Upon Exercise Under APB Opinion No. 25.*" Assuming the deferral does not permit diversification and the original number of shares at same exercise price is awarded, the action should not establish a new measurement date.

- 97-9 "*Effect on Pooling-of-Interests Accounting of Certain Contingently Exercisable Options or Other Equity Instruments.*" Indicated what type stock actions would not bar use of pooling-of-interests accounting.

- 97-12 "*Accounting for Increased Share Authorization in an IRS Section 423 Employee Stock Purchase Plan under APB Opinion No. 25.*" The discount at date of grant versus that permitted under IRC Section 423 determines if there is an earnings charge.

- 97-14 "*Accounting for Deferred Compensation Arrangements Where Amounts Earned are Held in a Rabbi Trust and Invested.*" Defined when company stock set aside for Rabbi Trusts is part of basic and/or diluted EPS.

- 99-6 "*Impact of Acceleration Provisions in Grants Made Between Initiation and Consummation of a Pooling-of-Interests Business Combination.*" Defined when grants would or would not preclude pooling-of-interests treatment.

- 00-12 "*Accounting by an Investor for Stock-Based Compensation Granted by an Investor to Employees of an Equity Method Investee.*" Described how the parent company and subsidiary company account for stock compensation.

- 00-15 "*Classification in the Statement of Cash Flows of the Income Tax Benefit Received by a Company Upon Exercise of a Nonqualified Employee Stock Option.*" Described the treatment of stock option income tax benefits is in cash flow statements.

- 00-16 "*Recognition and Measurement of Employer Payroll Taxes on Employee Stock Based Compensation.*" Described when a compensation cost and liability should be recognized by the company.

- 00-23 "*Issues Relating to the Accounting for Stock Compensation under APB 25 and FASB Interpretation No. 44.*" Addressed 31 rather technical issues raised by the SEC.

Source: Accounting Principles Board and Financial Accounting Standards Board

Index

ABOUT THE AUTHOR

Bruce R. Ellig holds his BBA and MBA from the University of Wisconsin-Madison, where he was elected Beta Gamma Sigma and Phi Beta Kappa. He retired at the end of 1996 after over 35 years of human resource experience, much of it doing executive compensation work with Pfizer Inc. The last 11 of those years he served as corporate vice president with worldwide responsibility for the total HR function reporting to the chairman and CEO of the company. During that period he was also secretary to the executive compensation committee of the board of directors.

Ellig has been a member of a long list of premier HR organizations and assumed leadership positions in many of these including serving as the Chairman of the National Board of Directors for the Society for Human Resource Management, an organization with well over 150,000 members. He has also served on the boards of directors for several companies and their compensation committees.

As a speaker, he has addressed over 300 organizations on human resource and compensation issues, and he has been widely quoted on human resource matters in general and executive compensation issues in particular throughout the world. Additionally, he has been interviewed on national radio and television programs. He is also a noted author of over 70 articles and four other books (in addition to having served on several editorial review boards).

Ellig has received numerous honors (including several "Man of the Year" awards) as well as the cherished lifetime achievement awards from WorldatWork (formerly the American Compensation Association) and the Society for Human Resource Management. He also was among the first elected to the National Academy of Human Resources.

He is listed in the prestigious *Marquis Who's Who in the East, Who's Who in Finance and Industry, Who's Who in America,* and *Who's Who in the World.*